Christopher R. Green
Somali Grammar

Mouton-CASL Grammar Series

Editors
Anne Boyle David
Claudia M. Brugman
Thomas J. Conners
Amalia Gnanadesikan

Volume 5

Christopher R. Green
Somali Grammar

Edited by
Nicola Lampitelli
Evan Jones

DE GRUYTER
MOUTON

ISBN 978-1-5015-2140-9
e-ISBN (PDF) 978-1-5015-0361-0
e-ISBN (EPUB) 978-1-5015-0351-1

Library of Congress Control Number: 2021942352

Bibliographic information published by the Deutsche Nationalbibliothek
The Deutsche Nationalbibliothek lists this publication in the Deutsche Nationalbibliografie;
detailed bibliographic data are available on the Internet at http://dnb.dnb.de.

© 2023 Walter de Gruyter, Inc., Boston/Berlin
This volume is text- and page-identical with the hardback published in 2021.
Cover photo: Muratani / iStock / Getty Images Plus
Printing and binding: CPI books GmbH, Leck

www.degruyter.com

for my mentors – Stuart Davis, Daniel Dinnsen, and Samuel Obeng

Foreword

It is remarkable that, in this age of unprecedented global communication and interaction, the majority of the world's languages are as yet not adequately described. Without basic grammars and dictionaries, these languages and their communities of speakers are in a real sense inaccessible to the rest of the world. This state of affairs is antithetical to today's interconnected global mindset.

This series, undertaken as a critical part of the mission of the University of Maryland Center for Advanced Study of Language (CASL), is directed at remedying this problem. One goal of CASL's research is to provide detailed, coherent descriptions of languages that are little studied or for which descriptions are not available in English. Even where grammars for these languages do exist, in many instances they are decades out of date or limited in scope or detail.

While the criticality of linguistic descriptions is indisputable, the painstaking work of producing grammars for neglected and under-resourced languages is often insufficiently appreciated by scholars and graduate students more enamored of the latest theoretical advances and debates. Yet, without the foundation of accurate descriptions of real languages, theoretical work would have no meaning. Moreover, without professionally produced linguistic descriptions, technologically sophisticated tools such as those for automated translation and speech-to-text conversion are impossible. Such research requires time-consuming labor, meticulous description, and rigorous analysis.

It is hoped that this series will contribute, however modestly, to the ultimate goal of making every language of the world available to scholars, students, and language lovers of all kinds. I would like to take this opportunity to salute the linguists at CASL and around the world who subscribe to this vision as their life's work. It is truly a noble endeavor.

Richard D. Brecht
Founding Executive Director
University of Maryland Center for Advanced Study of Language

Series Editors' Preface

This series arose out of research conducted on several under-described languages at the former University of Maryland Center for Advanced Study of Language. In commencing our work, we were surprised at how many of the world's major languages lack accessible descriptive resources such as reference grammars and bilingual dictionaries. Among the projects undertaken at the Center was the development of such resources for various under-described languages. This series of grammars presents some of the linguistic description we undertook to fill such gaps.

The languages covered by the series represent a broad range of language families and typological phenomena. They are spoken in areas of international significance, some in regions associated with political, social, or environmental instability. Providing resources for these languages is therefore of particular importance.

However, these circumstances often make it difficult to conduct intensive, in-country fieldwork. In cases where such fieldwork was impractical, the authors of that grammar have relied on close working relationships with native speakers, and, where possible, corpora of naturalistic speech and text. The conditions for data-gathering—and hence our approach to it—vary with the particular situation.

We found the descriptive state of each language in the series to be different from that of the others: in some cases, much work had been done, but had never been collected into a single overview; in other cases, virtually no materials in English existed. Similarly, the availability of source material in the target language varies widely: in some cases, literacy and media are very sparse, while for other communities plentiful written texts exist. The authors have worked with the available resources to provide descriptions as comprehensive as these materials, the native speaker consultants, and their own corpora allow.

One of our goals is for these grammars to reach a broad audience. For that reason the authors have worked to make the volumes accessible by providing extensive exemplification and theoretically neutral descriptions oriented to language learners as well as to linguists. All grammars in the series, furthermore, include the native orthography, accompanied where relevant by Romanization. While they are not intended as pedagogical grammars, we realize that in many cases they will supply that role as well.

Each of the grammars is presented as a springboard to further research, which for every language continues to be warranted. We hope that our empirical work will provide a base for theoretical, comparative, computational, and pedagogical developments in the future.

Claudia M. Brugman
Thomas J. Conners
Anne Boyle David
Amalia E. Gnanadesikan

Acknowledgements

This project began largely by accident in 2011 at the University of Maryland's former Center for Advanced Study of Language (CASL). As a new research scientist at CASL and fresh out of my PhD program, I was approached by Matt Heller. Matt had just finished a Somali course that was designed for adults learners of the language with previous success in learning another foreign language. Matt explained to me that he and his classmates had struggled for various reasons throughout their course, in large part because the materials available to them were in some ways written through the lens of European languages, rather than focused on the characteristics of Somali. As a result, their coursebooks treated certain fairly transparent features of Somali (e.g., verb inflection) in a very convoluted way while glossing over others that were much more tricky (e.g., negation strategies and subordination). Charged with coming up with new projects to propose to our Director of Research, I started delving into the literature on Somali to see what we could do to help, and shortly thereafter, I was hooked. My dissertation work was on Bambara, a Mande language spoken in Mali, which has very little morphology and very straightforward morphophonology. All of the sudden, I was faced with tons of morphology and an incredible array of alternations that were only mentioned in passing in the literature. As a phonologist, I was like a kid in a candy store, and my love affair with Somali began. To Matt Heller, I offer a heartfelt *Mahadsanid*!

Much of the early work that went into preparing to write this grammar would not have been possible without my "Team Africa" colleagues, Michelle Morrison and Nikki Adams. Michelle and Nikki were instrumental in teasing apart aspects of the Verb Complex and subordination/coordination, respectively, in our earlier draft technical report "teaching grammar" of Somali. This earlier manuscript provided an outline of sorts which I have expanded upon in creating this book. Unfortunately, upon leaving CASL, I lost access to the parallel Somali-English news corpus from which most of the examples in the teaching grammar were extracted. Thankfully, there are several Somali news corpora that have been cultivated since that time, notably the Norway Ministry of Education, Youth, and Sports *SoWaC* corpus and the University of Gothenburg *KORP* corpus. I have drawn on these fantastic resources in gathering examples and checking usage while creating the current, much expanded reference grammar.

In addition to Michelle and Nikki, other colleagues at CASL were instrumental in the early stages of this project. I am very grateful to Claudia Brugman who graciously provided us insights about a number of syntactic, semantic, and discourse matters during our weekly *Somali Reading Group* and to our research assistants Erin Smith Crabb and Valerie Novak for technical support. Evan Jones, one of the co-editors of this grammar, is also a former CASL research assistant. His encyclopedic knowledge of Somali (and well over a dozen other languages) has been invaluable. He was involved in proofing and editing the teaching grammar and kindly agreed to be involved in editing the current book. He has been not only a brilliant colleague, but also a great friend over the years.

Others who provided support in various ways for Somali research at CASL include Amy Weinberg, Mariah Bauer, Mike Bunting, Joe Danks, Anne David, Jared Linck, Carrie Bonilla, Ewa Golonka, Anton Rytting, Aric Bills, and Mike Maxwell. I should also note that I benefited a great deal from working with the IBM Watson team on their Somali learning platform prototype. Of course, this earlier research would not have been possible without the funding and support from the US Federal Government. I owe a special debt of gratitude to Tom Conners for the key role that he played in facilitating communication between me and the de Gruyter production staff in the year leading up to the completion of this book. Also a huge thank you to Amalia Gnanadesikan who kindly copy-edited the final draft of the manuscript.

The actual drafting of approximately half of the chapters in this book was completed during my 2019 research leave at the University of Gothenburg with the support of funding from the Wenner-Gren foundation. I owe a huge debt of thanks for my time in beautiful Gothenburg, Sweden, to incredible support and encouragement from Laura Downing and Morgan Nilsson. I am especially grateful to Laura for always asking tough questions that helped me to stay out of the analytical weeds and to ensure that this book would be useful to individuals other than Cushiticists and phonologists. I thank Morgan for his incredible patience with me during our *fikas* where I always seemed to have some wild idea to bounce off of him. I'm grateful to them both for their willingness to share data from their own project on Somali vowel harmony. Thanks also to Leora Bar-el for helpful chats about Somali tense and aspect and to Nick Mashkouri, Amanda Edmonds, and Eva-Marie Bloom Ström who always had time for a friendly conversation during my time at UGOT.

Also while in Gothenburg, I was honored to meet with many of the world's experts on Somali and Cushitic languages, including Giorgio Banti, David Le Gac, Martin Orwin, Maarten Mous, Sabrina Bendjaballah, and Francesa DiGarbo, as we presented at the Workshop on Somali Grammar. It was a transformative workshop that spurred inspiration, new perspectives, and collaborations. Indeed, it was at this workshop that I finally met Nicola Lampitelli in person, though we had communicated via email on several occasions in years prior. It was over a few beers in a Gothenburg pub that Nicola and I first discussed collaborating on Somali together. I am deeply indebted to him for taking on the role of co-editor of this grammar. His critical eye and thoughtful comments have been of tremendous benefit to this work.

I am also grateful to other colleagues with whom I've discussed matters related to this grammar and about Somali in general throughout the years. Many thanks to Ruth Kramer, Mary Paster, Sharon Rose, Larry Hyman, David Odden, Abbie Hantgan-Sonko, Michael Marlo, Mike Diercks, Wendell Kimper, Kristine Yu, Will Bennett, Kevin Gabbard, Kyle Jerro, Deborah Morton, and Chris Ehret. Special thanks go to Nina Kaldhol who kindly shared her data on Somali compounds with me and joined me for many long discussions on various aspects of Somali, both in person in Gothenburg and remotely from La Jolla, California. I'm also very grateful to Laura McPherson for sharing TEX files from her Seenku grammar and offering advice on formatting and other matters related to glossing, indexing, etc. Many thanks to Kirstin Börgen and Birgit Sievert at DeGruyter Mouton and to Simone and Charlotte at Konvertus for their assistance in the technical aspects of the publishing process. I am indebted to the external reviewer of this manuscript for their comments and critique.

At home, I thank Syracuse University, the Department of Languages, Literature, and Linguistics, and especially my colleagues in the Linguistic Studies Program for their support of my research. Also thanks to Chris Miller, John Craddock, Kevin Bailey, Ariel Servadio, Sam Castleberry, Natalie Gallagher, Patrick Smith, and others around Syracuse for their assistance in networking to connect me with local Somali speakers. Thanks also to my family and to Gary for tolerating my special brand of craziness and panic during the completion of this book, which took place during the COVID-19 crisis. An extra special thank you to Gary for his help with designing and editing several figures in the book.

Lastly, but most importantly, this work has only been possible with the patience and kindness of the consultants who have graciously shared their language with me over the years. A huge thank you to Deqa Salhan, Abdi Hussein, Abdullahi Ibrahim, Abduqadir Alqeys, Ahmed Sheikh, and Faadumo Warsame!!!

This material is based upon work supported, in whole or in part, with funding awarded to the University of Maryland, College Park, from the United States Government. Any opinions, findings and conclusions or recommendations expressed in this material are those of the author and do not necessarily reflect the views of the University of Maryland, College Park and/or any agency or entity of the United States Government. This material is being made available for personal or academic research use. If the intention is to use it for commercial reasons, please contact University of Maryland's Office of Technology Commercialization at otc@umd.edu or (301) 405-3947.

Figure 1.1: The *World Factbook* is in the public domain. Accordingly, it may be copied freely without permission. For more information, see `www.cia.gov/library/publications/the-world-factbook/docs/contributor_copyright.html`.

Figure 1.2: Used by permission of the Critical Threats Project at the American Enterprise Institute: `www.criticalthreats.org/analysis/somalia-conflict-maps-islamist-and-political`

Contents

Foreword —— VII

Series Editors' Preface —— IX

Acknowledgements —— XI

Abbreviations —— XXVII

1	**Introduction** —— 1	
1.1	Background —— 1	
1.2	Somali in Somalia and beyond —— 2	
1.3	Classification —— 6	
1.3.1	Ehret & Ali (1984) —— 8	
1.3.2	Lamberti (1984, 1986) —— 9	
1.3.3	Abdullahi (2000) —— 10	
1.3.4	Ismail (2011, 2015) —— 10	
1.4	Major Somali varieties —— 11	
1.4.1	Af-Maxaad Tidhi —— 11	
1.4.2	Northern Somali —— 12	
1.4.2.1	Djibouti Somali —— 13	
1.4.3	Central Somali —— 13	
1.4.4	Benaadir Somali —— 14	
1.5	Previous work on Somali —— 15	
1.5.1	Theoretical literature —— 15	
1.5.2	Reference and pedagogical materials —— 17	
1.6	Other languages of the Somali cluster —— 17	
1.6.1	Ashraaf (Marka, Shingani, Xamar) —— 17	
1.6.2	Maay (Maay-Maay) —— 18	
1.7	Somali in the diaspora —— 18	
1.8	Data sources —— 19	
1.9	Outline of this book —— 19	
2	**Orthography** —— 21	
2.1	Perso-Arabic —— 21	
2.2	Cismaaniya (Osmania) —— 21	
2.3	Gadabuursi —— 23	
2.4	Official orthography —— 23	

3	**Segmental Phonology —— 27**	
3.1	Consonants —— 27	
3.1.1	Establishing stop contrasts —— 31	
3.1.1.1	/b̥/ - (orthographic *b*) —— 34	
3.1.1.2	/d̥/ - (orthographic *d*) —— 34	
3.1.1.3	/g̥/ - (orthographic *g*) —— 35	
3.1.1.4	/tʰ/ - (orthographic *t*) —— 35	
3.1.1.5	/kʰ/ - (orthographic *k*) —— 36	
3.1.1.6	/q/ - (orthographic *q*) —— 37	
3.1.1.7	/ɖ/ - (orthographic *dh*) —— 37	
3.1.1.8	/ʔ/ - (orthographic *c*) —— 38	
3.1.1.9	/ʔ/ - (orthographic ') —— 39	
3.1.2	Other consonants —— 39	
3.1.2.1	/tʃ/ - (orthographic *j*) —— 39	
3.1.2.2	/m/ - (orthographic *m*) —— 40	
3.1.2.3	/n/ and /n̥/ - (orthographic *n*) —— 40	
3.1.2.4	/f/ - (orthographic *f*) —— 42	
3.1.2.5	/s/ - (orthographic *s*) —— 42	
3.1.2.6	/ʃ/ - (orthographic *sh*) —— 43	
3.1.2.7	/χ/ - (orthographic *kh*) —— 43	
3.1.2.8	/н/ - (orthographic *x*) —— 44	
3.1.2.9	/h/ - (orthographic *h*) —— 44	
3.1.2.10	/l/ and /l̥/ - (orthographic *l*) —— 45	
3.1.2.11	/r/ and /r̥/ - (orthographic *r*) —— 45	
3.1.2.12	/j/ - (orthographic *y*) —— 47	
3.1.2.13	/w/ - (orthographic *w*) —— 48	
3.1.3	Geminate consonants —— 48	
3.1.3.1	Geminate stops —— 49	
3.1.3.2	Geminate sonorants —— 50	
3.1.3.3	"Virtual geminates" —— 52	
3.2	Vowels —— 53	
3.2.1	[-ATR] short vowels - ɪ, ɛ, u, ɔ, a —— 59	
3.2.2	[+ATR] short vowels - i, e, ɯ, ɤ, æ —— 60	
3.2.3	[-ATR] long vowels - ɪɪ, ɛɛ, uu, ɔɔ, aa —— 60	
3.2.4	[+ATR] long vowels - ii, ee, ɯɯ, ɤɤ, ææ —— 61	
3.2.5	Diphthongs —— 61	
3.3	Vowel harmony —— 63	
3.3.1	In the nominal system —— 64	
3.3.2	In the verbal system —— 64	
3.3.3	Fronting/raising harmony —— 65	
3.4	Alternations —— 65	
3.4.1	Epenthesis —— 65	

3.4.2	Deaspiration —— 66	
3.4.3	Degemination —— 69	
3.4.4	Manner assimilation —— 70	
3.4.5	Consonant deletion —— 72	
3.4.6	Voicing —— 72	
3.4.7	Spirantization —— 73	
3.4.8	Vowel height alternations —— 74	
3.4.9	Debuccalization —— 75	
3.4.10	Assibilation —— 76	
3.4.11	Palatalization —— 78	
3.4.12	Metathesis —— 79	
3.5	V/Ø alternation —— 80	
4	**Syllable structure and phonotactics —— 85**	
4.1	Syllable structure —— 85	
4.2	Word shape and size requirements —— 86	
4.3	Phonotactics —— 87	
4.3.1	Word-initial and intervocalic consonant distribution —— 87	
4.3.2	Consonant distribution in codas —— 88	
4.3.3	Syllable contact sequences —— 89	
4.3.3.1	Sequences in roots —— 92	
4.3.3.2	Sequences created by V/Ø alternation —— 94	
4.3.3.3	Sequences in compounds and inflected forms —— 95	
4.3.3.4	Sequences in borrowings —— 95	
4.4	Loanword adaptation —— 96	
4.4.1	Segmental repair —— 96	
4.4.2	Phonotactic repair —— 97	
4.5	Poetic metrics —— 98	
5	**Tone —— 101**	
5.1	Introduction —— 101	
5.2	High tone assignment —— 102	
5.2.1	Nouns —— 102	
5.2.2	Verbs —— 105	
5.2.3	Other parts of speech —— 105	
5.3	Tone alternations —— 106	
5.3.1	Rightward H shift —— 106	
5.3.2	Premodifier H shift —— 109	
5.3.3	Other alternations —— 110	
5.4	Phrasal phenomena —— 110	
5.4.1	Subject Marking —— 110	
5.4.2	Associative High —— 111	

5.4.3	Vocative High —— 112	
5.5	Intonation —— 112	
5.5.1	High and Low boundary tones —— 113	
5.5.2	L tone of focalization —— 115	
5.5.3	Statements vs. questions —— 116	
6	**Nominal morphology —— 119**	
6.1	Gender and agreement —— 119	
6.2	Class and number —— 120	
6.2.1	Class 1: -ó plurals —— 121	
6.2.1.1	Class 1a: T singular / K plural —— 121	
6.2.1.2	Class 1b: K singular / T plural —— 122	
6.2.1.3	Class 1C: K singular / K plural —— 123	
6.2.2	Class 2: Reduplication plurals —— 123	
6.2.3	Class 3: Singular nouns ending in -e —— 124	
6.2.4	Class 4: Singular nouns ending in -o —— 125	
6.2.5	Irregular nouns —— 126	
6.2.5.1	Nouns using Arabic pluralization strategies —— 126	
6.2.5.2	'Prosodic plurals' —— 128	
6.2.6	Singulatives —— 129	
6.2.7	Double pluralization by -o-yaál —— 129	
6.2.8	Number marking summary —— 130	
6.3	Derivation —— 130	
6.3.1	Noun-to-noun derivation —— 131	
6.3.1.1	Abstract nouns with -nimó —— 131	
6.3.1.2	Abstract nouns with -iyád —— 131	
6.3.1.3	Abstract nouns with -tooyó —— 132	
6.3.1.4	Antonyms with -darró —— 133	
6.3.1.5	-éen —— 133	
6.3.2	Deverbal nouns —— 134	
6.3.2.1	-niin —— 134	
6.3.2.2	-n —— 134	
6.3.2.3	-ashó —— 134	
6.3.2.4	-itáan —— 134	
6.3.2.5	-aal —— 135	
6.3.2.6	Deverbal nouns with -tín —— 135	
6.3.2.7	Agentive nouns with -é —— 136	
6.3.2.8	Agentive nouns with -áa —— 136	
6.3.2.9	Instrumental nouns with -é —— 137	
6.3.2.10	Uncountable and collective nouns with -tó —— 137	
6.3.3	Ownership nouns with -le —— 137	
6.3.3.1	Collective nouns with -leý —— 138	

6.3.4	Abstract state nouns with *-aán* —— **139**	
6.3.5	Derivational morphology summary —— **139**	
6.4	Gerunds —— **139**	
6.5	Vocative marking —— **141**	
6.5.1	Noun vocative —— **141**	
6.5.2	Name vocative —— **142**	
6.5.3	Prosodic vocative —— **142**	
6.6	Associative marking —— **142**	
7	**Verbs and verbal morphology** —— **145**	
7.1	Stem types —— **146**	
7.1.1	Bare (Underived) —— **147**	
7.1.2	Experiencer —— **147**	
7.1.3	Inchoative —— **148**	
7.1.4	Reciprocal —— **149**	
7.1.5	Weak Causative —— **150**	
7.1.6	Factitive —— **151**	
7.1.7	Middle —— **153**	
7.1.8	Neuter —— **155**	
7.1.9	Strong Causative —— **156**	
7.1.10	Adjectival participles —— **158**	
7.2	Inflection —— **159**	
7.3	Infinitives —— **163**	
7.4	Auxiliary verbs —— **163**	
7.5	Main clause suffixing verbs —— **164**	
7.5.1	Realis contexts —— **166**	
7.5.1.1	Simple Present —— **166**	
7.5.1.2	Present Progressive —— **166**	
7.5.1.3	Simple Past —— **167**	
7.5.1.4	Past Progressive —— **168**	
7.5.1.5	Emphatic Past —— **169**	
7.5.2	Irrealis contexts —— **169**	
7.5.2.1	Simple Present Negative —— **169**	
7.5.2.2	Present Progressive Negative —— **170**	
7.5.2.3	Optative —— **171**	
7.5.3	Auxiliary constructions —— **172**	
7.5.3.1	Past Habitual —— **172**	
7.5.3.2	Conditional —— **173**	
7.5.3.3	Future —— **173**	
7.5.4	Other moods —— **174**	
7.5.4.1	Imperative —— **174**	
7.5.4.2	Potential —— **175**	

7.6	Main clause prefixing verbs —— 176	
7.6.1	Realis contexts —— 177	
7.6.1.1	Simple Present —— 177	
7.6.1.2	Present Progressive —— 178	
7.6.1.3	Simple Past —— 178	
7.6.1.4	Past Progressive —— 179	
7.6.1.5	Emphatic Past —— 180	
7.6.2	Irrealis contexts —— 180	
7.6.2.1	Simple Present Negative —— 180	
7.6.2.2	Present Progressive Negative —— 181	
7.6.2.3	Optative —— 182	
7.6.3	Auxiliary constructions —— 182	
7.6.3.1	Past Habitual —— 182	
7.6.3.2	Conditional —— 183	
7.6.3.3	Future —— 183	
7.6.4	Other moods —— 184	
7.6.4.1	Imperative —— 184	
7.6.4.2	Potential —— 184	
7.7	Irregular verbs —— 185	
7.7.1	Realis contexts —— 185	
7.7.1.1	Simple Present and Present Progressive —— 185	
7.7.1.2	Simple Past and Past Progressive —— 186	
7.7.2	Irrealis contexts —— 187	
7.7.2.1	Simple Present Negative —— 187	
7.7.2.2	Present Progressive Negative —— 187	
7.7.2.3	Optative —— 188	
7.7.3	Auxiliary constructions —— 188	
7.7.3.1	Past Habitual —— 188	
7.7.3.2	Conditional —— 189	
7.7.3.3	Future —— 189	
7.7.4	Other moods —— 190	
7.7.4.1	Imperative —— 190	
7.7.4.2	Potential —— 190	
7.8	Reduced agreement —— 191	
7.8.1	Prefixing and suffixing verbs —— 191	
7.8.2	Irregular verbs —— 194	
7.9	Subordinate clause verbs —— 196	
7.9.1	Complement, adverbial, and object relative clauses —— 196	
7.9.2	Suffixing verbs —— 198	
7.9.3	Prefixing verbs —— 199	
7.9.4	Irregular verbs —— 201	
7.9.5	Subject relative clauses —— 202	

7.9.6	Negation —— **204**	
7.10	Inflection summary —— **204**	
7.11	Hybrid verbs —— **207**	
8	**Compounds —— 211**	
8.1	Nominal compounds —— **211**	
8.1.1	Noun + Noun —— **212**	
8.1.2	Noun + Agentive Noun —— **213**	
8.1.3	Noun + Ownership Noun —— **214**	
8.1.4	Associative Compounds —— **214**	
8.1.5	Noun + Deverbal Noun —— **215**	
8.1.6	Noun + Gerund —— **215**	
8.1.7	Noun + Verb —— **216**	
8.1.8	Noun + Adjective —— **216**	
8.1.9	Noun + Adposition/Adverbial + Verb —— **216**	
8.2	Verbal compounds —— **217**	
8.2.1	Object Incorporation —— **217**	
8.2.2	Lexicalized compounds —— **219**	
8.2.3	Subject incorporation —— **220**	
8.3	Light verb constructions —— **220**	
8.4	Ideophones —— **221**	
8.5	Phrasal verbs —— **222**	
9	**The noun phrase —— 225**	
9.1	Noun categories —— **226**	
9.1.1	Count nouns —— **226**	
9.1.2	Corporate nouns —— **227**	
9.1.3	Uncountable nouns —— **228**	
9.1.3.1	Mass nouns —— **228**	
9.1.3.2	Collective nouns —— **229**	
9.1.3.3	Pluralia tantum —— **230**	
9.1.3.4	Summary of countable vs. uncountable nouns —— **231**	
9.1.4	Proper nouns —— **231**	
9.1.5	Color terms —— **232**	
9.1.6	Numerics —— **232**	
9.1.6.1	Cardinal numbers —— **232**	
9.1.6.2	Ordinal numbers —— **233**	
9.1.6.3	Approximate numbers —— **234**	
9.1.7	Ideophones —— **234**	
9.1.8	Independent personal pronouns —— **234**	
9.2	Subject marking —— **235**	
9.2.1	H tone loss —— **237**	

9.2.2	H tone loss with *-i*, *-yi*, or *-u* —— 238	
9.2.3	Vowel alternation —— 238	
9.2.4	No overt realization —— 238	
9.3	Determiners —— 239	
9.3.1	Possessive determiners —— 240	
9.3.2	Demonstrative determiners —— 241	
9.3.3	Remote definite determiner —— 242	
9.3.4	Definite determiner —— 244	
9.3.5	Interrogative determiner —— 245	
9.4	Lexical adjectives —— 246	
9.5	Associative constructions —— 248	
9.5.1	Prosodic associatives —— 249	
9.5.1.1	With possessive determiners —— 250	
9.5.2	Suffixing associatives with *-eéd*, *-oód*, *-aád* —— 250	
9.5.2.1	With count nouns —— 251	
9.5.2.2	Ordinal numbers —— 251	
9.6	Attributive relative clauses —— 252	
9.7	Other clitics —— 252	
9.7.1	Negative *-na* —— 252	
9.7.2	Intensifier *-ba* —— 253	
10	**The Verb Complex —— 255**	
10.1	The verb slot —— 256	
10.2	Pronoun clitics —— 257	
10.2.1	Subject pronoun clitics —— 258	
10.2.2	Impersonal subject pronoun —— 261	
10.2.3	First series object pronouns —— 264	
10.2.4	Reflexive/reciprocal pronoun —— 267	
10.3	Second series object pronouns —— 269	
10.4	Deictic particles —— 271	
10.4.1	Ventive *soó* —— 272	
10.4.2	Itive *sií* —— 273	
10.5	Adverbial particles —— 274	
10.5.1	*wada* —— 274	
10.5.2	*kala* —— 275	
10.6	Adpositions —— 276	
10.6.1	*ú* —— 278	
10.6.2	*kú* —— 279	
10.6.3	*ká* —— 280	
10.6.4	*lá* —— 281	
10.7	Adposition clusters —— 281	
10.7.1	Two adpositions —— 281	

10.7.2	Three adpositions —— 282	
10.7.3	OPC + one adposition —— 283	
10.7.4	OPC + two adpositions —— 284	
10.7.5	OPC + three adpositions —— 285	
10.7.6	Clusters with the ISP —— 286	
10.7.7	Clusters with the RRP —— 288	
10.8	Negative *má* —— 289	

11 Focus markers —— 293

11.1	Pre-verbal focus —— 294
11.1.1	báa —— 295
11.1.1.1	With a subject pronoun clitic —— 295
11.1.1.2	With negative *aán* —— 296
11.1.1.3	With interrogative *ma* —— 298
11.1.1.4	Coalescence with a preceding noun phrase —— 298
11.1.2	ayáa —— 299
11.1.2.1	With a subject pronoun clitic —— 299
11.1.2.2	With negative *aán* —— 300
11.1.2.3	With interrogative *ma* —— 301
11.1.2.4	With interrogative *ma* and negative *aán* —— 302
11.2	Post-verbal focus —— 303
11.2.1	With negative *aán* —— 306
11.2.2	With interrogative *ma* —— 307
11.2.3	With interrogative *ma* and negative *aán* —— 308
11.3	The subject focus condition —— 308
11.3.1	Verb inflection —— 309
11.3.2	Pronoun clitics —— 310
11.3.3	Subject marking —— 311
11.4	The object focus condition —— 311
11.4.1	Verb inflection —— 312
11.4.2	Pronoun clitics —— 312
11.4.3	Subject marking —— 313

12 Main clauses without focus marking —— 315

12.1	Declarative *waa* —— 316
12.1.1	wáaye ~ wéeye —— 318
12.2	Negative *má* —— 319
12.3	Interrogative *ma* —— 321
12.4	Optative —— 323
12.5	Potential —— 324
12.6	Imperative —— 325

13	**Information structure —— 327**
13.1	Broad Focus —— 327
13.2	Narrow focus —— 328
13.2.1	Narrow subject focus —— 329
13.2.2	Narrow object focus —— 329
13.3	Topicalization —— 330
13.3.1	Object topicalization / Subject focus —— 330
13.3.2	Subject topicalization / Object focus —— 330
13.4	Retopicalization via right dislocation —— 331
13.4.1	Subject dislocation —— 331
13.4.2	Object dislocation —— 332
13.4.3	Word order summary —— 332
13.5	Other discourse functions of focus —— 333
13.5.1	Contrastive focus —— 333
13.5.2	Cataphoric focus —— 334
13.5.3	Narrative focus —— 335
13.6	Focusing other constituents —— 337
13.6.1	Adverbs and adverbial clauses —— 337
13.6.2	Relative clauses —— 339
13.6.3	Complement clauses —— 340
13.6.4	Reported speech —— 341
13.6.5	Coordinated phrases and clauses —— 342
13.7	Focus without focus markers —— 343
13.8	Detopicalization strategies —— 343
14	**Subordination —— 347**
14.1	Relative clauses —— 347
14.1.1	Headedness —— 348
14.1.2	Relative/Antecedent relationship —— 349
14.1.2.1	Subject-Subject —— 349
14.1.2.2	Object-Subject —— 351
14.1.2.3	Subject-Object —— 352
14.1.2.4	Object-Object —— 354
14.1.3	Negation —— 356
14.1.4	Restrictive vs. non-restrictive —— 359
14.1.5	Attributive relative clauses with nominal complements —— 362
14.1.5.1	with 'be' —— 362
14.1.5.2	with 'have' —— 364
14.1.5.3	with 'lack' —— 366
14.1.5.4	with 'hold, possess' —— 366
14.1.6	Attributive relative clauses with hybrid verbs —— 367
14.1.7	Indirect counting —— 369

14.2	Complement clauses —— 369
14.3	Subordinating adverbial clauses —— 374
14.3.1	Time —— 374
14.3.2	Purpose and reason —— 377
14.3.3	Concession and condition —— 379
14.3.4	Manner —— 381
14.3.5	Location —— 382
15	**Coordination and other adverbials —— 383**
15.1	Coordination with coordinators —— 383
15.1.1	Conjunction with *iyo* —— 383
15.1.2	Disjunction with *ama* —— 385
15.1.3	Contrastive conjunction with *laakíin* —— 388
15.2	Coordination with clitics —— 389
15.2.1	Conjunction with *-na* —— 389
15.2.2	Disjunction with *-se* —— 390
15.3	Coordinating relative clauses —— 392
15.3.1	Non-restrictive coordination with *oo* —— 393
15.3.2	Restrictive coordination with *ee* —— 394
15.3.3	Restrictive/Non-restrictive coordination —— 395
15.4	Coordinating larger constituents —— 396
15.4.1	with *oo* —— 396
15.4.2	with *ee* —— 398
15.5	Coordinating adverbials —— 398
15.5.1	Time —— 399
15.5.2	Purpose and reason —— 400
15.5.3	Concession —— 401
15.5.4	Manner —— 401
15.6	Other adverbials —— 402
15.6.1	Time —— 402
15.6.2	Location —— 403
15.6.3	Manner —— 404
15.7	Comparatives and superlatives —— 404
16	**Questions —— 407**
16.1	Content questions —— 407
16.1.1	Who? / Whom? - *yáa, kúma/túma* —— 408
16.1.2	When? - *goórma* —— 410
16.1.3	Where? - *xaggeé, halkeé, meesheé* —— 411
16.1.4	What? - *maxá(a)* —— 413
16.1.5	Why? - *maxá(a)...ú* —— 415
16.1.6	How? - *sideé* —— 416

16.1.7	How much? / How many? - *ímmisa* —— 417	
16.1.8	How long? / How much? / From where? - *inteé* —— 419	
16.2	Polar questions —— 419	
16.2.1	*miyáa* as a general question marker —— 421	
16.3	Choice questions —— 422	
16.3.1	With an interrogative determiner —— 423	
16.3.2	With the interrogative clitic *=ma* —— 423	
16.3.3	With *meé* —— 423	
16.4	Tag questions —— 424	
16.4.1	*misé máya* - or not? —— 424	
16.4.2	*s(h)ów...má aha* - isn't it? —— 424	
A	**Appendix - Suffixing verb paradigms** —— 427	
A.1	Bare (underived) stems —— 428	
A.2	Experiencer stems —— 430	
A.3	Inchoative stems —— 433	
A.4	Reciprocal stems —— 436	
A.5	Weak causative stems —— 439	
A.6	Factitive stems —— 442	
A.7	Middle stems —— 445	
A.8	Neuter stems —— 448	
A.9	Strong causative stems —— 451	
A.10	Weak causative & middle stems —— 454	

Bibliography —— 459

Index —— 473

Abbreviations

1	first person
2	second person
3	third person
∅	null or unrealized morpheme
-	segmentable morpheme boundary
.	non-segmentable morpheme boundary, syllable boundary
:	morpheme coalescence
=	clitic boundary
#	word boundary
*	unattested form
~	variation, alternative pronunciation
/ /	underlying (phonological) form
[ ]	surface (phonetic) form
ADV	adverbial
AGT	Agentive
ASSOC	associative
C	consonant
COM	comparative
COMP	complementizer
CONJ	conjunction
DEC	Declarative
DEF	definite determiner
EXC	exclusive
FACT	Factitive
F	feminine
FOC	focus
FUT	future
G	glide consonant, geminate consonant
GER	gerundive
K	K-series agreement
IDEF	interrogative determiner
IDEO	ideophone
IMP	Imperative
INC	inclusive
INCH	Inchoative
INF	infinitive
INT	intensifier
IRR	irrealis
ISP	impersonal subject pronoun

ITV	itive
lit.	literal translation
LVC	light verb construction
M	Masculine
MID	Middle
NEU	Neuter
NEG	negative
NOM	Nominalizer
OBJ	object
OPC	object pronoun clitic
OPT	optative
orth.	orthographic
PL	Plural
POT	potential
PRES	Present
PROG	Progressive
PST	Past
PWd	Prosodic Word
QM	question marker
RDEF	remote definite determiner
Red	reduplicant
RED	reduced agreement
REL	relativizer
RECIP	Reciprocal
RRP	reflexive-reciprocal object pronoun
RSLT	Resultative
SCAUS	Strong Causative
SG	Singular
s.o.	someone
SPC	subject pronoun clitic
s.t.	something
STV	Stative
SUP	superlative
SUBJ	Subject Marker
T	T-series agreement
TBU	tone bearing unit
WCAUS	Weak Causative
V	vowel
VC	Verb Complex
VEN	ventive

1 Introduction

1.1 Background

Somali, or Af-Soomaali, is the official language of the Federal Republic of Somalia. Somali is also spoken in parts of neighboring Djibouti, Ethiopia, and in Kenya, as well as in diaspora communities concentrated in a growing number of cities in North America, Europe, and the Middle East. Somali is identified by the official registration authority for human languages with the International Organization for Standardization code [som] under ISO 639-3. Its Glottocode (`glottolog.org`) is *soma1255*.

It is estimated that there are approximately 16 million Somali speakers worldwide, most of whom are mother tongue (L1) speakers of the language (Eberhard et al., 2019). However, only approximately half of these individuals reside in Somalia itself. This distribution stems in large part from longstanding political instability and dangerous conditions in some parts of Somalia that have contributed to a flow of emigrants and refugees out of the Horn of Africa over many decades. Efforts aimed at partial repatriation supported by the United Nations Refugee Agency have met with only moderate success. The International Organization for Migration reports that thousands of migrants continue to flow each year out of South-Central Somalia in particular.

Linguistic research on Somali has enjoyed a long history, though the political situation in and around Somalia has hindered *in situ* research on the language for many years. Despite this, linguists have continued to work with speakers in diaspora communities around the globe, and there has been a noticeable uptick in new research emerging on Somali in the past decade. This research has primarily been undertaken by linguists whose consultants have resettled in different areas of the world. These diaspora varieties of Somali sometimes reveal subtle divergences from what is reported in the older descriptive linguistics literature and that is presumably representative of the Somali spoken (at least historically) in Somalia and its environs.

The research upon which this book is based grew out of such consultation with two diaspora Somali speakers living in the Washington, DC metro area. The primary goal of this earlier work conducted at the University of Maryland's former Center for Advanced Study of Language (CASL) was the creation of a teaching grammar for adult English-speaking learners of Somali. I served as the co-Principal Investigator overseeing the Somali project alongside Dr. Michelle Morrison. Upon leaving the University of Maryland, I began subsequent research aimed at reconfiguring and expanding the content contained in the teaching grammar, the product of which is the current book. This research was done in consultation with Somali speakers located in Sweden and facilitated by Professor Laura Downing and Senior Lecturer Morgan Nilsson at the University of Gothenburg, as well as with Somali speakers located in Syracuse, NY.

This book is about Somali grammar, but it does not pretend to be comprehensive. There is widespread variation among Somali speakers in many facets of the language, and there are many varieties that fall under the Somali umbrella that I have not encountered personally. As such, this book is not necessarily representative of all Somali varieties and all Somali speakers. In writing this book, I have focused on two modest goals. First, I aim to highlight findings that have emerged in the linguistics literature on Somali since Saeed's seminal 1999 reference grammar, such as in the areas of gender and number inflection, the connection between prosodic structure and morphophonological alternations, the language's tonal system, and compounding, among other topics. Of course, there is a great deal of new research that has emerged on Somali syntax as well. I hope that the reader will find the current work to be more comprehensive than Saeed (1999) in that it includes a number of topics that were not represented or otherwise not discussed in detail by Saeed. A second goal of this book is to bring into balance what we know about Somali phonology and morphology and the role that prosodic structure plays in its grammar relative to the much richer literature that has concentrated on the language's syntax and information structure.

1.2 Somali in Somalia and beyond

Compared to most other African countries where dozens, if not hundreds of indigenous languages are spoken, Somalia is, linguistically, fairly homogeneous. Somali is, by far, the most widely spoken first language in Somalia. Other Cushitic languages (e.g., Maay and Ashraaf, among others) are spoken in areas primarily in the southern part of the country. In addition, there are several ethnic minorities concentrated along Somalia's southern coast who speak other non-Cushitic languages, among these being *Somali Bantus* who speak coastal varieties of Swahili such as Zigula (also called Mushunguli or Mushungulu), ChiMwiini, and Bajuni. Even among these groups, Somali is a lingua franca, at least among some cross-section of the population. Lamberti (1984) reports that among minority ethnic groups, Somali is mostly spoken as a second language (L2) by men and children, while women tend not to use the language. It is without a doubt that longstanding unrest and the precarious state of the political climate in Somalia has also contributed greatly to its linguistic landscape.

Within Somalia itself, clan membership and a culture of nomadic pastoralism have contributed to the insular nature of certain populations and their languages. Though historical resources like Lewis (1955, 1999, 2002, 2010) describe a high degree of nationalist cohesion among Somalis, it is clan membership that forms the strongest ties within Somali society. There is an overarching emphasis on clan identity, and clan allegiance is often valued more highly than allegiance to the state itself. However, while clan allegiances are significant, so too are clan cleavages (Gajraj et al. 2005), which some suggest have historically been exploited by government officials for political gain (Kleist 2008).

Somali clans are patrineal and trace their origins to a single male ancestor (Hagi and Hagi 1998). The primary clan division in Somalia is between the Samaale and the

Sab. The term "Somali" itself has its roots in the name of the Samaale clan, though see Mansur (1984) for a different interpretation. Lewis (1955) and Abdullahi (2000) argue that the members of Sab sub-clans do not consider themselves to be Somalis owing to this etymological connection to the Samaale clan. As one might imagine, this further strains national cohesion.

It is important to arrive at some sense of the Somali clan structure as it sometimes pertains to linguistic description. For example, there are older works written about Somali that define a given variety based on clan name. See, for example, works on Isaaq Somali by Andrzejewski (1955, 1956). Also, and from a more practical standpoint, clan division has true linguistic correlates. That is, the Samaale group consists of four main clans – Isaaq, Hawiye, Dir, and Daarood. Individuals within these clans speak varieties or dialects that generally fall under the modern linguistic conception of the Somali language. Within the Sab clan, there are two major sub-clans - Digil and Rahanweyn (also called Maay) - whose members, as discussed in §1.3, speak language varieties that are contemporarily considered to be altogether different languages from Somali.

I have included a political map of what is generally thought of as the physical extent of Somalia in Figure 1.1, though the situation is far more complicated than this map would lead one to believe. This is unsurprising given that the political boundaries of most African nations were arbitrarily drawn by Europeans colonialists. As such, there are sizable populations of Somali speakers living in modern day eastern Kenya, in Djibouti, and in the Somali (formerly Ogaden) region of Ethiopia. Though Somalis are among the minority in these other nations, they enjoy benefits and protections not afforded to them in their homeland.

The arbitrary nature of Somalia's physical boundaries compared to the extent of what is historically ethnic Somali territory is still apparent today. This is because colonial Somalia was once divided into four administrative regions claimed by the United Kingdom, Italy, France, and Ethiopia. French claims ultimately became modern-day Djibouti, while Ethiopian claims were incorporated into Ethiopia and constitute that country's eastern Somali region mentioned just above. Land claimed by the United Kingdom constitutes the present day *de facto* sovereign territory of Somaliland which extends inland from the Gulf of Aden. The northern portion of the Italian-claimed area now constitutes another autonomous region of Somalia called Puntland. Remaining portions of the former Italian territory comprise the Federal Republic of Somalia, which includes the capital enclave, Mogadishu (Muqdisho), and other lands that technically remain under the oversight of the Somali federal government. Even within this area, however, governmental control is tenuous. There are other semi-autonomous regions, and some areas are controlled by warlords and militants, some of whom are known to be aligned with the jihadist organization Al-Shabaab. A rendering of the political areas of control as of February 2010 is in Figure 1.2, as reported by the American Enterprise Institute's Critical Threats Project (www.criticalthreats.org).

Fig. 1.1: Political map of Somalia (US Central Intelligence Agency 2020)

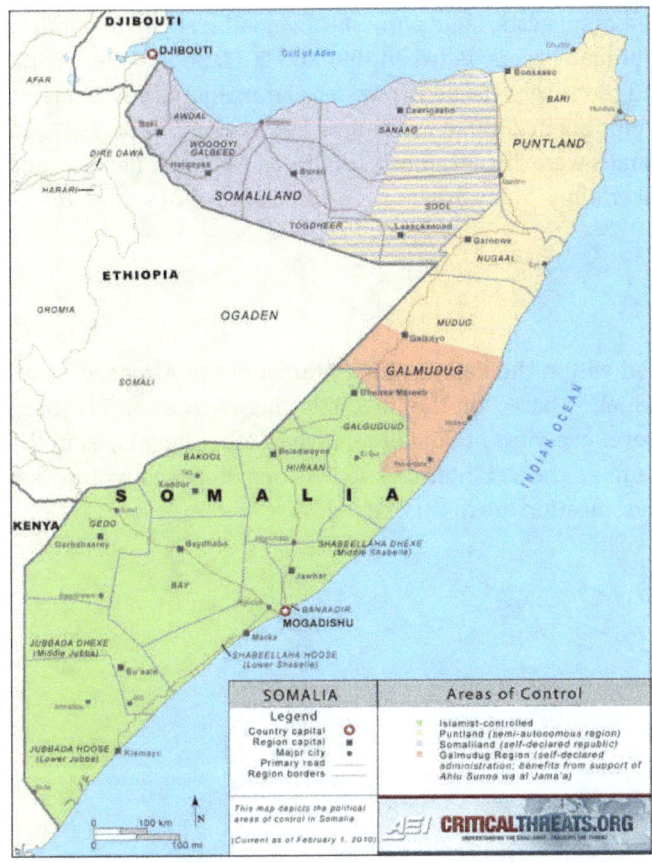

Fig. 1.2: Political areas of control, as of February 2010. Used with permission of the Critical Threats Project at the American Enterprise Institute.

As this territorial state of affairs suggests, large portions of Somalia remain in political turmoil and have been so for many years. Between 1991 and 2012, Somalia was without a democratically-elected central government. A series of transitional governments were in place, however, beginning in 2000. According to Putman and Noor (1993), in the early 1990s, 45% of Somalis were displaced from their homes or had fled Somalia altogether in the face of uncertainty. Many others were killed or died of starvation.

1.3 Classification

Somali is typically classified within the East Cushitic branch of the Afroasiatic language family. Figure 1.3, which is based on the linguistic classification in Eberhard et al. (2019), gives a high level overview of Somali relative to other languages in the family. This does not reflect finer-grained internal subdivisions proposed within East Cushitic. Other views on classification are discussed below.

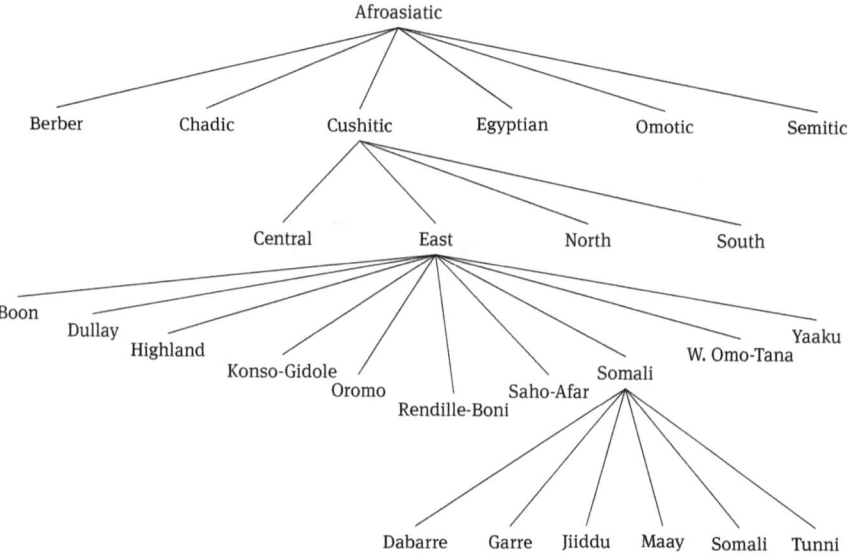

Fig. 1.3: Somali genetic tree (based on Eberhard et al. 2019)

Of those languages assigned codes by the ISO, Somali is mostly closely related to Dabarre [iso:dbr], Garre [iso:gex], Jiiddu [iso:jii], Tunni [iso:tqq], and Maay [iso:ymm]. In addition, Somali shares many similarities with Ashraaf, though this language has yet to be assigned an ISO code and is therefore absent from Eberhard et al.'s classification and, accordingly, from Figure 1.3. All of the aforementioned language varieties are spoken primarily in Somalia, but their mutual intelligibility with Somali is not always high.

Somali speakers have historically been in contact with speakers of other larger Cushitic languages like Afar and Oromo, and Semitic languages like Amharic and Harari. Arabic has had a notable influence on Somali, particularly in its lexicon, but also to some extent in its grammar and morphology (Banti, 2013; Zaborski, 1967), as a result of centuries of commercial and religious contact. In addition to many Arabic borrowings in its lexicon, there are also borrowed words from Italian, English, French, Persian, and Hindi found in Somali. Influence from English in particular continues to grow due to an influx of vocabulary in the areas of science, technology, medicine, and industry. The influence of French remains predominant in Djibouti.

Determining which language variety (or, better yet, varieties) one should properly consider to be 'Somali' is not always clear from the literature. This is because studies devoted to the classification of Somali and its linguistic kin sometimes approach the matter from differing perspectives and do not arrive at all the same conclusions. Classifications include Ehret and Ali (1984), Heine (1978), Lamberti (1984), and Moreno (1955). For a summary and discussion of these proposals, see Tosco (2012). More recent classifications are proposed by Abdullahi (2000) and Ismail (2011).

Four different perspectives on Somali classification are compared below. There are, of course, a number of other classifications that have been proposed that deal with higher-level groupings within the Afro-Asiatic family and the inter-relatedness between different phyla therein, among them Ehret (2011), Hetzron (1980), Sasse (1978), Tosco (2000), and famously Greenberg (1963). I limit my discussion to Somali and its closest kin, to the extent possible.

Classifications tend to recognize a distinction between two (though sometimes three) highly mutually intelligible *dialects* of Somali. The first, commonly called *Northern* Somali is cited as forming the basis of "standard" Somali, and its properties are historically reflected in literacy materials and in the language's official orthography. The counterpart of Northern Somali is sometimes referred to as *Benaadir* Somali and elsewhere as *Central* Somali.[1] Abdullahi (2000), however, proposes that Benaadir and Central Somali are different varieties and should be distinguished from one another. For Abdullahi, Central Somali refers to the variety of Somali spoken in non-coastal areas of geographic central and southern Somalia. It more closely resembles Northern Somali, differing from it mostly in fairly subtle phonological ways. Benaadir Somali, on the other hand, Abdullahi describes as being spoken in coastal areas and exhibits certain characteristics that render it less like Northern Somali. These distinguishing characteristics are said to have arisen due to a greater degree of mixing with Maay, Arabic, and dialects of Swahili spoken along the southern coast

---

[1] Several works purported to discuss "Central" Somali in fact discuss Rahanweyn (also called Maay). These include Angoujard (1989), Biber (1982, 1984b), and Saeed (1982a).

of Somalia (e.g., ChiMwiimi, Bajuni, and Zigula). Abdullahi suggests that Somali is best considered a dialect continuum whose major dialects (Northern, Central, and Benaadir) gradually diverge from one another in a roughly north to south direction.

Abdullahi is, of course, not the first scholar to recognize the many shared properties of these Somali varieties. Being highly mutually intelligible with one another, they are often collectively referred to as *Af-Maxaad Tidhi* in recognition of their relative homogeneity and to distinguish them from other languages of southern Somalia, such as Maay and those of the Digil (Dhigil) clans. *Af-Maxaad Tidhi* is derived from the question *Maxaad tidhi?* meaning 'What did you say?' The idea is that 'Somali' varieties that employ this term to mean 'What did you say?' are similar enough to one another to be considered under the umbrella of a singular Somali language.[2]

In addition to these varieties, I also briefly discuss Djibouti Somali. This particular variety does not often figure into classificatory discussions, which have been historically focused on Somali varieties within the political bounds of Somalia itself. Linguistic studies reporting details specific to Djibouti Somali have emerged in recent years (e.g., Lahrouchi and Lampitelli 2014; Lampitelli 2017, among others) that highlight some of its peculiarities relative to other varieties. The Somali entries in Morin (1995) are also representative of Djibouti Somali. Most scholars agree that Djibouti Somali is best considered a sub-dialect of Northern Somali, as suggested by Banti (2013).

The following sub-sections show that not all classifications converge upon a distinction solely between the Northern, Central, and Benaadir varieties of Somali. Some scholars once considered Maay to be a dialect of Somali, though it has since been designated as a separate language by the ISO. Similarly, some earlier classifications (e.g., Lamberti 1984) considered language varieties spoken by the Digil clans (namely, Dabarre, Tunni, Jiiddu, and Garre) to be Somali dialects. So, too, were even more distant cousins, like Boni and Rendille. These all have since been recognized as separate languages by the ISO, and their designations are reflected in the most recent Ethnologue (Eberhard et al., 2019).

1.3.1 Ehret & Ali (1984)

Ehret and Ali (1984) offer a classification based on a village by village survey of Somali language varieties in Somalia conducted between 1979 and 1982. This is supplemented by data from Somali speakers in Kenya. Dialects are largely pinned to particular towns or cities. The basis of the classification is on the presence of cognates in basic vocab-

---

[2] The equivalent phrase in Maay is *May artee?*, and in Ashraaf, it is *Maa doontee?*. As such, these languages are not typically considered to constitute varieties within Af-Maxaad Tidhi, though Ismail (2011) includes Ashraaf in this group. Most would consideration them members of a larger group which Banti (2013) calls the Somali "cluster."

ulary and shared lexical innovations. A schematization of their findings is in Figure 1.4.

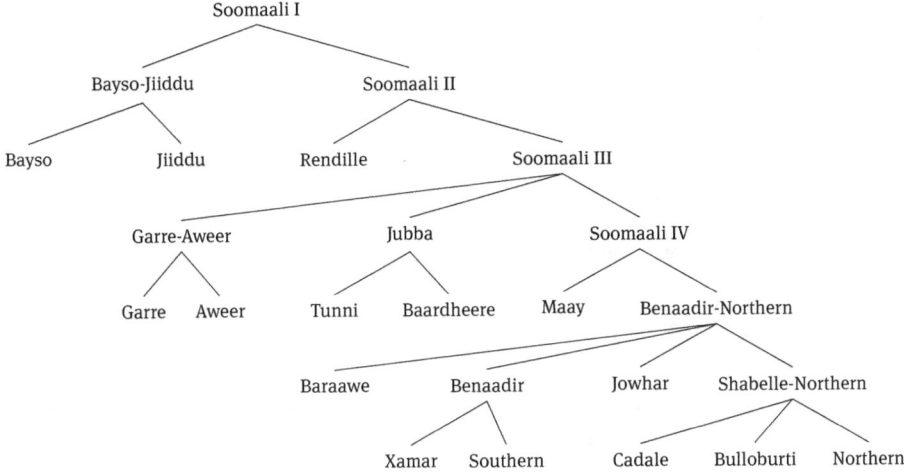

Fig. 1.4: Somali classification (based on Ehret and Ali 1984)

The aim of their larger classification project was to explore the historical divergence of Somali varieties earlier proposed by Sasse (1978). Ehret and Ali marvel at the sheer diversity of languages in the Somali cluster and the surprisingly low lexical similarity that exists even between languages claimed by Sasse to be closely related to one another. This work later became part of Ali's (1985) dissertation project.

1.3.2 Lamberti (1984, 1986)

The classification in Lamberti (1984, 1986) shares similarities with Ehret and Ali (1984). However, Lamberti takes issue with Ehret and Ali's choice to identify Somali "dialects" by the names of towns, rather than by regions. He argues that doing so leaves ambiguous the status of varieties spoken outside of said towns and cities within the surrounding region. Lamberti's classification is schematized in Figure 1.5. Lamberti proposes five Somali dialect groups: Northern, Benaadir, Ashraaf, May (Maay), and Digil. He leaves open the possibility that Jiiddu (classified alongside other Digil varieties) may itself constitute a separate dialect group. Northern Somali is defined as the most homogeneous and wide-reaching variety. Benaadir is said to have several (sub-)dialects which largely correlate with sub-national political boundaries. Ashraaf, which Ehret and Ali (1984) consider to be a sub-type of Benaadir, is granted status as a separate dialect.

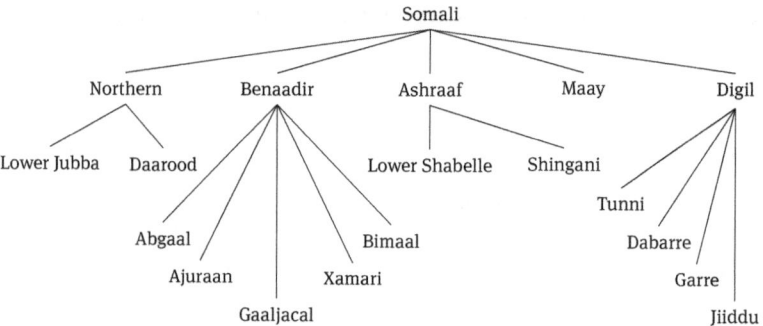

Fig. 1.5: Somali classification (based on Lamberti 1984, 1986)

1.3.3 Abdullahi (2000)

Abdullahi (2000) is a more comprehensive classification based on an amalgamation of phonological, morphological, and lexical characteristics. Abdullahi defines three main dialect groups – Northern, Central, and Benaadir – whose distribution aligns with geographic and/or administrative boundaries. These groups constitute the modern conception of *Af-Maxaad Tidhi* and coincide with what Eberhard et al. (2019) consider to be the Somali language, i.e., iso:[som]. Abdullahi diverges from his predecessors in clearly designating Maay and Digil as language outside of the Somali umbrella.

According to Abdullahi, the Northern, Central, and Benaadir dialects of Somali are mutually intelligible to a high degree and differ from one another only in fairly minor ways, whether phonological, lexical, or morphological. In the remainder of this book, I assume the classification proposed by Abdullahi (2000) and adopt the dialect designations suggested therein.

1.3.4 Ismail (2011, 2015)

Ismail (2011) and the published book derived from it (Ismail 2015) argue against clan-based classification, and even question the suitability of classification based on geography, at least to some extent. This is owing to the fact that modern Somali speakers have often been displaced from the traditional geographic center or region associated with their variety. As a result, he argues, geographic designators do not always reflect the reality of the contemporary Somali linguistic situation. He resigns to the fact, however, that geographic designations are perhaps the best choice to define major "dialects," but that there is richer diversity to be found in sub-dialects pinned to locations that "typify" a given variety. In this way, Ismail's approach echoes Lamberti's earlier method of classification in some ways. Notable is that Ismail defines *Af-Maxaad Tidhi* by three groups – Northern, Benaadir, and Ashraaf – with Central Somali being subsumed under Benaadir. The inclusion here of Ashraaf departs from other perspectives on *Af-Maxaad Tidhi*.

1.4 Major Somali varieties

1.4.1 Af-Maxaad Tidhi

Northern Somali is often cited as the basis for "standard" Somali, but the two are not the same. Banti (2013) argues that one must recognize and maintain a distinction between the variety (or dialect) of Somali spoken in northern regions of the country (i.e., Northern Somali) vs. that which serves as the basis for the official Somali orthography, is used in international news broadcasts, and, for all intents and purposes, constitutes the koiné that many refer to as Af-Maxaad Tidhi. According to Samarin (1971), a koiné is characterized by the incorporation of features from several dialects (i.e., the result of dialect mixing) into a single language variety. Others might instead call it a *lingua franca* of sorts (Andrzejewski 1971), or a language of wider communication. A similar sentiment is offered by Appleyard and Orwin (2008) who suggest that "standard Somali" best refers to a "range of varieties which are generally accepted as being understood by any other (Somali) speaker." They attribute this widespread familiarity to the use of this dialect by nomadic pastoralists and in poetry, which was also propagated by the same individuals.

What has historically been considered "standard" Somali, Af-Maxaad Tidhi, or Common Somali, has a tortuous history. The very idea of creating a standardized form of Somali stems, at least in the history of the Somali federal republic, from a 1972 mandate from the nation's federal government to select, standardize, and promote a variety of Somali for the purposes of literacy and education. Many of the challenges encountered in standardizing Somali grew from the choice of an appropriate and politically acceptable orthography. Somali's Romanized orthography was granted official constitutional status on October 21, 1972. For more on orthography, see Chapter 2.

Beyond orthography, Af-Maxaad Tidhi is characterized by a core vocabulary of Somali lexical items. In the years following independence, Somali witnessed a significant attempt at modernizing its vocabulary, some details of which are outlined in Caney (1984). In this work, Caney details four ways in which the Somali lexicon was modernized up until that point in time: i) semantic shift; ii) incorporation of borrowings and subsequent derivation; iii) formation of new compounds; and iv) the development of new "phrase groups" (i.e., idioms).

With these methods of innovation laid out, Caney provides numerous examples of new vocabulary items that fall within 18 subject areas. These include agriculture, armed forces, banking and finance, chemistry, commerce and industry, communications, education, geography, language, mathematics, medicine, the office, physics, politics and public affairs, press, printing and publishing, tourism, vehicles and vehicle parts, and work. Based on my work with Somali speakers in the US and Sweden over the last decade, it is clear that a sizable number of the so-called "modernized" vocabulary items cataloged by Caney are either not recognizable or otherwise sound archaic or awkward to today's speakers. For some of these terms or concepts, my speakers prefer to substitute foreign words, usually borrowed from English or sometimes from Arabic or French. In many instances, there are new lexical items that have been created to replace these archaic words, but also others. These are sometimes formed by compounds and phrases and have come to be widely used in contemporary Somali.

Following Caney (1984), another dissertation by Hared (1992) brought a different perspective on the modernization of Somali vocabulary and the standardization of the language itself. Unlike Caney, Hared presents a critical, quantitative analysis of these matters focused on lexical expansion of two types, namely nominal derivation and nominal compounding. He does so by examining the use of these devices, their variation, and changes in their frequency of use in three press registers (news reports, editorials, and feature articles) over a span of 17 years between 1973-1989.

There are, of course, many nativized borrowings from Arabic which pervade the Somali lexicon. Several major works are devoted to the subject of Arabic loanwords in Somali, including two dissertations: Callegari (1988) and Vasaturo (2012). To a lesser extent, there are borrowings that remain from Italian (see Mioni 1988), French (see Morin 1984), Persian, Hindi, other Ethiosemitic languages (e.g., Amharic and Oromo), but above all else, the influence of English continues to grow.

In the sub-sections that follow, I summarize the major points covered in approximately 300 pages of discussion in Abdullahi (2000) that detail characteristic distinctions between the Northern (§1.4.2), Central (§1.4.3), and Benaadir (§1.4.4) dialects of Somali. Because the aim here is to discuss Somali grammar, and not specifically dialectology, this summary is not intended to be exhaustive. I encourage the reader to consult Abdullahi (2000) directly for additional examples and further discussion.

It will become immediately clear that in most instances, the differences between Somali dialects, and particularly between Northern and Central Somali, are few in number and fairly minor. Benaadir Somali is somewhat more divergent and exhibits influences from other varieties. Djibouti Somali is considered to be a sub-dialect of Northern Somali.

After briefly introducing properties that distinguish the three major Somali dialects from one another, I turn in §1.6 to pointing out some characteristics of other members of the Somali language "cluster" that most linguists would agree are properly considered different languages, rather than dialects of Somali itself.

1.4.2 Northern Somali

For the purpose of making comparisons to other dialects, Northern Somali is an appropriate baseline at which to start. Generally speaking, there are two distinguishing characteristics of the dialect. One of these relates to pronunciation and the other to lexicon. The first is that Northern Somali has the retroflex implosive stop [ɖ] word-initially in words like *dhéer* 'long,' word-medially in words like *cadhó* 'anger,' and even word-finally in words like *gabádh* 'girl.' The latter two are instead pronounced with the rhotic [ɾ] in the Central and Benaadir Somali dialects.

Beyond this minor distinguishing phonological characteristic, Abdullahi (2000) points out a preponderance of borrowed words from English in Northern Somali, as well as a few (though not many) borrowings from Hindi. These sometimes reveal instances where a given referent is referred to with a word borrowed from English (or Hindi) in the North but with a borrowing from Italian in the geographically southern dialects. There are also dialect-specific Northern lexical items.

1.4.2.1 Djibouti Somali

I am aware of a few published works that draw upon data specifically from Djibouti Somali (DS), though there may be others forthcoming following from a 2016 workshop held at the University of Rouen (France) that brought together an international group of scholars to discuss matters particular to this variety.

Lahrouchi and Lampitelli (2014) discuss the syntax of gender, illustrating that *-yaál* pluralization is the default strategy in DS, as opposed to *-ó* pluralization in other NS varieties, though both strategies are found in DS. They illustrate that *-ó* pluralization involves only number and has no inherent gender. The opposing *-yaál* strategy instead enforces feminine gender in all instances. Lampitelli (2017) corroborates these findings. The paper illustrates that DS has two major pluralization strategies, with both strategies being acceptable to speakers for many (but not all) nouns. The paper also discusses the status of "pitch accent" in DS and its relationship to case marking relative to what is known to occur in NS. Examples in Morin (1995) are also from Djibouti Somali.

1.4.3 Central Somali

Central Somali exhibits (morpho-)phonological distinctions from Northern Somali other than the well-known [ɖ] vs. [ɾ] distinction mentioned above in §1.4.2.[3] This is simply a positional restriction. Whereas the stop [ɖ] is found in a variety of word positions in Northern Somali, it occurs only word-initially in content words in Central Somali, as well as in certain morphologically-derived environments. For example,

---

[3] Despite offering a three-way distinction between Northern, Central, and Benaadir dialects of Somali, Abdullahi (2000) later draws a secondary sub-division within Central Somali, pointing out some characteristics found particularly in what he calls *Central-South Somali*. I do not treat Central-South Somali separately here, but rather include its properties under the slightly broader category of Central Somali.

Abdullahi (2000) discusses that a sequence of /r#t/ across a morpheme boundary is realized [ɖ] in Central Somali. For example, Northern Somali *qortay* 'you(SG) wrote, she wrote' is realized *qodhay* in Central Somali.

Other minor distinguishing phonological characteristics include the presence of the auxiliary *-ah-* in the formation of progressive verb forms. Compare, Northern Somali *cunayaa* 'I am eating, he is eating' to Central Somali *cunahayaa*. Another difference is that sequences of [nt] in Northern Somali are instead realized as [ɲ] in Central Somali (cf. Northern Somali *inta* 'while' to *i[ɲ]a*). Lastly, there is vowel raising from [a] to [e] in some instances, an outcome that is more akin to what is observed in Benaadir Somali (cf. Northern Somali *saddex* 'three' to *seddex*). In addition, there are more substantive morphological and morphosyntactic peculiarities that distinguish Central Somali from its Northern counterpart. For example, there is a propensity for some vocalic or syllabic truncation, subject pronoun dropping, and different patterns of coalescence between adjacent morphemes in Central Somali compared to NS. As one might expect, there are also lexical differences between the varieties.

1.4.4 Benaadir Somali

Benaadir Somali is sometimes called Coastal Somali (Andrzejewski, 1971). Despite its divergent morphology and distinct phonological and lexical influences from Maay, Benaadir is considered a dialect of Somali. That said, the dialect is clearly within a convergence area where the lines between Somali and Maay are blurred to some degree. Notable resources discussing this particular dialect are Carcoforo (1912) and Moreno (1955).

Benaadir Somali exhibits many of the same phonological properties discussed just above for Central (e.g., [ɽ] in syllable codas and word-internal onsets, where Northern Somali has [ɖ]), but also others under influence from Maay. For example, pharyngeal consonant contrasts have neutralized in some instances, leading to the loss of [ʕ] (orth. *c*) and [ħ] (orth. *x*). Underlying diphthongs are also monophthongized. Under analogous influence from coastal varieties of Swahili spoken in southern Somalia, the labial consonants [f] and [v] sometimes replace [b]. There is also evidence of stricter phonotactics in Benaadir Somali, leading to the loss of some consonant clusters. This is seemingly due to the influence of Swahili and its maximal CV syllable shape.

There are distinct morphological differences in the formation of some verb tense/aspect combinations, such as in the formation of the present progressive. In the Benaadir verbal system, there is a leveling of characteristic inflectional irregularities found in Northern Somali, particularly the loss of prefixing verb inflection for person, number, and gender in favor of the far more robust and regularized pattern of inflection for these categories by suffixation.

In the nominal system, there is leveling seen in the loss of certain pluralization patterns. For example, while pluralization via *-ó* is arguably the default mechanism in Northern Somali, this is instead *-yaál* in Benaadir Somali. The latter *-yaál* pluralization is also found in Northern Somali, but only for a small set of nouns. This is not to say that *-ó* pluralization is entirely absent in Benaadir Somali. Rather, it has replaced so-called prosodic pluralization (see §6.2.5.2). Pluralization of another small class of nouns in Northern Somali via *-óyin* is instead by *-óshin* in the Benaadir dialect. Lastly, and of particular note from the standpoint of Benaadir morphology, is that it has borrowed its series of indefinite articles from Maay.

1.5 Previous work on Somali

Somali is among the better documented African languages and is certainly the best documented Cushitic language. For an annotated list of references, see Green et al. (2014) and Nilsson (2016b). Descriptive work on Somali and its constituent varieties (published in several European languages) dates back to the late nineteenth and early twentieth centuries (e.g., Hunter 1880; Kirk 1905; de Larajasse 1897; de Larajasse and de Sampont 1897; Palermo 1914; Reinisch 1903; de Sampont 1905; Schleicher 1892). There is also a rich history of research on Somali poetry and literature (e.g., Ahmed 1996; Andrzejewski and Lewis 1964; Antinucci and Cali 1986; Morin 1995), and more specifically on poetic meter, which has made particularly important contributions to the study of Somali phonology (notably, Banti and Giannattasio 1996; Johnson 1979; Orwin 1996, 2001; Orwin and Riiraash 1997).

1.5.1 Theoretical literature

In this section, I highlight some of the better-known works on Somali. What I include here is by no means comprehensive. I cite additional works, wherever relevant, in later chapters.

Perhaps the best-known scholar of Somali is Andrzejewski, who began his study of the language at the University of London School of Oriental and African Studies (SOAS) in 1948. Andrzejewski and colleague Muuse Galaal were recruited to develop a Somali orthography. Though their orthography was not ultimately selected for implementation, it greatly influenced the Ahmed orthography that became official in 1972; see Chapter 2. Andrzejewski wrote a series of highly influential papers on a variety of topics, including accentual patterns on verbs (Andrzejewski 1956), noun declensions (Andrzejewski 1964), case marking (Andrzejewski 1979), prepositions (Andrzejewski 1960), indicator (i.e., focus) particles (Andrzejewski 1975), and so-called hybrid verbs (Andrzejewski 1969), among other topics.

Saeed has also written on a variety of topics in Somali and its close cousins. Notable works on Somali proper include Saeed (1982b, 1984, 1993a, 1995, 1996, 2004). Other typological work on Somali varieties and Cushitic languages includes Saeed

(1992) and Saeed (1994). Saeed is perhaps best known for his 1993b pedagogical grammar, companion 1999 reference grammar, and his 2007 sketch of Somali morphology.

Banti has published on a range of topics including affixation (1984b), case marking (1984a), nominal structure (1988c), verbal structure (1988a; 1988b), relative clauses (2011a), loanwords (2013), among others. His 1985 monograph covers aspects of Somali phonology, morphology, and syntax.

Somali has held a particularly prominent place in the literature on formal syntax. Works pertaining to clause-level syntax include Antinucci (1980), Antinucci and Puglielli (1980), Antinucci et al. (1980), Frascarelli (2010b), Frascarelli and Puglielli (2003, 2007, 2009), Lecarme (1984, 1991, 1994, 1999a), Svolacchia and Puglielli (1999), and Svolacchia et al. (1995). Those on smaller phrase-level constituents, including the encoding of tense in nouns, are Lecarme (1995, 1996, 1999b, 2008).

Research on Somali phonology is not as extensive as that on the language's syntax. Early work on Somali phonology includes Armstrong (1934), Andrzejewski (1955), and Farnetani (1981). Hyman (1981) is the first formal analysis of Somali's tonal system. Another perspective on Somali tonology is found in Frid (1995). A series of descriptive works by Orwin (1993, 1994) explore segmental aspects of the language's phonology. Later works like Orwin (1996), Orwin and Riiraash (1997), and Orwin (2001) probe the relationship between poetry, metrical structure, and formal phonology. Green and Morrison (2016) discuss Somali tone in nouns and determiner phrases in light of contemporary perspectives on prosodic hierarchy theory. Green and Morrison (2018) later extend this line of inquiry to establish the prosodic structure of Somali verbs. Other recent work in the realm of prosodic phonology includes Downing and Nilsson (2019) and Kaldhol (2017). Lampitelli (2011, 2013) and Green and Lampitelli (2021) explore the interface between phonology and syntax in Somali, while Le Gac (2001, 2002, 2003a,b) presents some of the first experimental work aimed at establishing the phonetic correlates of intonation patterns in different prosodic domains relative to focus.

Other studies focus more narrowly on a particular topic or phenomenon. These include: noun incorporation (Tosco 2004), particular types of nouns (Serzisko 1992), color terminology (Maffi 1984, 1990), impersonal pronouns (Cabredo Hofherr 2004), reciprocal pronouns (Cabredo Hofherr 2007), deixis (Bourdin 2005; Morrison 2016), ideophones (Dhoorre and Tosco 1998), gender polarity (Lecarme 2002; Nilsson 2016a), gemination (Ségéral and Scheer 2001), vowel harmony (Mohamoud 2013; Kimper et al. 2018), verb inflection (Barillot et al. 2018), and computational approaches to manipulating Somali corpora (Hargreaves 2006; Hargreaves and Ramsay 2006; Nimaan et al. 2006).

1.5.2 Reference and pedagogical materials

There are three pedagogical grammars of Somali (Abdullahi 1996; Mansur and Puglielli 1999; Saeed 1993b), none of which are currently in print. Saeed's pedagogical grammar was later adapted as a reference grammar (Saeed 1999) and is still readily available from John Benjamins. An earlier reference grammar is Bell (1953). Materials with similar scope in German include Lamberti (1986) and Berchem (1991).

In addition, there is a truly exceptional Somali-Somali dictionary by Puglielli and Mansur (2012), as well as several others that are Somali-English (Hashi 1998; Orwin et al. 1999; Qoorsheel 2007; Zorc and Osman 1993). A variety of other dictionaries in various language combinations have been published but are out of print.

Lastly, there are a number of coursebooks and textbooks (Abdinoor 2007; Carter 1984; El-Somali-Mewis 1987; Orwin 1995; Osman and Zorc 1992), most of which are designed for use by English-speaking learners of Somali.

1.6 Other languages of the Somali cluster

1.6.1 Ashraaf (Marka, Shingani, Xamar)

The status of Ashraaf is perhaps the most precarious of all varieties in the Somali cluster. Among the classifications discussed in §1.3, it has been considered a sub-variety of Benaadir Somali (Ehret and Ali, 1984) and a dialect of its own on par with Northern and Benaadir Somali (Lamberti, 1984, 1986). It is clear, however, in Abdullahi (2000) that its status remains a matter of debate, particularly concerning whether Ashraaf refers to a people or a speech group. It is given status as a Somali dialect by Eberhard et al. (2019), despite the fact that it does not fall under the heading of *Af-Maxaad Tidhi*.

From a descriptive standpoint, Ashraaf has two distinct though highly mutually intelligible sub-dialects (Banti, 2011b), one of which is spoken primarily in the city of Marka (Merca). This is also sometimes called the Lower Shabelle variety of Ashraaf. The second Ashraaf variety is spoken by individuals residing in the Shingani district of Mogadishu. I am aware of a few works discussing the Shingani dialect (Abo 2007; Ajello 1984, 1988; Moreno 1953) which is also sometimes called Xamar (Hamar), the name that locals call the Somali capital Mogadishu.

Evan Jones and I have personally worked with speakers of the Marka dialect of Ashraaf in two diaspora communities in the United States (Minneapolis, MN and Phoenix, AZ, though we are aware of another community in Portland, OR) on several occasions over the span of 2009-2015. Some findings from this work are reported in Green and Jones (2018). While much work remains to be done, the speakers with whom we have worked note significant intelligibility issues between their language and Somali. Though anecdotal, these perspectives are arguably supported by descriptions of Ashraaf varieties by both Abo (2007) and Green and Jones (2018) where key divergences between Ashraaf, Somali, and Maay, particularly in terms of their morphology are discussed.

1.6.2 Maay (Maay-Maay)

There are a greater number of resources pertaining to the linguistic structure of Maay compared to those for Ashraaf, though nowhere near as many as for Somali. The availability of Maay resources is somewhat obscured by the fact that the most comprehensive of these, namely Saeed (1982a) and several others (e.g., Angoujard (1989), Biber (1982, 1984b)) are presented as studies of "Central" Somali. Thankfully, all of these scholars make it clear that the variety (or varieties) being described are in fact Rahanweyn or Maay.

There are some more recent studies of Maay, particularly on the Lower Jubba dialect, which include a series of works by Paster (2007, 2010, 2018) and her colleagues (Comfort and Paster 2009; Paster and Ranero 2015). Also available is an English-Maay dictionary by Mukhtar and Ahmed (2007) and more recently a comparative guide to linguistic work on Maay by Morrison and Abokor (2016) that summarizes the aforementioned works and includes new data from the second author of the study, who hails from Baidoa.

As Morrison and Abokor detail, the information in these resources is representative of speakers from a large geographic expanse. The details differ in many respects between sources. Notably, the Maay reported in Saeed (1982a) from Bur Hakaba, Somalia, and that in Biber (1982, 1984b) from the Mandera district of Kenya, are said to exhibit a type of accent-like tonal system that is akin to that found in Somali (Green and Morrison, 2016; Hyman, 1981). The Lower Jubba Maay covered by Paster, et al. is non-tonal and is suggested by Morrison and Abokor (2016) to be representative of a Southern Somalia lingua franca used as a second language by Somali Bantus.

1.7 Somali in the diaspora

There is a growing literature on the Somali diaspora, including the implications that it has for, and impacts that it has had on, particular nations or cities in which Somali refugees have resettled. See, for example, Abdile and Pirkkalainen (2011), Ahmed (2000), Bigelow (2010a,b), Houssein (2013), Issa-Salwe (2006), Kleist (2004, 2008), Olgac (2001), Al-Sharmani (2006, 2008), and Sheikh and Healy (2009), among many others. Linguists are just beginning to discover the effects that the diaspora is having on Somali and its structure. Notable studies highlighting some of these emerging differences, particularly in Scandinavian varieties of Somali, include Downing and Nilsson (2019) and Kaldhol (2017).

1.8 Data sources

The data represented in this book come from a variety of sources and were collected intermittently over a span of approximately seven years from 2013-2020. Some examples illustrating particular phenomena are drawn from the published literature and are indicated as such. Specific examples originally drawn from two published reference sources, Zorc and Issa (1990) and Zorc and Osman (1993), are abbreviated Z & I and Z & O, respectively, followed by page numbers. I have also gathered examples from the approximately 80 million token SoWac Somali Web Corpus (https://corpora.fi.muni.cz/habit/index.html), and the approximately 19 million token SpråkbankenText corpus (https://spraakbanken.gu.se/), as well as from news sources like BBC News Somali (https://www.bbc.com/somali). Examples from these corpora are cited throughout the grammar. Those examples from the SoWac and SpråkbankenText corpora include the original webpage source URL and document number, though in some instances the original webpages are no longer active. The interested reader should consult these corpora directly, as they are actively maintained, at least at the time of writing. Those data that are not specifically marked with a source are drawn from my own data collection with native speaker consultants. These data are representative of my work with six consultants whose gender, place of origin, and current place of residence are as follow: i) male, mid 40s from Hargeysa, residing in Virginia, USA, ii) female, mid 30s from Mogadishu, residing in Maryland, USA iii) male, early 30s from Mogadishu, residing in Gothenburg, Sweden, iv) male, late 30s from Mogadishu, residing in Gothenburg, Sweden, v) female, mid 30s from Mogadishu, residing in New York, USA vi) male, mid 40s from Bu'ale, residing in New York, USA.

1.9 Outline of this book

The remainder of this book is organized as follows: Chapter 2 provides a brief overview concerning the development of Somali's official orthography. Most examples in this grammar will be provided in Somali orthography with the exception of those in Chapter 3. This is because the focus of Chapter 3 is on establishing the language's consonant and vowel inventories and other matters related to segmental phonology. This includes information on allophony and on the many morphophonological alternations that occur in morphologically derived environments. Chapter 4 is devoted specifically to discussion of syllable structure, word shape requirements, and phonotactics. The language's tonal system, including tone assignment, distribution, and alternations, is covered in Chapter 5.

Chapter 6 is the first of three chapters devoted specifically to morphology, beginning with the nominal system. Chapter 7 then turns to the verbal system, with both derivational and inflectional morphology being discussed in turn. Chapter 8 covers compounds of different types, both nominal and verbal, as well as compound-like constructions like incorporation and phrasal verbs.

These are followed by Chapter 9, which covers noun categories and the construction of noun phrases. Chapter 10 then discusses the structure and elements of the Verb Complex. Having established the properties of noun phrases and the Verb Complex, Chapter 11 then turns to the construction of focus markers and the effects that different focus conditions have on other nominal and verbal elements in a clause. Chapter 12 discusses clause types that do not include focus markers.

The remaining chapters of this grammar cover other syntactic topics that involve larger constituents, subordination, and information structure. Chapter 13 covers focus and topicalization strategies that are manipulated for pragmatic and discursive purposes. Chapter 14 deals with clauses involving subordination. This includes relative clauses which, in some ways, behave similar to phrases involving subject focus, as well as complement clauses, adverbial clauses, and other clauses introduced by co-ordinators of various types. Chapter 15 discusses phrasal and clausal coordination, as well as non-subordinating adverbials. Finally, Chapter 16 covers question formation.

2 Orthography

The development of an orthography suitable for Somali has a long and complicated history dating back to the 13th century (Banti, 2013). Long before the adoption of the language's official Romanized orthography on October 21, 1972, Somali was written at various times and by various individuals in other scripts (see Labahn 1982). Given its proximity to the Arabic-speaking world and the fact that Somalis have long practiced Islam, the basis of some Somali orthographies is the Perso-Arabic script. Other orthographies can be considered indigenous scripts in that they were designed specifically for Somali by poets and folklorists. Of course, there were various Romanized scripts that were entertained before the adoption of the official orthography approximately 50 years ago. Those who took on the task of developing these were religious leaders, poets, political figures, and linguists.

2.1 Perso-Arabic

Tosco (2010, 2015) and Cerulli (1964) discuss script variants based on Perso-Arabic writing used by religious figure Sheekh Awees Baraawii. Examples of these are represented in his religious poetry and songs. Another Perso-Arabic-based script mentioned was developed by Sheekh Maxamed Makaahiil. Yet another script was proposed by folklorist Muuse Xaaji Ismaaciil Galaal (1954). This script, in particular, introduced Perso-Arabic-like vowel characters whose form differed according to location (i.e., word-initial, word-medial, word-final). The motivation for doing so, according to Galaal, "disposes the difficulty of the Arabic vowel system," such as the fact that in Arabic, a short vowel might be indicated only by a diacritic, or not at all.

One script of unclear origin is called Wadaad (i.e., learned man's) script, Wadaad's writing, or Wadaad Arabic and discussed by Lewis (1958). It has been described as more of a "broken Arabic" (Tosco, 2015) that utilizes Somali words. There are, of course, several proposed orthography variants based on the Perso-Arabic. Figure 2.1 is adapted from Lewis (1958) in order to simply illustrate a sample set of correspondences between Perso-Arabic characters, currently used characters in the Romanized Somali script, and their equivalents in the International Phonetic Alphabet (IPA).

2.2 Cismaaniya (Osmania)

In addition to scripts based on Perso-Arabic writing, there have been other indigenous scripts developed by Somali linguists, but also by poets and political figures. These are discussed to some extent in a series of works by Tosco (2010, 2012, 2015), and also by Warsame (2001). Two scripts among these are particularly notable, namely the *Cis-*

ى	ئ	ا	ئ	و	ئَ	أَى	آ	أو	و
i	e	a	o	u	ii	ee	aa	oo	uu
[i]	[e]	[a]	[o]	[u]	[i:]	[e:]	[a:]	[o:]	[u:]

ش	س	ف	ء	ق	ك	غ	ط	ت	د	ب
sh	s	f	'	q	k	g	dh	t	d	b
[ʃ]	[s]	[f]	[ʔ]	[q]	[k]	[g]	[ɖ]	[t]	[d]	[b]

ي	و	ل	ر	ن	م	ج	ه	ح	ع	خ
y	w	l	r	n	m	j	h	ch	c	kh
[j]	[w]	[l]	[r]	[n]	[m]	[tʃ]	[h]	[x]	[ʕ]	[ħ]

Fig. 2.1: Sample comparison of Somali Perso-Arabic script to Romanized script and IPA (adapted from Lewis 1958)

maaniya (Osmania) script, later called the *Far Soomaali* script, and the *Gadabuursi* script.

The Cismaaniya script was developed by Osman Yusuf Keenadiid in the early 1920s. Maino (1951, 1953) and Tosco (2015) discuss the history and fleeting success of its use. The script was developed without overt reference to any other script and was first used only privately among a group of politically-elite individuals and their followers. Its popularity rose for some time, and its use spread as it grew to be associated with a nationalist movement led by the Somali Youth League. One aim of the Somali Youth League was to revolt against a push towards a Pan-Islamic society and, in doing so, to lead a future, independent Somalia away from Arabic and the Perso-Arabic script. A representation of the Cismaaniya script extracted from Lewis (1958) is in Figure 2.2.

Fig. 2.2: Cismaaniya script (adapted from Lewis 1958)

2.3 Gadabuursi

The Gadabuursi script is discussed in Lewis (1958). This script enjoyed nowhere near the level of use and popularity as did the Cismaaniya script. According to Lewis, it was used only within a small circle of individuals. For the sake of comparison, a representation of the Gadabuursi characters is in Figure 2.3.

2.4 Official orthography

For the purpose of understanding certain aspects of Somali grammar and, in particular, its phonology and morphology, it is important to have a grasp on the creation, implementation, and use of its official Romanized orthography. In Chapter 3, I discuss Somali's segmental phonology relative to the International Phonetic Alphabet, but elsewhere in this grammar, examples will be presented orthographically.

According to Andrzejewski (1978), the first "practical steps" taken to develop a standard, Romanized Somali orthography began with Armstrong (1934), long before the 1960 unification of British Somaliland and Italian Somaliland into a single republic. Indeed, many of the early reference works on Somali, such as Armstrong (1934) and Bell (1953), are clearly written with a slant towards orthography development.

Fig. 2.3: Gadabuursi characters (adapted from Lewis 1958)

Despite this head start, even after independence, there was still no designated Somali script for many years.

The Somali Language Commission was formed after Somalia gained independence in 1960. One of its core charges was to choose an appropriate Somali script to promote education and literacy. After several years with little success, in 1966, the United Nations Educational, Scientific, and Cultural Organization (UNESCO) was called in to assist in the task. Even then, and for a few years thereafter, there was little movement or agreement on the matter. Following a 1969 military coup d'état led by Siad Barre, the Supreme Revolutionary Council (the ruling party) appointed another language commission in 1971 whose task was to finally choose an orthography. Despite fierce opposition, the leading choice emerged in a Romanized Somali orthography developed by Shire Jaamac Axmed. This orthography was based on Northern Somali and said by Andrzejewski (1977, 1978) to have been greatly influenced by many years worth of recommendations by Andrzejewski himself and also by Muuse Galaal.

According to Appleyard and Orwin (2008), Northern Somali was a popular choice for the dialect upon which to base "standard" Somali given its historical widespread use as a lingua franca and the prestige that it held among Somali poets. Other commentary concerning the development of this orthography is offered in Andrzejewski et al. (1966) and Laitin (1977). Axmed's Romanized orthography was granted official constitutional status on October 21, 1972. It is shown in 1.

(1) *Official Somali orthography, as of October 21, 1972*

b	t	d	dh	j	k	g	q
f	s	sh	kh	x	c	h	
m	n	r	l	w	y		
i/ii	e/ee	a/aa	o/oo	u/uu			

The selection and ratification of Axmed's new orthography introduced a Roman alphabet to efforts geared toward Somali literacy and finally opened the door to the creation of a unified, Somali-focused education system (Warsame, 2001). With the Northern-based orthography made official, the dialect became the *de facto* standard as it came to be used in official government and military communications. It also accordingly spread beyond the indigenous dialect area, particularly into the Somali capital, Mogadishu.

The official Somali alphabet contains 21 characters that correspond to consonants (three of which are digraphs) and five characters that correspond to vowels. Somali has a robust contrast between short and long vowels, which is indicated by doubled vowel characters. There is a far less widespread contrast between short and long consonants that is indicated by doubled consonant characters. The exception to this is *dh* which, when doubled, is sometimes written *ddh*, rather than *dhdh*, but is oftentimes rendered as a single digraph. It is more often the case that long consonants are created by morphological concatenation and subsequent alternations. These are indicated in the same way by doubled characters.

The relationship between written consonants in the Somali orthography and their equivalents in the International Phonetic Alphabet (IPA) is discussed further in §3.1. In most instances, there is a clear connection between a given symbol or character and its IPA equivalent. This stems from the fact that the Somali alphabet is largely phonemic. Each symbol roughly corresponds to one sound, though there are a few exceptions. In addition, a given sound may have predictable variants depending on where it occurs in a word (e.g., word-initial vs. word-medial position) or under the influence of an adjacent sound. More detail on the phonetic realization and morphophonological behavior of Somali consonants is in Chapter 3.

The relationship between written vowels and their IPA equivalents is not a clear mapping. It has been recognized, at least since Armstrong (1934), that Somali exhibits a distinction of some sort between tense and lax, or so-called "neutral" and "culus" (the word for 'heavy,' in Somali), vowels. This distinction is typically attributed to the phonological property Advanced Tongue Root (ATR). The contrast is on the one hand lexical, but the language also exhibits vowel harmony. A root containing one type of vowel will, depending on certain factors, cause the vowel of its affixes to harmonize. Likewise, some derivational affixes may even trigger harmonization of a root. This is discussed further in §3.3. Despite there being a distinction in this particular property of vowels, the Somali orthography does not encode the contrast. Both tense and lax vowels are indicated by the same symbols.

Of less significance is that the Somali orthography does not mark tone. The language makes use of tone, albeit to a limited degree, to signal some lexical and grammatical distinctions, but the location of tone is predictable in all but a few instances. Somali's tonal system is discussed in Chapter 5. In examples throughout this grammar, I mark the location of High tone with an acute accent. The realization of a word's tone is sometimes attenuated or altered at the phrase or clause level by boundary tones.

The official Somali orthography employs symbols that are able to easily capture the slight and predictable differences in pronunciation between the three major Somali dialects. For example, there is well-known dialectal variation between orthographic *dh* [ɖ] and *r* [ɾ], with the former reflecting the pronunciation in Northern Somali and the latter the pronunciation in Central and Benaadir Somali. Other dialectal differences in vowel pronunciation and, more broadly, patterns of vowel coalescence are also easily accommodated in the official orthography.

3 Segmental Phonology

This chapter covers the segmental phonology of Somali, including its phonemic consonant and vowel inventories, and segmental morphophonological alternations. The information in this chapter concerns itself primarily with establishing phonological contrasts and accounting for details of allophony and alternations. Somali's syllable structure and phonotactics are discussed in Chapter 4, and its tonal system is discussed in Chapter 5.

Other works devoted to describing aspects of the Somali segmental inventory include Armstrong (1934), Edmondson et al. (2004), Mohamoud (2013), Orwin (1994), and Pia (1965). These works collectively illustrate considerable variation between speakers of different regions, a fact that I have encountered in my own data collection. Unfortunately, there is no complete, contemporary phonetic study aimed at teasing apart the finer details of the Somali sound system. Farnetani (1981) presents some phonetic analysis of Somali segments, and more recently, an experimental study by Bendjaballah and Le Gac (2019) aims to elucidate acoustic aspects of singleton vs. geminate oral stops in different word positions.

3.1 Consonants

The Somali consonant inventory in Table 3.1 illustrates Somali's 25 short consonant phonemes. Somali also encodes a length contrast for some consonants, a matter discussed separately in §3.1.3. This section begins by discussing short consonants, including a description of the distribution of their allophones, where relevant. The phonemes in Table 3.1 are given in the International Phonetic Alphabet (IPA), and their orthographic equivalents are provided in parentheses when they differ from the IPA symbol.[1] This is necessary because the Somali orthography, despite generally being phonemic (see Chapter 2), does not always accurately represent the phonological status of all sounds that it represents. In other chapters, examples are given in the standard Somali orthography, but in this chapter, IPA equivalents in square brackets [ ] are provided to facilitate discussion and comparison of alternations. Where a comparison between phonemic and phonetic forms is necessary, the former is indicated in slash brackets / /.

---

[1] Place of articulation is abbreviated as follows: Lab.= Labial; Alv.= Alveolar; Vel.= Velar; Uv.= Uvular; Epi.= Epiglottal; Laryn.= Laryngeal.

Tab. 3.1: Somali consonant inventory

	Lab.	Alv.	Post-Alv.	Vel.	Uv.	Epi.	Laryn.
Stop	b̥ (b)	tʰ (t) d̥ (d)	ɖ (dh)	kʰ (k) g̥ (g)	q	ʡ (c)	ʔ (')
Affricate			tʃ (j)				
Nasal	m	ŋ̊ n (n)					
Fricative	f	s	ʃ (sh)		χ (kh)	ʜ (x)	h
Liquid		l̥ l (l) r̥ r (r)					
Glide	w		j (y)				

One challenge to accurately characterizing the Somali consonant inventory with IPA symbols pertains to oral stops. All descriptions of Somali that I have encountered recognize a contrast between three manners of articulation for oral stops, but there is significant disagreement concerning the best way to describe and to represent them. This is partly because the dimensions of contrast (at least historically) involve a combination of voicing, aspiration, and length but also because the contrasts are realized phonetically in different ways by speakers from different regions. A comparison between what has been earlier described about oral stops compared to what is observed in the productions of modern day Somali speakers suggests that conditions affecting the phonetic manifestation of these contrasts may have changed over time.

Briefly, in modern Somali, there are two series of oral stops that contrast with one another via a combination of voicing and aspiration. Given its multifaceted nature, and following perspectives offered by Pia (1965) and Orwin (1993, 1994), this seems best described phonologically as a fortis vs. lenis contrast. Other languages that have been described as encoding such a contrast typically have a series of strong, higher energy fortis consonants alongside another series of weaker, lower energy lenis consonants. The precise phonetic correlates of fortis vs. lenis consonants vary to some extent between languages. For Somali, fortis stops are voiceless and aspirated, though aspiration is not especially strong. Lenis stops are unaspirated and are typically voiced word-initially. I have observed, as have others, that lenis stops are often only weakly voiced in this position. Spectrograms comparing the initial consonants in *gád* 'sale' and *káb* 'shoe' are in Figures 3.1 and 3.2, respectively. The first represents a lenis stop while the second shows a fortis stop.

A third series of stops historically contrast with lenis stops in length, though only intervocalically. For some speakers, like those reported by Bendjaballah and Le Gac (2019), this phonemic length contrast has come to be realized only as a surface contrast in manner. That is, where they can be directly compared intervocalically, phonemic long lenis stops for some speakers have come to be realized as short stops while phonemic short lenis stops are now realized as fricatives. For others, including some speakers with whom I have worked, phonemic geminate stops maintain their length while phonemic short lenis stops are realized as fricatives. This relationship is seen

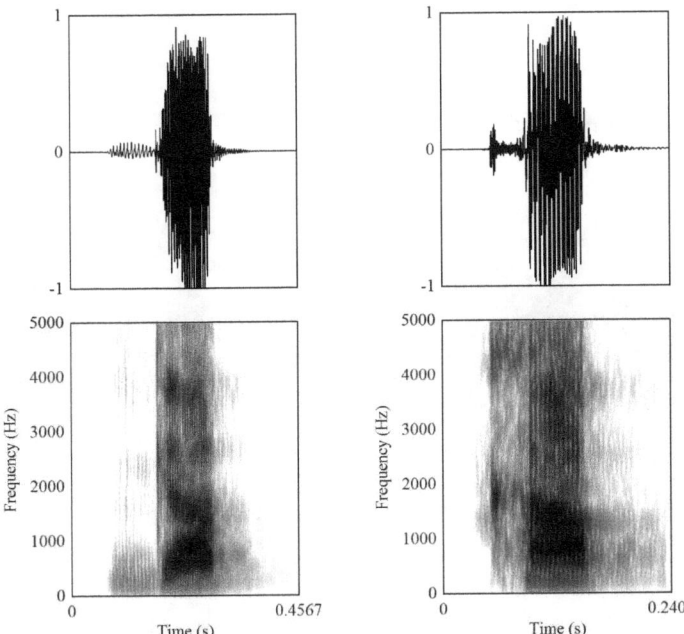

Fig. 3.1: *gád* 'sale' - spoken by Al   **Fig. 3.2:** *káb* 'shoe' - spoken by Al

in comparing *dábar* 'redness of the gums' and *dabbáal* 'fool' in Figures 3.3 and 3.4, as produced by a male speaker in his mid 30s from Mogadishu.

Given their variable realization and that there is no IPA diacritic to distinguish fortis vs. lenis stops, I use IPA symbols corresponding to voiceless aspirated vs. devoiced stops (i.e., t^h vs. $\d{d}$) to indicated fortis vs. lenis stops, respectively. This might appear contradictory to some, but the intent is to capture the fact that lenis stops are not equivalent to true voiced stops, nor to voiceless stops. In addition, despite the fact that fortis stops are not necessarily strongly aspirated, the fact that they are aspirated is key to understanding their phonological behavior.

30 — 3 Segmental Phonology

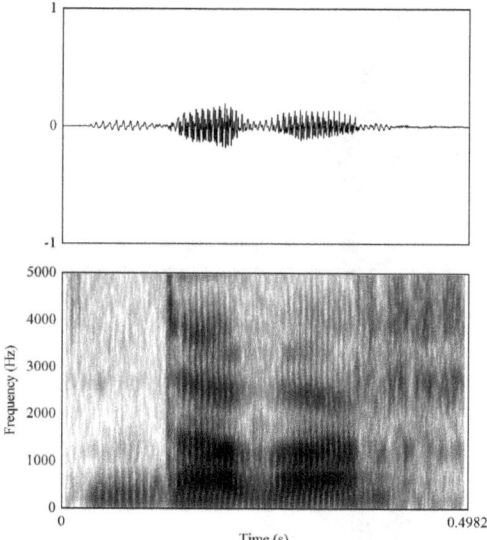

Fig. 3.3: *dábar 'redness of the gums'* - spoken by AS

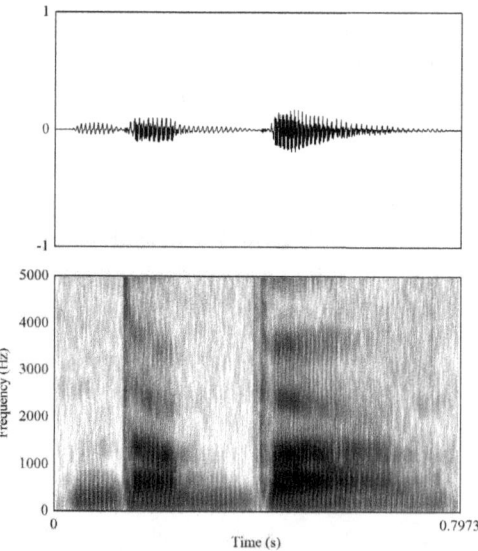

Fig. 3.4: dabbáal 'fool' - spoken by AS

Another matter of note concerns the status of the uvular fricative [χ] (orthographic *kh*). It is limited to loanwords, primarily from Arabic, and is not phonemic for all Somali speakers. Where [χ] is found in Northern Somali, [q] is used by Benaadir and Central Somali speakers. Compare Northern *taariikh* [tʰaariíχ] and Benaadir/Central *taariiq* [tʰaariíq] both meaning 'history.' A similar situation involves *dh* and *r*. The two sounds contrast for all speakers word-initially, being realized [ɖ] and [r], respectively. For Northern Somali speakers, this contrast persists in other positions. However, it is neutralized intervocalically and in codas (including word-finally) in favor of *r* (pronounced [ɾ]), for speakers of Benaadir and Central Somali. This dialectal difference is captured orthographically, including on international news websites. Compare, for example, Northern *cadho* [ʔáɖo] and Benaadir/Central *caro* [ʔáɾo], both meaning 'anger.'

3.1.1 Establishing stop contrasts

As introduced above, describing the nature of the contrast distinguishing Somali stops is a challenge. It has been inconsistently described even in the best cited resources on the language (e.g., Armstrong 1934; Saeed 1993a, 1999). Most works either take no clear stance on the nature of the stop contrast or instead assume that voicing is the primary contrast. Unfortunately, the assumption that voice is key to distinguishing these sounds from one another is problematic, despite what the orthography might suggest, and obscures important aspects of the language's phonology.

Stops that are typically described as "voiced" are often variably or intermittently voiced, even in word-initial position, and even in productions by the same speaker in successive tokens. Those that are typically described as "voiceless" are reliably realized with aspiration, except in syllable codas where they are deaspirated. Given these facts, Pia (1965) and Orwin (1993, 1994) notably call into question the suitability of a laryngeal contrast in Somali that is based solely on voicing, though this was earlier mentioned in passing by Armstrong (1934). Orwin argued that erstwhile "voiced" stops are not reliably voiced in most instances and only become so intervocalically under some conditions. "Voiceless" stops, however, he describes as aspirated, except in final positions whereat they become deaspirated. As such, Orwin argued that these facts do not point to voicing as the basis for Somali's laryngeal contrast but rather to a contrast based on aspiration or, according to his analysis, on the phonological feature [spread glottis]. In Orwin's view, voiceless aspirated stops are the marked series. The opposing series of stops is voiceless and unaspirated. Thus, the contrast between the two series of stops is neutralized in syllable codas, including word-finally, via loss of aspiration. Such a description is typologically better grounded than one based on voicing. Indeed, final deaspiration can be viewed as a type of lenition and one that is both phonetically natural and typologically well-attested. Viewed instead as a matter of voicing, one would have to assert that "voiceless" stops become "voiced" word-finally, an alternation that is typologically unexpected. The matter arises in a debate between Blevins (2004) and Iverson and Salmons (2006).

While I agree with Orwin in principle, Pia's proposal of a phonetically multifaceted fortis/lenis contrast better captures the Somali facts. Under such a view, Somali has a series of fortis stops (written *t* and *k*). These are voiceless and weakly aspirated, as seen above in Figure 3.2. The language's second series of lenis stops (written *b*, *d*, and *g*) are not realized in an acoustically consistent way, though they do correspond to Proto-East Cushitic voiced stops (Sasse, 1978). These stops vary in that while they are voiced, the degree of voicing varies considerably even between successive tokens of the same word produced by the same speaker. Consider two productions of *baád* 'extortion' by the same speaker (AI) in Figure 3.5. The first has almost non-existent voicing while the second has clear, though still fairly weak voicing. With voicing being inconsistent in this way, it would seem that the primary dimension of contrast seems best attributed to aspiration.

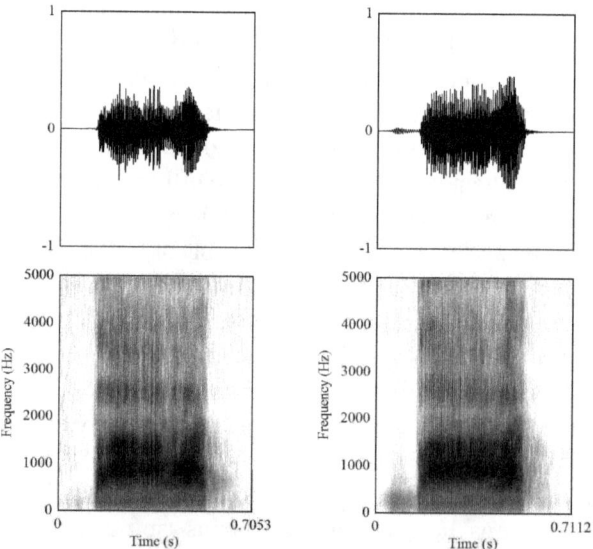

Fig. 3.5: *baád* 'extortion' - successive tokens spoken by AI

Descriptions of Somali segmental phonology also illustrate that lenis stops vary by dialect (or perhaps even by speaker) in their intervocalic realization. For the speakers of Northern Somali reported in Armstrong (1934), the realization of lenis stops depends on their location relative to H tone. They surface either as voiced stops [b, d, g] or corresponding spirants [β, ð, ɣ] depending on whether they appear in a syllable with stress (i.e., with H tone) or after such a syllable, respectively.[2] For the Central Somali speakers (with whom I have worked most extensively), however, these stops tend always to be realized as voiced spirants, regardless of their location relative to H tone. Morgan Nilsson (p.c.) has also brought to my attention that he knows of speakers who tend never to spirantize intervocalically. While the matter certainly deserves a great deal more attention, it should suffice here to recognize this variation and the realizations that might be encountered for these phones in this particular environment.

Somali's lenis stops have contrastive long counterparts, though this contrast is also realized in a phonetically inconsistent way. Some speakers maintain a phonetic length contrast, at least intervocalically, but others realize this synchronically as a surface manner contrast. That is, underlying geminate stops are realized as stops while singleton stops are realized as spirants. Regardless of their synchronic realization, it is undeniable that Somali maintains an underlying three-way stop contrast, e.g., *t* vs. *d* vs. *dd*, though only intervocalically. Section 3.1.3.2 discusses that an analogous and arguably more transparent length contrast is found in some of the language's sonorants.

In the remainder of this section, contrasts between Somali consonant phonemes are established and their allophones discussed. As motivated above, the contrast between stops at the same place of articulation is described as fortis vs. lenis. There is a series of lenis stops (/b̥, d̥, g̥/) and a series of fortis stops (/tʰ, kʰ/). Because the presence of voicing is variable in lenis stops, even word-initially, it may be that voicing is synchronically redundant. That said, lenis stops do reliably emerge as voiced in some environments, such as in a word-internal onset after a sonorant coda. To guide the discussion that follows, Table 3.2 summarizes the realizations of lenis and fortis stop phonemes in different word positions. These segments are compared: i) word-initially (or in an onset after a non-sonorant coda); ii) in final position (word-finally, or in a word-internal coda); iii) intervocalically; and iv) in an onset after a sonorant coda. The variable voicing of the lenis stops /b̥, d̥, g̥/ is not contrastive, and so both values are listed in the summary. Two variable realizations of intervocalic lenition are also shown.

This simple comparison illustrates that lenis stops pattern together as a natural class, as do their fortis counterparts. The behavior of other stops, namely /q, ɖ, ʔ, ʕ/, and also the affricate /tʃ/ are discussed in sections below relative to the extent to which they pattern (or not) with fortis and lenis stops.

---

[2] Several scholars have made passing reference to "stress" in Somali. Notably, Saeed (1999, 17) states that stress is correlated with High tone, though he makes no connection to metrification. As mentioned above, there is a significant literature on metrical structure relative to Somali poetics, but this has not yet extended substantively to the rest of the language's phonological grammar. As I hope to illustrate later in this chapter, there appears to be at least some evidence for metrical structure in segmental alternations observed in Somali. Importantly, however, there seems to be little evidence for a correlation between the metrical structure underlying these alternations and the distribution of High tone.

Tab. 3.2: Summary of stop allophony

	#_	_]σ	V_V	C._
/b̥/	p ~ b	p	β ~ b	b
/d̥/	t ~ d	t	ð ~ d	d
/g̥/	k ~ g	k	ɣ ~ g	g
/tʰ/	tʰ	t	tʰ	tʰ
/kʰ/	kʰ	k	kʰ	kʰ
/q/	q	q	q	ɢ
/ɖ/	ɖ	t	ɽ	ɖ
/ʔ/	ʔ	ʔ	ʔ	ʔ
/ʔ/	–	ʔ	ʔ	ʔ

3.1.1.1 /b̥/ - (orthographic *b*)

The bilabial stop /b̥/ has been described as "not much voiced," "weakly voiced," or with "slight or weak voicing" in word-initial position (cf. Armstrong 1934; Edmondson et al. 2004; Orwin 1994; Pia 1965; Saeed 1999). As illustrated above in Figure 3.5, this sound in word-initial position is pronounced with variable voicing. The same goes for /d̥/ and /g̥/. The pairs in (1) illustrate its contrast in place and manner of articulation word-initially.

(1) *Contrasts with /b̥/*

/b̥/ vs. /d̥/	bád	'sea'	dád	'people'
/b̥/ vs. /g̥/	bán	'diarrhea'	gán	'point (of a hook)'
/b̥/ vs. /ɖ/	báx	'exit'	dháx	'stay out'
/b̥/ vs. /q/	baád	'extortion'	qáad	'capacity'
/b̥/ vs. /m/	boóg	'scab'	moóge	'absent-minded one'

The stop /b̥/ is realized voiced as [b] after a sonorant consonant when it is in the onset of word-internal syllable, as in *carbuún* [ʔar.buún] 'deposit.' In other word-internal onsets, it may be weakly voiced or voiceless. In final positions, it is voiceless as in *cábdi* [ʔáp.ti] 'Cabdi (man's name)' and *qaýb* [qaɪ̯p] 'portion.' The intervocalic realization of /b̥/ varies. For some Northern Somali speakers, it is [b] or [β], depending on its location relative to H tone. The former is found when the stop is in the onset of H tone syllable while the latter is found when H tone precedes it. For other speakers, it is the bilabial fricative [β], regardless of its location relative to H tone, like in *habár* [ha.βár] 'old woman' and *dhában* [ɖá.βan] 'cheek.'

3.1.1.2 /d̥/ - (orthographic *d*)

Realizations of /d̥/ are like those for /b̥/. It is an alveolar stop for most speakers but tends to dentalize in faster speech. In word-initial position, it contrasts with other consonants in both place and manner of articulation. In addition, it contrasts with /tʰ/. Word-initially, /d̪/ is sometimes realized with voicing and elsewhere with little to no voicing. Examples in (2) show word-initial contrasts in place and manner of articulation, as well as in laryngeal specification, involving /d̪/.

(2) *Contrasts relative to /d̪/*

/d̪/ vs. /b̪/	dád	'people'	bád	'sea'
/d̪/ vs. /g/	dáb	'fire'	gádh	'chin'
/d̪/ vs. /ɖ/	deéq	'donation'	dhéeg	'camel's flank'
/d̪/ vs. /tʰ/	díb	'back'	tíg	'wheelbarrow'
/d̪/ vs. /tʃ/	díin	'turtle'	jíin	'edge'
/d̪/ vs. /n/	dácas	'sandals'	nácas	'fool'
/d̪/ vs. /s/	dáw	'path'	sów	'perhaps'

The phoneme /d̪/ is realized voiced in a syllable onset after a sonorant (*gúrdan* [gúr.dan] 'stomp'). It is voiceless in codas (*mádli* [mát.li] 'postpone'). For some speakers, it is voiced and spirantized intervocalically, regardless of where it is located relative to H tone. For others, it is [d] before a H tone or [ð] after it, as in *gudín* [gʊ.dín] 'axe' and *fádal* [fá.ðal] 'type of footprint.'

3.1.1.3 /g/ - (orthographic *g*)

The velar stop /g/ patterns with other lenis stops. Among the three, it is the most consistently realized with full voicing word-initially. It contrasts with stops at other places of articulation, as well as with its fortis counterpart /kʰ/. Examples in (3) illustrate various word-initial contrasts involving /g/.

(3) *Contrasts relative to /g/*

/g/ vs. /b̪/	gád	'sale'	bád	'sea'
/g/ vs. /d̪/	gán	'hook'	dán	'objective'
/g/ vs. /q/	gúb	'burn'	qúb	'spill'
/g/ vs. /kʰ/	gób	'fig tree'	kób	'locality'

In a word-internal syllable onset after a sonorant, it is voiced, but in codas, it is voiceless. Intervocalically, it is spirantized to [ɣ], as in *gogól* [gɤ.ɣɤ́l] 'carpet' and *mágac* [má.ɣaʔ] 'name,' for some speakers, regardless of where it occurs relative to H tone. For other speakers, it is [g] in the onset of a word-internal H-toned syllable and [ɣ] when immediately preceded by a H-toned syllable.

3.1.1.4 /tʰ/ - (orthographic *t*)

Somali has two fortis stop phonemes whose behavior differs markedly from that of the lenis stops discussed thus far. These stops are sometimes described in the literature as simply being voiceless. However, the fact that they are realized with aspiration is key to understanding their behavior and distribution. Examples in (4) show word-initial contrasts relative to /tʰ/ in both place and manner of articulation, as well as with /d̪/.

(4) *Contrasts relative to /tʰ/*

/tʰ/ vs. /d̪/	tír	'cancel'	dír	'dispatch'
/tʰ/ vs. /kʰ/	táx	'thread beads'	káx	'barren land'
/tʰ/ vs. /n/	toób	'dress'	nóog	'fatigue'
/tʰ/ vs. /s/	tún	'nape'	sún	'poison'
/tʰ/ vs. /l/	túr	'be lenient'	lúr	'pester'
/tʰ/ vs. /tʃ/	tír	'cancel'	jír	'body'

These examples show that /tʰ/ is aspirated in word-initial position. The phone remains aspirated when it appears in word-internal onsets, whether after another consonant (*ábti* [áp.tʰi] 'maternal uncle') or intervocalically (*kutaán* [kʰu.tʰaán] 'parasite'). The location of H tone relative to /tʰ/ does not affect its realization. There are no instances of [tʰ] in word-internal syllable codas or word-finally. This is due to deaspiration, which neutralizes the contrast between /tʰ/ and /d̪/ in these environments. For more on this, see §3.4.2.

3.1.1.5 /kʰ/ - (orthographic *k*)

Somali's other fortis stop is the velar stop /kʰ/. This stop forms a natural class with /tʰ/, as discussed in §3.1.1.4. Examples in (5) show key contrasts involving /kʰ/ along the lines of place and manner of articulation and laryngeal specification.

(5) *Contrasts relative to /kʰ/*

/kʰ/ vs. /g/	káb	'shoe'	gáab	'shortness'
/kʰ/ vs. /tʰ/	kág	'freeze'	tág	'go'
/kʰ/ vs. /q/	kúur	'proximity'	quúr	'disrespect'
/kʰ/ vs. /χ/	kásab	'achievement'	khásab	'sugarcane'

The realization of the phoneme /kʰ/ retains its aspiration when it appears in an onset, be it word-initially in the examples in (5) or word-internally after a coda (*márkab* [már.kʰap] 'ship (n.)'). Aspiration also persists intervocalically regardless of its location relative to H tone. Like [tʰ], [kʰ] is never realized in a coda syllable, including word-finally. When the sound might be expected to occur in such a final position, it is neutralized to [k] via the deaspiration rule discussed in §3.4.2. As such, the contrast between /kʰ/ and /g/ is neutralized in final positions.

3.1.1.6 /q/ - (orthographic *q*)

The voiceless uvular stop /q/ patterns partially with lenis stops and partially with fortis stops in terms of the alternations that it undergoes. It is aspirated word-initially and has a voice onset time similar to that of other fortis stops. It has no contrastive lenis counterpart. Like lenis stops, however, it is voiced in an onset after a sonorant (*qalqal* [qʰǽl.gæl] 'shocked'). Key word-initial contrasts in place and manner of articulation relative to /q/ are in (6).

(6) *Contrasts relative to /q/*

/q/ vs. /g/	qód	'tree stump'	gód	'hole'	
/q/ vs. /ʔ/	qás	'mix'	cás	'red'	
/q/ vs. /χ/	qabíil	'clan'	khabíir	'expert'	

Like fortis stops, /q/ is realized voiceless and is deaspirated in codas as in (*tárraq* [tʰár.raq] 'match.' It remains voiceless and aspirated intervocalically, as in *wáqaf* [wá.qʰaf] 'donation' and *duqád* [du.qʰát] 'dent.'

The uvular stop /q/ contrasts with the uvular fricative /χ/ (orthographic *kh*) in Northern Somali. However, Benaadir/Central Somali varieties have lost this contrast in favor of /q/. Thus, the geographically southern dialects have a phonemic inventory lacking /χ/. For more on this, see §3.1.2.7.

3.1.1.7 /ɖ/ - (orthographic *dh*)

Descriptions of the consonant written *dh* vary widely. It has been described as a voiced retroflex stop, a retroflex implosive stop, and a post-alveolar implosive stop. In historical reconstructions of the Proto-Cushitic consonant inventory like Sasse (1978), the sound corresponds to an implosive alveolar stop. See Heine (1978) and Hamann and Fuchs (2008) for other perspectives. Accounts converge on the fact that its pronunciation involves a complex gesture. Armstrong (1934), for example, states that the pronunciation of *dh* first involves the production of a voiced post-alveolar stop with a pharyngeal constriction. Upon the release of this constriction, the sound takes on characteristics of a implosive.

For most speakers with whom I have worked, it appears both implosive and retroflexed in initial positions. In codas, however, it is devoiced and no longer imploded, but still realized with retroflexion. It is also realized as a retroflex flap intervocalically. Though retroflexion is sometimes a gestural effect arising from the tendency for implosive stops to both lower the tongue body and raise the tongue tip (Mary Paster, p.c.), these realizations in Somali would be curious if one were to assume that retroflexion is a secondary articulation.

In full recognition that this matter deserves further attention, I analyze the phonemic form of *dh* in this grammar to be the implosive retroflex stop /ɖ/. The symbol adopted here is not officially recognized by the International Phonetic Association. As such, it is not included in the IPA, though it is well-recognized.[3]

The distribution and allophony exhibited by /ɖ/ most closely matches that of other lenis stops. When /ɖ/ occurs word-initially and after a sonorant, it is voiced, as in *dhéer* [ɖɛ́ɛr] 'long' and *indhó* [ɪn.ɖɔ́] 'eyes.' It is realized as a voiceless retroflex stop in codas, as in *xidhnaán* [ħɪʈ.naán] 'closed' and *qúdh* [qʰúʈ] 'self.' It may weaken for some speakers intervocalically, regardless of its location relative to H tone, becoming a retroflex flap, as in *siídhi* [sií.ɽi] 'whistle.' The examples in (7) show several word-initial contrasts in place and manner of articulation relative to /ɖ/.

(7) *Contrasts relative to /ɖ/*

/ɖ/ vs. /d̪/	dhár	'cloth'	dár	'watering hole'
/ɖ/ vs. /g/	dheél	'joke'	géel	'camel'
/ɖ/ vs. /tʃ/	dhaár	'swear'	jáad	'category'
/ɖ/ vs. /ʃ/	dhíg	'put down'	shíl	'accident'
/ɖ/ vs. /j/	dhoól	'front tooth'	yóol	'goal'

The implosive [ɗ] is found in all Somali varieties, but not in the same distribution. In intervocalic onsets and in codas, /ɖ/ is consistently realized as a retroflex flap [ɽ] in Benaadir and Central Somali varieties. These differing pronunciations are reflected in the Somali orthography, with written *dh* vs. *r* being used interchangeably on websites and in both reference and pedagogical materials.

3.1.1.8 /ʡ/ - (orthographic *c*)

A phonetic study by Edmondson et al. (2004) describes written *c* as an epiglottal stop with a pharyngeal offglide. This determination is echoed in work on closely-related Dahalo by Maddieson et al. (1993) where cognates also exhibit an epiglottal stop. Both Orwin (1994) and Saeed (1999) describe the sound as a voiced pharyngeal fricative with creaky phonation. Armstrong (1934), too, describes it as a pharyngeal fricative, but with "intermittent" voicing. In his historical reconstruction of East Cushitic, Heine (1978) determines that this sound is descendent from a pharyngeal stop, while Sasse (1978) instead proposes a pre-glottalized pharyngeal fricative. In this grammar, I adopt the determination of the phonetic studies on the matter that *c* is synchronically the epiglottal stop /ʡ/.

The epiglottal stop is realized in a fairly consistent manner regardless of the word position that it appears in or whether or not it occurs before or after H tone. Some word-initial contrasts are seen in the examples in (8).

---

[3] Given the variety of reported pronunciations of *dh*, it is worthwhile to note that some resources on Somali transcribe the sound simply as the retroflex stop [ɖ].

(8) *Contrasts relative to /ʡ/*

/ʡ/ vs. /ʜ/	cág	'foot'	xág	'side'
/ʡ/ vs. /h/	cíir	'rash'	híil	'root for a team'
/ʡ/ vs. /q/	cúud	'incense (n.)'	qúud	'provisions'
/ʡ/ vs. /k/	cás	'red'	gás	'mane'

The sound also occurs in word-internal onsets after a coda (*rafcáan* [raf.ʡáan] 'appeal (n.)'), intervocalically (*nácas* [ná.ʡas] 'fool'), and word-finally (*hólac* [hɤ́.læʡ] 'flame'). While both /ʡ/ and /ʔ/ occur intervocalically and word-finally, I have not encountered any true minimal pairs involving these segments.

3.1.1.9 /ʔ/ - (orthographic ')

The glottal stop /ʔ/ does not contrast with other consonants word-initially, though it does contrast with other phonemes (including stops) word-finally, as seen in (9). Despite this lack of initial contrast, the glottal stop does appear word-initially but only before a vowel. For discussion on this, see Orwin (1994).

(9) *Contrasts relative to /ʔ/*

/ʔ/ vs. /ḅ/	lá'	'lacking'	láb	'male'
/ʔ/ vs. /ḍ/	dá'	'age'	dád	'people'
/ʔ/ vs. /q/	bá'	'suffering (n.)'	báq	'fear'

The glottal stop also appears in word-internal syllable codas (*lo'jír* [lɔʔ.tʃɪr] 'herdsmen'), though most of such instances are compounds. Likewise, it can appear intervocalically before a vowel-initial suffix, as in deverbal nouns (*la'aán* [la.ʔaán] 'state of being without'). It also often appears in loanwords from Arabic (*khaá'in* [χaá.ʔɪn] 'traitor').

3.1.2 Other consonants

3.1.2.1 /tʃ/ - (orthographic *j*)

The only affricate in the Somali inventory is post-alveolar /tʃ/. It appears in word-initial and word-internal syllable onsets where it generally patterns with lenis stops. It is sometimes voiceless and other times realized with slight pre-voicing. Word-initial examples showing that /tʃ/ contrasts in place of articulation with various stops and in manner with other post-alveolar consonants are in (10).

(10) Contrasts relative to /tʃ/

/tʃ/ vs. /ḍ/	jaán	'circle'	daán	'cliff'
/tʃ/ vs. /ɡ/	jabán	'broken'	gaabán	'small'
/tʃ/ vs. /ɖ/	jáar	'neighbor'	dhaár	'oath'
/tʃ/ vs. /ʃ/	jír	'body'	shír	'assembly'
/tʃ/ vs. /j/	jádh	'chop'	yád	'beat'

The affricate /tʃ/ is absent in syllable codas, including word-finally, in native Somali words. It does, however, appear in final positions in loanwords (*xáj* [ħatʃ] 'Hajj, the pilgrimage to Mecca'). It is realized with voicing intervocalically (*cajúus* [ʔa.dʒúus] 'old person').

3.1.2.2 /m/ - (orthographic *m*)

The bilabial nasal /m/ can be seen in (11) as contrasting word-initially in place of articulation with /n/ but also in manner with other non-nasal consonants.

(11) Contrasts relative to /m/

/m/ vs. /n/	máqal	'hear'	núqul	'duplicate'
/m/ vs. /ḅ/	méher	'marriage contract'	báhal	'wild animal'
/m/ vs. /w/	meél	'place'	wéel	'vessel'
/m/ vs. /f/	maál	'pus'	fáal	'omen'

The bilabial nasal exhibits similar contrasts intervocalically and can also appear in a word-internal syllable coda (*shimbír* [ʃɪm.bír] 'bird'). It does not appear word-finally and is instead neutralized to [n]. Compare, *nimán* 'men' and *nín* 'man' where the stem-final consonant alternates word-finally. Edmondson et al. (2004) report that, for their speaker, intervocalic /m/ is sometimes pronounced as a nasalized bilabial fricative or approximant [ṽ].

There is a length contrast in Somali nasal consonants intervocalically, though this is not robust. Compare, for example, *cámal* 'behavior' and *cammoóle* 'blind person.' For more on the properties of geminate nasals, see §3.1.3.2.

3.1.2.3 /n/ and /ŋ/ - (orthographic *n*)

The alveolar nasal /n/ contrasts in place of articulation with /m/ word-initially and intervocalically. The two neutralize in favor of [n] word-finally. Word-initial contrasts with other alveolar consonants are exemplified in (12).

(12) *Contrasts relative to /n/*

/n/ vs. /m/	naág	'woman'	máag	'provoke'
/n/ vs. /t/	náb	'stick on'	dáb	'fire'
/n/ vs. /tʰ/	náas	'udder'	taas	'that, those'
/n/ vs. /s/	núur	'light'	suurád	'picture'
/n/ vs. /l/	náx	'be startled'	láx	'ewe'
/n/ vs. /r/	nóog	'fatigue'	róob	'rain'

There is a contrast word-finally between a voiced /n/ and a (partially) voiceless alveolar nasal, /n̥/, but this is not indicated orthographically. For speakers with whom I have worked, the voiced nasal is fully but not always strongly voiced for its entire duration. Its counterpart is no different in length but is consistently devoiced approximately half-way through its production. Unlike what is reported by Armstrong (1934), I have found no substantive difference in the length of these consonants based on the length of the preceding vowel. Pairs for comparison are: /ɗan/ *dhán* 'side' vs. /ɗan̥/ *dhán* 'drink milk' and /ɗaan/ *dáan* 'lower jaw' vs. /ɗææn̥/ *daán* 'cliff.' The first of these pairs is represented in Figures 3.6 and 3.7, as produced by the same speaker. For 'side,' the nasal is 137ms and voiced for nearly its entirety. For 'drink,' however, the nasal in total is 126ms, with 66ms being voiced and 60ms being devoiced.

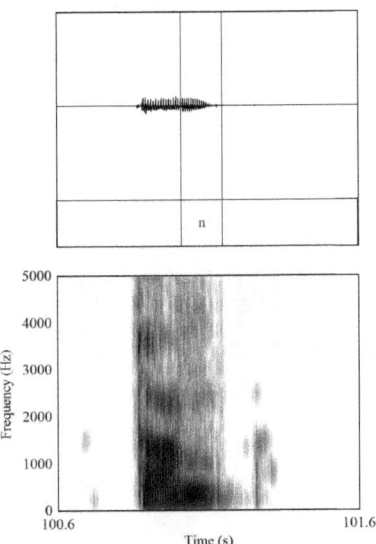

Fig. 3.6: *dhán* 'side' - spoken by AS

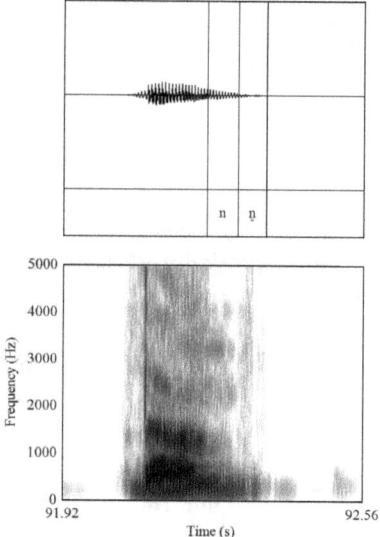

Fig. 3.7: *dhân* 'drink' - spoken by AS

Like with /m/ vs. /m:/, there is a length contrast between /n/ and /n:/ intervocalically. This can be seen in comparing words like *jánan* 'military general' vs. *jánno* 'paradise.' For more on geminate nasals, see §3.1.3.2.

3.1.2.4 /f/ - (orthographic *f*)

The labiodental fricative /f/ is realized [f] in initial (*fáas* [fǽæs] 'axe'), final (*qóf* [qʰɔ́f] 'person'), and intervocalic positions (*kifáax* [kʰi.fáaħ] 'struggle (n.)'). Word-initial contrasts relative to other labial and coronal consonants are in (13).

(13)   *Contrasts relative to /f/*

/f/ vs. /ɓ/	fáar	'sour milk'	báar	'peak'
/f/ vs. /m/	fáas	'axe'	móos	'dam'
/f/ vs. /w/	fíiq	'suck up a drink'	wíiq	'harm'
/f/ vs. /s/	fác	'age'	sác	'cow'
/f/ vs. /ʃ/	fín	'pimple'	shín	'time, due course'

3.1.2.5 /s/ - (orthographic *s*)

The alveolar fricative /s/ appears in all word positions, and its phonetic realization is consistent. Examples in (14) show key word-initial contrasts relative to /s/.

(14) Contrasts relative to /s/

/s/ vs. /ʃ/	sán	'nose'	shán	'five'
/s/ vs. /f/	sóoc	'sort out'	fóoc	'bulge'
/s/ vs. /n/	sábar	'waist'	nábar	'injury'
/s/ vs. /t/	sáb	'funeral meal'	dáb	'fire'
/s/ vs. /tʰ/	súke	'loner'	túke	'crow'

3.1.2.6 /ʃ/ - (orthographic *sh*)

Like other fricatives, the realization of the post-alveolar fricative /ʃ/ is consistent across all word positions, though it occurs far less frequently overall. The sound is well-attested in initial position, as in the examples in (15).

(15) Contrasts relative to /ʃ/

/ʃ/ vs. /s/	shíd	'kindle'	síd	'carry'
/ʃ/ vs. /χ/	shoód	'measuring cup'	khóof	'fear'
/ʃ/ vs. /tʃ/	shíl	'accident'	jíl	'imitate'
/ʃ/ vs. /ɖ/	shárad	'wager'	dhárab	'dew'
/ʃ/ vs. /j/	sháal	'shawl'	yéel	'obey'

The sound is found less often intervocalically (e.g., *buúshe* 'husk') and word-finally (e.g., *árbush* 'trouble') in native Somali words. It is more frequently found, however, in proper names and loanwords from various languages. For example, *komíshner* 'commissioner' and *Rúush* 'Russia.' The fricative [ʃ] also arises via assibilation when a sequence of /l+tʰ/ arises over some morpheme boundaries. For more on this, see §3.4.10.

3.1.2.7 /χ/ - (orthographic *kh*)

The voiceless uvular fricative /χ/ is phonemic, at least in Northern Somali. It appears almost exclusively in words borrowed from Arabic. The examples in (16) show that it contrasts word-initially in place of articulation with both /ʜ/ and /h/, as well as with the uvular and epiglottal stops, /q/ and /ʡ/, respectively.

(16) Contrasts relative to /χ/

/χ/ vs. /ʜ/	khóof	'fear'	xóog	'strength'
/χ/ vs. /h/	khásab	'force'	hár	'shadow'
/χ/ vs. /q/	khoorí	'canal'	qóor	'neck'
/χ/ vs. /ʡ/	kháyr	'goodness'	caýr	'poor people'

In addition to appearing in an onset, it appears in word-internal codas (*sakhráan* [saχ.ráan] 'drunk') and word-finally (*wasákh* [wasáχ] 'garbage'), as well as intervocalically (*dákhal* [dá.χal] 'mast (of boat)').

3.1.2.8 /ʜ/ - (orthographic *x*)

As with written *c*, descriptions concerning the nature of written *x* vary considerably. Saeed (1999) and Orwin (1994) echo proposals for Proto-Cushitic in asserting that the sound is the voiceless pharyngeal fricative /ħ/. However, two phonetic studies suggest epiglottal articulation. Armstrong (1934), for example, describes the sound as a voiceless epiglottalized pharyngeal fricative. Edmondson et al. (2004) asserts that the sound is synchronically realized as a voiceless epiglottal fricative. As I have done thus far, I adopt the findings of the more detailed phonetic analysis, treating and transcribing the sound as the epiglottal fricative /ʜ/. Examples in (17) illustrate key word-initial contrasts.

(17) *Contrasts relative to /ʜ/*

/ʜ/ vs. /χ/	*xásad*	'envy (n.)'	*khásab*	'force (n.)'
/ʜ/ vs. /h/	*xéer*	'custom'	*héer*	'rank (n.)'
/ʜ/ vs. /ʔ/	*xún*	'bad'	*cún*	'eat'
/ʜ/ vs. /q/	*xún*	'bad'	*qún*	'tonsil'

In addition to appearing word-initially, the sound is also found both in codas (*saddéx* [sad.déʜ] 'three') and in word-internal onsets (*suuxín* [suu.ʜín] 'anesthetic').

3.1.2.9 /h/ - (orthographic *h*)

The voiceless glottal fricative /h/ is found in both initial and final positions. In word-initial position, it is realized [h] and contrasts with fricatives at other places of articulation. Examples of word-initial contrasts are in (18).

(18) *Contrasts relative to /h/*

/h/ vs. /ʜ/	*héer*	'class, rank'	*xéer*	'custom'
/h/ vs. /χ/	*hóor*	'raindrops'	*khoóri*	'canal'

The voiceless glottal fricative contrasts with a variety of other sounds, as well as with /ʔ/, intervocalically. However, in this position, it is realized with voicing as /ɦ/ (*kuháan* [kʰu.ɦáan] 'diviner'). It also occurs lexically in word-final position, as clear from the language's orthography, but it is often unpronounced in this position (*káah* [kʰáah] ~[kʰáa] 'ray (of light)').

3.1.2.10 /l/ and /l̥/ - (orthographic *l*)

The lateral approximant /l/ is found word-initially and intervocalically. It is fully voiced in both positions. The examples in (19) illustrate word-initial contrasts with other coronal consonants, as well as with the rhotic /r/.

(19) *Contrasts relative to /l/*

/l/ vs. /r/	láb	'male'	ráb	'narrow place'
/l/ vs. /n/	lúr	'nuisance'	núur	'light'
/l/ vs. /s/	láx	'ewe'	sáx	'correctness'
/l/ vs. /t/	líx	'six'	tíx	'stanza'

This consonant also occurs word-finally, but there is a notable contrast in this position between voiced /l/ and partially devoiced /l̥/, similar to that described above for /n/ vs. /n̥/. There is no orthographic distinction made between the two phones. Voiced /l/ is voiced for its entire duration. Its voiceless counterpart is approximately the same length but is devoiced for the last 25% of its duration. There appears to be no substantive difference in duration in either of these based on the length of a preceding vowel. Pairs for comparison include: /dul/ *dúl* 'patience' vs. /dul̥/ *dúl* 'nostril' and /fool/ *fóol* 'face' vs. /fool̥/ *fóol* 'labor pain.'

Singleton /l/ and its geminate counterpart /l:/ contrast intervocalically, and this is captured in the language's orthography. Compare *salaán* [sa.laán] 'greeting' and *salláan* [sæl.lǽæn] 'staircase.' For more on geminate sonorants, see §3.1.3.2.

3.1.2.11 /r/ and /r̥/ - (orthographic *r*)

Somali's other liquid consonants are alveolar trills. The voiced trill appears word-initially, as in examples in (20), which show contrasts for place and manner of articulation.

(20) *Contrasts relative to /r/*

/r/ vs. /l/	rún	'truth'	lún	'be lost'
/r/ vs. /n/	rúug	'knee'	núug	'suckle'
/r/ vs. /t/	rág	'men'	tág	'go'
/r/ vs. /s/	rúux	'soul'	suúdi	'heat of sun'

Intervocalically, /r/ is realized as the flap [ɾ]. It is realized as such regardless of its location relative to H tone. Compare *Cárab* [ʔá.ɾap] 'Arab' and *biriír* [bi.ɾiír] 'forehead.'[4]

---

[4] Recall that orthographic *r* in Central/Benaadir Somali, in correspondence with Northern *dh*, is pronounced [ɽ].

This sound also occurs word-finally, but similar to what occurs for the alveolar nasal and the lateral approximant, it has a voiceless counterpart /r̥/ with which it contrasts in this position. Both are approximately the same length. There is no distinction made between them in the language's orthography. As seen in Figures 3.8 and 3.9, the phone that most scholars consider to be voiced /r/ is in fact partially devoiced. Its voiceless counterpart, however, is in fact clearly voiceless in its entirety. There is no apparent difference in length between them that depends on the length of the preceding vowel. Pairs for comparison include: /ʔir/ cír 'sky' vs. /ʔir̥/ cír 'bolus' and /ḇeer/ béer 'liver' vs. /ḇeer̥/ beér 'field.' In the latter, it is possible that there is some affect of H tone location on the realization of the liquid.

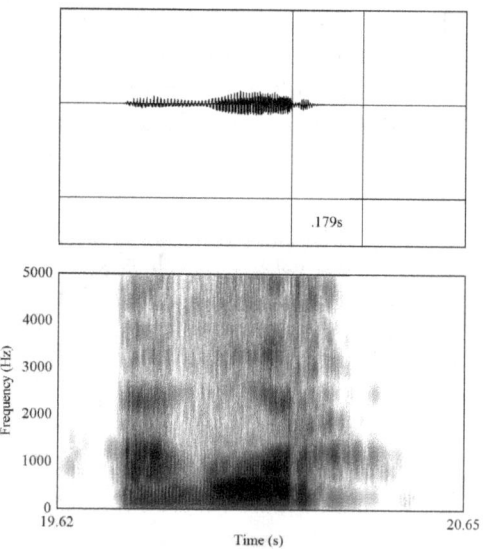

Fig. 3.8: *abúur* 'create' - spoken by AS

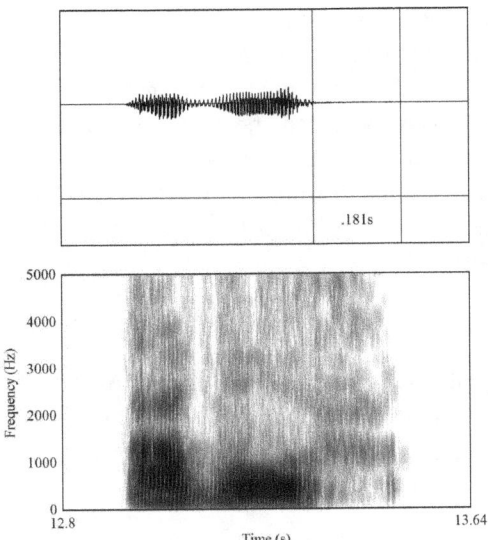

Fig. 3.9: *abúur* 'seed' - spoken by AS

Like with /l/, singleton /r/ contrasts with geminate /r:/ both intervocalically (cf. *cárrab* [ʔár.rap] 'tongue' and 'Arab,' above) and word-finally, but only the former is reflected in the language's orthography. Geminate sonorants are discussed in §3.1.3.2.

3.1.2.12 /j/ - (orthographic *y*)

The palatal glide /j/ contrasts with a variety of other consonants, and with the labiovelar glide /w/, in word-initial position. This is seen in (21). These same contrasts are found in word-internal syllable onsets where /j/ can occur intervocalically (*maayád* 'flood') and after another consonant (*nábyo* 'slander').

(21)   *Contrasts relative to /j/*

/j/ vs. /w/	yáab	'surprise'	wáab	'small hut'
/j/ vs. /l/	yúul	'bald'	lúr	'nuisance'
/j/ vs. /d/	yéel	'deed'	dhéel	'game'
/j/ vs. /ʃ/	yár	'small'	shár	'evil'
/j/ vs. /tʃ/	yúuc	'swell'	júuc	'laziness'

Written *y* is found before another word-final consonant in instances where it is typically described as the second member of the diphthongs *ay*, *ey*, and *oy*. Words like *qaýb* 'portion' show that it can carry H tone and accordingly that it counts as a tone bearing unit, at least in some instances. Exceptions to this are discussed in Section

3.2.5. Glides also appear word internally within a stem before another consonant that is syllabified into an onset (e.g., *dawlád* 'government') but never before a heterosyllabic C.C sequence. The restriction is relaxed before certain affixes, such as definite determiners, as in *qaýbta* 'the piece, the part.' This may reflect the fact that definite determiners prosodify outside of the word as clitics (Green and Morrison 2018), leaving them subject to somewhat different phonotactic requirements.

There are also orthographic words where *y* appears word-finally after a long vowel (e.g., *dhaáy* 'fresh milk' and *Báay*, the name of a city), but §3.2.5 discusses that these might be best considered phonetic offglides.

3.1.2.13 /w/ - (orthographic *w*)

Examples in (22) show that the labiovelar glide /w/ contrasts word-initially with labial consonants at other manners of articulation, as well as with the palatal glide /j/. These contrasts also hold when /w/ occurs intervocalically (e.g., *dáwo* /ḍawo/ 'medicine' vs. *dáyo* /ḍajo/ 'jackal').

(22) *Contrasts relative to /w/*

/w/ vs. /ɓ/	wéli	'saint'	beéni	'contradict'
/w/ vs. /m/	wán	'ram'	máro	'cloth'
/w/ vs. /f/	wáraf	'sling'	fáraq	'difference'
/w/ vs. /j/	wéel	'vessel'	yéel	'deed'

Similar to what is described above for written *y*, written *w* is typically described as the second half of the diphthongs *aw*, *ow*, and *uw*. This can be seen in monosyllabic words where a *vowel+w* sequence is followed by a word-final consonant, like in *haẃl* 'work' and *jówr* 'tyranny.' There are many instances where a phonetic [w] occurs word-finally after a short vowel. A comparison of words with final [w], like *qáw* 'ravine' and *qaẃ* 'thud,' once again show that *w* functions as a tone bearing unit, at least in some instances, in that it is able to host a H tone. There are exceptions to this discussed in Section 3.2.5. Unlike /j/, there are no instances that I have found in which *w* appears word-finally after a long vowel.

3.1.3 Geminate consonants

Somali has contrastive geminate stops and sonorants, though these are fairly limited in their distribution relative to their singleton counterparts. It is necessary to discuss these two groups of geminates separately as they differ both in their behavior and their distribution. Geminate oral stops are first discussed in §3.1.3.1, and geminate sonorants are later discussed in §3.1.3.2. In addition to the geminate consonants that are part of a word's lexical representation, there are also surface geminates that emerge in some instances upon the concatenation of two morphemes as the result of alternations. These are discussed in Sections 3.4.2 and 3.4.4. In §3.1.3.3, the matter of so-called "virtual geminates" is taken up, including whether there is evidence to include them into the language's consonant inventory.

3.1.3.1 Geminate stops

In addition to singleton fortis and lenis stops, Somali has a third series of stop consonants. These geminate stops stand in direct contrast with /ḅ/, /ḍ/, /g̣/, and /ɖ/ and are indicated in the Somali orthography by a written double consonant (i.e., *bb*, *dd*, *gg*). The exception to this is *dh* which may be written *dhdh* or sometimes simply as *ddh* or *dh*. There are instances, however, in which a written *CC* does not represent a lexical geminate but rather a morphologically-derived sequence of two consonants that may surface as a geminate due to assimilatory alternations.

There is abundant evidence for a historical contrast in length between geminate and singleton stops, though this is sometimes difficult to observe directly in modern Somali. Geminate stops do not occur word-initially, so no direct comparison can be made to singleton stops in that position. That these segments are absent word-initially is not surprising, of course, given that they are uncommon, though not entirely absent, in this position cross-linguistically. See discussion and evidence presented for geminate onsets in Topintzi (2014). One can find evidence for stem-final geminates, however, at least in some morphological environments, despite the fact that stem-final geminates are shortened via degemination word-finally (see §3.4.3). It is only when lexical geminates appear intervocalically that their true nature can be clearly witnessed. As introduced above, the precise realization of intervocalic geminates varies between speakers. For the speakers described by Bendjaballah and Le Gac (2019), they are realized phonetically as singleton stops. For some speakers with whom I have worked, they maintain their length. This is shown in Figures 3.3 and 3.4 above. Despite this variation, intervocalic lexical geminate stops can be directly compared to lexical singleton stops. The latter are easily distinguishable in that they are consistently realized as spirants in this position. Thus, in all instances, a contrast is maintained, but its synchronic phonetic realization has come to be realized differently over time.

Intervocalic geminate stops are voiced throughout their entire closure. The examples in (23) illustrate contrasts between geminate stops and both their fortis and lenis singleton counterparts. For the bilabial stop /ḅ/ and the implosive stop /ɖ/ there are no fortis singleton stops in the inventory.

(23) *Geminate stop contrasts*

/bː/ vs. /ɓ/	a.	gábbal	'daylight'	gábal	'portion'
	b.	sabbáar	'living expenses'	sábar	'waist'
/dː/ vs. /ɖ/	c.	qáddin	'prepay'	qádan	'fate'
	d.	múddac	'argument'	múdac	'awl'
/dː/ vs. /tʰ/	e.	saddéx	'three'	sáti	'woven bowl'
	f.	xaddáad	'blacksmith'	xátab	'rung of ladder'
/gː/ vs. /ɠ/	f.	óggol	'approval'	ogáal	'knowledge'
/gː/ vs. /kʰ/	g.	duggáal	'shelter'	dukáan	'shop (n.)'
/ɖ̡ː/ vs. /ɖ̡/	h.	cádhdho	'scabies'	cádho	'anger'

Verb stems present one piece of evidence for underlying stem-final geminate stops. When an underlying geminate occurs word-finally, as in the formation of the Imperative, it is simplified via degemination. This is seen with the verb *cáb* 'drink,' which is pronounced as such in isolation. However, when the word-final environment is removed, the geminate emerges. For example, the 1SG past form *cabbay* 'I drank,' is realized with a geminate stem-final consonant.[5]

3.1.3.2 Geminate sonorants

The consonant inventory also includes geminate sonorants. These are the geminate nasals, /mː/ and /nː/, and the geminate liquids, /lː/ and /rː/. Geminate sonorants are not found word-initially, but intervocalically they can be directly compared to singletons. Geminate sonorants are approximately twice as long as corresponding singletons. Compare Figures 3.10 and 3.11 with geminate vs. singleton *m*.

Other examples of singleton vs. geminate sonorants are seen in (24), some of which are true minimal pairs.

(24) *Intervocalic geminate sonorant contrasts*

/mː/	a.	damíin	'slow learner'	dammíin	'bail bond'
	b.	dúmar	'women'	dummád	'cat'
/nː/	c.	gunáad	'scab'	gunnád	'woven purse'
	d.	dhínac	'direction'	dhánnax	'tiny bit'
/lː/	e.	gálac	'kind of spear'	galládʼ	'gratitude'
	f.	hóloc	'flame'	hollób	'scaly skin'
	g.	jílib	'knee'	jíllab	'camel pasture'
/rː/	h.	bíre	'milk container'	bírre	'spear of grain'
	i.	cáro	'anger'	cárro	'dirt'
	j.	máro	'cloth'	márro	'sub-clan'

---

5 As discussed in §7.5, that the geminate can surface here can be seen as due to the presence of an open skeletal slot left unoccupied by the language's phonetically null (∅) 1SG person marker. In its corresponding 2SG form *cabtay* 'you (SG) drank,' the stop is not realized as a geminate, presumably because no such empty slot is present. The slot is instead occupied by the 2SG person marker *-t-*.

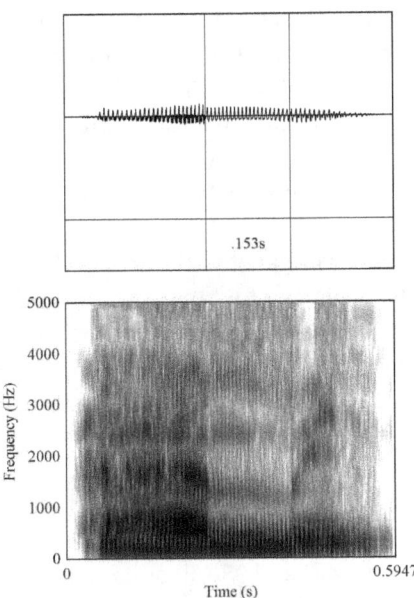

Fig. 3.10: *aámmin* 'trustworthy person' - spoken by AS

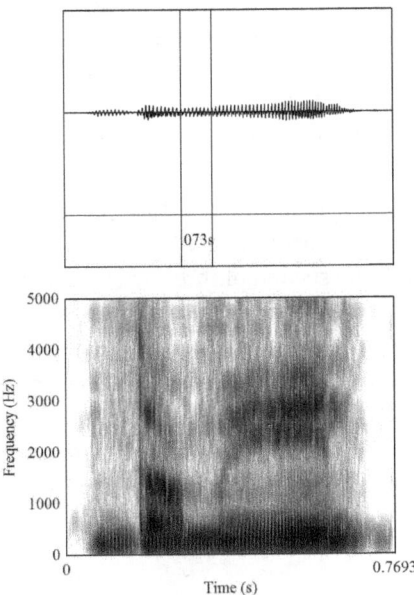

Fig. 3.11: *damíin* 'slow learner' - spoken by AS

3.1.3.3 "Virtual geminates"

Some scholars (Barillot 2002; Barillot and Ségéral 2005; Ségéral and Scheer 2001) have proposed that Somali's "voiceless" stops (i.e., written *t* and *k*) are best considered "virtual geminates." That is, these segments are argued to exhibit geminate-like behavior and to be lexically represented as geminates, despite the fact that they surface phonetically as singleton stops in all instances. Orwin and Gaarriye (2010) have also noted that these stops, but also several other segments, pattern in exceptional ways in poetic metrics compared to other consonants.

One piece of evidence offered in support of the proposal of virtual geminates relates to what Barillot and Ségéral (2005) call the "voicing of *t*," though this can be extended to *k* as well. Barillot & Ségéral argue that there is a rule in Somali whereby *t* (and *k*) are "voiced" and further spirantized when they occur intervocalically.[6] The basis of this argument stems from two specific instances in which *t* (and *k*) do indeed lenite intervocalically in this way. This can be seen, for example, when a noun ending in a vowel is followed by a definite determiner (compare *mindí* 'knife' and *mindída* 'the knife' [mindíða]). It also occurs in middle verbs in the 1SG and 3SG.M whose person/gender exponent is phonologically ∅ such as in *kabbadaa* 'I sip' (> kabb + at + ∅ + aa). The latter can be immediately compared to 2SG and 3SG.F forms where the presence of the person marker -*t*- – i.e., the presence of an underlying morphological geminate – blocks lenition. This is seen in *kabbataa* 'you (SG) sip' (> kabb + at + t + aa). Based on this blocking, Barillot & Ségéral argue that the failure of *t* to lenite intervocalically in comparable inflected forms of verbs like *matág* 'vomit,' *hitíq* 'walk slowly,' and others like them, is evidence for these stops being underlying geminates.

A challenge faced by this approach is that it fails to address the fact that lenition is possible only across morpheme boundaries and never within a stem. Green and Morrison (2018) have argued that lenition and other sandhi alternations are not possible within a prosodic word. Indeed, no such lenition can occur within or across two words in a compound, which also form a single prosodic word.

A second argument offered by Barillot et al. (2018) in favor of "virtual" geminates concerns the the outcomes of vowel/∅ alternation. As discussed in §3.5, Somali has many instances in which a short vowel nucleus in the second of three syllables in sequence alternates with ∅. For example, *diirsán* 'to warm oneself' emerges rather than *diirisán via loss of the Weak Causative extension's vowel (> diir + is + an). Vowel/∅ alternation is notably blocked by the presence of a geminate. This is understandably because reduction would yield a phonotactically disallowed sequence of "three" consonants (CCC); e.g., *kabbadaa* 'I sip' (> kabb + at + ∅ + aa), *kabbdaa. Tri-consonantal sequences are also avoided that do not involve geminates, so this is a general prohi-

---

[6] Recall from above that the matter of "voicing" is problematic given the behavior of Somali stops more broadly.

bition in the language. Compare, *gudubtaa* 'you (SG) cross' (> gudub + t + aa) and *gudbaa* 'I cross' (> gudub + ∅ + aa).

Barillot et al. compare these outcomes to the blocking of vowel/∅ alternation in the presence of stem-internal *t*, as in verbs like *matág* and *hitíq* (e.g., *matagaa* 'I vomit' (> matag + ∅ + aa), **matgaa*). They contend that blocking must be due to the fact that *t* is underlyingly geminate. However, there are least two other possible explanations for such blocking, both of which again relate to morphophonology and do not require an expansion of the underlying consonant inventory. As mentioned just above, Green and Morrison (2018) suggest that certain alternations – including vowel/∅ alternation – occur only in particular morphophonological domains. They contend that lenition processes like those affecting verbal suffixes upon inflection, and also determiners, occur at the word-level but *not* at the stem-level. Under such an approach, because the *t* in *matág* and *hitíq* is stem-internal, it would not be susceptible to lenition processes which act only in morphologically-derived environments. It may also be the case that instances of V/∅ alternation blocking are due to phonotactics. There may simply be a phonotactic constraint blocking V/∅ alternation in those instances where [tʰ] would be syllabified into a coda. Recall that this sound never occurs in a coda elsewhere in the language. From a standpoint of poetics, the exceptional behavior of these aspirated phones, but also *f, s, sh, j, y,* and *w*, may instead be due to their inherently longer duration.

With these thoughts in mind, I do not include geminate *t* or *k* in Somali's phonemic inventory of consonants. I instead attribute their exceptional behavior to constraints on the language's phonotactics and their ability (or not) to undergo alternations in certain prosodic domains.

3.2 Vowels

Somali has ten contrastive short vowel phonemes that are divided into two harmonic sets: /ɪ, ɛ, a, ɔ, u/ and /i, e, æ, ɤ, ɯ/. In addition to these short vowel phonemes, each vowel has a contrastive long counterpart, and there are five diphthongs. Somali does not have contrastive long diphthongs, though there will be more to say about this in §3.2.5.

Scholars have long been aware that Somali exhibits vowel harmony, though the phonological basis of the lexical contrast between the two harmonic sets of vowels has been debated. Most descriptions of the vowel system (e.g., Andrzejewski 1955; Angoujard and Hassan 1991; Armstrong 1934; Mohamoud 2013) assume an ATR (advanced tongue root) or tense/lax distinction between the harmonic sets, but there are exceptions. For example, Berchem (1991) proposes that Somali has "neutral" vs. "centralized" vowels. Edmondson et al. (2004) proposes that the distinction is instead based upon whether the supraglottal cavity is "sphinctered" or "expanded." Kimper et al.

(2018) aimed to begin to tease apart some finer-grained phonetic details of the two vowel harmony sets, but results were inconclusive.

Despite the contributions made by these works, further detailed study of Somali vowel harmony contrasts has been hindered in large part by the fact that no reasonably comprehensive list of which Somali words exhibit a given harmony series has been published. There is also no orthographic distinction made between vowels in the two series, and words whose vowels exhibit one vs. the other harmonic set of vowels are inconsistently marked, if at all, in the literature. A project undertaken by Laura Downing and Morgan Nilsson at the University of Gothenburg has recently made great strides to address this descriptive lacuna. As reflected in Nilsson and Downing (2019), the authors have revisited the Somali vowel system, reporting a variety of minimal and near minimal pairs that clearly substantiate the presence of a harmonic contrast (at least in long vowels) between what they and others call "neutral" vs. "culus" (heavy) vowels. Downing and Nilsson graciously shared data from their project with me, as well as lists of words that they compiled from various resources where words are marked according to harmonic set, totaling approximately 3,000 entries. Some examples that I provide below are entries extracted from the aforementioned lists. Other examples and all formant measurements provided below are drawn from my own data collection with three Somali speakers, two from Mogadishu and one from Bu'ale.

Based on the data available, and upon comparison to an array of African language harmony systems discussed in work by Casali (2003, 2008, 2016) and Rose (2017), it seems most appropriate to describe Somali vowels relative to the phonological feature [ATR]. This is done with the understanding, as discussed in the aforementioned works, that not all languages implement this feature in the same way phonetically. This distinction is, for all intents and purposes, captured in works by Saeed (1999) and Nilsson and Downing (2019). These works describe the two vowel series as neutral vs. culus, which equate here with the features [-ATR] and [+ATR], respectively. The former series contains /ɪ, ɛ, u, ɔ, a/ and the latter contains /i, e, ɯ, ɣ, æ/. One can clearly see in comparing the two series that not all vowel pairs are prototypical "tense" vs. "lax" counterparts, but rather, some pairs involve centralization instead of, or in addition to raising. The examples in (25) and (26) show harmonic pairs of short and long vowels, respectively.

(25) *Harmonic pairs for short vowels: [-ATR] vs. [+ATR]*

/ɪ/	díb	'back'	/i/	ríd	'hurl'
	íb	'orifice'		ibí	'afterbirth'
/ɛ/	dég	'peak'	/e/	dég	'alight'
	edéb	'politeness'		éb	'complete'
/a/	xád	'steal'	/æ/	xád	'border'
	cád	'white'		cád	'piece of meat'
/u/	búg	'forgery'	/ɯ/	búd	'grave'
	súg	'make clear'		súg	'wait'
/ɔ/	ór	'chant (n.)'	/ɤ/	ór	'rag'
	caáro	'spider'		caádo	'custom'

In exploring the behavior of Somali's vowel system, two facts become immediately clear. First, words whose vowels are from the [-ATR] series far outnumber those with vowels from the [+ATR] series. Second, minimal pairs are found but are not many in number, even within the same harmony series. That said, minimal or near minimal pairs are far easier to come by for *i*, *u*, and *a*, at least for short vowels. They are relatively few in number for *e* and *o*. Words of the shape *CeC* are especially infrequent in the language. Minimal and near minimal pairs for long vowels of different qualities are somewhat more prevalent.

(26) *Harmonic pairs for long vowels: [-ATR] vs. [+ATR]*

/ɪɪ/	díin	'religion'	/ii/	díin	'turtle'
	iimáan	'chief'		iimáan	'belief'
/ɛɛ/	feér	'rib'	/ee/	feér	'punch'
	eég	'look at'		éeg	'present time'
/aa/	ammáan	'security'	/ææ/	ammaán	'praise'
	saán	'animal hide'		saámi	'share (n.)'
/uu/	búuq	'noise'	/ɯɯ/	búug	'book'
	duúl	'fly'		duúl	'attack'
/ɔɔ/	doón	'want'	/ɤɤ/	doón	'boat'
	dóob	'bachelor'		doóbi	'milking vessel'

To begin, the distribution in vowel space of F1 vs. F2 for Somali's short [-ATR] vowels is provided in Figure 3.12 and that of short [+ATR] vowels is in Figure 3.13. Vowels are first presented separately here in order to illustrate that there are clear acoustic distinctions between different vowels within the same harmony set. The [-ATR] plot is representative of 191 tokens from three speakers and the [+ATR] plot represents 109 tokens from the same three speakers. Three tokens of a given monosyllabic word were elicited for each questionnaire entry, with one speaker also completing a second, longer questionnaire. Care was taken to control for the consonantal frame surrounding the vowels, to the extent possible, in hopes of arriving at a fairly clear picture of the vowel qualities themselves without deviations due to flanking consonants. Tokens containing noise or disfluencies were discarded. Vowels were selected via textgrid in Praat (https://www.fon.hum.uva.nl/praat/) and formants were extracted with Lennes' SpeCT formant extraction script (https://lennes.github.io/spect/). Outliers were corrected by hand, which is particularly applicable to high back vowels where F1 and F2 are close to one another and sometimes difficult to differentiate computationally. Vowel plotting was done using the University of Oregon NORM plotting suite (http://lingtools.uoregon.edu/norm/norm1.php) with Lobanov normalization. Vowel means are indicated with ellipses illustrating one standard deviation from the mean. These figures illustrate that there is some overlap in vowel space between [-ATR] front vowels, with similar overlap in vowel space between [+ATR] back vowels.

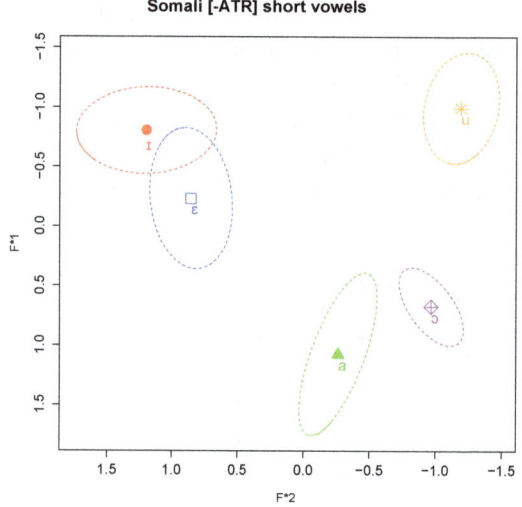

Fig. 3.12: Normalized F1 vs. F2 plot for three speakers - short, [-ATR] vowels

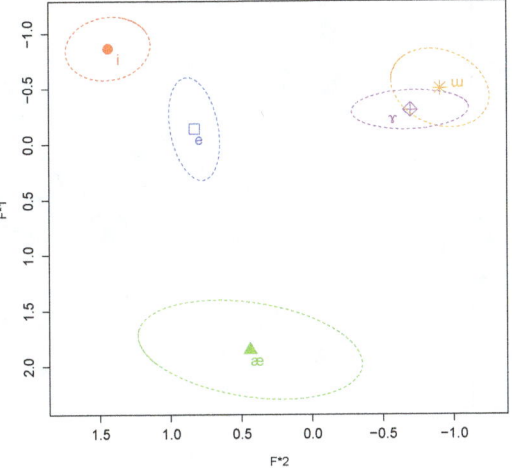

Fig. 3.13: Normalized F1 vs. F2 plot for three speakers - short, [+ATR] vowels

Generally speaking, [+ATR] vowels are raised and sometimes fronted relative to their [-ATR] counterparts. The high front vowels witnessed raising and fronting. The front mid vowels are distinguished primarily via fronting while the low vowels are primarily distinguished by raising. There is a remarkable degree of raising between [-ATR] and [+ATR] mid back vowels. For the high back vowels, the notable distinction between the two harmony series is that the [+ATR] vowel is centralized.

In comparing a given speaker's productions, there are individual differences in how one speaker implements the [ATR] contrast relative to another that are difficult to appreciate in a plot of averages across several speakers. It would be impractical to tease apart the various possibilities here. Rather, for reference here, Figure 3.14 shows how one of my consultants realizes [-ATR] vs. [+ATR] short vowels in his speech. I have chosen this speaker's vowel system because it appears to best approximate the generalizations captured in the amalgamated speaker averages above.

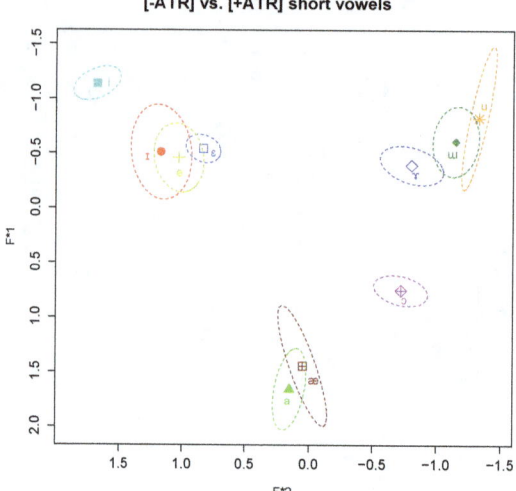

Fig. 3.14: Normalized F1 vs. F2 plot for short vowels - speech of Al

There is clearer differentiation in the quality of long vowels both within a harmony series and in a comparison of [-ATR]/[+ATR] harmony counterparts. Figure 3.15 shows F1 vs. F2 averages for long vowels for two speakers. Averages are representative of 18 tokens for each vowel. In each instance, there is a clear tendency for raising and fronting for each vowel. These findings for long vowels largely align themselves with what is reported by Nilsson and Downing (2019).

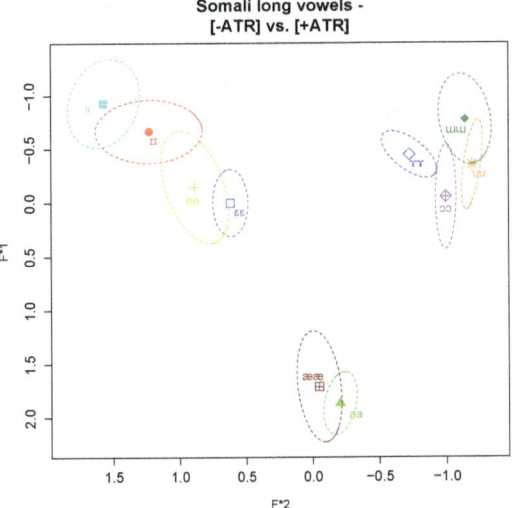

Fig. 3.15: Normalized F1 vs. F2 plot for long vowels for two speakers

Overall, contrasts between Somali vowels within the same harmony series can be established along the dimensions of height and backness. The dimension of ATR relates specifically to distinctions between harmonic pairs. Front vowel pairs ɪ/i and ɛ/e are redundantly unround. Back vowel pairs u/ɯ and ɔ/ɤ differ to some extent in their roundedness, but the distinction between them is multifaceted, also involving centralization and raising. As such, there is no apparent grounds for an independent contrast in roundness for low vowels. In attempting to motivate these contrasts directly in the sections below, CVC and CVVC words are used as exemplars. Doing so is most straightforward but also fraught with certain challenges. For example, though Somali has numerous CVC shaped words, the vocalic composition of these words is not evenly distributed. Words of this shape containing *i*, *u*, and *a* are far more widespread than those with *e* and *o*. This skewed distribution makes finding a diverse set of true minimal pairs a sizable challenge. This challenge is compounded by these limited sets being further sub-divided into the two harmonic series. Because contrasts between harmonic pairs were established just above, they will not be given below. As in §3.1, examples below use both orthography and the IPA.

3.2.1 [-ATR] short vowels - *ɪ, ɛ, u, ɔ, a*

Somali's neutral or [-ATR] vowels are /ɪ/, /ɛ/, /u/, /ɔ/, and /a/. With the exception of /u/, these vowels fall into a natural class that one might expect to encounter for prototypical "lax" vowels. However, perhaps due to the inability of the high back vowel /u/ to raise further, its [+ATR] counterpart is centralized instead of raised, being /ɯ/.

(27)   *[-ATR] vowel contrasts relative to height and backness*

/ɪ/ vs. /ɛ/	bɪ́r	'metal'	bɛ́d	'safety'
/ɪ/ vs. /u/	fɪ́r	'origin'	fúr	'open'
/ɪ/ vs. /a/	fɪ́n	'pimple'	fán	'art'
/ɛ/ vs. /ɔ/	bɛ́d	'safety'	qɔ́d	'tree stump'
/ɛ/ vs. /a/	hɛ́l	'find'	hál	'one'
/u/ vs. /ɔ/	dúl	'top, surface'	tɔ́l	'kinfolk'

3.2.2 [+ATR] short vowels - *i, e, ɯ, ʏ, æ*

Somali's culus or [+ATR] vowels are /i/, /e/, /ɯ/, /ʏ/, and /æ/. The front and low vowels form a natural class that might otherwise be expected for prototypical "tense" vowels. The back vowels are generally more centralized than their [-ATR] counterparts.

(28)   *[+ATR] vowel contrasts relative to height and backness*

/i/ vs. /e/	díbi	'bull'	dhegó	'ears'
/i/ vs. /ɯ/	rí'	'goat'	rúg	'thud'
/i/ vs. /æ/	díb	'tail'	dá'	'age'
/e/ vs. /ʏ/	lég	'brisket'	róg	'turn over'
/e/ vs. /æ/	déd	'cover with blanket'	kág	'freeze'
/ɯ/ vs. /ʏ/	gúb	'burn'	gób	'aristocracy'

3.2.3 [-ATR] long vowels - *ii, ɛɛ, uu, ɔɔ, aa*

The neutral [-ATR] long vowels are /ɪː/, /ɛː/, /uː/, /ɔː/, and /aː/, all of which are written orthographically with double vowels. These vowels are of comparable quality and approximately twice the length of their singleton counterparts.

(29)   *Long [-ATR] vowel contrasts relative to height and backness*

/ɪː/ vs. /ɛː/	mɪ́ɪr	'clear liquid'	meél	'place'
/ɪː/ vs. /aː/	dɪ́ɪg	'rooster'	daáq	'graze'
/ɪː/ vs. /uː/	lɪ́ɪn	'citrus fruit'	luúq	'voice'
/ɛː/ vs. /aː/	beér	'field'	báar	'tip'
/ɛː/ vs. /ɔː/	yéel	'deed'	yóol	'goal post'
/uː/ vs. /ɔː/	rúug	'knee'	róob	'rain'

3.2.4 [+ATR] long vowels - *ii, ee, ɯɯ, ʏʏ, ææ*

The culus [+ATR] long vowels are /iː/, /eː/, /ɯː/, /ʏː/, and /æː/, which are written orthographically with double vowels. These vowels are also of comparable quality and approximately twice the length of their singleton counterparts.

(30) *Long [+ATR] vowel contrasts relative to height and backness*

/iː/ vs. /eː/	*iíb*	'buy'	*éeg*	'now'
/iː/ vs. /æː/	*wiíq*	'harm'	*waáx*	'quarter'
/iː/ vs. /ɯː/	*gíir*	'spotted'	*guúl*	'victory'
/eː/ vs. /æː/	*béer*	'liver'	*báad*	'wing'
/eː/ vs. /ʏː/	*féer*	'punch'	*foód*	'forehead'
/ɯː/ vs. /ʏː/	*júuc*	'laziness'	*joóg*	'stay'

3.2.5 Diphthongs

Somali has five diphthongs, written *ay, ey, oy, aw*, and *ow*, all of which fall in sonority. Their tonal behavior is inconsistent and their ability to function as a tone bearing unit varies according to where they appear in a word and whether the word has one or more syllables. The pair of nouns *éy* 'male dog' and *eý* 'female dog' illustrates that both elements of a diphthong can function as a tone bearing unit, suggesting that they are both moraic. Despite their ability to bear a tone, the glide portion of a diphthong is not always counted in calculating the location of tone assignment. Recall that H tone is assigned to the final or penultimate mora of stems; for more on this, see Chapter 5. Words like *árday* 'student' illustrate that a word-final offglide is counted for tone assignment only when a word has two vocalic moras. If there are more than two moras, the final offglide is ignored in calculating the location of tone assignment.[7] Likewise, when word-internal in such longer words, the glide is ignored for the purpose of H tone assignment, as in *máwlac* 'place of worship,' *maẃlac.

Their tonal behavior aside, four of the language's diphthongs – *ay, ey, aw, ow* – form contrastive [-ATR] vs. [+ATR] pairs. Concerning *oy*, however, Saeed (1999) points out an apparent accidental gap such that *oy* is [+ATR] only. Taken on its own, this is a curious fact given that [+ATR] is the marked harmonic series (Casali 2003, among others). And, while it may be true, what seems most important to note is that there are remarkably few instances of the diphthong *oy* overall in the language. In a survey of Zorc and Osman (1993), I found only six stems containing this sequence. With this mystery unsolvable, other contrasts are shown between [-ATR] series diphthongs in (31) and [+ATR] series diphthongs in (32).

---

[7] Hyman (1981) makes a representational distinction between *Vi/Vu* and *Vy/Vw* sequences to capture this behavior. See further discussion in Orwin (1996).

(31) *Contrasts among [-ATR] series diphthongs*

/aw/ vs. /ow/	áwr	'he-camel'	aabbóow	'brother'
/aw/ vs. /ay/	haẃl	'work'	dabáyl	'wind'
/ey/ vs. /ay/	sháley	'yesterday'	árday	'student'

(32) *Contrasts among [+ATR] series diphthongs*

/aw/ vs. /ow/	cáws	'grass'	dhów	'nearby'
/aw/ vs. /ay/	daẃli	'cord for drawing water'	haýl	'animal branding'
/ow/ vs. /oy/	dhów	'nearby'	góy	'cut off'
/oy/ vs. /ey/	qóys	'household'	wéyl	'calf'
/oy/ vs. /ay/	qóy	'wet (v.)'	dáy	'look'
/ey/ vs. /ay/	éy	'dog'	dáy	'look'

As discussed further in §4.3.2, the distribution of diphthongs is similar, but not identical to, that of long vowels. Diphthongs appear more often word-finally than before a word-final consonant, as in *jówr* 'tyranny' and *adáyg* 'difficulty.' Word-finally before a coda, *w*-diphthongs appear more limited in their distribution than *y*-diphthongs. Diphthongs also appear in word-internal syllables, though only in an open syllable before another consonant that is syllabified into the onset of a following syllable. For example, *nay.naás* 'nickname' and *haw.raár* 'remark.' There are some, albeit fewer, restrictions on these combinations, the result being that the distribution of *w*- vs. *y*-diphthongs is more equivalent word-internally. In addition, and despite appearing word finally before a coda consonant, diphthongs do not occur word-internally before a sequence of two heterosyllabic consonants. This distribution is not surprising, as long vowels are also absent under the same conditions. However, while word-internal long vowels are not found within a stem before a C.C sequence, they are possible in instances of compounding (e.g., *goobjóog* 'witness') or following V/∅ alternation (e.g., *joogsatay* 'you (SG) stopped yourself' (> *joogisatay*). The same distribution applies to word-internal diphthongs.

There is no clear evidence that Somali has a contrast between short and long diphthongs, despite both the language's orthography including them in some instances and their inclusion in some reference resources (Saeed, 1999, 15). A survey of Zorc and Osman (1993) and Puglielli and Mansur (2012) reveals that headwords listed as containing long diphthongs fall into four categories, two of which are related. The first among these are morphologically-derived. For example, there are entries like *báay*, which is composed of the focus particle *báa* and the subject pronoun clitic *-ay*, and where the two morphemes coalesce with one another. Similar types of coalescence are seen with the declarative particle *waay* > *waa* + *ay*, among others. Related to this are entries containing the vocative suffix *-yahay* which is often truncated to *-áy/-éy/-óy*, which vary with long counterparts *-áay/-éey/-óoy*. A second type of potential long diphthong is seen as the result of allomorphy and notably involves verbs containing the inchoative suffix -óob which alternates to -ów or -óow under some conditions. A related outcome is seen in inflection for the imperative of the irregular verb aqoów 'know it!' A third type of apparent long diphthong is associated with loanwords, such as babbáay 'papaya' and kakáaw 'cacao.' The final and largest group of listed long diphthongs are all of the shape CVVy and are given as headwords or as alternatives to headwords either with a short vowel and glide CVy, as in dhaáy ~ dhaý 'fresh milk,' or simply with a long vowel and no glide CVV, though many of the latter are limited to verb stems. One possibility is that the emergence of an offglide in these words is purely phonetic, arising from a dispreference in Somali for word-final open syllables in content words. If this is true, it might suggest that written CVVy words are indicative of a contrast between underlying sequences with a long vowel /CVV/ versus those with a sequence of two non-identical vowels /CV$_1$V$_2$/, written CVy.

With these observations stated, I echo others (e.g., Armstrong 1934; Orwin 1994) in asserting that there is no phonological reality to Somali's written long diphthongs. If and when they do emerge, it is either purely a matter of phonetics or else a matter of allomorphy or borrowing.

3.3 Vowel harmony

I have not yet studied Somali vowel harmony extensively. The generalizations discussed in this section are based on a combination of my own ongoing work, as well as that reported in other contemporary work on this topic, including Nilsson and Downing (2019), Mohamoud (2013), and Aïm (1999). Note that there are other older works discussing Somali vowel harmony, including Armstrong (1934), Andrzejewski (1955), Hall et al. (1973), and Angoujard and Hassan (1991), but some findings reported in these works have been called into question.

Somali exhibits vowel harmony such that vowels within a word, including those that form a diphthong, must belong to the same harmonic series, either neutral (i.e., [-ATR]) or culus (i.e., [+ATR]). This is observed straightforwardly for monomorphemic words provided as examples above in Sections 3.2 and 3.2.5. In morphologically-complex words, the harmonic series exhibited depends on the word's particular morphological composition. ATR harmony, under those conditions where it occurs, is triggered by a [+ATR] series vowel, a fact that makes sense given that these vowels behave otherwise as marked relative to their [-ATR] counterparts.

ATR harmony can be progressive or regressive. As discussed below, progressive harmony is stem-controlled and is limited in the extent to which it can extend rightward. Regressive harmony, however, can be triggered by a [+ATR] derivational suffix or compound head, bringing about a [-ATR] → [+ATR] alternation on the stem itself. Such behavior supports the proposition that Somali prosodic words are right-headed (Green and Morrison 2016).

3.3.1 In the nominal system

In the nominal system, a [+ATR] noun stem will progressively harmonize plural suffixes with neutral vowels. This includes Class 1 plurals in *-ó*, Class 2 reduplication plurals, and Class 3 plurals in *-yaál*. Class 4 nouns taking plural *-óyin* differ, as the suffix itself is [+ATR] and triggers regressive harmony on the stem (Mohamoud 2013). I have also observed progressive [+ATR] harmony affecting several derivational suffixes in the nominal system, including *-nimó*, *-iyád*, *-itáan*, and *-aal*. Regressive harmony is possible from [+ATR] derivational suffixes like *-tooyó* and *-darró*. The gerundive suffix *-id* is also [+ATR] and brings about regressive harmony of the stem vowel (Nilsson and Downing 2019). This list of nominal suffixes is not exhaustive, and the matter merits further attention.

Progressive [+ATR] harmony also affects definite, remote definite, and demonstrative determiners. The behavior of possessive determiners differs in that 1SG, 3SG.M, 1PL, 2PL, and 3PL determiners in this category are [+ATR] and trigger regressive harmony on a stem with a neutral vowel. The 2SG and 3SG.F possessive determiners are [-ATR]. They neither affect a preceding stem, nor are they affected by progressive harmony from a [+ATR] stem. The interrogative determiner is also [-ATR] and does not affect, nor is affected by, the stem vowel.

In nominal compounds, harmony can proceed regressively from the rightmost element of the compound, but an initial [+ATR] element will not spread its value progressively. Nilsson and Downing (2019) report that a [+ATR] adjective will optionally spread its value regressively onto the noun that it modifies. They state that, generally speaking, harmony does not spread progressively from one lexical word onto another.

3.3.2 In the verbal system

The behavior of [ATR] vowel harmony in the verbal system shares some similarities to what is discussed above for the nominal system. There is limited stem-controlled [+ATR] harmony that extends rightward onto the verb's inflectional suffixes. In auxiliary constructions like the Present Progressive and Past Progressive, the auxiliary verb *hay-* is [+ATR] and will spread its value regressively onto the preceding main verb. However, a [+ATR] main verb will not progressively harmonize its auxiliary. Overall, regressive harmony is more extensive. Nilsson and Downing (2019) have illustrated that regressive harmony can extend from a [+ATR] stem leftward throughout the entire Verb Complex. In doing so, it will harmonize morphemes such as adverbial particles, adpositional particles, negative *má*, the ISP, and other subject pronoun clitics. Regressive harmony has also been shown to extend even onto the declarative clause type marker *waa*, as well as onto *ma* and *ha*. It does not, however, appear to spread onto focus markers. Reports that vowel harmony extends to full clauses as reported in

Andrzejewski (1955) and Hall et al. (1973) have been shown not hold for those speakers represented in Nilsson and Downing (2019).

3.3.3 Fronting/raising harmony

Both Armstrong (1934) and Nilsson and Downing (2019) discuss a second type of harmony involving fronting and raising that is triggered by [i] and [j]. This harmony has been little studied, though it appears to have a much different mechanism of spreading. It is reported to extend beyond the bounds of [ATR] harmony in that it can spread between lexical words.

3.4 Alternations

3.4.1 Epenthesis

Several types of epenthesis occur in Somali, two of which involve glides. One type involves the insertion of a glottal stop word-initially before a vowel. There are no alternations involved in this particular type of epenthesis. It is purely phonetic and satisfies a cross-linguistic tendency for languages to prefer syllables to have an onset (Orwin 1994). Thus, when an underlying string might not be prosodified with an onset, [ʔ] is epenthesized to create one. I will not discuss this particular type of epenthesis further here.

More interesting are cases of glide epenthesis. These occur in instances where the palatal glide [j] is epenthesized in a morphologically-derived environment, such as in noun pluralization. Here, epenthesis repairs hiatus between a stem-final vowel and the plural suffix -ó.[8] It also occurs in verbal inflection when verbs with a vowel-final stem are inflected for the first person singular or third person masculine singular. The epenthetic glide breaks a vowel-vowel sequence that arises due to the segmentally empty ∅ slot associated with inflection for these person/number combinations. In instances of noun pluralization, this strategy is also adopted for consonants that cannot geminate. One possibility is that a glide is inserted between stem-final /s, ʔ, tʃ, ħ/ (written s, c, j, x) and plural -ó to "reinforce" the plural suffix (Godon 1998; Nilsson 2016a).

---

[8] Stem-final i followed by plural -ó coalesce to y in instances like guri + o → guryó 'houses.'

(33) Glide epenthesis occurs between:
   a. a stem-final vowel and plural -ó (nouns)
   b. stem-final *s, c, j, x* and plural -ó (nouns)
   c. a stem-final vowel and a vowel-initial inflectional suffix (verbs)

An example of each of these is as follows:

(34) *koofiyó*
/kʰoofi-o/
hat-PL
'hats'

(35) *nacasyó*
/nacas-o/
fool-PL
'fools'

(36) *sameeyay*
/sam-ee-∅-aj/
make-FACT-1SG-PST
'I made'

There are other epenthetic alternations in Somali that do not involve glides. For example, within the Verb Complex, epenthesis occurs within some adposition clusters like *ú + ú → ugú*. When an adposition is joined by a pronoun clitic, however, the result is vowel coalescence, as in *i + ú → ií*. Green and Morrison (2018) suggest that these different epenthesis strategies relate to the prosodification of the elements in hiatus.

3.4.2 Deaspiration

The voiceless aspirated stops [tʰ] and [kʰ] do not appear phonetically in syllable codas. However, there is evidence that these stops occur underlyingly in stem-final positions, but when they come to be syllabified into a coda, they are deaspirated. Thus, while Somali encodes a contrast between aspirated and unaspirated voiceless stops in other word positions, this contrast is neutralized in syllable codas in favor of the unaspirated stop. Alternations that one can take as evidence of this neutralization are found in the language's verbal system.

Consider, for example, two past tense verbs inflected for the first person singular – *suntay* [sun.tʰay] 'I branded an animal' and *gunaanaday* [gu.naa.na.tay] 'I concluded' – compared to their second person singular forms: *sumadday* [su.mat.tay] 'you (SG) branded an animal' and *gunaanadday* [gu.naa.nat.tay] 'you (SG) concluded.' The two verbs behave differently concerning the realization of their stem-final consonant and person/gender suffix in the first vs. second singular. The outcomes for the 1SG forms allow us to be reasonably certain that the verb stem 'brand an animal' is /sumatʰ-/, with a final fortis, aspirated stop, while that for 'conclude' is /gunaanaḍ-/ with a final lenis stop. In the 1SG, the verb *suntay* has undergone a V/∅ alternation resulting in the syllabification of its stem-final consonant into an onset. There is also an alternation of /m/ → [n], but this is unrelated. Because the stem-final stop is syllabified in an onset upon reduction, it remains aspirated. The 1SG form *gunaanaday* also finds its stem-final consonant in an onset where it is either voiced or spirantized, the choice between which varies between speakers.

(37) *suntay*
 /sumatʰ-∅-aj/
 brand.an.animal-1SG-PST
 'I branded an animal'

(38) *gunaanaday*
 /gunaanaḍ̥-∅-aj/
 conclude-1SG-PST
 'I concluded'

In the 2SG, V/∅ alternation is blocked in *sumadday* to avoid creating a tri-consonantal sequence due to the presence of the inflectional suffix -*tʰ*-. As a result, the stem-final consonant must be syllabified into a coda where it is desaspirated. In turn, the following inflectional suffix is assimilatorily desaspirated. For *gunaanadday*, the stem-final consonant undergoes no alternation, though it also triggers deaspiration of the following inflectional suffix.

(39) *sumadday*
 /sumatʰ-tʰ-aj/
 brand.an.animal-2SG-PST
 'you (SG) branded an animal'

(40) *gunaanadday*
 /gunaanaḍ̥-tʰ-aj/
 conclude-2SG-PST
 'you (SG) concluded'

Deaspiration in examples like (39) and (40) falls under the heading of a larger set of alternations that Green and Morrison (2018) call sandhi effects. These word-level rules affect only inflectional affixes.

These inflected forms are helpful to motivate the nature of these stem-final consonants, but deaspiration is not necessarily triggered or conditioned by inflectional affixation. Forms like *aragtay* [arak.tʰay] 'you (SG) saw,' *arkay* [ar.kʰay] 'I saw,' and their corresponding imperative *arag* [arak] 'look!' demonstrate (this time for [kʰ] vs. [k]) that deaspiration occurs in syllable codas even in the absence of any inflectional suffix. Taken together, these show that deaspiration in verbs is not dependent on the creation of a morphologically-derived environment.

Deaspiration also occurs in the nominal system where it affects the initial consonant of the language's definite determiners. This occurs despite the fact that these consonants are syllabified into an onset. The conditions on deaspiration are slightly different for the two definite determiners. In (41), deaspiration affects the K/G series definite determiner after a noun like (41) whose stem ends in /i/, /u/, or /a/. Nouns with stem-final /e/ or /o/ yield a different set of alternations involving vowel height assimilation (§3.4.8) and debuccalization (§3.4.9). Example (42) shows that nouns ending in a lenis stop at the same place of articulation as the determiner also trigger an assimilatory deaspiration.

(41) *bériga*
/b̥eri=kʰa/
day=DEF
'the day'

(42) *rágga*
/raɡ=kʰa/
men=DEF
'the men'

In (43), deaspiration affects the T/D series definite determiner after stem-final /ʜ, χ, ʔ, ʡ, q/ (written x, kh, c, ', q, respectively). As with K/G definite determiners, a noun like (44) whose stem ends in an unaspirated stop at the same place of articulation will also cause progressive deaspiration.

(43) *káxda*
/kʰaʜ=tʰa/
desert=DEF
'the desert'

(44) *dersídda*
/d̥ersid̥=tʰa/
lecture=DEF
'the lecture'

As shown above, deaspiration of fortis stops when syllabified into an onset is not limited to the nominal system. In (39) and (40), we see that the 2SG/3SG.F suffix -*t*- is assimilatorily deaspirated in an onset after a stem final unaspirated stop. These instances of deaspiration are limited to affecting functional morphemes (i.e., affixes, determiners) across a boundary. In §3.4.7, deaspiration is shown to often feed a second process of spirantization.

3.4.3 Degemination

There are two instances in Somali in which one can observe active alternations that result in degemination. One of these affects underlying stem-final geminate stops. It is indeed these alternations that help one to motivate the presence of underlying geminates in the first place. The other type of degemination involves the simplification of sequences of morphologically-derived geminates in the verbal system.

It was introduced in §3.1.3 that Somali has both geminate stops and geminate sonorants. Only geminate stops are discussed here as the behavior of geminate sonorants is somewhat different. 1SG verbs like in (45) whose person/number slot is ∅ surface with a geminate stem-final stop. However, a comparable 2SG form with a /-t^h-/ person/number suffix like (46) has no such geminate. The presence of ∅ provides an empty slot into which the stem-final geminate can be syllabified. When this slot is unavailable, the geminate is simplified and realized as a singleton stop.

(45) *cabbay*
/ʔabb-∅-aj/
drink-1SG-PST
'I drank'

(46) *cabtay*
/ʔabb-t^h-aj/
drink-2SG-PST
'you (SG) drank'

An analogous outcome arises even in the absence of suffixation, such as in the formation of an imperative verb. When an underlying geminate stop finds itself in a word-final environment where it cannot be syllabified, it is again simplified, as in *cáb* 'drink!'

Degemination also occurs in morphologically-derived environments when a sequence of two stops arises upon the concatenation of the middle suffix /-át^h-/ and the 2SG suffix /-t^h-/. I assume that the middle suffix contains an aspirated stop, given the appearance of such a stop in verbs like *buub[t^h]ay* 'I ran away.' Recall from §3.4.2 that underlyingly unaspirated stops do not alternate to become aspirated, regardless of the syllable position into which they are prosodified. Evidence for degemination of such morphologically-derived sequences can be found in comparing a 2SG verb containing the morphological geminate like (47) to a verb with a ∅ 1SG slot like (48).⁹

(47) *joogsatay*
/tʃooq-is-atʰ-tʰ-aj/
stop-CAUS-MID-2SG-PST
'you (SG) stopped'

(48) *joogsaday*
/tʃooq-is-atʰ-∅-aj/
stop-CAUS-MID-1SG-PST
'I stopped'

Example (47) shows an underlying sequence of adjacent aspirated stops that undergoes degemination. What is key here is that the remaining stop is not deaspirated. Example (48) shows that when only a single stop is present underlyingly, however, the stop undergoes deaspiration. Green and Morrison (2018) have suggested that this can be viewed as a matter of rule ordering, as shown in (49). These outcomes obtain from a situation in which the deaspiration rule is ordered before the degemination rule. V/∅ reduction is also involved, as shown in the derivation.

(49) *Ordering of deaspiration and degemination*

	/tʃook-is-atʰ-tʰ-aj/	/tʃook-is-atʰ-∅-aj/
Deaspiration	tʃook-is-atʰ-tʰ-aj	tʃook-is-at-∅-aj
Degemination	tʃook-is-a-tʰ-aj	—
V/∅ reduction	tʃook-s-a-tʰ-aj	tʃook-s-at-∅-aj
	[tʃook.sa.tʰaj] (2SG/3SG.F)	[tʃook.sa.taj] (1SG/3SG.M)

The outcome seen here is opaque such that it appears that the deaspiration has underapplied. In essence, the presence of an underlying geminate sequence blocks deaspiration from applying.

3.4.4 Manner assimilation

There are several closely-related assimilatory processes that affect Somali suffixes and clitics. One such instance of assimilation was earlier discussed in §3.4.2. In this earlier

---

9 There are several forms of the Weak Causative extension. It is realized /is/ before a vowel and /i/ elsewhere, though its vowel is susceptible to V/∅ alternation in predictable instances. For an alternative view on the behavior of this morpheme, see Barillot et al. (2018).

section, it was shown that a stem-final unaspirated stop triggers progressive deaspiration of the initial consonant of a definite determiner. In this section, three additional instances of progressive assimilation involving manner of articulation from stem to suffix are discussed. The section ends by discussing one instance of regressive manner assimilation between suffixes.

One instance of progressive manner assimilation is caused by the stem-final implosive stop /ɖ/ and affects an adjacent aspirated stop /tʰ/. For example, in (50), the initial /tʰ/ of a determiner assimilates to [ɖ] when preceded by a noun ending with this stem-final consonant. The outcome is the same in verbs like (51) where a stem-final /ɖ/ yields the same affect on a following 2SG suffix /-tʰ-/.

(50) *feéd̪ha*
/feeɖ=tʰa/
rib=DEF
'the rib'

(51) *xidhdhay*
/ʜiɖ-tʰ-aj/
tie-2SG-PST
'you (SG) tied'

Two closely related instances of progressive manner assimilation are spurred by the stem-final liquids, /l/ and /r/, and affect the 1PL suffix /-n-/ in the language's verbal system. Examples (52) and (53) illustrate these alternations, respectively.

(52) *dillay*
/ɖil-n-aj/
kill-1PL-PST
'we killed'

(53) *barray*
/b̪ar-n-aj/
teach-1PL-PST
'we taught'

Last among the language's manner assimilations is regressive nasal assimilation that can also be observed within verbs. Example (54) shows that the same 1PL nasal suffix that was affected by liquids above is responsible here for assimilating a preceding /-tʰ-/ to its manner.

(54) *joogsannay*
   /tʃooq-is-atʰ-n-aj/
   stop-WCAUS-MID-1PL-PST
   'we stopped'

A similar alternation affects the Weak Causative in *karinnay* 'we cooked something.' In the string /kʰar-is-n-aj/, the 1PL nasal regressively assimilates the consonant of the Weak Causative to its manner.

3.4.5 Consonant deletion

Another alternation that illustrates the susceptibility of voiceless aspirated stops to the influence of adjacent sounds, and particularly those associated with the language's determiners, is seen in the deletion of /kʰ/ after [back] consonants. This occurs following /q, χ, ʜ, ʔ, h/. Examples are as follows:

(55) a. mádfa[ʔ] + kʰa → mádfaca 'the cannon'
   b. táa[h] + kʰa → táah 'the moan'
   c. míi[q] + kʰa → míiqa 'the thread'
   d. shée[χ] + kʰa → shéekha 'the sheikh'
   e. máda[ʜ] + kʰa → mádaxa 'the head'

It might be tempting to attribute this deletion to an Obligatory Contour Principle effect (Leben 1973) that removes sequences of adjacent dorsal consonants. However, because /h/ is also included in the class of consonants triggering deletion, this suggests the deletion is more general, though still articulatory in nature.

3.4.6 Voicing

Stem-internal lenis stops are either realized voiced or are spirantized intervocalically. Whether one or the other occurs differs between speakers from different areas. For some speakers, the underlying lenis stops /b̥, d̥, g̊/ (written *b, d, g*) are voiced intervocalically when they are in the onset of a syllable that carries H tone. Under these conditions, they are realized [b, d, g], respectively. Examples are in (56).

(56) a. *nabád* /nab̥ad̥/ → [na.bát] 'peace'
   b. *cudúd* /ʔud̥ud̥/ → [ʔu.dút] 'forearm'
   c. *magaálo* /mag̊aalo/ → [ma.gaá.lo] 'city'

Under opposing conditions, again at least for some speakers, when these underlying stops are in the onset of a syllable that is not associated with H tone, they are instead spirantized, being realized [β, ð, ɣ], respectively. Examples are provided below in §3.4.7. Both processes fall under the heading of lenition, but for some speakers, the location of the stop relative to H tone dictates the degree to which the stops are lenited.

As introduced above in §3.1.1, for most speakers with whom I have worked, underlying lenis stops are always realized intervocalically as spirants, regardless of the location of H tone. In addition, there are other speakers who exhibit an opposing strategy such that these stops are always realized intervocalically as voiced stops and never as spirants.[10]

3.4.7 Spirantization

Somali's underlying lenis stops /b̥, d̥, g̥/ (written *b, d, g*) are often spirantized intervocalically and realized [β, ð, ɣ], respectively. For some speakers, this is a general process, but for others it occurs only in the onset of a syllable after a H tone. Examples of intervocalic spirantization are as follows:[11]

(57) a. *hábar* /hab̥ar/ → [há.βar] 'old woman'
 b. *cúdur* /ʔud̥ur/ → [ʔú.ður] 'disease'
 c. *mágac* /mag̥aʔ/ → [má.ɣaʔ] 'name'

Spirantization also affects the initial consonant of the T/D class definite determiner under conditions similar to that described above. When this consonant finds itself between two vowels, the first of which has a H tone, it will spirantize from /tʰ/ → [ð]. Compare, for example, *mindí* 'knife' and its definite counterpart *mindí[ð]a* 'the knife.' Different alternations affect the K/G class definite determiner, however. It was shown in §3.4.2 that /kʰ/ at the beginning of a determiner is deaspirated intervocalically. This is the outcome in morphologically simplex nouns given that the default location of H tone on K/G series nouns is on the penultimate, rather than the final mora of the

---

10 It is important to bear in mind that these voicing alternations should be kept separate from others discussed in the literature concerning so-called "voicing" of written *t* and *k*. The alternations affecting these consonants in some intervocalic positions, though never within a stem, are instead cases of deaspiration; see discussion in §3.4.2.
11 One way of viewing voicing vs. spirantization might be to suppose that lenis stops are first voiced intervocalically in all instances. Then, a second rule of spirantization would either apply, or it would not, for some speakers. For those speakers whose grammars include this spirantization rule, some would apply it across the board, while others' application of the rule would depend on the presence of a preceding H.

stem. There are more morphologically complex nouns, however, that bring this same determiner into an environment immediately following H tone. The result is debuccalization, which is discussed in §3.4.9.

3.4.8 Vowel height alternations

Some stem-final vowels in nouns undergo height alternations under the influence of the vowel in a following word or determiner. These alternations do not affect stem-final /i, a, u/, but instead target only the mid vowels /e/ and /o/. Stem-final /e/ and /o/ have special status in Somali nouns given that nouns containing them behave as if they are morphologically complex, though this is not always easy to see. Indeed, there is reason to believe that stem-final /-e/ and /-o/ are suffixes.

Nouns ending in /-e/ and /-o/ behave as if they are morphologically complex in terms of the distribution of their H tone. For example, *báre* 'teacher' has a penultimate H when it occurs phrase-finally, but H is realized on the stem-final vowel upon the addition of a definite determiner, as in *baráha* 'the teacher.' The change in location of H is accompanied by an alternation of /e/ → [a], as well as an alternation in the consonant of the definite determiner. The latter is due to debuccalization and is discussed separately in §3.4.9. A similar outcome can be seen in nouns like *magaálo* 'city,' which witness a rightward shift in the location of H tone and a vowel alternation under the same conditions, as in *magaaláda* 'the city.'

These examples show that under the right conditions, either the stem or the suffix can be associated with H tone. It is illustrated below that when a morphologically-complex word has more than one morpheme on which H can be realized, H typically prefers to be realized on the rightmost of these morphemes. However, in nouns like those discussed above that end in /-e/ and /-o/, final H is avoided. H tone is instead realized earlier in the word. When the finality condition is removed, H tone shifts rightward.

In the nouns shown thus far, and indeed in many others with similar composition, /-e/ and /-o/ alternate in their height. The precise outcomes witnessed differ between Somali varieties, but generally speaking, the basic alternations are as follows:

(58) /e, o/ → [a] / _ C {e, o, a}
    a. *fúre* 'key' vs. *furáhéeda* 'her key'
    b. *báre* 'teacher' vs. *baráhóoda* 'their teacher'
    c. *guddoomíye* 'chairman' vs. *guddoomiyáha* 'the chairman'
    d. *eéddo* 'paternal aunt' vs. *eeddádeéd* 'her paternal aunt'
    e. *magaálo* 'city' vs. *magaaládóoda* 'their city'
    f. *meeló* 'places' vs. *meeláha* 'the places'

(59) /e, o/ → [i] / _ C {i}
   a. *fúre* 'key' vs. *furíhii* 'the (REM) key'
   b. *meeló* 'places' vs. *meelíhii* 'the (REM) places'

(60) /e, o/ → [u] / _ C {u}
   a. *madaxwéyne* 'president' vs. *madaxweynúhu* 'the president (SUBJ)'
   b. *meeló* 'places' vs. *meelúhu* 'the places (SUBJ)'

The alternations represented in (58) are ubiquitous, but those in (59) and (60) vary for some speakers. For example, one of my speakers from Mogadishu generalized the pattern in (58) to all vowels. Thus, she produced forms like *furáhii* 'the (REM) key' and *meeláhu* 'the place (SUBJ)' with an alternation to [a], rather than to [i] and [u], respectively.

Gabbard (2010, 2014) reports that quite the opposite outcome obtained for the speaker he interviewed in Columbus, Ohio. This speaker spent their childhood in Mogadishu and nine years in the Dadaab refugee camp in Kenya before coming to the US as an adult. For this speaker, rather than /e, o/ alternations resulting in [a, i, u], or collapsing entirely onto [a], the speaker instead had /e, o/ alternate precisely to the quality of the following vowel, resulting in a full range of possible vowels [i, u, e, o, a].

There are analogous vowel height alternations that occur outside the nominal system. For example, for some speakers, the conjunction *iyo* alternates to *iya*: *nín iya naág* 'man and woman.' The final *-o* seen in middle imperative verbs also alternates to *a* in other inflectional forms.

Despite these various alternations affecting stem-final /e/ and /o/, no such alternations affect other stem-final vowels. That is, underlying stem-final /i, u, a/ do not alternate. Lampitelli (2013) has suggested that this relates to the fact that /i, u, a/ are specified with a full set of vocalic features while /e, o/ are underspecified for height. As such, they regressively assimilate to the height features of a following vowel when given the chance to do so.

3.4.9 Debuccalization

Debuccalization is a fairly extreme instance of lenition in which a consonant loses its place features. It is arguably one step away from complete loss of a consonant. Debuccalization in Somali affects the initial consonant of K/G series determiners and results in an alternation of /k^h/ → [ɦ]. The process occurs intervocalically and occurs only when the targeted consonant is immediately preceded by a H tone.

In many instances, the /k^h/ of a determiner will simply undergo deaspiration when it is preceded by a stem-final /i, u, a/. This can be seen in words like *báriga* [bári=ka] 'the East.' In adding a determiner to such a morphologically-simplex noun from the K/G series, the word's H tone does not immediately precede the debuccalization target. A comparison of words like *meeló* 'places' and *meeláha* (> meel + o + kʰa) 'the places,' and indeed many examples given just above in §3.4.8, show morphologically-complex words whose H tone immediately precedes a K/G determiner. The result is debuccalization to [ɦ].

While it is often the case that debuccalization occurs between two identical vowels (perhaps due to vowel height assimilation affecting /e, o/), this is not a necessary condition for the process to occur. There are words like *furáhóoda* (> fur + e + kʰoo + tʰa) 'their key' that illustrate that debuccalization occurs between non-identical vowels, provided that the required tonal condition obtains.

3.4.10 Assibilation

Two alternations occur in Somali that fall under the heading of assibilation, a process that creates a sibilant. Both of these processes affect the realization of underlying /tʰ/, causing it either to be realized as [ʃ] or [s]. The conditions leading to one outcome versus the other are quite different.

One type of assibilation involves the alternation of an underlying sequence of /l + tʰ/ → [ʃ]. This type of assibilation occurs in both the nominal and verb systems and always involves the juxtaposition of a stem-final liquid and a suffix beginning with /tʰ/.[12] Representative examples are as follows:

(61) *dishay*
/ḍil-tʰ-aj/
kill-2SG-PST
'she killed (it)'

(62) *walaásháyda*
/walaal-tʰaj-tʰa/
sister-1SG.Poss-DEF
'my sister'

(63) *dadaashó*
/ḍaḍaal-tʰ-o/
strive-2SG-IRR
'you strive'

---

12 Assibilation fails to occur in a few notable instances. There is no alternation with i) the reciprocal extension *-tan*, ii) the deverbal suffix *-tin*, and iii) across lexical word boundaries, such as in compounding.

3.4 Alternations — 77

This might seem to be a rather unusual alternation, but there are other well-known cases of assibilation involving similar sequences. See Hall and Hamann (2006) for a typological overview. The difference in Somali is that the liquid seems to be secondarily removed. That /tʰ/ is otherwise assibilated in the absence of a preceding /l/ can be seen independently in the verb examples just below. One can also find evidence that sequences of *l.s* are avoided elsewhere in Somali, as in instances of metathesis in §3.4.12. It appears, therefore, that in examples like (61) through (63), and those like them, that rather than resorting to an arguably extreme process like metathesis to avoid *l.s*, the language instead chooses simply to delete the liquid.

There are other instances where one finds assibilation of /tʰ/ in the language's verbal system, where no preceding /l/ is involved. These are famously triggered by front vowels in two of the language's derivational extensions (Weak Causative and Factitive) and affect the now well-known target of alternations, the number/gender suffix /tʰ/. In these instances, /tʰ/ again alternates to [s].

To establish a baseline, consider the Weak Causative verbs below. We can see that the Weak Causative extension is realized [-i] in 1SG verbs like (64). This is its typical realization before another consonant. As noted above, it is realized [is] before a vowels, though V/∅ alternation may sometimes result in it being realized simply as -s.

(64) *kariyay*
      /kʰar-i-∅-aj/
      cook-WCAUS-1SG-PST
      'I cooked it/them'

The same verb in (65) inflected for the 2SG reveals that underlying /-tʰ-/ associated with the 2SG is realized as [s].

(65) *karisay*
      /kʰar-i-tʰ-aj/
      cook-WCAUS-2SG-PST
      'you (SG) cooked it/them'

Because the Weak Causative is also sometimes realized [-is] or [-s], we want to be reasonably certain that the [s] that emerges in (65) is not attributable to the extension itself. Examples like (66) and (67) can help in this regard. They illustrate that the other allomorphs of the Weak Causative arise only before another vowel-initial morpheme. It is realized [-is] in (66), but V/∅ reduction removes the suffix's vowel, yielding [-s] in (67), unless it is blocked from doing so by unfavorable phonotactics.

(66) *ergisaday*
/ereɢ-is-atʰ-∅-aj/
trust-WCAUS-MID-1SG-PST
'I entrusted it'

(67) *marsaday*
/mar-is-atʰ-∅-aj/
finish.off-WCAUS-MID-1SG-PST
'I finished (it) off'

Based on the conditions that are expected to obtain for [-is] to be selected, one can be reasonably certain that the sibilant that arises in (65) is due to assibilation of /tʰ/ rather than being from the Weak Causative extension. Thus, in the two instances of assibilation in Somali, one yielding [ʃ] is conditioned by a preceding stem-final /l/ while the other yielding [s] is triggered instead by the high front vowel /i/ of the weak causative extension. In the next section, we shall see that the Weak Causative is also implicated in alternations affecting consonants other than /tʰ/.

3.4.11 Palatalization

Palatalization in Somali can be seen in alternations where the stem-final dorsal stops /ɢ/ and /q/ are realized as the affricate [tʃ] under some conditions where they are followed by the Weak Causative extension. It is triggered by the addition of this derivational extension to the verb stem. This can be seen in Weak Causative verbs, but also in nouns derived from these verbs.[13] The palatalization is regressive in nature, though the Weak Causative also acts progressively to trigger analogous affects on the inflectional suffix /tʰ/, as discussed just above in §3.4.10. The outcomes of palatalization seen in verbs like (68) and (69) show that it is a stem-level rule.

(68) *joóji*
/tʃooɢ-i/
stop-WCAUS
'bring to a stop' (cf. *jóog* 'stop')

---

13 It seems best to describe palatalization as limited to the Weak Causative, as it does not occur before other morphemes beginning with -*i*, such as the subject marker (see §9.2). This likely relates to the fact that palatalization is a stem-level process while subject marking is accomplished by a phrase-level clitic.

(69) *báji*
/ḅaq-i/
fear-WCAUS
'frighten' (cf. *báq* 'fear')

There are instances, however, where palatalization is blocked from occurring where one might expect it. As seen in (70), a stem-final dorsal stop will not palatalize in stems that have undergone V/∅ alternation.

(70) *tífqi*
/tʰifiq-i/
drip-WCAUS
'cause to drip' (cf. *tífiq* 'drip')

The failure of palatalization to apply in such instances has been the subject of careful formal analysis in Bendjaballah (1998), but see also Barillot et al. (2018). Generally speaking, it appears to be grounded in phonotactics. As introduced in §3.1.2.1, the affricate [tʃ] (written *j*) is part of the Somali phoneme inventory and is found in both word-initial and word-internal syllable onsets. It does not regularly occur, however, in a word-internal onset after another consonant except in the formation of compounds like in the noun *goobjóog* 'witness' or the verb stem *afjíg* 'silence s.o.' It would seem, therefore, that palatalization fails to apply in those instances where it would create a disallowed phonotactic sequence within a single phonological word.

Palatalization of dorsal consonants also fails to occur in other segmentally identical, but morphologically distinct environments. For example, it does not occur before the infinitive suffix -*i* nor before the subject marker -*i*. This illustrates that the process does not apply at the word or phrase level.

3.4.12 Metathesis

There are instances of both short and longer distance metathesis where the linear order of two segments is reversed. Examples of short distance metathesis are clearly motivated by phonotactics and involve a reversal in the order of two segments that are brought into contact via V/∅ alternation. One such sequence that is avoided is **l.s*, which can be seen in a word like the adjective *shílis* 'fat' when it is nominalized by the suffix -*aán* yielding *shislaán* 'fatness (of an animal),' or sometimes *shishlaán*. Loss of the second vowel in the three syllable sequence would potentially bring about an *l.s* sequence, but this instead emerges [s.l] or [ʃ.l]. Recall from §3.4.10 that *l.s* is elsewhere avoided in Somali in instances where /l+tʰ/ → [ʃ]. This occurs in both nouns and verbs.

Another instance of metathesis repairs the creation of a sequence of **c.b*. This can be seen as the result of the same type of nominalization above, this time for *néceb* 'hate.' The nominalized form of this word is *nebcaán* 'hatred,' rather than *necbaán. These types of repairs, as well as instances in which V/Ø alternations do not occur where expected, can be attributed avoiding the creation of dispreferred C.C sequences. This speaks to the important role played by phonotactic constraints in Somali, despite the fact that such a wide variety of C.C sequences can be found. There is a clear distinction between the types of C.C sequences permitted in the language in a single word vs. in compounds. This is discussed in greater detail in Chapter 4.

There are also longer distance, more idiosyncratic instances of metathesis. A well-known example is variation between the realization of the word for 'elbow,' which is pronounced either *xúsul* or *súxul*.

3.5 V/Ø alternation

V/Ø alternation occurs in both the nominal and verbal systems and has been the subject of considerable debate in the literature. There are different approaches concerning how to treat such alternations, namely whether they are due to vowel loss or epenthesis. Proponents of a reduction approach include Puglielli (1981), Mioni (1988), Orwin (1994), Saeed (1999), and Green and Morrison (2018), while those who instead favor an insertion approach include Sasse (1978), Barillot (2002), and Barillot et al. (2018). Banti (1985) adopts somewhat different approaches for nouns vs. verbs. Mioni (1988) (without citing any particular study) suggests that approaches based on epenthesis are "provisional and disputable," but he does not necessarily take a strong stance on the matter. In the patterns discussed here, V/Ø alternations are described as being due to reduction. As such, alternations are attributed to the loss of a short vowel from the second of three syllables in sequence. Justifications for this choice are offered below, often in comparison to the epenthesis alternative, throughout the remainder of this section.

V/Ø alternations are morphologically-triggered, meaning that they do not affect monomorphemic words. In the nominal system, V/Ø alternation is often triggered by -ó pluralization. This is seen in comparing singular *ílig* 'tooth' and its plural *ilkó* 'teeth,' or singular *galáb* 'afternoon' and its plural *galbó* 'afternoons,' as well as *maalín* 'day' and its plural *maalmó* 'days.' Some analyses instead argue that words like *galáb* 'afternoon' have an underlying form ending in CC, /galb/. They contend that because the language disallows complex syllable margins, this forces epenthesis of a copy or "echo" vowel in order to avoid the creation of a syllable with a complex coda. When a suffix is added, and the *l.b* sequence can be syllabified across a syllable boundary, however, there is no epenthesis (*gal.bó* 'afternoons'). This approach might face certain challenges in outcomes like *maalín* 'day' vs. *maalmó* 'days' where the alternating vowel is not a copy. The same can be said of pairs like *xárig* 'rope' vs. *xargó* 'ropes,' *cedhíb* 'heel' vs. *cedhbó* 'heels,' and *xiídan* 'small intestine' vs. *xiidmó* 'intestines.' Although pairs like these are few in number, an epenthesis approach would need to treat these as exceptions or would instead need to propose epenthesis of a default vowel, though this vowel would not always be the same.

Similar alternations occur in the verbal system, as seen with the Weak Causative extension in *diirsán* 'to warm oneself' (**diirisán*) or the middle extension in *dubtay* 'you (SG) baked for yourself' (**dubatay*). Even a stem vowel can alternate, as seen in *hadlay* 'he spoke' (**hadalay*). These alternations are also found in longer words, as in *joogsatay* 'you (SG) stopped' (**joogisatay*).

One way that the alternations in both nouns and verbs can be unified is by an approach based on reduction whereby any failure to reduce is predicated on phonotactics. Indeed, reduction is proposed as a means to describe nearly identical alternations in other Cushitic languages like Iraqw (Mous 1993). These alternations might be somewhat more challenging to explain in an appeal to epenthesis, particularly given that the "echo vowel" condition does not always hold. One would need a secondary, default vowel epenthesis process, though this would also need to contend with choices between [a] and [i] as "defaults" in different circumstances.

What should be clear under any approach is that there is no inherent correlation between H tone and the susceptibility of a given vowel to alternate. By comparing *ílig/ilkó* 'tooth/teeth' and *galáb/galbó* 'afternoon/afternoons,' one can observe that stem vowels otherwise associated with H tone and those that are toneless are equally susceptible to alternation. In addition, V/∅ alternation also affects Present Habitual, Simple Past, and other verbs that never exhibit a H tone. In other words, V/∅ alternation and tone distribution have little bearing on one another. Concerning whether there is a connection between H tone and stress, Le Gac (2001, 2003a) has demonstrated that there is no correlation between H tone (Hz) and intensity (dB) in the language. As such, he claims that intensity is not a parameter of "accent" in Somali.

Despite intensity not appearing to play a role in characterizing Somali's speech rhythm, one might view V/∅ alternation as presenting some evidence for metrification, or the parsing of metrical feet in the language. A role for metrical feet in the language would be unsurprising given that foot structure is a well-established characteristic shown to be referenced and relied upon in Somali poetry (see §4.5). Despite this, metrical feet have not yet been entertained as a component of the language's prosodic phonology more broadly, as far as I am aware.

Though the matter deserves further inquiry, a possible metrically-conditioned view of V/∅ alternations in Somali is entertained in the examples below, where proposed feet are shown in parentheses. The primary goal here is to present generalizations concerning where and when these vocalic alternations appear, though there may be other ways to view them. As seen below, assuming a reduction approach, one could characterize observed outcomes by the parsing of quantity sensitive bimoraic feet. Under such a view, alternations appear to occur systematically and under predictable conditions.

In the examples below, I suggest that heavy (i.e., bimoraic) syllables are parsed into feet, with any remaining syllables parsed into feet from left to right.[14] Short stems best illustrate basic outcomes. Verbs like (71) and (72) show alternation of the second stem vowel. These and other examples might suggest that bimoraic feet parsed across two syllables exhibit a trochaic "strong + weak" rhythm, where the vowel in a weak foot position is lost.[15]

(71) *arkay*
(ara)(gay)
arag-∅-ay
'he saw'

(72) *hadleen*
(hada)(leen)
hadal-∅-een
'they spoke'

In words of different shapes, the alternating vowel is found in a syllable that could be viewed as unfooted, as in (73). Whether or not a stem-initial syllable is footed is unclear. Alternation of the first syllable vowel is never observed, presumably because this would create a complex onset, which would not accommodated by the language's phonotactics. This is shown in (74).

(73) *diirsan*
(dii)ri(san)
diir-is-an
'to warm oneself'

(74) *bilaabmay*
(bi(laa))ba(may)
bil-aab-am-ay
'it started'

If there is no heavy syllable in the stem, parsing of feet would appear to begin from the word's left edge. As such, when a choice between targets for reduction must be made, an unfooted vowel is chosen, as seen in (75).

---

14 The coda of CVVC syllables may be extrametrical, as is the case in certain other Afroasiatic languages, including Arabic (see Watson 2007).
15 Though trochaic feet in some languages exhibit a metrically-unbalanced CVV.CV shape, the *Rhythmic Harmony Scales* proposed by Prince (1990) define "ideal" trochees as being metrically balanced, e.g., CVV or CVCV.

(75) *quruxsán*
      (quru)xi(san)
      qurux-is-an
      'to embellish for oneself'

Other phonotactic preferences reveal themselves and appear to influence the phenomenon when words containing certain combinations of morphemes are formed. For example, in (76), reduction to *joogsatay* avoids the creation of three heavy syllables in a row, **joogistay*. An analogous outcome is seen in *balaqsanaa* in (77), as opposed to **balaqasnaa*, where a sequence of two heavy syllables in a row is avoided in favor of a sequence of heavy-light-heavy. Reduction yielding **balqisanaa* would be avoided perhaps because stem vowel deletion is dispreferred if an affixal vowel is available to delete.

(76) *joogsatay*
      (joo)(gisa)(tay)
      joog-is-at-t-ay
      'you (SG) stopped yourself'

(77) *balaqsanaa*
      (bala)(qisa)(naa)
      balaq-is-an-aa
      'it's flabby'

There are some words where two V/Ø alternations occur. This can be seen, for example, in *ergistay* 'he entrusted' (presumably, > *ereg-is-at-Ø-ay*). Words like this appear to follow from the same generalizations as above and are particularly revealing in that they show more about the types of structures that Somali prefers vs. permits vs. avoids at all costs. Here, the reductions yield three heavy syllables in a row, a situation that was avoided above in (76). Doing so here is presumably a reasonable option as it avoids a tri-consonantal sequence like in **ergsatay*.

(78) *ergistay*
      (ere)(gisa)(tay)
      ereg-is-at-Ø-ay
      'he entrusted'

Alternations in the nominal system are simpler owing in large part to the fact that noun stems are shorter. Also, stem shapes that would yield phonotactic conditions that are compatible with reduction are less common than those that occur in the verbal system. Most alternations in the nominal system involve CVCVC stems that take *-ó* pluralization. This is the case with pairs like *ílig/ilkó* 'tooth/teeth' and *galáb/galbó* 'afternoon/afternoons' where a foot appears to be parsed at the left edge of the stem, the weaker position of which is lost upon pluralization. It is not entirely clear whether the -*ó* suffix is footed, but alternations that occur when this suffix is followed by a definite determiner might suggest that it is parsed into a foot elsewhere: *galbó + ka → galbáha* 'the afternoons.'

(79) *ilkó*
(ili)go
ilig-o
'teeth'

(80) *galbó*
(gala)bo
galab-o
'afternoons'

As was the case with verbs, alternations in nouns are morphologically triggered, but not every morphological operation has the ability to initiate the process. Notably, cliticization by the definite determiner does not result in alternation. This can be seen in comparing the noun *gúri* 'house' and *gúriga* 'the house,' **gúrga*. There are also many instances in which V/Ø alternation appears to be blocked for phonotactic reasons. For example, one finds *mindiyó* 'knives' and not **mindyó*. Alternations that result in a word-internal long vowel+glide are also avoided, as in *aayadó* 'wonders' (**aaydó*). Similar outcomes obtain in the verbal system. For example, alternations that would result in an aspirated consonant in a syllable coda are avoided, as in *matagay* 'he vomited' (**matgay*). However, alternation will occur if an aspirated consonant can be syllabified into an onset, as in *arkay* 'he saw' (cf. *árag* 'see!' and *aragtay* 'she saw'). Beyond these examples, there are other prohibitions against alternation due to general phonotactic constraints in the language; these are outlined in §4.3.3.

4 Syllable structure and phonotactics

4.1 Syllable structure

Somali permits open and closed syllables both word-internally and word-finally. Its open syllable shapes include V, VV, CV, and CVV. CVV, in particular, represents a syllable containing a sequence of two vowels, which can either be identical or non-identical. Sequences of identical vowels result in a phonetic long vowel (CV:) while sequences of non-identical vowels (CV_1V_2) result in a diphthong whose second member is realized phonetically as an offglide, either [w] or [j].

Closed syllable shapes include VC, VVC, CVC, and CVVC. Syllables closed by the first half of a geminate, such as VG, VVG, CVG, and CVVG are also found, where G indicates a geminate. The geminate in such syllables can be either underlying or morphologically derived. Syllables with geminate stops surface only word-internally. Where a geminate stop might arise word-finally, it is simplified via degemination (see §3.4.3). Syllables closed by a geminate sonorant are also found word-internally. Like in open syllables, VVC, VVG, CVVC, and CVVG syllables may contain a sequence of identical or non-identical vowels. The former results in a phonetic long vowel while the latter results in a diphthong.

Onsetless syllables appear only word-initially, though speakers typically epenthesize a slight glottal stop [ʔ] to create an onset (*aragtí* [ʔaragtí] 'sight'). When a sequence of two morphemes arises that would result in vowel hiatus (i.e., a V.V or CV.V sequence) within a word, a variety of strategies are adopted to avoid the creation of a word-internal onsetless syllable. For example, a glide (typically [j]) is often epenthesized if the two vowels are non-identical (e.g., *mindí* 'knife' + -*ó* → *mindiyó* 'knives'). However, there are clusters of pronouns and function words within the Verb Complex that behave differently. In these instances, a diphthong may be created (e.g., *la* + *i* → *lay* 'one...me'), or the vowels may coalesce (e.g., *la* + *ú* → *loó* 'one...to'), with the precise outcome depending on the particular combination of vowels involved. There are also some instances in which two identical vowels arise in succession. Here, they simply form a long vowel (e.g., *calaámo* 'emblem' + -*óyin* → *calaamoóyin* 'emblems'). Examples illustrating various syllable shapes are in (1).

(1) *Syllable shapes*

a.	V	*ú*	'to, towards'
b.	VV	*oo.rí*	'wife'
c.	CV	*sú.bax*	'morning'
d.	CVV	*soo.míd*	'Ramadan fasting'
e.	CV_1V_2	*qaw.lád*	'room'
f.	VC	*ar.dáa*	'courtyard'
g.	VVC	*óog*	'twilight'
h.	CVC	*hár.gab*	'influenza'
i.	CVG	*bábbad*	'gust of wind'
j.	CVVC	*dhéer*	'tall'
k.	CV_1V_2C	*táwl*	'family lineage'
l.	VG	*ím.misa*	'how much'
m.	VVG	*eéb.be*	'God'
n.	V_1V_2G	*eyddín*	'muscle pain'
o.	CVVG	*saád.do*	'chest'
p.	CV_1V_2G	*tawl.lán*	'shapely'

Though there are many possible syllable shapes in Somali, there are no syllables with complex onsets or complex codas. When these might arise, such as in loanword incorporation, they are repaired by a variety of mechanisms. Examples of repairs in loanwords from English include deletion (*saajin* 'sergeant'), word-initial epenthesis (*iskaandhel* 'scandal'), and word-internal epenthesis (*taraabel* 'trouble'). Further discussion of these and other repairs observed in loanword incorporation is in §4.4.

Though complex syllable margins are not permitted, there are many instances in which two consonants do occur adjacent to one another. These are always found across a syllable boundary. This restriction can be seen in monomorphs like *war.qád* 'letter' and *jáb.ti* 'gonorrhea,' but also in the formation of compounds like *kaf.tan.dháb.le* 'truthful joke' (> *káftan* 'joke' + *dháb* 'truth' + 'have.RED'). There are further restrictions on the distribution of particular syllable types word-finally vs. word-internally discussed in §4.3.

4.2 Word shape and size requirements

Monomorphemic words are diverse in the combinations of syllable types that they permit, though most are mono- or disyllabic. Longer words are common, but they are morphologically complex, being formed by derivation or compounding. Verbs, in particular, are synthetic and may be more than two syllables in length. Other longer words are typically borrowings.

It seems clear that there is a minimal size requirement for lexical or content words. The smallest lexical words minimally contain a branching rhyme. This can be seen in CVC words like *dád* 'people' and VC words like *éy* 'dog,' but also in CVV words with a diphthong (*dhów* 'nearby'). Somewhat surprisingly, monomorphemic CVV content words whose stem vowels are identical are not found. Function words of this shape abound, however, such as the focus marker *báa* and the deictic particles *soó* and *sií*. What one could consider subminimal shapes (i.e., those without a branching rhyme) like V and CV exist, but they are largely limited to functional morphemes like adpositions (*ú*, *kú*, *ká*, and *lá*), pronominal clitics (e.g., *i*, *ku*, *na*), and definite determiners (*ka* and *ta*), none of which can occur independently.

Beyond these shapes, CVVC word shapes are widely found, though those with a long vowel (e.g., *doón* 'boat') far outnumber those with a diphthong (e.g., *déyn* 'debt'). There are stringent restrictions on which coda consonants can occur word-finally after a diphthong; see §4.3.2. Words of this shape that might be considered to have a final geminate come to be reduced in one of two ways.

In larger words, syllable shapes with a branching rhyme, namely CVC and CVV (whether a long vowel or a diphthong), are found preceding another syllable, as in *már.kab* 'ship,' *caá.to* 'thin person,' and *taw.bád* 'repentance.' CVVC syllable shapes (whether with a long vowel or diphthong) are absent word-internally before another syllable, except in the formation of compounds. CVVG syllables (closed by a geminate), however, are permitted before another syllable: e.g., *dhaaddán* 'healthy' and *kú hawllán* 'occupied.'

These facts taken together suggest that there is a minimal word condition, and that other factors (perhaps moraicity or syllable weight) come into play in dictating the distribution of syllable types in different word positions.

4.3 Phonotactics

4.3.1 Word-initial and intervocalic consonant distribution

There are few restrictions on the distribution of consonants in word-initial and intervocalic positions. Any singleton consonant phoneme, except for glottal stop /ʔ/, can appear word-initially. A phonetic [ʔ] does appear epenthetically when a vowel-initial stem occurs in word-initial position, but it is not contrastive. This restriction is relaxed in word-internal syllable onsets where any consonant, including /ʔ/, can occur intervocalically.

The lenis stops /ḅ, ḍ, g̣/ occur intervocalically, but they are realized either as voiced stops [b, d, g] or spirants [β, ð, ɣ] in word-internal onsets. For some speakers, this is conditioned by their location relative to H tone. For others, the position of H seems to have no effect on the realization of these consonants, though a slower speech rate sometimes yields voiced stops instead of spirants. The implosive stop /ɗ/ similarly alternates to [ɾ] intervocalically, and /h/ voices to [ɦ], but H tone location does not have an effect here. Geminate consonants do not appear word-initially, but both geminate stops and geminate sonorants can appear intervocalically. Geminates are discussed in Sections 3.1.3.1 and 3.1.3.2.

These restrictions on word-initial and word-medial consonant distribution are fairly loose, but there are more stringent conditions on consonant distribution in word-internal onsets after a coda. These are discussed in §4.3.3.

4.3.2 Consonant distribution in codas

The only word-final ban on consonant phonemes appears to pertain to the glides /j/ and /w/, though phonetic offglides are found as the second element of a diphthong both word-internally and word-finally; see §3.2.5. The affricate /tʃ/ does not occur in final positions in native Somali words, but it appears in this position in nativized loanwords, such as *rájmi* 'stoning' and *táaj* 'crown,' which are borrowed from Arabic. The nasal /m/ occurs stem-finally, though it also alternates to [n] in a word-final coda. Compare *ni.mán* 'men' and *nín* 'man.'

The fortis stops /tʰ/ and /kʰ/ are aspirated, as is /qʰ/, though aspiration is not contrastive in the last of these. These stops appear stem-finally, but they are deaspirated when they occur in a coda. Compare, for example, *ar.[kʰ]ay* 'I saw' and *ara[k].nay* 'we saw.'

Despite the fact that it appears as [ɾ] word-finally in the Central and Benaadir dialects, it seems unnecessary to posit that the implosive stop /ɗ/ is banned from occurring at the end of stems in these varieties.

The consonants that occur in a coda after a diphthong in word-final syllables are limited. I have found no instances in which any of Somali's consonants that one might associate with the phonological feature [back], namely /q, ʔ, ʜ, ʕ, h/ (written *q, ', x, c, h*, respectively), appear in such a coda, with one possible exception. The uvular fricative /χ/ (written *kh*) appears in borrowings like *shéekh* 'sheikh,' though some speakers pronounce this long vowel as a diphthong. Examples with consonants that appear word-finally after a [w]-diphthong or a [j]-diphthong are in (2) and (3), respectively. Instances of the latter outnumber the former, but such words are few in number overall. There are no comparable restrictions on consonants that can occur word-finally in a coda after a long vowel.

(2) *Word-final V[w]C*

a.	V[w]d	cáwd	'hot, stuffy place'
b.	V[w]s	cáws	'grass'
c.	V[w]l	qáwl	'pledge'
d.	V[w]r	jówr	'tyranny'

(3) Word-final V[j]C

a.	V[j]b	haýb	'genealogy'
b.	V[j]d	weýd	'thinness'
c.	V[j]dh	cáydh	'poor person'
d.	V[j]g	adáyg	'difficulty'
e.	V[j]n	dambeýn	'remainder'
f.	V[j]f	galléyf	'hardness'
g.	V[j]s	dubbéys	'hammering'
h.	V[j]sh	cáysh	'nourishment'
i.	V[j]l	héyl	'cardamom'
j.	V[j]r	déyr	'fence'

Closed CVVC syllables, whether containing a long vowel or a diphthong are not found word-internally before another syllable except in the formation of compounds. The exception to this is if the consonant closing such a syllable is the first half of a geminate.

4.3.3 Syllable contact sequences

When consonants come into contact across a syllable boundary, there are different sequences permitted depending on morphological composition. For example, phonotactic restrictions within a root are stricter than those in a stem containing derivational extensions. Constraints on permissible contact sequences are even looser in compounding and as the result of verbal inflection. There are additionally some sequences that appear limited to borrowed words. The distribution and generalizations presented below are based on an survey of two Somali dictionaries, Puglielli and Mansur (2012) and Zorc and Osman (1993), and supplemented by the approximately 71 million word online WaC corpus (https://corpora.fi.muni.cz/habit/run.cgi/). Of course, this survey does not pretend to be exhaustive, but nonetheless it reveals consistent generalizations about Somali phonotactics. There is also brief discussion on permitted syllable contact sequences in Somali in Cardona (1981) and Mioni (1988).

Figures 4.1 through 4.3 present a high level overview of the generalizations uncovered in the survey just mentioned. Consonants are represented by their orthographic equivalent, with codas on the y-axis and onsets on the x-axis. The figures summarize syllable contact sequences along the dimensions mentioned above, the details of which are explained in sections below.

Shaded cells are unattested in my survey. Those marked by L are found in loanwords, primarily from Arabic. Cells containing a particular C.C sequence indicate that the sequence is found in roots. Those having a hyphen (-) also appear in roots but are not widely distributed. They appeared in less than ten words in the survey. Cells with two asterisks (**) are found in compounds and as the result of inflectional affixation. Lastly, cells with a single asterisk (*) are found as the result of V/Ø alternations. Among the last three of these, C.C and hyphenated (-) sequences are also found in compounds, inflected forms, and as the result of V/Ø alternations. Those indicated by a single asterisk (*) are also found in compounds and inflected forms.

	b	d	dh	g	q	c	t	k	j
b	b.b	*	*	**	*	*	**	**	**
d	*	d.d	**	**	*	*	**	**	
dh	*		dh.dh			—	**	*	
g	**	**	**	g.g		—	**	**	**
q	**	*	**	**		—	**		**
c	*	*	**	**	L		**	**	**
f	**	**	**	**	**	**	**	**	**
s	*	*	**	**	—	**	**	**	**
sh	**		L	L	L	**	L	L	
kh	L	L			L		L		
x	*	**	**	**	**		**	**	**
h	L	L				L	**		L
m	m.b	L		**	*	*		**	**
n		n.d	n.dh	n.g	n.q	*	n.t	n.k	n.j
l	l.b	l.d	**	l.g	l.q	l.c	*	l.k	**
r	r.b	r.d	r.dh	r.g	r.q	r.c	r.t	r.k	r.j

Fig. 4.1: Syllable contact sequences - stop and affricate onsets

	f	s	sh	kh	x	h
b	**	*	–	L	–	*
d	*	*	**		**	
dh	*	*			*	
g	*	*	**		*	
q	–	*	–		**	**
c	*	*	**			
f		*	**		**	**
s	*				**	**
sh				L	**	**
kh		*	L			
x	**	*	**			
h	**	*				
m	**	*		**	**	L
n		*	**	**	**	L
l	l.f	*	*	**	l.x	**
r	r.f	r.s	r.sh	L	r.x	*

Fig. 4.2: Syllable contact sequences - fricative onsets

	m	n	l	r	w	y
b	*	–	b.l	b.r	**	**
d	*	*	d.l	d.r	*	*
dh	*	*	**			
g	*	*	*		**	**
q	*	*	*	*	L	**
c	*	*	*	*		
f	*	*	–	*	**	**
s	*	*	–	*	**	L
sh	*	*	*	*	–	L
kh	*	*	L	L	L	L
x	*	*	*	*	**	**
h	*	*	L	L	**	*
m	m.m	*	*	*		
n	*	n.n	**	**	**	**
l	l.m	*	l.l	**	l.w	*
r	r.m	*	**	r.r	r.w	*

Fig. 4.3: Syllable contact sequences - sonorant onsets

Missing from these charts are potential sequences beginning with consonants that are either entirely absent from codas (namely, *t.C* and *k.C*) or otherwise extremely restricted in such positions. The latter includes written *j* /tʃ/, which is found in sequences *j.g* and *j.k* in some compounds, and also in borrowings in the following combinations: *j.n*, *j.c*, *j.l*, and *j.r*. Also, glottal stop appears in a coda, but only before *d, g, j, n, l, w,* and *y,* in compounds or borrowings.

4.3.3.1 Sequences in roots

The abundance of possible syllable contact sequences in Figures 4.1 through 4.3 might suggest that Somali has fairly loose phonotactics. This might be true if one includes all of the language's morphologically-complex words and compounds, but looking specifically at monomorphemic words (i.e., within a root), as represented by cells including a particular C.C sequence, the picture is quite different. Among those sequences identified, the majority of C.C sequences include a coda nasal (4) or liquid (5). Nasal codas are with /n/ except before a bilabial, while the distribution of coda liquids is more evenly distributed between /l/ and /r/. Sonorant codas can occur before a wide variety of onset consonants, though there are occasional gaps. Of course, there are not many words that are clearly monomorphemic with word-internal C.C sequences to begin with.

(4) *Syllable contact in roots - nasal codas*

a.	m.b	kúm.bis	'meat cooked in ghee'
b.	n.d	qán.dac	'temperateness'
c.	n.dh	cán.dho	'udder'
d.	n.g	dan.gíig	'lay on a mat'
e.	n.q	hán.qal	'chest (body)'
f.	n.t	fán.to	'smallpox'
g.	n.k	kan.kóon	'circle'
i.	n.j	han.jábo	'threat'

(5) *Syllable contact in roots - liquid codas*

a.	l.b	*bél.bel*	'flame'
b.	l.d	*del.del*	'lynch'
c.	l.g	*macál.go*	'type of spoon'
d.	l.q	*wal.qál*	'naming ceremony'
e.	l.c	*wál.can*	'ancestry'
f.	l.k	*kal.káal*	'nurse'
g.	l.f	*qol.fáad*	'caulk'
h.	l.x	*kal.xán*	'collarbone'
i.	l.m	*mál.mal*	'myrrh'
j.	l.w	*bal.wád*	'unpleasant habit'
k.	r.b	*qúr.bac*	'young male camel'
l.	r.d	*ár.day*	'student'
m.	r.dh	*gár.dho*	'thick hair'
n.	r.g	*gór.gor*	'vulture'
o.	r.q	*hár.qad*	'pillow case'
p.	r.c	*búr.cad*	'butter'
q.	r.t	*tar.tiíb*	'slowness'
r.	r.k	*bar.kád*	'pool'
s.	r.j	*hár.jad*	'restlessness'
t.	r.f	*xar.fád*	'skill'
u.	r.s	*ir.saáq*	'nourishment'
v.	r.sh	*xór.shosh*	'decay'
w.	r.x	*qúr.xub*	'mammary gland'
x.	r.m	*ir.máan*	'livestock in milk'
y.	r.w	*wár.war*	'blunt spear'

Another smaller cluster of contact sequences appearing within monomorphemic words involve a bilabial or alveolar stop preceding a liquid, as in (6).

(6) *Syllable contact in roots - stop codas*

a.	b.l	*dub.lád*	'funnel'
b.	b.r	*sib.ráar*	'water skin'
c.	d.l	*dád.laq*	'extreme depth'
d.	d.r	*cad.rád*	'unmarried girl'

In addition, there are some contact sequences found in words that are not apparent borrowings or derivatives but that are limited in their distribution to just a few items. Examples are shown in (7).

(7) *Syllable contact in roots - other codas*

a.	b.sh	ráb.shi	'guano'
b.	b.x	kab.xán	'type of tree'
c.	b.n	áb.naq	'genealogy'
d.	g.c	shag.cád	'stride'
e.	q.c	waq.cád	'battlefield'
f.	q.f	shaq.fál	'armpit'
g.	q.sh	buq.shád	'envelope'
h.	f.l	áf.lax	'success'
i.	s.q	bis.qán	'pubic hair'
j.	s.l	was.lád	'portion'
k.	sh.w	xash.wád	'leak in a boat'

Lastly, the language's four geminate stops and four geminate sonorants are included in this group, though technically they represent a single segment that is syllabified into two adjacent syllables. Examples including these geminates are in Sections 3.1.3.1 and 3.1.3.2, respectively.

4.3.3.2 Sequences created by V/Ø alternation

The syllable contact sequences indicated by a single asterisk (*) in the tables above are found in native Somali words, but only where a V/Ø alternation is found. For example, the sequence *dh.b* arises when the word *cedhíb* 'heel' is pluralized. The addition of the plural suffix *-ó* results in V/Ø alternation and the noun *cedhbó* 'heels,' with a C.C sequence across a syllable boundary. If such an alternation does not occur, this is taken as evidence that the C.C sequence that would result is not permitted, at least within a stem. For example, we find words like *cuqúbo* 'curse,' as opposed to **cuqbo*, where there is no alternation to **q.b* occurs in the presence of *-o*. Some of these sequences that the language avoids creating within a stem via V/Ø alternation may be permitted elsewhere, however, such as in the formation of compounds and in loanwords.

The sequences permitted in a stem where V/Ø alternation is involved are diverse, but they largely reinforce the patterns already found in roots that are discussed in §4.3.3.1. That is, the alternations involve sonorant codas or sequences of a stop coda followed by a liquid onset. However, there are also some more diverse combinations, notably stop + stop sequences. Most striking are the abundance of *C.s*, *C.m*, and *C.n* sequences observed. These sequences would appear to arise due to the loss of vowels from highly productive suffixes, and often subsequent alternations. Examples are as follows:

(8) *ganacsáde*
/ganaʔ-is-aḍ-e/
sell-WCAUS-MID-AGT
'merchant'

(9) *duubmay*
/ḍuuḅ-an-∅-aj/
tie-INCH-1SG-PST
'he became tied (up)'

(10) *baduugnaa*
/ḅaḍuuq-an-∅-aa/
break-INCH-3SG-PST
'it was broken'

4.3.3.3 Sequences in compounds and inflected forms

Syllable contact sequences arising in compounds and upon inflection are indicated by cells with a double asterisk (**) in the figures above. These sequences are far more diverse than those seen in roots and stems. For compounds, this is intuitive given that, by definition, compounding involves two otherwise independent words that join to create a larger word. As such, one can safely assert that phonotactic restrictions across word boundaries are fairly loose. Examples of compounds showing a variety of syllable contact sequences are found in Chapter 8.

That there are looser phonotactic restrictions in inflected forms is less intuitive but nonetheless robustly attested in Somali. This can be seen in the abundance of syllable contact sequences involving what appears to be a word-internal onset with *t* or *k*. Sequences involving *t*, in particular, are prevalent as the suffix *-t-* is involved with the inflection of verbs for 2SG and 3SG.F. For example, a sequence of *g.t* is not permitted in roots or stems, but verbs like *aragtay* 'she saw' show that such a sequence is readily permitted upon inflection. Those involving onset *k* are found, for example, where a K-series definite determiner is added to a noun. For example, while a *b.k* sequence is not permitted in a root or in a stem after V/∅ alternation, it is found in *márkab=ka* 'the ship.' Green and Morrison (2018) have argued that morphemes like inflectional suffixes in verbs and definite determiners in the nominal system are clitics located outside of the phonological word. Such a view might help to explain why such exceptional heterosyllabic sequences occur in these instances.

4.3.3.4 Sequences in borrowings

Syllable contact sequences marked by L in the figures above are found in words that are clearly borrowings, many of which are from Arabic. These sequences, generally speaking, involve sounds that are less predominant overall in Somali content words but also sounds that are limited to borrowings altogether. These contact sequences tend to involve, "back" fricatives like written *kh*, *x*, and *h*, and also sometimes the uvular stop *q*, whether in the coda or in the following onset.

4.4 Loanword adaptation

A number of works offer surveys of loanwords borrowed into Somali from languages with which it has been in contact. Most of these focus on the presence and adaptation of Arabic loanwords into the language. They include, in chronological order, Zaborski (1967), Mioni (1988), Orwin (1991), Soravia (1994), Vasaturo (2012), and most recently Banti (2013). Banti (2013) is somewhat broader in that it also covers borrowings from Arabic and Southern Ethiosemitic languages. To these, one can add Tosco (2008), which focuses on Italian loanwords, and Mioni (1988), which discusses loanwords from both Italian and English. Kaldhol (2017) deals with the borrowing of Norwegian loanwords, and specifically compounds, within the Somali diaspora community in Oslo. These works focus primarily on phonological and morphological adaptation, as well as segmental "repairs" in borrowings from various languages. They should not be confused with other works whose goal is to survey efforts at lexicon expansion and modernization, namely Caney (1984) and Hared (1992).

The intent in this section is not to discuss specific borrowings or pathways of borrowing via commerce, religion, or technology, nor to provide lists of words believed to have been borrowed from a given language. Rather, common segmental adaptations made in loanword incorporation are first discussed. Then, attention is turned to phonotactic and metrical repairs that often occur in loanword adaptation. These offer some insight into the language's prosodic system that are not always immediately apparent from the structure or behavior of words in the indigenous Somali lexicon.

4.4.1 Segmental repair

Segmental repairs are found in words borrowed into Somali when the lending language's sound inventory contains a sound that does not occur in Somali's inventory. There are several well-attested and consistent repairs found in borrowings, at least for those languages with which Somali has long, or at least consistently been in contact, such as Arabic, French, Italian, and English. For example, instances of the voiceless bilabial stop [p] are realized in Somali as *b* (e.g., *monoboli* 'monopoly'). This repair stems from that fact that Somali has only a single bilabial stop phoneme. Of course, the precise phonetic realization of Somali stops varies widely, sometimes according to the syllable frame within which it appears. Other simple mappings include [v] → [f] (e.g., *Nofeembar* 'November'), [ʒ] → [ʃ] (e.g., *telefishan* 'television), [z] → [s] (e.g., *maarso*, Italian *marzo* 'March'), [θ] → [t] (e.g., *tayroodh* 'thyroid'), and [dʒ] → [tʃ] (e.g., *jaakád* 'jacket'), keeping in mind that orthographic *j* is pronounced [tʃ]. Arabic's pharyngealized "emphatic" consonants are simplified to their non-emphatic counterparts wherever there are equivalents. For example, [dˤ] → [d], [tˤ] → [t], and [sˤ] → [s] or [ʃ]. Emphatic [zˤ] (or [θˤ]) is usually mapped onto [d]. Mappings within the vowel system are far more variable given the complex interactions between tone and stress alongside long vs. short vowels and Somali's two harmonic series of vowels.

4.4.2 Phonotactic repair

Other adaptations observed in loanword incorporation have their basis in phonotactic constraints required by Somali syllables, rather than in incompatibilities between the lending and borrowing languages' sound inventories. Such repairs can be revelatory in that they present an opportunity to view unmarked or otherwise preferred structures that are not always apparent in the native lexicon. Given the relatively nascent nature of work on Somali prosodic phonology, and absent any substantive discussion in the literature on the possibility of metrical structure and stress in the language, how the language chooses to respond to incompatible phonotactic sequences has the ability to provide key insight into these topics.

One matter discussed in several of the aforementioned works on Somali loanword adaptation is that the language often incorporates loanwords in a way that is sensitive to the phonetic realization of stress in the lending language. More specifically, though vowel length is not phonemic in languages like Italian and English, it is apparent in the phonetic signal when a vowel is in a stressed syllable. Long vowels in borrowings are found word-initially (e.g., *baánki* 'bank') or in monosyllabic words (e.g., *búug* 'book'), but also in penultimate position in somewhat longer words (e.g., *agoósto*, Italian *agosto* 'August' and *shukulaáto*, Italian *cioccolàto* 'chocolate'). Long vowels can even be created word-finally (e.g., *dishibilíin* 'discipline'). However, this is not always the case, as seen in borrowings like *mítir* 'meter,' where one might expect *miitir* if the equation of stress and vowel length were to be consistently maintained upon borrowing. The same could be said of *korónto* 'electricity,' *koroonto*, as borrowed from Italian *corrente*.

There are several strategies adopted to accommodate disallowed consonant clusters that differ depending on whether the cluster is word-initial, word-internal, or word-final. There is also the special case of *s*-clusters. Word-initial #CC clusters are always repaired by epenthesis. In most instances, this involves the insertion of an epenthetic vowel between the two consonants, but with #sC clusters, epenthesis occurs before the first consonant. The latter repair is consistent, being realized with an epenthetic [i], as in *iskúul* 'school' and *istaádiyo*, from Italian *stadio* 'stadium.' Word-initial #CC repairs are more involved. The default strategy is arguably the epenthesis of a copy of the following vowel: #CCV$_1$ → #CV$_1$CV$_1$. This is seen in words like *galáas* 'glass,' and *borónso*, from Italian *bronzo* 'bronze.' In addition, however, there are other non-copy epenthetic repairs. For example, despite the exact vowel copy seen in 'bronze,' there are words like *buraash* 'brush' where this does not occur. Mioni (1988) attributes this to a "labializing effect" contributed by *b*, though one that is apparently not always consistent. In *bulukeeti*, from Italian *blocchetto* 'block,' there appears to be a combination of the repairs seen in 'bronze' and 'brush.' In other words like *barafúun* 'perfume,' there is no labializing effect at all. In still other words like *galóob* 'globe' and *dareéwal* 'driver,' the vowel copy generalization does not hold.

Borrowings that end in a single consonant are readily permitted, as seen in many of the examples provided thus far. Final CC#clusters, however, are avoided in all instances, being repaired either by deletion or epenthesis. Deletion can be seen in *báan* 'band' and *léysin* 'license,' while epenthesis occurs in words like 'bank,' shown above, but also when words end in #CCs. This can be seen in *dhokuméntis* 'documents,' *jornalístis* 'journalists,' and *ispórtis* 'sports.' Sometimes, the repair for such clusters is metathesis, as in *sáynis* 'science.' Clusters involving *r* are resolved in different ways, as in *rikóor* 'record' vs. *booskáadh* 'postcard.'

Just as was the case with the incorporation of words with initial clusters, the resolution of word internal clusters is more complex than it might first appear. Some sources report that epenthesis of a copy or "echo vowel" (Banti 2013) is the basic strategy or that this is "usually what occurs" (Zaborski 1967). Mioni (1988) notes, however, that while copy of an adjacent vowel is possible, epenthesis of a "neutral vowel," namely [a] is also found. Indeed, Tosco (2008) states that [a] insertion occurs "apparently more often" than copy vowel epenthesis, at least in borrowings from Italian. This neutral vowel epenthesis can also be seen in English loans like *elektaróon* 'electron' and *nayitaroojiin* 'nitrogen.'

While this matter deserves a great deal more attention, it seems that one cannot rest on the generalization of copy vowel epenthesis being the default strategy. Rather, it appears that there are at least two competing strategies for cluster repair whose governing factors are not yet entirely clear. As Mioni (1988) points out (citing discussion in Puglielli 1981), the fact that two strategies of consonant cluster repair are possible in loanword adaptation may have a bearing on approaches to and analyses of V/∅ alternations, as discussed in §3.5. That is, if Somali's default response to breaking consonant clusters is not copy vowel epenthesis, this could be seen as weakening perspectives that assume epenthesis, as opposed to reduction, to explain the outcome of V/∅ alternations that affect native Somali words in both the nominal and verbal systems. Under an epenthesis approach, all instances in which epenthesis does not result in vowel copy would have to be viewed as exceptions.

4.5 Poetic metrics

Linguistic studies of Somali poetic metrics have their origin in a series of articles by Maxamed Xaashi Dhamac 'Gaarriye' and Cabdullaahi Diiriye Guuleed 'Carraale' that were published in the Somali newspaper *Xiddigta Oktoobar* 'The October Star' in the 1970s. Gaarriye and Carraale set the stage for inquiry into the role of metrics in Somali phonology via their insightful discussion concerning the fact that the metrical structure of several of Somali's poetic genres is based on rhythmic units (i.e., moras) and not on syllables. A series of works over the next several decades by Antinucci and Cali (1986), Banti and Giannattasio (1996), Johnson (1979, 1984, 1988, 1996), Orwin and Riiraash (1997), Orwin (2001), and Orwin and Gaarriye (2010) expanded upon the contributions made in these earlier articles. Though originally focused solely on establishing the properties of different poetic genres, these scholars have increasing sought to make connections between poetic metrics and other components of Somali phonology. The remainder of this section briefly describes aspects of Somali poetic metrics that have implications for our understanding of the language's prosodic phonology more broadly.[1]

As stated above, one of the key insights of Gaarriye and Carraale's work was on the role of the mora in Somali poetic metrics. It is now well-established that different poetic genres make use of lines (i.e., quantitative scansions) with different numbers of moras and that these moras are organized into syllabic patterns that are unique to a given genre. For example, Orwin and Gaarriye (2010) discuss details of *jiifto*, one genre of Somali poetry, illustrating characteristics of its five metrical positions (MPs). These are schematized in Figure 4.4 where ⌣ equates with a single mora or short vowel. Thus, for MPs 1, 2, 4, and 5, each contains a sequence of two moras. MP3, however, contains only a single mora. The line below MPs 1, 2, 4, and 5 indicates that these positions may either be occupied by two light monomoraic syllables or instead by a single heavy unit composed of two moras, such as a long vowel or diphthong. Closed syllables generally pattern with light syllables, though there are restrictions on where in the line they can appear.

⌣⌣	⌣⌣	⌣	⌣⌣	⌣⌣
MP1	MP2	MP3	MP4	MP5

Fig. 4.4: Schematization of a *jiifto* line

For the purpose of this overview, the issue of *ancep* syllables is set aside. These are primarily associated with function words which, though phonologically composed of two moras, may be artistically manipulated in the construction of certain scansion types such that they are realized short (i.e., monomoraic).

Much has been revealed throughout the years about finer details of *jiifto* and other scansion patterns, particularly concerning how syllable final consonants and diphthongs participate in the metrical system. Beginning with glides, studies have shown that CVGC words with a diphthong like *daýr* 'autumn rain' are heavy (i.e., they contain

---

[1] I am incredibly grateful to Martin Orwin for his input concerning which characteristics of Somali poetic metrics would be best to include here.

two moras) and pattern with syllables containing a long vowel, like CVVC. The same bimoraic behavior applies to a VG word like *éy* 'dog.' A syllable containing a vowel-final diphthong in a word like *árday* 'student,' however, behaves as if it were light, or monomoraic. These facts easily align with perspectives outlined above in §4.2 concerning word size requirements. The behavior of other consonants is different.

Though CVC and CV syllables, each containing a short vowel, have long been treated as quantitatively equivalent (i.e., both being light or monomoraic), their distribution differs to some extent. A collaboration between Gaarriye and Orwin solidified the fact that within a *jiifto* line, there are only certain MPs wherein a syllable can end in a consonant. This distribution is shown in Figure 4.5 where a superscript *c* indicates those instances where a closed syllable can occur.

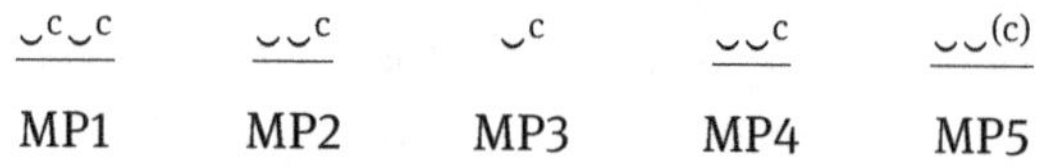

⌣ᶜ⌣ᶜ	⌣⌣ᶜ	⌣ᶜ	⌣⌣ᶜ	⌣⌣(ᶜ)
MP1	MP2	MP3	MP4	MP5

Fig. 4.5: Closed syllable distribution in a *jiifto* line

The limited distribution of closed syllables, and importantly their avoidance medially in some metrical positions, might suggest that coda consonants have the ability to contribute quantitatively to the syllable, at least in some instances. Notably, such syllables are avoided within MPs 2, 4, and 5, but can appear at their right edge. Orwin and Gaarriye (2010) point out that MP1 is more flexible from a metrical perspective in that it may accommodate two closed syllables. MP5 also varies in its behavior, as it is subject to special constraints by virtue of being at the end of the line. Whether this behavior of closed syllables is best analyzed as being due to a contribution of weight or simply length, however, is yet unclear.

Along these same lines, Orwin and Gaarriye (2010) have shown that there are even some singleton consonants, namely *t, k, j, f, s, sh, j,* and *w*, that are avoided in the same medial MP 2, 4, and 5 positions as closed syllables and geminates. They suggest that there is something unique about these consonants that contributes to their limited distribution. In the spirit of Ségéral and Scheer (2001) and Barillot (2002), they entertain a connection between these consonants and the presence of "virtual geminates." For more on this idea, as §3.1.3.3.

5 Tone

5.1 Introduction

Somali is a tone language from the standpoint of contemporary perspectives on prosodic typology. Following discussion in Hyman (2006) and references cited therein, a tone language is a language "in which an indication of pitch enters into the lexical realisation of at least some morphemes." While this is certainly true of Somali, its tone system is reduced and non-prototypical. This is a matter made abundantly clear by Klingenheben (1949), who asks very pointedly, "Ist das Somali eine Tonsprache?" [Is Somali a tone language?]. The unusual status of Somali's tonal system is also discussed in Hyman (2019a,b).

The Somali tone system is characterized by the presence of a High (H) tone that is culminative on a single (phonological) word (Hyman 1981; Green and Morrison 2016). This fact has led some to refer to Somali as a "tonal accent" language. However, because this H tone is not obligatory in all instances, an approach based on accent is undesirable. H tone in Somali is limited in its distribution and is realized on a mora tone bearing unit (TBU). It is illustrated below that the location of H tone is morphologically-conditioned. In morphologically-simplex words (i.e., within roots), H is found on either the final or penultimate mora of a root. In more complex words, some affixes can bear a H tone, while others do not. H tone in these words surfaces on the rightmost tone bearing affix, though there are exceptions. The overarching generalization is that H tone demarcates the right edge of a Somali prosodic (or phonological) word. Any TBU that is not associated with H is best considered phonologically toneless (∅). Toneless TBUs are realized as phonetically Low (L).

As introduced earlier, it is important to recognize that a string constituting an orthographic word may be associated with more than one H tone. Green and Morrison (2016) have showed that phonological, morphological, and orthographic wordhood in Somali do not necessarily correlate with one another in all instances. Though the bounds of a phonological and morphological word do sometimes correlate, there are instances in which one phonological word corresponds to more than one morphological word, and vice versa. They suggest that it is best to consider most Somali orthographic words as corresponding to a phonological phrase.

In this chapter and elsewhere, reference will be made to prosodic structures assumed in contemporary Prosodic Hierarchy Theory (Nespor and Vogel, 1985; Selkirk, 1978, 1981, 1984), as schematized in Figure 5.1.

Work on Somali has tended not to make explicit reference to these prosodic categories until fairly recently. The exception to this is descriptions of syllable shape and distribution that are found in most reference and pedagogical resources, and discussion of the mora which, to my knowledge, began with Hyman's (1981) analysis of Somali's tonal system. Saeed (1999) also mentions the mora to some extent, citing

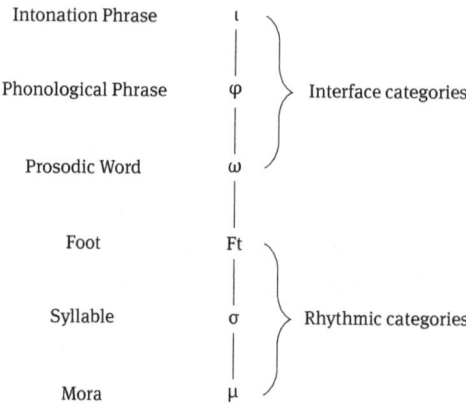

Fig. 5.1: Prosodic Hierarchy

Hyman's work, as does work by Orwin, Banti, and their colleagues on Somali metrics and poetry. Interface categories – prosodic word, phonological phrase, and intonation phrase – are invoked much later, beginning notably with works by Le Gac (2002, 2003b,a), and later in various works by Green and Morrison (2016, 2018), Kaldhol (2017), Downing and Nilsson (2019), and Green and Lampitelli (2021), though this list is not exhaustive.

5.2 High tone assignment

5.2.1 Nouns

Since Hyman (1981), the mora is understood as being the relevant unit of tone assignment in Somali. It is the language's tone bearing unit (TBU). This is clear in words whose final syllable contains a long vowel or diphthong, both of which are bimoraic sequences. H tone can associate to either mora. The role of the mora is clear in the assignment of H tone to nouns, though there are only limited instances where the presence of H on the penultimate vs. final mora is lexically-contrastive. For example, consider the segmentally identical but tonally distinct nouns *gées* 'horn' and *geés* 'side.' They differ in whether H is located on the penultimate or final mora of a long vowel. A similar distinction is seen on diphthongs in *éy* 'male dog' and *eý* 'female dog' (or also, 'dogs'). These suggest that diphthongs function phonologically like a sequence of two vowels (and, therefore, two moras) in H tone assignment, at least in some instances.[1]

---

[1] As discussed in Section 3.2.5, this is not always the case. The distribution of H tone on words like *árday* suggests that the offglide portion of a diphthong is counted for H tone assignment only in monosyllabic words.

The noun pairs just introduced can also be used to illustrate that H tone location (at least in morphologically-simplex words) correlates with a word's grammatical gender. This can be seen in the determiner that a given noun selects, being either from the K-series or T-series. Nouns with a H tone on their penultimate mora select a K-series determiner. Compare, for example, *gées=ka* 'the horn' and *éy=ga* 'the male dog.' Those with a H tone on their final mora instead select a T series determiner. Compare, in this instance, *geés=ta* 'the side' and *eý=da* 'the female dog.' Traditionally, these are referred to as "masculine" and "feminine" gender, respectively, but I refer to them as K-series and T-series. I do so for two main reasons. First, in most instances, the invocation of masculine and feminine to refer to nouns selecting one or the other determiner has no objective reality in the language. As the 'dog' examples show, however, grammatical gender does sometimes correlate with biological gender, but this is the exception rather than the rule. Second, and along similar lines, some (but not all) Somali nouns exhibit what has long been called "gender polarity" between the singular and plural (see Lecarme 2002; Meinhof 1912). For example, the noun 'woman' takes T-series, "feminine" gender in the singular *naágta* 'the woman,' but instead takes K-series, "masculine" gender in the plural *naagáha* 'the women.' As such, one would have to state that 'women' is a masculine noun. Abstracting away from the terms masculine and feminine in favor of another means by which to describe Somali's grammatical gender system avoids these issues to some extent.

Returning specifically to H tone distribution, the generalizations introduced above are easily observed in the singular, morphologically-simplex nouns of the same shape from opposing grammatical genders in (1). Monosyllabic nouns have H assigned to their vowel, being the only moraic tone bearing unit, in both genders. The penultimate H/K-series vs. final H/T-series distribution applies across word shapes and extends to longer monomorphemic words. For example, K-series CVVCV nouns have a H on the second mora of their first syllable. H tone distribution in more complex words is discussed in §5.3.

(1)

a.	CVC	*jíd*	'road'	*jídka*	'the road'
b.		*káb*	'shoe'	*kábta*	'the shoe'
c.	CVVC	*béer*	'liver'	*béerka*	'the liver'
d.		*qoór*	'neck'	*qoórta*	'the neck'
e.	CVCV	*hílib*	'meat'	*hílibka*	'the meat'
f.		*galáb*	'afternoon'	*galábta*	'the afternoon'
g.	CVVCV	*maroódi*	'elephant'	*maroódiga*	'the elephant'
h.		*maalín*	'day'	*maalínta*	'the day'
i.	CVCVVC	*insáan*	'human'	*insáanka*	'the human'
j.		*carbuún*	'deposit'	*carbuúnta*	'the deposit'

There are also a small number of nouns where moras and, accordingly, H tone location are implicated in the assignment of singular vs. plural number (or sometimes collectivity; see Nilsson 2018). This is seen in *díbi* 'bull' and *dibí* 'bulls,' where penultimate H indicates singular and final H plural. As expected, there are accompanying differences in grammatical gender agreement. Singular *díbi=ga* 'the bull' selects a K series determiner while plural *dibí=da* 'the bulls' selects its determiner from the T series.

Some scholars (Le Gac, 1997; Godon, 1998; Lampitelli, 2011; Green and Lampitelli, 2021) have proposed a correlation between H tone assignment, grammatical gender, and root structure. They suggest that "feminine," T-series nouns have an additional skeletal slot appended to their right edge. This has been called the "feminine exponent," as "masculine," K-series nouns lack it. Though there are different perspectives on the matter, the generalization under this view is that the form of a T-series noun like *geés* 'side' would be /kees+V/. A K-series nouns like *gées* 'horn' would instead simply be /kees/. The additional V of the feminine exponent would associate with a mora that gets counted in calculating the location of H tone assignment. That the word's H tone surfaces on what appears to be its final mora would therefore be due to the fact that there is no segmental material realized on the V. Such an approach is attractive in that H tone in morphologically-simplex words is always assigned to the penultimate mora of a stem.[2]

There is variation observed in the realization of H tone on nouns such that not all speakers consistently produce a word-final phonetic [HL] vs. [LH] contour in K-series vs. T-series words, respectively. These contours are characteristic of the speech of Northern and Central Somali, but speakers from the Benaadir Somali area tend instead to pronounce T-series words with a flat, H sequence. Thus, while Northern and Central speakers would typically produce *naág* 'woman,' Benaadir speakers would produce *náág* under the same conditions. Banti (1988c) refers to this as a "natural decontouring effect."

The basic mora-based calculation for H tone assignment described thus far applies to simplex nouns, but the assignment of tone to morphologically complex words is different, though still predictable. As discussed in §5.3.1, some morphemes (e.g., derivational suffixes) attract H tone, while others (e.g., inflectional suffixes and clitics) do not. Thus, depending on the morphological composition of a given word, H tone may occur before the penultimate mora. Despite this, however, the overarching

---

2 The presence of the feminine exponent has also been implicated in explaining at least two other characteristics of Somali nouns. Though their perspectives differ in some ways, both Godon (1998) and Green and Lampitelli (2021) have argued that it plays a role in conditioning stem-final consonant doubling under *-ó* pluralization in some nouns (cf. *sánnad* 'year' and *sannaddó* 'years' vs. *irbád* 'needle' and *irbadó* 'needles'). In addition, they suggest that the feminine exponent provides a skeletal slot for the realization of the subject marker. The subject marker *-i* appears only in "feminine" nouns (e.g., *naag=i* 'woman (SUBJ),' cf. *naág*). "Masculine" nouns lacking the feminine exponent realize subject marking only by the loss of their H tone (e.g., *nin* 'man (SUBJ),' cf. *nín*). For more on subject marking, see §9.2.

generalization is that a word's H tone will surface on the rightmost tone bearing morpheme.

5.2.2 Verbs

Morphologically simplex verbs consisting solely of a root and no derivational extensions have H tone assigned to their penultimate mora. In monosyllabic roots with a single short vowel, this is on the verb's only vowel (*cún* 'eat!'). On longer roots, this can be on the first half of a long vowel (*kéen* 'bring!') or even on the penultimate syllable (*fásax* 'let go!'). The location of H tone shifts rightward when a tone bearing extension is added to the root. This includes most derivational extensions whose tonal behavior is discussed in §5.3.1. Other suffixes involved in inflection bear H tone only in certain syntactic configurations, namely when they take irrealis paradigm inflection. See §7.10 for a summary of the conditions governing this behavior.

The behavior of H tone in verbs presents some reason to question the precise mechanism of H tone assignment, namely whether it is based on moras or some other structural calculation. Compare, for example, the imperative and infinitival forms of the CVC verb *cún* 'eat!' and *cúni* 'to eat' to those of the CVVC verb *kéen* 'bring!' and *keéni* 'to bring.' As otherwise expected, H remains on the same TBU in the first verb, but shifts rightward by one TBU in the second in order to maintain the penultimate mora generalization established above. However, we can further compare this outcome to corresponding imperative and infinitive forms of Weak Causative verbs like *kári* 'cook!' and *karín* 'to cook.' Here, H is not uniformly attracted to the weak causative extension but rather shifts to the extension only in the presence of the word-final nasal required in the infinitive. On direct comparison, it might appear that the final nasal of 'to cook' is behaving as moraic, while that of 'bring!' is not.

5.2.3 Other parts of speech

Somali has a closed set of basic adjectives (see §9.4) whose pattern of H tone assignment mirrors that of nouns. Each appears associated with either K-series or T-series agreement and, as such, is assigned either a penultimate or final mora H, respectively. A much larger class of adjectival participles are derived by one of two tone-bearing suffixes (see §7.1.10). The situation is similar for adverbs. Simplex adverbs have idiosyncratic tone assignment while derived adverbs have a H tone on their suffix.

Somali's four adpositional particles (§10.6) are associated with a H tone. When they occur in clusters, the cluster has a single H tone which appears on the rightmost adposition in the cluster. Deictic particles (§10.4) are also tonal, while other adverbial particles located within the Verb Complex are not. Other constituents within the Verb Complex like pronominal clitics (Sections 10.2.1 and 10.2.3) are not associated with a

H tone, though independent subject pronouns (§9.1.8) behave like nouns and have a H tone, as do "second series" object pronouns (§10.3).

Focus markers are associated with a H tone, but the tonal specification of other particles like clause type markers is determined by the presence or absence of H tone on an adjacent word. Clitics are also toneless in most circumstances, though they may be associated with a boundary tone in some discourse contexts.

5.3 Tone alternations

The location of a word's H tone alternates, changing location under predictable circumstances. In §5.3.1, alternations are discussed in which H tone shifts rightward following the addition of certain derivational suffixes. Most derivational suffixes in both the nominal and verbal systems are tone bearing. When present, the rightmost of these carries the word's H tone. H tone also shifts rightward in the 'pre-modifier' form of two closed classes of nouns that are morphologically-complex even in their singular form. These are discussed in §5.3.2.

5.3.1 Rightward H shift

Every morphologically simplex word is assigned a H tone on either its penultimate or final mora. Morphologically complex words are different in this respect owing to the fact that some suffixes involved in word formation can bear tone while others cannot. Derivational suffixes in both the nominal and verbal systems are tone bearing, though there are a few notable exceptions. For example, most derivational extensions in the verbal system attract H tone, but the reciprocal/co-participatory suffix -*tan* fails to do so. The various affixes in the nominal system that are involved in pluralization (which one might think of as inflectional) also attract H tone. This coupled with the fact that some plural affixes encode gender suggests that pluralization in Somali has certain derivation-like properties, a matter discussed previously by Lecarme (2002). Inflectional suffixes and clitics, on the other hand, tend not to exhibit H tone. Again, however, there are notable exceptions to this generalization found in particular syntactic constructions, such as in the formation of associative constructions (see §9.5). In these constructions, a phrasal H boundary tone comes to be realized on the rightmost TBU of a phrase, regardless of the morphological or prosodic status of the TBU. H tone is also found on inflectional suffixes in the irrealis paradigm.

When a tone bearing suffix is added to a noun stem, the location of H tone shifts from stem to suffix. Examples showing rightward H tone shift adapted from Green and Morrison (2016, 2018) are shown in (2). This is not an exhaustive list of the morphemes that trigger rightward shift, but rather an illustration of the phenomenon. The behavior of specific morphemes is discussed in Chapter 6.

(2) a. sán 'nose' + -án → sanán 'noses'
 b. masíix 'messiah' + -iyád → masiixiyád 'Christianity'
 c. díg 'announce' + -niín → digniín 'warning'
 d. díl 'kill' + -áa → diláa 'killer'

Green and Morrison (2016) attribute rightward H tone shift to the formation of a recursive prosodic word (PWd). Under their view, tone-bearing derivational suffixes project a PWd, with the two PWds adjoining to create a recursive structure. An example of this is shown in Figure 5.2. Here and elsewhere, Somali permits only a single H to be expressed on the larger, newly created PWd. H is located on the second of the two morphemes, suggesting that these larger PWds are phonologically right-headed.

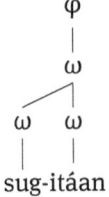

sug-itáan

Fig. 5.2: Prosodic word recursion - *sugitáan* 'waiting (n.)'

Rightward H shift is also seen in compounding as two PWds adjoin to create a larger PWd. Some examples are in (3), but more detail on nominal compounds is found in §8.1.

(3) a. gár 'justice' + yaqáan 'one who knows' → garyaqáan 'judge (n.)'
 b. háwl 'work' + qáran 'nation' → hawlqáran 'civic duty'
 c. dáb 'fire' + damís 'extinguished' → dabdamís 'fireman'
 d. caloól 'stomach' + xanúun 'pain' → caloolxanúun 'stomach ache'

H tone will continue to shift rightward upon the addition of another tone bearing suffix to a word or another element to a compound. Figure 5.3 shows a pluralized compound composed of four tone attracting morphemes. H tone surfaces only on the last of these: *madaxweynayaál* 'presidents.' Related words like *madaxweynáha* 'the president' substantiate the tone bearing status of other morphemes within the word and the gradual rightward movement of H tone as the word grows more morphologically complex.

 A comparison of *madaxwéyne* 'president' and *madaxweynáha* 'the president' shows that Somali sometimes avoids H tone on a short word-final open syllable. When the word final condition is removed in the second word, H is found on -*é*, in-

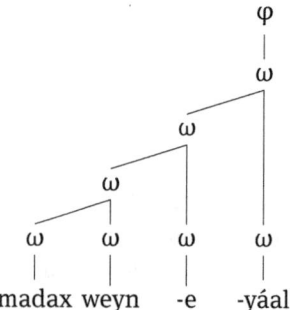

Fig. 5.3: Rightward H shift in complex words - *madaxweynayáal* 'presidents'

dicating that it is indeed a potential tone bearing suffix. This is often referred to as "pre-modifier" H tone alternation; see §5.3.2. Complex words like *madaxweynáha* 'the president' also show that not all morphological operations lead to rightward H tone shift. The last morpheme in this word is a definite determiner, which is not typically associated with H tone (recall, however, the exception of associative constructions that involve a phrasal boundary tone).

The same generalizations pertaining to H tone shift also apply to verbs. This can be seen in (4) in the derivation of denominal verbs and in the creation of new stems by the addition of an extension to an existing base.

(4) a. *abaár* 'drought'+ *-óob* → *abaaróob* 'become drought stricken'
b. *dác* 'spilled water' + *-éyn* → *dacéyn* 'cause to overflow'
c. *jiíd* 'drag away' + *-án* → *jiidán* 'drag oneself away'
d. *cáb* 'drink' + *-síin* → *cabsíin* 'make drink'

More complex stems containing multiple extensions have a single H tone on their rightmost extension. For example, the verb *bilaabín* 'cause to begin' contains a root followed by two extensions, the inchoative *-áab* and the weak causative *-ín*. The stem containing all three has a H tone on the rightmost of these – the weak causative. Thus, the principles dictating rightward H tone shift in nouns and verb stems are closely related.

Rightward H shift is also seen in the formation of adposition clusters in the Verb Complex. Each adposition, *ú*, *kú*, *ká*, and *lá* can independently carry H tone (see §10.6), but a cluster like *kagalá* (> *ká + ká + lá*) has a H tone on only the rightmost adposition.

5.3.2 Premodifier H shift

Another alternation that involves H tone movement is found on nouns that appear to behave as if multimorphemic even in their singular form. The stems of such nouns appear to have been relexicalized along with one of two suffixes, either *-e* or *-o*. Nouns of these types are discussed in Sections 6.2.3 and 6.2.4, respectively. They have non-transparent meanings and are non-decomposable. They can be compared to nouns formed productively from two segmentally identical suffixes, agentive *-é* and plural *-ó*, whose composition and meaning are transparently derived from a related base.

Relexicalized nouns containing the *-e* and *-o* suffixes are unique tonally in that, when they occur phrase-finally, H tone is found on the root, but when modified by another suffix or clitic, H tone shifts rightward onto the suffix.

Consider, for example, *dáwo* 'medicine' (also sometimes spelled *daáwo*). Phrase-finally or in isolation, H tone is located on the root, but its 'pre-modifier' form before the definite determiner is *dawáda* 'the medicine' where the location of H tone is on the *-o* suffix. Alternations in vowel quality here and elsewhere are unrelated to the tonal phenomenon. The same behavior is seen in a noun like *báre* 'teacher' which also witnesses a change in the location of its H tone when modified, as in *baráha* 'the teacher.' Note that subject marking (§9.2) does not provide a suitable environment for pre-modifier H shift. In these instances, H tone is present and remains on the root under subject marking (cf. *dáwo* 'medicine' and *dáwo* 'medicine.SUBJ').

There is considerable variation in the application of pre-modifier H tone. For example, I have worked with a speaker from Mogadishu who sometimes applies this alternation, by extension, to synchronic *-ó* plurals. For most speakers, synchronic *-ó* plurals have a H tone on the plural suffix even phrase-finally, as in *naagó* 'women' (cf. *naág* 'woman'). However, this speaker appears to avoid this H phrase-finally in favor of a form like *naágo*. But, when modified, H shifts to its expected location on the suffix, *naagáha* 'the women.' Another speaker with whom I have worked (who is bilingual in Somali and Maay) from Bu'ale does not exhibit the pre-modifier H alternation. For him, 'medicine' is *dawó* and 'the medicine' is *dawáda*, with H tone remaining in place. Thus, for this speaker, the generalization is in the opposite direction such that he applies the *-ó* pluralization tonal pattern to all nouns ending in *-o*.

It is unclear how robust these outcomes are among Somali speakers in different areas. They may be a the result of paradigmatic extensions or reflect a change in progress in some varieties. Downing and Nilsson (2019) discuss prosodic restructuring that affects the realization of H tone in other nominal constructions, as observed in the productions of speakers in certain diaspora populations. The variation just discussed may be another reflex of such restructuring, but it would be premature to say so for sure.

5.3.3 Other alternations

Two other tonal phenomena defy clear categorization as to whether they should be described alongside other word level or phrase level tonal outcomes. The first of these concerns a type of tone polarity witnessed in alternations involving the declarative (DEC) sentence type marker *waa* and the interrogative (QM) marker *ma* as well as their various inflections; see §12.1. These are realized with a H tone if immediately followed by a toneless word but are instead realized without a H tone if it is followed by a word with H tone. These outcomes are closely tied to another tonal alternation that affects verbs, but only in some morphosyntactic contexts. While most Somali verb contexts find a verb realized with a H tone, affirmative realis mood verbs inflected for the Present Simple, Simple Past, and Potential are toneless. For example, when the DEC occurs immediately before such a verb, as in (5), the DEC is realized with a H tone. Elsewhere, it is toneless, as in (6).

(5) Idínku wéydin cunteen.
    idin=k=u w=eydin cun-t-ee-n
    you.PL=K.DEF=SUBJ DEC=2PL eat-2-PST-PL
    'You (PL) have eaten.'

(6) Naágtu wey gaabántahay.
    naag=t=u w=ey gaab-an-t-ah-ay
    woman=T.DEF=SUBJ DEC=3SG.F short-STV-3SG.F-be-PRES
    'The woman is short.'

One way to view this might be that these morphemes prosodify with material that follows them (e.g., within the same phonological phrase) such that this prosodic constituency is reflected in its tonal behavior. If the material following them has a H tone, no tone is required. However, if the material is toneless, then a H tone emerges on them. While works by Le Gac and by Green and Morrison have begun to explore the prosodification of constituents within and related to the Somali Verb Complex, the precise status of these elements relative to others is yet unclear.

5.4 Phrasal phenomena

5.4.1 Subject Marking

Subject marking is a phrase level phenomenon by which the last morpheme in a subject noun phrase in certain syntactic configurations undergoes a variety of interrelated alternations that collectively indicate the subjecthood of the phrase. Subject marking has several exponents, one of which is the loss of H tone. Loss of H tone may also be accompanied by other segmental alternations in some instances. Despite these generalizations, subject marking is known to be highly variable and sometimes inconsistently realized (Banti 1984a). It appears most intact among Northern Somali speakers who employ a full range of its exponents – tonal, segmental, or both. Tonal manifestations of subject marking are being lost in geographically southern varieties, and this is reflected in the speech of some individuals in the diaspora. These speakers employ subject marking, but only in a subset of instances where it is realized segmentally. This section is concerned primarily with describing the basic tonal outcomes of subject marking.

Subject marking is realized by H deletion alone in monomorphemic K-series nouns. Compare H tone *nín* 'man' and toneless *nin* 'man.SUBJ.' Compounds ending in a K-series noun are affected similarly (cf. *magaalamadáx* 'capital city' and *magaalamadax* 'capital city.SUBJ'), as are nouns ending in a derivational suffix that requires K-series agreement (cf. *sugitáan* 'waiting' and *sugitaan* 'waiting.SUBJ').

H deletion under subject marking affects other parts of speech like morphologically-simplex adverbs (cf. *kalé* 'other' and *kale* 'other.SUBJ') and remote definite determiners (cf. *naágtií* 'the (REM) woman' and *naágtii* 'the (REM) woman.SUBJ'). Nouns pluralized by *-ó* typically behave in the same way (cf. *irbadó* 'needles' and *irbado* 'needles.SUBJ'). Note, however, that the published literature reports variation in this regard for *-ó* plurals. I discuss these details in §9.2.

Monomorphemic T-series nouns realize both H deletion and the addition of *-i* under subject marking. Compare *naág* 'woman' and *naagi* 'woman.SUBJ.' Like K-series selecting morphemes just above, compounds ending in a T-series noun also witness H deletion + *-i* (cf. *buuglacág* 'cash ledger' and *buuglacagi* 'cash ledger.SUBJ'), as do derivational suffixes requiring T-series agreement (cf. *jamciyád* 'union' and *jamciyadi* 'union.SUBJ'). The same outcome is found with adjectival participles that require T-series agreement; cf. the basic and subject marked pairs like *wanaagsán* 'good' and *wanaagsani* 'good.SUBJ' or *weýn* 'big' and *weyni* 'big.SUBJ.' A combination of H tone loss and the addition of segmental material under subject marking also affects all demonstrative determiners (§9.3.2), consonant-final dependent clause verbs (§7.9), and some verbs that require reduced paradigm inflection (§7.8).

One curious exception is that the relexicalized *-e* and *-o* nouns introduced above in Section 5.3.2 are not affected by subject marking. They neither lose their tone nor witness segmental alternation.

5.4.2 Associative High

Associative *Noun of Noun* constructions are used in Somali to express ownership, possession, and other types of attribution. Discussion of different types found in the language and their morphosyntactic properties is in §9.5. Here, the focus is only on their tonal properties.

Each noun in an associative construction exhibits a H tone. An unusual phonological characteristic of these constructions, however, is that H tone on the last member of the construction is located on its final TBU, even if this is a definite determiner. Recall that definite determiners are otherwise prosodically inert and typically do not have a H tone. Consider, for example, the associative construction *mídabka gurigá* which can be translated either as 'the house's color' or 'the color of the house.' The construction contains two noun phrases, each of which is definite. The H tone of the first noun phrase is located, as expected, on the penultimate TBU of the noun stem. For the second member of the construction, H tone is on the definite determiner, rather than on its typical location on the noun stem: *gúriga* 'the house.' Tone is analogously distributed on all types of associative constructions, including those containing more than two nouns in sequence. This behavior is sometimes attributed to the presence of a H boundary tone located at the right edge of the phrase comprised of the construction. In essence, this H boundary tone serves to distinguish such constructions from a simple sequence of two noun phrases. It has the ability to override (and thereby overwrite) word level tonal properties.

5.4.3 Vocative High

Somali employs three types of vocative or direct address constructions. Two of these are explicitly morphological while one, the prosodic vocative, involves a H tone overlay such that H tone is invariably realized on the initial TBU of a given word. For more on this, see §6.5.

5.5 Intonation

Few studies on Somali have been devoted to clause level intonation patterns or to the interaction of tones between adjacent clauses. Those that are available primarily include a series of related studies by Le Gac (1997, 2001, 2002, 2003a,b) and more recently Le Gac (2016). Le Gac's works center upon the interaction between word level H tone "accent" and the effect that focus marking has on its realization. Another study in this realm is Nagano-Madsen et al. (2019) which presents findings related to declarative vs. interrogative intonation contours. Notably, they report variation in the realization of H tones in succession that may ultimately reflect different prosodic constituencies within larger clauses. To these, one might also add an unpublished manuscript by Frid (1995) that was concerned mainly with tonology, but offers passing comments on phrasal boundary tones. This section highlights a few intonative characteristics that have been discussed in the published and unpublished literature. For the purpose of this grammar, I have collected data primarily aimed at confirming earlier findings. However, in doing so, I have sometimes found divergences that might be explored

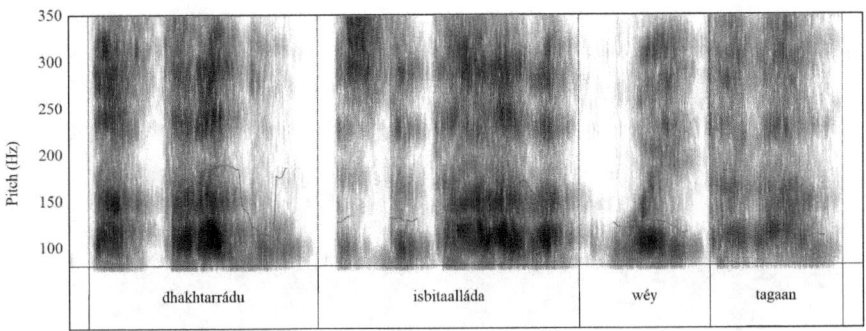

Fig. 5.4: Pitch track of 'The doctors go to the hospitals.' - spoken by Alb

in more detail in future research. This is undoubtedly an area of research on Somali phonology that deserves a great deal more attention, particularly given the complex nature of the language's information structure. For more on this, see Chapter 13.

5.5.1 High and Low boundary tones

The role of H tone in delimiting Somali word and phrase boundaries is well-established. It is well-known that H tone is culminative, but not obligatory, on phonological words and that it alternates predictably as the result of various types of word formation (e.g., compounding, derivation, inflection, and cliticization). What is less clear are the ways in which tones interact across higher structural boundaries, namely across phrase and clause boundaries of different types.

Generally speaking, adjacent H tones are realized at different pitches, with each successive H being realized at a slightly lower pitch than the one before it. In works by Le Gac cited above, this is explored primarily in successive noun phrases where it is attributed to downdrift. Downdrift, also called automatic downstep, is a natural declination of successive H tones under the influence of one (or more) intervening L tones. Such an outcome can be seen in Figure 5.4 which involves two adjacent noun phrases in a clause without focus. There is downdrift between the first (189 Hz) and second H tone (175 Hz). There is a more significant decline in pitch between the second H tone and that of the declarative clause type marker. According to Le Gac, the second and third H tones would be separated by an intonation phrase boundary.

In general, Le Gac treats Somali noun phrases as being delimited at their right edge by an intonational boundary tone. When such a phrase is not in focus, this is a L_{ι} tone, which contributes to downdrift. He has shown that this declination is either blocked or attenuated when a noun phrase is in focus by the presence of an intonational H_l tone. Figure 5.5 shows that not only is H declination blocked in such a context, but the H_l tone reveals itself at the right edge of the focused phrase on a definite determiner, which is elsewhere toneless.

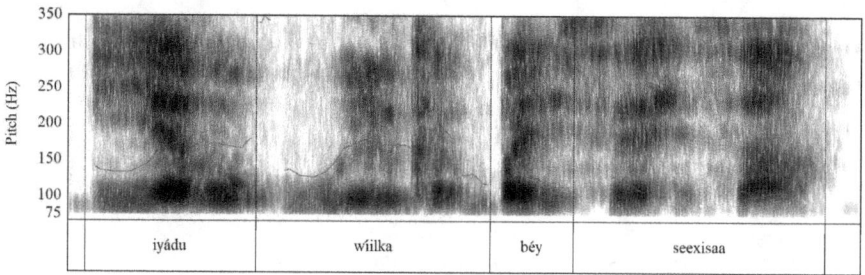

Fig. 5.5: Pitch track of 'She puts the boy to sleep.' - spoken by Alb

Declination of H tones has not been explored in detail in a wider array of Somali phrase types. I have found that it occurs between successive H tones associated with a noun and its modifying relative clause, even within a focused phrase. This is shown in Figure 5.6 where, once again, there is approximately 12-15 Hz declination between successive H tones in the noun phrase *kóob sháah áh*. Such outcomes reveal that a more nuanced analysis might need to be explored concerning precisely which types of boundaries are associated with a L_l tone.

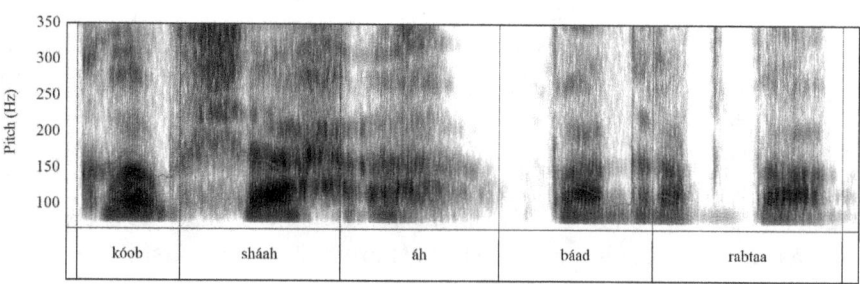

Fig. 5.6: Pitch track of 'You want a cup of tea.' - spoken by AS

The behavior of H tones across intonation phrase boundaries varies. In some instances, there is downdrift-like declination. This was seen in Figure 5.4 above between

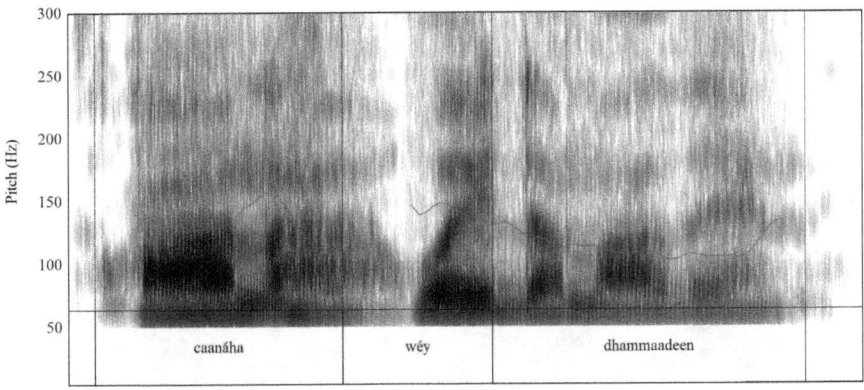

Fig. 5.7: Pitch track of 'The milk was finished.' - spoken by AS

the second noun phrase and the declarative clause type marker. In other instances, there is either the maintenance of H tone level or a complete upward pitch reset at the beginning of a new intonation phrase. This can be seen in Figure 5.7 where the pitch of the H tone is reset on the declarative marker to the same height as the preceding H tone. The conditions governing these outcomes are not well-established, but most certainly have their basis in information structure.

5.5.2 L tone of focalization

In addition to a focus-marked noun phrase possessing a H boundary tone that renders it immune to downdrift, Le Gac has discussed the presence of a "Low tone of focalization" (L_{Foc}). According to Le Gac, the role of L_{Foc} is to delimit the prosodic boundary between an intonation phrase encompassing the focused noun phrase and the intonation phrase that follows it. He shows that L_{Foc} is unlike phonetic Low tones supplied by default to otherwise toneless TBUs in that it entails a dramatic pitch drop that far surpasses other Low tones in the clause. This tone is shown to be realized either on the noun phrase itself or on the focus marker that immediately follows the noun. The factors dictating this depend on the prosodic composition of the focused noun phrase, but in addition, outcomes vary between speakers.

An outcome that I have observed for some speakers that may prove to be related to the presence of L_{Foc} is that the H tone of a focus marker seems to be present, but highly attenuated in some instances. This was seen above in Figure 5.5 where the expected HL contour is apparent on the focus marker, but its height is markedly decreased relative to the two preceding H tones. This behavior is even more striking in Figure 5.8 where the focus marker is flanked by two noun phrases, each with H tones being at much higher pitch levels than that of the focus marker.

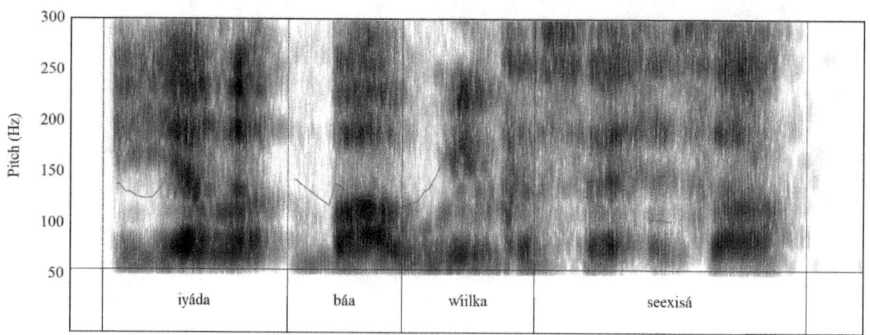

Fig. 5.8: Pitch track of 'It is she who puts the boy to bed.' - spoken by Alb

5.5.3 Statements vs. questions

One intonational phenomenon discussed by Nagano-Madsen et al. (2019) concerns differences in pitch range in statements vs. questions. In addition to confirming that Somali interrogative clauses do not display pitch rise, they show that corresponding H tones in question/statement pairs differ in that those in questions are consistently higher than their counterparts in statements. Along these same lines, they illustrate that questions are generally in a higher pitch register than corresponding statements.

Figure 5.9 compares pitch traces for the question *Búugga máad qortey?* 'Did you write the book?' (solid line) and the corresponding statement *Búugga wáan qoray.* 'I wrote the book' (speckled line). Both the H tone on the noun *búuga* and that on the clause type marker are noticeably higher in the question.

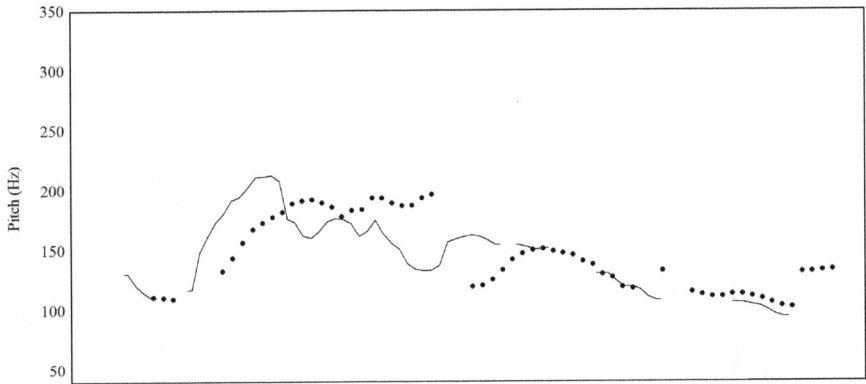

Fig. 5.9: Pitch traces comparing question (solid) / statement (speckled) pair - spoken by Alb

6 Nominal morphology

This chapter covers nouns and the morphemes involved in their construction. Somali nouns share a common template, shown in Figure 6.1. The root occurs first and may be followed by one or more derivational suffixes. A plural marker, where present, will occur next. Somali pluralization has certain derivation-like qualities. For example, plural suffixes are tone attracting, and some have inherent gender. Others have also suggested that number marking is derivational, both in Somali and in Cushitic more broadly. See, for example, discussion in Lecarme (2002) and Mous (2012).

root   +   derivation   +   plural   +   determiner(s)   +   clitic(s)

Fig. 6.1: Basic noun template

Determiners and clitics are included in this noun template to reflect the fact that orthographic nouns include these elements. Determiners and clitics are, of course, elements of the noun phrase rather than proper suffixes. Of Somali's five types of determiners, all behave as independent grammatical words, and four are also prosodically independent. The exception is the definite determiner, which is prosodically inert and perhaps best considered a clitic. For more on the relationship between grammatical and phonological wordhood in Somali, see Green and Morrison (2016).

Recall from Chapter 5 that a monomorphemic Somali noun is associated with a H tone that is realized on either its penultimate or final mora. In more morphologically-complex nouns, still only a single H tone is expressed, and this H tone is typically realized on the rightmost morpheme of the stem. There are conditions, however, that result in exceptions to these generalizations. For example, under subject marking (see §9.2), a noun may fail to exhibit a H tone. Also, under the influence of a phrasal boundary tone, H tone may be realized on an enclitic instead of on the stem.

6.1 Gender and agreement

Every nominal root is associated with one of two grammatical genders. Grammatical gender correlates with the location of the noun's H tone (see §5.2) and the pattern of agreement that it requires on determiners that modify it. A noun's grammatical gender is also responsible for governing subject-verb agreement on a verb if the noun is the subject of that verb.

Traditionally, Somali nouns are designated as being either "masculine" or "feminine" gender. In this grammar, erstwhile masculine agreement is referred to as K-series agreement, while feminine agreement is T-series agreement. These designators refer to the initial consonant of the basic form of agreeing determiners in each series. For example, *hílib* 'meat' is a K-series noun as seen in the form of its definite determiner in *hílibka* 'the meat.' Likewise, *gacán* 'hand' is a T-series noun. Its form with the same determiner is *gacánta* 'the hand.' These consonants – *k* and *t* – serve as exemplars to define agreement patterns, but they undergo predictable morphophonological alternations. The K-series definite determiner can be realized *-ka*, *-ga*, *-ha*, or simply *-a* while the T-series definite determiner can be realized *-ta*, *-da*, *-dha*, or *-sha*. These alternations extend to other determiners as well. The conditions under which each occurs are summarized in Table 6.1. Gender agreement series is shown in glosses by abbreviations like K.DEF, which would indicate a definite determiner in the K-series.

Tab. 6.1: Gender agreement alternations summary

Gender series	Realization	Environment		
K	g	$V_x \_ V_y$	bériga	'the day'
	h	$V_x \_ V_x$	baráha	'the teacher'
	∅	q, x, kh, c, h _	mádaxa	'the head'
	k	elsewhere	sánnadka	'the year'
T	d	V _ V	mindída	'the knife'
	dh	dh _	gabáddha	'the girl'
	sh	l _ → sh	úsha	'the stick'
	t	elsewhere	galábta	'the afternoon'

Another term related to grammatical gender that is encountered in the Somali literature (notably, Lecarme 2002; Meinhof 1912) is "gender polarity," or the idea that nouns change grammatical genders between singular and plural. While it is true that some Somali nouns do this (cf. *sánnadka* 'the year' vs. *sannaddáda* 'the years,' which take K- and T-series agreement, respectively), this does not occur for all types of pluralization (cf. *sánka* 'the nose' vs. *sanánka* 'the noses,' which both take K-series agreement). Godon (1998) and Nilsson (2018) have independently argued that Somali collapses gender distinctions when verbs are inflected for plural. They suggest that the grammatical gender of plural nouns is not inherent, but rather predictable by a combination of suffixal morphology and the shape of the noun stem itself.

6.2 Class and number

Somali nouns are traditionally divided into "declension classes" according to their morphophonological behavior. There are many competing proposals for the best set of principles on which to do so (see Andrzejewski and Lewis 1964; Andrzejewski 1979; Banti 1988c; Hyman 1981; Lampitelli 2013; Le Gac 2003b; Lecarme 2002; Maniscalco

2015; Morin 1991; Orwin 1995; Saeed 1993b, 1999; Zorc and Osman 1993, among others). In this grammar, nouns are classified based primarily on the following characteristics:

(1) a. strategy for pluralization
    b. grammatical gender of the singular
    c. stem shape

The primary factor used to define class membership here is pluralization strategy. There are four main noun classes that form their plural via suffixation. Further subdivisions are justified in a few instances such as when nouns take the same plural suffix but behave differently in terms of the agreement that they require thereafter. This is dictated by a combination of the grammatical gender of the singular and stem shape. In addition to these major classes, the properties of irregular nouns are discussed, such as those borrowed from Arabic that sometimes retain word-internal pluralization strategies characteristic of the source language. These and other nouns with irregular pluralization strategies typically have a second suffixing plural that looks like that of other Somali nouns. It is not uncommon in East Cushitic languages for nouns to have more than one plural form (Lecarme 2002; Lampitelli 2013). Lastly, there is one peculiar noun whose basic form is conceptually plural and is made singular by a singulative suffix. In each instance, the gender agreement series required by each noun is indicated by including its definite determiner.

6.2.1 Class 1: -ó plurals

Class 1 nouns form their plural by the addition of the H tone suffix -ó. This can be considered a default class of sorts, as newer borrowed nouns are typically placed into this class. In addition, nouns from other classes often have a second Class 1 plural. Class 1 contains singular nouns that are specified for either K- and T-series grammatical gender. Though all of these nouns take the same plural suffix, the resulting plural nouns differ in the grammatical gender agreement that they require. As such, three sub-classes are defined – Class 1a, 1b, and 1c – into which the broader group of Class 1 nouns is subdivided. Despite the necessity of this descriptive subdivision, a given plural noun's behavior is predictable based on the gender of its singular and its stem shape.

6.2.1.1 Class 1a: T singular / K plural

Class 1a nouns take T-series gender agreement in the singular and have a H tone on their final (or only) mora. They are pluralized by -ó, and these plurals have a H tone on the plural suffix and no H on the root. The plurals take K-series agreement.

(2) Class 1a nouns

a.	káb	'shoe'	kábta	'the shoe'
	kabó	'shoes'	kabáha	'the shoes'
b.	naág	'woman'	naágta	'the woman'
	naagó	'women'	naagáha	'the women'
c.	irbád	'needle'	irbádda	'the needle'
	irbadó	'needles'	irbadáha	'the needles'
d.	mindí	'knife'	mindída	'the knife'
	mindiyó	'knives'	mindiyáha	'the knives'
e.	galáb	'afternoon'	galábta	'the afternoon'
	galbó	'afternoons'	galbáha	'the afternoons'

If the singular noun ends in a vowel, an epenthetic glide [j] (written *y*) is inserted between this vowel and the *-ó* suffix. When a Class 1a plural is further modified, the suffixal vowel alternates. These alternations are described in §3.4.8.

6.2.1.2 Class 1b: K singular / T plural

Class 1b nouns take K-series agreement in the singular. They have H tone on their penultimate mora. They are pluralized by *-ó*, and H tone is found on this suffix. There is no H on the root in the plural. Plurals take T-series agreement. If the singular noun ends in a vowel, an epenthetic glide is inserted between this vowel and the plural suffix.

(3) Class 1b nouns

a.	albáab	'door'	albáabka	'the door'
	albaabbó	'doors'	albaabbáda	'the doors'
b.	sánnad	'year'	sánnadka	'the year'
	sannaddó	'years'	sannaddáda	'the years'
c.	ciídan	'army'	ciídanka	'the army'
	ciidammó	'armies'	ciidammáda	'the armies'
d.	abwáan	'scholar'	abwáanka	'the scholar'
	abwaannó	'scholars'	abwaannáda	'the scholars'
e.	gantáal	'arrow'	gantáalka	'the arrow'
	gantaalló	'arrows'	gantaalláda	'the arrows'
f.	górgor	'vulture'	górgorka	'the vulture'
	gorgorró	'vultures'	gorgorráda	'the vultures'
g.	ábti	'maternal uncle'	ábtiga	'the maternal uncle'
	abtiyó	'maternal uncles'	abtiyáda	'the maternal uncles'
h.	nácas	'fool'	nácaska	'the fool'
	nacasyó	'fools'	nacasyáda	'the fools'

If the noun stem ends in *b, d, m, n, l, r* (keeping in mind that word-final /m/ alternates to [n]), the consonant is doubled upon pluralization. If the noun ends in a consonant that is not part of this set, an epenthetic glide is inserted instead. The -*ó* suffix alternates in quality when the plural is further modified. See §3.4.8 for more on these alternations.

As Nilsson (2018) has shown, the fact that Class 1b plurals have more than two syllables is key in predicting their behavior relative to agreement. Class 1b plurals like those above have three syllables and take T-series agreement. They can be compared to the Class 1c nouns in §6.2.1.3 that also take the plural -*ó* suffix but whose plurals are disyllabic. Class 1c nouns are K-series in the singular and remain K-series in the plural.

6.2.1.3 Class 1C: K singular / K plural

Class 1c nouns also take plural -*ó*. They require K-series agreement in both the singular and the plural. In the singular, they have a H tone on their penultimate mora, and on the plural suffix in their corresponding plural forms. There is no H on the root in the plural.

(4) *Class 1c nouns*

a.	hílib	'meat'	hílibka	'the meat '
	hilbó	'meats'	hilbáha	'the meats'
b.	nábar	'wound'	nábarka	'the wound'
	nabró	'wounds'	nabráha	'the wounds'
c.	ílig	'tooth'	íligga	'the tooth'
	ilkó	'teeth'	ilkáha	'the teeth'
d.	gúri	'house'	gúriga	'the house'
	guryó	'houses'	guryáha	'the houses'
e.	náas	'breast'	náaska	'the breast'
	naasó	'breasts'	naasáha	'the breasts'

Some Class 1c nouns undergo V/Ø reduction when they are pluralized. If the stem ends in a vowel, an epenthetic glide is inserted between a stem-final vowel and the plural suffix before reduction, which results in a consonant-glide sequence, like in *guryó* 'houses.' For more on V/Ø alternations, see §3.5. As with other -*ó* plurals, the suffixal vowel alternates upon the addition of a determiner. See §3.4.8 for details of these alternations.

6.2.2 Class 2: Reduplication plurals

Class 2 contains a comparatively small set of nouns whose plurals are formed via partial suffixing reduplication of their stem. All singular nouns in this class are monosyllabic and end in a consonant. Most of these take K-series agreement and have a H tone on their penultimate or only mora. However, there are a few that instead take T-series agreement and accordingly have a H tone on their final or only mora. Plurals in Class

2 are formed by a copy of the final consonant of the singular noun, preceded by the vowel -á, the combination of which is added as a suffix: -áC.

(5) Class 2 nouns

a.	áf	'language'	áfka	'the language'
	afáf	'languages'	afáfka	'the languages'
b.	sán	'nose'	sánka	'the nose'
	sanán	'noses'	sanánka	'the noses'
c.	míis	'table'	míiska	'the table'
	miisás	'tables'	miisáska	'the tables'
d.	túug	'thief'	túugga	'the thief'
	tuugág	'thieves'	tuugágga	'the thieves'
e.	nín	'man'	nínka	'the man'
	nimán	'men'	nimánka	'the men'
f.	búd	'tomb'	búdda	'the tomb'
	budád	'tombs'	budádka	'the tombs'
g.	qoór	'neck'	qoórta	'the neck'
	qoorár	'necks'	qoorárka	'the necks'
h.	wíil	'boy'	wíilka	'the boy'
	wiilál	'boys'	wiilásha	'the boys'
i.	báal	'feather'	báalka	'the feather'
	baalál	'feathers'	baalásha	'the feathers'

H tone is located on the reduplicated suffix in the plural, and in most instances, the plural takes K-series agreement. However, there are a few exceptions to these generalizations, all of which involved singular K-series nouns of the shape CVV[l]. These form their plural via reduplication just like the other nouns, but their plural takes T-series agreement.

Another exception that belongs in this class is the borrowed word *búug* 'book,' which is K-series in the singular (*búugga* 'the book'). Rather than the usual partial reduplication pattern, the vowel of the reduplicant is lengthened yielding *buugaág* 'books,' rather than **buugág*, though some speakers accept this alternative. The plural takes T-series agreement, as in *buugaágta* 'the books.'

6.2.3 Class 3: Singular nouns ending in -e

Singular Class 3 nouns are composed of a noun stem followed by the suffix *-e*. These nouns take K-series agreement in the singular. H tone on these nouns in isolation is on the stem, rather than on the suffix, but H shifts rightward onto the suffix when the noun is further modified, such as by a definite determiner. Compare, for example, *báre* 'teacher' and *baráha* 'the teacher' with a K-series definite determiner. This premodifier H tone shift is discussed in §5.3.2. The *-e* suffix itself alternates in quality when it is not word final. See §3.4.8 for more on these alternations.

The *-e* suffix is elsewhere involved in the productive derivation of agentive and instrumental nouns (see Sections 6.3.2.7 and 6.3.2.9, respectively), but the meaning that it contributes to Class 3 nouns is non-compositional and may point to relexification. For example, *beége* 'gauge' has an unsuffixed counterpart *béeg*, but this refers specifically to a unit of measurement for grain.

Class 3 nouns are pluralized by the suffix *-yaál*. This suffix carries H tone on its second mora and there is no H expressed on the nominal base or *-e* suffix. Plural Class 3 nouns with *-yaál* require T-series agreement.

(6) *Class 3 nouns*

a.	*abbaanduúle*	'commander'	*abbaanduuláha*	'the commander'
	abbaanduulayaál	'commanders'	*abbaanduulayaásha*	'the commanders'
b.	*beége*	'gauge'	*beegáha*	'the gauge'
	beegayaál	'gauges'	*beegayaásha*	'the gauges'
c.	*guddoomíye*	'chairman'	*guddoomiyáha*	'the chairman'
	guddoomiyayaál	'chairmen'	*guddoomiyayaásha*	'the chairmen'
d.	*madaxweýne*	'president'	*madaxweynáha*	'the president'
	madaxweynayaál	'presidents'	*madaxweynayaásha*	'the presidents'

Some speakers use the *-yaál* suffix to derive collective 'double plurals' from plural nouns ending in *-ó*. This is discussed in §6.2.7.

6.2.4 Class 4: Singular nouns ending in *-o*

Class 4 nouns are grammatically singular (i.e., they entail singular verb agreement), but otherwise behave morphologically like plurals. They contain what appears, in many instances, to be a fossilized plural *-o* suffix, yet they have no corresponding 'singular' that can be created by removing this suffix. Other nouns in this category are similarly-shaped borrowings that also behave grammatically as singular. Singular Class 4 nouns take T-series agreement. A historical explanation for their form and behavior is also suggested by Saeed (1999, 57). Their H tone is on the nominal base, but H shifts to *-o* when the noun is modified via pre-modifier H tone shift. See §5.3.2. As elsewhere, *-o* alternates in quality when followed by a determiner or another suffix; see §3.4.8.

(7) *Class 4 nouns*

a.	baáko	'package'	baakáda	'the package'
	baakoóyin	'packages'	baakoóyinka	'the packages'
b.	calaámo	'symbol'	calaamáda	'the symbol'
	calaamoóyin	'symbols'	calaamoóyinka	'the symbols'
c.	hoóyo	'mother'	hooyáda	'the mother'
	hooyoóyin	'mothers'	hooyoóyinka	'the mothers'
d.	dooxáto	'gang'	dooxatáda	'the gang'
	dooxatoóyin	'gangs'	dooxatoóyinka	'the gangs'

These nouns are pluralized by *-óyin*, after which they take K-series agreement. This suffix carries the word's H tone, with any preceding H tone being removed.

Caney (1984) mentions that there are some singular nouns of this type that instead take the suffix *-w* to form their plural. I have found only two words in Zorc and Osman (1993) that might fit this characterization, both of which are collectives: cf. *xooló, xoolów* 'livestock' and *carsaanyó, carsaanyów* 'crustaceans.' Neither of these supposed "plurals" in *-w* were acceptable to my speakers.

6.2.5 Irregular nouns

6.2.5.1 Nouns using Arabic pluralization strategies

Some borrowed nouns from Arabic retain their pluralization strategy from the source language. One of these is 'broken' or internal pluralization that involves vocalic alternations within the word's templatic root, rather than suffixation. For example, the singular noun *kúrsi* 'chair' is built upon the root K-R-S. Its plural is *kuraasí* 'chairs.' Not all instances of broken pluralization exhibit the same alternations. There are over a dozen strategies for this type of pluralization exhibited in Arabic itself.

For Somali, most instances of broken pluralization involve singular nouns with a penultimate H tone and K-series agreement. When pluralized, they have a final H and take T-series agreement.[1] It is notable, however, that some (but not all of these) have a second Class 1 *-ó* plural: *kursiyó* is an alternative plural form of 'chairs.'

---

[1] One instance where this does not hold is for singular *sabáb* 'reason' (cf. *sabábta* 'the reason'). Its broken plural is *asbaabó*, rather than simply *asbáab*, suggesting that it is doubly pluralized in a way. It also takes T-series agreement in the singular and K-series in the plural, which is the reverse of other broken plurals.

(8) *Nouns with 'broken' plurals*

a.	búnduq	'rifle'	búnduqa	'the rifle'
	banaadíiq	'rifles'	banaadíiqda	'the rifles'
b.	qálin	'pen'	qálinka	'the pen'
	qalmaán	'pens'	qalmaánta	'the pens'
c.	kitáab	'book'	kitáabka	'the book'
	kutúb	'books'	kutúbta	'the books'
d.	báqal	'mule'	báqalka	'the mule'
	buquúl	'mules'	buquúsha	'the mules'
e.	sícir	'price'	sícirka	'the price'
	ascaár	'prices'	ascaárta	'the prices'
f.	báxri	'sailor'	báxriga	'the sailor'
	baxaarí	'sailors'	baxaarída	'the sailors'

Some Arabic borrowings instead form a suffixal 'sound' plural. These are morphologically consistent in that they take the suffix *-iín*. Singular nouns that take suffixal sound pluralization follow K-series agreement and have a H tone on their penultimate mora. Upon pluralization, H is on the plural suffix, and the resulting noun takes T-series agreement.

(9) *Nouns with 'sound' plurals*

a.	siyaási	'politician'	siyaásiga	'the politician'
	siyaasiyiín	'politicians'	siyaasiyiínta	'the politicians'
b.	Múslin	'Muslim'	Múslinka	'the Muslim'
	Muslimiín	'Muslims'	Muslimiínta	'the Muslims'
c.	caábid	'worshipper'	caábidka	'the worshipper'
	caabidiín	'worshippers'	caabidiínta	'the worshippers'
d.	caájis	'lazy person'	caájiska	'the lazy person'
	caajisiín	'lazy people'	caajisiínta	'the lazy people'
e.	faásid	'immoral person'	faásidka	'the immoral person'
	faasidiín	'immoral people'	faasidiínta	'the immoral people'

A final set of nouns with Arabic pluralization are singular nouns that refer to people, titles, or professions, but specifically to "feminized" versions of these. For example, the noun *saaxíib* 'friend' can be general or can refer specifically to a male friend; it takes K-series agreement. To specify that the friend is female, there is a suffixed form *saaxiibád*, and this takes T-series agreement. One strategy to pluralize these feminized nouns is through sound pluralization, which gives *saaxiibaád* 'female friends' and still takes T-series agreement. However, these nouns also alternatively take an *-ó* plural, as in *saaxiibadó*, which instead take K-series agreement. Other examples are in (10).

(10) *Feminine nouns with 'broken' plurals*

a.	*dhakhtarád*	'female doctor'	*dhaktarádda*	'the female doctor'
	dhakhtaraád	'female doctors'	*dhakhtaraádda*	'the female doctors'
	dhakhtaradó	'female doctors'	*dhakhtaradáha*	'the female doctors'
b.	*fannaanád*	'female artist'	*fannaanádda*	'the female artist'
	fannaanaád	'female artists'	*fannaanaádda*	'the female artists'
	fannaanadó	'female artists'	*fannaanadáha*	'the female artists'
c.	*faranjiyád*	'female foreigner'	*faranjiyádda*	'the female foreigner'
	faranjiyaád	'female foreigners'	*faranjiyaádda*	'the female foreigners'
	faranjiyadó	'female foreigners'	*faranjiyadáha*	'the female foreigners'

Nilsson (2018) illustrates that Somali speakers do not consistently treat pluralized Arabic borrowings as plural nouns in the same sense as they do native Somali nouns, including sound plurals that are pluralized via suffixation. He notes variation in these Arabic plurals in terms of their number agreement. Nouns pluralized by one of the aforementioned Arabic strategies may require either singular or plural agreement on pronouns and verbs.

6.2.5.2 'Prosodic plurals'

Another small class of nouns has been traditionally described as being inflected for plural number only by a change in its grammatical gender and an accompanying change in the location of its H tone. A classic example of this is *díbi* 'ox' which, like other penultimate H nouns, takes K-series agreement (*díbiga* 'the ox'). Its counterpart *dibí* 'oxen' takes no overt plural suffix, requires T-series agreement (*dibída* 'the oxen'), and has a H tone on its final mora. Such nouns can have a plural interpretation and accordingly take plural agreement, but they can just as easily be interpreted as collectives, instead taking singular agreement. The following examples from Nilsson (2018) illustrate this point. The same noun takes plural agreement on the verb in (11) and singular agreement on the verb in (12).

(11) *Dibídu   waa ay   daáqayaan.*
      dibi=d=u   waa ay   daaq-ay-∅-aa-n
      ox=T.DEF=SUBJ DEC 3PL graze-PROG-3-PRES-PL
      'The oxen are grazing.'

(12) *Dibídu   waa ay   daáqaysaa.*
      dibi=d=u   waa ay   daaq-ay-s-aa
      ox=T.DEF=SUBJ DEC 3SG graze-PROG-3SG.T-PRES
      'The oxen are grazing.'

Nouns in this category typically have a second morphological plural formed with the -*ó* suffix. Thus, *dibiyó* also means 'oxen.' These alternative plurals behave in some ways like other Class 1b nouns in that they have H tone on the -ó suffix and take T-series agreement, but with no final consonant gemination (where relevant). Examples of other nouns that behave similarly are in (13).

(13) *Nouns with 'prosodic' plurals*

a.	áwr	'male camel'	áwrka	'the male camel'
	aẃr	'male camels'	aẃrta	'the male camels'
	awró	'male camels'	awráda	'the male camels'
b.	mádax	'head'	mádaxa	'the head'
	madáx	'heads'	madáxda	'the heads'
	madaxyó	'heads'	madaxyáda	'the heads'
c.	Soomaáli	'Somali person'	Soomaáliga	'the Somali person'
	Soomaalí	'Somali people'	Soomaalída	'the Somali people'
	Soomaaliyó	'Somali people'	Soomaaliyáda	'the Somali people'

6.2.6 Singulatives

I am aware of only one plural noun *hawéen* 'women' whose singular is formed via suffixation. This noun takes the singulative suffix *-eý*, resulting in *haweeneý* 'woman.' The plural takes K-series agreement, while the suffixed singular takes T-series agreement.

6.2.7 Double pluralization by *-o-yaál*

The plural suffix *-yaál* used to pluralize Class 3 nouns is also used to form collective double plural or "plural of plural" nouns (Lecarme 2002) from morphologically plural Class 1 nouns ending in *-ó*. The resulting nouns sometimes have fairly idiomatic meanings, and the productivity of this mechanism varies among speakers. Some speakers readily apply double pluralization to a wide variety of nouns, while other speakers categorically reject its use in nearly every instance. As in Class 3, the *-yaál* suffix attracts H tone, with any H tone on the already plural base being lost. These double plurals take T-series agreement.

(14) Double plurals with -yaal

a.	naagó	'women'	naagáha	'the women'
	naagayaál	'groups of women'	naagayaásha	'the groups of women'
b.	ilkó	'teeth'	ilkáha	'the teeth'
	ilkayaál	'sets of teeth'	ilkayaásha	'the sets of teeth'
c.	fardó	'horses'	fardáha	'the horses'
	fardayaál	'herds of horses'	fardayaásha	'the herds of horses'
d.	lafó	'bones'	lafáha	'the bones'
	lafayaál	'piles of bones'	lafayaásha	'the piles of bones'

6.2.8 Number marking summary

Table 6.2 summarizes the facts presented above concerning different groups of nouns and their morphological behavior. The table includes the morphological elements associated with singular vs. plural nouns in each group (where relevant) as well as the gender agreement series that each requires.

Tab. 6.2: Number marking summary

Type		Singular		Plural	
		Affix	Gender series	Affix	Gender series
Class 1	a	–	T	-ó	K
	b	–	K	-ó	T
	c	–	K	-ó	K
Class 2		–	K	-áC	K
Class 3		-e	K	-yaál	T
Class 4		-o	T	-óyin	K
Arabic	broken	–	K	various	T
	sound	–	K	-iín	T
	feminine	-ád	T	-aád	T
Prosodic		penult H	K	final H	T
Singulative		-eý	T	–	K

6.3 Derivation

Many Somali nouns and verbs share the same root, but the two categories sometimes differ tonally. The location of H tone on a nominal stem is determined by its grammatical gender: penultimate mora H for K-series nouns and final mora H for T-series nouns. For example, the noun *carbuún* 'deposit' is from the T-series (*carbuúnta* 'the deposit') and accordingly has a H on its final mora. On verb stems, there is a single tonal pattern. For example, the corresponding verb stem *carbúun* 'deposit' has H on the penultimate mora, which will shift predictably upon suffixation, such as when forming the infinitive *carbuúni* 'to deposit' so that it again appears on the penultimate mora. Compare this outcome to the K-series noun *go'dóon* 'isolation' (cf. *go'dóonka* 'the isolation') which has a penultimate mora H. The corresponding verb stem *go'doomée* 'isolate' has a H once again on the penultimate mora.

6.3.1 Noun-to-noun derivation

6.3.1.1 Abstract nouns with -*nimó*

The suffix -*nimó* is added to some animate nouns to create an abstract noun that represents a state (15) or a concept (16).

(15) *State nouns with -nimó*

a.	*Muslinnimó*	'Muslimhood'	*Múslin*	'Muslim'
b.	*Kirishtaannimó*	'Christianity'	*Kirishtáan*	'Christian'
c.	*musharraxnimó*	'candidacy'	*mushárrax*	'candidate'
d.	*jaalnimó*	'friendship'	*jáal*	'comrad'

(16) *Concept nouns with -nimó*

a.	*xornimó*	'independence'	*xór*	'free person'
b.	*midnimó*	'unity'	*míd*	'someone'
c.	*ilbaxnimó*	'civilization'	*ílbax*	'civilized person'
d.	*maalinnimó*	'daytime'	*maalín*	'day'

These nouns have a H tone on the final mora of the abstract suffix and take T-series agreement, e.g., *xornimáda* 'the independence.' The final vowel of the suffix alternates when followed by a determiner, just as final -*ó* does elsewhere (see §3.4.8). In some instances, abstract nouns in -*nimó* can be pluralized. These plurals pattern with other Class 4 nouns (§6.2.3) in taking the -*óyin* suffix and K-series agreement, e.g., *waayaaragnimoóyinka* 'the experiences.'

6.3.1.2 Abstract nouns with -*iyád*

The suffix -*iyád* is borrowed directly from Arabic and is used to derive abstract nouns. It is added to animate nouns, but also to adjectives to create state and concept nouns.[2]

---

[2] The noun *shuuciyád* is also sometimes pronounced (and written) *shuyuuciyád*, which is representative of a more conservative form of the original Arabic loan.

(17) *Abstract nouns with -iyád*

a.	insaaniyád	'humanity'	insáan	'human'
b.	Masiixiyád	'Christianity'	Masíix	'Messiah'
c.	shuuciyád	'communism'	shuúci	'communist'
d.	mas'uuliyád	'responsibility'	mas'úul	'responsible'
e.	jamciyád	'union'	jámac	'group'
f.	jinsiyád	'nationality'	jínsi	'race'

These abstract nouns have a H on their final mora and take T-series agreement, e.g., *jamciyádda* 'the union.' Those that can be pluralized follow a Class 1 pattern in taking the *-ó* suffix, as in *mas'uuliyaddó* 'responsibilities.' Unlike other Class 1 nouns with a T-series singular, these plurals also require T-series agreement: *mas'uuliyaddáda* 'the responsibilities.'[3]

6.3.1.3 Abstract nouns with *-tooyó*

The suffix *-tooyó* derives abstract nouns from a variety of other nouns, including those with animate referents and even other abstract nouns. The abstract nouns created by this suffix are associated with feelings and concepts.

(18) *Abstract nouns with -tooyó*

a.	kalgacaltooyó	'affection'	kalgácal	'love'
b.	gacaltooyó	'kindness'	gácal	'dear person'
c.	dhaxaltooyó	'inheritance'	dháxal	'legacy'
d.	boqortooyó	'kingdom'	bóqor	'king'
e.	saaxiibtooyó	'friendship'	saaxíib	'friend'

These nouns have a H tone on the final mora of their suffix and take T-series agreement, as in *boqortooyáda* 'the kingdom.' The final vowel of the suffix undergoes alternations in its quality like those discussed in §3.4.8. Nouns with this suffix that can be pluralized take *-óyin* and pattern with Class 4 nouns. They take K-series agreement, as in *boqortooyoóyinka* 'the kingdoms.'

---

[3] Though nouns like these are not very frequent and accordingly do not appear in some corpora, they appear to be in use more broadly, such as on internet news sites and fora. See https://www.bbc.com/somali/war-46972570 for *mas'uuliyaddó* and https://www.somaliaonline.com/community/topic/38661-hoodaaddada-faroole-iyo-hungada-ssc/ for *mas'uuliyaddáda*. Forms without gemination of the stem final consonant are also possible.

6.3.1.4 Antonyms with -darró

The suffix -darró derives antonyms from other nouns. The resulting nouns have a H tone on their final mora.

(19) Antonyms with -darró

a.	nasiibdarró	'bad luck'	nasíib	'luck'
b.	naxariisdarró	'unkindness'	naxariís	'mercy'
c.	nidaamdarró	'chaos'	nidáam	'order'
d.	dhiigdarró	'anemia'	dhíig	'blood'
e.	gardarró	'wrongdoing'	gár	'justice'
f.	guuldarró	'failure'	guúl	'success'

Antonyms formed by -darró can be made definite and take T-series agreement, as in guuldarráda 'the failure.' They behave like other Class 1 nouns ending in -ó in that their final vowel alternates when further modified. See §3.4.8. Those antonyms formed by -darró that can be pluralized pattern with Class 4 nouns in taking the plural suffix -óyin and K-series agreement. This is seen in guuldarroóyinka 'the failures.'

6.3.1.5 -éen

The suffix -éen derives nouns from deverbal nominal compounds. The nouns that it creates often refer to pathways or repositories.

(20) Deverbal nouns with -éen

a.	badmaréen	'seaway'	(pathway of sea)
b.	biyaxiréen	'dammed water'	(closure of water)
c.	caanaggaléen	'breast, udder'	(holder of milk)
d.	cunnammaréen	'digestive system'	(processor of food)
e.	hantiqabéen	'wealthy person'	(holder of wealth)
f.	jawrfaléen	'tyrant'	(doer of tyranny)
g.	maalqabéen	'capitalist'	(holder of finances)

Deverbal nouns with -éen take K-series agreement (e.g., maalqabéenka 'the capitalist') and have a H tone on their penultimate mora. Those that can be pluralized follow Class 1b behavior in that they are pluralized with -ó and thereafter take T-series agreement: cf. maalqabeennó 'capitalists' and maalqabeennáda 'the capitalists.'

6.3.2 Deverbal nouns

6.3.2.1 -niin

The suffix *-niin* creates deverbal nouns from underived (bare) verb stems. The resulting nouns have the meaning 'act of X-ing' where X is the verb. Deverbal nouns with *-niin* are not entirely consistent in their tonal behavior and agreement, though most have a penultimate H tone and accordingly take K-series agreement, as in *saxníinka* 'the act of correcting' (cf. *sáx* 'correct'). There are only four entries among several dozen in Zorc and Osman (1993) where nouns with the same suffix instead take T-series agreement and have a H tone on their final mora, as in *digniínta* 'the act of warning' (cf. *díg* 'announce'). Some deverbal nouns of this type have become lexicalized. For example, *furníin* means 'divorce' as a concept. The corresponding gerund *furís* instead refers to the act of divorcing or opening.

6.3.2.2 -n

Deverbal nouns derived from weak causative verbs are created by the addition of *-n* to the verbal base. The resulting nouns are homophonous with the infinitival form of these verbs. For example, there are pairs like *joóji* 'halt' and *joojín* 'ban (n.)' or *alaakoódi* 'flirt' and *alaakoodín* 'flirting, courtship.' These nouns have a H tone on their final mora and take T-series agreement, e.g., *joojínta* 'the ban.'

6.3.2.3 -ashó

Deverbal nouns are formed from middle verbs by the addition of *-ashó* to the verbal base. This can be seen in simple middle verbs by comparing *madhó* 'empty (v.)' and *madhashó* 'emptiness,' but also when a middle verb is formed from a weak causative base. For example, compare *raagsó* 'be impatient' (> *raag-is-o*) and *raagsashó* 'impatience.' These nouns behave like others ending in *-ó* in that they undergo vowel height alternations (see §3.4.8) when further modified. They also take T-series agreement, as in *raagsasháda* 'the impatience.'

6.3.2.4 -itáan

The deverbal suffix *-itáan* is added only to bare verbal bases and creates nouns that refer to actions and concepts. Examples are in (21).

(21) *Deverbal nouns with -itáan*

a.	buuxitáan	'overflow'	búux	'be full'
b.	qoditáan	'excavation'	qód	'dig'
c.	helitáan	'discovery'	hél	'find'
d.	tiritáan	'cancellation'	tír	'cancel'
e.	cabbitáan	'beverage'	cáb	'drink'
f.	duulitáan	'flight'	dúul	'fly'

Deverbal nouns with -*itáan* have H tone on their penultimate mora and take K-series agreement, as in *cabitáanka* 'the beverage.' Those that can be pluralized behave like Class 1b nouns. They take the plural suffix -*ó* and require T-series agreement: cf. *cabitaannó* 'beverages' and *cabitaannáda* 'the beverages.'

6.3.2.5 -aal

The suffix -*aal* derives deverbal nouns from a variety of verbal bases. As such, it is arguably more productive than other suffixes described thus far in this section. The nouns that it creates generally refer to states and concepts.

(22) *Deverbal nouns with -áal*

a.	diráal(ka)	'emissary'	dír	'send'
b.	dhigáal(ka)	'savings'	dhíg	'put away'
c.	jiráal(ka)	'existence'	jír	'exist'
d.	qiráal(ka)	'acknowledgment'	qír	'admit'
e.	socdáal(ka)	'travel'	socó	'walk, proceed'
f.	xalaál(/sha)	'purity'	xál	'wash, cleanse'
g.	dhacsaál(/sha)	'fatigue'	dhacsáal	'become tired'

The examples in (22) illustrate that deverbal nouns with -*aal* are not totally consistent in their tonal and agreement behavior. That said, those with a H tone on their penultimate mora and taking K-series agreement appear to far outnumber those with a H on the final mora that take T-series agreement.

6.3.2.6 Deverbal nouns with -*tín*

Yet another means by which to create deverbal nouns is by the addition of the suffix -*tín* to verbal bases of several types. Its use is fairly infrequent, based on the corpora searches that I have conducted. Some nouns that I have come across have a meaning similar to that of nouns derived by -*niín* in that they refer to the 'act' corresponding to the verb base. For example, *gelín* 'insertion' is derived from *géli* 'put into,' while *cabatín* 'complaint,' is derived from verb *cabó* 'complain.' Some take K-series agreement (*cabatínka* 'the complaint') while others take T-series agreement (*baqdínta* 'the act of being afraid'). I have not come across plurals of these deverbal nouns.

6.3.2.7 Agentive nouns with -é

It was shown above that Class 3 nouns ending in *-e* behave as if they are composed of two morphemes, though the two morphemes are not typically separable, at least not transparently so. There are other nouns, however, where the same suffix is synchronically productive in deriving deverbal agentive nouns. Examples of such nouns are in (23).

(23) *Agentive nouns with -é*

a.	baaré	'investigator'	báar	'examine'
b.	kaxeeyé	'delivery person'	kaxée	'deliver, drive'
c.	hoggaamiyé	'leader'	hoggáam	'lead'
d.	ganacsadé	'merchant'	ganacsó	'trade (v.)'

Unlike Class 3 nouns, agentive nouns formed productively by *-é* have a H tone on their suffix and take K-series agreement, as in *ganacsadáha* 'the merchant.' Class 3 nouns have the same *-é* suffix, but on their own have a H tone on their stem (e.g., *abbaanduúle* 'commander'). It is only upon further modification, such as the addition of a determiner, that H tone shifts rightward onto the agentive suffix.

These agentive nouns are pluralized by the addition of *-yaál* and thereafter take T-series agreement: *ganacsadayaásha* 'the merchants.' They are closely related to the instrumental nouns discussed in §6.3.2.9 that are formed by the same suffix.

6.3.2.8 Agentive nouns with -áa

Another means by which to derive agentive nouns is via *-áa*, though this strategy seems to be fairly unproductive. Agentive nouns formed by this suffix have a H tone on their penultimate mora and take K-series agreement, as in *diláaga* 'the killer.' Other examples are in (24).

(24) *Agentive nouns with -áa*

a.	diláa	'killer'	díl	'kill'
b.	gabayáa	'poet'	gabáyi	'recite a poem'
c.	heesáa	'singer'	hées	'sing a song'
d.	jiláa	'imitator'	jíl	'imitate'
e.	qoráa	'writer'	qór	'write'

These nouns pattern with other Class 3 nouns in taking the plural suffix *-yaál* and subsequent T-series agreement, as seen in *dilaayaásha* 'the killers.'

6.3.2.9 Instrumental nouns with -é

Deverbal instrumental nouns are formed by -é and pattern in some ways with Class 3 nouns, but more closely with the agentive nouns discussed in §6.3.2.7 that are formed by the same suffix. These instrumental nouns have a H tone on the -é suffix and take K-series agreement.

(25) *Instrumental nouns with -é*

a.	dabé	'oven'	dáb	'bake'
b.	daabecé	'printer'	daábac	'print'
c.	dalooliyé	'hole punch'	daloóli	'pierce'
d.	qarxiyé	'fuse'	qárxi	'explode'
e.	burburiyé	'bulldozer'	búrbur	'crush'

Deverbal instrumental nouns that can be pluralized do so via the *-yaál* plural suffix and take T-agreement, as in *burburiyayaásha* 'the bulldozers.'

6.3.2.10 Uncountable and collective nouns with -tó

Another group of deverbal nouns is formed by the addition of *-tó* to verb stems of a variety of types. This suffix is fairly multipurpose in the types of nouns that it derives under the broader heading of uncountables. For example, it forms nouns for living things (e.g., *xamaarató* 'crawling reptiles,' cf. *xamaaró* 'crawl on one's belly'), liquids (e.g., *dhiintó* 'juice,' cf. *dhíim* 'ooze'), terms associated with medical conditions (e.g., *xuurtó* 'exhaustion,' cf. *xuurtée* 'be exhausted'), but also abstract concepts or states (e.g., *haftó* 'breathlessness,' cf. *háf* 'suffocate').

Nouns in this category follow T-series agreement, as in *dhiintáda* 'the juice.' There are also nouns of this type that can be pluralized and which do so by taking the suffix *-óyin*. The resulting nouns take K-series agreement. For example, the uncountable noun *goosató* 'secessionists' is derived from the verb *goosó* 'secede.' Its definite plural is *goosatoóyinka* 'the groups of secessionists.'

This suffix creates nouns that refer to a collective group, but oftentimes the same noun can also refer specifically to an individuated female of that group. This is in line with perspectives raised by Nilsson (2018) concerning Somali collectives discussed in §9.1.3.2. For example, *xoogsató* can refer to a collective 'workforce' or simply to a 'female worker.' This noun is derived from the verb *xoogsó* 'work for someone.'

6.3.3 Ownership nouns with -le

The suffix *-le* is derived from the reduced paradigm verb *léh* 'have.' The addition of *-le* to a noun does not affect the noun's H tone. This presents some evidence of its status here as a suffix or clitic, rather than a word. We shall see elsewhere that Somali compounds behave uniformly in having H tone on their last element. Thus, the synchronic form of this morpheme bears signs of grammaticalization in comparison to *léh* such as loss of segmental content and loss of H tone.

(26) *Nouns with -le*

a.	*biyóole*	'water-owner'	*biyó*	'water'
b.	*dukáanle*	'shopkeeper'	*dukáan*	'shop (n.)'
c.	*sáwirle*	'photographer'	*sáwir*	'portrait'
d.	*caanóole*	'milkman'	*caanó*	'milk'
e.	*beeróole*	'farmer'	*beeró*	'farm'
f.	*rayíisle*	'barber'	*rayíis*	'barber shop'

The examples in (26) show that *-le* is added to concrete nouns to derive nouns that denote possession, ownership, craft/profession, or some semblance of authority over the concrete noun. They pattern in some ways with Class 3 nouns, though not all these derived ownership nouns behave the same way. Some pattern with Class 3 in taking K-series agreement in the singular, as in *biyóolaha* 'the water-owner.' These are pluralized by *-yaál* and thereafter take T-series agreement, as in *biyoolayaásha* 'the water-owners.'

Others form Class 2b collectives with the addition of *-ý*, as in *caanooleý* 'milkmen.' These take T-series agreement: *caanooleýda* 'the milkmen.'

6.3.3.1 Collective nouns with *-leý*

Closely related to the nouns just above are collective nouns formed by the suffix *-leý*. These are collective counterparts to ownership nouns ending in *-le*. They can take either singular or plural agreement. The only H tone on these is on the suffix itself, and the resulting nouns take T-series agreement. For more on the behavior of these nouns, see 'Guri-Barwaaqo' (2018).

(27) *Collective nouns with -leý*

a.	*geélle*	'camel owner'	*geelláha*	'the camel owner'
	geelleý	'camel owners'	*geelleýda*	'the camel owners'
b.	*ariíle*	'goat merchant'	*ariiláha*	'the goat merchant'
	ariileý	'goat merchants'	*ariileýda*	'the goat merchants'
c.	*beeraále*	'farmer'	*beeraaláha*	'the farmer'
	beeraaleý	'farmers'	*beeraaleýda*	'the farmers'
d.	*fardoóle*	'horseman'	*fardooláha*	'the horseman'
	fardooleý	'horsemen'	*fardooleýda*	'the horsemen'

6.3.4 Abstract state nouns with *-aán*

The suffix *-aán* creates abstract nouns referring to states (of being) from adjectives (28), from adjectival participles derived from verbs via the stativizing suffixes *-án* and *-óon* (29), and also directly from stative verbs (30). The examples below illustrate that in each instance, the resulting noun exhibits a H tone on the final mora of the suffix itself, and when made definite, takes T-series agreement.

(28)　*Abstract nouns from adjectives*

a.	*casaán*	'redness'	*cás*	'red'
b.	*nuglaán*	'softness'	*nugúl*	'soft'
c.	*oggolaán*	'state of being in agreement'	*oggól*	'consenting'
d.	*roonaán*	'state of being better off'	*róon*	'better off, improved'

(29)　*Abstract nouns from adjectival participles*

a.	*hagoognaán*	'state of having a covered head'	*hagoogán*	'covered, veiled'
b.	*maahsanaán*	'absent-mindedness'	*maahsán*	'absent-minded'
c.	*miirnaán*	'state of being filtered'	*miirán*	'filtered'
d.	*qurxoonaán*	'state of being beautiful'	*qurxóon*	'beautiful'

(30)　*Abstract nouns from stative verbs*

a.	*habboonaán*	'state of being correct'	*habbóon*	'be correct'
b.	*qoyaán*	'wetness'	*qóy*	'become wet'
c.	*habaarraán*	'state of being cursed'	*habáar*	'be cursed'
d.	*doorsoonaán*	'state of being changed'	*doorsóon*	'be transformed'

6.3.5 Derivational morphology summary

As shown in the sections above, the primary division between derivation within the Somali nominal system is between those suffixes that derive abstract nouns of various types from other nouns and those that are explicitly deverbal. The morphology involved in creating these derived nouns, their pluralization strategy (where relevant), and associated gender agreement requirements are summarized in Table 6.3.

6.4 Gerunds

Somali gerunds are verbal nouns formed either via the addition of a suffix to a verbal base or directly via conversion (also called zero derivation). Gerunds function as nouns in that they exhibit grammatical gender, take nominal morphology, and can

Tab. 6.3: Derivational morphology summary

Type	Affix	Basic Gender series	Affix	Plural Gender series
N to N	-nimó	T	-óyin	K
	-iyád	T	-ó	T
	-tooyó	T	-óyin	K
	-darró	T	-óyin	K
	-éen	K	-ó	T
Deverbal	-niin	K/T	–	–
	-n	T	–	–
	-ashó	T	–	–
	-itáan	K	-ó	T
	-aal	K/T	–	–
	-tín	K/T	–	–
	-é	K	-yaál	T
	-áa	K	-yaál	T
	-tó	T	-óyin	K
	-le	K	-yaál/-ý	T
	-aán	T	–	–

serve as a verbal argument. They also govern patterns of agreement on verbs. This is shown in (31) where a gerund requiring a T-series determiner is the subject of the clause's verb. The verb accordingly takes T-series agreement.

(31) ... oo   fahmíddu   ká míd tahay.
      ... oo   fahm-id=d=u   ka mid t-ah-ay
      ... CONJ understand-GER=T.DEF=SUBJ of one 3SG.T-be-PRES
      '... and understanding is one of them.' (tooshnews.net: 124864)

That gerunds retain some of their verbal properties is clear, however, from the fact that they can take an object. This is seen in (32) for the gerund *sheegídda* '(the) telling' which takes the object *sheekó* 'stories.'

(32) *Maxámed sheekó   sheegídda   wuu   kú wanaagsányahay.*
      Maxamed sheek-o   sheeg-id=da   w=uu   ku wanaag-san-y-ah-ay
      Maxamad story-PL tell-GER=T.DEF DEC=3SG.M in good-STV-3SG.M-be-PRES
      'Maxamed is good at telling stories.' (Z & O: 605)

Another retained verbal property of gerunds is that they can be modified by an adverb, as seen in (33).

(33) *Cunísta   dhaqsó badán ama wáx badán ...*
      cun-is=ta   dhaqso badan ama wax badan ...
      eat-GER=T.DEF quickly very   or   thing many
      'Eating too quickly or too much ...'

Somali gerunds are formed from verb stems of different types, though not all gerunds are formed via suffixation. A bare or underived verbal base forms its gerund with *-íd* and take T-series agreement (e.g., *baaríd(da)* 'searching,' cf. *báar* 'search'). A weak causative base instead takes *-ís*, but these gerunds do not behave uniformly in terms of agreement series that they require. Some take T-series agreement (e.g., *duulís(ta)* 'flying,' cf. *duúli* 'fly a plane') while others take K-series (e.g., *karís(ka)* 'cooking,' cf. *kár* 'cook'). Gerunds formed from middle bases take *-ád* and consistently require K-series agreement (e.g., *baxsád(ka)* 'escaping,' *baxsó* 'escape'). In each instance, the gerund has a H tone on the suffix.

Gerunds derived from other verbal bases are not formed morphologically. In some instances, they are formed via conversion. Those from experiencer verbs take K-series agreement (e.g., *doorsóon(ka)* 'transformation,' cf. *doorsóon* 'become transformed'). Those from inchoative verbs (e.g., *duqów(ga)* 'aging process,' cf. *duqóob* 'age (v.)') and reciprocal verbs (e.g., *últan(ka)* 'game involving a fight with sticks,' cf. *últan* 'fight e.o. with sticks') take K-series agreement. The location of their H tone does not change from verb to noun in these instances. Lastly, those formed from factitive verbs take T-series agreement (e.g., *fududeýn(ta)* 'simplification,' cf. *fududée* 'simplify'). H tone is on the penultimate mora in the verb (as otherwise expected), but this shifts to the final mora in the gerund.

6.5 Vocative marking

Vocative, or direct address marking is discussed here because it is accomplished morphologically. It occurs on nouns, including proper names. There are three types of vocative marking. The first of these, the *noun vocative*, does not occur with proper names. It involves only the addition of a non-tonal suffix to the noun. The second, the *name vocative* is found both on names and on a limited set of nouns. It involves the addition of a tonal suffix. The third, which I call the *prosodic vocative*, has a distribution like that of the name vocative and is accomplished solely by a tonal alternation but no accompanying suffix.

6.5.1 Noun vocative

The noun vocative is formed by the addition of a non-tonal suffix to a noun. The addition of this suffix does not affect the realization of the noun's H tone. The suffixes used in the formation of noun vocatives are *-yohow* for K-series nouns and *-yahay* for T-series nouns. Examples are *dádyohow* 'Oh, people' (cf. *dádka* 'the people') and *gabád-hyahay* 'Oh, daughter' (cf. *gabádha* 'the daugher'). Note that the nouns meaning 'father' and 'mother' pattern instead with the name vocatives; see §6.5.2.

6.5.2 Name vocative

The name vocative is formed by the addition of one of four tonal suffixes to a name. The suffix *-ów* is added to names that follow K-series agreement, which typically involves male names like *Muúse* which is realized *Muúsów* 'Oh, Muuse.' The same suffix is also used for *aábbe* 'father' which is realized *aábbów* 'Oh, father.' The location and realization of H tone on the modified name does not change, and there is a H on the vowel of the vocative suffix.

Names that follow T-series agreement, typically female names, take one of three suffixes: *-éey*, *-áay*, or *-óoy*. The first of these has the widest distribution, while the latter two are found only after names ending in *-a* and *-o*, respectively. For example, *Cánab* is realized *Cánabéey* 'Oh, Canab,' while *Nadiífa* is realized *Nadiífáay* 'Oh, Nadiifa.' The behavior of the last of suffix can be demonstrated for *hoóyo* 'mother' which is realized *hooyóoy* 'Oh, mother.'

In each instance, the vocative suffix has a H on its penultimate mora, keeping in mind that the orthographic word-final *y* is a phonetic off-glide and does not behave as if moraic. In general, the H tone of the modified element is not altered, but if this H is located on a stem-final vowel, there is only a single H expressed on the penultimate mora once the vocative suffix is added.

6.5.3 Prosodic vocative

The prosodic vocative involves the overlay of a H tone on the first mora of the modified noun. The same strategy is used for both K-series and T-series nouns. Consider the male name *Maxámed* which is *Máxamed* 'Oh, Maxamed' when marked with a prosodic vocative. The female name *Faadúmo* becomes *Fáadumo* 'Oh, Fadumo.'

6.6 Associative marking

Associative marking, also sometimes called genitive marking in the literature (Andrzejewski 1979; Saeed 1999), is found in the formation of associative constructions. In general, these constructions indicate a particular relationship that holds between two nouns (e.g., possessive, partitive, etc.). Several different associative constructions are found in Somali, the details of which are discussed in §9.5. Associative marking is introduced here because it involves morphology added to a noun. The formation of any associative construction involves the addition of a H boundary tone on the last noun in the construction. See §5.4.2. In some associative constructions, this noun is additionally marked by one of the following suffixes: *-eéd*, *-oód*, and *-aád*.

The first of these suffixes, *-eéd*, can be considered the basic form. The suffix *-oód* is found on some nouns ending in *-ó*, and *-aád* has idiosyncratic uses with some nouns referring to domesticated animals. Because this is a phrase-level phenomenon, examples and more detailed discussion appears in §9.5. Note that the formation of ordinal numerals also involves associative marking; see §9.1.6.2.

7 Verbs and verbal morphology

This chapter covers verbs and the morphology associated with their construction. The highly synthetic nature of Somali's verbal morphology, sometimes opaque morphophonological interactions between morphemes, and the bearing of information structure on verbal inflection render verbs a complex category to describe in a systematic way. This chapter is primarily concerned with verbal morphology, leaving matters related to morphosyntax and syntax for later chapters.

The verb itself is just one element of Somali's clausal Verb Complex, which is discussed as a unit in Chapter 10. The morphemes that comprise Somali verbs are organized into one of two structural templates. The vast majority of Somali verbs (all but five, or maybe up to seven, depending on one's perspective) are inflected by suffixation and exhibit the basic structure shown in Figure 7.1.

$$\text{verb stem} + \begin{Bmatrix} \text{person} \\ \text{gender} \end{Bmatrix} + \begin{Bmatrix} \text{tense} \\ \text{number} \end{Bmatrix}$$

Fig. 7.1: Suffixing verb template

Those few verbs that do not follow this suffixing verb template are instead inflected in some instances by a combination of prefixation and ablaut and follow the template in Figure 7.2. These verbs have sometimes been called 'strong' verbs in the Somali literature based on comparison to the ablaut behavior seen in the inflection of verbs in Germanic languages. The exceptional nature of these verbs' morphology is clear in that speakers of some Somali varieties are losing or have lost this pattern of prefixing/root-changing inflection in favor of suffixing inflection alternatives.

$$\begin{Bmatrix} \text{person} \\ \text{gender} \end{Bmatrix} + \text{verb stem} + \begin{Bmatrix} \text{tense} \\ \text{number} \end{Bmatrix}$$

Fig. 7.2: Root-changing verb template

Person/gender and tense/number are given in brackets in these templates based on the fact that there is not always an overt exponent of a given inflectional category realized on a verb. Compare, for example, the 1SG and 2SG past tense forms *sheegay* 'I spoke' and *sheegtay* 'you (SG) spoke,' respectively. Here, the verb stem is *sheeg-* and the past tense suffix is *-ay*. In the 2SG, there is additionally the person suffix *-t-* while there is no overt exponent for person in the 1SG.

In addition to discussing lexical verbs of many types in this chapter, the chapter ends by discussing what Andrzejewski (1969) famously defined as "hybrid" verbs.

These verbs are formed by the concatenation of an adjective or adjectival participle and an inflected form of the verb 'to be.' They are discussed here alongside other verbs because they exhibit verbal morphology. They also behave syntactically like other verbs.

7.1 Stem types

From a morphological perspective, there are eleven basic verb stem types, including what are referred to below as bare or underived stems. Other stem types are created through the addition of suffixes that I follow Andrzejewski (1968, 1969) in calling derivational *extensions*. It is also possible to derive more complex stems via the concatenation of more than one derivational extension, though not in all combinations. There are five extensions – weak causative, strong causative, middle, neuter passive, and factitive – that derive verb stems from other verbs. Three extensions – experiencer, inchoative, and reciprocal – derive verbs either primarily or exclusively from nouns. Beyond these, there are two stativizing suffixes -*án* and -*óon* that are involved in the creation of adjectival participles which, in turn, form the foundation of the hybrid verbs mentioned above. Some reference resources, notably Bell (1953) and Saeed (1993b, 1999), focus in large part on defining the characteristics of only a subset of these categories and relegate others to passing remarks, based perhaps on supposed productivity. A more holistic view of Somali verbs is adopted here in which each stem type is treated equally and their behavior discussed in turn.

To discuss the properties of Somali verbs in more detail, I expand upon the template in Figure 7.1, and in particular, the slot designated as the *verb stem*. The verb stem itself is also templatic in that it can be further subdivided into slots in which particular extensions are found. A Somali verb stem must obligatorily contain the verb's root, but a verb stem may also contain one or two, but rarely more than two, derivational extensions. These extensions occur only in certain combinations, and they must occur in a strict order. The language's verb stem template is in Figure 7.3.

root ⟨stativizers⟩ { experiencer / inchoative / reciprocal } { factitive / weak causative } { middle / neuter passive } ⟨strong causative⟩

Fig. 7.3: Verb stem template

The way that this template is presented reflects the fact that the root is the only obligatory element of the verb stem. All other elements given in brackets are involved in derivation. Examples are provided below illustrating that extensions listed within a single set of brackets do not co-occur in the same stem. Extensions that are found in different slots can co-occur within the same stem and occur in the order shown.

In the sections below and elsewhere, verbs are given in their usual citation form, with the morphology summarized in Table 7.1, unless otherwise noted. These forms are shown relative to a CVVC root for the sake of exposition. This is the form that one will encounter in most Somali dictionaries. Corresponding infinitival forms are included in this table for comparison.

Tab. 7.1: Verb citation form and infinitive summary

Stem type	Citation	Infinitive	Section
Bare	cv́vc-∅	cvv́c-i	7.1.1
Experiencer	cvvc-óod	cvvc-óon	7.1.2
Inchoative	cvvc-óob	cvvc-oóbi	7.1.3
Reciprocal	cv́vc-tan	cvv́c-tan	7.1.4
Weak Causative	cvv́c-i	cvvc-ín	7.1.5
Factitive	cvvc-éyn	cvvc-éyn	7.1.6
Middle	cvvc-ó	cvvc-án	7.1.7
Neuter	cvvc-án	cvvc-án	7.1.8
Strong Causative	cvvc-síi	cvvc-síin	7.1.9

7.1.1 Bare (Underived)

A verb root forms the simplest verb stem. These are referred to as bare (i.e., underived) stems throughout this grammar. Many Somali verbs share a common root with a noun, and as such, they also share semantic similarities. For example, there is a close connection between the noun *kár* 'steam' and the verb *kár* 'cook.' Bare stem verbs form their infinitive with the suffix *-i*, e.g., *kári* 'to cook.'

H tone is always located on the penultimate mora of a bare verb stem. As such, a given verb and its corresponding noun do not necessarily exhibit H tone on the same location of the stem. H tone location is correlated in pairs like *fóof* 'go out to graze' and *fóof* 'grazing land' (here, a K-series noun), but not so in pairs like *xíiq* 'pant (v.)' and *xiíq* 'panting' (a T-series noun). For more on H tone assignment to nouns vs. verbs, see §5.2.

7.1.2 Experiencer

Experiencer verbs are intransitive verbs derived primarily from abstract nouns by the addition of *-óon*, *-óod*, or *-óo*. The resulting verbs have the sense of 'to feel X,' 'to experience X,' or 'to have X,' where X is the noun from which the verb is derived. For example, the experiencer verb *murugóod* 'feel worried' is derived from the noun *murúg* 'worry.' Experiencer verbs form their infinitive with the suffix *-óon*.

(1) *The experiencer extension is realized:*
    a. *-óon* word-finally, as in *cadhóon* 'to feel anger,' except in the imperative
    b. *-óod* before a vowel, as in *riyooday* 'I had a dream'
    c. *-óo* before a consonant, as in *gaajootay* 'you (SG) felt hungry,' and in the imperative, as in *cadhóo* 'be angry!'

In forming an experiencer verb, H tone appears on the experiencer extension rather than on the nominal base. This is not always apparent, however, given that H tone is not realized on most realis mood verbs.

(2) *Experiencer verbs vs. nouns*

a.	*cidlóod*	'feel lonely'	*cídlo*	'empty place'
b.	*dhaxamóod*	'feel cold'	*dhaxán*	'cold'
c.	*geeriyóod*	'experience death'	*geerí*	'death'
d.	*jiriiricyóod*	'get goosebumps'	*jiriiríco*	'goosebumps'
e.	*murugóod*	'be worried'	*murúg*	'worry'
f.	*saliilyóod*	'shudder'	*saliílyo*	'sound causing shudders'

It is possible to derive more complex bases from an experiencer verb. For example, there are examples of experiencer + weak causative, as in *dibboódi* 'keep cattle outdoors overnight' (cf. *dibbóod* 'be left out overnight') and experiencer + middle, as in *geeriyoodó* 'meet one's death' (cf. *geeriyóod* 'die').

7.1.3 Inchoative

Inchoative verbs are typically derived from concrete and abstract nouns via the addition of *-ów* or *-óob* to the nominal base. There is variation, however, such that some speakers pronounce these *-áw* and *-áab*. The resulting verbs are intransitive and have a sense of 'to become X,' where X is the noun from which the verb is derived. This can be seen in the inchoative verb *duqóob* 'become old,' which is derived from the noun *dúq* 'elder.' Inchoative verbs form their infinitive with *-oóbi*.

(3) *The inchoative extension is realized:*
    a. *-óob* before a vowel, as in *beloobay* 'he became troublesome'
    b. *-ów* elsewhere, as in *nacasów* 'become a fool!'

The addition of the inchoative extension causes a shift of H tone from the nominal base, rightward onto the extension. Of course, this is keeping in mind that most of Somali's realis mood verbs fail to express H tone.

(4) *Inchoative verbs vs. nouns*

a.	abaaróob	'become drought stricken'	abaár	'drought'
b.	collóob	'become the enemy'	cól	'enemy'
c.	fayóob	'become healthy'	fáyo	'good health'
d.	hungóob	'become disappointed'	húngo	'disappointment'
e.	suuróob	'become possible'	suúro	'possibility'

Inchoative verbs can also be derived from adjectives, as in *caddóob* 'become white' (cf. *cád* 'white'), as well as from adjectival participles, as in *dhiirranóob* 'have courage' (cf. *dhiirrán* 'brave') and *habboonóob* 'be suitable' (cf. *habbóon* 'suitable'). Inchoative verbs can also serve as a base for further derivation by the weak causative, as in *bilaábi* 'cause to start' and the middle, as in *bilaabó* 'start s.t. for oneself' (cf. *bilóob* 'begin').

7.1.4 Reciprocal

The extension *-tan* (and its alternant *-tam*) derive verbs from nouns that convey a sense of reciprocity.[1] In most instances, these verbs entail reciprocated action between two or sometimes more individuals, but there is also a small set of these that are autobenefactive in nature. Reciprocal verbs forms their infinitive with *-tan*.

(5) *The reciprocal extension is realized:*
   a. *-tam* before a vowel, as in *kaltamayeen* 'they were taking turns with one
   b. *-tan* elsewhere, as in *xafiiltan* 'to compete with one another' another'

An unusual characteristic of this extension compared to others is that it does not attract H tone from the morpheme that precedes it. When the reciprocal is added, H tone remains in place rather than shifting rightward onto the reciprocal extension.

(6) *Reciprocal verbs vs. nouns*

a.	cilaáqtan	'argue with one another'	cilaáq	'argument'
b.	jikáartan	'quarrel with one another'	jikáar	'counter-argument'
c.	sháratan	'make a bet with each other'	shárad	'wager'
d.	baáyactan	'negotiate with one another'	baáyac	'bargaining'

---

[1] Andrzejewski (1968) claims that the reciprocal suffix has other allomorphs, *-lan/-lam* and *-ran/-ram*, that occur after stems ending in a liquid. I have not come across these in my data.

The examples in (6) are representative of the majority of verbs containing the reciprocal extension. These are more prototypical reciprocal verbs in that they involve two (or more) individuals that are simultaneous participants in the verbal action. This is seen in (7), where the minister is also involved in the activity of joking, and in (8), where the group of men are arguing amongst themselves.

(7) *Maalíntaás wasíirka   ayáannu kaftannay   ...*
    maalin-taas wasiir=ka   aya-annu kaf-tan-n-ay   ...
    day-T.that   minister=K.DEF FOC=we joke-RECIP-1PL-PST

   'That day, we joked with the minister ...' (somaliland.org: 21198)

(8) *kóox rág áh   oo kú sharatamay   ...*
    koox rag ah   oo ku shara-tam-∅-ay   ...
    group men be.RED REL on bet-RECIP-3SG-PST

   'A group of men who were betting on ...' (geeska.net: 240060)

Other verbs containing the reciprocal extension in (9) are autobenefactive reciprocals. The subject of these verbs undertakes some action from which they can benefit, but where there is also second, understood object that is also affected by the verbal action.

(9) Autobenefactive reciprocal verbs vs. nouns

a.	*gáatan*	'stalk'	*gáad*	'ambush (n.)'
b.	*shabbáaxtan*	'practice shooting'	*shabbáax*	'target practice'
c.	*túugtan*	'plead with someone'	*túug*	'begging (n.)'
d.	*xáqtan*	'claim one's rights'	*xáq*	'right (n.)'

7.1.5 Weak Causative

There are two causative extensions in Somali. The highly productive weak causative is discussed in this section, while the strong causative is covered separately in §7.1.9. The weak causative has several allomorphs: *-ís, -í, -s,* and *-ín*, each of which occurs in predictable instances. The weak causative is responsible for triggering alternations like palatalization (§3.4.11) and assibilation (§3.4.10.) Verbs ending with this extension form their infinitive by *-ín*.

(10) *The weak causative extension is realized:*
   a. *-ín* word-finally, as in *karín* 'to cook' (except in the imperative), and before a nasal
   b. *-ís* before a vowel, as in *ergisaday* 'I entrusted'
   c. *-s* following V/Ø alternation, as in *marsaday* 'I finished (it) off
   d. *-í* elsewhere, as in *kariyay* 'I cooked,' including in the imperative

The weak causative is valency enhancing. It typically adds a causer subject to an intransitive verb. In turn, it demotes the intransitive verb's subject to the object of the weak causative verb.

(11) *Weak causative vs. Bare verbs*

a.	buúbi	'chase s.t. away'	búub	'run away'
b.	dhoófi	'send abroad'	dhóof	'travel abroad'
c.	mári	'allow s.o. to pass'	már	'pass through'
d.	ummúli	'deliver a baby'	úmmul	'give birth'

It is also possible to derive a transitive weak causative verb from an already transitive verb, but the resulting verb often has a more idiosyncratic meaning which seems indicative of lexicalization. For example, the transitive verb *dáah* 'hide' can take the weak causative suffix becoming *daáhi*, meaning 'delay, hinder' rather than 'to hide s.o.'

A weak causative verb can also serve as the basis for the derivation of more complex stems. This occurs productively with the middle, as in *diirsó* 'warm oneself' (cf. *diíri* 'make warm,' *díir* 'become warm'), the neuter passive, as in *buuxsán* 'become full' (cf. *buúxi* 'fill s.t. up'), and even the strong causative, as in *gaardisíin* 'cause s.o. to train' (cf. *gaárdi* 'train').

7.1.6 Factitive

Factitive (sometimes called resultative) verbs are derived from nouns and adjectives, as well as from adjectival participles. In each instance, the suffix *-eýs*, or one of its allomorphs *-ée* or *-éyn*, is added to the nominal or adjectival base. There is variation, however, as *-eýs* and *-éyn* are pronounced by some speakers as *-áys* and *-áyn*, respectively. The factitive extension attracts H tone from the base that precedes it. Factitive verbs forms their infinitive with *-éyn*.

(12) *The factitive extension is realized:*
  a. *-éyn* word-finally, as in *shaqéyn* 'to make s.t. function'
  b. *-éys* before a vowel, as in *daruureysán* 'clouded'
  c. *-ée* before a consonant, as in *dambeeyay* 'I made s.o. late,' and in the imperative

Factitive verbs derived from nouns, adjectives, and adjectival participles can be either transitive or intransitive. In each instance, they involve action that typically brings about a change of state or location. Transitive factitive verbs have a direct object and an object complement, though these might not be overtly expressed in all instances. For example, in (13), the factitive verb has an implied reflexive object and an object complement such that the action 'making a reservation' brings about a change of state in the direct object, namely being 'reserved' or 'having a reservation.' The state or location itself is encoded in the verb.

(13) Miyáad   carbuún   sameysateen?
     m=iy=aad   carbuun   sam-eys-a-t-ee-n
     QM=FOC=2SG   reservation make-FACT-MID-2-PST-PL
     'Did you make yourself a reservation?' (Z & O: 96)

Other examples of factitive verbs of this type (i.e., those that are derived from nouns) are in (14).

(14) *Transitive factitive verbs derived from nouns*

a.	*baadiyéyn*	'cause s.o. to lose s.t.'	*baadí*	'lost person'
b.	*cagéyn*	'trample s.o.'	*cág*	'foot'
c.	*dambaséyn*	'cover with ashes'	*dámbas*	'ashes'
d.	*nabarréyn*	'wound s.o.'	*nábar*	'wound'

Transitive factitive verbs are also derived from adjectives and adjectival participles where the verb encodes a change of state brought about on the object. Examples of these are in (15).

(15) *Transitive factitive verbs derived from adjectives/adjectival participles*

a.	*caddéyn*	'make white'	*cád*	'white'
b.	*roonéyn*	'make better'	*róon*	'better'
c.	*toolmoonéyn*	'make handsome'	*toolmóon*	'handsome'
d.	*cusboonéyn*	'renew'	*cusbóon*	'renewed'

Intransitive factitive verbs are derived from nouns like those in (16) and involve changes in state and location. Those derived from adjectives and adjectival participles as in (17) typically involve changes in location or orientation.

(16) *Intransitive factitive verbs derived from nouns*

a.	geeséyn	'stand to one side'	gées	'side'
b.	jarcéyn	'tremble'	járco	'trembling'
c.	qaxwéyn	'have a coffee break'	qáxwo	'coffee'
d.	rucléyn	'run slowly'	rúcle	'jogging'

(17) *Intransitive factitive verbs derived from adjectives/adjectival participles*

a.	horréyn	'be first'	hór	'front, before'
b.	sarréyn	'be highest in rank'	saré	'high, upper'
c.	ladnéyn	'become well'	ladán	'healthy'
d.	fiicnéyn	'make good'	fiicán	'nice'

7.1.7 Middle

Middle verbs are derived from other verbs, and often from bare and weak causative bases. There is reason to consider the underlying or basic form of the middle to be -*at*, though it has five allomorphs and therefore seldom appears as such. Like other verbal extensions (other than the reciprocal), the middle is associated with H tone when it is the last extension in the stem. Stems ending with the middle extension form their infinitive with -*án*.

(18) *The middle extension is realized:*
  a. -*ó* in imperatives, as in *baaró* 'look for yourself!'
  b. -*án* word-finally, as in *badán* 'to multiply,' and before nasals, as in *joogsannay* 'we stopped ourselves'
  c. -*ád* between vowels, as in *joogsaday* 'I stopped myself'
  d. -*t* following V/Ø alternation, as in *qabtay* 'I held myself'
  e. -*át* elsewhere, as in *joogsatay* 'you (SG) stopped yourself'

Forming middle verbs is highly productive. A middle verb can be derived from both transitive and intransitive verbs and also derives verbs in both of these categories. It is not consistently valency-enhancing nor valency-reducing, but rather, this depends on the semantic content of the verbal base to which the middle extension is added. Its complex semantics and inconsistent syntactic behavior have led scholars to analyze it variously as deriving reflexive, reciprocal, autobenefactive, and indeed middle verbs, among other categories (see Abu-Manga and Jungraithmayr 1988; Andrzejewski 1968; Puglielli and Bruno 1988; Saeed 1995). Saeed (1995), in particular, illustrates that these verbs cross-cut both syntactic and semantic categories and have characteristics best understood on a cline, from one-participant to two-participant events, with characteristics of middle voice and reflexivity, but also with some outliers. Briefly, Saeed defines six major semantic categories of verbs containing the middle extension, as shown in (19), though some of these can be further sub-divided.

(19) *'Middle'* verb categories:
    a. inherent reciprocals: *dhexsó* 'have a business relationship'
    b. autobenefactives: *danaysó* 'pursue one's interests'
    c. inherent reflexives: *diirsó* 'warm oneself'
    d. those affecting the body: *libiqsó* 'blink one's eyes'
    e. those affecting the mind/emotions: *cabsó* 'be afraid'
    f. subject is an undergoer: *bogsó* 'heal'

From a morphophonological perspective, middle verbs display consistent behavior, though the middle extension itself has several allomorphs. The examples in (20) are of middle verbs derived from bare stems. It would be impractical to provide examples of middle voices from all six categories here and below. The reader is directed to Saeed (1995) for additional examples that are designated within each of the categories introduced above.

(20) *Middle verbs derived from bare stems*

a.	hafó	'drown, suffocate'	háf	'drown s.o.'
b.	jiidó	'drag oneself away'	jíid	'drag away'
c.	miisó	'balance oneself'	míis	'balance'
d.	qasó	'do s.t. in a complicated way'	qás	'complicate'

Middle verbs are also derived productively from bases containing the weak causative extension, as in (21). The weak causative is realized *-s* here due to V/∅ alternation. Middle verbs derived instead from a base containing the factitive extension are in (22).

(21) *Middle verbs derived from weak causative bases*

a.	baansó	'regain one's strength'	baáni	'nourish'
b.	gaabsó	'stop short of s.t.'	gaábi	'shorten'
c.	hubsó	'make certain for oneself'	húbi	'make certain'
d.	leexsó	'turn s.t. toward oneself'	leéxi	'turn to one side'

(22) *Middle verbs derived from factitive bases*

a.	habeysó	'organize for oneself'	habéyn	'organize'
b.	hogeysó	'bake for oneself'	hogéyn	'bake'
c.	kaxeysó	'take s.o. with you'	kaxéyn	'take s.o.'
d.	libeysó	'be victorious'	libéyn	'bring success'

7.1.8 Neuter

Neuter or neuter-passive (Andrzejewski 1969) verbs in Somali are formed via the addition of the suffix *-ám* to a bare or weak causative base, though it has other allomorphs. The suffix attracts a H tone when it is the last extension in the stem.

(23) *The neuter extension is realized:*
   a. *-ám* before a vowel, as in *kulkamay* 'it was kindled'
   b. *-m* after V/∅ alternation, as in *bilaabmay* 'it started'
   c. *-án* elsewhere, as in *beerán* 'to be planted'

The neuter extension is valency-decreasing and forms intransitive verbs that share similarities with prototypical passive verbs in other languages. For example, the only argument of a Somali neuter verb is a non-agent subject. However, unlike with passive verbs in other languages where an agent might be readily expressed obliquely, it is ungrammatical to do so with a neuter verb. In (24), the underived verb 'dig' takes an agent subject and a patient direct object. However, in (25), the neuter verb requires a patient subject, but the former agent 'the child' cannot be expressed, even as an oblique.

(24) *Cúnuggu   wúxuu   qódayay   dhúlka.*
     cunug=g=u   wux=uu   qod-ay-∅-ay   dhul=ka
     child=K.DEF=SUBJ DEC=3SG.M dig-PROG-3SG.M-PST   ground=K.DEF
     'The child was digging the ground.'

(25) *Dhúlka   wúu   qodmay.*
     dhul=ka   w=uu   qod-m-∅-ay
     ground=K-DEF   DEC=3SG.M   dig-NEU-3SG.M-PST
     'The ground was dug.'

In trying to compel a passive reading with an oblique agent, my speaker suggested the sentence in (26) as an alternative. Though this sentence is structurally different and does not have an oblique agent, it is clear that the verb must once again be made active in an attempt to express the agent.

(26) Dhúlka   wáxa qoday   cúnugga.
    dhul=ka   waxa qod-∅-ay   cunug=ga
    ground=K-DEF FOC dig-3SG.M-PST   child=K.DEF
    'What the child dug was the ground.'

The examples in (27) show other neuter verbs derived from bare bases, while those in (28) show neuter verbs derived from weak causative bases.

(27) *Neuter verbs derived from bare bases*

a.	diirán	'be peeled'	díir	'peel'
b.	jabán	'get broken'	jáb	'break'
c.	hodán	'become rich'	hód	'cheat'
d.	shidán	'be ignited'	shíd	'ignite'

(28) *Neuter verbs derived from weak causative bases*

a.	buuxsán	'become full'	buúxi	'fill up'
b.	doorsán	'become transformed'	doóri	'transform'
c.	hoggaansán	'be guided'	hoggaámi	'guide'
d.	iibsán	'be sold'	iíbi	'sell'

7.1.9 Strong Causative

The second of Somali's causative extensions is the strong causative. Strong causative verbs are derived by the addition of the suffix *-sii* or its word-final allomorph *-siin* to another verbal base. The strong causative, when present, is always the last element of the verb stem. This suffix attracts H tone.

(29) *The strong causative is realized:*
   a. *-siin* word-finally, as in *yeelsiin* 'to convince'
   b. *-sii* elsewhere, as in *tartansiiyey* 'I caused s.o. to compete'

There is a difference in meaning between the strong causative and weak causative, but this is not always consistent. In general, most verbs appear to take one or the other, but not both causatives, so the precise difference between them is sometimes difficult to discern. However, there are a few verbs that can take either causative, and in such verbs, there appears to be difference in the participation of the causer in the action. Generally speaking, for the weak causative, the causer is a participant in the action, whereas for the strong causative, the causer initiates the action but is not an active participant in it. Sentences (30) vs. (31) illustrate this distinction. In the first, the subject is 'playing along with' the children, perhaps ensuring that they continue playing. In the second, the subject is 'entertaining' the children but not necessarily interacting directly with the childrens' play.

(30) *Waan lá cayaariyaa ilmáha.*
w=aan la cayaar-i-y-aa ilma=ha
DEC=1SG with play-WCAUS-1SG-PRES children=K.DEF
'I am playing (along) with the children.'

(31) *Waan lá cayaarsiinayaa ilmáha.*
w=aan la cayaar-siin-ay-∅-aa ilma=ha
DEC=1SG with play-SCAUS-PROG-1SG-PRES children=K.DEF
'I am entertaining the children.'

Another related instance is seen in comparing (32) and (33). In the first, the subject is instructing the participants to reconcile their issue, but in the second, the subject is actively causing them to do so, perhaps by acting as a mediator between them.

(32) *Wáxaan idhi ká heshíiya doódda.*
wax=aan ∅idh-i ka heshi-iy-a doód=da
FOC=1SG 1SG-tell-PSG to reconcile-WCAUS-IMP.PL argument=T.DEF
'I told (them) to reconcile the argument.'

(33) *Wáad heshiisiisey labádaás qóf.*
w=aad heshi-i-sii-s-ey laba-daas qof
DEC=2SG reconcile-WCAUS-SCAUS-2SG-PST two-T.those people
'You made those two people reconcile.'

The examples in (34) show the derivation of strong causative verbs from bare, underived bases.

(34) *Strong causative verbs derived from bare bases*

a.	*cabsíi*	'make drink'	*cáb*	'drink'
b.	*dheelsíi*	'make dance'	*dhéel*	'dance'
c.	*gaadhsíi*	'make reach'	*gáadh*	'reach'
d.	*jiirsíi*	'push through'	*jíir*	'push'
e.	*taabsíi*	'cause to touch'	*táab*	'touch'

The weak causative and strong causative extensions can also co-occur in the same verb stem, although in limited instances like *barisíi* 'cause to beg' (cf. *bári* 'beg'). A strong causative verb can also be derived from a base containing a middle extension, as in *socodsíi* 'cause to proceed' (cf. *socó* 'continue on'), a factitive, as in *mideysíi* 'unify' (cf. *midéyn* 'unite'), a reciprocal, as in *tartansíi* 'make compete with one another' (cf. *tártan* 'compete with one another'), an inchoative, as in *dambaabsíi* 'to cause to err' (cf. *dambóob* 'err'), and an experiencer, as in *guddoonsíi* 'cause to accept, to deliver' (cf. *guddóon* 'accept').

7.1.10 Adjectival participles

Somali has only a small, closed class of approximately 40 lexical adjectives (see §9.4). Beyond this, the language productively derives adjectival participles by the addition of one of two stativizing suffixes, *-án* and *-óon*, to a verbal base. For example, the adjectival participle *feydán* 'uncovered' is derived from the verb *féyd* 'uncover' via the addition of *-án*. Likewise, *doorsóon* 'altered' is derived from the weak causative verb *doóri* 'transform' via the suffix *-óon*.

Examples of adjectival participles derived by *-án* from different verbal bases are in (35). The first group are from bare stems, the second from weak causative stems, and the third from factitive stems. Adjectival participles derived instead by *-óon* are in (36).

(35) *Adjectival participles formed by -án*

a.	hoolán	'scraped'	hóol	'scrape'
b.	jallaadán	'bound'	jalláad	'bind'
c.	lulán	'shaken'	lúl	'shake'
d.	qasaalán	'laundered'	qasáal	'wash'
e.	qallafsán	'obstinate'	qalláfi	'make coarse'
f.	sahansán	'surveyed'	sahámi	'survey'
g.	seexsán	'extinguished'	seéxi	'extinguish'
h.	galeysán	'covered'	galéyn	'put a cover on s.t.'
i.	hubeysán	'armed'	hubéyn	'arm'
j.	nimceysán	'prosperous'	nimcéyn	'bring about prosperity'

(36) *Adjectival participles formed by -óon*

a.	garansóon	'knowledgeable'	garansíi	'make understand'
b.	jilcóon	'loose'	jílci	'stretch out'
c.	warróon	'informed'	wári	'ask for information'
d.	xasillóon	'tranquil'	xásil	'become calm'

Adjectival participles cannot take a full complement of verbal inflection on their own (nor can lexical adjectives). They instead form a hybrid verb with *aháan* 'to be' which will encode any inflection for agreement in person, number, and gender. Among the simplest instances of this can be seen in examples like (37).

(37) *Waan   fiicánahay.*
    w=aan   fiic-an-∅-ah-ay
    DEC=1SG good-STV-1SG-be-PRES
    'I am fine.'

More detail on the behavior of adjectival participles in hybrid verbs is found in §7.11.

7.2 Inflection

Somali verbs are inflected for person, number, and grammatical gender though not all verbs do so identically.[2] Some inflectional behavior is dictated by stem type. Most verbs fall into the category of *suffixing* verbs (§7.5) given that they are inflected for person, number, and grammatical gender exclusively via suffixation. A small number of verbs are instead in a group of *prefixing* verbs (§7.6). These are inflected for person, number, and grammatical gender via a combination of prefixation, suffixation, and alternation to their root vowel.

Syntactic context also plays a significant role in verb inflection. Somali exhibits two major inflectional paradigms that I will call the *realis* and *irrealis* paradigms. The realis paradigm is associated with verbs in affirmative, tensed main clauses and in relative clauses whose head is the subject of the main clause verb that is not in focus. The irrealis paradigm is associated with negative main clause verbs, verbs in most subordinate clauses, and modalities like the conditional and potential. Another key distinction in the Somali verbal system is between *full* vs. *reduced* agreement. In most instances, a verb will inflect for a full complement of person, number, and grammatical gender distinctions. However, in specific instances – under subject focus and in subject relative clauses – the inflectional distinctions exhibited by verbs collapse such that only a subset of person, number, and grammatical gender distinctions remain uniquely encoded. Another consideration to be discussed below is whether verbs exhibit a H tone or are instead toneless.

The perspective offered on the Somali verbal system in this chapter differs in some respects from that found in other literature on the language. One way is in the invocation of realis and irrealis modalities in reference to the language's inflectional paradigms. Doing so highlights correlations in verbal behavior in several otherwise challenging to define contexts (negative main clause verbs, subordinate clause verbs, etc., as mentioned just above), all of which relate in some way to unknown or unrealized actions or states. Realis paradigm inflection occurs instead only in limited contexts, all of which relate in some respect to given (i.e., known, topical, defined) in-

---

2 Though 1PL pronouns are inflected for clusivity (i.e., inclusive vs. exclusive), verbs are not inflected for this distinction.

formation. Another way that the approach taken here differs is in its treatment of verb tone. The discussion below highlights the fact that realis mood present and past tense main clause verbs and verbs in relative clauses whose subject is also the main clause subject are toneless, while other verbs are toned. There appears, once again, to be a correlation of sorts between tonelessness and givenness, though one that is admittedly difficult to address adequately in this grammar. It is notable, however, that the only other instances in which a Somali content word appears toneless is as the result of subject marking. Only subjects that are not in focus can be subject marked, suggesting therefore that they are known, given, or topical to some degree (Tosco 2002). Of course, these differing perspectives are conceptual in nature, but they do not change the facts of the language. Rather, the hope is that they might help to bring transparency to the description that follows while setting the stage for future, more detailed inquiry into their underpinnings.

In order to set the stage for the remainder of this chapter, and to offer a preview of the major inflectional distinctions introduced just above, consider the summary in (38) for the suffixing verb *búub* 'fly.' This display directly compares the affirmative Simple Present, which takes realis paradigm inflection, to its negative counterpart, which instead takes the irrealis paradigm. The latter also happens to be the same verb form found in most subordinate clause verbs. These negative and subordinate clause verbs have in common that they refer to unrealized or unknown events, actions, or states.

(38) *Comparing realis vs. irrealis inflectional paradigms*

	Realis		Irrealis	
1SG	buubaa	'I fly'	buubó	'that I fly, I don't fly'
2SG	buubtaa	'you fly'	buubtó/buubtíd	'that you fly, you don't fly'
3SG.M/K	buubaa	'he flies'	buubó	'that he flies, he doesn't fly'
3SG.F/T	buubtaa	'she flies'	buubtó	'that she flies, she doesn't fly'
1PL	buubnaa	'we fly'	buubnó	'that we fly, we don't fly'
2PL	buubtaan	'you(PL) fly'	buubtáan	'that you(PL) fly, you(PL) don't fly'
3PL	buubaan	'they fly'	buubáan	'that they fly, they don't fly'

Several properties of the two paradigms are immediately clear. In these instances, Somali verbs are inflected for three persons, singular vs. plural number, and for grammatical gender in the third person singular. Moreover, within a given paradigm, inflection for 1SG and 3SG.M (K-series agreement) are identical, as is inflection for 2SG and 3SG.F (T-series agreement). There are two variants of the 2SG in the irrealis paradigm.

Another major inflectional distinction in Somali is between those contexts requiring full vs. reduced inflectional agreement. Using the same verb as above, two agreement patterns for the realis inflectional paradigm in the Simple Present (full vs. reduced) are shown in (39). Full agreement is required in declarative clauses without focus, as well as in instances of object focus. Reduced agreement is specific to subject focus and subject relative clauses. Full vs. reduced agreement also occurs in irrealis paradigm inflection.

(39) *Comparing full vs. reduced agreement (realis paradigm)*

	Full agreement	Reduced agreement
1SG	buubaa	buuba
2SG	buubtaa	buuba
3SG.M/K	buubaa	buuba
3SG.F/T	buubtaa	buubta
1PL	buubnaa	buubna
2PL	buubtaan	buuba
3PL	buubaan	buuba

In (39), reduced agreement entails that most person, number, grammatical gender combinations collapse into one form, with the exception of 3SG.F/T and 1PL, which retain unique forms. Slight differences are found between suffixing and prefixing verbs under the conditions of reduced agreement, which will be discussed in detail below.

Beyond these major inflectional characteristics, there are some combinations of tense, aspect, and mood that involve only suffixation on a main verb. This can be seen, for example, in a Simple Past verb like *sheegtay* 'you (SG)/she spoke' where the main verb is followed by the suffix *-t-*, which encodes 2SG or 3SG.F. This verb also takes the suffix *-ay*, which is specific to the Simple Past. Other inflectional categories are expressed by the combination of a main verb infinitive followed by an inflected auxiliary verb. For example, the Future is formed by the infinitive of the main verb followed by the Simple Present form of the auxiliary verb *dóon*, as in *Waan cúni doonaa.* 'I will eat.'

Table (40) summarizes the tense, aspect, and mood combinations found in Somali's main clause verbs and their basic morphological construction. The first group contains those contexts that take realis paradigm inflection. The second group takes irrealis paradigm inflection. Most subordinate clause verbs also fall into this category. The third group is composed of contexts that are formed by an auxiliary construction. The last group contains a few outliers whose behavior and morphology do not fit well within one particular group. Each of these contexts and details specific to them are discussed in turn in sections below.

(40) *Tense, aspect, mood summary*

Simple Present	stem + *-aa(n)*
Present Progressive	stem + *-ayaa(n)*
Simple Past	stem + *-ay/-een*
Emphatic Past	Simple Past variant w/ H tone
Past Progressive	stem + *-ay(C)ay/ -ay(C)ee(n)*
Present Simple Negative	stem + *-ó/áan*
Present Progressive Negative	stem + *-ayó/-ayáan*
Optative	subject clitic ... *-o/-een* w/ H stem
Past Habitual	infinitive + Simple Past of *jir-*
Conditional	infinitive + Simple Present of *lah-*
Future	infinitive + Simple Present of *doon-*
Imperative	stem (+ *-a*)
Potential	*shów* ... stem + *-ee(n)*

Verbal negation typically involves a combination of suffixation and the presence of a clause type classifier. In most instances, this is either *má* or *aán*, though some contexts instead require *ha* or *yáan*. Some clauses containing a pronominal subject have two negative classifiers that form a periphrastic sequence – *má...aán* – which flanks the subject pronoun. In contexts formed by an auxiliary construction, the negative classifier may directly precede the main verb or instead the auxiliary verb.

Some verbs do not inflect fully when negated, but rather take a single form for all person, number, gender combinations. This form will contain the negative suffix *-n*. The Simple Present and Present Progressive are exceptions to this in that their negative counterparts are fully inflected for person, number, and gender using the irrealis inflectional paradigm, alongside a negative clause type classifier.

Due to the highly synthetic nature of Somali verbs, many segmental alternations occur upon inflection owing to the concatenation of morphemes of different shapes and sizes. This includes epenthesis, degemination, assibilation, deaspiration, manner assimilation, palatalization, and V/∅ alternation, the details of which are are described in §3.4.

In the sections below, different verb types are discussed in turn. This begins with infinitives in §7.3, followed by auxiliary verbs in §7.4. Attention is then turned to the behavior of suffixing verbs, followed by prefixing verbs and irregular verbs in main clauses. Within each of these types, contexts that take realis inflection are discussed, followed by those that take irrealis inflection. These are followed by contexts formed by an auxiliary construction and, lastly, other contexts that behave in a unique way compared to others. After discussing the morphology of main clauses verbs, focus turns to subordinate clause verbs and then to those contexts requiring reduced agreement. Lastly, the characteristics of hybrid verbs are discussed.

7.3 Infinitives

The infinitival form of a verb is found only in combination with an inflected auxiliary verb. In some cases, the auxiliary verb has been grammaticalized and no longer expresses any lexical content. For example, the Present and Past Progressive are formed, at least historically, with the auxiliary verb *háyi* 'hold.' In other constructions, the inflected auxiliary verb retains its lexical content. For example, the Future is formed with the auxiliary verb *dóon* 'want.' In every instance, the infinitive precedes the inflected auxiliary verb, as in *bilaábi doonnaa* 'we will begin.'

The infinitive is formed via suffixation, with the suffix used being particular to a given stem type. A verb's infinitive is dictated by the last extensional element in the verb stem except, of course, in underived verbs. Infinitival suffixes are given in (41). All of these suffixes attract H tone when they are stem-final, with the exception of the suffixes associated with the bare, underived base and the reciprocal.

(41) *Infinitive suffixes by stem type*

Bare	-*i*	Experiencer	-*óon*
Inchoative	-*oóbi/-aábi*	Reciprocal	-*tan*
Weak Causative	-*ín*	Factitive	-*éyn/-áyn*
Middle	-*án*	Neuter	-*án*
Strong Causative	-*síin*		

The infinitive itself has no gerundive use as a verbal noun. Gerunds are derived uniquely via suffixation or via conversion, as discussed in §6.4.

The four prefixing verbs and the three irregular verbs shown in (42) do not take derivational extensions. Each has only a single infinitival form, though there are sometimes dialectal differences in the form of the infinitive used and its pronunciation.

(42)

imán	'to come'	*odhán*	'to say'
oólli/ooláan	'to be (exist)'	*aqoón/oqoón*	'to know'
ahaán	'to be'	*lahaán*	'to have'
		la'ahaán	'to lack'

7.4 Auxiliary verbs

There are seven auxiliary verbs in Somali shown in (43) that occur alongside an infinitive and convey modal distinctions of different types. Four of these contribute grammatical rather than lexical meaning. These infinitive + inflected auxiliary constructions are involved in the encoding of aspect and mood distinctions in the verbal system. The other three auxiliaries retain much of their lexical integrity.

(43) *Auxiliary verbs*

	Root form	Auxiliary meaning	Lexical meaning	Context(s)
a.	*jir-*	'used to'	'be in a place, exist'	Past Habitual
b.	*lah-*	'could, should, might'	'have'	Conditional
c.	*doon-*	'will, shall'	'want'	Assumptive
d.	*hay-*	'is/was X-ing'	'have, hold, possess'	Present Progressive
				Past Progressive
e.	*kar-*	'be able, can do'	'know how to'	
f.	*waa-*	'cannot'	'fail, be unable'	
g.	*gaadh-*	'almost do, nearly do'	'arrive'	

Auxiliary verbs are involved in the formation of clauses with an infinitival complement. Such clauses have an inflected auxiliary verb preceded by a main clause infinitive. They are sometimes included alongside subordinate clauses because they are translated as such in languages like English. However, they are formally auxiliary constructions.

(44) Gaárigií   ayáan   soó   iibsán   karay.
     gaari-gii ay=aan   soo   iib-s-an   kar-∅-ay
     car-K.RDEF FOC=1SG   VEN   buy-WCAUS-MID.INF   be.able-1SG-PST
     'I was able to buy the car.'

(45) Máanta waan   dhimán   gaadhay.
     maanta w=aan   dhim-an   gaadh-∅-ay
     today DEC=1SG   die-MID.INF   almost.do-1SG-PST
     'Today, I almost died.'

7.5 Main clause suffixing verbs

Main clause suffixing verbs exhibit a full inflectional paradigm, meaning that they inflect for a full complement of person, number, and grammatical gender distinctions. The exception to this is in instances of subject focus, which are discussed separately in §7.8, where they instead exhibit reduced agreement. A typical example of such full inflection is seen in the Simple Present affirmative and negative in (46), which require realis vs. irrealis inflection, respectively.

(46) *Sample main clause suffixing verb paradigm*

	Affirmative	Negative
1SG	buubaa	buubó
2SG	buubtaa	buubtó or buubtíd
3SG.M/K	buubaa	buubó
3SG.F/T	buubtaa	buubtó
1PL	buubnaa	buubnó
2PL	buubtaan	buubtáan
3PL	buubaan	buubáan

In 1SG, 3SG.M, and 3PL forms, there is an empty slot (∅) in the verb template where other persons have an overtly expressed exponent. The integrity of this slot becomes apparent in that a glide is epenthesized to fill it in some contexts (cf. *buubiyay* 'I chased away' and *buubisay* 'you (SG) chased away,' keeping in mind that 2SG /t/ predictably alternates to [s] after [i]). 2SG, 3SG.F, and 2PL have in common that they are inflected with *-t-*, and 1PL is inflected with *-n-*.

The inflectional paradigms above can be reconfigured to more clearly illustrate the morphological simplicity of the Somali verbal system. While Somali inflects for typical person, number, and gender combinations, it does not do so in the same way that we find, for example, in most Indo-European languages. As shown in (47), inflection for 1SG and 3SG.M are identical, as are 2SG and 3SG.F. 1PL patterns with other singular number categories, while 3PL and 2PL pattern with 1SG/3SG.M and 2SG/3SG.F, respectively, with plural number being indicated by *-n*.

(47) *Reorganized suffixing verb paradigm*

1SG/3SG.M	buub-∅-aa	3PL	buub-∅-aa-n
2SG/3SG.F	buub-t-aa	2PL	buub-t-aa-n
1PL	buub-n-aa		

Verbs, in general, inflect for grammatical gender only in the 3SG, where there are unique forms for masculine and feminine for human referents. This extends to non-human referents as well in that masculine aligns with K-series agreement and feminine aligns T-series agreement, as dictated by the verb's subject.

In the sections that follow, it will be shown that different tense, aspect, and mood distinctions are encoded either exclusively by suffixation or sometimes by an auxiliary construction involving the infinitive of a main verb followed thereafter by an inflected auxiliary verb. Inflection for negation is consistently indicated by suffixation on the verb, though negation is indicated more broadly by clause type classifiers that are specific to a given context and/or modality. Because it would be impractical to provide a paradigm for every verb stem type, one exemplar is given representing each of three major stem types – bare, weak causative, and middle. For reference, complete paradigms for other stem types are in the appendix.

7.5.1 Realis contexts

7.5.1.1 Simple Present

Simple Present verbs convey information that is considered factual to the speaker at the present time. These verbs do not provide aspectual contextualization for how the action is done or how often the action is occurring. Both active and stative verbs can be inflected for the Simple Present. These verbs are characterized by their -*aa(n)* suffix, where the final nasal reflects plural number and is found only in 2PL and 3PL forms. In the affirmative, Simple Present verbs are toneless.

(48) *Simple Present suffixing verbs - affirmative*

	Bare 'fly away'	Weak Causative 'chase away'	Middle 'run away'
1SG/3SG.M	*buubaa*	*buubiyaa*	*buubtaa*
2SG/3SG.F	*buubtaa*	*buubisaa*	*buubataa*
1PL	*buubnaa*	*buubinnaa*	*buubannaa*
2PL	*buubtaan*	*buubisaan*	*buubataan*
3PL	*buubaan*	*buubiyaan*	*buubtaan*

2SG/3SG.F and 2PL verbs with a weak causative stem witness assibilation of their person suffix; see §3.4.10. These same forms are subject to degemination but not deaspiration in the middle; see §3.4.3. 1SG/3SG.M and 3PL in middle voice verbs lose a suffixal vowel via V/Ø alternation; see §3.5. Weak causative and middle suffixes also undergo manner alternation in 1PL forms; see §3.4.4. To express negation of the Simple Present requires irrealis paradigm inflection, which is discussed in §7.5.2.1.

7.5.1.2 Present Progressive

Present Progressive verbs convey information about actions that the speaker knows to be underway at the present time. The Present Progressive is typically used only with active verbs, though if the action entailed in an otherwise stative verb is contextualized adverbially, a stative verb can be inflected for the Present Progressive. For example, the stative verb *fadhiisó* 'sit oneself down' cannot be used on its own in the progressive: **Waan fadhiisánayaa.* 'I am sitting.' However, the addition of a deictic, adposition, or other contextualizing adverbial results in grammaticality: *Waan síi fadhiisánayaa.* 'I am sitting (away).' or *Waan kú fadhiisánayaa.* 'I am sitting on it.'

Present Progressive verbs are similar to the Simple Present in that they have an -*aa(n)* suffix. They differ, however, in that they are formed by an auxiliary-like construction where the infinitive of the main verb (except in bare stems) is followed by the auxiliary verb *(h)ay-* which carries present tense inflection. This context, and the Past Progressive formed like it, differ from other auxiliary verb constructions in Somali in that the infinitive and auxiliary prosodify together as a single word. The two components in other auxiliary constructions are prosodified separately as two words. Like other auxiliary constructions, however, H tone is found on the stem, and inflectional *-t-* undergoes assibilation after *i*.

(49) *Present Progressive suffixing verbs - affirmative*

	Bare 'flying away'	Weak Causative 'chasing away'	Middle 'running away'
1SG/3SG.M	buúbayaa	buubínayaa	buubánayaa
2SG/3SG.F	buúbaysaa	buubínaysaa	buubánaysaa
1PL	buúbaynaa	buubínaynaa	buubánaynaa
2PL	buúbaysaan	buubínaysaan	buubánaysaan
3PL	buúbayaan	buubínayaan	buubánayaan

Negation of the Present Progressive requires irrealis paradigm inflection. This is discussed in §7.5.2.2.

7.5.1.3 Simple Past

The Simple Past is used to convey information about a completed event that occurred only a single time in the past. These verbs are generally characterized by the suffix *-ay*, though in Central/Coastal dialects, its pronunciation is closer to *-ey*. In 2PL and 3PL forms, the suffix is instead *-een* where the final nasal indicates plural number. In the affirmative, these verb forms are toneless. Alternations due to assibilation and V/Ø reduction occur where expected. In affirmative main clauses, Simple Past verbs are toneless.

(50) *Simple Past suffixing verbs - affirmative*

	Bare 'flew away'	Weak Causative 'chased away'	Middle 'ran away'
1SG/3SG.M	buubay	buubiyay	buubtay
2SG/3SG.F	buubtay	buubisay	buubatay
1PL	buubnay	buubinnay	buubannay
2PL	buubteen	buubiseen	buubateen
3PL	buubeen	buubiyeen	buubteen

There is no inflection for person, number, or gender in the negative Simple Past verbs. All combinations shown in (51) simply involve the infinitive associated with a given stem type, except bare stems which take *-in*. Negation is marked, as elsewhere, outside the verb by the negative clause type marker *ma*, and the nature of the verb's subject is recoverable from subject pronouns.

(51) *Simple Past suffixing verbs - negative*

	Bare 'didn't fly away' *buubín*	Weak Causative 'didn't chase away' *buubín*	Middle 'didn't run away' *buubán*
all p/n/g			

7.5.1.4 Past Progressive

Past Progressive verbs describe events that were ongoing in the past. They do not express whether or not the action is still underway. These verbs are similar in construction to Present Progressive verbs in that they are formed by an auxiliary-like construction involving the infinitive of the main verb (except in bare stems). They are followed by the auxiliary verb *(h)ay-* which is inflected for the Simple Past. The two prosodify together as a single word with H tone being on the main verb stem, rather than on the auxiliary.

(52) *Past Progressive suffixing verbs - affirmative*

	Bare 'was flying away'	Weak Causative 'was chasing away'	Middle 'was running away'
1SG/3SG.M	*buúbayay*	*buubínayay*	*buubánayay*
2SG/3SG.F	*buúbaysay*	*buubínaysay*	*buubánaysay*
1PL	*buúbaynay*	*buubínaynay*	*buubánaynay*
2PL	*buúbayseen*	*buubínayseen*	*buubánayseen*
3PL	*buúbayeen*	*buubínayeen*	*buubánayeen*

Negative Past Progressive verbs are shown in (53). They do not inflect for person, number, or gender, but rather have a single form for all of these inflectional combinations. There are, however, two forms of the negative. One of these involves the simple addition of *-éyn* to the verb stem, and the other adds *-eynín*. Andrzejewski (1956) describes these as optional variants, at least in Isaaq (Northern) Somali. My speakers from Mogadishu recognize both as grammatical, but they indicate that the former "sounds more Northern" and that they would not produce it themselves.

(53) *Past Progressive suffixing verbs - negative*

	Bare 'wasn't flying away' *búubéyn* or *búubeynín*	Weak Causative 'wasn't chasing away' *buubínéyn* or *buubíneynín*	Middle 'wasn't running away' *buubánéyn* or *buubáneynín*
all p/n/g			

Both of these negative suffixes bear a H tone, the result being that the verb carries two H tones, one being on the verb stem and the other on the negative suffix itself.

7.5.1.5 Emphatic Past

The Emphatic Past (or Independent Past, as it is sometimes called) is reported in the literature, but no speaker with whom I have worked recognizes it, nor can I find examples of its use in web corpora. According to Banti (2019), it is "a tense used in poetry, proverbs, curses, and contemporary fiction for marking moments of heightened tension." It stands alone and is used as a means of affirmative or emphatic response. From a morphological standpoint, it is fully inflected for person/number/gender, has a H tone, and has no negative form.

(54) *Emphatic Past suffixing verbs*

	Bare 'flew away'	Weak Causative 'chased away'	Middle 'ran away'
1SG	búubay	buubíyay	buubáday
2SG/3SG.F	búubtay	buubísay	buubátay
3SG.M	búub	buubí	buubáy
1PL	búubnay	buubínay	buubánay
2PL	buubté	buubisé	buubaté
3PL	buubé	buubiyé	buubadé

The Emphatic Past bears some similarity to the Simple Past, at least in its 1SG, 2SG/3SG.F, and 1PL forms. The 3SG.M is simply the verb stem. In each of these forms, H tone is reported to occur on the stem. The 2PL and 3PL differ in that H tone occurs on the suffix.

7.5.2 Irrealis contexts

7.5.2.1 Simple Present Negative

Simple Present Negative verbs are inflected with irrealis paradigm suffixes. They require the same suffixal inflection as do the present tense subordinate clause verbs discussed in §7.9. That these verbs pattern with verbs in other irrealis contexts makes sense if one considers that the actions or activities that they describe are yet unrealized or have not occurred. Under this view, one might consider the inflectional suffixes associated with these contexts to be the morphological exponents of the irrealis mood, with negation itself being expressed instead by an obligatory negative clause type marker that precedes the verb, though not always directly.

In forming the Simple Present Negative, alternations due to assibilation, manner assimilation, and V/Ø reduction occur as otherwise expected. An epenthetic glide fills the empty person slot in weak causative 1SG/3SG.M and 3PL forms. All Simple Present verbs have a H tone on their final syllable. In 2PL and 3PL forms, this H tone is the only difference distinguishing them from their toneless affirmative counterparts.

(55) *Simple Present suffixing verbs - negative*

	Bare 'don't fly away'	Weak Causative 'don't chase away'	Middle 'don't run away'
1SG/3SG.M	*buubó*	*buubiyó*	*buubtó*
2SG	*buubtó* or *buubtíd*	*buubisó* or *buubisíd*	*buubató* or *buubatíd*
3SG.F	*buubtó*	*buubisó*	*buubató*
1PL	*buubnó*	*buubinnó*	*buubannó*
2PL	*buubtáan*	*buubisáan*	*buubatáan*
3PL	*buubáan*	*buubiyáan*	*buubtáan*

7.5.2.2 Present Progressive Negative

There are two strategies used to form a Present Progressive Negative verb. One of these – the short form – involves a typical auxiliary construction with a main verb infinitive and a negatively inflected auxiliary verb. The other – the long form – uses the same auxiliary-like construction seen in the affirmative Present Progressive where the main verb and auxiliary prosodify together as a single word. The use of one strategy vs. the other depends on whether the verb is part of a simple, clause-final declarative statement or otherwise part of a larger string of discourse.

The short form of the Present Progressive Negative, as seen in (56), is used clause-finally. It is formed by the infinitive of a main verb (including with bare stems) followed by an inflected form of the auxiliary verb *hay-* to which the negative marker *má-* has been added. The auxiliary takes the irrealis inflectional paradigm. In addition to expected alternations, there are three H tones on these verbs. The first is on the main verb, the second on the negative marker, and the third on the auxiliary verb suffix.

(56) *Present Progressive suffixing verbs - negative (short form)*

	Bare 'not flying away'	Weak Causative 'not chasing away'	Middle 'not running away'
1SG/3SG.M	*buúbi máayó*	*buubín máayó*	*buubán máayó*
2SG	*buúbi máaysó* or *buúbi máaysíd*	*buubín máaysó* or *buubín máaysíd*	*buubán máaysó* or *buubán máaysíd*
3SG.F	*buúbi máaysó*	*buubín máaysó*	*buubán máaysó*
1PL	*buúbi máaynó*	*buubín máaynó*	*buubán máaynó*
2PL	*buúbi máaysáan*	*buubín máaysáan*	*buubán máaysáan*
3PL	*buúbi máayáan*	*buubín máayáan*	*buubán máayáan*

A second, long form of the present progressive negative is used elsewhere and is closer in structure to the affirmative present progressive discussed in §7.5.1.2. The main verb infinitive (except in bare stems) is followed by the auxiliary *(h)ay-* which in turn takes irrealis paradigm inflection. The negative particle *má* is not prosodified within the Verb Complex itself but rather occurs earlier in the clause. There is one H tone on the stem and one on the inflectional suffix.

(57) *Present Progressive suffixing verbs - negative (long form)*

	Bare 'not flying away'	Weak Causative 'not chasing away'	Middle 'not running away'
1SG/3SG.M	búubayó	buubínayó	buubánayó
2SG	búubaysó or búubaysíd	buubínaysó or buubínaysíd	buubánaysó or buubánaysíd
3SG.F	búubaysó	buubínaysó	buubánaysó
1PL	búubaynó	buubínaynó	buubánaynó
2PL	búubaysáan	buubínaysáan	buubánaysáan
3PL	búubayáan	buubínayáan	buubánayáan

7.5.2.3 Optative

Optative verbs express wishes and hopes and are fully inflected for person, number, and gender. They are characterized by a non-tonal variant of the irrealis inflectional paradigm introduced above. These verbs do exhibit a H tone, but this tone is located on the verb stem, rather than on the inflectional suffix. Another minor difference is that 2PL and 3PL forms are pronounced *-een*, rather than *-aan*. In the affirmative, Optative verbs are preceded by one of the subject pronoun clitics in §10.2.1, with the exception of third person forms, which are preceded by *ha*. These clitics do not necessarily immediately precede the verb, so they are not include them in the paradigm.

(58) *Optative suffixing verbs - affirmative*

	Bare 'may X fly away'	Weak Causative 'may X chase away'	Middle 'may X run away'
1SG/3SG.M	búubo	buubíyo	buubádo
2SG/3SG.F	búubto or búubtid	buubísid	buubátid
1PL	búubno	buubínno	buubánno
2PL	búubteen	buubíseen	buubáteen
3PL	búubeen	buubíyeen	buubádeen

Negative forms of the Optative are not inflected for person, number, and gender. Rather, this information is encoded in the subject clitics that precede the verb in their clause. The verb occurs in its infinitive form, with the exception of those with bare stems which take -*in* rather than simply -*i*. Negative Optative verbs also co-occur with the clause type marker *yáan* which hosts the relevant subject clitic.

(59) *Optative suffixing verbs - negative*

	Bare 'may X not fly away' *buubín*	Weak Causative 'may X not chase away' *buubín*	Middle 'may X not run away' *buubán*
all p/n/g			

7.5.3 Auxiliary constructions

The auxiliary constructions described in this section differ from those constructions used to form the Present Progressive, Past Progressive, and the long form of the Past Progressive Negative in that they involve a main verb infinitive followed by an inflected auxiliary verb where the two remain prosodified as separate words.

7.5.3.1 Past Habitual

The Past Habitual describes completed events and actions that happened more than one time in the past. Forming the Past Habitual involves an auxiliary construction where the main verb infinitive is followed by the auxiliary verb *jir-* inflected for the Simple Past. The main verb infinitive has a H tone, but the inflected auxiliary verb is toneless.

(60) *Past Habitual suffixing verbs - affirmative*

	Bare 'used to fly away'	Weak Causative 'used to chase away'	Middle 'used to run away'
1SG/3SG.M	*buúbi jiray*	*buubín jiray*	*buubán jiray*
2SG/3SG.F	*buúbi jirtay*	*buubín jirtay*	*buubán jirtay*
1PL	*buúbi jirnay*	*buubín jirnay*	*buubán jirnay*
2PL	*buúbi jirteen*	*buubín jirteen*	*buubán jirteen*
3PL	*buúbi jireen*	*buubín jireen*	*buubán jireen*

There is only a single form of the negative Past Habitual used for all person, number, grammatical gender combinations. This is formed by the main verb infinitive and a negatively inflected form of the auxiliary verb. The verb's subject is elucidated elsewhere by subject pronouns.

(61) *Past Habitual suffixing verbs - negative*

	Bare 'didn't used to fly away' *buúbi jirín*	Weak Causative 'didn't used to chase away' *buubín jirín*	Middle 'didn't used to run away' *buubán jirín*
all p/n/g			

7.5.3.2 Conditional

Conditional verbs express information that speakers are reasonably but not entirely certain would obtain if some set of conditions were met. They are formed by an auxiliary construction composed of the infinitive of the main verb followed by the auxiliary verb *leh-* inflected for the Simple Past. The main verb infinitive has a H tone while the inflected auxiliary verb is toneless. As an irregular verb, the auxiliary involved here is inflected somewhat differently from other verbs discussed thus far; see Section 7.7 for more detail.

(62) *Conditional suffixing verbs - affirmative*

	Bare 'would fly away'	Weak Causative 'would chase away'	Middle 'would run away'
1SG/3SG.M	*buúbi lahaa*	*buubín lahaa*	*buubán lahaa*
2SG/3SG.F	*buúbi lahayd*	*buubín lahayd*	*buubán lahayd*
1PL	*buúbi lahayn*	*buubín lahayn*	*buubán lahayn*
2PL	*buúbi lahaydeen*	*buubín lahaydeen*	*buubán lahaydeen*
3PL	*buúbi lahaayeen*	*buubín lahaayeen*	*buubán lahaayeen*

Inflection for the negative conditional collapses into a single form. This context is formed by a main verb infinitive and the auxiliary takes the tonal negative suffix *-aýn*.

(63) *Conditional suffixing verbs - negative*

	Bare 'wouldn't fly away' *buúbi laháyn*	Weak Causative 'wouldn't chase away' *buubín laháyn*	Middle 'wouldn't run away' *buubán laháyn*
all p/n/g			

7.5.3.3 Future

The Future expresses information that speakers are positive would obtain if some set of conditions were met. It is also formed by an auxiliary construction, this time composed of the infinitive of the main verb followed by the auxiliary verb *doon-*, that is inflected fully for the Simple Present. As in other auxiliary constructions, there is H tone on the infinitive, but the inflected auxiliary remains toneless.

(64) *Future suffixing verbs - affirmative*

	Bare 'will fly away'	Weak Causative 'will chase away'	Middle 'will run away'
1SG/3SG.M	buúbi doonaa	buubín doonaa	buubán doonaa
2SG/3SG.F	buúbi doontaa	buubín doontaa	buubán doontaa
1PL	buúbi doonnaa	buubín doonnaa	buubán doonnaa
2PL	buúbi doontaan	buubín doontaan	buubán doontaan
3PL	buúbi doonaan	buubín doonaan	buubán doonaan

Negating the Future is also accomplished with an auxiliary construction. The main verb remains in the infinitive and the auxiliary verb *doon-* is inflected fully for person/number/gender following the irrealis inflectional paradigm. These suffixes have a H tone, as does the infinitive. Like in other instances, there are two variants for 2SG.

(65) *Future suffixing verbs - negative*

	Bare 'won't fly away'	Weak Causative 'won't chase away'	Middle 'won't run away'
1SG/3SG.M	buúbi doonó	buubín doonó	buubán doonó
2SG	buúbi doontó or buúbi doontíd	buubín doontó or buubín doontíd	buubán doontó or buubán doontíd
3SG.F	buúbi doontó	buubín doontó	buubán doontó
1PL	buúbi doonnó	buubín doonnó	buubán doonnó
2PL	buúbi doontáan	buubín doontáan	buubán doontáan
3PL	buúbi doonáan	buubín doonáan	buubán doonáan

7.5.4 Other moods

7.5.4.1 Imperative

Verbs in the Imperative mood are used for commands of different degrees of intensity, whether intended as authoritative or as a light suggestion. They are not inherently considered rude. These verbs inflect for number but not for person or gender. Plural number is indicated by the addition of the suffix *-a* to the verb stem. This involves glide epenthesis in the weak causative. In the middle, it is important to keep in mind that the proposed basic form of the extension is *-át*. Vowel-finally the middle is realized as *-o*, but in the plural, upon the addition of *-a*, V/∅ alternation results in a consonant cluster. There is a H tone on the stem in all Imperative forms.

(66) *Imperative suffixing verbs - affirmative*

	Bare 'fly away!'	Weak Causative 'chase away!'	Middle 'run away!'
SG	búub	buubí	buubó
PL	búuba	buubíya	buubtá

Imperative mood verbs are negated in the singular by the addition of the suffix *-(i)n*. This is added directly to the stem in the singular but is followed by *-a* in the plural. H tone is on the stem in the singular and on the negative suffix in the plural. In addition to this suffixal inflection, negative Imperative mood verbs are preceded by the clause type marker *ha*.

(67) *Imperative suffixing verbs - negative*

	Bare 'don't fly away!'	Weak Causative 'don't chase away!'	Middle 'don't run away!'
SG	buubín	buubín	buubán
PL	buubína	buubinína	buubanína

7.5.4.2 Potential

Verbs in the Potential mood encode information that could possibly (but not certainly) occur if some set of conditions were to obtain. Their behavior is in some ways reminiscent of affirmative vs. negative Simple Present and Simple Past verbs. Both affirmative and negative are fully inflected for person, number, and gender and are characterized by the suffix *-ee(n)*, with the final *n* occurring only in the 2PL and 3PL. The verbs themselves are toneless in the affirmative and are sometimes preceded by the clause type marker *shów* (or its variant *sów*).

(68) *Potential suffixing verbs*

	Bare 'perhaps ... fly away'	Weak Causative 'perhaps ... chase away'	Middle 'perhaps ... run away'
1SG/3SG.M	buubee	buubiyee	buubadee
2SG/3SG.F	buubtee	buubisee	buubatee
1PL	buubnee	buubinee	buubanee
2PL	buubteen	buubiseen	buubateen
3PL	buubeen	buubiyeen	buubadeen

Negative potential verbs additionally contain the negative suffix *-n* in all instances. They also differ from their affirmative counterparts in that they have a H tone on the Potential suffix.

(69) *Potential suffixing verbs - negative*

	Bare 'wouldn't fly away'	Weak Causative 'wouldn't chase away'	Middle 'wouldn't run away'
1SG/3SG.M	*buubéen*	*buubiyéen*	*buubtéen*
2SG/3SG.F	*buubtéen*	*buubiséen*	*buubatéen*
1PL	*buubnéen*	*buubinéen*	*buubanéen*
2PL	*buubtéen*	*buubiséen*	*buubatéen*
3PL	*buubéen*	*buubiyéen*	*buubtéen*

7.6 Main clause prefixing verbs

Four verbs are inflected for person, number, and gender through a combination of prefixation, suffixation, and changes to their root vowel. These verbs are: *imán* 'to come,' *odhán* 'to say,' *oólli* 'to be (exist),' and *aqoón* 'to know.'[3] Prefixing/root-changing inflection only occurs in those contexts that do not involve an auxiliary construction. This includes the Simple Present, Simple Past, Potential, and Optative. Other inflectional contexts behave in an identical way to suffixing verbs.

There is also evidence to suggest that the inflectional properties of these verbs are unstable to some extent. For example, two of the four verbs optionally omit tense marking altogether in the Simple Present. Three of the four verbs have optional, suppletive suffixing inflectional variants in the Simple Past. In approaching a description of these verbs, I do so from a conservative perspective. In the remainder of this section, the focus is on what most would consider to be their basic forms, with other optional forms or variants indicated where relevant. With this in mind, and for an initial comparison, (70) shows Simple Present paradigms for the prefixing verb *imán* 'come' alongside the suffixing verb *búub* 'fly' introduced above. The same differences seen in realis vs. irrealis paradigm inflection seen in suffixing verbs also apply to prefixing verbs.

---

[3] Some speakers instead pronounce 'to know' as *oqoón*. Also, the verb 'to say' is *orán* in Central and Benaadir Somali.

(70) *Prefixing vs. suffixing realis inflection - Simple Present*

	Prefixing 'come'	Suffixing 'fly away'
1SG	imaadaa	buubaa
2SG	timaadaa	buubtaa
3SG.M/K	yimaadaa	buubaa
3SG.F/T	timaadaa	buubtaa
1PL	nimaadaa	buubnaa
2PL	timaadaan	buubtaan
3PL	yimaadaan	buubaan

In prefixing verbs, 2SG, 3SG (both grammatical genders), and 1PL are encoded by a prefix. 2PL and 3PL are encoded by a similar prefix but also the plural suffix *-n* which is also found in suffixing verbs. Thus, the substantive difference between the two paradigms is that prefixing verbs take person marking via prefixation.

7.6.1 Realis contexts

7.6.1.1 Simple Present

The Simple Present is one context in which both prefixation and a change in the root vowel are observed. Prefixing verbs do not behave uniformly, however, as *oólli* 'to exist' and *aqóon* 'to know' optionally occur without their tense suffixes. Though these verbs take person marking via prefixation, they retain a slot in the verb template where person marking would otherwise be found in suffixing verbs. This is clear in that either the stem-final consonant lengthens or a consonant is inserted (e.g., in 'say,' where stem-final *h* cannot be lengthened) to fill the empty slot. As elsewhere, Simple Present verbs in the affirmative are toneless.

(71) *Simple Present prefixing verbs - affirmative*

	'say'	'come'	'exist'	'know'
1SG	idhaahdaa	imaaddaa	aal(laa)	aqaan(naa)
2SG/3SG.F	tidhaahdaa	timaaddaa	taal(laa)	taqaan(naa)
3SG.M	yidhaahdaa	yimaaddaa	yaal(laa)	yaqaan(naa)
1PL	nidhaahdaa	nimaaddaa	naal(laa)	naqaan(naa)
2PL	tidhaahdaan	timaaddaan	taal(laan)	taqaan(naan)
3PL	yidhaahdaan	yimaaddaan	yaal(laan)	yaqaan(naan)

The negative counterpart to the Simple Present for prefixing verbs is discussed in §7.6.2.1.

7.6.1.2 Present Progressive

Present Progressive prefixing verbs are inflected like the suffixing verbs in §7.5.1.2. They do not exhibit prefixation for number/grammatical gender in this context. Rather, they form an auxiliary-like construction composed of the main verb infinitive and the auxiliary *hay-* which is inflected for the Simple Present in the affirmative. The infinitive and auxiliary are prosodified as a single word.

(72) *Present Progressive prefixing verbs - affirmative*

	'saying'	'coming'	'existing'	'knowing'
1SG/3SG.M	odhánayaa	imánayaa	oólayaa	aqoónayaa
2SG/3SG.F	odhánaysaa	imánaysaa	oólaysaa	aqoónaysaa
1PL	odhánaynaa	imánaynaa	oólaynaa	aqoónaynaa
2PL	odhánaysaan	imánaysaan	oólaysaan	aqoónaysaan
3PL	odhánayaan	imánayaan	oólayaan	aqoónayaan

Negative forms of the Present Progressive for prefixing verbs are covered in §7.6.2.1.

7.6.1.3 Simple Past

Prefixing verbs in the Simple Past form a paradigm where inflection involves a combination of prefixation for number, stem vowel change, and suffixation. However, three of the four prefixing verbs vary in their use, or have fallen out of use for some speakers, in favor of another semantically-related suffixing verb. For example, i) *odhán* varies with *dháh* 'say'; ii) *oólli* varies with *jír* 'exist'; and iii) *aqoón* varies with a hybrid verb based on the adjective *óg* 'aware, knowing.' For more on hybrid verbs, see Section 7.11. For each of these, there is a suffixing paradigm based on a second verb stem. Even *imán* 'to come' has a second, suffixing paradigm, but its basis is the same stem.

The basic, prefixing inflectional paradigm for these verbs is in (73). For each verb, inflection for number and grammatical gender is accomplished by prefixation, along the lines of that introduced above in the Simple Present. 2PL and 3PL inflect for number by an additional *-n* plural suffix. The verbs are toneless.

(73) *Simple Past prefixing verbs - affirmative*

	'said'	'came'	'existed'	'knew'
1SG	idhi	imid	iil	iqiin
2SG/3SG.F	tidhi	timid	tiil	tiqiin
3SG.M	yidhi	yimid	yiil	yiqiin
1PL	nidhi	nimid	niil	niqiin
2PL	tidhaahdeen	timaaddeen	tiilleen	tiqiinneen
3PL	yidhaahdeen	yimaaddeen	yiilleen	yiqiinneen

The inflectional paradigm for the suffixing alternatives of these verbs shown in (74) and generally follows that of suffixing verbs in the Simple Past. The exception to this is 'to know,' whose inflectional paradigm is more akin to that of the irregular verbs *aháan* 'to be' and *laháan* 'to have.' Their behavior is discussed in §7.7.

(74) *Simple Past 'prefixing' verbs - affirmative suffixing forms*

	'said'	'came'	'existed'	'knew'
1SG	dhahay	imaaday	jiray	ogaa
2SG/3SG.F	dhahday	timaaday	jirtay	ogayd
3SG.M	dhahay	yimaaday	jiray	ogaa
1PL	dhahnay	nimaaday	jirnay	ogayn
2PL	dhahdeen	timaaddeen	jirteen	ogadeen
3PL	dhaheen	yimaaddeen	jireen	ogayeen

Simple Past verbs are not inflected for person, number, and gender in the negative. There is a single form with the suffix *-(i)n*. Person, number, and gender information is otherwise recoverable from subject pronouns. Negative Simple Past forms of basic prefixing verbs, and their alternative suffixing counterparts, are as follows in (75).

(75) *Simple Past prefixing verbs - negative*

	'didn't say'	'didn't come'	'didn't exist'	'didn't know'
all p/n/g	odhannín	imannín	oollín	aqoonín
	dhahín	imannín	jirín	ogáyn

7.6.1.4 Past Progressive

Past Progressive prefixing verbs are inflected in a way that is identical to the suffixing verbs in §7.5.1.4. They form an auxiliary-like construction with the auxiliary verb *hay-* that is inflected for the Simple Past. The main verb is in its infinitival form.

(76) *Past Progressive prefixing verbs - affirmative*

	'was saying'	'was coming'	'was existing'	'was knowing'
1SG/3SG.M	odhánayay	imánayay	oólayay	aqoónayay
2SG/3SG.F	odhánaysay	imánaysay	oólaysay	aqoónaysay
1PL	odhánaynay	imánaynay	oólaynay	aqoónaynay
2PL	odhánayseen	imánayseen	oólayseen	aqoónayseen
3PL	odhánayeen	imánayeen	oólayeen	aqoónayeen

These verbs are fully inflected in the affirmative, but these distinctions are collapsed into a single form in the negative, though there are two variants. As introduced above for suffixing verbs, my speakers from Mogadishu accept both variants, but they identify the shorter variant ending in *-éyn* as being characteristic of Northern Somali. Andrzejewski (1956) describes them as optional variants.

(77) *Past Progressive prefixing verbs - negative*

	'wasn't saying'	'wasn't coming'	'wasn't existing'	'wasn't knowing'
all p/n/g	*odhánéyn* or *odháneynín*	*imánéyn* or *imáneynín*	*oóléyn* or *oóleynín*	*aqoónéyn* or *aqoóneynín*

7.6.1.5 Emphatic Past

As introduced above for suffixing verbs, the Emphatic (or Independent) Past is mentioned in the literature. It seems to have fallen out of contemporary use, at least for the speakers that I have consulted. Reported forms for prefixing verbs resemble those in the Simple Past, though the suffixal paradigm that they take differs in the 2PL and 3PL. 'To exist' and 'to know' also take suffixes in addition to their person prefixes. All forms have a H tone, either on the verb stem or on the suffix in 2PL and 3PL forms.

(78) *Emphatic Past prefixing verbs*

	'said'	'came'	'existed'	'knew'
1SG	*ídhi*	*ímid*	*aállay*	*iqiínay*
2SG/3SG.F	*tídhi*	*tímid*	*taálay*	*tiqiínay*
3SG.M	*yídhi*	*yímid*	*yaálay*	*yiqiínay*
1PL	*nídhi*	*nímid*	*naálay*	*niqiínay*
2PL	*tidhaahdé*	*timaaddé*	*taallé*	*tiqiinné*
3PL	*yidhaahdé*	*yimaaddé*	*yaallé*	*yiqiinné*

7.6.2 Irrealis contexts

7.6.2.1 Simple Present Negative

Negative Simple Present verbs combine their prefixation for person with suffixation following the irrealis *-ó/-áan* paradigm. 'Exist' and 'know' obligatorily take suffixes here (unlike in the affirmative Simple Present in §7.6.1.1), and all suffixes have a H tone.

(79) *Present Simple prefixing verbs - negative*

	'say'	'come'	'exist'	'know'
1SG	idhaahdó	imaaddó	aalló	aqaannó
2SG	tidhaahdó or	timaaddó or	taalló or	taqaannó or
	tidhaahdíd	timaaddíd	taallíd	taqaanníd
3SG.M	yidhaahdó	yimaaddó	yaalló	yaqaannó
3SG.F	tidhaahdó	timaaddó	taalló	taqaannó
1PL	nidhaahnó	nimaadnó	naalló	naqaannó
2PL	tidhaahdáan	timaaddáan	taallíin	taqaanníin
3PL	yidhaahdáan	yimaaddáan	yaallíin	yaqaanníin

7.6.2.2 Present Progressive Negative

In negative contexts, there are short and long forms of the Present Progressive Negative that differ in whether the negative marker *má* joins the auxiliary verb or is found elsewhere in the clause. Along the lines introduced in §7.5.2.2, the short forms in (80) are used clause-finally in simple declarative statements.

(80) *Present Progressive prefixing verbs - negative (short form)*

	'not saying'	'not coming'	'not existing'	'not knowing'
1SG/3SG.M	odhán máayó	imán máayó	oólli máayó	aqoón máayo
2SG	odhán máaysó or	imán máaysó or	oólli máaysó or	aqoón máaysó or
	odhán máaysíd	imán máaysíd	oólli máaysíd	aqoón máaysíd
3SG.F	odhán máaysó	imán máaysó	oólli máaysó	aqoón máaysó
1PL	odhán máaynó	imán máaynó	oólli máaynó	aqoón máaynó
2PL	odhán máaysáan	imán máaysáan	oólli máaysáan	aqoón máaysáan
3PL	odhán máayáan	imán máayáan	oólli máayáan	aqoón máayáan

Likewise, the corresponding long forms in (81), in which negative *má* does not immediately precede the auxiliary, are used in non-clause-final instances.

(81) *Present Progressive prefixing verbs - negative (long form)*

1SG/3SG.M	odhánayó	imánayó	oólayó	aqoónayó
2SG	odhánaysó	imánaysó	oólaysó	aqoónaysó
	odhánaysíd	imánaysíd	oólaysíd	aqoónaysíd
3SG.F	odhánaysó	imánaysó	oólaysó	aqoónaysó
1PL	odhánaynó	imánaynó	oólaynó	aqoónaynó
2PL	odhánaysáan	imánaysáan	oólaysáan	aqoónaysáan
3PL	odhánayáan	imánayáan	oólayáan	aqoónayáan

7.6.2.3 Optative

Optative prefixing verbs are fully inflected in the affirmative with irrealis -o/-een suffixes, with the latter being found only in the 2PL and 3PL. Person and gender marking remain prefixal, and there is a H tone on the verb stem. These verbs are preceded in their clause by a subject marker clitic (see §10.2.1), or the clitic *ha* for all 3rd person forms.

(82) *Optative prefixing verbs - affirmative*

	'may X say'	'may X come'	'may X exist'	'may X know'
1SG	*idhaáhdo*	*imaáddo*	*aállo*	*aqaánno*
2SG/3SG.F	*tidhaáhdo*	*timaáddo*	*taállo*	*taqaánno*
3SG.M	*yidhaáhdo*	*yimaáddo*	*yaállo*	*yaqaánno*
1PL	*nidhaáhno*	*nimaánno*	*naállo*	*naqaánno*
2PL	*tidhaáhdeen*	*timaáddeen*	*taálleen*	*taqaánneen*
3PL	*yidhaáhdeen*	*yimaáddeen*	*yaálleen*	*yaqaánneen*

Optative verbs are not inflected for person, number, and gender in the negative. Rather, these verbs occur in their infinitive form. Person, number, and gender are recoverable from subject clitics. Negation itself is indicated by the clause type marker *yáan*.

7.6.3 Auxiliary constructions

7.6.3.1 Past Habitual

Prefixing verbs are inflected for the Past Habitual like the suffixing verbs in §7.5.3.1. They form a true auxiliary construction composed of the main verb infinitive and the auxiliary verb *jir-* inflected for the Simple Past. Here, and in other auxiliary constructions in this section, the infinitive and inflected auxiliary verb are prosodified separately as two words.

(83) *Past Habitual prefixing verbs - affirmative*

	'used to say'	'used to come'	'used to exist'	'used to know'
1SG/3SG.M	*odhán jiray*	*imán jiray*	*oólli jiray*	*aqoón jiray*
2SG/3SG.F	*odhán jirtay*	*imán jirtay*	*oólli jirtay*	*aqoón jirtay*
1PL	*odhán jirnay*	*imán jirnay*	*oólli jirnay*	*aqoón jirnay*
2PL	*odhán jirteen*	*imán jirteen*	*oólli jirteen*	*aqoón jirteen*
3PL	*odhán jireen*	*imán jireen*	*oólli jireen*	*aqoón jireen*

Past Habitual verbs do not inflect for person, number, and gender in the negative. There is a single form composed of the infinitive of the main verb followed by a negatively inflected form of the auxiliary verb.

(84) *Past Habitual prefixing verbs - negative*

	'didn't ... say'	'didn't ... come'	'didn't ... exist'	'didn't ... know'
all p/n/g	odhán jirín	imán jirín	oólli jirín	aqoón jirín

7.6.3.2 Conditional

Conditional mood prefixing verbs are formed by the same mechanism found in suffixing verbs in §7.5.3.2. Affirmative forms involve an auxiliary construction with the infinitive of the main verb and the auxiliary verb *leh-* inflected for the Simple Past.

(85) *Conditional prefixing verbs - affirmative*

	'would say'	'would come'	'would exist'	'would know'
1SG/3SG.M	odhán lahaa	imán lahaa	oólli lahaa	aqoón lahaa
2SG/3SG.F	odhán lahayd	imán lahayd	oólli lahayd	aqoón lahayd
1PL	odhán lahayn	imán lahayn	oólli lahayn	aqoón lahayn
2PL	odhán lahaydeen	imán lahaydeen	oólli lahaydeen	aqoón lahaydeen
3PL	odhán lahayeen	imán lahayeen	oólli lahayeen	aqoón lahayeen

Negative conditional prefixing verbs have a single form for all person, number, and grammatical gender combinations.

(86) *Conditional prefixing verbs - negative*

	'wouldn't ... say'	'wouldn't ... come'	'wouldn't ... exist'	'wouldn't ... know'
all p/n/g	odhán laháyn	imán laháyn	oólli laháyn	aqoón laháyn

7.6.3.3 Future

Forming the Future for prefixing verbs follows the same strategy used for suffixing verbs in §7.5.3.3. The infinitive of the main verb is followed by the auxiliary verb *doon-* that is fully inflected for person, number, and gender in the Simple Present.

(87) *Future prefixing verbs - affirmative*

	'will say'	'will come'	'will exist'	'will know'
1SG/3SG.M	odhán doonaa	imán doonaa	oólli doonaa	aqoón doonaa
2SG/3SG.F	odhán doontaa	imán doontaa	oólli doontaa	aqoón doontaa
1PL	odhán doonnaa	imán doonnaa	oólli doonnaa	aqoón doonnaa
2PL	odhán doontaan	imán doontaan	oólli doontaan	aqoón doontaan
3PL	odhán doonaan	imán doonaan	oólli doonaan	aqoón doonaan

Negative forms in this mood consist of the main verb infinitive followed by the same auxiliary, but the auxiliary is inflected with the irrealis inflectional paradigm, including a H tone.

(88) *Future prefixing verbs - negative*

	'won't say'	'won't come'	'won't exist'	'won't know'
1SG/3SG.M	odhán doonó	imán doonó	oólli doonó	aqoón doonó
2SG	odhán doontó or odhán doontíd	imán doontó or imán doontíd	oólli doontó or oólli doontíd	aqoón doontó or aqoón doontíd
3SG.F	odhán doontó	imán doontó	oólli doontó	aqoón doontó
1PL	odhán doonnó	imán doonnó	oólli doonnó	aqoón doonnó
2PL	odhán doontáan	imán doontáan	oólli doontáan	aqoón doontáan
3PL	odhán doonáan	imán doonáan	oólli doonáan	aqoón doonáan

7.6.4 Other moods

7.6.4.1 Imperative

Imperative mood verbs inflect for plural number via the suffix *-a*, but they do not inflect for person and gender. In addition to the typical Imperative form for 'come,' there is another defective form that is used in the affirmative, but not in the negative.

(89) *Imperative prefixing verbs - affirmative*

	'say!'	'come!'	'be!'	'know!'
SG	dhéh	imów / kaálay	óol	aqóow
PL	dháha	imaáda / kaálaya	oólla	aqoóda

In the negative, singular verbs take the suffix *-ín*, and plurals add the *-a* suffix mentioned above. H tone is on the stem in both the singular and plural. Negative imperative verbs are also preceded in their clause by the clause type marker *ha*.

(90) *Imperative prefixing verbs - negative*

	'don't say!'	'don't come!'	'don't be!'	'don't know!'
SG	odhanín	imanín	oollín	aqoonín
PL	odhanína	imanína	oollína	aqoonína

7.6.4.2 Potential

Potential prefixing verbs are formed by prefixation for person/gender and suffixation by *-ee(n)*, with the final *-n* being attributed to plural number and occurring only in the 2PL and 3PL. These verbs may also occur in a clause preceded by the clause type marker *shów* (or its variant *sów*). These verb are toneless.

(91) *Potential prefixing verbs - affirmative*

	'perhaps ... say'	'perhaps ... come'	'perhaps ... be'	'perhaps ... know'
1SG	idhaahdee	imaaddee	aallee	aqaanee
2SG/3SG.F	tidhaahdee	timaaddee	taallee	taqaanee
3SG.M	yidhaahdee	yimaaddee	yaallee	yaqaanee
1PL	nidhaahnee	nimaaddee	naallee	naqaanee
2PL	tidhaahdeen	timaaddeen	taalleen	taqaaneen
3PL	yidhaahdeen	yimaaddeen	yaalleen	yaqaaneen

Negative forms of the Potential take the same *-éen* suffix in all person, number, and gender combinations. Person and grammatical gender, in particular, are still encoded via prefixes.

(92) *Potential prefixing verbs - negative*

	'wouldn't say'	'wouldn't come'	'wouldn't exist'	'wouldn't know'
1SG	idhaahdéen	imaadéen	oolléen	oqoodéen
2SG/3SG.F/2PL	tidhaahdéen	timaadéen	taalléen	oqootéen
3SG.M/3PL	yidhaahdéen	yimaadéen	yaalléen	oqoodéen
1PL	nidhaahdéen	nimaadéen	naalléen	oqoonnéen

7.7 Irregular verbs

There are two closely related irregular verbs, *ahaán* 'to be' and *lahaán* 'to have,' that share many inflectional similarities with root-changing verbs but have properties that merit their being treating separately from other verbs. To this, one might also add *la'aán* 'to lack,' which generally behaves like 'to be' and 'to have.' 'To have' and 'to lack' are derived from 'to be,' as they are formed by inflected forms of 'to be' to which *leh-* or *la'* are added. This section covers the behavior of 'to be' and 'to have,' which behave in a particularly irregular way in relative clauses. For more on this, see §14.1.5.

7.7.1 Realis contexts

7.7.1.1 Simple Present and Present Progressive

The Simple Present of *ahaán* 'to be' is inflected like other prefixing verbs. These verbs are toneless. Comparable forms for *lahaán* 'to have' look like a quasi-auxiliary construction in that a static form of this verb, *lée-*, is added to an inflected form of 'to be.' The corresponding Present Progressive is also formed by an auxiliary-like construction composed of the main verb infinitive followed by the auxiliary verb *hay-* inflected for the Simple Present where the two are prosodified as a single word.

(93) *Present tense irregular verbs - affirmative*

	'am/are'	'have'	'am/are being'	'am/are having'
1SG	ahay	léeyahay	ahaánayaa	lahaánayaa
2SG/3SG.F	tahay	léedahay	ahaánaysaa	lahaánaysaa
3SG.M	yahay	léeyahay	ahaánayaa	lahaánayaa
1PL	nahay	léenahay	ahaánaynaa	lahaánaynaa
2PL	tihiin	léedihiin	ahaánaysaan	lahaánaysaan
3PL	yihiin	léeyihiin	ahaánayaan	lahaánayaan

The negative counterparts to these verb contexts are discussed separately in Sections 7.7.2.1 and 7.7.2.2, respectively.

7.7.1.2 Simple Past and Past Progressive

Inflection for the Simple Past affirmative for 'to be' and 'to have' is unique. One finds neither the tense suffix seen in suffixing verbs, nor the person/gender prefixes seen in prefixing verbs. Rather, inflection for person, number, and grammatical gender is suffixal. Corresponding progressive forms, however, are more prototypical. They are, as elsewhere, formed by an auxiliary-like construction involving *hay-* fully inflected for the Simple Past.

(94) *Simple Past and Past Progressive irregular verbs - affirmative*

	'was/were'	'had'	'was/were being'	'was/were having'
1SG/3SG.M	ahaa	lahaa	ahaánayay	lahaánayay
2SG/3SG.F	ahayd	lahayd	ahaánaysay	lahaánaysay
1PL	ahayn	lahayn	ahaánaynay	lahaánaynay
2PL	ahaydeen	lahaydeen	ahaánayseen	lahaánayseen
3PL	ahaayeen	lahaayeen	ahaánayeen	lahaánayeen

Full inflection is lost in the negative. For the Simple Past, the forms are *aháyn* and *laháyn*. In the Past Progressive, they are *aháyneýn/aháynaynín* 'not being' and *laháyneýn/laháynaynín* 'not having.' The same dialectal distribution (or preference) pertaining to short vs. long forms applies here as well.

7.7.2 Irrealis contexts

7.7.2.1 Simple Present Negative

Simple Present irregular verbs in the negative are inflected for person and number, though there is only one third person form for both genders and for singular and plural number. Alternate pronunciations in which vowels within the verb stem alternate to match that of the suffix are also listed. Third person forms are particularly irregular in that they may consist only of the verb stem itself.

(95) *Simple Present irregular verbs - negative*

	'am/are not'	'don't have'
1SG	ahí/ihí	lehí/lihí
2SG	ahíd/ihíd	lehíd/lihíd
3SG.M/3SG.F/3PL	ahá/áh	lahá/léh
1PL	ahín/ihín	lehín/lihín
2PL	ahidín/ihidín	lehidín/lihidín

7.7.2.2 Present Progressive Negative

The Present Progressive Negative of irregular verbs follows a pattern similar to that found in other verbs. It is formed by an auxiliary-like construction with *hay-*, but there are two forms, short and long, whose use differs by context (see discussion above in §7.5.2.2). For the short forms in (96), the negative marker *má* is prefixed onto the inflected auxiliary verb.

(96) *Present Progressive Negative irregular verbs - short form*

	'not being'	'not having'
1SG/3SG.M	ahaán máayó	lahaán máayó
2SG	ahaán máaysó or	lahaán máaysó or
	ahaán máaysíd	lahaán máaysíd
3SG.F	ahaán máaysó	lahaán máaysó
1PL	ahaán máaynó	lahaán máaynó
2PL	ahaán máaysáan	lahaán máaysáan
3PL	ahaán máayáan	lahaán máayáan

For the long forms in (97), the negative marker occurs earlier in the clause, rather than directly preceding the auxiliary verb. Though there are two options, both follow regular inflectional patterns seen elsewhere.

(97) *Present Progressive Negative irregular verbs - long form*

	'not being'	'not having'
1SG/3SG.M	*ahaánayó*	*lahaánayó*
2SG	*ahaánaysó* or *ahaánaysíd*	*lahaánaysó* or *lahaánaysíd*
3SG.F	*ahaánaysó*	*lahaánaysó*
1PL	*ahaánaynó*	*lahaánaynó*
2PL	*ahaánaysáan*	*lahaánaysáan*
3PL	*ahaánayáan*	*lahaánayáan*

7.7.2.3 Optative

Irregular verbs in the Optative are fully inflected for person/number/gender just as in other verbs. They involve suffixation of *-o/-een* and the verbs are preceded in their clause (though not always immediately) by a subject pronoun clitic. H tone is on the stem.

(98) *Optative irregular verbs - affirmative*

	'may X be'	'may X have'
1SG/3SG.M	*ahaádo*	*lahaádo*
2SG/3SG.F	*ahaáto*	*lahaáto*
1PL	*ahaáno*	*lahaáno*
2PL	*ahaáteen*	*lahaáteen*
3PL	*ahaádeen*	*lahaádeen*

These verbs are not fully inflected for person/number/gender in the negative. There is a single form for each – *ahaannín* 'may X not be!' and *lahaannín* 'may X not have!' – with other agreement information recoverable from subject pronouns. The verbs are also preceded in their clause by the clause type marker *yáan*.

7.7.3 Auxiliary constructions

7.7.3.1 Past Habitual

The irregular verbs form their Past Habitual by an auxiliary construction with the main verb infinitive and *jir-* fully inflected for the Simple Past. In the negative, there is a single form for all person/number/gender combinations.

(99) *Past Habitual irregular verbs*

	'used to be'	'used to have'
1SG/3SG.M	ahaán jiray	lahaán jiray
2SG/3SG.F	ahaán jirtay	lahaán jirtay
1PL	ahaán jirnay	lahaán jirnay
2PL	ahaán jirteen	lahaán jirteen
3PL	ahaán jireen	lahaán jireen
	'didn't used to be'	'didn't used to have'
all p/n/g	ahaán jirín	lahaán jirín

7.7.3.2 Conditional

Irregular verbs form their Conditionals like other verbs. In the affirmative, this is via an auxiliary construction with the Past Simple of *leh-*. There is only a single form of the negative conditional for each verb.

(100) *Conditional irregular verbs - affirmative*

	'would ... be'	'would ... have'
1SG/3SG.M	ahaán lahaa	lahaán lahaa
2SG/3SG.F	ahaán lahayd	lahaán lahayd
1PL	ahaán lahayn	lahaán lahayn
2PL	ahaán lahaydeen	lahaán lahaydeen
3PL	ahaán lahaayeen	lahaán lahaayeen

(101) *Conditional irregular verbs - negative*

	'wouldn't ... be'	'wouldn't ... have'
all p/n/g	ahaán laháyn	lahaán laháyn

7.7.3.3 Future

To form the Future of irregular verbs, the language follows the same strategy as in all other verbs. In the affirmative, this involves an auxiliary construction with the main verb infinitive and the Simple Present of the auxiliary verb *doon-* seen in §7.5.3.3. Likewise, for the negative, the auxiliary verb is inflected for the Simple Present Negative, as seen in §7.5.2.1.

(102) *Future irregular verbs*

	'will be'	'will have'	'won't be'	'won't have'
1SG/3SG.M	ahaán doonaa	lahaán doonaa	ahaán doonó	lahaán doonó
2SG	ahaán doontaa	lahaán doontaa	ahaán doontó or ahaán doontíd	lahaán doontó or lahaán doontíd
3SG.F	ahaán doontaa	lahaán doontaa	ahaán doontó	lahaán doontó
1PL	ahaán doonnaa	lahaán doonnaa	ahaán doonnó	lahaán doonnó
2PL	ahaán doontaan	lahaán doontaan	ahaán doontáan	lahaán doontáan
3PL	ahaán doonaan	lahaán doonaan	ahaán doonáan	lahaán doonáan

7.7.4 Other moods

7.7.4.1 Imperative

The Imperative of irregular verbs bears a resemblance to other verbs. In the affirmative singular, these verbs look like prefixing verbs. In the negative, their structure is even more general, simply taking *-ín*. Both the affirmative and negative are inflected for plural number by the addition of the suffix *-a*.

(103) *Imperative irregular verbs*

	'be!'	'have!'	'don't be'	'don't have'
SG	aháw	laháw	ahaannín	lahaannín
PL	ahaáda	lahaáda	ahaannína	lahaannína

7.7.4.2 Potential

Irregular verbs are inflected fully for person, number, and grammatical gender in the Potential and also take *-ee(n)*, to which the nasal suffix in parentheses is added in the 2PL and 3PL. For the Potential Negative, person and grammatical gender marking are maintained, and all forms take the same suffix *-eén*.

(104) *Potential irregular verbs - affirmative*

	'perhaps ... be'	'perhaps ... have'
1SG/3SG.M	ahaadee	lahaadee
2SG/3SG.F	ahaatee	lahaatee
1PL	ahaanee	lahaanee
2PL	ahaateen	lahaateen
3PL	ahaadeen	lahaadeen

(105) *Potential irregular verbs - negative*

	'wouldn't be'	'wouldn't have'
1SG/3SG.M/3PL	ahaadeén	lahaadeén
2SG/3SG.F/2PL	ahaateén	lahaateén
1PL	ahaaneén	lahaaneén

7.8 Reduced agreement

There are two conditions under which verbs lose the ability to inflect fully for person, number, and grammatical gender agreement. These are: i) when the verb is in a main clause whose subject is morphologically marked as in focus; and ii) when the verb is in a subject relative clause. In these instances, a verb instead exhibits *reduced agreement* meaning that it inflects only for a subset of the aforementioned categories. Some works, like Saeed (1999) and Banti (2011b), have called this phenomenon "reduced paradigm inflection," but this is somewhat misleading. While the inflectional paradigm is the same, it is simply the number of distinctions made that is reduced.[4] This section first discusses reduced agreement in prefixing and suffixing verbs before turning to irregular verbs, whose behavior diverges markedly from others.

7.8.1 Prefixing and suffixing verbs

In an attempt to begin with a fairly simple comparison of 'full' vs. 'reduced' agreement, consider the verbs in Table (106). This table shows Simple Present verbs as they occur in subject and object relative clauses, and particularly in relative clauses whose head is not the subject of the main clause verb. In this particular configuration, the verbs follow two different inflectional paradigms, with verbs in object relative clauses taking the *irrealis* paradigm and those in subject relative clauses taking a truncated form of the *realis* paradigm that is unique to the Simple Present and other contexts derived from it. In both instances, the verbs bear H tone on their suffix. What is more important here is that object relative clause verbs require full agreement within its inflectional paradigm, while subject relative clause verbs instead require reduced agreement.

---

[4] Others have called it the "restrictive paradigm" (Ajello 1984; Andrzejewski 1968, 1975; Antinucci and Puglielli 1984; Frascarelli and Puglielli 2003; Hayward and Saeed 1984; Lecarme 1995), "partial agreement" (Antinucci and Puglielli 1980), and the "convergent paradigm" (Andrzejewski 1968).

(106) *Agreement in relative clause verbs - main clause object*

	Object RC (full agreement)	Subject RC (reduced agreement)
1SG	qodó	qodá
2SG	qoddó	qodá
3SG.M	qodó	qodá
3SG.F	qoddó	qoddá
1PL	qodnó	qodná
2PL	qoddáan	qodá
3PL	qodáan	qodá

Table (107) shows these same verbs as they occur in subject and object relative clauses whose head noun is the main clause subject. In this configuration, all relative clause verbs are inflected for the *realis* paradigm and are toneless. However, subject relative clause verbs once again take reduced agreement while object relative clause verbs again take full agreement. Thus, the requirement for reduced agreement in subject relative clause verbs holds in all instances.

(107) *Agreement in relative clause verbs - main clause subject*

	Object RC (full agreement)	Subject RC (reduced agreement)
1SG	qodaa	qodaa
2SG	qoddaa	qodaa
3SG.M	qodaa	qodaa
3SG.F	qoddaa	qoddaa
1PL	qodnaa	qodnaa
2PL	qoddaan	qodaa
3PL	qodaan	qodaa

Reduced agreement is also required on main clause verbs whose subject is morphologically marked as in focus. These reduced agreement verbs under subject focus bear H tone.

The full vs. reduced agreement patterns shown thus far for suffixing verbs are equally applicable to prefixing verbs, with one slight adjustment. In full agreement contexts, suffixing verbs make a five-way inflectional distinction for person, number, grammatical gender combinations. These verbs collapse person, number, gender distinctions in favor of the 1SG/3SG.M form, except in the 3SG.F and 1PL, which retain the same inflectional suffixes found elsewhere. Prefixing verbs instead make a six-way distinction under reduced agreement. The generalization is much the same as for prefixing verbs, though 1SG additionally retains a unique form. For the sake of comparison, Table (108) shows suffixing and prefixing verb paradigms alongside one another. These particular verb forms are found in object (Full) and subject (Reduced) relative clauses whose head noun is not a main clause subject.

(108) *'Full' vs. 'reduced' agreement in suffixing vs. prefixing verbs*

	Suffixing		Prefixing	
	Full	Reduced	Full	Reduced
1SG	qodó	qodá	imaaddó	imaaddá
2SG	qoddó	qodá	timaaddó	yimaaddá
3SG.M	qodó	qodá	yimaaddó	yimaaddá
3SG.F	qoddó	qoddá	timaaddó	timaaddá
1PL	qodnó	qodná	nimaadnó	nimaadná
2PL	qoddáan	qodá	timaaddáan	yimaaddá
3PL	qodáan	qodá	yimaaddáan	yimaaddá

In order to contextualize these possibilities, first consider the verbs in (109) and (110). Both examples contain a main clause verb whose subject is in focus. As expected of subject focus, the verbs exhibit H tone and take reduced agreement.

(109) *Xanúun báa i   hayá.*
      xanuun baa i   hay-a
      pain   FOC 1SG.OBJ hold-PRES.RED

'I am in pain.' i.e., 'Pain is on me.' (Z & O: 298)

(110) *Wáxaa dábkii   shidaý   nimánkii.*
      waxaa dab-kii   shid-ay   nim-an-kii
      FOC   fire-K.RDEF start-PST.RED man-PL-K.RDEF

'The men started the fire.' (Z & I: 180)

Example (111) contains a subject relative clause that is the subject of the main clause. The subject is not in focus. Thus, the finite relative clause verb is toneless (though the stem is toned, as expected in the progressive) and exhibits reduced agreement – *keénayaa*, rather than *keénayaan*. As elsewhere, relative clauses are offset by square brackets.

(111) *Nimánka   [keénayaa]   waa askár.*
      nim-an=ka   keen-ay-aa   waa askar
      man-PL=K.DEF bring-PROG-PRES.RED   DEC soldier

'The men who are bringing it are soldiers.'

Example (112) also contains a subject relative clause that is the subject of the main clause verb. Here, however, the subject noun phrase containing the relative clause is in focus. The relative clause verb requires H tone on its suffix (as well as on the stem, as this too is a progressive verb) and it also requires reduced agreement. The main clause verb is also accordingly toned and exhibits reduced agreement due to the subject focus condition.

(112) *Naagáha*   *[imánayá]*   *báa raáci*
naag-a=ha   iman-ay-a   baa raac-i
woman-PL=K.DEF come-PROG-PRES.RED FOC accompany-INF
dooná.
doon-a
FUT-PRES.RED

'The women who are coming will accompany them.' (Orwin 1995: 192)

Examples (113) and (114) each have a subject relative clause, but their head is not the subject of the main clause verb. As such, the relative clause verb is toned and exhibits reduced agreement. The inflectional behavior of these relative clause verbs and that of the relative clause verb in (112) are identical.

(113) *Nimánka*   *[keénayá]*   *ma aragtay?*
nim-an=ka   keen-ay-a   ma arag-t-ay
man-PL=K.DEF bring-PROG-PRES.RED QM see-2SG-PST

'Have you seen the men who are bringing it?'

(114) *Ma igú*   *toosín*   *kartaa*   *dukáan [iibiyá*
ma i=gu   toos-in   kar-t-aa   dukaan iib-i-ya
QM 1SG.OBJ=to direct-INF be.able-2SG-PRES store   sell-WCAUS-PRES.RED
sháah]?
shaah
tea

'Can you direct me to a store [that sells tea]?' (Z & O: 639)

These examples show that reduced agreement applies to any main clause verb under subject focus, as well as to any subject relative clause verb. Main clause verbs that are not under subject focus and verbs in object relative clauses require full agreement. Full agreement forms are covered in §7.5. Further discussion concerning the inflectional distinctions between subject and object relative clauses is in §7.9.

7.8.2 Irregular verbs

The same principles concerning the distribution of full vs. reduced agreement defined above for prefixing and suffixing verbs also generally apply to irregular verbs. That said, there is a difference in the behavior of Simple Past vs. Simple Present contexts. The reduced agreement forms of Simple Past irregular verbs (found with subject focus and in subject relative clauses) are shown in (115). The verbs in this table are further sub-divided into their toned vs. toneless forms, for comparison. They behave much like the verbs discussed just above in §7.8.1.

(115)   *Reduced agreement irregular verbs - Simple Past*

	'be'		'have'	
	Toned	Toneless	Toned	Toneless
1SG, 2SG, 3SG.M, 2PL, 3PL	*ahaá*	*ahaa*	*lahaá*	*lahaa*
3SG.F	*ahaýd*	*ahayd*	*laháyd*	*lahayd*
1PL	*ahaýn*	*ahayn*	*laháyn*	*lahayn*

In the Simple Present, the irregular nature of these verbs reveals itself. Rather than reducing to the three-way inflectional distinction seen in (115), these verbs further collapse onto a single value. This is *áh* for 'be' and *léh* for 'have.'

Example (116) shows such an outcome for a Simple Present irregular verb in a subject relative clause and (117) for a main clause verb under subject focus.

(116)   *Kóob [sháah áh]   báad   rabtaa.*
koob shaah ah   b=aad   rab-t-aa
cup tea   be.PRES.RED FOC=2SG want-2SG-PRES
'You want a cup of tea.' (S93: 300)

(117)   *Soomaalíya iyo Somaliland ayáa máanta kúlan   kú léh*
Soomaaliya iyo Somaliland ayaa maanta kulan   ku leh
Somalia   and Somaliland FOC   today meeting in have.PRES.RED
magaaláda Jabuutí.
maagala=da Jabuuti
city-T.DEF Djibouti
'Somalia and Somaliland have a meeting today in Djibouti city.' (fposts: 113)

These irregular Simple Present verbs are also unique in that they can be morphologically subject marked. They lose their H tone and take the subject marker *-i*, being realized *ahi* and *lehi*, though some speakers may pronounce them *ihi* and *lihi*, respectively. Subject-marked irregular verbs in relative clauses are shown in (118) and (119).

(118)   *Habéen báa ... nín [socóta ahi]   ú yimid.*
habeen baa ... nin socota ah-i   u y-imid
night FOC ... man traveler be.PRES.RED-SUBJ to 3SG.M-come.PST
'One night...a traveling man came.' (Z & I: 371)

(119) *Wáxa mahád [kú lehi]*   *labáda   muwaadín ee*
       waxa mahad ku   leh=i   laba=da   muwaadin ee
       FOC thanks to have.PRES.RED=SUBJ   two=T.DEF citizens   REL
       [qorbajóogta   áh]   ...
       qorbajoog=ta   ah
       living.abroad=T.DEF   be.PRES.RED

'Thanks are given to two citizens living abroad...' (somaliland.org: 11655)

7.9 Subordinate clause verbs

Subordinate clause verbs are those that occur in complement clauses, adverbial clauses, and relative clauses. Subordinate clause verbs, as a class, behave differently from main clause verbs, particularly in terms of their tonal and segmental morphology. Some subordinate clause verbs (e.g., Simple Present and Present Progressive) require a different inflectional paradigm than their corresponding main clause verbs do. Others (e.g., Simple Past) differ tonally but not segmentally from their main clause counterpart. Generally speaking, subordinate clause verbs are tonal while main clause verbs are toneless.

One challenge to describing the morphological behavior of subordinate clause verbs is that the morphology that they require depends on two additional factors. First, if a subordinate clause is the subject of the main clause verb, its verb behaves in a way that morphologically resembles a main clause verb. In addition, if the subordinate clause verb is in a subject relative clause, it requires reduced agreement. This requirement holds whether the head of such a subject relative clause is also the subject of the main clause verb or not. The conditions on reduced agreement and verb forms attributed to it were discussed above in §7.8.

In order to describe their properties, subordinate clause verbs are divided below into two groups. In the remainder of this section, the focus is primarily on the behavior of verbs in complement clauses, adverbial clauses, and object relative clauses. The inflectional properties of subject relative clause verbs will be only briefly summarized, as they were discussed in detail in §7.8 relative to their requirement for reduced agreement.

7.9.1 Complement, adverbial, and object relative clauses

Subordinate clause verbs, generally speaking, are inflected for a different paradigm than are main clause verbs. For some tense, aspect, mood, and polarity contexts, the only distinction between the two paradigms is tonal. For others, the distinction is both tonal and segmental. Inflection for present tense verbs, in particular, is markedly different in main vs. subordinate clauses. A key distinction can also be made between the basic behavior of subordinate clause verb vs. that seen when the subordinate clause functions as the subject of a main clause.

To demonstrate their basic behavior, compare the sentences in (120) and (121), adapted from Saeed (1999, p. 224). The first of these shows a complement clause that is the object of the main clause verb. This complement clause verb requires irrealis paradigm inflection, taking the H toned suffix *-ó*. The second example contains a nearly identical complement clause that is instead the subject of the main clause. Here, the present progressive complement clause verb looks no different from a typical main clause verb. It exhibits the same toneless realis paradigm *-aa* suffix that would be found on a main clause verb. The complement clauses are indicated by square brackets.

(120) *[Ínuu imánayó] ayáan ógahay.*
 in=uu ∅-iman-ay-o ay=aan og-∅-ah-ay
 COMP=3SG.M 3SG.M-come-PROG-IRR FOC=1SG aware-1SG-be-PRES
 'I know that he is coming.'

(121) *[Ínuu imánayaa] waa hubáal.*
 in=uu ∅-iman-ay-aa waa hubaal
 COMP=3SG.M 3SG.M-come-PROG-PRES DEC certainty
 'That he is coming is certain.'

Thus far, the *-ó/-áan* inflectional paradigm found in subordinate clauses like these has been described as related to irrealis modality, broadly construed. The reason for this is because this paradigm (though sometimes with a slight difference in vowel quality) is also required on main clause verbs in the Simple Present Negative, Present Progressive Negative, and the Future Negative. A closely related, though non-tonal, inflectional paradigm is found in the formation of Optative verbs. Each of these contexts bears a relationship to irrealis modality in that the action or state that they encode is somehow yet unrealized or inferential from the standpoint of the speaker. The same logic might be extensible to subordinate clauses. Past tense subordinate clause verbs do not exhibit the same segmental paradigm, though they do exhibit H tone.

In (120), the main clause verb encodes an expression of certainty, but the action expressed by the subordinate clause verb is yet to be realized. When such a clause is the subject in a main clause, however, its verb exhibits the same inflectional behavior (both segmentally and tonally) as do most main clause verbs. Such alternations suggest a possible connection in Somali between subjecthood and givenness or perhaps factuality, which appears to align itself with the use of an inflectional paradigm that is otherwise associated with verbs in the indicative or declarative mood (i.e., realis, broadly construed). There is indeed a rich and complex literature on the matter of "realis" vs. "irrealis" modalities. Scholars have debated even the suitability of the terms themselves, the ways that the two supposed modalities can be subdivided into finer-grained categories, and the distribution of phenomena attributed to the distinction between them. See, for example, Bybee (1998), Elliott (2000), Givón (1994), and Mithun (1995), among many others. Furthermore, Somali is not alone in the complex ways that it employs its realis vs. irrealis marking on verbs in subject vs. object subordinate clauses, respectively. For more on this, see discussion in Mauri and Sansò (2012, 2016).

Though the matter deserves a great deal more inquiry, it is important here to note that the alternation between these two inflectional paradigms has traditionally been considered in the Somali literature to be a reflex of morphological subject marking (see §9.2). If this is true, it would differ markedly from other exponential realizations of subject marking in the language. With this in mind, I have suggested that realis vs. irrealis is perhaps a better way to conceive of this phenomenon, though whether it is the *best* way to do so deserves further consideration.

7.9.2 Suffixing verbs

Simple Present and Present Progressive verbs in the subordinate clauses discussed in this section exhibit the realis inflectional paradigm if their clause is the subject of the main clause. Otherwise, they exhibit irrealis *-ó/-áan* inflection. Full inflectional agreement is required in both instances. These distinctions are shown in (122) for the Simple Present and in (123) for the Present Progressive.

(122) *Subordinate clause inflection - Simple Present - 'fly'*

	Main Clause Subject	Main Clause Object
1SG/3SG.M	buubaa	buubó
2SG	buubtaa	buubtó or buubtíd
3SG.F	buubtaa	buubtó
1PL	buubnaa	buubnó
2PL	buubtaan	buubtáan
3PL	buubaan	buubáan

(123) *Subordinate clause inflection - Present Progressive - 'flying'*

	Main Clause Subject	Main Clause Object
1SG/3SG.M	buúbayaa	buúbayó
2SG	buúbaysaa	buúbaysó or buúbaysíd
3SG.F	buúbaysaa	buúbaysó
1PL	buúbaynaa	buúbaynó
2PL	buúbaysaan	buúbaysáan
3PL	buúbayaan	buúbayáan

Examples (120) and (121) above illustrated this subject vs. non-subject distinction for complement clause verbs. Example (124) shows an additional example in which the Present Progressive form of the verb 'eat' in a subordinate clause introduced by a subordinating conjunction takes irrealis paradigm inflection.

(124) *Márkaan wáx cúnayó,   caanó báan   cabbaa.*
mark=aan wax cun-ay-o   caano b=aan   cabb-∅-aa
time=1SG thing eat-PROG-1SG.IRR milk FOC=1SG drink-1SG-PRES
'When I eat, I drink milk.' (Z & I: 166)

Verbs in certain other contexts do not make such a marked distinction between main and subordinate clauses. In the Simple Past, for example, both subject and object subordinate clause forms are segmentally identical to their main clause counterparts. However, object subordinate clauses have a final H tone, while subject forms are toneless. This is seen in (125).

(125) *Subordinate clause inflection - Simple Past*

	Main Clause Subject	Main Clause Object
1SG/3SG.M	buubay	buubaý
2SG/3SG.F	buubtay	buubtaý
1PL	buubnay	buubnaý
2PL	buubteen	buubtéen
3PL	buubeen	buubéen

Example (126) shows a Simple Past verb introduced by the same subordinating conjunction as the verb in (124). The subordinate clause is not the subject of the main clause verb and accordingly takes *tageý*, rather than toneless *tagey*.

(126) *Márkaan tageý,   búu   dhintey.*
mark=aan tag-∅-ey   b=uu   dhin-t-∅-ey
time=1SG go-1SG-PST FOC=3SG.M die-MID-3SG.M-PST
'When I left, he died.' (Z & I: 163)

7.9.3 Prefixing verbs

The same principles defined above for suffixing verbs also apply to Somali's four prefixing verbs. In the Simple Present and Present Progressive, these verbs exhibit full agreement for the irrealis -*ó*/-*áan* inflectional paradigm when they occur in a subordinate clause that is not the main clause subject. The verbs in (127) and (128) represent these forms.

(127) *Simple Present prefixing verbs in subordinate clauses*

	'say'	'come'	'exist'	'know'
1SG	*idhaahdó*	*imaaddó*	*aalló*	*aqaannó*
2SG	*tidhaahdó* or *tidhaahdíd*	*timaaddó* or *timaaddíd*	*taalló* or *taallíd*	*taqaannó* or *taqaanníd*
3SG.M	*yidhaahdó*	*yimaaddó*	*yaalló*	*yaqaannó*
3SG.F	*tidhaahdó*	*timaaddó*	*taalló*	*taqaannó*
1PL	*nidhaahnó*	*nimaadnó*	*naalló*	*naqaannó*
2PL	*tidhaahdáan*	*timaaddáan*	*taalláan*	*taqaannáan*
3PL	*yidhaahdáan*	*yimaaddáan*	*yaalláan*	*yaqaannáan*

(128) *Present Progressive prefixing verbs in subordinate clauses*

	'saying'	'coming'	'existing'	'knowing'
1SG/3SG.M	*odhánayó*	*imánayó*	*oóllayó*	*aqoónayó*
2SG	*odhánaysó* or *odhánaysíd*	*imánaysó* or *imánaysíd*	*oólaysó* or *oólaysíd*	*aqoónaysó* or *aqoónaysíd*
3SG.F	*odhánaysó*	*imánaysó*	*oólaysó*	*aqoónaysó*
1PL	*odhánaynó*	*imánaynó*	*oólaynó*	*aqoónaynó*
2PL	*odhánaysáan*	*imánaysáan*	*oólaysáan*	*aqoónaysáan*
3PL	*odhánayáan*	*imánayáan*	*oólayáan*	*aqoónayáan*

Example (129) shows an instance of a Present Progressive prefixing verb being used in a clause introduced by the subordinating conjunction *iláa* 'until.'

(129) Iláa aan ká   imánayó,   hálkán jóog!
      ilaa aan ka   iman-ay-∅-o   halkan joog
      until 1SG from come-PROG-1SG-IRR   here   stay.IMP
      'Until I am back, stay here!' (S93: 329)

When Simple Present and Present Progressive verbs appear instead in a subordinate clause that is a main clause subject, their suffixes are toneless, and they they are inflected fully for the realis paradigm. As such, these verbs are identical to their main clause counterparts. See Sections 7.6.1.1 and 7.6.1.2.

Simple Past forms for subordinate clauses that are not a main clause subject are in (130). They are segmentally identical to their main clause counterparts but have a H tone. See §7.6.1.3. They lose this tone when their clause is a main clause subject.

(130) *Simple Past prefixing verbs in subordinate clauses*

	'said'	'came'	'existed'	'knew'
1SG	idhí	imíd	iíl	iqiín
2SG/3SG.F	tidhí	timíd	tiíl	tiqiín
3SG.M	yidhí	yimíd	yiíl	yiqiín
1PL	nidhí	nimíd	niíl	niqiín
2PL	tidhaahdéen	timaaddéen	tiilléen	tiqiinnéen
3PL	yidhaahdéen	yimaaddéen	yiilléen	yiqiinnéen

The Past Progressive verbs in (131) behave in the same way. They are segmentally identical to their main clause counterparts, though they have an additional suffixal H tone. This H tone is lost when their clause is a main clause subject.

(131) *Past Progressive prefixing verbs in subordinate clauses*

	'was saying'	'was coming'	'was existing'	'was knowing'
1SG/3SG.M	odhánayaý	imánayaý	oólayaý	aqoónayaý
2SG/3SG.F	odhánaysaý	imánaysaý	oólaysaý	aqoónaysaý
1PL	odhánaynaý	imánaynaý	oólaynaý	aqoónaynaý
2PL	odhánayséen	imánayséen	oólayséen	aqoónayséen
3PL	odhánayéen	imánayéen	oólayéen	aqoónayéen

7.9.4 Irregular verbs

Present tense irregular verbs also occur in the subordinate clauses under discussion in this section. These verbs are segmentally identical to their main clause counterparts. When the subordinate clause is not a main clause subject, these verbs have a H tone. This tone does not appear when the subordinate clause is the subject of the main clause.

(132) *Simple Present and Simple Past irregular verbs in subordinate clauses*

	'be'	'have'	'been'	'had'
1SG	ahaý	leeyahaý	ahaá	lahaá
2SG/3SG.F	taháy	leedahaý	ahaýd	lahaýd
3SG.M	yahaý	leeyahaý	ahaá	lahaá
1PL	nahaý	leenahaý	ahaýn	lahaýn
2PL	tihíin	leedihíin	ahaydéen	lahaydéen
3PL	yihíin	leeyihíin	ahaayéen	lahaayéen

Present Progressive forms differ in that they require the irrealis inflectional pattern, as shown in (133). However, when the subordinate clause functions as the main clause subject, these verbs revert back to a form that is segmentally identical to their main clause counterparts. See §7.7.1.1.

(133) *Present Progressive irregular verbs in subordinate clauses*

	'being'	'having'
1SG/3SG.M	ahaánayó	lahaánayó
2SG	ahaánaysó or	lahaánaysó or
	ahaánaysíd	lahaánaysíd
3SG.F	ahaánaysó	lahaánaysó
1PL	ahaánaynó	lahaánaynó
2PL	ahaánaysáan	lahaánaysáan
3PL	ahaánayáan	lahaánayáan

Example (134) shows a Present Progressive form of 'be' in a subordinate clause introduced by the subordinating conjunction *iláa* 'until.' It requires the irrealis inflectional paradigm and has a suffixal H tone. The subordinate clause verb in (135) is in the Simple Present. The subordinate clause is not the main clause subject in either of these examples.

(134) Iláa 2017 uu   kagá   sií mid aháanayó
       ilaa 2017 uu   ka=ga   sii mid ahaan-ay-∅-o
       until 2017 3SG.M with=on ITV same be-PROG-3SG.M-IRR
       kóoxdíisa.
       koox-diis-a
       team-T.3SG.M.POSS=DEF

   'Until 2017 he is remaining on the same team.' (soomalidamaanta: 16248)

(135) Maxáa   lagú   gartey   Soomaáli ínaad   taha*y*?
       ma-xaa la=gu   gar-t-∅-ey   Soomaali in=aad   t-ah-ay
       QM-FOC ISP=on discover-MID-3SG.M-PST Somali   COMP=2SG   2SG-be-PRES

   'How was it discovered that you are a Somali?' (Z & I: 363)

7.9.5 Subject relative clauses

Subject relative clause verbs behave uniquely compared to other subordinate clauses in Somali in that they require reduced agreement for person, number, and grammatical gender in all instances. This means that reduced agreement is required regardless of whether or not the head of the subject relative clause functions as the main clause subject. There is an inflectional difference, however, between subject-subject relative clause verbs and object-subject relative clause verbs. Subject-subject relative clause verbs are toneless while object-subject relative clause verbs are toned, as are all subject relative clause verbs under subject focus. Another distinction between these two classes is that the former takes realis paradigm inflection, while the latter requires a truncated form of this paradigm, but only in the Simple Present and other contexts derived from it. Characteristics specific to reduced agreement were discussed in detail above in §7.8.

The verbs in (136) are representative of those found in subject relative clauses in suffixing and prefixing verbs in the Simple Present. In each instance, reduced agreement can be seen in that suffixing verbs make just a three-way distinction, and prefixing verbs a four-way distinction for person, number, and grammatical gender.

(136) *Subject relative clause verbs - main clause subject vs. object (Simple Present)*

	Suffixing Verb		Prefixing Verb	
	Main Cl Subj	Main Cl Obj/Subj Focus	Main Cl Subj	Main Cl Obj/Subj Focus
1SG	qodaa	qodá	imaaddaa	imaaddá
2SG	qodaa	qodá	yimaaddaa	yimaaddá
3SG.M	qodaa	qodá	yimaaddaa	yimaaddá
3SG.F	qoddaa	qoddá	timaaddaa	timaaddá
1PL	qodnaa	qodná	nimaadnaa	nimaadná
2PL	qodaa	qodá	yimaaddaa	yimaaddá
3PL	qodaa	qodá	yimaaddaa	yimaaddá

In addition, this table highlights the inflectional differences introduced above between subject-subject relative clause verbs (where the head noun is also the main clause subject) vs. object-subject relative clause verbs (where the head noun is not the main clause subject) and all subject relative clause verbs under subject focus. The latter group are toned and truncated relative to the former.

Comparable forms showing subject relative clauses in the Present Progressive are in (137). The pattern represented here can be extended to all suffixing and prefixing verbs. The same principles pertaining to subject-subject vs. object-subject relative clauses and subject focus hold here as well.

(137) *Subj relative clause verbs - main clause subject vs. object (Present Progressive)*

	Suffixing Verb		Prefixing Verb	
	Main Cl Subj	Main Cl Obj/Subj Focus	Main Cl Subj	Main Cl Obj/Subj Focus
1SG	qódayaa	qódayá	imánayaa	imánayá
2SG	qódayaa	qódayá	imánayaa	imánayá
3SG.M	qódayaa	qódayá	imánayaa	imánayá
3SG.F	qódaysaa	qódaysá	imánaysaa	imánaysá
1PL	qódaynaa	qódayná	imánaynaa	imánayná
2PL	qódayaa	qódayá	imánayaa	imánayá
3PL	qódayaa	qódayá	imánayaa	imánayá

Inflection for both *aháan* 'to be' and *laháan* 'to have' is highly irregular in subject relative clauses. A complete illustration of the facts pertaining to their behavior is found in §7.8.2.

7.9.6 Negation

Inflection for negation on subordinate clause verbs is identical to what occurs for main clause verbs. The substantive difference between the two scenarios, however, is in the clause type marker that precedes the verb. Whereas *má* is used exclusively in main clauses, either *aán* or a periphrastic combination of *má...aán* flanking a subject pronoun is found in subordinate clauses. For details, see §14.1.3.

7.10 Inflection summary

The inflectional behavior of Somali verbs is complex, but there are several correlations and consistencies that emerge within the larger system. At the highest level, one can draw a comparison between main clause and subordinate clause verbs. Within subordinate clauses, a key distinction is between subject relative clause verbs and all other subordinate clause verbs in that the former require reduced agreement. A further distinction can be made depending on whether a clause is, or at least modifies, the main clause subject. Another characteristic, but one that crosses the divide between main and subordinate clause, is whether verbs require the realis or irrealis inflectional paradigm. Lastly, one can also draw a distinction between toned vs. toneless verb contexts.

To more clearly summarize these various characteristics and their correlations, this section provides a direct comparison of a single verb form across several contexts. Such a summary is helpful because viewing entire inflectional paradigms at once, as done in the sections above, sometimes has the effect of obscuring certain systematicities of the grammar. With this in mind, Figure 7.4 shows the 2SG form of the verb *kéen* 'bring' across a number of key contexts in the Simple Present, with the Simple Past shown for comparison.

This figure draws a distinction between main clause and subordinate clause verbs, though there is an unmistakable connection in some instances between main clause verbs and those subordinate clause verbs that are not in subject relative clauses. The Simple Present examples given show toneless fully inflected realis mood vs. toned fully inflected irrealis mood forms across these two categories. This distinction is not found in all contexts. It is absent, for example, in the Simple Past.

For subordinate clause verbs, a secondary distinction can be drawn between a group consisting of complement clauses (Comp), adverbial clauses (Adv), and object relative clauses (Obj RC) and a second group containing just subject relative clauses

	Main Clause	Subordinate Clause				
		Comp, Adv, non-Subj RC		Subj RC		
		Pres	Past	Pres	Past	
Toneless	keentaa	keentaa	keentay	keenaa	keenay	MC Subj
Toned	keentó/keentíd Irrealis	keentó/keentíd	keentaý	keená	keenaý	MC non-Subj/ Subj Focus

Fig. 7.4: Inflection summary - *kéen* 'bring,' 2SG Simple Present/Simple Past

(Subj RC). For relative clauses, object vs. subject refers specifically to the head of the relative clause itself. For example, *the man [you introduced]* is an Object RC while *the man [who introduced you]* is a Subject RC. The primary factor distinguishing between these groups is full vs. reduced agreement. In the former, one can observe that 2SG agreement is maintained by *-t-*, while in the Subj RC form, reduced agreement results in this suffix not being expressed. For more on reduced agreement, see Section §7.8.

Another substantive distinction in subordinate clause verbs can be drawn between those appearing in a clause that either functions as the subject of a main clause (for Comp clauses) or modifies a noun that is the subject of the main clause (for RCs). These verbs are toneless and require realis inflection. Note that the full vs. reduced agreement generalizations described above still hold here.

When a subordinate clause verb does not fit this "main clause subject" condition, or if the main clause involves subject focus, the subordinate clause verb exhibits a H tone. Realis paradigm inflection (albeit reduced) is once again required for subject relative clauses, though the paradigm in the Simple Present and related contexts has a short final vowel. In other subordinate clause types, the distribution of realis vs. irrealis inflection is as expected, with the latter being limited to the Simple Present and those contexts structurally related to it.

For the sake of further comparison, Figure 7.5 shows the same summary of contexts, but this time for 3PL of *kéen* in the Present Progressive, with the Past Progressive shown for comparison.

As stated above, a subject relative clause verb and a main clause verb are both toned under subject focus. While this might appear somewhat counterintuitive, consider the verbs in (138) and (139), which are adapted from Orwin (1995: 193).

		Main Clause	Subordinate Clause				
			Comp, Adv, non-Subj RC		Subj RC		
			Pres	Past	Pres	Past	
Toneless		keénayaan	keénayaan	keénayeen	keénayaa	keénayay	MC Subj
Toned		keénayâan Irrealis	keénayâan	keénayéen	keénayá	keenayaý	MC non-Subj/ Subj Focus

Fig. 7.5: Inflection summary - *kéen* 'bring,' 3PL Present/Past Progressive

(138) *Naagáha   [imánayá]   báa raáci*
      naag-a=ha   iman-ay-a   baa raac-i
      woman-PL=K.DEF come-PROG-PRES.RED FOC accompany-INF
      dooná.
      doon-a
      FUT-PRES.RED
      'The women who are coming will accompany them.'

(139) *Naagáha   [imánayaa]   wáa raáci*
      naag-a=ha   iman-ay-aa   waa raac-i
      woman-PL=K.DEF come-PROG-PRES.RED DEC accompany-INF
      doonaan.
      doon-∅-aa-n
      FUT-3-PRES-PL
      'The women who are coming will accompany them.'

Both examples contain a subject relative clause whose head is the subject of the main clause. As such, reduced agreement is found on both relative clause verbs. What should be clear, however, is that the relative clause verb in (138) under subject focus is inflected paradigmatically just like the main clause verb. Both verbs are toned and require reduced agreement in the realis paradigm. Example (139) does not involve subject focus. Both verbs are again inflected identically, this time having toneless suffixes that are fully inflected for the realis paradigm. Thus, there is an agreement of sorts between the relative clause and main clause verbs in terms of the inflection that they require.

7.11 Hybrid verbs

Hybrid verbs are Somali's main strategy for expressing attribution. These verbs are 'hybrid' in that they are formed by an adjective or adjectival participle to which an inflected form of *ahaán* 'to be' is added. Hybrid verbs are adjectival in that they are used for attribution, but they are verbal in that they take a full complement of verbal derivation and inflection, including person, number, and gender.[5]

A lexical adjective can modify a noun directly (see §9.4), but to be used predicatively, an adjective must form a hybrid verb with 'to be.' These possibilities are seen in (140) and (141), respectively, for the lexical adjective *cusúb* 'new.'

(140) Wáxaan soó iibsaday   gaádhi cusúb.
      wax=aan soo iib-s-ad-∅-ay   gaadhi cusub
      FOC=1SG VEN buy-WCAUS-MID-1SG-PST car   new
      'I bought myself a new car.'

(141) Wúxu   wuu   cusúbyahay.
      wux=u   w=uu   cusúb-y-ah-ay
      thing=DEF.SUBJ DEC=3SG.M new-3SG.M-be-PRES
      'The thing is new.' (Z & I: 108)

Adjectival participles, on the other hand, can modify a noun only predicatively. Within a noun phrase, this is accomplished with a subject relative clause whose verb is a reduced form of *ahaán* 'to be,' as in (142). Here, the participle *deggán* 'living' is derived from the verb *dég* 'live' and is joined by a reduced past tense form of 'to be.'

(142) dádkií   [deggánaa]
      dad-kii   degg-an-∅-aa
      people-K.RDEF live-STV-be-PST.RED
      'the inhabitants' (people who are living)

When not in a subject relative clause, an adjectival participle will join a fully inflected form of 'to be.' In (143), the adjectival participle *dhaawacán* 'injured' is derived from the verb *dhaáwac* 'injure' via the stativizing suffix *-án*. The adjectival participle is joined by a 1SG Simple Present verb.

---

[5] I follow Andrzejewski (1969) and Ajello (1988) in calling these "hybrid verbs." Other terms found in the literature include "adjectival verbs" (Ajello, 1984), "stative verbs" (Antinucci et al. 1980; Gebert 1988), and "C4 (conjugation 4) verbs" (Bell 1953). Saeed (1999) simply calls them adjectives, but distinguishes them from "basic" or lexical adjectives.

(143) *Waan dhaawacánahay.*
w=aan dhaawac-án-∅-ah-ay
DEC=1SG injure-STV-1SG-be-PRES
'I am injured.'

Example (144) shows a hybrid verb involving an adjectival participle derived by the stativizing suffix *-óon*.

(144) *Waan nabdóonahay.*
w=aan nabd-oon-∅-ah-ay
DEC=1SG wellness-STV-1SG-be-PRES
'I am well.'

In the Simple Past, *-ah-* is regularly truncated from the hybrid verb, as in (145), yielding *fiícnaa* rather than **fiícnahaa*.

(145) *Waan fiícnaa.*
w=aan fiic-an-∅-∅-aa
DEC=1SG good-STV-1SG-be-PST
'I was fine.'

Hybrid verbs in the affirmative Simple Present are typically formed with a full form of 'to be' (*ahay*, *tahay*, etc.). This is seen in examples like (143) and (144). Saeed (1999, pp. 104-105) claims that in informal speech, the verb may be truncated such that the *-ah-* is omitted, similar to what occurs in the Simple Past. Such an outcome is seen in the following example.

(146) *Waa asáas xúnyay.*
waa asaas xun-y-∅-ay
DEC ancestry bad-3SG.M-be-PRES
'He comes from a bad lineage.'

My speakers categorically reject such Simple Present hybrid verbs with truncation. As seen below, however, other instances of truncation are possible in the Simple Present when forming negatives.

Hybrid verbs are fully inflected for person, number, gender in main clauses, as in (147). This also applies to hybrid verbs in subordinate clauses, though these exhibit the irrealis inflectional paradigm and appear only in the progressive, as in (148).

(147) Dádka   Soomaaliyeéd wey   wanaagsányihiin.
       dad=ka   Soomaali-yeed w=ay wanaag-s-an-y-ih-ii-n
       people=K.DEF Somali-ASSOC DEC=3PL good-WCAUS-STV-3-be-PRES-PL
       'The Somali people are kind.' (Z & I: 148)

(148) Wáxay   márag   cád ú   tahay   [ín wáx lá
       wax=ay   marag   cad u   t-ah-ay   in   wax la
       FOC=3SG.F evidence clear with 3SG.F-be-PRES COMP thing ISP
       qarsánayó].
       qar-s-an-ay-∅-o
       hide-WCAUS-STV-PROG-3SG.M-IRR
       'It is clear evidence that something is being hidden." (dharaaro.com: 145)

Like other verbs, hybrid verbs require reduced agreement when they occur in a subject relative clause, like in (149). Here, if not for the reduced agreement requirement, we would otherwise expect the verb to have 3PL agreement.

(149) Somaliland iyo Ethiopia oo [márkii horé wanaagsánaa]...
       Somaliland iyo Ethiopia oo   markii hore wanaag-s-an-∅-aa
       Somaliland and Ethiopia REL then first good-WCAUS-STV-be-PST.RED
       'Somaliland and Ethiopia, which were good at the time ... (tooshnews: 55500)

Likewise, when their subject is marked for focus by a focus marker, a hybrid verb requires reduced agreement, as in (150). Here, again, one would expect 3PL agreement in other syntactic contexts.

(150) Mindiyáha   báy   meél kú daadsánaa.
       mindi-ya=ha   b=ay   meel ku daad-s-an-aa
       knife-PL=K.DEF FOC=3PL place out spill-WCAUS-STV-∅-PST.RED
       'The knives spilled out everywhere.'

Negation of hybrid verbs in both present and past tenses involves truncation of *-ah-*. While the usual negative Past Simple form of 'to be' is *aháyn*, hybrid verbs take the truncated form *-aýn*, as in (151).

(151) Má fiicnaýn.
       ma fiic-n-∅-ayn
       NEG good-STV-be-PST.NEG
       'It was not good.'

'To be' is also truncated in negative Simple Present hybrid verbs. Example (152) shows a negative hybrid verb with the suffix -*á*. The negative Simple Present of 'to be' found elsewhere is *ahá*.

(152) *Waxáy   yidhaahdaan   má   wanaagsaná.*
wax=ay   y-idhaahd-aa-n ma   wanaag-s-an-∅-a
FOC=3PL 3-say-PRES-PL   NEG good-WCAUS-STV-3SG.M-be.RED
'They say it isn't good.'

8 Compounds

Somali has both nominal and verbal compounds, as well as light verb constructions and phrasal verbs. The characteristics and the strategies employed to form these are quite different from one another. Nominal compounds are first discussed in §8.1 followed by verbal compounds in §8.2. Within each, there are several sub-types. Later in the chapter, light verb constructions and phrasal verbs are covered.

8.1 Nominal compounds

Nominal compounds are formed by several strategies, but these various types have certain characteristics in common. For example, nominal compounds are realized with a H tone on their rightmost element. This indicates that they are phonologically right-headed. There is a mismatch between their phonology and syntax, however, in that nominal compounds are syntactically left-headed. The leftmost element of a nominal compound is a noun that functions as its syntactic head. Syntactic left-headedness is most apparent when the compound is the subject of a verb. In such instances, the grammatical gender of the syntactic head is consistently manifested in the grammatical gender agreement required on the verb. For example, in (1), K-series agreement is found on the verb whose subject is a nominal compound with a K-series first element (cf. *áfka* 'the mouth'). In (2), T-series agreement is found on the verb whose subject has a T-series first element (cf. *haẃsha* 'the work').

(1) *Afmiinshaárku*   *waa xúnyahay.*
    af-miinshaar=k=u   waa xun-y-ah-ay
    mouth-saw=K.DEF=SUBJ DEC bad-3SG.K-be-PRES
    'The lobbyist is bad.' (Kaldhol 2019)

(2) *Hawlgacmeéddu*   *waa adágtahay.*
    hawl-gacm-eed=d=u   waa adag-t-ah-ay
    work-hand-ASSOC=T.DEF=SUBJ DEC hard-3SG.T-be-PRES
    'Manual labor is hard.' (Kaldhol 2019)

Arriving at a generalization concerning the grammatical gender of compounds themselves is a more complex task. This is because speakers sometimes adopt different strategies for assigning grammatical gender on modifiers, such as on determiners. Kaldhol (2019) shows that, for different speakers, grammatical gender agreement on modifiers is sometimes governed by the first element of the compound while other times it appears governed by the element immediately preceding the modifier. Viewed another way, speakers appear either to assign grammatical gender based on syntactic headedness or instead based on linear adjacency. Complicating matters further, however, is that there is even intraspeaker variation in the choice of strategy adopted.

Generally speaking, if both elements of a nominal compound are similarly gendered (K+K or T+T), there is no mismatch on any modifier. The gender of the resulting compound will match the gender of its components. For example, the compound *afgúri* 'dialect' is composed of two K-series nouns, *áf* 'mouth' and *gúri* 'home.' As such, it always takes K-series agreement, as seen in *afgúriga* 'the dialect.' Likewise, *lacagbixín* 'payment' is composed of two T-series nouns, *lacág* 'money' and *bixín* 'act of issuing.' The compound always requires T-series agreement, as seen in *lacagbixínta* 'the making of a payment.'

For noun + noun compounds where the second noun is not deverbal, if there is a grammatical gender mismatch between the elements of a compound, the gender agreement observed on modifiers varies. For example, the compound *magaalamádax* 'capital city' is composed of T-series *magaálo* 'city' followed a K-series *mádax* 'head.' Sometimes this compound appears with T-series agreement (*magaalamádaxda* 'the capital city'), but other times with K-series agreement (*magaalamádaxa* 'the capital city'). One of my speakers offered an insightful, albeit anecdotal observation that the choice for him depends on "how far ahead" he is thinking. Generally speaking, in our elicitations, if he was less familiar with a given word, paused, or was otherwise disfluent, gender was determined via linear adjacency. However, in a fluid production or in a full sentence, he was more apt to choose gender according to the syntactic head. A careful study of this phenomenon will appear in Kaldhol's forthcoming dissertation.

Though different strategies for assigning grammatical gender to determiners are observed in some compound types, speakers are more consistent in their choice of grammatical gender on modifiers when the final element of the compound is a verb or if the final element is modified by a derivational suffix. In noun + verb compounds, the verb is the syntactic head and is also found immediately before a modifier. As such, both conditions point toward grammatical gender being predicated on the verb. Bare deverbal nouns take K-series agreement in compounds. In other instances, derivational suffixes entail their own grammatical gender, and by the same logic just described (i.e., their stem-finality), gender on modifiers and in subject-verb agreement is consistently dictated by the suffix.

8.1.1 Noun + Noun

The simplest nominal compounds are formed by two morphologically-simplex (i.e., underived) nouns. Endocentric compounds of this type are consistently semantically left-headed, though sometimes only metaphorically. These compounds sometimes vary in the grammatical gender that they require on modifiers and in subject-verb agreement, as discussed above, as based either on linear adjacency or syntactic headedness.

(3) *Semantically left-headed endocentric compounds*

T	magaálo 'city'	K	mádax 'head'	magaalamádax	'capital city'
K	búug 'book'	T	lacág 'money'	buuglacág	'cash ledger'
K	fóol 'front tooth'	K	maroódi 'elephant'	foolmaroódi	'ivory'
K	gód 'burrow'	T	shinní 'bee'	godshinní	'beehive'
T	hamuún 'hunger'	K	górgor 'vulture'	hamuungórgor	'insatiable hunger'

Endocentric compounds that might instead appear to be right-headed are deverbal. These are discussed in §8.1.5.

Exocentric compounds are also formed by a concatenation of noun + noun, as in (4). Speakers vary here, too, in the grammatical gender that they assign to modifiers and in subject-verb agreement.

(4) *Exocentric noun + noun compounds*

K	áf 'mouth'	K	máal 'loan'	afmáal	'orator'
T	bír 'iron'	T	danáb 'electricity'	birdanáb	'magnet'
K	búr 'flour'	T	saliíd 'oil'	bursaliíd	'fritter'
K	hílib 'meat'	K	táhan 'power'	hilibtáhan	'carnivore'
K	béer 'liver'	K	kúrus 'hump'	beerkúrus	'liver disease'

8.1.2 Noun + Agentive Noun

Compound nouns referring to professions are formed by joining two nouns, the second of which is a deverbal agentive noun ending in the suffix -*é*. This suffix is discussed further in §6.3.2.7. Examples of these compounds are in (5). Like other nouns ending in -*é* (see §6), these compounds consistently require K-series agreement. For example, the definite form of the first example in (5) is *taariikhqoráha* 'the historian,' which has a K-series definite determiner.

(5) *Noun + agentive noun compounds*

taariíkh	'history'	qoré	'writer'	taariikhqoré	'historian'
áf	'mouth'	hayé	'possessor'	afhayé	'spokesperson'
lacág	'money'	hayé	'possessor'	lacaghayé	'cashier'
wár	'news'	geeyé	'escort'	wargeeyé	'announcer'

Similar compounds are formed with a deadjectival noun. For example, the compound *madaxweyné* 'president' is composed of the noun *mádax* 'head' and the adjective *wéyn* 'big.' Like the agentive compounds above, these require K-series grammatical gender agreement.

8.1.3 Noun + Ownership Noun

There are nominal compounds formed by joining a noun and another noun or deverbal noun to which the suffix *-le* has been added. In §6.3.3, the nouns created by this suffix were defined as ownership nouns, but in compounds the nouns created have more figurative or relational meanings. For example, the compound *labacánle* refers to the condition of having stuffed cheeks while eating. It is composed of the numeric *lábo* 'two' and the noun *cán* 'cheek' to which the suffix *-le* is added. Thus, the meaning is non-compositional. Other examples are as follows in (6).

(6) *Noun + ownership noun compounds*

dabaál	'swimming'	jóog	'act of standing'	dabaaljóogle	'treading water'
dhaqáaq	'movement'	jóog	'act of standing'	dhaqaaqjóogle	'hesitant walking'
fúruq	'smallpox'	bíyo	'water'	furuqbiyóle	'chicken pox'
kábbo	'sip'	qáb	'have'	kabbaqáble	'lukewarm liquid'

These compounds pattern with other Class 3 nouns discussed in §6.2.3 in that they take K-series grammatical gender agreement.

8.1.4 Associative Compounds

Associative compounds are composed of a noun followed by another noun or adjective to which one of the associative suffixes *-eéd* or *-oód* is added (for discussion of these suffixes, see §6.6). I have not come across any compounds with Somali's third associative suffix *-aád*, but such compounds might certainly be possible. The resulting compounds have the basic meaning 'Noun 1 of Noun 2,' but they may also have more figurative meanings in some instances. For example, *shaqagacmeéd*, composed of *sháqo* 'work' and *gacán* 'hand,' can mean 'work of (the) hand' or instead 'manual labor.' Other examples are as follows in (7).

(7) *Associative compounds*

nín	'man'	hawĺ	'labor'	ninhawleéd	'hardworker'
libáax	'lion'	bád	'sea'	libaaxbadeéd	'shark'
sún	'poison'	indhó	'eyes'	sunindhoód	'tear gas'
bíyo	'water'	yár	'small'	biyayaroód	'water shortage'

Associative compounds, despite having a suffix that assigns its own grammatical gender attached to their final element, often behave like other noun + noun compounds. That is, they tend to vary in the grammatical gender that they trigger on modifiers and in subject-verb agreement based either on syntactic headedness or linear adjacency.

8.1.5 Noun + Deverbal Noun

Somali derives deverbal nouns either by conversion or by suffixation. Many such nouns can join another noun to create a compound. Some examples are as follows in (8), but these are by no means representative of all types:

(8) Noun + deverbal noun compounds

bád	'sea'	maréen	'route'	badmaréen	'sea route'
gár	'law'	aqáan	'knowledge'	garyaqáan	'judge'
dhúl	'land'	dhaqashó	'conservation'	dhuldhaqashó	'conservancy'
bíyo	'water'	beége	'gauge'	biyabeége	'water meter'
caloól	'stomach'	xanúun	'pain'	caloolxanúun	'stomach ache'
tácab	'product'	khasaáro	'loss'	tacabkhasaáro	'profit loss'

These compounds consistently take the grammatical gender agreement that is required by their particular deverbal noun. Because of the many different possibilities, it is impractical to list all of them here. For specifics on deverbal noun formation and the grammatical gender required by type of deverbal noun, see §6.3.2.

8.1.6 Noun + Gerund

Gerunds are formed either by suffixation or by conversion, the details of which depend on the verb stem from which they are derived. These derived nouns can join another noun in the formation of nominal compounds.

(9) Noun + verbal noun compounds

aábo	'attention'	yeelíd	'causing'	aabayeelíd	'being concerned about s.t.'
dáb	'fire'	damís	'extinguishing'	dabdamís	'fire department'
qálin	'pen'	jebín	'breaking'	qalinjebín	'graduation'
wádne	'heart'	doorín	'changing'	wadnadoorín	'heart transplant'
áb	'ancestor'	tirís	'counting'	abtirís	'genealogy'
abáal	'reward'	dhurád	'scooping up'	abaaldhurád	'pension'

Noun + gerund compounds require grammatical gender agreement based on what is required by their particular gerundive suffix. For example, those taking -íd require T-series agreement, while those instead appearing with -ís take either K- or T- series agreement. Those taking the suffix -ád require K-series. For more detail on these and other gerundive suffixes and their grammatical gender requirements, see §6.4.

8.1.7 Noun + Verb

Nominal compounds are also created by a combination of noun and a bare verb stem. Similar combinations also create verbal compounds, as discussed in §8.2. Nominal compounds formed by this strategy consistently require K-series agreement, which likely relates to the fact that bare verb stems otherwise have a H tone on their penultimate mora. Elsewhere, it has been shown that there is a correlation between penultimate H tone and K-series agreement.

(10)   Noun + verb compounds

dád	'person'	cún	'eat'	dadcún	'cannibal'
indhó	'eyes'	sharéer	'block'	indhasharéer	'veil'
ádhi	'sheep'	jír	'be with'	adhijír	'shepherd'
bíyo	'water'	xídh	'contain'	biyaxídh	'dam'

8.1.8 Noun + Adjective

Similar to the noun + verb compounds in §8.1.7, there are also nominal compounds formed with one of the language's closed class of lexical adjectives. Examples are in (11), and for more on adjective, see §9.4).

(11)   Noun + lexical adjective compounds

bád	'sea'	wéyn	'big'	badwéyn	'ocean'
dán	'means'	yár	'small'	danyár	'needy person'
dúl	'patience'	xún	'bad'	dulxún	'impatient one'
wár	'news'	móog	'unaware'	warmóog	'uninformed one'

8.1.9 Noun + Adposition/Adverbial + Verb

More complex deverbal compounds are composed of a noun followed by a verb and its associated adposition and/or adverbial. These functional morphemes intervene between the noun and verb. Unlike most other deverbal compounds, the grammatical gender of these compounds is dictated by the noun. This likely reflects the fact that the noun is not incorporated into the verb, which it otherwise appears to be in the deverbal compounds in Sections 8.1.5 and 8.1.7. This fact is reinforced by the presence of the intervening adposition and/or adverbial. In other instances of noun incorporation, the incorporated noun immediately precedes the verb. Noun incorporation is discussed in §8.2.

(12) *Noun + (Adposition/Adverbial + Verb) compounds*

cíd	'family'	*lá jóog*	'stay with'	*cidlajóog*	'pet'
dál	'country'	*kú gál*	'enter into'	*dalkugál*	'entry visa'
dhíig	'blood'	*kú shúb*	'pour into'	*dhiigkushúb*	'transfusion'
derís	'neighbor'	*kú nóol*	'living with'	*deriskunóol*	'scrounger'
cír	'sky'	*ká soó dhác*	'happen'	*cirkasoodhác*	'sudden event'
mídab	'color'	*kalá sóoc*	'separate from'	*midabkalasóoc*	'racism'

Such compounds also form the basis for other types of compounds discussed in sections above. There are many possibilities, but one that is often encountered involves the creation agentive nouns like *gacankudhíigle* 'murderer' (> gacan-ku-dhiig-le, 'one who has blood on their hand').

8.2 Verbal compounds

Verbal compounds are also formed by several strategies. The first and seemingly most productive strategy discussed first in §8.2.1 is via object incorporation. This can involve incorporation of either a direct or oblique object. There are also some instances of subject incorporation discussed in §8.2.3.

8.2.1 Object Incorporation

Somali verbs can form a verbal compound via incorporation of a noun. These sequences look similar to some of the nominal compounds discussed in sections above, but they instead form verbs. One type of incorporation involves a transitive verb incorporating its direct object. Incorporation of this type is typically valency-reducing, with the resulting verbal compound being intransitive. Verbs created by noun incorporation of this type tend to have a transparent compositional meaning. There are exceptions to this discussed in §8.2.2, however, where a transitive verb appears to incorporate its direct object but remains transitive. These exceptions seem best attributed to lexicalization.

To illustrate object incorporation, consider first the sentence in (13). Here, the transitive verb *béel* 'lack' takes the noun phrase 'talent and conscience' as its direct object.

(13) Waan   nécbahay   nimánka   [táyo iyo damíir
     w=aan   necb-∅-ah-ay   nim-an=ka   tayo iyo damiir
     DEC=1SG hate-1SG-be-PRES   man-PL=K.DEF   talent and conscience
     beeshay].
     beesh-ay
     lack-PST.RED
     'I hate men who lack talent and conscience.' (keydmedia: 247189)

The same verb in (14) instead incorporates its direct object and accordingly becomes intransitive. That incorporation has occurred is made clear by the fact that i) the noun *míyir* 'consciousness' is located within the Verb Complex (between the verb and its adposition), and ii) the noun loses its H tone.

(14) Wúu   kú celiyey   hálkaás ayúu   marxúumku
     w=uu   ku celi-y-ey   halkaas ay=uu   marxuum=k=u
     time=3SG.M in put-3SG.M-PST there   FOC=3SG.M deceased=K.DEF=SUBJ
     kú   miyir   beelay.
     ku   miyir   beel-∅-ay
     there consciousness lack-3SG.M-PST
     'When he continued like that, the deceased became unconscious.'
     (qaawane: 1934)

In order to make such a verbal compound transitive once again, a valency-enhancing extension must be added. This can be seen in (15) where the verb *dháaf* 'surpass' incorporates the object *búux* 'fullness' to yield *buuxdháaf* 'overflow.' This verb can take a direct object when the Weak Causative extension is added to it.

(15) Wáan   buuxdhaafiyay   dhaláda.
     w=aan   buux.dhaaf-i-y-ay   dhala=da
     DEC=1SG overflow-WCAUS-1SG-PST   bottle=T.DEF
     'I overfilled the bottle.'

There are also verbal compounds where a verb incorporates an oblique object, as in *maalinsocán* 'travel for a day.' This compound is formed from the intransitive verb *socán* 'travel,' which incorporates the oblique object *maalín* 'day.'

Other work discussing Somali noun incorporation includes Ajello (1995), Sasse (1984), Svolacchia and Puglielli (1999), and Tosco (2002, 2004).

8.2.2 Lexicalized compounds

There are other verbal compounds that look like a direct object has been incorporated into a transitive verb but where the resulting verb remains transitive. For example, the transitive verb *dhíg* 'place' incorporates the noun *búd* 'grave' to yield *buddhíg* 'bury.' The compound can still take a direct object, as seen in (16).

(16) *Wáan   buddhigay   mídkii.*
     w=aan   bud.dhig-∅-ay   mid-kii
     DEC=1SG grave.put-1SG-PST person-K.RDEF
     'I buried the person.'

In many instances, these verbs have an idiomatic or non-compositional meaning. For example, the verb *afdúub* 'kidnap' is formed from *dúub* 'bind' and the incorporated object *áf* 'mouth.' Tosco (2004) suggests that these idiosyncrasies and the residual transitivity of these verbs has arisen due to lexicalization. He defines three types of such compounds. The first type of these relate to body parts: *jílib* 'knee' + *dhíg* 'put down' becomes *jilibdhíg* 'assume the position to fight.' The second type relates to locative or spatial terms: *dábo* '(a) place behind something else' + *dhéh* 'say' becomes *dabadhéh* 'repeat something after someone.' The last group involves culture-specific or domain-specific activities: *áb* 'ancestor' + *tirsán* 'count for oneself' becomes *abtirsán* 'trace one's genealogy.'

    Tosco (2004) also provides several examples of verbs that have incorporated their direct object that can either have their valency reduced or maintained, though with a difference in meaning between the two. One such examples pertains to the verb *raadráac*, which as a transitive verb means 'investigate' and as an intransitive verb means 'track.' It is composed of the transitive verb *ráac* 'follow' and the noun *ráad* 'trail.' Example (17) shows that on its own, *ráac* is transitive.

(17) *Wáan   ku   raacay.*
     w=aan   ku   raac-∅-ay
     DEC=1SG 2SG.OBJ follow-1SG-PST
     'I followed you.'

The incorporated form in (18) is intransitive, while that in (19) is transitive but has a different meaning.

(18) *Wáan   raadraacay.*
     w=aan   raad.raac-∅-ay
     DEC=1SG trail.follow-1SG-PST
     'I traced a trail.'

(19) Wáy   i   raadraaceen.
    w=ay   i   raad.raac-∅-ee-n
    DEC=3PL 1SG.OBJ trail.follow-3-PST-PL
    'They investigated me.'

8.2.3 Subject incorporation

Other instances of incorporation are found in which an intransitive or stative verb incorporates its subject. The resulting verbal compound remains intransitive. Examples of these compounds are in (20).

(20) *Subject Incorporation*

daacaqúrun	'be gassy'	lit. the belch stinks
hiyikác	'become excited'	lit. the heart rises
dabakannáax	'be self-made'	lit. the backside gets fat
dhegaculusán	'be hard of hearing'	lit. the ears harden
beercaddów	'be worn out'	lit. the liver whitens

8.3 Light verb constructions

Somali, like other Cushitic languages (Darmon 2012; Vanhove 2007), has light verb constructions (LVC). LVCs have been noted for Somali in Sasse (1984) and Saeed (1999), though not by this term. Rather, these scholars characterize these constructions as instances of noun incorporation involving a restricted set of semantically attenuated verbs. I have found five verbs in Somali that appear to form the basis of LVCs. These are: *báx* 'bring out, exit,' *gál* 'bring in, enter,' *qáad* 'take,' *síi* 'give,' and *béel* 'lose.' Each of these verbs is transitive and can also occur outside of an LVC with no semantic reduction.

The formation of an LVC is valency decreasing. This is seen in (21) where *qaadán* 'accept, adopt' (derived from *qáad* 'take') incorporates the noun *dúl* 'patience' and thereafter does not require a direct object. One indication that an LVC has been formed is that the incorporated noun retains its H tone. Recall that in other instances of incorporation which do not form an LVC, the incorporated noun loses its H tone. In (21), the noun is also clearly located within the Verb Complex, occurring between a deictic particle and the verb itself.

(21) *Múusan   ú   síi dúlqaadán   karín.*
    m=uus=an   u   sii dul.qaad-an   kari-n
    NEG=3SG.M=NEG with ITV patience.accept-INF be.able-NEG
    'He couldn't remain patient.'

It is also possible to create a transitive LVC, but this requires the addition of a valency-increasing extension, as seen with the weak causative extension in (22).

(22) *Wáan   ku   ífbixiyay.*
    w=aan   ku   if.bix-i-y-ay
    DEC=1SG 2SG light.bring.out-WCAUS-1SG-PST
    'I made you famous.'

Other examples involving each of the light verbs mentioned above are as follows in (23).

(23) *Light verb constructions*

rúux	'soul'	*báx*	'bring out'	*rúuxbíx*	'die'
wár	'news'	*báx*	'bring out'	*wárbíx*	'give a statement'
hár	'shade'	*gál*	'enter'	*hárgál*	'shade oneself'
magán	'sanctuary'	*géli*	'make enter'	*magángéli*	'give sanctuary'
martí	'guest'	*qáad*	'take'	*martíqáad*	'host a banquet'
jáan	'sole of foot'	*qáad*	'take'	*jáanqáad*	'make footsteps'
bów	'punch'	*síi*	'give'	*bówsíi*	'land a punch'
yáab	'surprise'	*síi*	'give'	*yáabsíi*	'surprise'
cíil	'grief'	*béel*	'lose'	*cíilbéel*	'vent one's anger'
indhó	'eyes'	*béel*	'lose'	*indhábéel*	'become blind'

8.4 Ideophones

Somali also behaves like other Cushitic languages in forming ideophones with a light verb construction (Appleyard 2001). These are categorized and analyzed in detail in Dhoorre and Tosco (1998). In forming these light verb constructions, the ideophone itself behaves as a noun while the verb is an inflected form of one of two semantically-reduced verbs, either *odhán* 'say' or *síi* 'give.' Some examples of ideophones are as follows in (24).

(24) *Ideophones*

a.	*bagagáx*	something being shattered
b.	*báf*	something being smashed by a blow
c.	*búg*	a snap or explosion
d.	*buluqbulúq*	swishing
e.	*daláq*	sudden or unexpected entrance
f.	*fagáx*	action of running
g.	*fashkáx*	being scattered all at once

The following sentential examples from Dhoorre and Tosco (1998) illustrate the use of ideophones in light verb constructions. In each, the ideophone occurs before the Verb Complex and has a H tone.

(25) *Irríddií   ayáa qáb tidhí.*
     irrid-dii   ayaa qab t-idhi
     door-T.RDEF FOC Ideo 3SG.F-say.PST.RED
     'The door banged.'

(26) *Maxáad   wásh iigú   siisay?*
     m=ax=aad   wash i=u=gu   sii-s-ay
     QM=FOC=2SG Ideo me=to=for give-2SG.F-PST
     'What did you hit me like that for?'

8.5 Phrasal verbs

Phrasal verbs are formed by a verb and one or more elements preceding it within the Verb Complex. This can include one or more adpositions, a deictic particle, or an adverbial particle. Phrasal verbs are distinguished from other verbs in that their meanings are non-compositional and, thus, seldom transparent. Consider, for example, the verb *jéed* 'look at,' which forms the basis for several phrasal verbs. The phrasal verb *kú jéed* means 'move toward s.t./s.o.,' while *ú jéed* means 'understand.' The phrasal verb *ulá jéed*, with two adpositions, means 'intend for s.t. to happen.' With a deictic particle, *ú soó jéed* means 'be vigilant.' Clearly, there are many possible combinations, all of which are semantically related to some degree, but their precise denotation is not recoverable from meanings typically associated with the relevant adpositions, deictics, etc.

Besides their non-compositional meaning, one characteristic that distinguishes phrasal verbs in Somali from an otherwise transparent sequence of a verb and other preceding elements is that the adpositions that form phrasal verbs do not govern an object pronoun or noun phrase. From a diagnostic standpoint, this is only so helpful, given that third person object pronouns in Somali have no segmental exponent. The following examples built upon the middle verb *noqán* 'become, return oneself' illustrate such a distinction. Sentence (27) contains the phrasal *ká noqán* 'abandon.' Taken literally, this would mean something along the lines of 'return oneself from,' which could be construed metaphorically as 'abandon,' but is certainly not transparent.

(27) *Xildhibaanó Soomaalí áh   ayáa ká   noqdaý*
     xildhibaan-o Soomaali ah   ayaa ka   noq-d-ay
     official-PL   Somali   be.PRES.RED FOC from return-MID-PST.RED
     moóshin.
     mooshin
     motion
     'Some Somali lawmakers have abandoned a motion.'

In (28), however, the adposition *ká* governs the oblique object 'several press conferences,' and there is a transparent connection to the subject's action of 'returning' expressed via the verb *noqán*.

(28) *Dhówr úrur   saxafadeéd   ayúu   odáy   ká*
     dhowr urur   saxafad-eed   ay=uu   oday   ka
     several meeting journalist-ASSOC FOC=3SG.M witness at
     noqday.
     noq-d-∅-ay
     return-MID-3SG.M-PST
     'He has returned as a witness in several press conferences.' (alshahid.net: 2395)

The adpositions involved in the formation of phrasal verbs behave just like any others in terms of their ability to cluster with pronoun clitics and negative *má*. See Chapter 10 for further details on the segmental and tonal properties of these clusters, as well as the relative order of the elements that they contain.

9 The noun phrase

Chapter 6 introduced the morphological characteristics of nouns. The current chapter concerns itself with syntactic properties exhibited by different types of nouns and with the formation of noun phrases. Describing Somali noun phrases presents at least two immediate challenges. The first of these is that orthographic nouns are often coextensive with a full noun phrase. This can be seen in that determiners of different types join the noun that they modify to form a single orthographic word regardless of their prosodic status as an independent phonological word or as a clitic. Compounds are also written as a single orthographic word, but other modifiers like adjectival participles and relative clauses are rendered as separate written words.

Another challenge to describing Somali noun phrases is that, from a syntactic perspective, they are not verbal arguments (Frascarelli and Puglielli 2003; Lecarme 1999a; Saeed 1994). A number of studies have illustrated that the valency of a given verb is satisfied by pronomimal clitics within the Verb Complex, rather than by noun phrases themselves. Based on this fact, the Verb Complex is often described as a miniature version of a Somali sentence, with noun phrases being syntactic adjuncts whose primary function is to contribute to information structure (e.g., focus and topicality). As such, noun phrases are described as being located outside of the Verb Complex.

Regardless of their argument status, noun phrases do have the ability to affect patterns of agreement on the verb in some instances. This is clear when a noun phrase is placed into focus by a focus marker. If such a noun phrase is co-referential with the verb's subject, the verb requires reduced agreement (see §7.8) whereby it expresses fewer person, number, and gender categories.

Within noun phrases themselves, the head noun governs patterns of agreement on its determiners, though there are exceptions to this involving compounds (see §8.1).

Figure 9.1, repeated here from Chapter 6, shows the basic structure of a Somali noun phrase. Though this template illustrates the basic ordering of constituents within such a phrase, there are many permutations of these elements that would be impossible to capture within a single schematic. This basic template shows that the noun occurs first in a noun phrase and may be followed by one or more derivational suffixes and/or a plural suffix. Of course, in the formation of nominal compounds, more than one nominal root may be joined before suffixes are added.

root + derivation + plural + determiner(s) + other modifier(s) + clitic(s)

Fig. 9.1: Basic noun template

The slot occupied by determiners can be further subdivided given that there are morphosyntactic constraints on the distribution and co-occurrence of different determiners within a given noun phrase. Finer-grained distinctions can also be made concerning clitics. The definite determiner clitic, for example, occurs in the clitic slot, rather than alongside other determiners. It selects a noun or another determiner as its host. Other clitics like the subject marker clitic more indiscriminately attach to the rightmost element of the larger noun phrase, including to a relative clause. Other nominal modifiers like lexical adjectives and relative clauses, if present, follow determiners but will precede the subject marker clitic.

9.1 Noun categories

As a lexical class, nouns exhibit fairly coherent syntactic behavior in terms of their function as the head of a noun phrase and in the patterns of agreement that they govern. However, nouns can be divided into several categories based on their ability to be made definite, their semantic interpretation as singular vs. plural, and their countability. In this section, major categories of count vs. non-count nouns are first covered. Discussion then turns to other nominal categories that exhibit more idiosyncratic properties, such as numerals, proper nouns, color terms, and independent personal pronouns.

9.1.1 Count nouns

The largest category of nouns is count nouns. Count nouns can be counted directly by numerics. In order to do so, a numeric immediately precedes the noun that it modifies. This is a fairly odd characteristic of Somali noun phrases, as other attributes and modifiers otherwise follow the noun being that they modify. However, the reason for this oddity is that the numeric and noun form an associative construction (see §9.5). Thus, examples like (1) and (2) might be more transparently glossed 'four of men' and 'three of knives,' respectively.

(1) afár nín
    four man
    'four men'

(2) saddéx mindí
    three   knife
    'three knives'

Most count nouns have a singular form and also a plural that is formed via suffixation. One possible exception to this is so-called "prosodic plurals" whose purported plurality is encoded only by a rightward H tone shift with no accompanying segmental material added to the noun. However, these have been argued by Nilsson (2018), among others, to be better defined as collectives rather than as plurals. For more on this, see §6.2.5.2. Another exception to pluralization via suffixation is found in some Arabic loanwords that maintain a non-concatenative pluralization pattern, being borrowed directly from the source language. See §6.2.5.1 for more on these nouns.

Count nouns require different number agreement on verbs depending on whether they are morphologically singular or plural. Example (3) shows a singular noun that takes singular verb agreement, while (4) shows its corresponding plural, which accordingly takes plural verb agreement.

(3) *Naágtu   wáxay   kú jirtaa   gúriga.*
    naag=t=SUBJ   wax=ay   ku jir-t-aa   gúri=ga
    woman=T.DEF=SUBJ FOC=3SG.T in exist-3SG.T-PRES   house=K.DEF
    'The woman is in the house.'

(4) *Naagúhu   wáxay   kú jiraan   gúriga.*
    naag-u=h=u   wax=ay   ku jir-∅-aa-n   guri=ga
    woman-PL=K.DEF=SUBJ FOC=3PL in exist-3-PRES-PL   house=K.DEF
    'The women are in the house.'

9.1.2 Corporate nouns

Corporate nouns refer to groups of people, animals, or objects whose morphologically singular form can be interpreted semantically as either singular or plural. Examples include: *koóx* 'team,' *ciídan* 'army,' and *géel* 'herd of camels.' As such, they may take plural agreement on pronouns and verbs even when singular. Nilsson (2018) offers the following examples illustrating behavior of the corporate noun *qóys* 'family.' In (5), there is singular verbal agreement with the singular noun. However, (6) shows that plural agreement is also grammatical after the very same noun when the noun is interpreted as semantically plural.

(5) *Qóyskiisu   wáxa uu ká koobán   yahay   shán*
    qoys-kii=s=u   waxa uu ka koob-án   y-ah-ay   shan
    family-K.his=T.DEF=SUBJ FOC 3SG of consist-STV   3SG.K-be-PRES five
    ruúx.
    ruux
    person
    'His family consists of five people.'

(6) *Faárax qóyskiisu   wáxa ay dhaqdaan   géel.*
    Faarax qoys-kii=s=u   waxa ay dhaq-d-aa-n   geel
    Faarax family-K.his=DEF=SUBJ FOC   3.PL breed-3-PRES-PL camel
    'Faarax's family breeds camels.'

Corporate nouns have regular singular and plural forms. For example, *qóys* has a morphological plural, *qoysás* 'families.' These morphological plurals require plural agreement.

Like count nouns (§9.1.1), corporate nouns can be counted directly. For example, a phrase like *saddéx qoýs* 'three families' shows the noun can be counted directed by a numeral. However, corporate nouns can also be counted indirectly by being placed into a subject relative clause. This is seen in *saddéx [qóys áh]* 'three (which are) families.' Countability is an important factor distinguishing corporate nouns from the collective nouns discussed in §9.1.3.2. While corporate nouns can be counted both directly and indirectly, collective nouns can only be counted indirectly.

9.1.3 Uncountable nouns

9.1.3.1 Mass nouns

Mass nouns refer to unindividuable substances and require singular agreement, even when they appear to be morphologically plural in having the suffix *-o*. Examples include liquids (*málab* 'honey,' *dhíig* 'blood'), powders (*búr* 'flour,' *bús* 'dust'), seeds and grains (*baríis* 'rice,' *qamádi* 'wheat'), some words related to food (*cúnto* 'food,' *canjeéro* 'flatbread,' *hílib* 'meat'), minerals (*bír* 'iron,' *cúsbo* 'salt'), and other items that would be difficult to quantify (*qíiq* 'smoke,' *cáws* 'grass,' *dhiíqo* 'mud,' *tímo* 'hair'). Mass nouns cannot be counted directly by numerals, but rather must be counted indirectly by way of some unit of measurement. For example, in (7), the mass noun for 'flour' must be counted by cup.

(7) *hál koób oo [búr áh]*
    one cup   REL flour be.RED
    'one cup of flour'

For some mass nouns, there are apparent exceptions to this restriction against direct counting and singular interpretation, though this results in idiosyncratic interpretations. For example, *hál búr*, literally meaning 'one flour,' refers to one piece of a type of fried bread (made from flour) but not to an individual grain of flour.

Mass nouns require singular verb and pronoun agreement as in (8). They do not typically have regular plural forms, but in some instances, it is possible to pluralize a mass noun to indicate an excessive amount. For example, *digír* 'beans' can take the plural suffix *-yaál* to yield *digiryaál* whose interpretation is 'a lot of the same beans,' rather than 'different kinds of beans.'

(8) *Málabku   wúu   dhammaaday.*
     malab=k=u   w=uu   dhamm-aad-∅-ay
     honey=K.DEF=SUBJ DEC=3SG.M finish-INCH-3SG.M-PST
     'The honey is finished.'

Though they do not refer to masses, per se, monomorphemic nouns referring to abstract concepts often behave like mass nouns. This is also true for those abstract nouns ending in *-o*. In both instances, the noun behaves as singular from the standpoint of syntactic agreement. Examples containing such abstract nouns are in (9) and (10).

(9) *Xanáaqu   ma fiicnó.*
     xanaaq=∅=u   ma fiic-n-o
     bitterness=K.DEF=SUBJ NEG good-STV-IRR
     'Bitterness isn't good.'

(10) *Carádu   way   xúntahay.*
     cara=d=u   w=ay   xun-t-ah-ay
     anger=T.DEF=SUBJ   DEC=3SG.F bad-3SG.T-be-PRES
     'Anger is bad.'

9.1.3.2 Collective nouns

Collective nouns have referents that are treated as an unindividuable group and cannot be counted directly. They are morphologically singular and do not have a regular plural form. Examples include nouns *carruúr* 'children,'[1] *shinní* 'bees,' and *ló* 'cattle.'

Collective nouns are counted indirectly by being placed into a relative clause. The collective noun itself is within a relative clause that modifies a numeric. This is seen in *shán [carruúr áh]* 'five children' or, more transparently, 'five (who are) children.'

Collective nouns differ from mass nouns in that they can be interpreted semantically as either singular or plural, and, as such, they can take either pattern of syntactic agreement on pronouns and verbs. This is shown in (11) and (12), respectively, for the collective noun *dhír* 'plants.'

---

[1] One of my speakers indicated that plural forms of some collective nouns are possible, but they result in idiosyncratic meanings. For example, *carruuró* is a pluralized form of *carruúr* that means 'small children' but not 'groups of children.' I have not explored this matter in detail with other speakers.

(11) Faa'iidoóyinka   dhírtu   ú   léedahay...
      faa'iido-oyin=ka dhir=t=u   u   lee-d-ah-ay
      benefit-PL=K.DEF plants=T.DEF=SUBJ   for have-3SG.T-be-PRES
      'The plants have benefits...'

(12) iyo dhírtu   ay   kú noolaadaan.
      iyo dhir=t=u   ay   ku nool-aad-∅-aa-n
      and plants=T.DEF=SUBJ   3PL at thrive-INCH-3-PRES-PL
      'and the plants are thriving.'

There are other collective nouns that are morphologically plural in that they have an *-o* suffix. These include *duúnyo* 'livestock' and *ílmo* 'children.' These can have either singular or plural interpretation, as reflected in agreement.

9.1.3.3 Pluralia tantum

Pluralia tantum nouns are a type of mass noun that are inherently plural. This is evidenced from plural morphology, namely the suffix *-o*, from the fact that they have no singular counterpart, and also that they always require plural agreement. Two common nouns that belong in this category are *bíyo* 'water' and *caáno* 'milk.'

Pluralia tantum nouns cannot be counted by numerals, but rather, they must be counted by some unit of measure. Example (13) shows that the noun is placed within a relative clause that modifies a countable noun referring to some unit of measure.

(13) saddéx liitír [oo bíyo   áh]
      saddex liitir oo biyo   ah
      three liter   REL water be.PST.RED
      'three liters of water'

Pluralia tantum nouns require plural agreement, as in (14).

(14) Caanáha   wáy   dhammaadeen.
      caana=ha   w=ay   dhamm-aad-∅-ee-n
      milk=K.DEF DEC=3PL   finish-INCH-3-PST-PL
      'The milk is finished.'

Two other nouns appear to belong in this category, namely *háblo* 'girls' and *ído* 'flock of sheep.' Both appear morphologically plural and require plural agreement in all instances. This separates them from morphologically plural collectives that can readily be interpreted as either singular or plural.

9.1.3.4 Summary of countable vs. uncountable nouns

Table 9.1 summarizes the properties of the different noun categories described thus far. Included here is whether a noun can be pluralized or not, or if it is otherwise inherently plural, as well as the strategy used for counting (direct vs. indirect) and number agreement.

Tab. 9.1: Countable vs. uncountable noun summary

Type	Pluralization	Counting	Agreement
Count	yes	direct	SG/PL, based on morphology
Corporate	yes	direct or indirect	SG/PL; SG may take PL AGR
Mass	no	indirect	SG only
Collective	no	indirect	SG or PL
Pluralia Tantum	inherent	indirect	PL only

9.1.4 Proper nouns

Proper nouns refer to the names of people and places, clan names, and holidays. Also included in this group are days of the week (15), months of the Roman calendar (16), and months of the Somali lunar calendar (17). Forms in the following tables are provided alongside their definite determiners; alternations affecting stem-final vowels and H tone are also indicated.

(15) *Days of the week*

Isniín(ta)	'Monday'	*Júmce(/áha)*	'Friday'
Talaádo(/áda)	'Tuesday'	*Sabtí(da)*	'Saturday'
Arbáco(/áda)	'Wednesday'	*Axád(da)*	'Sunday'
Khamiís(ta)	'Thursday'		

(16) *Months of the Roman calendar*

Janaáyo(/áda)	'January'	*Luúlyo(/áda)*	'July'
Febraáyo(/áda)	'February'	*Agoósto(/áda)*	'August'
Maárso(/áda)	'March'	*Sibtambár(ta)*	'September'
Abriíl(sha)	'April'	*Oktoobár(ta)*	'October'
Maájo(/áda)	'May'	*Noofembár(ta)*	'November'
Juún(ta)	'June'	*Disembár(ta)*	'December'

(17) *Months of the lunar calendar*

Dágo(/áda) or *Séko(/áda)*	'first month'	*Awcismáan(/ka)* or *Sabuúx(da)*	'seventh month'
Miirá(da)	'second month'	*Gasayár(/ta)*	'eighth month'
Mowlíid(ka)	'third month'	*Sóon(ka)*	'ninth month'
Maalmaddoóne(/áha)	'fourth month'	*Soónfur(ka)*	'tenth month'
Ban Hóre(/áda)	'fifth month'	*Sidataál(/sha)*	'eleventh month'
Ban Dámbe(/áda)	'sixth month'	*Arráfo(/áda)*	'twelfth month'

These nouns behave like other nouns in some ways. They can function as the head of a noun phrase and have a H tone. They also have their own grammatical gender and accordingly require gender and number agreement on pronouns and verbs. However, proper nouns cannot co-occur with most modifiers, with the exception of definite determiners in some instances. They are not typically pluralized.

9.1.5 Color terms

Somali has three basic color terms: *caddaán* 'white, whiteness,' *madów* 'black, darkness,' and *casaán* 'red, redness.' These can function as nouns but also have closely related counterparts that function as hybrid verbs, similar to other adjectivals. Other color terms are related, by extension, to nouns associated with some color. For example, *huruúd* 'saffron' is a word used for 'yellow, yellowness.' Likewise, *dóog* 'green' is the same as one word for 'grass.' Other color terms are borrowed, like *bulúug* 'blue.' Color terms have a H tone like other nouns. They also have grammatical gender and govern verbal agreement patterns, where relevant. In addition to these basic color terms, there are others related specifically to human skin color and cattle hide color. These are discussed by Maffi (1984, 1990).

9.1.6 Numerics

Numerics share characteristics with other nouns. They can be modified by determiners, have grammatical gender, and are associated with H tone. Numerics are unusual, however, in that they occur at the head of a phrase and are modified by the noun that they refer to within an associative construction. For more on the properties of associative constructions, see Sections 6.6 and 9.5.

9.1.6.1 Cardinal numbers

Cardinal numbers are shown in (18) along with their definite determiners. The numbers one through eight take T-series agreement while nine and ten take K-series agreement.

(18)

1.	koẃ(da)	6.	líx(da)
2.	lábo(/áda)	7.	toddobá(da)
3.	saddéx(da)	8.	siddeéd(da)
4.	afár(ta)	9.	sagáal(ka)
5.	shán(ta)	10.	tóban(ka)

The forms of 'one' differ by context: *koẃ* is used in counting, while *koób* is used in forming larger numbers (e.g., *koób iyo sóddon* '31'). In noun phrases, *hál* is used (e.g., *hál markáb* 'one ship').

Multiples of ten between 20 and 90 are shown in (19). These are formed by the addition of *-tan*, or *-atan* after a vowel. The forms for 30 and 50 are irregular in that they are formed from a stem that does not correspond to a cardinal number. All multiples of 10 ending in *-tan* or *-atan* take K-series agreement. The initial consonant of the suffix undergoes sandhi alternations where relevant (see §3.4), but H tone remains on the stem.

(19)

20.	labaátan	60.	líxdan
30.	sóddon	70.	toddobaátan
40.	afártan	80.	siddeétan
50.	kónton	90.	sagaáshan

Numerals between multiples of ten (e.g., 21, 22, etc.) are additive. A numeral between 1 and 9 is joined to a multiple of 10 with the conjunction *iyo*. For example, 23 is *saddéx iyo labaátan*. Because these end in a multiple of ten, they take K-series agreement. This is the strategy used in Northern Somali. Speakers of other varieties, including Central and Benaadir Somali, use the opposite order. For example, 23 would instead be *labaátan iyo saddéx*, with subsequent agreement predicated on the grammatical gender series of the final numeral.

Other multiples include *bóqol* '100,' *kún* '1,000,' and the borrowing *malyúun* '1,000,000.' Hundreds, thousands, and millions are multiplicative. For example, 300 is *saddéx boqól*. H tone shifts to the final tone bearing unit on the second noun, illustrating that these are also in an associative construction. More complex numbers are formed by a combination of these strategies, both multiplicative and additive, as appropriate. For example, *líx kún, saddéx boqól, labá iyo labaátan* is '6,322.'

9.1.6.2 Ordinal numbers

Ordinal numbers are formed by the addition of the suffix *-aád* to a given numeral. Examples include: *kowaád* '1st,' *boqolaád* '100th,' and *afár iyo kontonaád* '54th.' These represent another type of associative construction; see §6.6. When modified by a determiner, ordinal numbers take T-series agreement. For example, *labaádda* 'the second.'

9.1.6.3 Approximate numbers

Approximate numerals are created by the addition of *-eéyo* or *-eéye* to a cardinal number in some multiple of ten, to create a noun meaning 'approximately X' or 'not more than X,' where X is the numeral. For example, *kontameéyo* 'approximately 50.' Approximate numerals act like other numerals in that they can function as the head of a phrase: *tobaneeyó dumár* '(approximately) ten women.'

Use of the two forms is largely restricted by dialect: *-eéyo* is typical in Central and Benaadir Somali, while *-eéye* is more common in Northern Somali. One of my speakers from Hargeysa (Northern Somali) considered both acceptable, while another from Mogadishu (Central Somali) found *-eéye* totally ungrammatical. Both suffixes attract H tone, with H tone shifting rightward when the approximate is phrase medial. Those nouns formed by *-eéyo* take T-series agreement, while K-series agreement is required with *-eéye*.

9.1.7 Ideophones

Ideophones behave morphologically like other nouns, but they are only used in light verb constructions. For more on the construction of ideophones, see §8.4.

9.1.8 Independent personal pronouns

Independent personal pronouns function in many ways like nouns. They differ from other pronouns and are "independent," however, in that they occur outside of the Verb Complex, just as nouns and noun phrases do. Pronouns found within the Verb Complex are clitics (see §10.2). Also like nouns, independent personal pronouns are associated with a H tone, exhibit grammatical gender, and can be modified by a determiner.

Somali's independent personal pronouns are given in (20), each in its full form followed by a definite determiner and also its corresponding short form without a determiner. The short forms do not occur on their own, but rather only when the pronoun is joined by another morpheme, such as a focus particle.

(20) *Independent personal pronouns*

a.	aníga	aní	'I, me'
b.	adíga	adí	'you (SG)'
c.	isága	isá	'he, him'
d.	iyáda	iyá	'she, her'
e.	annága	anná	'we, us (excl)'
f.	innága	inná	'we, us (incl)'
g.	idínka	idín	'you (PL)'
h.	iyága	iyá	'they, them'

With the exception of the third person feminine singular, independent personal pronouns take K-series agreement. All of these pronouns have a H tone on their final mora (before the determiner, where relevant). There is a clusivity distinction in independent personal pronouns, but the 1PL inclusive is largely restricted to the written medium.

Example (21) shows that an independent personal pronoun can function either as the subject or object of a verb and, where applicable, can be subject marked. It also shows that the pronoun, as a T-series subject, requires T-series agreement on the verb.

(21) *Iyádu   way   ká   lacág badnayd   isága.*
     iya=d=u   w=ay   ka   lacag badn-ay-d   isa=ga
     she=T.DEF=SUBJ DEC=3SG.F COM money much-be.PST-3SG.F he=K-DEF
     'She had more money than him.' (Z & O: 42)

Example (22) shows a sentence in which an independent personal pronoun occurs in its short form upon coalescence with a focus particle.

(22) *Adáa   i   daartay.*
     ad:aa   i   daar-t-ay
     2SG:FOC 1SG strike-2SG-PST
     'You struck me.' (Z & O: 121)

9.2 Subject marking

The matter of subject marking in Somali is fairly controversial. Some consider subject marking to be accomplished by a morpheme that is an exponent of syntactic nominative or subject case. Whether or not Somali exhibits a system of grammatical case marking, however, has long been debated. Several seminal works (Andrzejewski and Lewis 1964; Andrzejewski 1979; Banti 1984a, 1988c; Le Gac 2001; Saeed 1999, among others) assume that Somali nouns encode case. Some describe four cases (nominative, absolutive, genitive, and vocative), while early works by Andrzejewski refer only to *Case A* and *Case B*, with the latter aligning with others' description of the nominative. Some have called this perspective into question (e.g., Tosco 1994) and recent work has rekindled the debate (Green and Morrison 2015; Green 2019; Lampitelli 2019; Nilsson 2017, 2019). These later works collectively argue that if Somali does inflect for syntactic case, it does so in non-canonical and typologically unusual ways. Green and Lampitelli (2021) argue that the various realizations of the morpheme long associated with subject marking are influenced by its status as a clitic. It is treated as a clitic here. Accordingly, the element that it joins is referred to as its host.

In order to remain agnostic, to the extent possible, the focus here is on the exponents of so-called subject marking and the realization of what will simply be called the subject marker (SUBJ) morpheme. The use of this term has two inherent shortcomings that should be kept in mind: i) not all subjects are associated with the SUBJ, and ii) the full extent of the SUBJ's function is yet unclear.

The SUBJ can occur on some but not all verbal subjects and has several realizations – loss of H tone, H tone loss *and* addition of a segmental exponent (*-i*, or sometimes *-u*), and vowel alternation. In some instances where it might be expected, it also appears to have no overt realization. Precisely how the SUBJ is realized depends on several factors, including: i) the syntactic category of its host (noun, determiner, etc.); ii) the grammatical gender of its host (where relevant); iii) the segmental shape of its host; and iv) how it prosodifies with its host.

The SUBJ does not occur on a subject that is marked as "in focus" by a focus marker. Where present, subject marking occurs on the last morpheme of a noun phrase that functions as a subject. This can be on the noun stem itself, but also on a suffix, a determiner, and on some dependent clause verbs. Consider, for example, the two simple sentences in (23) and (24).

(23) *Idínku   Afgoóye báad   tagteen.*
     idin=k=u   Afgooye b=aad   tag-t-ee-n
     you=K-DEF=SUBJ Afgooye FOC=2PL go-2-PST-PL
     'You (PL) went to Afgooye.'

(24) *Idínka   báa Afgoóye tageý.*
     idin=ka   baa Afgooye tag-ey
     you=K.DEF FOC Afgooye go-PST.RED
     'You (PL) went to Afgooye.'

In (23), the oblique object is indicated as in focus by the focus marker that follows it. The non-focused subject noun phrase is marked by the SUBJ. The SUBJ is realized on the definite determiner. In (24), the subject is in focus and, accordingly, its phrase cannot be marked by the SUBJ. This is, of course, just one instantiation of SUBJ. Others are discussed in the sub-sections below.[2]

Use of the SUBJ varies to some extent by dialect. Speakers of Northern Somali are more apt to utilize the full complement of SUBJ strategies introduced just above. However, speakers of other varieties tend to use the SUBJ only when it has a segmental exponent. This can co-occur with H tone loss, but these speakers tend not to subject-mark by loss of H tone alone. Because the realization of the SUBJ is so diverse and multifaceted, it would be impossible here to list every morpheme that can associate with the SUBJ. Rather, the sub-sections below summarize four ways that SUBJ is realized and provide exemplars for each.

9.2.1 H tone loss

The most ubiquitous realization of the SUBJ is the loss of H tone. For example, the noun *nín* 'man' is realized *nin* 'man.SUBJ' in the presence of the SUBJ. The SUBJ is realized by the loss of H tone with no segmental exponent on:

(25) a. monomorphemic, singular K-series nouns in Classes 1b, 1c, and 2
  b. nouns with consonant-final derivational suffixes that require K-series agreement (e.g., *-éen*, *-itáan*, *-níin*, *-áal*, and plural *-óyin*)
  c. compounds whose last element is a noun from a. or b.
  d. remote definite determiners
  e. adverbs with penultimate H tone (e.g., *kále* 'other')

Another instance in which the SUBJ may be realized via H tone loss is on nouns pluralized by *-ó* from Class 1. This is the outcome most widely reported in the literature (see Frid 1995; Le Gac 2003a; Orwin 1995) and is indeed what I have observed for my speakers. However, there is variation reported elsewhere in the literature regarding such outcomes. For some speakers, the H tone of *-ó* plural is only optionally lowered by the SUBJ (see Hyman 1981; Banti 1988c). For others, H is instead lowered to Mid (M) tone (see Andrzejewski 1964, 1979) or only lowers before a pause (see Saeed 1999). As shown in the next section, H tone loss is sometimes accompanied by the addition of another segmental exponent.

---

[2] There are alternations between irrealis and realis inflection in dependent clause verbs that have traditionally been considered to be another reflex of subject marking. While it is certainly true that a dependent clause verb alternates from irrealis paradigm to realis paradigm inflection when the clause is the subject of a main clause verb, this connection may be epiphenomenal. That is, the paradigmatic alternation that occurs may not necessarily be due to the presence of the same SUBJ morpheme discussed in this section, but rather to an incompatibility between subjecthood and irrealis modality. For further discussion, see §7.9.

9.2.2 H tone loss with -*i*, -*yi*, or -*u*

H tone loss via SUBJ is often accompanied by the segmental exponent -*i*. For example, the noun *naág* 'woman' is realized *naagi* 'woman.SUBJ' in the presence of the SUBJ. When a morpheme marked in this way ends in a vowel, an epenthetic glide [j] (written *y*) is inserted between the stem and the SUBJ yielding -*yi*: compare *mindí* 'knife' and *mindíyi* 'knife.SUBJ.' This also applies to distal demonstrative determiners. For example, *koó* and *toó* are realized *kooyi* and *tooyi*, respectively, when the SUBJ is present. Morphological items that realize the SUBJ in this way include:

(26)   a. monomorphemic, singular T-series nouns in Class 1a
      b. nouns with consonant-final derivational suffixes that require T-series agreement (e.g., derivational -*iyád*, -*aán*, -*niín*, -*aál*, and plural -*yaál*)
      c. compounds whose last element is a noun from a. or b.
      d. demonstrative determiners
      e. dependent clause verbs ending in a consonant and a final H tone (cf. *aháyn* 'not be' and *ahayni*)

The segmental exponent may be -*u*, in variation with -*i*, after proximal and medial demonstrative determiners. See §9.3.2. These have been described as "optional variants" (Saeed 1999). My consultants seem willing to accept either variant, but prefer the variant in -*i*. In consulting the SoWac Somali Web Corpus, it is abundantly clear that forms in -*i* far outnumber those in -*u* in all instances.

9.2.3 Vowel alternation

Presence of the SUBJ does not lead to the loss of H tone when the morpheme joins another phrase-final clitic, such as the definite determiner or the intensifier -*ba*. These clitics intervene between the SUBJ clitic and its host. When these clitics are also present, the SUBJ is instead realized via vowel alternation. For example, the definite determiners -*ka* and -*ta* are realized -*ku* and -*tu*, respectively. Likewise, the intensifier -*ba* is realized -*bu*. In each instance, the noun being modified retains its H tone. For example, K-series *búugga* 'the book' becomes *búuggu* under subject marking.

9.2.4 No overt realization

Recall from Sections 6.2.3 and 6.2.4 that singular nouns from Classes 3 and 4 appear to be morphologically-complex even in their singular form. Their tonal behavior suggests that they contain concretized suffixes such that the location of their H tone shifts from stem to suffix under certain conditions. Phrase-finally, or in isolation, H tone is located on the stem, but phrase-medially in the "pre-modifier form," H tone shifts rightward. For example, the H tone on *dáwo* 'medicine' shifts when the noun is made definite: *dawáda* 'the medicine.' For these nouns, under those conditions where one would expect the SUBJ, H tone on Class 3 and 4 nouns remains on the stem: *dáwo* 'medicine.SUBJ.'

An analogous effect is seen on bare possessive determiners (see §9.3.1) in the presence of the SUBJ. Briefly here, presence of the SUBJ on bare possessive determiners (i.e., inalienable forms not followed by a definite determiner) interacts with phrasal marking of associative relationships (indicated by H tone at the right edge of a noun phrase). Consider, for example, the noun phrases *búugga* 'the book' and *wíilka* 'the boy.' When the two join in an associative relationship, the result is *búugga wiilká* 'the boy's book' where H tone occurs on the final tone bearing unit of the larger phrase, overwriting the tonal pattern on 'the boy.' The associative H also affects bare possessive determiners when they are not under subject marking, as in *aabbáhaý* 'my father.' H tone is on the final mora of the possessive determiner in these instances, but under subject marking, H tone shifts back to its usual, or default location on the penultimate mora, as in *aabbaháy*. In addition, the noun in such instances loses its H tone. See Green and Lampitelli (2021) for an analysis of these patterns.

9.3 Determiners

There are five types of determiners discussed in this section – possessive determiners, demonstrative determiners, remote definite determiners, definite determiners, and interrogative determiners. Taken together, these generally accomplish similar syntactic functions but have distinct phonological and morphological properties. A given noun need not be accompanied by a determiner, but also more than one determiner can modify a noun. When more than one determiner is present, they occur in a fixed order. Possessive determiners occur closest to the noun, followed by demonstrative determiners and then remote definite determiners. Definite determiners are clitics and always occur last in the phrase among other determiners, though they may be followed by other clitics. Interrogative determiners can co-occur with other determiners, except with the definite determiner.

Determiners have in common that they agree in grammatical gender and number (where relevant) with the noun that they modify. Grammatical gender agreement is indicated by the initial consonant of each determiner, whether K-series or T-series, though each of these alternate predictably depending on the segmental environment surrounding them. K-series determiners alternate between *k, g, h,* and ∅. T-series determiners alternate between *t, d, dh,* and *sh*. The sandhi alternations leading to these outcomes are discussed in §3.4. As such, each determiner has multiple phonologically-conditioned allomorphs.

From a tonal perspective, possessive determiners have a penultimate H tone under most conditions. Demonstrative determiners, remote definite determiners, and interrogative determiners have a final H tone. Definite determiner clitics are toneless. These determiners also differ from one another in terms of the tonal relationship they have with elements that precede them in a phrase. Three determiners – possessive, demonstrative, and remote definite – behave similarly from the standpoint of their tonology. Definite determiners and interrogative determiners are different from these other determiners and from one another.

9.3.1 Possessive determiners

Possessive determiners agree with the noun that they modify in grammatical gender and number. They also inflect for biological gender in the third person singular. Some speakers, particularly of Northern Somali, maintain a distinction between inclusive and exclusive first person plural, but this distinction is increasingly lost in favor of the exclusive form.

Somali's full paradigm of possessive determiners is in (27). Bare possessive determiners are those that occur without an accompanying definite determiner. These are limited in their use to define family members, close relations, and body parts. In this way, their use equates in some ways to what one might consider inalienable possession. These bare forms are given alongside a second *full* possessive determiner that includes a definite determiner (see §9.3.4) that also agrees with a modified noun in grammatical gender. These full possessive determiners have broader use and generally equate to what one might consider alienable possession.

(27) *Possessive determiners*

	Bare	Full	Bare	Full	
1SG	káy	káyga	táy	táyda	'my, mine'
2SG	káa	káaga	táa	táada	'your, yours (SG)'
3SG.M	kíis	kíisa	tíis	tíisa	'his'
3SG.F	kéed	kéeda	téed	téeda	'her'
1PL.ex	káyo	kayága	táyo	tayáda	'our, ours (exc.)'
1PL.in	kéen	kéenna	téen	téenna	'our, ours (inc.)'
2PL	kíin	kíinna	tíin	tíinna	'your, yours (PL)'
3PL	kóod	kóoda	tóod	tóoda	'their, theirs'

For full possessive determiners, the definite determiner appears in its CV form only after a possessive determiner ending in a vowel or nasal. Otherwise, it is simply realized *-a*, regardless of grammatical gender agreement. Possessive determiners occur immediately following the noun that they modify, even when more than one determiner occurs in the phrase.

Possessive determiners are best analyzed as having a penultimate H tone in their basic form, despite the fact that the location of their H tone sometimes alternates. These alternations occur when a noun and possessive determiner form an associative construction (see §6.6). This can easily be seen on a phrase containing a bare possessive determiner. In such a phrase, the noun has its H tone realized as expected, while the possessive determiner's H is realized on the final TBU: for example, *aabbáhaý* 'my father.' Under the influence of the SUBJ, the noun loses its H tone and H on the possessive shifts leftward by one TBU: *aabbaháy* 'my father.SUBJ.' These are the only instances in which the possessive determiner is directly affected by the SUBJ.

For full possessive determiners, both the noun and possessive have a H tone. H on the noun is found where expected based on grammatical gender and associated suffixes. H on the possessive determiner is on the penultimate mora: for example, *qálinkáyga* 'my pen.' Neither the noun nor possessive are affected tonally in the presence of the SUBJ. Rather, the SUBJ is realized on the definite determiner via a vowel alternation: *qálinkáygu* 'my pen.SUBJ.'

Note that possessive determiners can be used pronominally, such as in simple declaratives like *Waa káyga.* 'It's mine.'

9.3.2 Demonstrative determiners

Demonstrative determiners agree with the noun that they modify in grammatical gender. Their initial consonant undergoes expected sandhi alternations; see §3.4. There are four demonstrative determiners, though their use varies by dialect and by medium (i.e., written vs. spoken). There is a proximal demonstrative *kán/tán* 'this, these' that is used by all speakers. Another demonstrative that appears widely is *kaás/taás* 'that, those.' Speakers of Northern Somali maintain an additional distal demonstrative *koó/toó* 'that (yonder), those (yonder),' which was not acceptable to my speakers from Mogadishu. In written Somali, there is a medio-distal demonstrative *keér/teér*, but this is rare. These demonstratives can modify a noun but can also be used pronominally or impersonally, e.g., *kán/tán* 'this one.' When used impersonally in reference to a plural entity, they modify the noun *kú* 'someone, something' and begin with *w*, e.g., *kúwán* 'these ones.' Demonstrative determiners are in (28).

(28) *Demonstrative determiners*

		w/ the SM		
Proximal	kán	kani	kanu	'this, these'
	tán	tani	tanu	
	wán	wani	wanu	'these'
Medial	kaás	kaasi	kaasu	'that, those'
	taás	taasi	taasu	
	waás	waasi	waasu	'those'
Medio-Distal	keér	keeri		'that, those'
	teér	teeri		
	weér	weeri		'those'
Distal	koó	kooyi		'that, those'
	toó	tooyi		
	woó	wooyi		'those'

Demonstrative determiners do not affect the expression of H tone on the noun that they modify. Regardless of their gender agreement pattern, they exhibit a H tone on their final mora in their basic form. For example, *búuggaás* 'that book' has an expected K-series penult H on the noun but a final H on the determiner. These determiners lose their H tone and are also marked segmentally under subject marking, with segmental variation being attested for some forms. For example, with subject marking, 'that book' is either *búugaasu* or *búugaasi*. As stated above, there is reason to believe that the -*i* variant in each instance has a much wider distribution.

A demonstrative determiner can be separated from the noun that it modifies only by a possessive determiner: for example, *gúrigáygán* 'this house of mine' is a sequence of noun + possessive + demonstrative.

9.3.3 Remote definite determiner

Somali's remote definite determiners (RDEF) are *kií* and *tií*. They are sometimes referred to as "tensed definite articles" (Lecarme 1996, 2008) and "anaphoric determiners" (Tosco, 1994). Generally speaking, they are used to select a known or understood referent but one that is not necessarily physically present. Their use has been argued by Lecarme (2008) to be connected with tense in that, when used as a subject (at least for some speakers), they require past tense marking on verbs. Examples (29) and (30), adapted from Lecarme (2008), illustrate two closely-related contexts.

(29) *Ardayádda*   *[Soomaalída áh]*   *way*
ardayad=da   Soomaali=da áh   w=ay
female.student=T.DEF Somali=T.DEF be.PRES.RED DEC=3SG.F
imaáneysaa.
imaan-ey-s-aa
come-PROG-3SG.F-PRES
'The Somali student is coming.'

(30) *Ardayáddii*   *[Soomaalída aháyd]*   *wáy*
ardayad-dii   Soomaali=da ah-ay-d   w=ay
female.student-T.RDEF Somali=T.DEF be-PST-3SG.F DEC=3SG.F
timid.
t-imid
3SG.F-come.PST
'The Somali student came.'

Example (29) shows a subject noun made definite by a definite determiner clitic. This determiner does not require past tense agreement. Example (30), however, has a subject noun with a remote definite determiner. This determiner is compatible with past tense inflection on both the verb in the relative clause modifying the RDEF-marked noun and on the main clause verb.

Though the requirement for past tense with remote definite determiners appears true for some speakers, as reported in the literature, for other speakers with whom I have worked and in some examples I have found in corpora, the requirement is not necessarily absolute. Examples (31) and (32) help to illustrate this point.

(31) *Dhábtii*   *waa laácib [cajiib*   *áh].*
dhab-tii   waa laacib cajiib   ah
truth-T.RDEF DEC player wonderful be.PRES.RED
'In truth, he's a wonderful player.'

(32) *Jilayaáshii*   *[ay macallimádda*   *ú*   *aháyd]*   *ayáa baráha*
jila-yaa-shii   ay macallin-ad=da   u   ah-ay-d   ayaa bara=ha
actor-PL-T.RDEF 3PL teacher-PL=T.DEF for be-PST-3SG.T FOC trainer=K.DEF
bulshadá   *ugú*   *tartámayá*   *tacsídéeda.*
bulsha=da   u-gu   tar-tam-ay-a   tacsi-dee=da
society=T.DEF on-for compete-RECIP-PROG-PRES.RED cause-T.her=T.DEF
'The actors who she taught are competing with community educators to offer condolences.' (bbc somali: 53266547)

Example (31) shows a noun modified by a remote definite determiner in an equative sentence. Its predicate counterpart contains a subject relative whose verb is in the present tense. One might expect to find a past tense relative clause verb if there were an absolute connection between remote definite determiners and past tense. Likewise, in (32), the sentence's subject is modified by a remote definite determiner. While the relative clause that it modifies contains a past tense verb, the main clause verb that the subject governs is in the present tense. Once again, the connection between remote definite determiners and past tense agreement appears not to be absolute.

The examples thus far show that a remote definite determiner agrees with the noun that it modifies in grammatical gender. As elsewhere, this is reflected in the first consonant of the determiner. And, as with other determiners, these consonants undergo predictable sandhi alternations. These determiners, either *kíí* or *tíí*, can also be used pronominally, meaning simply 'the one (that we saw, that we were speaking of, etc.).' When used impersonally in this way, and in reference to some plural entity, *kúwíí* 'the ones (that we saw, that we were speaking of, etc.)' is used.

A remote definite determiner and the noun that it modifies each express a H tone. The noun's H tone is found wherever expected based on its class and number, and the determiner's H tone is on its final mora: for example, *márkabkíí* 'the ship' and *aroórtíí* 'the morning.' In the presence of the SUBJ, the noun retains its H tone as is, but the determiner loses its H tone. Thus, the forms of the preceding phrases in the presence of the SUBJ are *márkabkii* 'the ship.SUBJ' and *aroórtii* 'the morning.SUBJ.'

A remote definite determiner can be separated from the noun that it modifies by a possessive determiner, as in *gúrigáygíí* 'the house of mine,' or by a demonstrative determiner, as in *dádkoógíí* 'that country.' I have not encountered any instances in which a noun can be followed by a sequence of possessive + demonstrative + remote definite determiner.

9.3.4 Definite determiner

The definite determiners *-ka* and *-ta* agree with the noun that they modifier in grammatical gender. As with other determiners, they undergo predictable sandhi alternations in certain environments (see §3.4). Other forms of *-ka* are *-ga*, *-ha*, and *-a* while the other forms of *-ta* are *-da*, *-dha*, and *-sha*. Examples are as follows where the second definite marked form is subject-marked:

(33) *Alternations in definite determiners*

			w/o SUBJ	w/ SUBJ	
a.	qálin	'pen'	qálinka	qálinku	'the pen'
b.	díbi	'bull'	díbiga	díbigu	'the bull'
c.	mácne	'meaning'	macnáha	macnúhu	'the meaning'
d.	mádax	'head'	mádaxa	mádaxu	'the head'
e.	maalín	'day'	maalínta	maalíntu	'the day'
f.	gabádh	'girl'	gabádha	gabádhu	'the girl'
g.	úl	'stick'	úsha	úshu	'the stick'

Definite determiners cannot stand alone. They occur only alongside the noun that they modify (e.g., *irbádda* 'the needle'), though as discussed in §9.3.1, they can also follow a possessive determiner, as in *irbáddáyda* 'my needle.' The examples above show that a definite determiner has no effect on the noun's H tone, but a definite determiner also does not have a H tone of its own. Green and Morrison (2016) consider them to be free clitics, given that they appear to be prosodified at the level of the phrase, rather than into the word itself. The only condition under which a definite determiner can exhibit a H tone is in an associative construction; see §9.5.

When a noun phrase ending in a definite determiner is followed by the SUBJ, the SUBJ is realized only by a vowel alternation, rather than by the loss of a H tone. For example, *dábka* 'the fire' becomes *dábku* 'the fire.SUBJ.' The noun retains its H tone, and the vowel of the determiner alternates.

9.3.5 Interrogative determiner

Interrogative determiners agree with the noun that they modify in grammatical gender. Grammatical gender agreement is indicated by the first consonant of the determiner, which undergoes sandhi alternations where relevant. These determiners, which in their basic forms are *keé* and *teé*, follow the noun they modify. They have a H tone on their final mora and the preceding noun loses its H tone: e.g., *markabkeé* 'which ship?' and *irbaddeé* 'which needle?' Interrogative determiners can also be used pronominally on their own, as in *keé* or *teé* to mean 'which (one)?' Used impersonally in this way for plural referents, the form is *kuweé* 'which (ones)?'

An interrogative determiner can be separated from the noun that it modifies by a possessive determiner, as in *gurigaageé* 'which house of yours?,' but not by a demonstrative, remote definite determiner, or definite determiner. Whenever an interrogative determiner is present, it will have a H tone on its final mora. These determiners are not affected by subject marking.

9.4 Lexical adjectives

Somali has a fairly small, closed set of lexical adjectives that can be used to modify nouns. Other adjectival words are adjectival participles derived from verbs and are discussed separately in Section 7.1.10. Example (34) shows nominal attribution via a lexical adjective. As discussed in §14.1.5, one way to treat such constructions formally, as discussed by Saeed (1988, 1993b, 1999), is to consider them subject relative clauses which, in the present tense, lose their verb 'to be' via "copula reduction." Under this view, in this example, 'new airplane' might instead be translated 'airplane that is new.'

(34) *Dayuurád cusúb báy   ahayd.*
 dayuurad cusub b=ay   ah-ay-d
 airplane new   FOC=3SG.T be-PST-3SG.T
 'It was a new airplane.' (Z & O: 17)

An alternative approach might be to treat these as associative constructions, akin to those discussed below in Section 9.5, though there is perhaps some reason to question such an approach. Associative constructions typically encode a genitive 'X of Y' or 'X's Y' relationship, which might be difficult to capture in sequences involving a lexical adjective. That is, rather than *dayuurád cusúb* 'new airplane' being translated literally as 'airplane that is new' under a relative clause approach, under an alternative associative approach, one might expect a reading like 'airplane of newness,' which seems stilted. There is no doubt that the matter merits further inquiry.

When more than one lexical adjective modifies a noun, the two are coordinated by *oo*. Elsewhere, this functions as a relativizer coordinating more prototypical relative clauses, as later discussed in §15.3. Example (35) shows the same phrase from (34) modified by a second lexical adjective.

(35) *Dayuurád cusúb oo weýn báy   ahayd.*
 dayuurad cusub oo   weyn b=ay   ah-ay-d
 airplane new   SUB big FOC=3SG.T be-PST-3SG.T
 'It was a new, big airplane.'

Other combinations are possible, such as when a noun is modified by a lexical adjective and another nominal. In these instances, the nominal requires 'to be' to be expressed, similar to what is seen in relative clauses. In (36), the particle *oo* once again coordinates two attributive modifiers, but the second one, being a nominal, requires the verb *áh*.

(36) *Dayuurádda   cusúb oo   faransíiska   áh   báy*
     dayuurad=da   cusub oo   faransiis=ka   ah   b=áy
     airplane=T.DEF new   SUB French=K-DEF be.PRES.RED FOC=3SG.T
     ahayd.
     ah-ay-d
     be-PST-3SG.T
     'It was the new French airplane.'

There appears not to be a restriction on the relative order of attributes of different types, at least in simple instances. For example, *cáshar weýn oo labaád áh* 'a big, second lesson' in which a lexical adjective precedes a numeric is grammatical, as is *cáshar labaád áh oo weýn* where the order of attributes is reversed. Speakers I consulted about this note no substantive difference in meaning between the two options.

The list in (37) is a fairly complete set of Somali's lexical adjectives. If the adjective ends in a short vowel, that vowel has H tone. Otherwise, H tone is on the penultimate vocalic mora. Pronunciation variants are indicated where relevant.

(37) Lexical Adjectives

a.	adág	'hard, strong, difficult'
b.	bisíl	'cooked, ripe'
c.	cabsí	'dangerous, frightening'
d.	cád	'white'
e.	cás	'red, pink'
f.	culús	'heavy, serious'
g.	cusúb	'new, fresh'
h.	dambé	'recent, next'
i.	dháw/dhów	'near, close by'
j.	dhéer	'tall, long, deep, loud'
k.	feejíg/feeyíg	'careful, alert, cautious'
l.	fóg	'far, distant, remote'
m.	fudúd	'easy, simple, relaxed'
n.	idíl	'complete, all'
o.	jecél	'loving, fond'
p.	kulúl	'hot'
q.	le'ég	'equal in size'
r.	mác	'sweet, plump, well-said'
s.	madów	'black, gloomy, sad'
t.	móog	'ignorant, unaware, lacking'
u.	necéb	'hated, disliked'
v.	nég	'permanent, stable, calm, serene'
w.	nóol	'alive, cheerful, lively'
x.	nugúl	'soft, delicate, weak, docile'
y.	óg	'aware, knowledgeable, informed'
z.	qabów	'cold'
aa.	róon	'good, excellent, superior'
bb.	saré	'topmost, upper, supreme'
cc.	shilís	'fat, plump, stout (of animals)'
dd.	ugúb	'childless, virginal, fresh'
ee.	úun	'sole, only, merely'
ff.	wál	'each, every'
gg.	wéyn	'big, large, important'
hh.	xún	'bad, evil, worthless'
ii.	yár	'small, slight, young, few'

9.5 Associative constructions

Associative constructions are a productive means by which to express attribution in Somali. These are sometimes called genitive constructions elsewhere in the Somali literature, under the view that the language has a system of grammatical case marking. The relationships that they entail are varied, but generally convey the meaning 'noun 1 of noun 2' or 'noun 1's noun 2.' Some uses include: i) simple attribution, like in *gacánta midíg* 'the right(side) hand'; ii) the expression of part/whole relationships, like *hílib lo'aád* 'meat of a cow'; iii) the expression of ownership, as in *gúriga Ibraahím* 'Ibraahim's house'; and iv) describing the composition of a group, as in *wágan fardoód* 'a herd of horses.'

All associative constructions have in common that, all else being equal, any member of the construction can be made definite, and each exhibits a H tone. Their phonological behavior is indicative of the fact that each element of the construction forms its own phrase. That both elements can host determiners reinforces their biphrasal nature syntactically. That said, associative constructions form a left-headed syntactic constituent. The first noun in the construction governs patterns of subject-verb agreement. Though the construction as a whole is syntactically left-headed, both members of the construction dictate their own grammatical gender requirements on the determiners that modify them.

Consider the phrase *cílmiga bulshadá* 'social science' (the science of society) formed by an associative construction in (38). Agreement on the verb follows the K-series pattern which matches the head noun's K-series definite determiner. However, the second noun in the construction has a T-series definite determiner, illustrating that the grammatical gender of the head noun is not distributed over both phrases.

(38) *Haddíi cílmiga   bulshadá   wáx [lagú   qiimeeyó]*
     haddii cilmi=ga   bulsha=da   wax la=gu   qiim-ee-y-o
     if   science=K.DEF society=T.DEF thing ISP=with value-FAC-3SG.K-IRR
     'If social science is something one values' (somalithinktank.org: 43064)

I show in the sections below that these constructions form two main categories – prosodic associatives and suffixing associatives.

9.5.1 Prosodic associatives

Associative marking by H tone alternation alone occurs in phrases like *furáha gurigá* 'the key of the house' and *heés Soomaalí* 'a Somali song.' The H tone of the first noun occurs where expected for its gender agreement class and any associated morphology. The H tone of the second noun, however, is located on the final TBU of the noun phrase, even if this is a definite determiner. For the first example, we would otherwise expect *gúriga* 'the house' to have a H tone on the penultimate mora of the nominal root if this phrase were not the second member of an associative construction. Prosodic associatives are one of the few instances where a H tone can occur on a definite determiner.

Prosodic associatives are formed when: i) the final noun of the construction is definite, or ii) the final noun is non-definite but takes K-series agreement. Consider the following examples in (39).

(39) *Prosodic associative constructions*

a.	búugga wiilká	'the boy's book' (lit. the book of the boy)
b.	mídabka gurigá	'the house's color' (lit. the color of the house)
c.	qurúxda gabadhá	'the girl's beauty' (lit. the beauty of the girl)
d.	arrimáha bulshadá	'social issues' (lit. the issues of society)
e.	hílibka orgigá	'goat meat' (lit. the meat of the goat)
f.	heés Soomaalí	'a Somali song' (cf. *Soomaáliga* 'the Somali language')

Because prosodic associatives involve only a tonal alternation, the syntactic relationship can be indicated unambiguously on the final TBU of a noun modified by a definite determiner. This is because a definite determiner is otherwise toneless, and thus the presence of a phrasal H boundary tone is perceptible. The situation is analogous for a non-definite K-series noun. These nouns have H tone on their penultimate mora. Thus, rightward shift of H tone to the noun's final mora alone is sufficient to mark the associative relationship. Non-definite T-series nouns behave differently.

9.5.1.1 With possessive determiners

A prosodic associative is formed when a bare possessive determiner modifies a noun (see §9.3.1). For example, the phrase *saaxíibkaý* 'my friend' has a H tone where expected on the noun *saaxíib* 'friend' but a H on the final mora of the possessive determiner. Elsewhere, we would expect H tone on the penultimate mora of the possessive determiner, as in *qálinkáyga* 'my pen.'

Bare possessive determiners are also used in forming partitives. Consider, for example, the phrase *iyága shántoód* 'the five of them.' Here, the numeric *shán* is modified by a T-series 3PL bare possessive determiner with a H on its final mora. Again, we would otherwise expect H on the penultimate mora. Additional examples are in (40).

(40) *Partitive associative constructions*

a.	iyága qáarkoód	'some of them' (lit. they, their portion)
b.	góbolkaás qáarkoód	'part of that region' (lit. that region, its portion)
c.	labádeén	'the two of us' (lit. our two)
d.	shántiín	'the five of you (PL)' (lit. your five)
e.	afártan shílin dhammaántiís	'forty shillings in all' (lit. forty shillings, its whole)

9.5.2 Suffixing associatives with *-eéd, -oód, -aád*

Forming an associative construction requires a suffix when: i) the final noun of the construction is non-definite and takes T-series agreement, or ii) the final noun of the construction takes K-series agreement and ends in *-ó*. The generalization, as stated above, is that in both these instances, H tone is typically located on the noun's final mora. Thus, prosodic marking of the associative by final H tone alone would be redundant.

Associative marking by suffixation is accomplished in most instances via the addition of *-eéd* to the second of two nouns in sequence. Examples are in (41). The suffix *-eéd* is used when the noun to which it attaches ends in a consonant or in a vowel other than *-ó*.[3]

(41) *Suffixing associatives with -eéd*

a.	*búrbur maaliyadeéd*	'fragments of wealth'	cf. *maaliyád* 'wealth'
b.	*gácanka Cadmeéd*	'the Gulf of Aden'	
c.	*sháqo macallimeéd*	'work of a (female) teacher'	cf. *macallín* 'teacher'
e.	*beeraláyda Soomaaliyeéd*	'the farmers of Somalia'	cf. *Soomaaliyá* 'Somalia'

When a noun instead ends in plural *-ó*, the suffix *-oód* is used, as in *wágan fardoód* 'a herd of horses.' In addition, there are some idiosyncratic, lexically-specific instances in which *-aád* is instead used. These are limited to occurring with terms for certain animals, as in *hílib lo'aád* 'meat of a cow.'

9.5.2.1 With count nouns

Suffixing associatives are a strategy used for counting plural nouns ending in *-ó*.

(42) *Counting associatives*

a.	*afárta meeloód*	'the four places'	cf. *meeló* 'places'
b.	*shán daqiiqadoód*	'five minutes'	cf. *daqiiqadó* 'minutes'
c.	*saddéxda maalmoód*	'the three days'	cf. *maalmó* 'days'
d.	*afár biloód*	'four months'	cf. *biló* 'months'
e.	*saddéx geesoód*	'three sides'	cf. *geesó* 'sides'
f.	*labáda sannaddoód*	'the two years'	cf. *sannaddó* 'years'

9.5.2.2 Ordinal numbers

It was introduced in §9.1.6.2 that *-aád* is used to form ordinal numbers when it is suffixed to a numeric noun. The following examples in (43) show that these ordinal number associatives can be used to modify a noun.

---

[3] One exception is *baabuúr Mareykaneéd* 'an American car,' which takes *-eéd* but is a K-series noun ending in a consonant. N. Lampitelli has suggested to me that perhaps this is because the interpretation is instead 'a car of the Americans.'

(43) *Ordinal number associatives*

a.	cáshar labaád	'a second lesson'
b.	dariishádda afaraád	'the fourth window'
c.	booqashádéydii kowaád	'my first visit'
d.	fásalka lixaád	'the sixth grade'
e.	qófka kowaád	'the first person'
f.	bísha shanaád	'the fifth month'

9.6 Attributive relative clauses

I showed in §9.4 that Somali can express attribution of a noun directly only by a closed class of approximately 40 lexical adjectives and does so via what some might consider to be relative clauses. Subject relative clauses are employed in attribution more broadly and are formed via a closed set of verbs taking a noun complement or otherwise by a hybrid verb. These are discussed in detail alongside other relative clauses in §14.1.5.

9.7 Other clitics

In addition to the definite determiner discussed in §9.3.4, there are two additional enclitics that can occur at the right edge of a noun phrase.

9.7.1 Negative -na

The nominal enclitic -na negates the content of the noun to which it attaches. It does not appear to be productive, but rather forms negative pronouns and adverbs like those below. It has no affect on the tonal behavior of the noun that precedes it and does not exhibit a H tone itself.

(44) *Negative enclitic -na*

a.	cídna	'no one, nobody'
b.	meélna	'nowhere'
c.	mídna	'neither'
d.	wáxna	'nothing'
e.	qófna	'no one'
f.	márna	'never'

9.7.2 Intensifier -*ba*

The phrasal enclitic -*ba* is an intensifier that reinforces the content of the phrase to which it attaches. It is non-tonal and does not affect the tone of the phrase to which it attaches. It often appears in the creation of pronouns like *wáxba* 'anything' (cf. *wáx* 'thing') and *wálba* 'every' (cf. *wál* 'each'), but its use is far more productive.

That the intensifier is phrase final is clear in instances like *toddobáadkiíba* 'each week' and *afártaba* 'the four of them,' the latter of which shows that it follows a definite determiner. It can just as easily intensify negation, as seen in *márnaba* and *goórnaba*, both of which mean 'never.' In these instances, it appears after the negative enclitic -*na*. The intensifier is also affected by the SUBJ, becoming -*bu*. Its vowel alternates in the same manner seen in definite determiners.

10 The Verb Complex

The basis of every Somali clause is the Verb Complex (VC). The VC is a constituent that is composed minimally of a verb, but it also typically contains other elements such as pronoun clitics, adpositions, and deictic particles. Considerable attention has been given to the VC (e.g., Appleyard 1990; Gebert 1986; Hyman 1981; Saeed 1999; Svolacchia et al. 1995; Svolacchia and Puglielli 1999, among others), though it is sometimes alternatively called the "verbal piece," "verbal group," or "verbal complex." Some have described the VC as a miniature version of the Somali sentence (e.g, Gebert 1988; Puglielli 1981). This perspective stems, at least in part, from the fact that pronoun clitics within the VC satisfy the verb's valence, even in the absence of overt coreferential noun phrases. Of course, one must bear in mind that not all pronoun clitics have segmental exponents and that some syntactic operations appear to trigger movement of subject pronoun clitics (located at the left edge of the VC) and other VC elements outside of the VC itself. Along these lines, some scholars have described noun phrases (located outside of the VC) as syntactic adjuncts or "satellites" whose presence and location relative to the VC is dictated by information structure (Frascarelli and Puglielli 2003; Lecarme 1999a; Saeed 1994). Others analyze them formally as constituents within syntactic XPs associated with focus and topic (see, e.g., Frascarelli 2010b,a; Frascarelli and Puglielli 2009).

Figure 10.1 provides a representation of the Somali VC's templatic structure. This figure illustrates that the verb must appear within the VC. Other elements that may or may not appear under certain conditions are in parentheses. When other elements are present, the verb always appears last relative to them.[1]

$\langle SP \rangle$ $\langle ISP \rangle$ $\left\{ \begin{array}{c} OBJ_1 \\ RRP \end{array} \right\}$ $\langle ADP(s) \rangle$ $\langle NEG \rangle$ $\langle OBJ_2 \rangle$ $\langle DEIC \rangle$ $\langle ADV \rangle$ verb

Fig. 10.1: Verb Complex template

When other VC elements are present, they precede the verb and occur in a fairly rigid templatic order, with only a few phonotactic and morphotactic constraints being responsible for any variation in this regard. The relative order of elements within the VC can also be altered slightly upon the coordination of clauses, where often there is insertion of a clausal conjunction clitic (see §15.2). Also, it is important to note that nouns do not occur within the VC except in instances in which they have been incorporated by the verb. For more on this, see Sections 8.2.1 and 8.2.2. Details about the

---

[1] SP = Subject pronoun; ISP = Impersonal subject pronoun; OBJ_1 = first series object pronoun; RRP = reflexive/reciprocal object pronoun; ADP = adposition; NEG = Negative; OBJ_2 = second series object pronoun; DEIC = deictic; ADV = adverbial

behavior of individual components of the VC are covered in turn in sections below. In examples throughout this chapter, the VC is indicated in square brackets.

From a phonological perspective, Le Gac (2002) proposes that the VC comprises an intonation phrase. It can be separated by a pause from any noun phrase that comes before or after it, but a pause is not grammatical between elements of the VC itself. Under this view, and depending on the type and number of elements within it, one could further divide the VC into one or two phonological phrases. One of these contains the verb itself, which forms a phonological phrase with its inflectional suffixes. Elements within the VC before the verb form another phonological phrase.

In addition to the verb, elements such as adpositions, second position object pronouns, and deictic particles are associated with their own H tone. Adpositions, in particular, display certain word-like properties. When more than one adposition is present, they cluster together, appearing to form a single phonological word with just one H tone. Adpositions (whether singular or in a cluster) serve as a host to pronominal proclitics, where relevant. Subject pronoun clitics are enclitics, and as such, they do not cliticize with other pronoun clitics but rather they join the morpheme that precedes them (e.g., a clause type particle or focus particle) or otherwise may be drawn out of the VC in the formation of questions and clefts.

10.1 The verb slot

Though it is found in the last slot of the VC, description of the VC begins here with the verb because it is the only truly obligatory element found within the constituent. Several types of verbs can occupy the verb slot. These include an inflected finite verb (1), an inflected auxiliary verb preceded by an infinitive (2), a hybrid verb (3), and, in the case of attributive relative clauses, solely an adjective (4) or adjectival participle (5).

(1) *Wa[annu lá   soconnay]   hawlgálka.*
    wa=annu la   soc-on-n-ay   hawl.gal=ka
    DEC=1PL about be.apprised-MID-1PL-PST work.commit=K-DEF
    'We were told about the mission.'

(2) *Waláalkaá   sideé b[áan   ulá   xiriíri   karaa]?*
    walaal-kaa   sidee b=aan   u-la   xiriir-i   kar-∅-aa
    sibling-K.your how FOC=1SG for-with contact-INF be.able-1SG-PRES
    'How can I get in touch with your brother?' (Z & O: 696)

(3) *Áad ay[áan   ugú faraxsánahay].*
    aad ay=aan   ugu farax-s-an-∅-ah-ay
    very FOC=1SG SUP happy-WCAUS-STV-1SG-be-PRES
    'I am very happy about it.'

(4) *naág [wanaagsán]*
 naag wanaag-s-an-∅
 woman good-WCAUS-STV-be.PRES.RED
 'a good woman' (lit. a woman who is good)

(5) *wáqtiga [dhów]*
 waqti=ga dhow
 time=K-DEF near
 'the near future' (the time that is near)

Also possible are verbs that have incorporated a noun, as in (6).

(6) *oo sheegey ín aán Kénya [loogú dulqaadán doonin].*
 oo sheeg-∅-ey ín aán Kénya lo=o-gú dul-qaad-án doon-in
 REL say-3SG.M-PST COMP NEG Kenya ISP=for-on patience-take-INF will-NEG
 'who said that Kenya will not be tolerated.' (allbadweyn.net: 126507)

The VC can contain only a single verb (or hybrid verb, etc.). As such, in more complex sentences, verbs cannot simply be conjoined within a VC. Rather, entire VCs are coordinated. This is seen in (7) where the superlative adposition cluster *ugú* is repeated in three successive VCs.

(7) *sí waafaqsán shuruúcda [ugú adág], [ugú*
 si waafaq-s-an shuruuc=da ugu adag ugu
 way in.accordance-WCAUS-STV law=T.DEF SUP difficult SUP
 hufán], [ugúna macquulsán].
 huf-an ugu=na macquul-s-an
 transparent-STV SUP=CONJ credible-WCAUS-STV
 'according to the most robust, transparent, and credible laws.'

10.2 Pronoun clitics

Pronoun clitics occur within the VC and function as verbal arguments, thereby satisfying the verb's valence. This is sometimes obscured by the fact that third person object pronouns have no overt exponent. Subject pronouns can be co-referential with a full NP outside of the VC, but an external NP cannot occur independent of a co-referential pronoun clitic unless the NP is marked as "in focus" by a focus marker.

This section first discusses subject pronoun clitics, including the impersonal subject pronoun (ISP) *la*. After this, object pronoun clitics are discussed, including the reflexive/reciprocal object pronoun (RRP) *is*. Whether or not subject pronoun clitics should be in included in the VC is a matter of considerable debate (see Frascarelli

2010b; Lecarme 1991; Saeed 1999; Svolacchia et al. 1995). Subject pronoun clitics (SPC) are included within the VC here because, in the vast majority of cases, they occur at what is arguably the left edge of the VC. They precede object pronoun clitics, which are undoutedbly within the VC. If the VC is in fact a miniature version of a Somali sentence, and Somali has a default SOV word order (Gebert 1986; Svolacchia et al. 1995), this is precisely the position in which one might expect to find them. The debate surrounding SPCs concerns the presence of certain exceptions where, at the surface level, a SPC does not appear at VC's left edge. These exceptions likely stem from the fact that SPCs are enclitics, as opposed to object pronoun clitics, which are proclitics, and that SPCs must cliticize onto a functional projection, rather than onto a lexical projection. As such, though they typically prosodify with an immediately preceding focus marker or clause type marker, these elements may appear elsewhere for discourse purposes. Accordingly, they attract the SPC away from its usual location. It is also possible, in the absence of such an element, for their host to be a clause-initial question marker, complementizer, subordinator, or the post-verbal, cleft-forming focus marker *waxa*, which may not necessarily immediately precede the VC. In these instances, the subject pronouns may ultimately be separated from the VC itself by another element, such as a noun phrase or adverbial.

10.2.1 Subject pronoun clitics

Subject pronoun clitics (SPC) are typically found at the left edge of the VC where they are enclitic to a preceding function word. There are, however, some instances in which they can be attracted outside the VC, such as in the formation of Wh-questions, clefts, and upon subordination. As shown in (8), there are unique SPCs for most person, number, and grammatical gender combinations, as well as for clusivity in 1PL, at least for some speakers. Inclusive 1PL refers to the speaker, hearer, and other relevant individuals. Exclusive 1PL instead refers just to the speaker and hearer, and excludes other relevant individuals. Those speakers who do not make this distinction for clusivity utilize the 1PL exclusive form.

It is often the case that there is no overt number distinction in the first and second person, as indicated in parentheses. This means that first and second person singular forms are used even for corresponding plural referents. The forms for 3SG.F and 3PL are identical.

(8) *Subject pronoun clitics*

1SG	=aan	1PL.exc	=aannu (=aan)
		1PL.inc	=aynu
2SG	=aad	2PL	=aydin (=aad)
3SG.M	=uu		
3SG.F	=ay	3PL	=ay

The following examples illustrate cliticization of a SPC onto each of Somali's three focus markers.

(9) *Áad yár b[áan ú akhriyey].*
    aad yar b=aan u akhri-y-ey
    very slow FOC=1SG with read-1SG-PST
    'I read it carefully.'

(10) *Nínkaás miy[áad aqoónaysey]?*
     nin-kaas m=iy=aad aqoon-ay-s-ey
     man-K.that QM=FOC=2SG know-PROG-2SG-PST
     'Did you recognize that man? (Z & O: 25)

(11) *Wúx[uu dhaxlay] arígii aabbíhiis?*
     wux=uu dhaxl-∅-ay ari-gii aabbi-hiis
     FOC=3SG.M inherit-3SG.M-PST sheep-K.RDEF father-K.his
     'He inherited his father's sheep.' (Z & O: 182)

The focus marker *báa*, in particular, may fuse with a preceding NP, making it appear that a SPC has cliticized directly onto the NP itself. This is seen in (12). The presence of the focus marker is clear from its contribution of H tone which is otherwise absent on definite determiners and on SPCs.

(12) *Géesk[úu ká soó galay].*
     gées=k:∅=uu ká soo gal-∅-ay
     side=K.DEF:FOC=3SG.M from VEN enter-3SG.M-PST
     'He entered from the side.'

SPCs cliticize onto focus markers only when the subject of a clause is not morphologically marked as in focus. Such cliticization occurs when the subject is pronominal, as in (9) through (12), as well as when a subject noun phrase is present that is not marked as in focus, as in (13). In this example, the oblique object is in focus, thereby compelling the 3PL SPC to cliticize onto the focus marker.

(13) *Inammádií   iyo   gabdhíhií   súuqa   b[áy   tageen].*
     inam-ma-dii iyo   gabdh-i-hii   suuq-a   b=ay   tag-∅-ee-n
     boy-PL-T.RDEF and girl-PL-K.RDEF market-K.DEF FOC=3PL go-3-PST-PL
     'The boys and girls went to the market.' (Z & I: 140)

For comparison, consider (14), where the subject NP is marked as in focus. Here, the focus marker does not host a corresponding 3SG.M SPC.

(14) *Macállinka   báa   buugág   [na   siiyeý].*
     macallin=ka   baa   buug-ag na   sii-y-ey
     teacher=K.DEF FOC   book-PL 1PL.OBJ   give-PST.RED
     'The teacher gave books to us.' (Z & I: 88)

SPCs also cliticize onto clause type markers like *waa*, as in (15), and *ma*, as in (16).

(15) *W[aad   fiicnáyd].*
     w=aad   fiic-n-ay-d
     DEC=2SG good-STV-PST-2SG
     'You were fine.'

(16) *M[aynu   naqaannó]   iyága.*
     m=aynu   n-aqaan-no   iyaga
     NEG=1PL.inc 1PL-know-IRR   them
     'We don't know them.'

They can also clicitize onto the complementizer *ín*, as in (17), as well as onto other subordinators, as in (18).

(17) *Isú   diyaaríya   ín[aad   fuushaan].*
     is=u   diyaar-i-ya   in=aad   fuu-sh-aa-n
     RRP=for prepare-WCAUS-INF COMP=2PL mount-2-PRES-PL
     'Prepare yourselves for boarding.' (Z & O: 340)

(18) *Xágg[aad   ká   heshay]   lacágtan?*
     xagg=aad   ka   he-sh-ay   lacag-tan
     where=2SG   from find-2SG-PST money-T.this
     'Where did you get this money from?' (Z & O: 680)

In each of these instances, the SPC maintains its location at the left edge of the VC, though these same functional morphemes have the ability to attract a SPC out of the VC, as in (19) and (20). In these and related instances, they are separated from the VC by a noun or adverbial. The displaced SPCs are underlined in these examples.

(19) *Waa inaad   hádda [iská   qashó].*
     waa in=aad   hadda is=ka   qa-sh-o
     DEC COMP=2SG now RECIP=at have.operation-2SG-IRR
     'You must have an operation now.'

(20) *Muxúu   Cáli [ká   hadley]?*
     m=ux=uu   Cali ka   hadl-∅-ey
     QM=FOC=3SG.M Cali about speak-3SG.M-PST
     'What did Cali talk about?' (Z & I: 158)

10.2.2 Impersonal subject pronoun

In addition to the enclitic SPCs described in §10.2.1, there is the impersonal subject pronoun (ISP) proclitic *la*. This pronoun is used only for human referents, and its use introduces a passive reading to the clause.[2] The ISP is a toneless proclitic that occurs in a slot between other SPCs and object pronoun clitics (OPC) within the Verb Complex. The simplest illustrations of the ISP are found in clauses that do not contain a focus marker, like (21) and (22). The ISP always requires 3SG.M verbal agreement.

(21) *Wáa [la qorey].*
     waa la qor-∅-ey
     DEC ISP write-3SG.M-PST
     'It was written.'

(22) *Shów lacágta   [la igá   xadee].*
     show lacag=ta   la i=ga   xad-∅-ee
     what.if money=T.DEF ISP 1SG.OBJ=from steal-3SG.M-POT
     'Suppose that the money is stolen from me.' (Z & I: 396)

The ISP is limited in its use to functioning as the subject of a transitive verb. Compare the examples just above to (23) where the impersonal subject of an intransitive verb must instead be expressed by *qóf* 'someone.'

(23) *Qóf   Af-Carábi   ma [kú hadlaa]?*
     qof   af-Carabi   ma ku hadl-∅-aa
     someone language-Arabic QM in speak-3SG.M-PRES
     'Does anyone speak (in) Arabic?' (Z & O: 534)

---

[2] Some have called this morpheme an "arbitrary subject pronoun" (Svolacchia and Puglielli 1999) or a "non-specific subject pronoun" (Saeed 1999). Others (Appleyard 1990; Cabredo Hofherr 2004; Gebert 1986), however, use the term "impersonal subject pronoun," as adopted here.

It is not possible to use the ISP to refer impersonally to an object. Example (24) shows that the OPC *ku* in the first clause is co-referential with the ISP *la* in the second clause. Having the latter in both clauses is ungrammatical.

(24)   *Háddii gaajó [ku haysó],   cúntáa   [la cunaa].*
       haddii gaajo   ku hay-s-o,   cun=t:aa   la cun-∅-aa
       if   hunger 2SG seize-2SG-IRR food=T-DEF:FOC ISP eat-3SG.M-PRES
       'If one gets hungry, one eats food.'

The ISP cannot cliticize onto a focus marker, even in a clause with a focus-marked object, like in (25). Recall from §10.2.1 that under such conditions, other SPCs obligatorily cliticize onto the focus marker. In fact, when the subject of a clause is the ISP, a focus marker must be bare. This is seen in each of the examples in this section.

(25)   *Búuggán   ayáa [la soó gatay].*
       buug-gan   ayaa la   soo gat-∅-ay
       book-K.this FOC   ISP VEN buy-3SG.M-PST
       'This book was bought.' (Cabredo Hofherr 2004)

Likewise, (26) shows that the ISP cannot be attracted out of the VC in instances when other SPCs might be. These facts are in support of the prosodic status of the ISP as a proclitic.

(26)   *Ímmisa sáac báa bángiga   [la xidhaa]?*
       immisa saac baa bangi=ga   la xidh-∅-aa
       which time FOC bank=K.DEF ISP close-3SG.M-PRES
       'What time is the bank closing?' (Z & O: 695)

That the ISP is a proclitic is also clear in instances in which it cliticizes onto a first series object pronoun or an adposition. Both lead to segmental alternations. ISP + first series object pronoun clusters are in (27). These clusters are toneless.

(27)   *Impersonal subject pronoun + 1st series object pronoun*

la = i	lay	'one...me'
la = ku	lagu	'one...you (SG)'
la = na	nala	'one...us (exc)'
la = ina	layna	'one...us (inc)'
la = idin	laydin	'one...you (PL)'

Forms where the ISP joins a third person object pronoun are not included here given that the latter have no segmental exponent. Note, also, that there is metathesis involving the ISP and the 1PL exclusive object pronoun. Examples of these clusters in context are in (28) and (29).

(28) *Wáa [lay   arkay].*
     waa la=i   ark-∅-ay
     DEC ISP=1SG.OBJ see-3SG.M-PST
     'Someone saw me.'

(29) *Má [lagu   siiyay]?*
     ma la=gu   sii-y-ay
     QM ISP=2SG.OBJ give-3SG.M-PST
     'Did someone give it to you?'

ISP + adposition clusters are in (30). These clusters have a H tone on the adposition and often result in segmental alternations.

(30) *Impersonal subject pronoun + adposition*

la + ú	loó	'one…to, for'
la + kú	lagú	'one…into, on'
la + ká	lagá	'one…from, out of'
la + lá	lalá	'one…with'

The following examples show that when an ISP and adposition occur in the same VC, the adposition does not govern the ISP. In (31), the adposition governs the oblique object. In (32), the adposition governs the passive subject.

(31) *Hálkiyo Xámar   inteé [loó socdaa]?*
     halk=iyo Xamar intee lo=o soc-d-∅-aa
     here=and Mogadishu how.far ISP=to proceed-MID-3SG.M-PRES
     'And, how far from here does one go towards Mogadishu?' (Z & O: 288)

(32) *Lacág baa [lalá   tagay].*
     lacag baa la=la   tag-∅-ay
     money FOC ISP=with go-3SG.M-PST
     'Money was taken away.' (Z & I: 173)

The ISP must remain within the VC, even when other elements to which it typically clicitizes move outside of the VC. For example, the ISP typically clusters with the negative particle *má* within the VC, yielding *lamá*, as in (33).

(33) Wéli [lamá   arkín]   wáxan   oo   kále.
     weli la=ma   ark-in   wax-an   oo   kale
     yet ISP=NEG see-PST.NEG   thing-K.this REL else

   'Nothing like this has been seen before.' (Z & I: 382)

Example (34), however, shows that while the negative particle can move outside the VC, the ISP does not move along with it. Other clitics, like object pronouns and adpositions, can be drawn outside the VC by movement of the negative. For more on this, see §10.8.

(34) Má [la aqoóneynín].
     ma la aqoón-eyn-in
     NEG ISP know-PST.PROG-NEG

   'It wasn't known.' (Z & O: 25)

10.2.3 First series object pronouns

There are two object pronoun paradigms in Somali. These are the first series and second series object pronouns. The first series object pronouns covered in this section are pronominal proclitics that typically (though not always) occur in a slot in the VC between subject pronoun clitics and adpositions. Second series object pronouns are found in a separate slot, closer to the verb and are discussed separately in §10.3.

Somali's first series object pronoun clitics (OPC) are shown in (35). Some speakers maintain a clusivity distinction in 1PL OPCs, though many speakers collapse this in favor of the exclusive form. There are no third person object pronoun clitics, either in the singular or plural.

(35) *First series object pronoun clitics*

1SG	i=	1PL.exc	na=
		1PL.inc	ina=
2SG	ku=	2PL	idin=
3SG	∅	3PL	∅

Because of the third person gap in the object pronoun paradigm, a clause with a transitive verb that has no expressed object pronoun, like in (36) and (37), has an understood third person reading. Its precise referent, however, is ambiguous out of context. In other instances, no such ambiguity arises, as OPCs have distinct forms for other person/number combinations.

(36) *Súuqa   b[áan   kú arkay].*
     suuq=a   b=aan   ku ark-∅-ay
     market=K.DEF FOC=1SG in see-1SG-PST
     'I saw him/her/it/them in the market.'

(37) *W[áy   maqashay].*
     w=ay   maqa-sh-ay
     DEC=3SG.F hear-3SG.F-PST
     'She heard him/her/it/them.'

OPCs can function as a verb's direct object (38), indirect object (39), or oblique object (40), just like full NPs can.

(38) *Waan   ká   xúmahay   ín[aan   ku dhibó].*
     w=aan   ka   xum-∅-ah-ay   in=aan   ku dhib-o
     DEC=1SG with sorry-1SG-be-PRES COMP=1SG you trouble-IRR
     'I am sorry to trouble you.' (Z & O: 189)

(39) *Áad báan   ugú fárxayaa   haddáad   caawinaád*
     aad b=aan   ugu farx-ay-∅-aa   hadd=aad   caawina-ad
     very FOC=1SG SUP be.happy-PROG-1SG-PRES if=2SG   assistance-PL
     [i   siisó].
     i   sii-s-o
     1SG.OBJ give-2SG-IRR
     'I would be most happy if you give me assistance.' (Z & O: 216)

(40) *Hálka waxáannu ú   nimid   ín[aan   kulá   hadalló].*
     halka waxa=annu u   n-imid   in=aan   ku=la   hadal-l-o
     here FOC=1PL   to 1PL-come.PST   COMP=1PL 2SG.OBJ=with speak-1PL-IRR
     'We came here to speak with you.' (Z & O: 288)

SPCs, as enclitics, do not cluster with OPCs within the VC. OPCs do, however, cluster with the ISP, as seen in (41). The clusters formed and additional examples of these clusters in context are provided in §10.2.2.

(41) *Wáa [nala   kalá gooyay].*
     waa na=la   kala goo-y-ay
     DEC 1PL.exc.OBJ=ISP   apart sever-3SG.M-PST
     'We were disconnected from one another.' (Z & O: 267)

First series OPCs can also cluster with one or more adposition. An OPC joined by a single adposition was shown in (40), but a more complex cluster containing two adpositions is seen in (42). A full list of possible OPC+adposition clusters and additional examples in context are found in §10.7.

(42) Sí xún ay[áy noolá dháqmayaan].
si xun ay=ay no=o-la dhaq-m-ay-∅-aa-n
way bad FOC=3PL 1PL.OBJ=to-with care.for-NEU-PROG-3-PRES-PL
'They are going to treat us badly.'

In addition to clustering with the ISP and adpositions, OPCs also cluster with negative *má* within the VC in the combinations shown in (43). Again, because there are no overt third person OPCs, no third person forms are listed.

(43) *First series object pronoun clitics + negative*

1SG	imá	1PL.exc	namá
		1PL.inc	inamá
2SG	kumá	2PL	idinmá

A typical example of an OPC + negative cluster within the VC is shown in (44). In other instances, an OPC can move along with a negative to the left edge (or perhaps outside) the VC, as in (45) and (46). In this position, the cluster can host the SPC enclitic.

(44) Cáli [kumá sheegín].
Cali ku=ma sheeg-in
Cali 2SG.OBJ=NEG tell-NEG
'Cali did not tell you.' (Z & O: 390)

(45) Wáxba imá [ay siinín].
waxba i=ma ay siin-in
anything 1SG.OBJ=NEG 3SG.F give-NEG
'She didn't give anything to me.' (Z & O: 325)

(46) Sháley kum[áan arkín].
shaley ku=ma=an ark-in
yesterday 2SG.OBJ=NEG=1SG see-NEG
'I didn't see you yesterday.' (Z & I: 218)

Examples like (38) showed that a SPC and OPC can co-occur in the VC; the OPC need not move leftward outside of the VC. Thus, the ability of the OPC to move appears conditioned by its prosodification with the negative. In §10.8, additional examples make clear that the negative does not move out of the VC in all instances. However, it does so obligatorily in the presence of a SPC that has no other host, as was seen in examples like (45) and (46). The negative can also move on its own (i.e., not in a cluster with another element), but only around the ISP. This was seen in (34). The negative will instead remain within the VC if it forms a cluster that contains more than two syllables.

10.2.4 Reflexive/reciprocal pronoun

Occurring in the same slot in the VC as other first series object pronoun clitics is the reflexive/reciprocal pronoun (RRP) *is*. This pronoun is toneless and can form clusters with adpositions and the negative marker *má*. The RRP can have a reflexive meaning like 'oneself' as in (47) or a reciprocal meaning like 'each other,' as in (48).

(47) *Bíyo b[áy   iskú   shubtey].*
    biyo b=ay   is=ku   shub-t-ay
    water FOC=3SG.F RRP=on pour-3SG.F-PST
    'She poured water onto herself.' (Z & O: 610)

(48) *Aabbáháa   iyo anígu   wá[annu is   niqiin].*
    aabba-haa   iyo ani=g=u   wa=annu is   n-iqiin
    father-K.your and I=K.DEF=SUBJ DEC=1PL RRP 1PL-know.PST
    'Your father and I knew each other.' (Z & I: 316)

The RRP has a second allomorph *isa* which occurs before the deictic markers *soó* and *sií*, and before verbs beginning with *s*, in avoidance of a *s#s* sequence.

(49) *Míd   walbá [isa soó abaabúlayaan].*
    mid   walba isa soo abaabul-ay-∅-aa-n
    person each RRP VEN organize-PROG-3-PRES-PL
    'Each person is organizing himself.'

Like other OPCs, the RRP can function as a verb's direct object (50), indirect object (51), or oblique object (52).

(50) *Miy[áad   is aqoóneyseen]?*
    m=iy=aad   is aqoon-ey-s-ee-n
    QM=FOC=2SG   RRP know-PROG-2-PST-PL
    'Do you know one another?' (Z & I: 318)

(51) *W[áy is nabadgaliyeen].*
w=ay is nabad.gal-i-y-ee-n
DEC=3PL RRP peace.enter-WCAUS-3-PST-PL
'They said goodbye to one another.'

(52) *Labádaás baabuúr w[ay iskú dheceen].*
laba-daas baabuur w=ay is=ku dhec-∅-ee-n
two-T.those car DEC=3PL RRP=into collide-3-PST-PL
'Those two cars collided with each other.' (Z & O: 171)

The examples given thus far show that the RRP is used to refer to both singular or plural referents. It can also be used to refer to nouns in other countability categories, such as collectives, as in (53).

(53) *Ló'da súuqa b[áy iskú aragtay].*
lo'=da suuq=a b=ay is=ku arag-t-ay
cattle=T.DEF market=K.DEF FOC=3SG.T RRP=at see-3SG.T-PST
'The cattle saw each other in the market.'

The RRP can also occur in clusters with one (54) or more adpositions (55), with the rightmost adposition exhibiting a H tone. It does not cluster with the ISP, as seen in (56).

(54) *W[ay islá galeen] dambiyádii.*
w=ay is=la gal-∅-ee-n dambi-ya-dii
DEC=3PL RRP=with commit-3-PST-PL crime-PL-T.RDEF
'They committed the crimes with one another.'

(55) *Wáxaa kále oo goóbtaás [la iskulá qaatay]* ...
waxaa kale oo goob-taas la is=ku=la qaa-t-∅-ay
FOC other REL area-T.that ISP RRP=to=with confine-MID-3SG.T-PST
'It had also confined itself to that other area ...' (jeexdin.net:14732)

(56) *Wáa [la is dul taágayaa].*
waa la is dul taag-ay-∅-aa
DEC ISP RRP up fix-PROG-3SG.M-PRES
'It's being fixed up.' (booramaonline: 196)

Other clusters with the RRP can contain the negative marker *má*, as in (57) and (58).

(57) *Bulshádani*   *[ismá*   *weydiisó]*   *su'áashaás.*
bulsha-dan=i   is=ma   weydi-is-o   su'aash-aas
community-T.this=SUBJ RRP=NEG ask-WCAUS-MID-IRR question-T.that
'This community does not ask itself that question.' (badso.org: 913)

(58) *laakiin wáli rásmi áh*   *[la iskumá*   *afgarán].*
laakiin wali rasmi ah   la is=ku=ma   afgar-an
but   each official be.PRES.RED ISP RRP=on=NEG commit-NEG
'but, each official has not been committed to it.' (daawo.net: 3603)

For symmetric predicates that semantically entail reciprocity, it is not possible to use the RRP (Cabredo Hofherr 2007). This is shown in (59).

(59) *Nimánku*   *w[áy*   *kulmeen].*
nim-an=k=u   w=ay   kulm-∅-ee-n
man-PL=K.DEF=SUBJ DEC=3PL meet-3-PST-PL
'The men met.' (Cabredo Hofherr 2007)

10.3 Second series object pronouns

Second series object pronouns are far less frequently encountered in Somali. This stems from the fact that very specific conditions need to obtain in order for them to be used. These pronouns are shown in (60). Like the first series object pronouns discussed in §10.2.3, second series object pronouns form a gapped paradigm in which third person pronouns have no segmental form.

(60) *Second series object pronouns*

1SG	kaý	1PL.exc	kayó
		1PL.inc	keén
2SG	kaá	2PL	kiín
3SG	∅	3PL	∅

Second series object pronouns have a H tone on their final mora and occur in a slot within the VC between the object/adposition cluster and the verb itself. They are undeniably derived from Somali's possessive determiners (see §9.3.1). Biber (1984a) has suggested that they developed as a way to disambiguate object referents and to simultaneously avoid having more than one object pronoun clitic within the same VC.

In order for a second series object pronoun to appear in the VC, the sentence must require two overt pronominal objects. Because of the gapped paradigms in both first and second series object pronouns, this means that neither of the two object pronouns can have a third person referent. Consider the example in (61) that contains a 2PL direct object and a 1PL oblique object.

(61) W[uu   idinká   keén   qaaday].
w=uu   idin=ka   keen   qaad-∅-ay
DEC=3SG.M 2PL.OBJ=from 1PL.OBJ take-3SG.M-PST
'He took you from us.'

Example (62) shows that a second series object pronoun will also emerge when one of the two overt objects pronouns is the RRP. This illustrates that the condition is not necessarily on first series OPCs, but rather on OPCs in general.

(62) [Iská   kaý   dhíci]!
is=ka   kay   dhic-i
RRP=from 1SG.OBJ defend-IMP
'Defend yourself from me!' (Z & O: 190)

Regardless of whether it is a direct object, indirect object, or oblique object, if one of two object pronouns is third person (and therefore ∅), the other pronominal argument is expressed by a first series OPC. This is seen in (63) and (64). Thus, there is no inherent connection between second series pronouns and a particular type of object. The language will express a first series OPC whenever possible.

(63) Ma [lagú   siiyay]?
ma la=gu   sii-y-ay
QM ISP=2SG.OBJ give-3SG.M-PST
'Did someone give him/her/it to you?'

(64) W[aan   idinká   qaaday].
w=aan   idin=ka   qaad-∅-ay
DEC=1SG 2PL=from take-1SG-PST
'I took it from you (PL).'

One implication of the arbitrary connection between pronoun series and object type is that when both a first series and a second series object pronoun are present in the same VC, speakers vary between which pronoun is used for a given object. Thus, there is the potential for ambiguity such that the sentence in (65), for example, has two possible interpretations.

(65) W[ay   nagá   kaá   qaadeen].
      w=ay   na=gá   kaá   qaad-∅-ee-n
      DEC=3PL 1PL.OBJ=from 2SG.OBJ take-3-PST-PL

   'They took us from you.' or 'They took you from us.'

10.4 Deictic particles

The slot within the VC following the object/adposition cluster and before the verb is associated with four particles, two of which are the deictic particles *soó* and *síi*. The first of these indicates ventive deixis (motion toward) while the latter indicates itive deixis (motion away). The deictic particles have a H tone on their final mora and do not prosodify with other elements of the VC. Simple examples of their use are in (66) and (67), respectively, and show motion that is relative to a deictic center explicitly defined within the sentence.

(66) Shakhsiyáadka   ayáa [soó galaý].
      shakhsi-aad=ka   ayaa soo gal-ay
      individual-PL=K.DEF FOC VEN enter-PST.RED

   'The individuals entered.' (Morrison 2016)

(67) isága oo   [ká síi báxayay]   másjid [kú yaal]
      isaga oo   ka   sii bax-ay-∅-ay   masjid ku y-aal
      he   SUB from ITV leave-PROG-3SG.M-PST mosque in 3SG.M-exist.PRES
      Boosaáso.
      Boosasso
      Boosasso

   '...as he was leaving a mosque in Boosasso.'

Somali's deictic particles have been discussed on several occasions in the literature (e.g., Appleyard 1990; Andrzejewski 1960; Biber 1984a; Saeed 1994; Svolacchia et al. 1995), with seminal works on the subject being those by Bourdin (2002, 2005). Bourdin established that, in addition to entailing motion towards or away from some deictic center, deictic particles require some knowledge of the *process* encoded by the verb and the role of the *participant* in the action, in order to be properly interpreted. Examples like (68) show that the interpretation is not always as simple as direction toward or away from some defined location. Here, the ventive particle is used in describing action that would otherwise seem to be itive in nature.

(68) *Qófkan   ayáa [ká   soó   duulaý]   Tansaaníya.*
     qóf-kan   ayaa ká   soó   duul-ay   Tansaaníya.
     person-K.that FOC from VEN   fly-PST.RED Tanzania
     'That person had flown (away) from Tanzania.'

Morrison (2016) more recently proposed that the key to interpreting the use of Somali deictic particles is speaker orientation. That is, use of the ventive *soó* involves egocentric orientation, whether literally or figuratively. The itive *sií*, on the other hand, entails orientation away from the speaker, again, whether literally or figuratively. Thus, in cases like (68), the physical motion may be away from some location, but the flying involves motion oriented around the speaker; the speaker is moving along with the direction of motion. Example (69) illustrates a more metaphorical use of the ventive where the motion is towards a state, rather than a location. Some common uses of each of the two deictic particles are summarized in sub-sections below.

(69) *Xitáa gaadíidka   dadweynahá waa [uu   soó laabtay.]*
     xitaa gaadiid=ka   dad-weyna=ha waa uu   soó laab-t-∅-ay
     even transport=K.DEF   public=K.DEF DEC 3SG.M VEN return-MID-3SG.M-PST
     'Even public transportation is back to normal.' (Morrison 2016)

10.4.1 Ventive *soó*

In its simplest uses, the ventive particle *soó* conveys physical motion towards some actual or metaphorical deictic center.

(70) *Wáxaa se   hádda   [ká   soó   noqday]*   ...
     waxaa se   had=da   ka   soo   noq-d-∅-ay...
     FOC   CONJ time=T.DEF   from VEN   return-MID-3SG.M-PST
     'But, I've just returned ...' (geeska.net: 12927)

It is used in orienting the participant alongside the action taking place, with the participant being the literal or figurative deictic center. The verbal motion itself, however, can be away from some physical location as encoded by an adposition, like in (68), or in the semantics of the verb itself, as in (71).

(71) *Wáx[aan lá   soó   cararay]   carruúrtáyda.*
     wax=aan lá   soó   carar-∅-ay   carruúr-táy=da
     FOC=1SG with VEN   flee-1SG-PST children-1SG=T.DEF
     'I fled with my children.' (Morrison 2016)

The ventive particle is also used in establishing temporal deixis pertaining to a past (72) or forthcoming event (73).

(72) *Líxdií biloód ee [la soó dhaafay]* ...
lix-dii bil-ood ee la soo dhaaf-∅-ay
six-T.RDEF month-ASSOC SUB ISP VEN pass.by-3SG.M-PST
'In the six months that have passed ...' (qaawane.net: 12063)

(73) *Xílligií roobkuná waa [soó dháwyahay].*
xilli-gii roob-k=u=na waa soo dhaw-y-ah-ay
season=K.RDEF rain=K.DEF=SUBJ=CONJ DEC VEN soon-3SG.M-be-PRES
'And the rainy season is coming soon.' (Morrison 2016)

10.4.2 Itive *sií*

The itive deictic particle *sií* encodes physical motion away from an actual (74) or undefined deictic center (75).

(74) *Ayáa xággií jirrída [ú sií dhutiyey].*
ayaa xag-gii jirri=da u sii dhut-i-y-ey
FOC direction-K.RDEF trunk=T-DEF to ITV limp-WCAUS-3SG.M-PST
'He limped away in the direction of the trunk.' (Morrison 2016)

(75) *Cádowgu waa [uu sií carárayaa].*
cadow=g=u waa uu sii carar-ay-∅-aa
enemy=K.DEF=SUBJ DEC 3SG.M ITV flee-PROG-3SG.M-PRES
'The enemy is fleeing.' (Morrison 2016)

Temporally, it can refer to motion away from the current time, even in the presence of an adposition like *kú*.

(76) *Maalínba maalín ay[áan kú sií gudbinaa]* ...
maalin=ba maalin ay=aan ku sii gudb-i-n-aa
day=INT day FOC=1PL on ITV pass-WCAUS-1PL-PRES
'Day by day, we pass it by ...' (aflax.net: 610)

The itive marker is also used in conveying intensification of some action in that the action is "coming out" from some metaphorical deictic center.

(77) *Máanta míddaas waa [ay   sií wiíqmaysaa].*
     maanta mid-aas   waa ay sii wiiq-m-ay-s-aa
     today one-T.that DEC 3SG.T ITV weak-STV-PROG-3SG.T-PRES

'Today, this one is getting weaker.' (rajonews.net: 342028)

10.5 Adverbial particles

The final slot in the VC before the verb and after deictic particles is the location in which two adverbial particles, *wada* 'together' and *kala* 'apart,' appear. They are toneless and can appear either with or without the deictic particles *soó* and *sií*.

10.5.1 *wada*

The adverbial particle *wada* is derived from the verb *wád* 'continue, keep with.' One function of this particle is to reinforce that the action entailed by the verb involves the entire group referenced by the subject, rather than some subset of this group. This sense is applicable when the VC's verb has a plural subject.

In (77), the addition of the adverbial illustrates that the car should be shared by all five of the individuals being spoken to, rather than, perhaps, by a pair of them.

(78) *Baabúurkan [wada lahaadá]   shántiinnu!*
     baabuur-kan wada lahaad-a   shan-tiin=n=u
     car-K.this ADV have-IMP.PL five-T.your=T.DEF=SUBJ

'The five of you are sharing this car (together)!' (Z & O: 408)

In (79), the adverbial instead expresses that neither of the individuals involved is talking to the other, as opposed to the entailed silence being caused by just one person.

(79) *Má[annu wada hadalnó].*
     ma=aanu wada hadal-n-o
     NEG=1PL ADV speak-1PL-IRR

'We do not speak to each other.' (Z & I: 198)

The adverbial *wada* can also appear alongside either *soó* (80) or *sií* (81).

(80) ín   ay [ká soó wada muuqdáan]   shírarka
     in   ay ka soo wada muuq-d-∅-aa-n   shir-ar=ka
     COMP 3PL at VEN ADV appear-MID-3-PRES-PL meeting-PL=K-DEF
     magaaladá.
     magaala=da
     town=T-DEF

'that they appear with one another at the town assembly meetings.'

(81) Má [sií wada nooláan   karaan],   qabíilka   iyo qarannimáda.
     ma sii wada nool-aan   kar-aan,   qabiil=ka   iyo qarannima=da
     NEG ITV ADV living-STV.INF be.able-IRR clan=K-DEF and nationality=T.DEF

'They can no longer live together, clan and nationality.' (Somalilandpost:11283)

When used either with a singular (82) or a plural subject (83), *wada* can function as an intensifier, indicating that the action of the verb was done fully or to a high degree.

(82) Háddii aánan   sáa [ú   gaajáysnayn],   [má wada cúni
     haddii aan=an   saa u   gaaj-ays-an-ayn   ma wada cun-i
     if   NEG=1SG   thus COM hunger-FAC-STV-NEG   NEG ADV eat-INF
     laháyn]   cuntáda.
     lah-ayn   cunta=da
     have-NEG food=T-DEF

'If I hadn't been so hungry, I wouldn't have eaten up all the food.' (Z & O: 409)

(83) Iyága kumá   [ay wada odhanéyn].
     iyaga ku=ma   ay   wada odhan-eyn
     they 2SG.OBJ=NEG 3PL ADV tell-NEG

'They weren't telling everything to you.' (Z & I: 294)

10.5.2 *kala*

A second adverbial particle *kala* is a grammaticalized combination of the adpositions *ká* 'off' and *lá* 'with.' The particle is used alongside verbs with either singular or plural subjects and adds subtleties to the verbal semantics such as 'alone' or 'apart,' as in (84) and (85).

(84) Dhaqaalúhu   w[úu   kala daatay].
     dhaqaalu=h=u   w=uu   kala daa-t-∅-ay
     economy=K-DEF=SUBJ   DEC=3SG.K ADV spill-MID-3SG.K-PST

'The economy fell apart.'

(85) W[áy   kala tageen].
     w=ay   kala tagØ-ee-n
     DEC=3PL ADV go-3-PST-PL
     'They went separately.'

The adverbial *kala* can appear alongside either *sií* or *soó*, as in the following examples.

(86) Arrimáhaás   ayáa [sií kala jajabínayá]
     arrim-a-haas   ayaa sii kala ja-jab-in-ay-a
     matter-PL-K.these FOC ITV ADV Red-break-WCAUS-PROG-PRES.RED
     koóxda.
     koox=da
     group=T.DEF
     'These matters are breaking apart the group.'

(87) Xiisád weýn ayáa [soó kala dhexgashaý]   Rúushka   iyo
     xiisad weyn ayaa soo kala dhex-gash-Ø-ay   Ruush=ka   iyo
     crisis large FOC VEN ADV between-enter-3SG.T-PST.RED Russia=K.DEF and
     Túrkiga.
     Turki=ga
     Turkey=K.DEF
     'A great crisis came about between Russia and Turkey.' (dhacdo.org:2561)

10.6 Adpositions

There are four adpositional particles which can be found in a slot within the VC after pronoun clitics. These are shown in (88) where they are listed with common meanings. Adpositions govern indirect and oblique objects and their associated object pronouns. This includes both first and second series object pronouns, where appropriate, which are also located within the VC. This fact is not always apparent, however, given that third person object pronouns in both the first and second series have no segmental form. Of course, object pronouns may be co-referential with a full NP outside of the VC. Because these morphemes can follow a first series OPC, precede a second series object pronoun, or even (in the case of third person objects) not have an overt referent at all, referring to these functional morphemes as adpositions covers all of these scenarios.

(88) *Adpositional particles*

ú	'to, for, towards, on behalf of'
kú	'at, in, into, on, onto, concerning, with (instrumental)'
ká	'from, about, away from, out of'
lá	'with (comitative), about'

That these are particles and not clitics is clear from several facts. First, each is associated with H tone. Second, adpositions form clusters with one another within which alternations occur that are otherwise found in Somali only across word boundaries. Third, adposition clusters have just a single H tone on the final adposition. This suggests that they form a recursive structure as do other complex structures like compounds (Green and Morrison 2016).

In the simplest instances, as in (89), the object governed by an adposition is overtly realized within the VC. Here, the adposition *ú* governs the 1PL OPC *na*, with the two clustering together. It is shown in sections below that these clusters come in many combinations and can contain more than one adposition. In (90), the adposition *ká* governs the second series object pronoun *keén*.

(89) Dhakhaatíirta   ayáa [noó   sheegeén]   ín   ...
      dhakhaatiir=ta ayaa no=o sheeg-∅-ee-n in   ...
      doctor.PL=T.DEF FOC   1PL=to say-3-PST-PL COMP

      'The doctors told us that...'

(90) Bulsháda   w[ay   iská   keén   dhiciyeen].
      bulsha=da   w=ay   is=ka   keen   dhici-y-ee-n
      community=T.DEF DEC=3SG.T RRP=from 1PL.OBJ   defend-3-PST-PL

      'The community defended itself from us.'

Adpositions do not always cluster with an OPC. This is seen, for example, when third person objects are involved. Such a scenario is shown in (91), in which the verb has an unexpressed pronominal 3SG direct object and a 3PL oblique object. Here, the adposition *ú* governs the oblique object, despite the object having no overt pronoun within the VC. The adposition is co-referential, however, with a full NP located outside the VC.

(91) Ilmáháaga   [ú shéeg]!
      ilma-haa=ga   u sheeg
      child-K.your=K.DEF to tell-IMP

      'Tell (it) to your child!'

In the remainder of this section, properties of each of the four individual adpositions are introduced in turn. Later, discussion turns to the formation of adposition clusters of increasing levels of complexity.

10.6.1 *ú*

The adposition *ú* is associated with several spatial or directional meanings (e.g., 'to, towards, for, on behalf of') that represent physical or metaphorical destinations. This adposition governs pronouns and their co-referential NPs that fill several thematic roles, including beneficiary (92), goal (93), and purpose (94).

(92) *Dowláddu   ... wáx[ay   ú   shaqeeysaa]*
 Dowlad=d=u   ... wax=ay   u   shaq-eey-s-aa
 government=T.DEF=SUBJ ... FOC=3SG.F for work-FACT-3SG.F-PRES
 shácabka.
 shacab=ka
 citizens=K.DEF

 'The government ... works for the citizens.' (keydmedia.net)

(93) *Dabadéed ínta uu   kór [ú booday]   Núur ...*
 dabadeed inta uu   kor u bood-∅-ay   Nuur
 after   then 3SG to up jump-3SG-PST Nuur

 'After that, he jumped up to Nur...' (somalilandpost.net: 49847)

(94) *Daáwo   ma [ú baahántahay]?*
 daawo   ma ú baah-an-t-ah-ay
 medicine QM for need-STV-2SG-be-PRES

 'Are you in need of medicine?' (Z & O: 37)

This adposition can also govern manner adverbials, as seen in (95) and (96).

(95) *Tartiíb b[áan   ú   akhriyay].*
 tartiib b=aan   u   akhri-y-ay
 care   FOC=1SG with read-1SG-PST

 'I read it carefully.' (with care)

(96) *Sída   daméerk[úu   ú shaqeeyaa].*
 sí=da   daméer=k:∅=uu   ú shaq-ee-y-aa
 way=T.DEF donkey=K.DEF:FOC=3SG.M in work-FACT-3SG.M-PRES

 'He works like a donkey.' (in the way of a donkey) (Z & O: 133)

The presence of *ú* in a main clause can govern a complement clause that expresses a purpose or reason, as in (97). This sequence of *ú...ín* can be translated as 'in order to' or 'so that.'

(97) *Wáxay   wáx [ú   baránaysaa]   ín   ay*
     wax=ay   wax u   bar-an-ay-s-aa   in   ay
     FOC=3SG.F thing in.order study-MID-PROG-3SG.F-PRES COMP 3SG.F
     heshó   shahaádo.
     hesh-∅-ó   shahaádo
     receive-3SG.F-IRR degree
     'She is studying (something) in order to receive a degree.' (Z & O: 53)

10.6.2 *kú*

The adposition *kú* has several meanings, including 'in,' 'into,' 'on,' and 'at,' among others. It governs pronouns and their co-referential NPs related to locations that do not necessarily involve physical or metaphorical movement, but rather indicate where the verbal action is taking place. These are associated with the thematic roles of location (98) and goal (99).

(98) *Ma [kú xanuúnaysaa]   hálkan?*
     ma ku xanuun-ay-s-aa   halkan
     QM at hurt-PROG-2SG-PRES   here
     'Are you hurting here?' (at this place) (Z & O: 684)

(99) *Baríiska   máraq [kú dár]!*
     bariis=ka   maraq ku dar
     rice=K.DEF broth on put.IMP
     'Put broth on the rice!'

This adposition also governs pronouns and NPs that express the instrument with which (100) or the means by which (101) an action is carried out. In these instances, it is best translated as 'with' or 'by,' respectively.

(100) *Úl   b[áan   iskú   dhuftey].*
      ul   b=aan   is=ku   dhuf-t-∅-ey
      stick FOC=1SG RRP=with hit-MID-1SG-PST
      'I hit myself with a stick.' (Z & I: 175)

(101) *Dayuurád m[éey   kú imán].*
dayuurád m=eey   kú iman
plane   NEG=3PL by come.NEG
'They didn't come by plane.' (Z & O: 325)

Like *ú*, *kú* can also govern manner adverbials. The former is associated with purpose or reason, as shown above in (95), while the latter, seen in (102), simply expresses the manner in which some event is occurring at some location.

(102) *Waxyár kádib waaba [kú dhaafay].*
waxyar   kadib waa=ba   with pass.by-3SG.PST
little.bit after DEC-INT with pass.by-3SG.K-PST
'After just a little while, it passed by.' (onechelsea.net: 128824)

10.6.3 *ká*

The adposition *ká* governs pronouns and NPs that fill the thematic role of origin or source, whether physically, as in (103), or metaphorically, as in (104).

(103) *Waan   ógahay   ínaydin   Márka [ká timaaddaan].*
w=aan   og-∅-ah-ay   in=aydin   Marka ka   t-imaad-d-aa-n
DEC=1SG aware-1SG-be-PRES COMP=2PL Marka from 2PL-come-2PL-PRES-PL
'I know that you come from Marka.'

(104) *Telefisyóonka   b[áannu ká   maqallay].*
telefisyoon=ka   b=aannu ka   maqal-l-ay
television=K.DEF FOC=1PL from hear-1PL-PST
'We heard it from the television.' (Z & I: 155)

It is also used to refer to topics of interest or conversation (105) and is accordingly translated as 'about.'

(105) *Anígu   wáxba   [kamá   fekeró].*
ani=g=u   wax=ba   ka=má   feker-∅-o
I=K.DEF=SUBJ thing=INT about=NEG think-1SG-IRR
'I'm not thinking about anything.'

This adposition is also used to express a physical (106) or metaphorical (107) separation from something. In (106), *ká* clusters with a second instance of the same adposition, which is a component of the phrasal verb *ká baxsán* 'escape' (cf. *báx* 'exit').

(106) *Dírqi b[áan kagá baxsaday].*
dirqi b=aan ka-ga bax-s-ad-∅-ay
just FOC=1SG out-from go-WCAUS-MID-1SG-PST
'I just escaped from it.' (Z & O: 154)

(107) *Hílib b[úu ká caaggányahay].*
hílib b=uu ká caagg-án-y-ah-ay
meat FOC=3SG.M from abstain-STV-3SG.M-be-PRES
'He is abstaining from meat.' (Z & O: 80)

This adposition is also used in the formation of comparatives, as discussed in §15.7.

10.6.4 *lá*

The last of Somali's four adpositions, *lá*, is a comitative. It governs pronouns and NPs that refer to one of two participants in an event.

(108) *Kú tashó ín[aad ilá joogtó].*
ku tash-∅-o in=aad i=la joog-t-o
on plan-2SG-IRR COMP=2SG 1SG.OBJ=with stay-2SG-IRR
'Plan on staying with me.' (Z & O: 627)

(109) *... wáxaana [aan lá shaqáyn doonnaa] maámulka.*
... waxaa=na aan la shaq-ayn doon-n-aa maamul=ka
... FOC=CONJ 1PL with work-INF will-1PL-PRES administration=K.DEF
'... and we will work with the administration.' (risaala.net: 103555)

10.7 Adposition clusters

Adpositions cluster with one another, as well as with preceding object pronoun clitics (OPCs), the ISP, the RRP, and even with a following negative marker to form a single phonological word. These clusters have a single H tone located on the rightmost morpheme in the cluster. In the sections below, the various types of clusters that are found in Somali are discussed, beginning with the simplest adposition + adposition clusters, and then turning to more complex combinations of the elements just mentioned.

10.7.1 Two adpositions

When two adpositions form a cluster, they always maintain the same linear order relative to one another: *ú* - *kú* - *ká* - *lá*. This is the case, bearing in mind, that two of the same adposition can also cluster with one another, with the exception of *lalá; a double comitative is ungrammatical. Attested adposition + adposition clusters are in (110), with unattested sequences marked with a dash. Though each adposition is associated with a H tone on its own, there is a single H tone on these clusters found on the rightmost adposition. Various alternations are witnessed: i) *k* alternates with *g*; ii) *g* is inserted epenthetically between two instances of *ú*; iii) *u* alternates to *a* across a velar.

(110) *Adposition + adposition clusters*

	ú	kú	ká	lá
ú	ugú	ugú	ugá	ulá
kú	–	kagá	kagá	kulá
ká	–	–	kagá	kalá

In some instances, both adpositions in a given cluster have expressed pronominal or NP referents. This is seen for *kulá* in (111) where *kú* governs *isága* 'him' and *lá* governs *warqádda* 'the letter.'

(111) Warqádda báan isága [kulá noqday].
 warqad=da b=aan isaga ku-la noq-d-∅-ay
 letter=T.DEF FOC=1SG him to-with return-MID-1SG-PST
 'I returned to him with the letter.' (Z & O: 389)

In other instances, however, one of the two adpositions forming the cluster is part of a phrasal verb. This is seen in (112) for *kalá*, where the first adposition forms the phrasal verb *ká tág* 'go away,' while the second governs the NP 'the boy's pen.'

(112) Wíilka qálinkiisá b[áan kalá tagay].
 wiil=ka qalin-kiis=a b=aan ka-la tag-∅-ay
 boy=K.DEF pen-K.his=K.DEF FOC=1SG away-with go-1SG-PST
 'I went away with the boy's pen.'

10.7.2 Three adpositions

Clusters of three adpositions are also possible in the combinations shown in (113). The alternations mentioned above sometimes obscure the precise nature of the adpositions involved. A single H tone is typically located on the rightmost of the three adpositions, with a few notable exceptions discussed below.

(113) *Three adposition clusters*

		ú	*kú*	*ká*	*lá*
ugú	(ú+ú)	*ugugú*	*ugugú*	*ugugá*	*ugulá*
ugú	(ú+kú)	*ugugú*	*ugugú*	*ugugá*	*ugulá*
ugá	(ú+ká)	*ugugá*	*ugugá*	*ugagá*	*ugala*
ulá	(ú+lá)	*ugulá*	*ugulá*	*ugalá*	–
kugú	(kú+kú)	*ugugú*	*kú kugú*	*kú kagá*	*kugulá*
kagá	(kú+ká)	*ugagá*	*kú kagá*	*kú kagá*	*kagalá*
kulá	(kú+lá)	*ugulá*	*kugulá*	*kagalá*	–
kagá	(ká+ká)	*ugagá*	*kagagá*	*kagagá*	*kagalá*

One surprising fact is that two instances of *kú* cannot cluster together with another *kú*, nor with *ká*. The first adposition in these sequences is prosodified separately, having its own H tone. Alternations also fail to occur between the first and second adposition in the sequence, thus substantiating their prosodic separability. This is also reflected in written Somali, where the first adposition in the sequence is separated from the other two. Note, also, that while sequences like *ulalá*, *kulalá*, and *lagulá* can appear, one of the two *la*s is the ISP. There is metathesis to avoid sequences like **laulá*.

Sentence (114) contains a VC with a cluster of three adpositions. The first adposition *ú* refers to the city 'Ceel Barde,' the second *kú* to 'fear,' and the last *lá* to 'her family.'

(114) *Faadúmo wáxay   sheegtay   ínay   cábsi darteéd*
      Faadumó wax=ay   sheeg-t-ay   ín=ay   cabsi dar-teed
      Faadumo FOC=3SG.F say-3SG.F-PST COMP=3SG.F fear   reason-T.her
      [*ugulá   soó carartay*]   *qóyskéeda*   *Céel Bardé.*
      u-gu-lá   soó carar-t-ay   qóys-kee=da   Ceel Barde
      to-in-with VEN flee-3SG.F-PST family-K.her=T.DEF Ceel Barde
      'Fadumo said that she fled in fear with her family to Ceel Barde.'

10.7.3 OPC + one adposition

Adpositions cluster together with object pronoun clitics (OPCs) in all possible combinations, as shown in (115). In most instances, the linear order of the two elements is such that the OPC precedes the adposition. There are only two exceptions (*idiín* and *kaá*) where this order is disrupted or otherwise unclear due to coalescence. Because third person object pronouns have no segmental form, they are not included in this table.

(115) *OPC + adposition clusters*

		ú	*kú*	*ká*	*lá*
1SG	*i*	*ií*	*igú*	*igá*	*ilá*
2SG	*ku*	*kuú*	*kugú*	*kaá*	*kulá*
1PL.ex	*na*	*noó*	*nagú*	*nagá*	*nalá*
1PL.in	*ina*	*inoó*	*inagú*	*inagá*	*inalá*
2PL	*idin*	*idiín*	*idinkú*	*idinká*	*idinlá*

An OPC + adposition cluster can be formed by an adposition that governs the OPC with which it clusters, as in (116). However, this is not always the case, as seen in (117), where the third person pronominal object governed by the adposition is unexpressed.

(116) *W[uu   ilá   hadlay].*
      w=uu   i=la   hadl-Ø-ay
      DEC=3SG.M 1SG.OBJ=with speak-3SG.M-PST
      'He spoke with me.'

(117) *Mux[úu   kugú   dhuftay]?*
      m=ux=uu   ku=gu   dhuf-t-Ø-ay
      QM=FOC=3SG.M 2SG.OBJ=with hit-MID-3SG.M-PST
      'What did he hit you with?' (Z & I: 350)

10.7.4 OPC + two adpositions

More complex clusters are formed by an OPC followed by two adpositions, in that order. As in the formation of other clusters, there are some consonantal and vocalic alternations that occur and there is a single H tone for the cluster found on the rightmost adposition.

(118) *OPC + two adposition clusters*

		ugú	*ugá*	*ulá*	*kugú*	*kagá*	*kulá*	*kalá*
1SG	*i*	*iigú*	*iigá*	*iilá*	*ikugú*	*igagá*	*igulá*	*igalá*
2SG	*ku*	*kuugú*	*kaagá*	*kuulá*	*kugugú*	*kaagá*	*kugulá*	*kaalá*
1PL.ex	*na*	*noogú*	*noogá*	*noolá*	*nagugú*	*nagagá*	*nagulá*	*nagalá*
1PL.in	*ina*	*inoogú*	*inoogá*	*inoolá*	*inagugú*	*inagagá*	*inagulá*	*inagalá*
2PL	*idin*	*idiinkú*	*idiinká*	*idiinlá*	*idinkugú*	*idinkagá*	*idinkulá*	*idinkalá*

An example of such a cluster is in (119). Here, the first adposition governs an oblique object while the second is part of the phrasal verb *ká tág* 'bring s.t. out of s.o.'

(119)   ... wáxay   [iigá   tageen]   tiiraányo.
        ... wax=ay   i=i-ga   tag-∅-ee-n   tiiraanyo
        ... FOC=3PL 1SG.OBJ=in-out go-3-PST-PL sorrow
        '... they have left me with sorrow.' (voiceofsomalia: 133517)

10.7.5 OPC + three adpositions

The most complex clusters that I have encountered contain an OPC followed by a sequence of three adpositions. The types of alternations seen here are similar to those described in §10.7.4 for sequences containing just two adpositions. There are some combinations that prosodify into two clusters that behave as separate prosodic words. Each has its own H tone, and there are no sandhi alternations between the adjacent clusters. For others, a single cluster appears possible with only a single H on the rightmost adposition and with sandhi alternations occurring throughout the cluster. Given their sheer complexity, this variation is not surprising.

I have not been able to find or elicit clusters with all imaginable combinations of elements. Only those that I have been able to elicit or locate in the Somali WaC corpus, the Korp corpus, or elsewhere on the internet are included below. Given the length of these clusters, they are split into two tables. Clusters beginning with a combination of *OPC + ú* are in (120) while those beginning with *OPC + kú* or *ká* are in (121).

(120)   OPC + three adposition clusters (1)

		ugugú	ugagá	ugalá	ugulá
1SG	i	–	iigagá	iigalá	iigulá
2SG	ku	kuú kugú	kuú kagá	kuú kalá	kuugulá
1PL.ex	na	–	noogagá	noogalá	noogulá
1PL.in	ina	–	inoogagá	inoogalá	inoogulá
2PL	idin	idiinkugú	idiinkagá	idiinkalá	idiinkulá

(121)   OPC + three adposition clusters (2)

		kugulá	kagagá	kagalá
1SG	i	igú kulá	igá kagá	igá kalá
2SG	ku	kugú kulá	kagá kagá	kagá kalá
1PL.ex	na	nagú kulá	nagá kagá	nagá kalá
1PL.in	ina	inagú kulá	inagá kagá	inagá kalá
2PL	idin	idíin kulá	idíin kagá	idíin kalá

Example (122) shows a sentence with a complex cluster containing one OPC followed by three adpositions. The cluster *idiinkugú* is formed of the sequence *idin+ú+ú+kú*. One *ú* governs the indirect object, which is the OPC *idin* itself. The second *ú* is part of the phrasal verb *ú gudbín* 'present s.t. to s.o.,' and the final adposition *kú* governs the locative adverbial *hálkan*.

(122)   *Wáxaan   hálkan [idiinkugú   soó   gudbínaynaa]*
        wax=aan halkan idiin=ku-gu   soo gudb-in-ay-n-aa
        FOC=1PL here   2PL.OBJ.to=about-at VEN present-WCAUS-PROG-1PL-PRES
        barnaámij aad ú   xiisó   bádan.
        barnaamij aad u   xiis-∅-o   badan
        program   very about interest-3SG.K-IRR many

        'What we are presenting to you here is a program that is very interesting.' (vidinfo.org: 273858)

10.7.6 Clusters with the ISP

Adpositions form clusters with the impersonal subject pronoun *la* (ISP) in a way similar to that described above for object pronoun clitics. The ISP is always the leftmost element in the sequence, regardless of the complexity of the cluster. The cluster's H tone remains on its rightmost element.

(123)   *ISP + adposition clusters*

	ú	kú	ká	lá
la	loó	lagú	lagá	lalá

Example (124) illustrates a fairly simple case in which the ISP joins an adposition that governs a questioned oblique object. Given that adpositions govern objects, it is never the case that an adposition will govern the ISP.

(124)   *Máxaa   [lagú   kariyey]?*
        m=axaa la=gú   kar-i-y-ey
        QM=FOC ISP=with cook-WCAUS-3SG.M-PST

        'What was it cooked with?' (Z & I: 172)

Table (125) shows clusters containing the ISP followed by two adpositions.

(125)   *ISP + two adposition clusters*

	ugú	ugá	ulá	kugú	kagá	kulá	kalá
la	loogú	loogá	loolá	lagugú	lagagá	lagulá	lagalá

An example illustrating such a cluster in context is in (126). Here, the ISP is the impersonal subject of the transitive verb. The first adposition *ú* (realized *o* after alternation) governs the oblique object *isbitáal* 'hospital,' while the second adposition *lá* is part of the phrasal verb *lá cárar* 'rush off with.'

(126) Dádkií   dhaáwaca   ahaa   wáxa [loolá
       dad-kii   dhaawac=a   ah-aa   waxa lo=o-la
       people-K.RDEF injury=K.DEF be-PST.RED FOC ISP=to-with
       cararay]   isbitáal sí   [loó   daaweeyó].
       carar-∅-ay   isbitaal si   lo=o   daaw-ee-y-o
       rush.off-3SG.K-PST hospital way ISP=to treat-FACT-3SG-IRR
       'The injured people were rushed off to the hospital in order to be treated.'

Clusters with three adpositions and the ISP are also possible in any combination, as shown in (127).

(127) ISP + three adposition clusters

	ugugú	ugagá	ugalá	ugulá	kugulá	kagagá	kagalá
la	loogugú	loogagá	loogalá	loogulá	lagugulá	lagagagá	lagagalá

Other clusters are found in which an OPC is present alongside the ISP and one or more adpositions. It is impractical to list all of these, but to illustrate basic combinatory possibilities, (128) shows clusters of the ISP followed by an OPC and a single adposition. As in most other instances, forming these clusters results in sandhi alternations, and there is a single H tone on the rightmost element of the cluster.

(128) ISP + OPC + adposition clusters

	ú	kú	ká	lá
la + i	layií	laygú	laygá	laylá
la + ku	laguú	lagugú	lagaá	lagulá
la + na	lanoó	lanagú	lanagá	lanalá
la + ina	laynoó	laynagú	laynagá	laynalá
la + idin	laydiín	laydinkú	laydinká	laydinlá

A contextual example of ISP + OPC + one adposition is in (129) while a similar example with two adpositions is in (130).

(129) Annága báa [lanoó   soó órdayay].
       annaga baa la=no=o   soo ord-ay-∅-ay
       1PL.exc FOC ISP=1PL.exc.OBJ=at VEN run-PROG-3SG.M-PST
       'Someone was running toward us.'

(130) Xaqiíqdu   wáxay   tahay   waa [naloogá
       xaqiiq=d=u   wax=ay   t-ah-ay   waa na=lo=o-ga
       fact=T.DEF=SUBJ FOC=3SG 3SG.T-be-PRES DEC 1PL.OBJ-ISP-to-for
       yeeray].
       yeer-∅-ay
       call-3SG.M-PST
       'The fact is that we were called upon.' (voiceofsomalia.net: 176574)

10.7.7 Clusters with the RRP

The reflexive/reciprocal object pronoun *is* (RRP) occupies the same slot as OPCs do. Clusters with the RRP exhibit the same types of alternations and tonal behavior as the other clusters described thus far in sections above. In some of the simplest instances, the RRP joins a single adposition, resulting in the clusters in (131). The RRP always precedes adpositions here and in more complex clusters.

(131) RRP + adposition clusters

	ú	kú	ká	lá
is	isú	iskú	iská	islá

In examples like (132), the adposition governs the RRP itself. However, this is not always the case. As seen in (133), the adposition *ká* instead governs the oblique object 'the mirror.'

(132) Sháah b[áan   iskú   daadiyey].
       shaah b=aan   is=ku   daad-i-y-ey
       tea   FOC=1PL RRP=on   spill-WCAUS-1SG-PST
       'I spilled tea on myself.' (Z & I: 175)

(133) Muraayádda waa [la iská   arkaa].
       muraayad=da waa la is=ka   ark-∅-aa
       mirror=T.DEF DEC ISP RRP=from see-3SG.M-PRES
       'You can see yourself in the mirror.' (Z & I: 352)

Clusters formed by the RRP and two adpositions are given in (134). As elsewhere, these clusters have a H tone on the second of the two adpositions.

(134) RRP + two adposition clusters

	ugú	ugá	ulá	kugú	kagá	kulá	kalá
is	isugú	isugá	isulá	iskugú	iskagá	iskulá	iskalá

An example of such a cluster in context is in (135). Here, neither of the two adpositions governs the RRP.

(135) Askárta   búr b[áy   iskagá   celiyeen].
      askar=ta   bur b=ay   is=ka-ga   celi-y-ee-n
      soldiers=T.DEF club FOC=3PL RRP=with-from protect-3-PST-PL
      'They protected themselves from the soldiers with a club.' (Z & O: 336)

As with other object pronouns, even more complex clusters are possible such as those with the RRP and three adpositions. Also possible are clusters where the RRP is preceded by the ISP and followed by one or more adpositions. Possibilities like this formed with one adposition are in (136).

(136) ISP + RRP + adposition clusters

	ú	kú	ká	lá
la + is	laysú	layskú	layská	layslá

An example of such a cluster in context follows in (137).

(137) Waa goób aán wáxba   [laysú   qarín].
      waa goob aan wax-ba la=is=u   qar-i-n
      DEC place NEG thing-INT ISP=RRP=from hide-WCAUS-NEG
      'It is a place where nothing is hidden.'

10.8 Negative *má*

The distributional behavior of the negative particle *má* is more complex than that of other components of the VC. The negative marker is associated with H tone and is found in a slot before the verb. A simple illustration of negative *má* relative to the verb is in (138).

(138) Carruúrta   aabbáhoód   [má shaqeeyó].
      carruur=ta   aabba-hood   ma shaqee-yo
      children=T.DEF father=K.their   NEG work-3SG.IRR
      'The children's father does not work.'

In what might be viewed as its canonical distribution, negative *má* will appear following an adposition but before a second series object pronoun, deictic particle, or adverbial particle. Example (139) shows that negative *má* will typically follow an adposition, while (140) shows that it precedes other immediately pre-verbal elements like a deictic particle.

(139) *Meéshaás [kamá arkó] máabka.*
 meesh-aas ka-ma ark-o maab=ka
 place-T.that from-NEG see-1SG.IRR map=K.DEF
 'I can't find that place on the map.' (Z & O: 26)

(140) *Máanta farxáddéyda [má soó koóbi karó].*
 maanta farxad-dey=da ma soo koob-i kar-o
 today happiness-T.my=T.DEF NEG VEN contain-INF be.able-1SG.IRR
 'Today, I cannot contain my happiness.'

The challenge in describing the behavior of the negative particle, however, is that it often migrates leftward, away from its typical slot in the VC. For example, it can move leftward to host a subject pronoun clitic that has no other functional projection on which to cliticize, as in (141), including when no other noun phrase precedes the VC, as in (142).

(141) *Basál m[éy cunáan].*
 basal m=ey cun-aa-n
 onion NEG=3PL eat-3.IRR-PL
 'They don't eat onions.'

(142) *M[éynu tagnó].*
 m=eynu tag-n-o
 NEG=1PL go-1PL-IRR
 'We aren't going.'

The various combinatory clusters of negative *má* + SPC are shown in (143). For some speakers, the number distinction between first and second person singular and plural collapses in favor of the singular. There is variation between forms with *a* vs. *e* before a glide.³

---

3 The ISP and negative can cluster within the VC, but if the negative moves leftward, the ISP does not migrate along with it. See §10.2.2.

(143) *Negative má + subject pronoun clitic*

má=aan	máan	1SG
má=aad	máad	2SG
má=uu	múu	3SG.M/K
má=ay	máy ~ méy	3SG.F/T
má=annu *or*	máannu	1PL.exc
má=aan	máan	
má=aynu	máynu ~ méynu	1PL.inc
má=aydin *or*	máydin ~ méydin	2PL
má=aad	máad	
má=ay	máy ~ méy	3PL

In instances where negative *má* moves leftward, an OPC (or a sequence of OPC + adposition) with which *má* has prosodified can migrate along with it. This is seen in (144) and (145), but more examples are given in §10.2.3.

(144) *Ánigu   márnaba [kumáan   odhán].*
       ani=g=u   marna=ba ku-ma=aan   odh-an
       I=K.DEF=SUBJ never=INT 2SG.Obj-NEG=1SG   say-PST.NEG
       'I never said it to you.' (Z & O: 507)

(145) *Wáqti dheér is   má[annu   arkín].*
       waqti dheer is   ma=aanu   ark-in
       time long RRP   NEG=1PL.exc see-PST.NEG
       'We haven't seen each other for a long time.' (Z & O: 426)

As one might expect, given the many examples of VC clusters introduced in sections above, more complex clusters involving negative *má* are possible. It would be impractical, in the interest of space, to list all possible combinations here. Rather, the following examples show some possibilities.

(146) *Saás   [noogumá   yimaaddáan].*
       saas   no=o-gu-ma   y-imaad-daan
       like.that 1PL.OBJ=to-about-NEG   3PL-come-PRES.NEG
       'They don't come to us about it like that.' (Z & O: 499)

(147) *Laakíin wada-shaqaýn   dambé   [isugumá   kaaya hadhín].*
       laakiin wada-shaqayn   dambe   is=u-gu-ma   kaaya hadh-in
       but   together-working no.longer   RRP=to-with-NEG 1PL remain-NEG
       'But, we no longer have to remain together, working together with one another.'
       (somaliland.org: 13430)

11 Focus markers

The encoding of focus in Somali is a morphological means by which some sentential constituent is indicated as either being new information entered into the discourse or is highlighted in order to increase its salience relative to other constituents. Generally speaking, a constituent that is not marked in this way is assumed to be topical, meaning that it is known or already active in the discourse. As shown later, in Chapter 13, constituents are brought into focus via co-occurrence with a focus marker. It is also possible to make a constituent explicitly topical, but this instead involves a manipulation of word order.

Somali is like some, but not all, Cushitic languages in that it utilizes specific particles to indicate focus. This chapter discusses the characteristics of three focus markers: *báa*, *ayáa*, and *wáxa(a)*. Some scholars (e.g., Andrzejewski 1975; Frascarelli and Puglielli 2003; Gebert 1986; Saeed 2004) have also treated declarative *waa* as a verb or predicate focus marker, but there is some reason to question this approach given that *waa* is commonly found in verbless sentences. The particle *waa* is not included here alongside other focus markers, but rather is discussed separately in Chapter 12 with other clause type particles.

Elsewhere in the literature, Somali's focus markers have been called *indicator particles* (Andrzejewski 1975; Antinucci and Puglielli 1980; Bell 1953; Livnat 1983, 1984), *foregrounding particles* (Tosco 2002), and *emphatic particles* (Hetzron 1965). Their behavior is among the best-studied aspects of Somali grammar (Andrzejewski 1975; Gebert 1986; Lecarme 1999a; Saeed 1984; Tosco 2002, among others). Generally speaking, focus markers are found in sentences where new information is being introduced, re-introduced, highlighted, or emphasized in the discourse. More specifically, focus markers are found only in tensed main clauses and never within subordinate clauses.

In a tensed main clause, a subject or object noun phrase can be focus marked, as can an adverbial, a subordinate clause, and even a series of coordinated clauses. Recall from Chapter 10 that the Verb Complex contains a verb and all the necessary pronouns to fill the verb's valence. As such, noun phrases act as *satellites* (Saeed 1999) or *syntactic adjuncts* (Lecarme 1999a; Svolacchia and Puglielli 1999) whose relative order can vary based on different discourse conditions. Given that the order of constituents like noun phrases and adverbials in Somali is not rigid relative to the Verb Complex (VC), focus markers contribute to information structure by highlighting, foregrounding, or emphasizing select information. That said, most scholars would agree that the basic, pragmatically neutral order of constituents in a Somali sentence is Subject NP + (Object NP) + Verb Complex (see Gebert 1986).

This chapter begins by discussing the morphosyntactic characteristics of focus markers and reserves more detailed discussion of their role in information structure for Chapter 13. The basic morphological characteristics and the distribution of Somali's three focus markers are first introduced. Two of these, *báa* and *ayáa*, focus constituents that occur before the Verb Complex. The third, *wáxa(a)*, focuses a constituent that occurs after the Verb Complex. Also in this chapter, the basic properties of clauses in which the verb's subject vs. one of its objects is morphologically marked as in focus are compared. Important here will be those instances in which the subject of a main clause verb is focus marked. Focus marking of a subject i) requires that the main clause verb exhibit reduced agreement, ii) precludes the use of resumptive subject pronoun clitics, iii) is incompatible with morphological subject marking, and iv) licenses an additional, optional strategy for negation. Another characteristic of subject focus is that associated main clause verbs exhibit H tone on their inflectional suffix, a trait that distinguishes them main clause verbs under most other conditions. No such requirements are associated with clauses with object focus, nor of those that do not contain a focus marker but rather contain a clause type particle. In examples throughout this chapter, the constituent that is in focus is indicated by square brackets [ ].

Note that in addition to the morphological focus markers discussed in this chapter, there are other lexical strategies discussed by Banti (2019) that Somali employs to encode focus in clauses where focus markers are not permitted. These are discussed later in §13.7. For an overview on focus marking elsewhere in Cushitic, see Mous (2012).

11.1 Pre-verbal focus

The pre-verbal focus markers *báa* and *ayáa* are largely interchangeable, though the latter is associated with a higher register than the former and more often encountered in written Somali. These are called pre-verbal focus markers because they and the constituent that they place into focus occur before the VC. A pre-verbal focus marker immediately follows the constituent that it places into focus. For example, in (1), the subject 'the teacher' is placed into focus by the focus marker *báa*.

(1) *[Macállinka]   báa buugág ná   siiyeý.*
    macallin=ka   baa buug-ag na   sii-y-ey
    teacher=K.DEF FOC book-PL 1PL.OBJ give-3SG.K-PST.RED
    '[The teacher] gave the books to us.' (Z & I: 88)

Such a sentence is an appropriate response to a question like 'Who gave us the books?' where clarifying information about the subject is being sought. Of course, there are other instances in which this would also be a licit response such as 'What happened?' where the response is expected to contain all new information. It is illustrated below that despite their nearly identical function, the two pre-verbal focus markers differ in the ways in which they coalesce or fuse with other elements around them.

11.1.1 báa

The pre-verbal focus marker *báa* occurs independently in two circumstances and coalesces with a subject pronoun clitic (SPC) elsewhere. It obligatorily occurs on its own when it focuses a subject. This can be seen in examples like (2) and (3), both of which involve subject focus. The subject is sentence-initial in the first example and not so in the second. The subject focus condition is discussed further detail in §11.3.

(2) *[Dayuurád] báa kú dhacdaý taalládii.*
    dayuurad baa ku dhac-d-ay   taala-dii
    airplane FOC into fall-3SG.T-PST.RED statue-T.RDEF
    '[An airplane] crashed into the statue.'

(3) *Nínkií   [naágtii]   báa aragtaý.*
    nin-kii   naag-tii   baa arag-t-ay
    man-K.RDEF woman-T.RDEF FOC see-3SG.F-PST.RED
    '[The woman] saw the man.' (Z & I: 95)

The focus marker *báa* may also optionally occur on its own under one particular object focus condition where a subject is syntactically topicalized. See §13.3.2 for further discussion and examples.

11.1.1.1 With a subject pronoun clitic

The focus marker *báa* coalesces with a SPC when an object is in focus, though there are exceptions to this when a subject is topicalized (see §13.3.2). Combinations of *báa* + SPC are shown in (4). 1PL and 2PL subjects are sometimes expressed with the corresponding singular SPC. There is dialectal variation in vowel quality in some forms, as indicated by ~ here and below. These focus marker + SPC clusters have a H tone contributed by *báa* on their first mora.

(4) *báa + subject pronoun clitic*

báa=aan	báan	1SG (~1PL)
báa=aad	báad	2SG (~2PL)
báa=uu	búu	3SG.M/K
báa=ay	báy ~ béy	3SG.F/T
báa=annu	báannu	1PL.exc
báa=aynu	báynu ~ béynu	1PL.inc
báa=aydin	báydin ~ béydin	2PL
báa=ay	báy ~ béy	3PL

When *báa* coalesces with a SPC, one can be certain the verb's subject is not in focus. Compare (3) just above and (5) where the word order is identical, but the presence of an SPC cliticized onto *báa* in the latter is indicative of object focus. Notice that in (3), the focused subject retains its expected tonal profile, but the unfocused subject in (5) loses its final H tone due to subject marking (see §9.2).

(5) *Nínkii   [naágtií]   búu   arkey.*
    nin-kii   naag-tii   b=uu   ark-∅-ey
    man-K.RDEF.SUBJ woman-T.RDEF FOC=3SG.M see-3SG.M-PST
    'The man saw [the woman].' (Z & I: 95)

Other examples of *báa* + SPC coalescence under object focus are in (6) and (7), both of which have pronominal subjects with no co-referential subject NP outside the Verb Complex.

(6) *[Meeshéé]   báan   ká   fuulaa?*
    mee-sh-ee   b=aan   ka   fuul-∅-aa
    place-T.IDEF FOC=1SG from board-1SG-PRES
    'From [where] should I board?' (Z & O: 462)

(7) *[Rá'yigaás] báy   diideen.*
    ra'yi-gaas   b=ay   diid-∅-ee-n
    idea-K.that FOC=3PL refuse-3-PST-PL
    'They refused [that idea].' (Z & O: 550)

11.1.1.2 With negative *aán*

Somali has two negative particles, *má* and *aán*. The first of these has a wide distribution (see §12.2) but does not occur in clauses with focus marking. Rather, in a negative clause containing a focus marker, *aán* is used instead and cliticizes onto the focus marker. Under subject focus, given that there are no SPCs present, negative *aán* clusters with *báa* yielding *baán*, as in (8). Note that H tone is on the second mora in *baán* whereas it is on the first mora in *báan*, which is FOC + 1SG. As elsewhere, the verb is also inflected for negative.

(8) *[Cábdi] baán   qabán.*
    Cabdi   b-aan   qab-an
    Cabdi   FOC-NEG catch-PST.NEG
    '[Cabdi] did not catch him.'

Under object focus, *báa* still clusters with negative *aán*, but an SPC is also present. There is dialectal variation in the formation of these focus/*aán*/SPC clusters. Though the focus marker always occurs first, the relative order of the negative marker and SPC varies. As discussed in various works (e.g., Andrzejewski 1975, Banti 1985, Moreno

1955, Saeed 1999), Northern Somali speakers prefer FOC + NEG + SPC, as in (9). In these forms, there is a H tone on the first mora of the first syllable. As introduced above, 1PL and 2PL subjects may be expressed with a corresponding singular SPC. Variations in vowel quality are indicated by ~ where relevant.

(9) *báa + aán + subject pronoun clitic*

báa-aán=aan	*báanan*	1SG (~ 1PL)
báa-aán=aad	*báanad*	2SG (~ 2PL)
báa-aán=uu	*báanu*	3SG.M/K
báa-aán=ay	*báanay ~ báaney*	3SG.F/T
báa-aán=annu	*báannan*	1PL
báa-aán=aydin	*báanayd ~ báaneyd*	2PL
báa-aán=ay	*báanay ~ báaney*	3PL

Speakers of more geographically southern varieties use FOC + SPC + NEG, as in (10). In these forms, there are two H tones: the first is on the first mora of the first syllable, with the other being on the last syllable.

(10) *báa + subject pronoun clitic + aán*

báa=aan-aán	*báanán*	1SG (~ 1PL)
báa=aad-aán	*báadán*	2SG (~ 2PL)
báa=uu-aán	*búusán*	3SG.M/K
báa=ay-aán	*báynán ~ béynán*	3SG.F/T
báa=annu-aán	*báannán*	1PL
báa=aydin-aán	*báydnán ~ béydnán*	2PL
báa=ay-aán	*báynán ~ béynán*	3PL

An example of such a cluster is in (11) where the oblique object is in focus. Here, the subject is pronominal, and the verb takes an infinitival complement as its direct object.

(11) [*Magaaládán*] *búusán   doóneynín   ínuu*
       magaala-dan   b=uus-an   doon-eyn-in   in=uu
       city-T.that   FOC=3SG.M-NEG   want-PST.PROG-NEG COMP=3SG.M
       degó.
       deg-o
       live-3SG.M-IRR
       'He did not want to live in [that city].' (Z & I: 379)

11.1.1.3 With interrogative *ma*

Question formation in clauses containing *báa* does not involve clustering of the focus marker and the interrogative marker *ma*. As seen in both (12) and (13), *ma* directly precedes the focused constituent, whether it is a subject or object.

(12) Ma *[Cáli] báa keenaý?*
 ma Cali baa keen-∅-ay
 QM Cali FOC bring-3SG.M-PST.RED
 'Did [Cali] bring it?'

(13) Ma *[caanáha] báy Maryam cabtay?*
 ma caana-ha b=ay Maryam cab-t-ay
 QM milk=K.DEF FOC=3SG.F Maryam.SUBJ drink-3SG.F-PST
 'Did Maryam drink [the milk]?'

This outcome differs from what occurs with *ayáa* where the interrogative marker cliticizes onto the focus marker. Details of this second scenario are discussed in §11.1.2.

11.1.1.4 Coalescence with a preceding noun phrase

A unique characteristic exhibited by *báa* is its ability to coalesce with another element that precedes it, an outcome observed in both written and spoken Somali. As a result of this coalescence, the initial consonant of the focus marker is lost, though its presence is still realized in the retention of its H tone, but also sometimes by vowel length. The same generalizations introduced above also hold here concerning the presence vs. absence of SPCs under different focus conditions. When it is not easily segmentable, coalescence of *báa* is indicated with ∅ in examples here and elsewhere.

(14) *[Géesk]úu ká soó galay.*
 gees=k-∅=uu ka soo gal-∅-ay
 side=K.DEF-FOC=3SG.M from VEN enter-3SG.M-PST
 'He entered from [the side].'

(15) *[Biyá]a meél kú balaqsánaá.*
 biya-a meel ku balaq-s-an-aa
 water-FOC place out spilled-W.CAUS-STV-PST.RED
 '[Water] spilled out there.' (Z & O: 46)

(16) *[Ad]áa i daartaý.*
 ad-aa i daar-t-ay
 you-FOC 1SG-OBJ disturb-2SG-PST.RED
 '[You] disturbed me.' (Z & O: 121)

11.1.2 ayáa

Many characteristics of the pre-verbal focus marker *ayáa* closely parallel those discussed above for *báa*, though the former is associated with a more formal register. For both pre-verbal focus markers, the focus marker itself immediately follows the constituent that it places into focus. Both also occur before the VC, and *ayáa* appears on its own in instances of subject focus, as in (17), meaning that it does not coalesce with a SPC. This follows from requirements of the subject focus condition (§11.3).

(17) [Akhbaártií] ayáa tuuládií kú shaacday.
akhbaar-tii ayaa tuula-dii ku shaac-d-ay
news-T.RDEF FOC village-T.RDEF around spread-MID.3SG.F-PST.RED

'[The news] spread around the village.' (Z & I: 428)

This focus marker may also appear on its own under one particular object focus configuration, as discussed in §13.3.2. In other instances, it will coalesce with a SPC.

11.1.2.1 With a subject pronoun clitic

Under most object focus scenarios, the focus marker *ayáa* joins with an enclitic SPC in the combinations shown in (18). Each of these clusters has a H tone contributed by the focus marker that is realized on the first mora of the second syllable. As in many other instances, 1PL and 2PL forms optionally collapse onto the corresponding singular. There is also variation in vowel quality in some forms, as indicated by ~, where relevant.

(18) *ayáa + subject pronoun clitic*

ayáa=aan	ayáan	1SG (~ 1PL)
ayáa=aad	ayáad	2SG (~ 2PL)
ayáa=uu	ayúu	3SG.M/K
ayáa=ay	ayáy ~ ayéy	3SG.F/T
ayáa=annu	ayáannu	1PL.exc
ayáa=aynu	ayáynu ~ ayéynu	1PL.inc
ayáa=aydin	ayáydin ~ ayéydin	2PL
ayáa=ay	ayáy ~ ayéy	3PL

Instances of object focus in which *ayáa* is joined by a SPC are as follows in (19) and (20). In (19), focus is on a direct object, while in (20), it is on an oblique object.

(19) *[Bíir] ayáannu cabney.*
biir aya=annu cab-n-ey
beer FOC=1PL.exc drink-1PL-PST
'We drank [beer].' (Z & I: 182)

(20) *[Isága] ayáy ú égtahay.*
isa=ga ay=ay u eg-t-ah-ay
he=K.DEF FOC=3SG.F to resemble-3SG.F-be-PRES
'She bears resemblance to [him].' (Z & O: 205)

11.1.2.2 With negative *aán*

In clauses with focus marking, the negative marker *aán* is used, rather than *má*. The negative marker joins *ayáa* directly, yielding *ayaán* when the subject is in focus. This is because SPCs do not occur in the subject focus configuration. H tone in these instances is on the final mora, rather than on the penultimate mora, as would be the case in *ayáan* when the focus marker is instead followed by the 1SG SPC. An example of *ayáa* + negative *aán* is shown in (21). As expected, the clause's verb is inflected for negation as well.

(21) *[Al-Shabáab] ayaán wali ká hadlín qáraxán máanta*
Al-Shabaab ay=aan wali ka hadl-in qarax-an maanta
Al-Shabaab FOC=NEG yet about speak-PST.NEG explosion-K.that today
ká dhacay.
ka dhac-∅-ay
on occur-3SG.K-PST
'[Al-Shabaab] has not yet spoken about the explosion that occurred today.' (kalsantv: 530)

Under most object conditions, the combination of *ayáa* + *aán* is joined by a SPC. As was the case with *báa*, the focus marker always comes first in the sequence, but speakers vary in the relative order of the negative and SPC that they employ. Northern Somali speakers prefer FOC + NEG + SPC, as in (22). In these clusters, H tone remains on the first mora of the second syllable. 1PL and 2PL forms have optional variants that match their singular counterparts and there are dialectal differences in vowel quality for some forms.

(22) *ayáa + aán + subject pronoun clitic*

ayáa-aán=aan	ayáanan	1SG (~ 1PL)
ayáa-aán=aad	ayáanad	2SG (~ 2PL)
ayáa-aán=uu	ayáanu	3SG.M/K
ayáa-aán=ay	ayáanay ~ ayáaney	3SG.F/T
ayáa-aán=annu	ayáannan	1PL
ayáa-aán=aydin	ayáanaydin ~ ayáaneydin	2PL
ayáa-aán=ay	ayáanay ~ ayáaney	3PL

Speakers of geographically southern dialects instead prefer the order FOC + SPC + NEG, as in (23). There are two H tones on these forms: one H on the the first mora of the second syllable and the other on the last syllable.

(23) *ayáa + subject pronoun clitic + aán*

ayáa=aan-aán	ayáanán	1SG (~ 1PL)
ayáa=aad-aán	ayáadán	2SG (~ 2PL)
ayáa=uu-aán	ayúusán	3SG.M/K
ayáa=ay-aán	ayáynán ~ ayéynán	3SG.F/T
ayáa=annu-aán	ayáannán	1PL
ayáa=aydin-aán	ayáydnán ~ ayéydnán	2PL
ayáa=ay-aán	ayáynán ~ ayéynán	3PL

Example (24) shows a FOC + SPC + NEG cluster in a sentence where a time adverbial is in focus.

(24) [*Hádda 20 maálmoód*] *ayúusán   masaájidka   ká*
      hadda   20 maalm-ood ay=uus-an   masaajid=ka   ka
      since   20 day-ASSOC FOC=3SG.M-NEG mosque=K.DEF   from
      bixín.
      bix-in
      leave-WCAUS.NEG
      'He hasn't exited the mosque [for 20 days].' (allbadweyn: 16041)

11.1.2.3 With interrogative *ma*

In those instances where a SPC is not present (e.g., under subject focus), interrogative *ma* joins *ayáa* yielding *miyáa*. Such an outcome is seen in (25). Here, the subject is in focus, a fact made clear by reduced agreement on the verb. In §12.3, it is shown that there is another instantiation of *miyáa* used in forming some yes/no questions that does not entail focus marking.

(25) *[Wiiláshaás] miyáa keenaý.*
wiil-a-shaas m=iyaa keen-ay
boy-PL-t.those QM=FOC bring-PST.RED

'Did [those boys] bring it?' (Antinucci 1980)

Under most other focus conditions, *miyáa* is joined by a SPC in the combinations shown in (26). Variation that is otherwise expected in 1PL and 2PL forms (vs. their singular counterparts), as well as in vowel quality, occurs here too. H tone in these clusters remain on the first mora of the second syllable.

(26) *ma+ ayáa + subject pronoun clitic*

ma-ayáa=aan	*miyáan*	1SG (~ 1PL)
ma-ayáa=aad	*miyáad*	2SG (~ 2PL)
ma-ayáa=uu	*miyúu*	3SG.M/K
ma-ayáa=ay	*miyáy ~ miyéy*	3SG.F/T
ma-ayáa=annu	*miyáannu*	1PL.exc
ma-ayáa=aynu	*miyáynu ~ miyéynu*	1PL.inc
ma-ayáa=aydin	*miyáydin ~ miyéydin*	2PL
ma-ayáa=ay	*miyáy ~ miyéy*	3PL

Examples of these clusters in context are in (27) and (28). In (27), focus is on the direct object, and in (28), it is on an oblique object.

(27) *[Nínkaás] miyáad aqoóneysey?*
nin-kaas m-iy=aad aqoon-ey-s-ey
man-K.that QM-FOC=2SG know-PROG-2SG-PST

'Did you recognize [that man]?' (Z & O: 25)

(28) *[Dukáanka] miyáad wáx ugá baahántahay?*
dukaan=ka m-iy=aad wax u-ka baah-an-t-ah-ay
store=K.DEF QM-FOC=2SG thing of-from needy-STV-2SG-be-PRES

'Are you in need of anything from [the store]? (Z & O: 472)

11.1.2.4 With interrogative *ma* and negative *aán*

The focus marker *ayáa* can combine directly with both interrogative *ma* and negative *aán*, yielding *miyaán*. This is shown in (29). Note that H tone is realized here on the final mora.

(29) *Maryan miyaán   tegín?*
    Maryan mi-ya-aan   teg-in
    Maryan QM-FOC-NEG   go-PST.NEG
    'Wasn't it Maryan who went?' (Z & O: 472)

Elsewhere, an SPC is added to *ma + ayáa*, forming the clusters shown in (30) and (31). In these clusters, the order of the interrogative and focus marker is consistent, but there is dialectal variation in the order of the SPC and negative relative to one another. As discussed elsewhere, Northern Somali speakers form clusters shown in (30) in which the negative precedes the SPC. There is one H tone located on the first mora of the second syllable.

(30)   *ma+ ayáa + aán + subject pronoun clitic*

ma-ayáa-aán=aan	miyáanan	1SG (~ 1PL)
ma-ayáa-aán=aad	miyáanad	2SG (~ 2PL)
ma-ayáa-aán=uu	miyáanu	3SG.M/K
ma-ayáa-aán=ay	miyáanay ~ miyáaney	3SG.F/T
ma-ayáa-aán=annu	miyáannan	1PL.exc
ma-ayáa-aán=aynu	miyáanaynu	1PL.inc
ma-ayáa-aán=aydin	miyáanaydin	2PL
ma-ayáa-aán=ay	miyáanay ~ miyáaney	3PL

Other speakers use the opposite order, shown in (31), where the SPC precedes the negative marker. These differ in a variety of expected ways, including that the clusters have two H tones.

(31)   *ma+ ayáa + subject pronoun clitic + aán*

ma-ayáa=aan-aán	miyáanán	1SG (~ 1PL)
ma-ayáa=aad-aán	miyáadán	2SG (~ 2PL)
ma-ayáa=uu-aán	miyúusán	3SG.M/K
ma-ayáa=ay-aán	miyáyán ~ miyéyán	3SG.F/T
ma-ayáa=annu-aán	miyáannán	1PL.exc
ma-ayáa=aynu-aán	miyáynán ~ miyéynán	1PL.inc
ma-ayáa=aydin-aán	miyáydán ~ miyéydán	2PL
ma-ayáa=ay-aán	miyáyán ~ miyéyán	3PL

11.2 Post-verbal focus

A third focus marker, *wáxa(a)* is involved in cataphoric focalization (Svolacchia et al. 1995) of a constituent that follows the Verb Complex. This is often, but not always, a "heavy" constituent like a subordinate clause, quotation, or a series of coordinated clauses. *Wáxa(a)* is often translated as a cleft or pseudo-cleft construction, but the speakers with whom I have worked tend to reject such readings. Examples of its use in focusing a long vs. short constituent are seen in (32) and (33), respectively. As above, the constituent in focus is indicated by square brackets.

(32) Wáxa róon [ínaannu dhaqsó tagnó].
waxa roon in=aannu dhaqso tag-n-o
FOC better COMP=1PL quickly go-1PL-IRR
'It is better [that we go quickly].' (Z & O: 328)

(33) Wáxa tagaý [Cáli].
waxa tag-∅-ay Cali
FOC go-3SG.M-PST.RED Cali
'[Cali] went.'

As the parentheses thus far in *wáxa(a)* might suggest, there are two variants of this focus marker that differ only in the length of the final vowel: *wáxa* is purportedly more common in Northern Somali, while *wáxaa* is more common elsewhere. Both are used in many sources from different areas as well as by speakers from different regions. As such, they appear to be essentially interchangeable in contemporary Somali.

The interaction of *wáxa(a)* with other morphemes parallels that of the pre-verbal focus markers discussed in Sections 11.1.1 and 11.1.2. For example, the post-verbal focus marker appears on its own when it places a subject into focus. See, for example, the sentences above in (32) and (33). This behavior follows from one requirement of the subject focus condition, namely that SPCs do not occur when a subject is in focus (see §11.3). There is, of course, the exceptional instance involving one type of object focus introduced above and discussed further in §13.3.2.

In other focus conditions instances, *wáxa(a)* is joined by an SPC in the combinations shown in (34). In each instance, there is a single H tone found on the first syllable.

(34) *wáxa(a) + subject pronoun clitic*

wáxa(a)=aan	wáxaan	1SG (~ 1PL)
wáxa(a)=aad	wáxaad	2SG (~ 2PL)
wáxa(a)=uu	wáxuu ~ wúxuu	3SG.M/K
wáxa(a)=ay	wáxay ~ wáxey	3SG.F/T
wáxa(a)=annu	wáxaannu	1PL.exc
wáxa(a)=aynu	wáxaynu ~ wáxeynu	1PL.inc
wáxa(a)=aydin	wáxaydin ~ wáxeydin	2PL
wáxa(a)=ay	wáxay ~ wáxey	3PL

Examples of several different combinations of *wáxa(a)* + SPC in context are as follows. In each instance, a clausal object complement is placed into focus.

(35) *Wáxay   tahashay   [ínay   shaqáda   qabató].*
    wax=ay   taha-sh-ay   in=ay   shaqa=da   qab-a-t-o
    FOC=3SG.F try-3SG.F-PST COMP=3SG.F work=T.DEF do-MID-3SG.F-IRR
    'She tried [to do the work].' (Z & O: 619)

(36) *Wúxuu   tahliyay   [ínuu   kacó].*
    wux=uu   tahl-i-y-ay   in=uu   kac-o
    FOC=3SG.M urge-W.CAUS-3SG.M-PST COMP=3SG.M get.up-IRR
    'He urged himself [to get up].' (Z & O: 620)

(37) *Sánnadkán wáxaan rabaa   [Yúrub ínaan   fásax   ú   tagó].*
    sannad-kan wax=aan rab-Ø-aa   Yurub in=aan   fasax   u   tag-o
    year-K.this FOC=1SG want-1SG-PRES Europe COMP=1SG vacation for go-IRR
    'This year, I want [to go to Europe for vacation].'

It is worth noting here that there are other instances in which forms like *wáxaan*, *wáxaad*, and the like might arise that are not connected to post-verbal focus. In sentences like (38), *wáxaad* occurs in a sentence containing the declarative clause type marker. Here, *wáx* 'thing' is a noun that is the head of a relative clause and that functions as the direct object of the main clause verb.

(38) *Wáydin taqaannaan   wáxaad   doóneysaan.*
    w=aydin t-aqaan-n-aa-n   wax=aad   doon-ey-t-aa-n
    DEC=2PL 2PL-know-2-PRES-PL thing=2PL want-PROG-2-PRES-PL
    'You (PL) know what you want.' (Z & O: 624)

Its role as a simple noun, rather than a focus marker, is also seen in (39). This sentence also contains the declarative clause type marker, with *wáxa* being the defined head of a complex noun phrase.

(39) *Húbka   atamká   waa wáxa   wélwelka   weýn kú*
    hub=ka   atam-ka   waa wax=a   welwel=ka   weyn ku
    war=K.DEF atom=K.DEF DEC thing=K.DEF concern=K.DEF large of
    hayá   aadámiga.
    hay-a   aadami=ga
    have-PRES.RED humanity=K-DEF
    'Atomic war is humanity's greatest concern.'

11.2.1 With negative *aán*

Like other clauses containing a focus marker, those with *wáxa(a)* are negated by *aán* and also have a negatively inflected verb. The focus marker and negative particle combine to yield *waxaán* in instances where an SPC cannot occur (e.g., under subject focus). Such an example is shown in (40) where the focused subject is a coordinated series of relative clauses.

(40) Waxaán muuqanín [adéeggií aasaasigá ahaa ee
wax=aan muuq-an-in adeeg-gii aasaasi=ga ah-aa ee
FOC=NEG visible-MID-NEG service-K.RDEF basic=K.DEF be-PST.RED REL
dégmo].
degmo
district

'[The basic services of the district] are not visible.' (ceelwayne: 126)

In other focus conditions, the combination of focus marker and negative *aán* may be joined by an SPC. As already seen for other focus markers in sections above, the relative order of the negative and SPC varies among speakers from different areas. The position of the focus marker itself is constant. The order that is most prevalent in Northern Somali is FOC + NEG + SPC, as seen in the clusters in (41). Besides an expected optional collapse of 1PL and 2PL forms onto their singular counterparts and vocalic alternations, 3PL and 3SG.F share the same form. There remains a single H tone, but it is realized on the first mora of the second syllable.

(41) *wáxa(a) + aán + subject pronoun clitic*

wáxa(a)-aán=aan	waxáanan	1SG (~ 1PL)
wáxa(a)-aán=aad	waxáanad	2SG (~ 2PL)
wáxa(a)-aán=uu	waxáanu	3SG.M/K
wáxa(a)-aán=ay	waxáanay ~ waxáaney	3SG.F/T
wáxa(a)-aán=aannu	waxáannu	1PL.exc
wáxa(a)-aán=aynu	waxáanayn ~ waxáaneyn	1PL.inc
wáxa(a)-aán=aydin	waxáanayd ~ waxáaneyd	2PL
wáxa(a)-aán=ay	waxáanay ~ waxáaney	3PL

The opposing order, more commonly used by speakers of the Central and Benaadir dialects, is shown in (42). Here, the SPC precedes the negative. Two H tones are found in these instances, one on the first syllable and the other on the last or only mora of the final syllable.

(42) *wáxa(a) + subject pronoun clitic + aán*

wáxa(a)=aan-aán	wáxaanán ~ wáxanán	1SG (~ 1PL)
wáxa(a)=aad-aán	wáxaadán ~ wáxadán	2SG (~ 2PL)
wáxa(a)=uu-aán	wáxuusán ~ wúxuusán	3SG.M/K
wáxa(a)=ay-aán	wáxaayán ~ wáxayán	3SG.F/T
wáxa(a)=aannu-aán	wáxaannaán ~ wáxannaán	1PL.exc
wáxa(a)=aynu-aán	wáxaynaán	1PL.inc
wáxa(a)=aydin-aán	wáxaydaán	2PL
wáxa(a)=ay-aán	wáxaayán ~ wáxayán	3PL

Examples in context are shown in (43) and (44). The first of these shows the NEG + SPC order while the second instead shows SPC + NEG.

(43) *Waxáanan   hilmaámáyn   [rúntií   darajoóyinka*
      wax-aan=an hilmaam-ay-n   run-tii   darajo-oyin=ka
      FOC-NEG=1SG forget-PROG-PST.NEG detail-T.RDEF ranking-PL=K.DEF
      ciidammaddá].
      ciidamm-ad=da
      military-PL=T.DEF
      'I've not forgotten [the details of the military's rankings].'
      (somaliland.org: 11516)

(44) *Laakíin wáxaadán   márna warbaahínta Soomaalidá   kú árkáyn*
      laakiin wax=aad-an   marna warbaahin=ta soomaali=da ku ark-ay-n
      but   FOC=2SG-NEG never media=T.DEF Somali=T.DEF in see-PROG-NEG
      [mashrúuc ballaarán].
      mashruuc ballaar-an
      project   large-STV
      'But, you've never seen [a large project] in the Somali media.' (alkhabiir: 520)

11.2.2 With interrogative *ma*

Questions are formed in clauses with *wáxa(a)* via the addition of the interrogative particle *ma* before the focus marker. The two do not coalesce. These look similar to, but are distinct from, sentences formed with the question word *maxáa* 'what.'

In subject focus contexts, the focus marker is bare, as in (45). It may be also joined by a subject pronoun clitic, yielding the clusters in (34), when an object is in focus. An example of this is shown in (46).

(45) Ma wáxaa wada hádlayá   [dawlád   iyo maámul]?
      ma waxaa wada hadl-ay-a   dawlad   iyo maamul
      QM FOC   ADV speak-PROG-PRES.RED government and administration
      'Is it that the government and administration are speaking together?
      (somaliland.org: 53013)

(46) Háddaba madaxweynúhu   ma wúxuu   qorsháystay
      hadda=ba madaxweynu=h=u   ma wux=uu   qorsh-ays-t-∅-ay
      now=INT president=K.DEF=SUBJ QM FOC=3SG.M plan-FACT-MID-3SG.M-PST
      [ín   uu   wareejiyó]?
      in   uu   wareej-i-y-o]
      COMP 3SG.M take.into.account-WCAUS-3SG.M-PRES.IRR
      'And just now, is the president planning to take it into account?'
      (rakaadnews.com: 220206)

11.2.3 With interrogative *ma* and negative *aán*

The post-verbal focus marker can also form questions when negated. Once again, the question marker *ma* precedes the focus marker. The focus marker itself is joined by the negative marker *aán* and often by a subject pronoun clitic, but only when an object is in focus. In the interest of space, the various combinations are not repeated here, but see §11.2.1 for a full list of possibilities.

(47) Ma waxaánad   garánáyn   [masuuliyádda   aad
      ma wax-aan=ad   garan-ayn   masuuliyad=da   aad
      QM FOC-NEG=2SG understand-PRES.NEG responsibility=T.DEF 2SG
      noó   haysó]?
      no=o   hay-s-o
      1PL.OBJ=to have-2SG-PRES.IRR
      'Are you not aware of the responsibility that you have to us?'
      (somaliland.org: 325132)

11.3 The subject focus condition

In clauses with focus marking, there are morphosyntactic and tonological requirements characteristic of what is referred to here as the *subject focus condition* that serve as the key diagnostic for teasing apart the formal properties of focus markers vs. other clause type markers. In this section, it is illustrated that subject focus has a bearing on verb inflection, precludes the use of subject pronoun clitics, affects the choice of negative particle, and prevents morphological subject marking. There are also certain word orders that are associated with subject focus, but these are discussed separately in Chapter 13 as they serve particular discursive functions.

11.3.1 Verb inflection

A main clause verb whose subject is morphologically marked as in focus by a focus marker exhibits a reduced agreement paradigm. Recall from §7.8 that this entails an inflectional pattern in which certain combinations of number and person collapse onto a single form. In addition, these verbs are unique relative to most other main clause verbs in that they have H tone on their inflectional suffix. For the sake of convenience, a summary of the forms of main clause verbs found under the subject focus condition, compared to those found under other conditions, are shown here in (48).

(48) *'Full' agreement vs. agreement under subject focus - Simple Past*

	Suffixing		Prefixing	
	Full	Subj Focus	Full	Subj Focus
1SG	qoday	qodaý	imid	imíd
2SG	qodday	qodaý	timid	yimíd
3SG.M	qoday	qodaý	yimid	yimíd
3SG.F	qodday	qoddaý	timid	timíd
1PL	qodnay	qodnaý	nimid	nimíd
2PL	qoddeen	qodaý	timaaddeen	yimíd
3PL	qodeen	qodaý	yimaaddeen	yimíd

As shown, even in the full agreement paradigm, forms for 1SG and 3SG.M are segmentally identical in suffixing verbs, as are those for 2SG and 3SG.F. Thus, there are five inflectional forms in full agreement. This collapses onto only three forms in the reduced agreement paradigm. More specifically, 2SG, 2PL, and 3PL merge with 1SG/3SG.M. The outcome is much the same in prefixing verbs, though a unique 1SG form is maintained in both the full and reduced agreement patterns. Full agreement forms are toneless while those found in the subject focus condition exhibit a H tone.

Sentences (49) and (50) offer a clear and simple comparison between these inflectional paradigms. The first contains the declarative clause type particle *waa* which does not have the same effect that pre-verbal focus markers do on a preceding subject. The verb in this sentence takes full agreement and is toneless. The second sentence instead contains the pre-verbal focus marker *báa* which marks the subject as in focus. The verb in this sentence accordingly requires reduced agreement and is toned. Other distinguishing characteristics of the subject focus condition seen in comparing these examples are discussed further below.

(49) *Adígu   wáad   rabtaa.*
adi=g=u   w=aad   rab-t-aa
2SG=K.DEF=SUBJ DEC=2SG want-2SG-PRES
'You want it.'

(50) *[Adíga]   báa rabá.*
adi=ga   baa rab-a
2SG=K.DEF FOC want-PRES.RED
'[You] want it.'

Comparable examples of the subject focus condition involving *ayáa* and *wáxa(a)* are as follows in (51) and (52), respectively.

(51) *Íntaan   ká   bogsánayó,   [ádiga]   ayáa i*
int=aan   ka   bog-s-an-ay-o   adi=ga   ayaa i
while=1SG from recover-W.CAUS-MID-PROG-IRR 2SG=K.DEF FOC 1SG.OBJ
baanánayá.
baan-an-ay-a
take.care-MID-PROG-PRES.RED
'While I am recovering, [you] will take care of me.' (Z & O: 69)

(52) *Wáxa jabaý   [kóobkéyga].*
waxa jab-ay   koob-key=ga
FOC break-PRES.RED cup-K.my=K.DEF
'[My cup] broke.' (Z & I: 178)

11.3.2 Pronoun clitics

Subject pronoun clitics are not found when a subject is focused by a focus marker. This restriction is seen in examples (50) through (52) above. The focus marker in each stands alone without a cliticized subject pronoun. In most other focus conditions, this restriction does not hold. One possibility to explain this prohibition against the presence of SPCs under the subject focus condition might be that it arises from the fact that subject focus necessarily entails the presence of an overt subject noun phrase, thus obviating the need for a resumptive, co-referential pronoun.

It has also been suggested that the absence of a SPC within the Verb Complex is responsible for the reduced agreement seen under these and related conditions (e.g., in subject relative clauses). Proposals raised in several works (e.g., Frascarelli 2010b; Frascarelli and Puglielli 2003; Puglielli 1981) appeal to the presence of an "anti-agreement effect" (Ouhalla 1993). Briefly, for Somali, the argument is that the presence of a null subject precludes the verb from expressing the morphological feature [person], but [gender] and [number] features are retained. There are some potential shortcomings in such an approach, however, such as the fact that what we think of as 1PL forms are not inflected for number in the same way as 2PL and 3PL. The latter two of these require suffixal -*n* while 1PL does not (see discussion in §7.5). One might argue, therefore, that simply appealing to the inability of the verb to inflect [number] does not adequately capture the phenomena.

11.3.3 Subject marking

Another defining characteristic of the subject focus condition is that subject marking via the subject marker clitic (see §9.2) does not occur on a morphologically-focused subject. Thus, a subject cannot simultaneously be focus marked and subject marked. Compare, for example, (49) and (50) above. The subject of the declarative clause in (49) bears subject marking on its definite determiner. The same subject under focus marking cannot be subject-marked in the same way.

11.4 The object focus condition

The characteristics of the object focus condition provide a clear counterpoint to the various restrictions brought into play in the subject focus condition. Under object focus, a focus marker is still present within the clause. This means that the restrictions discussed in the preceding section can undeniably be linked to focus being on a subject constituent, rather than being connected to focus marking in general. Recall that object focus applies to objects of any type, be they direct, indirect, or oblique. Such an object can be marked by a pre-verbal focus marker that immediately follows it or by the post-verbal focus marker. Though the post-verbal focus marker focuses an object that occurs after the Verb Complex, the focus marker itself occurs before the Verb Complex.

Most characteristics that obtain in the object focus condition can be said to represent an unmarked or default state of affairs. That is, they can be seen applying even in clauses that do not contain a focus marker. Furthermore, they even apply in instances in which adverbials and dependent clauses, are in focus. Both under object focus and in other non-focus clauses, verbs exhibit full agreement in their inflectional paradigm. Likewise, in both instances, SPCs are permitted, and a subject can be morphologically subject-marked. The generalization that can be made is that the subject focus condition represents a marked or specialized set of conditions.

11.4.1 Verb inflection

When the object of a main clause verb is morphologically marked as in focus, the verb exhibits full agreement within its inflectional paradigm. This means that the verb will inflect for a full array of person, number, and grammatical gender exponents. This can be readily compared to the subject focus condition described in §11.3 where instead one observes reduced agreement in verb inflection. The following examples show a cross-section of object focus types employing the three focus markers.

(53) *[Furáha gurigá] báad haysaa.*
fura=ha guri=ga b=aad hay-s-aa
key=K.DEF house=K.DEF FOC=2SG have-2SG-PRES
'You have [the house key].' (Z & I: 45)

(54) *[Afár maalmó dabadeéd] ayáy tágayaan.*
afar maalm-o dabadeed ay=ay tag-ay-∅-aa-n
four day-PL after FOC=3PL go-PROG-3-PRES-PL
'They are going [after four days].'

(55) *Wáxaydin aragteen [saaxíibkaý].*
wax=aydin arag-t-ee-n saaxiib-kay
FOC=2PL see-2-PST-PL friend-K.my
'You (PL) saw my friend.'

Example (53) shows object focus with *báa* where the direct object is in focus. Example (54) shows focus on an oblique object with *ayáa*. Lastly, (55) shows direct object focus with *wáxa(a)*. In each instance, the verb is inflected with full agreement.

11.4.2 Pronoun clitics

In the subject focus condition, the presence of a resumptive SPC is ungrammatical. Under the object focus condition, however, SPCs are required in nearly every instance. This can be seen in examples (53) through (55) above where the focus marker is followed in each instance by a SPC.

The situation with object pronoun clitics is much different. Their presence is obligatory within the Verb Complex, arguably in all instances. This, of course, is keeping in mind that there is a gap in Somali's object pronoun paradigms such that third person (both singular and plural) has no overt form. However, one can observe for non-third person objects that an object pronoun must be present whether an object is in focus (56), the subject is in focus (57), or when some other constituent like an adverbial is in focus, as in (58).

(56) [Ániga]   ayúu   Cabdi   iigá   warramay
     ani=ga   ay=uu   Cabdi   i=i-ga   warr-am-∅-ay
     1SG=K.DEF FOC=3SG.M Cabdi.SUBJ 1SG.OBJ=to-about inform-NEU-3SG.M-PST
     arríntan.
     arrin-tan
     issue-T.this
     'Cabdi informed [me] about this issue.'

(57) [Waláalkeéd] báa ií   sheegeý.
     walaal-keed   baa i=i   sheeg-ey
     brother-K.her FOC 1SG.OBJ=to tell-PST.RED
     '[Her brother] told me.' (Z & I: 104)

(58) [Shálay] báa lay   dilay.
     shalay   baa la=y   dil-∅-ay
     yesterday FOC ISP=1SG.OBJ beat-3SG.M-PST
     'Someone beat me [yesterday].' (Svolacchia et al. 1995)

11.4.3 Subject marking

Whereas morphological subject marking is prohibited under the subject focus condition, it readily occurs on subjects under the object focus condition. This is shown, for example, in (59).

(59) Coomaádigu   wúxuu   eryánayaa   [bakayláha].
     coomaadi=g=u   wux=uu   ery-an-ay-∅-aa   bakayla=ha
     vulture=K.DEF=SUBJ FOC=3SG.K chase-MID-PROG-3SG.M-PRES rabbit=K.DEF
     'The vulture is chasing [the rabbit].' (Z & O: 206)

It is important to keep in mind, as discussed in §9.2, that the use of morphological subject marking differs markedly between dialects in ways that are not clearly understood. Subject marking has both tonal and segmental exponents whose realization is influenced by a combination of factors. Its presence is seen most consistently when it has a segmental exponent, like in (59). In other instances, segmental realization of the subject marker may be accompanied by the loss of H tone. Those instances in which subject marking might only be seen by H tone loss, with no accompanying segmental exponent, are less consistently realized.

12 Main clauses without focus marking

This chapter deals specifically with the structure of main clauses that do not contain a phrase, adverbial, or subordinate clause that is morphologically marked as 'in focus' by one of Somali's three focus markers: *báa*, *ayáa*, and *wáxa(a)*. Main clauses with focus marking are treated separately in Chapter 13 because they have distinct syntactic properties. This is particularly apparent when a subject noun phrase is in focus. As introduced in §11.3, subject focus entails reduced agreement on the main clause verb, precludes the use of a resumptive subject pronoun clitic within the Verb Complex, and is also incompatible with morphological subject marking on the focused noun phrase. No such restrictions are observed in the main clauses discussed in this chapter.

This chapter is divided into sections based on the presence (or absence) of what have often been referred to as "classifiers" in the Somali literature. These morphemes are in complementary distribution with the focus markers discussed in Chapter 11 and are associated with clausal modality. In the broader linguistics literature, the term classifier is used to refer to a type of word or affix found in a language's nominal system that contributes information of various types about a noun's referent. This use is not applicable to the function of so-called "classifiers" in Somali, and as such, these are referred to here instead as *clause type particles*.

The chapter begins in §12.1 by discussing main clauses containing the declarative particle *waa*. In §12.2, main clauses containing the negative particle *má* are discussed, and, in §12.3, attention turns to those with the interrogative particle *ma*. Section 12.4 covers main clauses containing optative mood verbs. These have no clause type particle in the affirmative but require the negative clause type marker *yaan* in the negative. Section 12.5 discusses clauses containing potential mood verbs. Though these are seldom used in speech, they occur in written Somali and are optionally accompanied by the particle *show* or its dialect variant *sow*. Lastly, in §12.6, the properties of clauses containing imperative mood verbs are discussed. There is, once again, no particular clause type particle associated with these clauses in the affirmative, but they require the negative marker *ha* in the negative.[1]

---

[1] Some works (e.g., Andrzejewski 1975; Frascarelli and Puglielli 2003; Gebert 1986; Saeed 2004) describe declarative *waa* as a verb or predicate focus marker (or indicator particle). This viewpoint has been called into question given that *waa* is commonly found in verbless sentences. Likewise, Andrzejewski (1975) describes other clause type markers like interrogative *ma*, potential *show* (*sow*), and negative optative *yaan* as focus markers, but this is not widely accepted.

12.1 Declarative *waa*

The declarative clause type particle is *waa*. It occurs in affirmative declarative clauses containing an indicative mood verb, as well as in verbless equative sentences. Importantly, it does not occur in a clause alongside another constituent that is morphologically marked as in focus. Descriptions of declarative *waa* differ concerning whether or not it plays a role in predicate and/or verbal focus. Those works contesting that it is a focus marker include Andrzejewski (1975), Frascarelli (2010b), Gebert (1986), Puglielli (1981), and Svolacchia et al. (1995), while those arguing against this viewpoint include Frascarelli and Puglielli (2007, 2009), Lecarme (1991), Saeed (1984), and Tosco (2002). In this grammar, I adopt the latter point of view as *waa* differs from Somali's other focus markers in at least three substantive ways. First, the presence of *waa* does not require reduced agreement on the clausal verb in any instance. Second, the presence of *waa* does not prohibit the use of resumptive subject pronoun clitics (SPC). Rather, SPCs are typically found in clauses with *waa*, while their absence is a marked choice employed for the purpose of emphasis (Gebert 1986). Lastly, the subject of a clause containing *waa* is not prohibited from being morphologically subject-marked. Another strong argument against the status of *waa* as a verbal focus marker in particular is that it can occur in verbless clauses. For example, it joins two elements in equative sentences like (1) and (2).

(1) *Tani   waa xáaskáygií.*
    tan=i   waa xaas-kay-gii
    T.this=SUBJ DEC wife-K.my-K.RDEF
    'This is my wife.'

(2) *Waa aníga.*
    waa ani=ga
    DEC I-K.DEF
    'It is I.'

Another common use of *waa* is in declarative sentences with an unexpressed subject as in (3).

(3) *Waa sháqo dhíb   léh.*
    waa shaqo dhib   leh
    DEC work trouble have-PRES.RED
    'It is difficult work.'

The use of *waa* on its own is largely limited to simple constructions such as these, but it is more often the case that *waa* hosts a subject pronoun enclitic, yielding the forms shown in (4). These forms reveal expected variation. For example, the number distinction between 1PL and 2PL collapses in favor of their singular counterparts for some speakers. There is also variation between forms with *a* and *e* before the glide [j] in the 3SG.F, 3PL, 2PL, and 1PL.inc.

(4) *Declarative + subject pronoun clitic*

waa=aan	waan	1SG
waa=aad	waad	2SG
waa=uu	wuu	3SG.M/K
waa=ay	way ~ wey	3SG.F/T
waa=annu *or*	waannu	1PL.exc
waa=aan	waan	
waa=aynu	waynu ~ weynu	1PL.inc
waa=aydin *or*	waydin ~ weydin	2PL
waa=aad	waad	
waa=ay	way ~ wey	3PL

Clusters of the declarative + SPC are found in a wide variety of instances, such as when there is a pronominal subject solely expressed by the SPC, as in (5), but also when the SPC is co-referential with a NP, as in (6). These and other examples illustrate that *waa* typically appears immediately preceding a Verb Complex.

(5) Waan   filayaa   ínaad   jeclatéen.
    w=aan   fil-ay-∅-aa   in=aad   jecl-a-t-ee-n
    DEC=1SG hope-PROG-1SG-PRES COMP=2SG like-MID-2-PST-PL
    'I am hoping that you liked it.'

(6) Af-Faransíisku   wuu   adágyahay.
    af-Faransiis=k=u   w=uu   adag-y-ah-ay
    language-French=K.DEF=SUBJ DEC=3SG.K difficult-3SG.K-be-PRES
    'French is difficult.'

The combination of *waa* + SPC is the arguable default choice in pragmatically neutral contexts. That said, the absence of an SPC is not ungrammatical, though this choice is more appropriate for emphasis or confirmation. Compare, for example, (7) and (8).

(7) Nimánku   wáy   yimaaddeen.
    nim-an=k=u   w=ay   y-imaad-d-ee-n
    man-PL=K.DEF=SUBJ DEC=3PL 3-come-3-PST-PL
    'The men came.'

(8) *Nimánku   wáa yimaaddeen.*
    nim-an=k=u   waa y-imaad-d-ee-n
    man-PL=K.DEF=SUBJ DEC 3-come-3-PST-PL
    'The men did come.'

These examples show that declarative *waa* occurs in clauses with verbs of different types, including hybrid verbs, and that these verbs are fully inflected for person, number, and grammatical gender. Examples like (1), and (6) through (8), show that the subject noun phrase in clauses with *waa* is morphologically subject-marked.

Also shown in the examples thus far is that declarative *waa* does not consistently manifest a H tone. For example, it has no H tone in (6) but has a H tone in (8). This stems from *waa* being underlyingly toneless. It receives its tonal specification based on the tone of the word that follows it. If the word following it has a H tone, as in (6), *waa* surfaces toneless. However, if the word following *waa* is toneless, as in (8), *waa* surfaces with a H tone on its first mora. Because SPCs are also toneless, their presence has no influence on tone assignment. Whether or not the cluster of *waa* + SPC has a H tone still depends on the tone of the following word.

12.1.1 wáaye ~ wéeye

Closely related to *waa* is another declarative marker, *wáaye*, which may alternatively be pronounced *wéeye*. According to Tosco (2002), while *waa* and *wáaye/wéeye* tend to be acceptable to all speakers, *wáaye/wéeye* is more prevalent in Central and Benaadir Somali. Both declaratives accomplish a similar function, but the distribution of *wáaye/wéeye* is notable in that it occurs clause-finally in most instances, as in (9), which is a verbless equative sentence. This declarative is also used informally as a greeting or to voice one's agreement with some proposition.

(9) *Beeréle wéeye.*
    beerale weeye
    farmer   DEC
    'He is a farmer.'

Beyond its use in such simple declaratives, *wáaye/wéeye* is often found in conjunction with *wáxa* 'the thing.' The two function together to construct declarative statements involving a full "heavy" clause, as in (10) and (11). Recall that elsewhere, closely related *wáxa(a)* functions as a focus marker for "heavy" constituents (see §11.2).

(10) Cabashádayádu   waxa wéeye ínaanu   bulsháda   réer
     cabasha-daya=d=u   waxa weeye in=aanu   bulsha=da   reer
     complaint-T.our=T.DEF=SUBJ it is COMP=1PL society=T.DEF people
     Puntlánd ... sheegnó   ín   ...
     Puntland ... sheeg-n-o   in
     Puntland ... inform-1PL-IRR COMP

     'Our complaint, it is that we inform the people of Puntland that ... '
     (dhaymoolenews: 176)

(11) Háddaba su'aáshu   waxa wéeye fálkaá   yáa
     haddaba su'aa=sh=u   waxa weeye falkaa   yaa
     therefore question=T.DEF=SUBJ it is   deed-K.that who
     gaystay?
     gay-s-t-∅-ay
     bring.about-W.CAUS-MID-3SG.M-PST

     'Therefore, the question, it is who did the deed?' (qaawane.net: 1934)

In a related way, the combination *waxa wéeye* acts as a conjunction joining two clauses, often being translated as 'therefore' or 'because,' as in (12).

(12) Wár   cusúb kumá   siin   karó
     war   cusub ku-ma   sii-n   kar-o
     information new   2SG.SUBJ-NEG give-NEG be.able-1SG.IRR
     sabábtuna   waxa wéeye weli má maqlín   wáx   cusub.
     sabab=t=u=na   waxa weeye weli ma maql-in   wax   cusub
     reason=T.DEF=SUBJ=and it   is   yet NEG hear-PST.NEG thing new

     'And the reason I cannot give you new information is because I have not heard anything new yet.' (Z & O: 669)

12.2 Negative *má*

The negative counterpart to the indicative declarative clause type particle *waa* is *má*. This clause type particle appears in clauses without morphological focus marking which, of course, must also contain a verb that is inflected for negative. Negative *má* is associated with a H tone, a characteristic that differentiates it from the segmentally identical interrogative particle *ma* discussed below in §12.3.

Negative *má* was first introduced in §10.8, where its location in the Verb Complex was discussed, as was its behavior relative to other clitics and particles with which it can cluster. These include subject pronoun clitics, object pronoun clitics, and adpositional particles. There are indeed many instances like that seen in (13) where negative *má* is located within its usual slot in the Verb Complex. In this example, *má* clusters with an adpositional particle and precedes an auxiliary construction. These clusters come in many combinations and are discussed throughout Chapter 10.

(13) *Sídaas umá xirxíri kartíd.*
sidaas u-ma xirxir-i kar-tid
like.that to-NEG tie.up-INF be.able-2SG.PRES.NEG
'You cannot tie it up like that.' (Z & O: 646)

Elsewhere, *má* can occur on its own, rather than clustering with another clitic or particle. This is seen in (14).

(14) *Gúriga míis má yaalló.*
guri=ga miis ma y-aal-lo
house=K.DEF table NEG 3SG.K-be-PRES.NEG
'There is no table in the house.' (Z & O: 706)

Among the more notable characteristics of negative *má* that set it apart from other elements of the VC is its ability to move leftward from its typical location, whereafter it serves as a host for a subject pronoun enclitic. This typically occurs in instances where a SPC has no other functional morpheme on which to cliticize. For example, in (15), one might otherwise expect *má* to form a cluster with the object pronoun clitic as it did above in (12). However, it instead moves leftward, serving as a host for the 3SG.M SPC.

(15) *Múu kú aqoónéyn.*
m=uu ku aqoon-eyn
NEG=3SG.M 2SG.OBJ know-PST.NEG
'He didn't recognize you.'

Negative *má* is also found in subordinate clauses, but only when it forms a periphrastic construction with negative *-aán*. This occurs when the subject of a negative subordinate clause verb is pronominal, as in (16). For further details and the forms of other *má* + SPC + *aán* clusters, see §14.1.3.

(16) *Wáxaan ogaaday macállin muusán ká aha\u0301yn*
wax=aan ogaa-d-∅-ay macallin m=uu=aan ka ah-ayn
FOC=1SG know-MID-1SG-PST teacher NEG=3SG.M=NEG in be-PST.NEG
dúgsigaas.
dugsi-gaas
school-K.that
'I knew (that) he was not a teacher in that school.'

It is important to keep in mind, as introduced in Chapter 11, that *má* does not occur in a main clause with focus marking. Rather, negative *aán* is found in such instances. It will cliticize onto a focus marker, often in combination with an SPC.

12.3 Interrogative *ma*

The toneless interrogative particle *ma* is used in the formation of yes/no, or polar questions. It is found in clauses without a focus marker in those instances where information is being sought about something or someone that is topical. For example, in (17), *ma* occurs at the beginning of a sentence that seeks confirmation about the entirety of the proposition.

(17)   *Ma ií   doóri   kartaa   qáar?*
       ma i=i   door-i   kar-t-aa   qaar
       QM me=for choose-INF be.able-2SG-PRES some
       'Can you choose some for me?' (Z & O: 157)

The situation is only slightly different in (18) where the information to be confirmed pertains to one particular expressed topical item, in this case, 'the house.'

(18)   *Gúriga   ma la   iibiyey?*
       guri=ga   ma la   iib-i-y-ey
       house=K.DEF QM ISP sell-W.CAUS-3SG.M-PST
       'Has the house been sold? (Z & I: 171)

In both instances, interrogative *ma* can appear on its own without a pronominal subject. This is possible provided that the subject is recoverable elsewhere or otherwise understood. In the first example, the 2SG subject is clear from verb inflection while, in the second, the subject is the ISP found within the Verb Complex.

     Interrogative *ma* may also occur in a cluster with a subject pronoun enclitic in the combinations seen in (19). Expected variation in the number distinction between 1PL and 2PL forms and their singular counterparts, as well as dialectal differences in vowel pronunciation are observed here, as they have been elsewhere. The resulting clusters are toneless.

(19) *Interrogative ma + subject pronoun clitic*

ma=aan	maan	1SG
ma=aad	maad	2SG
ma=uu	muu	3SG.M/K
ma=ay	may ~ mey	3SG.F/T
ma=annu *or*	maannu	1PL.exc
ma=aan	maan	
ma=aynu	maynu ~ meynu	1PL.inc
ma=aydin *or*	maydin ~ meydin	2PL
ma=aad	maad	
ma=ay	may ~ mey	3PL

The presence vs. absence of a SPC appears not to introduce any significant difference in meaning, though speakers with whom I have worked have suggested to me that the presence of an SPC serves to emphasize the subject or to make the question more pointed. Examples with interrogative + SPC clusters are as follows.

(20) Lacág maad   amaahánaysaa?
     lacag m=aad   amaah-an-ay-s-aa
     money QM=2SG   borrow-STV-PROG-2SG-PRES

     'Are you borrowing money?' (Z & I: 194)

(21) Maan kuulá   hadlaa   iyáda?
     m=aan ku=u-la   hadl-Ø-aa   iyada
     QM=1SG 2SG.OBJ=for-with   speak-1SG-PRES her

     'Shall I speak with her for you?' (Z & I: 350)

Interrogative *ma* can also occur in a clause with a focus marker. In these instances, the focus marker indicates that new information is being sought about a non-topical constituent. See examples pertaining to the presence of *ma* in clauses with each of Somali's three focus markers in Chapter 11.

Note that speakers appear generally unwilling to simply negate yes/no interrogative clauses formed with *ma*. Rather, to do so, it is preferred to use a focus construction. This is perhaps done to preclude a potentially ambiguous response. Consider, for example, that the question 'Are you a student?' can be answered affirmatively or negatively without ambiguity. However, a yes/no answer to a question like 'Are you not a student?' is potentially ambiguous. Answers of 'yes (I'm not a student)' vs. 'no (I'm not a student)' could both be interpreted as meaning that the respondent is not a student.

For more on the use of interrogative *ma* in the formation of polar questions, including the special case of *miyáa* as a general question marker, see §16.2.

12.4 Optative

A main clause containing an affirmative optative mood verb does not have a particular clause type marker. It is instead characterized by the irrealis verb inflection paradigm (see §7.5.2.3) and H tone on the verb stem. These optative clauses also contain a subject pronoun clitic. In some instances, the 1SG and 2SG SPCs may be shortened, and there is a unique third person SPC *ha*. SPCs found in clauses with affirmative optative verbs are shown in (22).

(22) *Subject pronoun clitics - optative affirmative*

an ~ aan	1SG, 1PL
ad ~ aad	2SG, 2PL
ha	3SG.M/K, 3SG.F/T, 3PL
annu	1PL.exc
aynu	1PL.inc

Optative clauses require no special syntax. The SPC is found at the left edge of the Verb Complex, as otherwise expected, and it may be separated from the verb by other elements such as an adpositional, deictic, or adverbial particle. These clauses may also have one or more overt noun phrases and/or adverbials that appear on either side of the Verb Complex. Examples are as follows in (23) through (25).

(23) *Dayuurádda ha ráaceen.*
dayuurad=da ha raac-∅-ee-n
plane=T.DEF 3PL go.along-3-IRR-PL
'May they go by plane!'

(24) *Bál an iskaá báro.*
bal an is-ka=a bar-∅-o
just 1SG RRP-2SG.OBJ=to introduce-1SG-IRR
'Just let me introduce myself to you.' (Z & O: 335)

(25) *An kala beddelánno meeláha.*
an kala beddel-an-n-o meel-a=ha
1PL ADV change-NEU-1PL-IRR place-PL=K.DEF
'Let's change places.' (Z & O: 58)

The structure of negative optative clauses is somewhat different. They require a shortened SPC, as shown in (26), but third person forms do not converge onto a single exponent. The verb must also be inflected for negation.

(26) *Subject pronoun clitics - optative negative*

an	1SG, 1PL
ad	2SG, 2PL
u	3SG.M/K
ay	3SG.F/T, 3PL

The shortened SPCs above are enclitic to a clause type marker *yáan* in negative optative clauses, yielding the combinations in (27). This clause type marker has a H tone on its penultimate mora which remains in place following cliticization by an SPC.

(27) *Optative negative + subject pronoun clitic*

yáan=an	yáanan	1SG, 1PL
yáan=ad	yáanad	2SG, 2PL
yáan=u	yáanu	3SG.M/K
yáan=ay	yáanay	3SG.F/T, 3PL

The clusters in (27) appear before the Verb Complex but may be separated from it by a noun phrase or adverbial. This is not surprising given that SPCs are elsewhere attracted out of their usual position at the left edge of the VC and thereafter cliticize onto a host functional morpheme. Example (28) shows a negative optative clause whose subject is pronominal. Example (29) instead shows a cluster in which the SPC is co-referential with a subject noun phrase.

(28) *Yáanad aqoón beéntiisa!*
yaan=ad aqoon been-tiisa
OPT.NEG=2SG know-OPT.NEG lie-T.his
'May you not know his lies!' (Z & I: 322)

(29) *Afádu yáanay nínkéeda ká tégin.*
afa=d=u yaan=ay nin-keeda ka teg-in
wife=T.DEF=SUBJ OPT.NEG=3SG.T man-K.her from go-OPT.NEG
'May the woman not leave her husband!' (codkanoloshacusub.info: 731)

12.5 Potential

Main clauses containing a verb inflected for the potential mood are accompanied by the clause type marker *shów* in Northern Somali and *sów* in southern varieties. In both instances, there is a H tone on the penultimate mora of the clause type marker. In describing the characteristics of these clauses, I have relied primarily on written Somali gathered from corpora and other print sources, as my speakers from both major dialect regions find potential verb forms to be old fashioned and do not readily produce them. Some speakers suggested alternatives to the potential inflectional paradigm, instead using the adverbial *maláha* 'maybe, perhaps.'

What can be considered prototypical instances of potential clauses in (30) and (31) contain one of the potential clause type markers mentioned above and a verb inflected for the potential.

(30) *Shów baabúurkóoda amaahannee?*
 show baabuur-kooda amaah-an-n-ee
 POT car-K.their borrow-MID-1PL-POT
 'What if we borrow their car?' (Z & O: 22)

(31) *Sów cuntádu taallee?*
 sow cunta=d=u t-aall-ee
 POT food=T.DEF=SUBJ 3SG.T-be-POT
 'Perhaps there is food there?' (Z & O: 615)

Potential *shów/sów* always appears in its clause before the Verb Complex. It can be separated from the Verb Complex by another noun phrase or adverbial, as in the preceding examples, or it can immediately precede the Verb Complex, as in (32). This example shows that the potential clause type marker is also used in a clause with a negatively inflected verb.

(32) *Yuúsuf búugga sów múu akhrinéen?*
 Yuusuf buug=ga sow m=uu akhr-in-ee-n
 Yuusuf book=K.DEF POT NEG=3SG.M read-W.CAUS-POT-NEG
 'Didn't Yuusuf read the book?'

The potential clause type marker is also found in the formation of one particular type of tag question *sów má ahá?*, meaning 'isn't it?' or 'wasn't it?,' which is discussed in §16.4.

12.6 Imperative

Imperative clauses do not require a clause type marker, but are instead recognizable by verb inflection, including inflection for number. An example of an affirmative singular imperative is in (33), while an example of a plural imperative is in (34).

(33) *Makhaayádda   cúnto iigá   kéen!*
     makhaayad=da   cunto i=i-ga   keen
     restaurant=T.DEF food 1SG.OBJ=to-from bring.IMP
     'Bring food to me from the restaurant!'

(34) *Na   soó boóqda   márkaad   doontaan!*
     na   soo booq-d-a   mark=aad doon-t-aa-n
     1PL.OBJ VEN visit-MID-IMP.PL   time=2PL want-2-PRES-PL
     'Come visit us whenever you want!'

In a negative imperative clause, the negative particle *ha* is used, rather than *má*. Unlike *má*, *ha* never clusters with other elements within the Verb Complex, but rather is always located at its left edge. Singular and plural examples of the negative imperative are as follows:

(35) *Shírka   ha   ká   baaqán!*
     shir=ka   ha   ka   baaq-an
     meeting=K.DEF   IMP.NEG   from   miss-MID.IMP.NEG
     'Don't miss the meeting!'

(36) *Bérri   dúgsiga   ha   imanína!*
     berri   dugsi=ga   ha   iman-in-a
     tomorrow school=K.DEF   IMP.NEG   come-IMP.NEG-PL
     'Tomorrow, don't come to the school!'

13 Information structure

This chapter covers information structure and the organization of constituents within a Somali sentence. Somali has been described as a *discourse-configurational* language (see, e.g., Lecarme 1991; Svolacchia et al. 1995) in that it employs specific syntactic, morphological, and prosodic strategies for marking information as being in focus vs. topical. Focused or 'discourse new' information, be it a noun phrase, adverbial, a whole clause, or series of clauses, is primarily indicated by one of the language's three focus markers discussed in Chapter 11. Banti (2019) also illustrates that Somali employs a variety of strategies by which information can be brought into focus without one of these focus markers. Topical (i.e., given or known) information, on the other hand, is not focus marked. Rather, in clauses that contain a focus-marked element, topicality can be introduced or reinforced syntactically via constituent shifting or may be re-established via right dislocation.

13.1 Broad Focus

Broad focus is associated with a discourse context in which all information is known, or believed to be new. Its use is appropriate, for example, in response to a general or thetic question like 'What happened?' where no element can be taken as explicitly topical. Such a response is associated with an SF(O)V word order, where F indicates the position of the focus marker, and the object is indicated in parentheses, given that an object may not always be present. In response to such a question, a sentence like (1) would be appropriate. The subject, object, and the action entailed by the verb are all assumed to be new information.

(1) *[Wíilka] báa shimbírta dilaý.*
    wiil=ka   baa shimbir=ta dil-∅-ay
    boy=K.DEF FOC bird=T.DEF kill-3SG.M-PST.RED
    '[The boy] killed the bird.'

This particular configuration is appropriate in clauses containing one of the two preverbal focus markers, *báa* and *ayáa*. A comparable clause that instead uses the postverbal focus marker *wáxa(a)* involves cataphoric focus and is appropriate in somewhat different discourse contexts discussed separately below in §13.5.2.

That the focus marker in the broad focus configuration follows the subject indicates that this is formally a type of subject focus. As such, the requirements of the Subject Focus Condition (SFC) discussed in §11.3 are observed. This includes reduced agreement in verb inflection, use of a toned verb paradigm, as well as a prohibition on the presence of a resumptive subject pronoun clitic and on morphological subject marking.

That SFOV order is most appropriate in broad focus contexts is one argument in favor of SOV being the language's default word order (see Gebert 1986; Svolacchia et al. 1995). It is also the word order that has been reconstructed for Proto-Cushitic (Saeed 2004). As typologically expected of SOV languages, when a broad focus context involves an indirect or oblique object, this additional constituent tends to precede the direct object (DO), as in (2). Even when there is no DO, as in (3), the indirect/oblique object still tends to precede the VC.

(2) *[Cáli] báa Máryam warqád ú keenaý.*
Cali baa Maryam warqad u keen-Ø-ay
Cali FOC Maryam letter to bring-3SG.M-PST.RED
'[Cali] brought the letter to Maryam.'

(3) *[Aníga iyo saaxíibkaý] báa isbitáalka tagnaý.*
ani=ga iyo saaxiib-kay baa isbitaal=ka tag-n-ay
1SG=K.DEF and friend-K.my FOC hospital=K.DEF go-1PL-PST.RED
'[My friend and I] went to the hospital.'

It is also worth noting for comparison, that SOV is the order in which elements appear within the Verb Complex (VC) itself. The verb occurs last within the VC and is preceded by other elements as appropriate, including subject pronoun and object pronoun clitics, the first of which I have suggested occurs at the VC's left edge. As mentioned in Chapter 10, scholars like Gebert (1988) and Puglielli (1981) have described the VC as a miniature version of the sentence.

13.2 Narrow focus

Another possible response to a thetic question like 'What happened?' – where any and all information to be provided is assumed to be new – involves narrow focus on either the subject or on an object. The effect is that one particular constituent is brought into focus relative to others. This narrow focus configuration is also used to focus a subject or object in instances where another constituent is topical and/or included in a content question. In both instances, whether the subject or an object is placed into narrow focus, the order of constituents remains SOV. The difference, however, is in the location of the focus marker, which will always be immediately following the focused constituent.

13.2.1 Narrow subject focus

In addition to its use in broad focus contexts discussed just above, a SFOV word order is used for narrow subject focus. Thus, while a sentence like (4), repeated from (1), is an appropriate response to a thetic question like 'what happened?', it is also appropriate in response to a question like 'Who killed the bird?' Here, the object included in the content question is topical, and the identity of the subject is new to the discourse.

(4) [Wíilka]   báa shimbírta   diláy.
    wiil=ka   baa shimbir=ta dil-∅-ay
    boy=K.DEF FOC bird=T.DEF kill-3SG.M-PST.RED
    '[The boy] killed the bird.'

As stated above, such a configuration follows the Subject Focus Condition (§11.3). It requires i) reduced agreement verb inflection, ii) a toned inflectional paradigm, iii) no resumptive subject pronoun clitic, and iv) no morphological subject marking.

13.2.2 Narrow object focus

Narrow object focus is also associated with the language's canonical word order configuration SOFV. This order is the same as with broad focus and narrow subject focus, with the only difference being the place of the focus marker, which is now immediately after the object. This configuration, seen in (5), is possible in response to a thetic question, but also to one like 'What did the boy kill?' where the subject is included in the content question and is therefore topical or given information. New information about the object is being sought.

(5) Wíilku   [shimbírta] búu   dilay.
    wiil=k=u   shimbir=ta b=uu   dil-∅-ay
    boy=K.DEF=SUBJ bird=T.DEF FOC=3SG.M kill-3SG.M-PST
    'The boy killed [the bird].'

The narrow object focus configuration exhibits all expected characteristics of the Object Focus Condition (§11.4). These include: i) the verb takes full paradigm inflection, ii) the subject bears morphological subject marking, and iii) there is a 3SG subject pronoun clitic cliticized onto the focus marker that is co-referential with the subject noun phrase.

13.3 Topicalization

There are other word order configurations that depart slightly from the language's canonical SOV word order via a shift in constituents to OSV. A constituent, whether a subject or object, can still be marked as in focus under this configuration, but the non-focus marked constituent is highlighted as being topical. As such, sentences of this type are not an appropriate response to thetic questions like 'What happened?' where no particular constituent is explicitly mentioned and is therefore presumed to be topical. Rather, these responses make explicit the topical nature of one constituent while simultaneously marking the other as new to the discourse.

13.3.1 Object topicalization / Subject focus

An object can be made topical relative to a focused subject by way of the word order configuration OSFV. This configuration is appropriate in response to a pointed question like 'Who killed the bird?' where the object is explicitly topical and where the subject is expected to be new information. This is a departure from Somali's basic SOV word order in that the topical object is fronted. The focus-marked subject still precedes the Verb Complex. This configuration is seen in (6).

(6) *Shimbírta [wíilka]   báa dilaý.*
     shimbir=ta wiil=ka   baa dil-∅-ay
     bird=T.DEF boy=K.DEF FOC kill-3SG.M-PST.RED
     'The bird, [the boy] killed it.'

Though the topical nature of the object is made explicit, sentences like these still involve a focused subject and accordingly exhibit characteristics of the Subject Focus Condition. As seen in (6), the focused subject is not morphologically subject-marked (*wiilku* 'the boy.SUBJ'), and no subject pronoun clitic joins the focus marker (*buu*). Lastly, the verb requires reduced agreement and is tonal.

13.3.2 Subject topicalization / Object focus

Just as an object could be made explicitly topical under subject focus, it is illustrated below that a subject can just as easily be made explicitly topical under object focus. The word order associated with this configuration is OFSV, where the focus marker immediately follows the clause-initial object, and the topical subject remains before the Verb Complex. This is in some ways not a prototypical instance of topicalization in that the topicalized constituent is not clause-initial. However, given that a clause-initial subject without focus marking is already associated with narrow object focus, it is perhaps not unexpected that the language adopts another strategy to encode topicality. This is accomplished by simply shifting the order of the two constituents; such a configuration is seen in (7). This is appropriate in response to a question like 'What did the boy kill?' where the subject is known and therefore topical and where the object is new information. Such a response would be inappropriate in response to a thetic question where the verb's subject is not known.

(7) [Shimbírta] búu/báa wíilku dilay.
    shimbir=ta b=uu wiil=k=u dil-∅-ay
    bird=T.DEF FOC=3SG.M boy=K.DEF=SUBJ kill-3SG.M-PST
    'The boy, he killed [the bird].'

As in other instances of object focus, the subject is morphologically subject-marked, and the verb takes full paradigm inflection. What is somewhat unusual about this particular configuration is that the presence of a subject pronoun clitic is possible but not necessarily required. One possible reason for this optionality may stem from the fact that the subject is topical and expressed by a noun phrase that is already morphologically marked by the subject marker. In this way, the presence of a subject pronoun clitic would be redundant. Thus, given that the argument status of the two noun phrases is unambiguous, this may obviate or at least render optional the use of an SPC.

13.4 Retopicalization via right dislocation

Another departure from Somali's canonical SOV word order is witnessed in instances of right dislocation, where either a subject or object noun phrase moves rightward beyond the Verb Complex. The resulting word orders are OVS and SVO, respectively. A constituent can be right dislocated if it is topical. An opposing focus-marked constituent remains in place, preceding the Verb Complex. Such a strategy can perhaps be thought of as re-introducing or re-establishing the topicality of the moved constituent. It is important to keep in mind that it is also possible for a focus-marked constituent to occur to the right of the Verb Complex, but this occurs only with the post-verbal focus marker *wáxa(a)* in instances of cataphoric, or presentational focus. This focus condition is discussed in §13.5.2.

13.4.1 Subject dislocation

Dislocation of a topical subject to the right of the Verb Complex results in an OVS word order and is possible under object focus. The focused object noun phrase remains in place, preceding the VC. An example of this situation is seen in (8).

(8) [Shimbírta] búu   dilay   wíilku.
    shimbir=ta b=uu   dil-∅-ay   wiil=k=u
    bird=T.DEF FOC=3SG.M   kill-3SG.M-PST   boy=K.DEF=SUBJ
    'He killed [the bird], the boy did.'

Despite the marked word order seen here, the usual characteristics of the Object Focus Condition are observed. The object is focused by a pre-verbal focus marker to which a subject pronoun is cliticized. The subject pronoun is co-referential with the dislocated subject noun phrase. The post-verbal subject noun phrase is morphologically subject-marked, and the verb itself takes full paradigm inflection.

13.4.2 Object dislocation

It is also possible to right dislocate a topical object, resulting in a SVO word order. This is possible under subject focus, with the focused subject remaining before the Verb Complex. An example of this is in (9).

(9) [Wíilka]   báa dilaý   shimbírta.
    wiil=ka   baa dil-∅-ay   shimbir=ta
    boy=K.DEF   FOC kill-3SG.M-PST.RED   bird=T.DEF
    '[The boy] killed it, the bird.'

As expected in instances of subject focus, the Subject Focus Condition is required here as well. This subject noun phrase is not morphologically subject-marked, and there is no co-referential subject pronoun clitic associated with the pre-verbal focus marker. The verb, as elsewhere, requires reduced agreement and is toned.

13.4.3 Word order summary

Table 13.1 provides a summary of word orders associated with the basic focus and topicalization strategies discussed in the sections above, all of which involve a pre-verbal focus marker. These cover instances where two overt noun phrases – one subject, one direct object – are present. Given the number of word order combinations possible upon introducing one or more additional objects (i.e., indirect or oblique), I have not gone into further detail on this matter. Other discourse functions of focus, as well as the use of the cataphoric focus marker *wáxa(a)*, are discussed in §13.5.

Tab. 13.1: Basic focus/topicalization word word summary

Focus condition	Word order	
Broad Focus	S F O V	Section 13.1
Narrow Subject Focus	S F O V	Section 13.2.1
Narrow Object Focus	S O F V	Section 13.2.2
Object Topicalization	O S F V	Section 13.3.1
Subject Topicalization	O F S V	Section 13.3.2
Subject Retopicalization	O F V S	Section 13.4.1
Object Retopicalization	S F V O	Section 13.4.2

13.5 Other discourse functions of focus

Thus far, this chapter has been concerned primarily with canonical uses of Somali focus marking and its role in organizing 'new' vs. 'topical' information within fairly simple sentences and in reference to constituent arrangement relative to the Verb Complex. In particular, the connection between *broad* focus relative to other focus configurations was discussed. Scholars like Tosco (2002) and Saeed (1999) have attributed the broad focus configuration to "event reporting" given that it can be used to introduce information that is presumed to be new to the listener/reader in its entirety. Also discussed was *narrow* focus and some pragmatic implications involved in moving subject or object noun phrases relative to one another while remaining before the Verb Complex, as well as right dislocation of a phrase beyond the Verb Complex. The principles discussed using these exemplars extend to many other more complex clause and sentence types. In addition, however, there are certain other discourse-related functions of focus marking that extend beyond those covered above. Five such uses are discussed in the remainder in this section.

13.5.1 Contrastive focus

Contrastive focus is a mechanism by which information that is already activated or topical in the discourse can be highlighted, reintroduced, or otherwise disambiguated. This differs somewhat from narrow focus in that the information being contributed is not entirely new but rather offered in contrast to something else. Consider the question and response in (10) and (11), respectively.

(10) *Fúre ma haysaa?*
 fure ma hay-s-aa
 key QM have-2SG-PRES
 'Do you have a key?'

(11) [Furáha   gurigá]   báan   hayaa.
      fura=ha   guri=ga   b=aan   hay-∅-aa
      key=K.DEF house=K.DEF FOC=1SG have-1SG-PRES
      'I have the house key.'

In (11), contrastive focus is placed on the object, presumably to disambiguate it from other possible keys that the speaker might have. This is done despite the fact that 'the key' is topical information.

Another related instance of contrastive focus can be seen in the response to question (12). In (13), the response confirms but further clarifies the content of the question.

(12) Guryáha   ma dhágax báa lagá   dhisaa?
      gury-a=ha   ma dhagax baa la=ga dhis-∅-aa
      house-PL=K.DEF QM stone   FOC ISP=of build-3SG.M-PRES
      'Are the houses built of stone?'

(13) Dhágax iyo qóryo báa lagá   dhisaa.
      dhagax iyo qoryo baa la=ga dhis-∅-aa
      stone and wood FOC ISP=of build-3SG.M-PRES
      'They are built of stone and wood.'

13.5.2 Cataphoric focus

The vast majority of the examples provided in this chapter have illustrated focus using one of Somali's two pre-verbal focus markers, *báa* or *ayáa*. Somali's third focus marker *wáxa(a)* is widely used but is unusual in that the constituent that it places into focus is obligatorily located post-verbally and therefore at a distance from the focus marker itself. I follow Svolacchia et al. (1995) in calling this *cataphoric* focus in that *wáxa(a)* signals that focus is on forthcoming (specifically, post-verbal) information. The focus marker acts as a cataphor that is co-referential with the downstream constituent. Others have instead referred to such constructions as "heralding sentences" (Andrzejewski 1975) in that they signal to the listener/reader that important information is yet to be spoken. Another term for the construction that appears in the literature is "presentational focus" (Hetzron 1965).

As shown in §11.2, cataphoric focus with *wáxa(a)* exhibits the same behavior as pre-verbal focus with *báa* and *ayáa* regarding requirements for subject focus vs. object focus. The difference, however, is that the constituent in focus remains post-verbal, though other pre-verbal constituents may be organized relative to one another in different ways for the purposes of topicalization.

The cataphoric focus configuration is often used to place focus on a "heavy" constituent like an entire clause, quotation, or even a string of coordinated phrases or clauses, but this is not always the case. Example (14) shows cataphoric focus on a single noun. Notice here that it is a post-verbal subject that is in focus. There is no resumptive pronoun clitic on the focus marker, the verb exhibits reduced agreement, and there is no morphological subject marking.

(14) *Wáxa nalá   joogtá   [gabádh].*
     waxa na=la   joog-t-a   gabadh
     FOC 1PL.OBJ=with stay-3SG.F-PRES.RED girl
     'The girl is staying with us.'

In (15), the same strategy is adopted, but for a much larger clause. Here, focus is placed on an entire post-verbal complement clause. Because this is not a case of subject focus, we find a resumptive subject pronoun clitic on the focus marker and full paradigm inflection on the main clause verb.

(15) *Wáxaan rejéynayaa   [ínaad   nagá   raáli*
     wax=aan rej-eyn-ay-∅-aa   in=aad   na=ga   raali
     FOC=1SG hope-FACT-PROG-1SG-PRES COMP=2PL 1PL.OBJ=with satisfaction
     ahaatáan].
     ahaa-t-aa-n
     be-2-IRR-PL
     'I hope that you will be satisfied with us.'

Sentences like these are often described and translated as wh- or pseudo-clefts where the syntactically postposed information is fronted in translation to capture the fact that it is in focus or otherwise emphasized. I have found over the years that this practice is problematic in the opinion of Somali speakers. That is, consultants from various areas of Somalia with whom I have worked often reject such cleft translations, or at least find such translations awkward or only marginally acceptable. As such, I do not suggest cleft translations for sentences involving cataphoric focus.

13.5.3 Narrative focus

In longer stretches of discourse, including in storyline narration, news broadcasts, and the like, strategies adopted for manipulating focus on and topicalization of particular constituents are more diverse. While it is generally the case that there is only a single focus-marked constituent within a main clause, this constraint does not always hold in more complex discourse contexts. Focus can indeed be placed on a single constituent in order to introduce or re-introduce individuals or participants in the story or to highlight a time or location.

For example, the text in (16) is extracted from an article on BBC News Somali during the COVID-19 crisis. It reports on some of the first scientific findings concerning the virus as published in a journal article by Professor KK. A quotation from the article is provided, with the professor's name first introduced in post-verbal focus. After discussion centering around other individuals, KK is reintroduced to the story in (17) with pre-verbal focus.

(16) *"Xógtan shaacá lagá qaaday waa muhíim..."*
xog-tan shaac-a la=ga qaad-∅-ay waa muhiim...
issue-T.this revelation-K.DEF ISP=about find-3SG.M-PST DEC important...
sidáas wáxaa tirí   Prof KK
sidaas waxaa t-iri   Prof KK.
thus   FOC 3SG.F-say.PST.RED Prof KK

'To have found out about this is important ... said Professor KK.'

(17) *Prof K ayáa BBC-da ú sheegtaý ...*
Pro K ayaa BBC=da u sheeg-t-ay
Prof K FOC BBC=T.DEF to say-3SG.F-PST.RED

'Professor K said to BBC that ...' (bbc somali/52535102)

Such examples involving a single focus marker parallel those already discussed. The remainder of this section highlights a few instances in which the structuring of information is more complex in that it involves two focus markers. For additional examples and other analyses of narrative focus, see Ajello (1995), Hetzron (1965), Lecarme (1999a), Saeed (1999), and Tosco (2002), among others.

It is often the case that focus can be placed on a sentence-initial adverb or adverbial clause with a pre-verbal focus marker which is then followed by post-verbal focus on some other constituent. In a similar way, pre-verbal focus may instead be placed on a noun phrase that refers to a time or location. Such double focus marking is not found with two pre-verbal focus markers. One such example is seen in (18). Preceding this sentence is discussion of whether soybean oil is safe for cooking. The locative adverbial clause 'in other countries' is placed into contrastive focus by the pre-verbal focus marker *ayáa*. It is followed thereafter by the post-verbal focus marker which highlights discourse new information about food safety testing.

(18) *[Waddamó kalé] ayáa wáxaa lagú sameeyeý   [baadhitaanó*
waddam-o kale ayaa waxaa la=gu sam-ee-y-ey   baadhitaan-o
country-PL other FOC FOC ISP=in do-FACT-3SG-PST.RED research-PL
saliidó kalá duwán].
saliido ka-la duwan
oil   in-with various

'In other countries, various oil tests have been conducted.' (naaf.no: 25)

In (19), pre-verbal focus is instead on an adverbial noun phrase 'the event.' Post-verbal focus is simultaneously on a specific individual who was in attendance at the event. In such instances, the constituent that is in post-verbal focus is the "new" information. The event being focused is already topical, having been mentioned a few sentences earlier. It is reintroduced as under focus to add continuity or "coherence" (to use a term suggested by Tosco 2002) to the storyline.

(19) *[Munaasabádda] ayáa wáxaa ká qeyb   galaý   [Wasíir*
     munaasabad=da ayaa waxaa ka qeyb   gal-ay   wasiir
     event=T.DEF   FOC FOC by portion enter-PST.RED minister
     ku-xigéenka   Wasaarádda   Warfaafínta].
     ku-xigeen=ka   wasaarad=da   warfaafin=ta
     deputy=K.DEF   ministry=T.DEF information=T.DEF
     'The event was attended by the Deputy Minister of Information.'
     (xamarcadde.com: 10)

13.6 Focusing other constituents

The discussion of focus marking thus far has centered upon simple noun phrase exemplars. Many other constituents like location, time, and manner adverbials can be placed into focus by a focus marker. The same can be said for larger constituents like dependent clauses of various types, including relative clauses, complement clauses, a series of conjoined or coordinated clauses, and even entire utterances or quotations in instances of reported speech.

Important in each instance is how each of these constituents functions relative to others in a main clause. Though these constituents are longer and/or more complex than the noun phrases discussed thus far, the requirements of the subject focus condition and object focus condition still hold. Of course, the object focus condition can perhaps still be viewed here as the basic or default state of affairs. However, if one of these other constituents functions as the main clause verb's subject, deviations associated with the subject focus condition (§11.3) will apply. It is often but not always the case that these longer, "heavier" constituents are placed into focus by the post-verbal focus marker.

13.6.1 Adverbs and adverbial clauses

Adverbial information is often conveyed by phrase- or clause-sized constructions. There is additionally a fairly small class of lexical adverbs, as well as other smaller adverbials derived from other parts of speech. Adverbials of different types are discussed further in Sections 14.3, 15.5, and 15.6. The goal of this section is to provide some examples of various types of focused adverbials based on their co-occurrence with different focus markers, rather than based on their function. Thus, this is by no means an exhaustive representation of the many types of adverbials found in the language.

It is often the case that shorter adverbials are focused by a pre-verbal focus marker. This is seen in (20) for the time adverbial *márkaas* 'then' (> mar + kaas, 'that time') and in (21) for *berrí* 'tomorrow.'

(20) *[Márkaas] báannu cunnaa.*
markaas ba=aanu cun-n-aa
then FOC=1PL eat-1PL-PRES
'And then, we eat.'

(21) *[Berrí] báan idiín imánayaa.*
berri b=aan idiin iman-ay-∅-aa
tomorrow FOC=1SG 2PL.OBJ.to come-PROG-1SG-PRES
'Tomorrow, I am coming to you.'

Somewhat longer subordinate temporal clauses like that in (22) can also be placed into focus by a pre-verbal focus marker. Here, the temporal clause is introduced by *márka* 'when' (> mar + ka, 'the time'). Formally, such a clause is an object relative clause whose head is the adverbial ('he died *at the time*'). Because the main clause does not involve subject focus, a subject pronoun cliticizes onto the focus marker.

(22) *[Márkuu dhinteý], béy tageen.*
mark=uu dhin-t-ey b=ay tag-∅-ee-n
when=3SG.M die-MID-PST FOC=3PL go-3-PST-PL
'When he died, they left.' (Z & I: 163)

There are other adverbial clauses that are formally subject relative clauses. This is seen, for example, in (23), where the head noun *iyága* 'they' is joined by the relativizer *oo*: 'they who are teaching.' As a subject relative clause, the relative verb requires reduced agreement and is toned.

(23) *[Iyágoo baraya], béy ardéydu*
iyag=oo bar-ay-a b=ey ardey=d=u
they=REL teach-PROG-PRES.RED FOC=3PL student.PL=T.DEF=SUBJ
tagtey.
tag-t-ey
go-3PL-PST
'While they were teaching, the students left.' (Z & I: 184)

In other instances, an adverbial can be focused by the post-verbal focus marker. This is seen in (24), where a clausal manner adverbial is in focus.

(24) *Wúxuu   is   arkay   [iságoo xaaládiis   faráxa   ka*
       wux=uu is   ark-∅-ay   isag=oo xaalad-iis   faraxa   ka
       FOC=3SG RRP see-3SG-PST he=REL situation-T.his happiness out
       baxdaý].
       bax-d-∅-ay
       leave-MID-3SG.M-PST.RED
       'He found himself being a person in a happy situation.' (qaawane.net: 124812)

As one might expect, an adverbial does not function as the subject of a main clause verb. As such, in instances where an adverbial is in focus, the main clause verb takes full paradigm inflection. A subject pronoun clitic is also possible, as is morphological subject marking.

13.6.2 Relative clauses

A relative clause can modify a main clause subject noun phrase or an object noun phrase. Such a phrase behaves just like other simpler noun phrases and may be marked as in focus in its entirety. Recall from §7.10 that the inflectional patterns required on relative clause verbs often (but not always) differ from that required for main clause verbs.

When the head of a relative clause is also the subject of the main clause verb, the inflectional paradigm required on the relative clause verb depends on whether or not the subject is in focus. In instances of subject focus, the relative clause verb is toned, otherwise it is toneless. In addition, and in all instances, a subject relative clause verb takes reduced agreement, regardless of its tonal status. Consider the following examples.

In (25), a subject relative clause that is also the main clause subject is in focus. The verb *tagá* within this relative clause has a H tone and takes reduced agreement (cf. *tagaa*). As in other instances of subject focus, the main clause verb is also toned and requires reduced agreement.

(25) *[Xámsa [oo Rúush tagá]]   báa gabádh [Rúush   áh]*
       Xamsa   oo   Ruush tag-a   baa gabadh Ruush   ah
       Xamsa   REL Russia go-PRES.RED   FOC girl   Russian be.PRES.RED
       guursadaý.
       guur-s-a-d-ay
       marry-W.CAUS-MID-3SG.M-PST.RED
       'Xamsa, who goes to Russia, married a Russian girl.' (Z & I: 346)

This can be compared to the examples in (26) and (27). In (26), a subject relative clause is the subject of the main clause verb. As a subject relative clause verb, it takes reduced inflection, but here, it is toneless, owing to the fact that the larger subject noun phrase is not in focus. Recall from above that a subject relative clause verb would be toned (cf. *arkaý*) if its subject noun phrase were the main clause subject. The main clause verb also takes full inflection.

(26) *Nínkií*   [*náagta*   *arkay*]   *wúu*   *qoslay.*
     nin-kii   naag=ta   ark-∅-ay   w=uu   qosl-∅-ay
     man-K.RDEF woman=T.DEF see-3SG.M-PST.RED DEC=3SG.M laugh-3SG.M-ay
     'The man who saw the woman laughed.' (Livnat 1984: 55)

In (27), a subject relative clause is in focus, but it is not the main clause subject. Without main clause subjecthood preventing it from doing so, the relative clause verb will take reduced agreement and will be toned (cf. *hurdaa*). Because this is not an instance of main clause subject focus, the main clause verb is toneless (cf. *xadaý*, which would obtain under subject focus).

(27) *Aníg[oo hurdá]*   *ayáa la xaday*   *lacágtií.*
     anig=oo hurd-a   ayaa la xad-∅-ay   lacag-tii
     I=REL sleep-PRES.RED FOC ISP steal-3SG.M-PST money-T.RDEF
     'While I slept, someone stole the money.' (Saeed 1993b)

Of course, there are other possibilities when it comes to a relative clause being in focus (e.g., object relative clauses of different types). However, the examples above illustrate a key distinction in focused relative clauses, namely the requirements for full vs. reduced inflection and tone in subject relative clauses based on how the relative clause functions in the main clause itself.

13.6.3 Complement clauses

A complement clause functions as a single constituent and can be marked in its entirety as being in focus. These clauses are recognizable by the complementizer *in*, which is joined by a subject pronoun clitic. Such a construction cannot be rendered as a main clause subject and therefore matters related to the Subject Focus Condition are not applicable. The verb in a focused complement clause always requires the irrealis inflectional paradigm.

Given the "weight" of a complement clause, it is often the case that they are focused by the post-verbal focus marker and therefore appear after the Verb Complex. This is seen in (28).

(28) Dowláddu   wáxay   garwaaqsatay
      dowlad=d=u   wax=ay   garwaaq-s-at-∅-ay
      government=T.DEF=SUBJ FOC=3SG.T agree-WCAUS-MID-3SG.T-PST
      [ínay   lá   xaajootó   AM].
      in=ay   la   xaajoot-o   AM
      COMP=3SG.T with negotiate-IRR AM

   'The government has agreed to negotiate with AM.' (rasmimedia: 267685)

It is sometimes the case, however, that a complement clause can be focused by one of the pre-verbal focus markers. Accordingly, it appears immediately followed by its focus marker and before the Verb Complex, as in (29).

(29) [Ínaan   imánayó]   ayúu   ógyahay.
      in=aan   iman-ay-o   ay=uu   og-y-ah-ay
      COMP=1SG come-PROG-IRR FOC=3SG.M know-3SG.M-be-PRES

   'He knows that I am coming.'

13.6.4 Reported speech

In instances of reported speech, it is possible to place an entire quotation in focus. Despite these potentially being relatively longer stretches of discourse, they tend to be focused with a pre-verbal focus marker. As one might expect, in written discourse, this is usually *ayáa*. Like the case of focused complement clauses with *ín*, reported speech functions as the object of the main clause verb: 'X said Y.' This is seen in (30).

(30) "[Tanina   waa geeddi-sócodka aanu
      tan=i=na   waa geeddi-socod=ka aanu
      this=SUBJ=CONJ DEC process=K.DEF 1PL
      higsánaynó],"   ayáy   kú   tiri   L.
      hig-s-an-ay-n-o   ay=ay   ku   t-iri   L.
      aim.for-WCAUS-MID-PROG-1PL-IRR FOC=3SG.F about 3SG.F-say L

   'And this is the process that we are aiming for, said L.' (sagalradio.org: 99424)

Of course, not all instances of reported speech are necessarily focused. Rather, another component of the clause may instead be in focus, with the reported span of discourse still functioning as the object of the main clause verb. Such a situation is seen in (31).

(31) [Iságoo faraxsán]   ayúu   yidhi   ...
     isag=oo farax-s-an   ay=uu   y-idhi   ...
     he=REL happy-WCAUS-STV FOC=3SG.M 3SG.M-say.PST

'And being happy he said ...' (haatuf.net: 223)

13.6.5 Coordinated phrases and clauses

It has been shown thus far that constituents of a vast array of sizes can be placed into focus. In the sections above, the examples provided pertain to individual phrases, clauses, and even sentences (in the case of reported speech) being in focus. It is also the case that coordinated phrases and clauses can be placed into focus by a focus marker. As one might imagine, such constructions occur in countless combinations, but the grammatical principles pertaining to their construction are just like those of smaller constituents.

For example, in (32), a sequence of two coordinated subject relative clauses modifies the compound noun *isu-sócodka*. This noun is also the subject of the main clause verb and is marked as in focus by *ayáa*. As expected, based on the Subject Focus Condition, the focus marker has no cliticized pronoun, is not morphologically subject-marked, and the main clause verb requires reduced agreement.

(32) [Isu-sócodka waddoóyinka   waawéyn ee góbolka]   ayáa
     isu-socod=ka waddo-oyin=ka waa-weyn ee gobol=ka   ayaa
     traffic=K.DEF street-PL=K.DEF Red-large REL state=K.DEF FOC
     xayírmi   dooná.
     xayir-m-i   doon-a
     block-STV-INF will.be-PRES.RED

'Traffic on the large roads in the state will be blocked.' (batalaalenews: 4447)

Compare this to (33) where the phrase containing conjoined relative clauses focused by *báa* is not the subject of the main clause verb. Here, the focus marker is joined by a subject pronoun clitic, and the main clause verb takes full paradigm inflection.

(33) Wáxa [ífka   kú   nóol oo dhán] báan   rabaa
     waxa if=ka   ku   nool oo dhan b=aan   rab-∅-aa
     FOC   universe=K.DEF within living REL all   FOC=1SG want-1SG-PRES
     ínaan   bartó.
     in=aan   bar-t-o
     COMP=1SG learn-MID-IRR

'I want to learn about all living things in the universe.' (Z & O: 318)

13.7 Focus without focus markers

Banti (2019) is perhaps the first to propose that Somali has strategies that it uses to place focus on constituents in clauses where canonical focus markers cannot be used. Among these strategies are two cleft-like constructions that he defines as *pseudo-clefts* and *predicate-only clefts*. In addition, he proposes several "focus-linked" words and clitics that function in a manner similar to focus markers in highlighting key information within the clause. The examples below are extracted from this source.

To begin, (34) shows what Banti calls a pseudo-cleft. The example contains a declarative main clause with *waa*. The relative clause indicated in brackets is a pseudo-cleft which provides a counterpart to *kuwán* 'these.' As mentioned previously, though clauses with *waa* do not behave canonically like other clauses containing one of the focus markers discussed in Chapter 11 (i.e., *báa*, *ayáa*, *wáxa(a)*), some scholars (including Banti) consider *waa* to be a focus marker.

(34) [*Wíxii   máanta la   i   siiyaý*]   *waa kuwán.*
     wix-ii   manta la   i   sii-y-ay   waa kuwan
     thing-K.RDEF today ISP 1SG.OBJ give-3SG.M-PST DEC these
     'What I was given today are these.'

An example of what Banti calls a predicate-only cleft is in (35). This also involves a declarative main clause with *waa*, but here the predicate has no subject counterpart.

(35) *Wáa [ta   Cábdi arkay].*
     waa ta   Cabdi ark-∅-ay
     DEC T.DEF Cabdi see-3SG.M-PST
     'It is that Cabdi saw it.'

In addition to these two cleft strategies, Banti cites seven function words and clitics that, at least in some instances, can be implicated in focus-like behavior. They are either used in non-indicative clauses where other focus markers are not permitted or otherwise alongside a focus marker in an indicative clause to add further detail to the focus-marked element. These include: *uun* 'just, only,' *xataa* 'even,' *keliya* 'only,' *qudha* 'only,' *laf* 'self,' and also the clausal conjunction clitic *=na* and intensifier clitic *=ba*.

13.8 Detopicalization strategies

There appear to be several degrees of topicality that can be exploited in Somali discourse. In the simplest cases, one might consider a constituent to be topical by virtue of the fact that it is not marked overtly as 'in focus,' new, or highlighted information by a focus marker (Tosco 2002). However, as illustrated above, there are syntactic means by which to more explicitly mark a constituent as being topical. In Sections 13.3.1 and 13.3.2, it was shown that topicalization is possible by shifting the arrangement of subject and object constituents from their unmarked SOV order to OSV. It was also shown in Sections 13.4.1 and 13.4.2 that constituents can be retopicalized by right dislocation.

Though topical information is often expressed overtly by a full noun phrase, Somali also has syntactic strategies to detopicalize subject and object constituents. In these instances of detopicalization, the noun phrase referent remains active in the discourse but is morphologically attenuated in some way. For example, Tosco (2002, 2004) analyzes some instances in which an object noun is incorporated into the verb as a type of detopicalization. Compare sentences (36) through (38).

(36) *Waan   dharárka   tolay.*
    w=aan   dhar-ar=ka   tol-∅-ay
    DEC=1SG cloth-PL=K-DEF sew-1SG-PST
    'I sewed the fabric.'

(37) *Wáan   tolay.*
    w=aan   tol-∅-ay
    DEC=1SG sew-1SG-PST
    'I sewed it.'

(38) *Wáan   dhartolay.*
    w=aan   dhar-tol-∅-ay
    DEC=1SG fabric-sew-1SG-PST
    'I sewed.' (fabric-sewed)

In (36), 'the fabric' is an expressed topical noun phrase that functions as the direct object of a transitive verb. In (37), however, in the absence of an overt object noun phrase, the same transitive verb's valence is satisfied by a forced third person reading (recall that third person object pronouns are not overt). Lastly, in (38), the verb's valence is instead satisfied by an explicit but incorporated object. This permits a more generic reading without even an understood object. For more on noun incorporation in Somali, see §8.2.2.

While this strategy has been noted for objects, a subject can also be detopicalized. This is accomplished formally under an object focus configuration in which the subject is expressed only via the impersonal subject pronoun (ISP) *la*. Recall from §10.2.2 that sentences whose subject is the ISP are sometimes translated as passive. Examples are as follows in (39) and (40).

(39) *[Waxyaabó badán] báa la soó bandhígayaa.*
 wax-yaab-o badan baa la soo bandhig-ay-∅-aa
 thing-PL-PL many FOC ISP VEN display-PROG-3SG.M-PRES
 '[Many things] are being displayed.' (i.e., 'One is displaying [many things].')

(40) *[Búugga] báa la akhrínayaa.*
 buug=ga baa la akhr-in-ay-∅-PRES
 book=K.DEF FOC ISP read.W.CAUS-PROG-3SG.M-PRES
 '[The book] is being read.' (i.e., 'One is reading [the book].')

Constructions like these are discussed by Gebert (1986) under the heading of "extreme" subject detopicalization, as well as by Hetzron (1965). Hetzron attributes the subject detopicalization via this mechanism as a means by which to simultaneously highlight the object and predicate while backgrounding the subject.

14 Subordination

This chapter is devoted to discussing the properties of subordinate clauses (also called dependent clauses). The chapter is divided into three major sections: relative clauses, complement clauses, and subordinating adverbial clauses.

14.1 Relative clauses

Relative clauses are treated first because they have unique properties compared to other subordinate clause types. Subject relative clauses, in particular, display properties that closely parallel those associated with the Subject Focus Condition in main clauses (see §11.3). This includes special requirements for verb inflection, the absence of resumptive subject pronoun clitics, and the absence of morphological subject marking. No such restrictions are found in other subordinate clauses. The close parallels between subject relative clauses and main clause subject focus have attracted a great deal of attention in the literature. Research on this topic includes Antinucci and Puglielli (1980), Antinucci and Puglielli (1984), Lecarme (1995), and Banti (2011b), among others.

Though certain distinctions can be drawn between relative clauses and other subordinate clauses, all Somali subordinate clauses have some properties in common. For example, clause type markers (e.g., declarative *waa*) and focus markers do not occur within a subordinate clause. Also, subordinate clause verbs are compatible only with a subset of tense/aspect/mood distinctions compared to main clause verbs. Relative clause verbs, in particular, are inflected for tense. Subordinate clauses also have in common that negation entails the negative particle *aán*, though this is not obligatory. Negation being obligatorily marked on verbs may ultimately contribute to the optionality of the negative particle. Each of these characteristics are discussed further below.

In addition to the division that can be drawn between subject and object relative clauses, another matter discussed in this chapter concerns the fact that Somali makes morphological and syntactic distinctions between restrictive vs. non-restrictive (or appositive) relative clauses. Briefly here, restrictive relative clauses provide essential disambiguating information about the head noun that they modify. They *restrict* the set of possible referents that the noun might have. These relative clauses immediately follow the head noun that they modify with no intervening relativizer. Non-restrictive relative clauses instead provide non-essential information. Their role, therefore, is not to restrict the set of possible noun referents. These relative clauses differ in two main respects from restrictive relative clauses: i) they are introduced by the relativizer *oo*, and ii) they can appear at a distance from the head noun that they modify. It is important to bear in mind that the relativizer *oo* is homophonous with the coordinating conjunction *oo* which conjoins two or more clauses modifying the same indefinite head. This conjunction and its counterpart *ee* are discussed in Chapter 15.

14.1.1 Headedness

Somali relative clauses are externally headed, except in one particular context discussed below. This means that the noun modified by the relative clause (i.e., the head noun) is located outside of the relative clause itself. This fact is not always apparent given that not all relative clauses in Somali have an overt relativizer. However, given that the head noun always appears before any other elements of the relative clause and that, if a relativizer is present, the head noun precedes it, this is a safe assertion to make. Sentence (1) contains a restrictive relative clause in which there is no relativizer. The noun *gabárta* 'the girl' is both the subject of the relative clause verb and the subject of the main clause. The head noun immediately precedes the relative clause in its entirety. Somali subject relative clauses are gapped such that there is no pronoun that is co-referential with the head noun included within the relative clause.

(1) Gabárta [múuska cuntay] waa waláasháy.
 gabar=ta muus=ka cun-t-ay waa walaa-shay
 girl=T.DEF banana=K.DEF eat-3SG.F-PST.RED DEC sister-T.my
 'The girl who ate the banana is my sister.' (Antinucci & Puglielli 1980)

A related example is seen in (2) which instead contains a non-restrictive relative clause introduced by the relativizer *oo*. Here, the head noun *nín* 'man' is the subject of the relative clause and immediately precedes the relativizer.

(2) Ma garáneyó ínta nín [oo hálkaa kú
 ma gar-an-ey-o in=ta nin oo halkaa ku
 NEG know-MID-PROG-IRR amount=T.DEF man REL there at
 dhimatáy].
 dhim-at-ay
 die-MID-PST.RED
 'I don't know the amount of men that died there.' (Z & O: 327)

While these and most Somali relative clauses can be categorized as externally headed, Banti (2011b) brings to light that internally-headed relative clauses are possible in literary genres. One such example is in (3).

(3) Waar [nínkii   hádalkuu   ina   yidhí]   ma
    well nin-kii   hadal=k=uu   ina   y-idhi   ma
    well man-K.RDEF word=K.DEF=3SG.M 1PL.OBJ 3SG.M-say.PST QM
    máqlayseen?
    maql-ay-s-ee-n
    hear-PROG-2-PST-PL
    'Well, did you hear the words this man told us?'

As Banti explains, sentences like this contain a relative clause whose head noun is inside the relative clause itself. In the case of (3), the head noun of the relative clause *hádal* is preceded by subject of the relative clause verb.

14.1.2 Relative/Antecedent relationship

A relative clause can modify an antecedent of any type, regardless of the constituent's function in the main clause. That is, the relative clause antecedent can function either as the subject or as an object of the main clause verb. The role of the head noun within the relative clause can likewise be either a subject or an object. Somali makes use of any combination of these options. For example, a subject-subject relative clause is one in which the head noun is both the subject of the main clause verb and of the relative clause verb. An object-subject relative clause is instead one in which the head noun is the subject of the relative clause verb and an object of the main clause verb. The same principles apply for object-object and subject-object relative clauses. Of course, the relationships are somewhat more diverse when an object is involved given that objects may be direct, indirect, or oblique. Though any of these combinations are possible, there are structural differences that distinguish them from one another. I discuss each combination in turn in the sub-sections below. For expository purposes, this section is limited to covering restrictive relative clauses. These differ structurally from their non-restrictive counterparts only in fairly subtle ways. Non-restrictive relative clauses are discussed separately in §14.1.4.

14.1.2.1 Subject-Subject

A subject-subject (SS) relative clause is one in which the head noun functions as both the subject of the main clause and the subject of the relative clause verb. Subject relative clauses in Somali are formed by a gap, meaning that there is no co-referential noun or pronoun within the relative clause itself that corresponds to the head noun. Subject relative clauses exhibit behavior that largely parallels the Subject Focus Condition (see §11.3).

(4) *Within a subject-subject relative clause:*
 a. the verb requires reduced inflectional agreement
 b. the verb requires realis paradigm inflection
 c. a subject pronoun clitic does not appear

Example (5) shows that there is no resumptive subject pronoun clitic within the subject relative clause. Indeed, the presence of such a clitic is ungrammatical (*Wiilásha [ay búugga akhriyey] way óoynayaan.). This prohibition differs markedly from what occurs in object relative clauses, where the presence of a subject pronoun clitic is grammatical, and in some instances obligatory. The relative clause verb also exhibits reduced agreement within the realis inflectional paradigm. Its form is *akhriyey* rather than *akhriyeen*.

(5) Wiilásha [búugga akhriyey] way
 wiil-ash=a buug=ga akhriy-ey w=ay
 boy-PL=T.DEF book=K.DEF read-PST.RED DEC=3PL
 oóynayaan.
 ooy-n-ay-Ø-aa-n
 cry-WCAUS-PROG-3-PRES-PL
 'The boys who read the book are crying.'

Though these verbs taking realis inflection have no H tone on their inflectional suffix, they may have a H tone elsewhere on the verb. As seen in (6), the relative clause verb takes reduced agreement for the present progressive *imánayaa* rather than full paradigm *imánayeen*. There is always a H tone on the stem in progressive aspect verbs.

(6) Naagáha [imánayaa] waa raáci doonaan.
 naag-a=ha iman-ay-aa waa raac-i doon-Ø-aa-n
 woman-PL=K.DEF come-PROG-PRES.RED DEC accompany-INF FUT-3-PRES-PL
 'The women who are coming will accompany them.' (Orwin 1995: 192)

When a subject relative clause's head noun is also a focus-marked main clause subject, the relative clause verb bears a suffixal H tone. Compare (6) with its focused counterpart in (7). In the latter, both the relative clause verb and main clause require a truncated, toned form of the realis paradigm with reduced agreement.

(7) Naagáha   [imánayá]   báa raáci   dooná.
    naag-a=ha   iman-ay-a   baa raaci   doon-a
    woman-PL=K.DEF come-PROG-PRED.RED FOC accompany FUT-PRES.RED
    'The woman who are coming will accompany them.' (Orwin 1995: 193)

Given that the subject in a subject-subject relative clause is outside the relative clause itself, there is no possibility of morphological subject marking within the relative clause.

14.1.2.2 Object-Subject

An object-subject (OS) relative clause is one in which the head noun functions as the subject of the relative clause verb while being an object (or non-subject) of the main clause. Like the SS relative clauses discussed in §14.1.2.1, these relative clauses have a gap such that the head noun is located outside of the relative clause. As part of a larger natural class of subject relative clauses, OS relative clauses exhibit many, but not all of the same properties as do SS relative clauses.

(8) *Within an object-subject relative clause:*
   a. the verb requires reduced agreement
   b. the verb requires realis paradigm inflection
   c. a subject pronoun clitic does not appear

Each of these properties can be seen in an example like (9). This sentence contains an OS relative that modifies the direct object of the main clause verb. The relative clause verb *oóyayá* is in the present progressive. It has a final H tone and a shortened vowel. This verb also shows reduced agreement relative to its 3PL subject *wiilásha* 'the boys.' Lastly, there is no co-referential subject pronoun permitted within the relative clause itself. A sentence like **Waan jecéylyahay wiilásha [ay oóyayá]* containing such a pronoun would be ungrammatical.

(9) Waan   jecéylyahay   wiilásha   [oóyayá].
    w=aan   jeceyl-Ø-ah-ay   wiil-ash=a   ooy-ay-a
    DEC=1SG love-1SG-be-PRES boy-PL=T.DEF   cry-PROG-PRES.RED
    'I love the boys [who are crying].'

Since the head of an OS relative clause is outside the relative clause itself, there is no possibility of morphological subject marking. Of course, this does not preclude subject marking elsewhere in the sentence. For example, (10) contains an OS relative clause modifying the main clause direct object *wáxa* 'the thing.' It exhibits the hallmark characteristics of these relative clauses introduced just above. Notice, however, that the main clause subject *adígu* is morphologically subject marked.

(10) *Adígu   wáxa   [socdá]   má taqaannaa?*
      adi=g=u   wax=a   soc-d-a   ma t-aqaann-aa
      you=K.DEF=SUBJ thing=K.DEF happen-MID-PRES.RED QM 2SG-know-PRES
      'Do you know what is happening?' (Z & I: 316)

Along similar lines, because the head noun is an object (i.e., a non-subject) of the main clause, there are no complicating factors related to focus in the main clause. Example (11) contains an OS relative clause on the main clause direct object that is in focus. The relative clause verb takes reduced agreement and is toned. The main clause verb instead takes full agreement, and its suffix is toneless.

(11) *Ma wáx [basbáas léh]   báad   doóneysaan?*
      ma wax   basbaas leh   b=aad   doon-ey-s-aa-n
      QM thing spicy   have.PRES.RED FOC=2PL want-PROG-2-PRES-PL
      'Do you want something that is spicy?' (Z & O: 55)

14.1.2.3 Subject-Object

A subject-object (SO) relative clause is one in which the head noun functions as an object of the relative clause verb while also being the subject of the main clause. Object relative clauses are markedly different from subject relative clauses in several ways. For example, the verb in an object relative clause takes full agreement in all instances. In the case of SO relative clauses, the verb is typically toneless and fully inflected, making it look identical to most main clause verbs. The exception to this, however, is when the head noun, being the subject of the main clause, is in focus. Here, the verb is toned, as is the main clause verb. Another general property of object relative clauses is that the subject of the relative clause verb must be expressed, whether by a noun phrase, a subject pronoun clitic, or both. The conditions governing this are discussed in more detail below. When a subject noun phrase is found within an object relative clause, it will be morphologically subject marked.

(12) *Within a subject-object relative clause:*
      a. the verb requires full inflectional agreement
      b. the verb is toneless, except under subject focus
      c. a subject noun phrase, clitic, or both occur are required
      d. a subject noun phrase is subject marked when present

In (13), the main clause subject *buugágga* 'the books' is the direct object of the relative clause verb. The relative clause verb is fully inflected for 3PL and has no H tone. The subject of the relative clause verb is expressed and its definite determiner bears subject marking.

(13) *Buugágga   [nimánku   keenaan]   waa kúwán.*
     buug-ag=ga   nim-an=k=u   keen-∅-aa-n waa kuwan
     book-PL=K.DEF man-PL=K.DEF=SUBJ bring-3-PRES-PL DEC these
     'The books that the men bring are these. (Saeed 1999: 213)

A sentence like (14) illustrates a similarly constructed example in which the subject of the relative clause is pronominal and accordingly expressed by a subject pronoun clitic.

(14) *Gaádhiga [uu   keenay]   wáa jabay.*
     gaadhi=ga uu   keen-∅-ay   waa jab-∅-ay
     car=K.DEF 3SG.M bring-3SG.M-PST   DEC break-3SG.M-PST
     'The car that he brought broke.'

It is also possible for both a subject noun phrase and a subject pronoun clitic to occur within an SO relative clause. Moreover, as shown in the following three examples from Antinucci and Puglielli (1980), there are three orders in which they can appear relative to one another that generally convey the same meaning but likely entail subtle pragmatic nuances that I have not explored in detail. In (15), the SPC precedes the noun phrase. In (16), the noun phrase precedes the SPC. In both these instances, the two precede the relative clause verb. In (17), we can see that it is also possible for the noun phrase to follow the relative clause verb, but it is ungrammatical for the SPC to do so (**Cali qoray uu*).

(15) *Warqádda   [uu   Cali   qoray]   máanta báy   tégi*
     warqad=da   uu   Cali   qor-∅-ay   maanta b=ay   teg-i
     letter=T-DEF 3SG.M Cali.SUBJ write-3SG.M-PST today FOC=3SG.T leave-INF
     doontaa.
     doon-t-aa
     FUT-3SG.T-PRES
     'The letter that Cali wrote will leave today.'

(16) *Warqádda [Cali   uu   qoray]   máanta báy   tégi*
    warqad=da Cali   uu   qor-∅-ay   maanta b=ay   teg-i
    letter=T-DEF Cali.SUBJ 3SG.M write-3SG.M-PST today FOC=3SG.T leave-INF
    doontaa.
    doon-t-aa
    FUT-3SG.T-PRES
    'The letter that Cali wrote will leave today.'

(17) *Warqádda [uu   qoray   Cali]   máanta báy   tégi*
    warqad=da uu   qor-∅-ay   Cali   maanta b=ay   teg-i
    letter=T-DEF 3SG.M write-3SG.M-PST Cali.SUBJ today FOC=3SG.T leave-INF
    doontaa.
    doon-t-aa
    FUT-3SG.T-PRES
    'The letter that Cali wrote will leave today.'

Because the head noun of a SO relative clause is the main clause subject, it may be marked as in focus by a focus marker. In these instances, the requirements of Subject Focus Condition apply, and the relative clause verb is toned, as is the main clause verb. However, because the relative clause is an object relative clause, its verb takes full agreement.

(18) *Baríiska   [uu   nínku   iibiyó]   báa fiicán.*
    bariis=ka   uu   nin=k=u   iibiy-o   baa fiic-an
    rice=K-DEF 3SG.M man=K.DEF=SUBJ sell-PRES.IRR FOC good-STV
    'The rice that the man sells is good.' (Livnat 1984: 70)

14.1.2.4 Object-Object

An object-object (OO) relative clause is one in which the head noun functions as an object of the relative clause verb and as an object of the main clause verb. Like the object relative clauses discussed in §14.1.2.3, the verb in an OO relative clause takes full agreement. However, unlike SO relative clauses where there is the complicating matter of main clause subjecthood, the verb in an OO relative clause is always toned. A subject must be expressed in these relative clauses, whether by a noun phrase, a subject pronoun clitic, or both. A subject noun phrase will be morphologically subject marked when it occurs within an OO relative clause.

(19) *Within an object-object relative clause:*
   a. the verb requires full inflectional agreement
   b. the verb is toned
   c. a subject noun phrase, clitic, or both are required
   d. a subject noun phrase is subject marked when present

Example (20) shows an object-object relative clause on *buugágta* 'the books.' This is the direct object of the main clause verb as well as the direct object of the relative clause verb. Within the relative clause, the verb is fully inflected for 3PL, and its suffix is toned. It is indicated using parentheses that the subject pronoun clitic within the relative clause is optional. The relative clause subject can occur alongside this coreferential SPC, but its absence is not ungrammatical. The subject noun phrase within the relative clause is morphologically subject marked.

(20) Waan   jecéylyahay   buugágta   [(ay) wiiláshu
     w=aan   jeceyl-y-ah-ay   buug-ag-ta   ay   wiil-a=sh=u
     DEC=1SG   love-1SG-be-PRES book-PL=T.DEF 3PL   boy-PL=T.DEF=SUBJ
     akhriyéen].
     akhri-y-ee-n
     read-3-PST-PL
     'I love the books that the boys read.'

Because the head noun of an OO relative clause is also a main clause object, its inflectional behavior is unaffected by subject focus marking or main clause subjecthood. Example (21) shows a scenario in which the head noun is an oblique object of both the main clause and relative clause verbs. The relative clause verb exhibits full agreement and is toned. Once again, the optionality of the subject pronoun clitic within the object relative clause is indicated by parentheses.

(21) Áxmed wúxuu   kú nóolyahay   meésha   [(uu) Cáli kú
     Axmed wux=uu   ku nool-y-ah-ay   meesh=a   uu   Cali ku
     Axmed FOC=3SG   in live-3SG.M-be-PRES place=T.DEF   3SG.M Cali in
     nóolyahaý].
     nool-y-ah-ay
     live-3SG.M-be-PRES
     'Axmed lives in the place where Cali lives.' (Livnat 1984: 77)

14.1.3 Negation

The formation of negative relative clauses entails many of the same principles defined above for affirmative relative clauses. All four of the major head-antecedent relationships (SS, OS, SO, and OO) are found in negative relative clauses. There is a restriction against the presence of a subject pronoun clitic in both SS and OS relatives. The presence of such a pronoun is obligatory in some SO and OO relatives, with the exception of those with a third person head noun. In such instances, a subject pronoun clitic is optional, but its absence is not ungrammatical. In some ways, however, the structure of negative relative clauses is less complex. For example, the TAM contexts found in these clauses encode verbal negation by a single invariant form for all person, number, grammatical gender combinations. In addition, and although all four of the major head-antecedent relationships can be found in negative relative clauses, subject-subject combinations of this type are difficult to express under main clause subject focus. They are instead typically expressed using a declarative clause, thereby precluding the marked behavior attributed to subject focus.

One recognizable characteristic of negative relative clauses is the negative marker *aán*. This is found only in negative subordinate clauses and in main clauses with subject focus. Though it is typically present, it is not obligatory, as seen in a comparison of (22) and (23). This optionality is likely due to the fact that negation is also encoded on the relative clause verb.

(22) *díl [qíil laháyn]*
 dil qiil lah-ayn
 murder reason have-PST.NEG
 'a murder without reason'

(23) *meél [aán búuq laháyn]*
 meel aan buuq lah-ayn
 place NEG noise have-PST.NEG
 'a place without noise'

In those instances where a subject pronoun clitic appears in the relative clause, it will form a cluster with negative *aán*. These clusters are shown in (24), which also illustrates that the order of the SPC and *aán* relative to one another is variable.

(24)   *Subject pronoun clitic + aán*

aan=aán	aanán	or	aán=aan	aánan	1SG
aad=aán	aadán	or	aán=aad	aánad	2SG
uu=aán	uusán	or	aán=uu	aánu	3SG.M/K
ay=aán	ayán	or	aán=ay	aánay ~ aáney	3SG.F/T
aanu=aán	aannán	or	aán=aanu	aánnan	1PL.exc
aynu=aán	aynán	or	aán=aynu	ánayn ~ áneyn	1PL.inc
aydin=aán	eydnán	or	aán=aydin	ánaydin ~ áneydin	2PL
ay=aán	ayán	or	aán=ay	aánay ~ aáney	3PL

Such a cluster in context is in (25) in the OO relative clause on *cuntáda* 'the food.' The head noun modified by this relative clause is in focus. As expected of object focus, the main clause verb takes full inflection and is toneless.

(25)   Cuntáda   [aánay   cunín]   báan   keenay.
       cunta=da   aan=ay   cun-in   b=aan   keen-∅-ay
       food=T.DEF NEG=3SG.T eat-PST.NEG FOC=1SG take-1SG-PST

       'I took the food that she did not eat.' (Orwin 1995: 229)

Another related possibility is to find a subject pronoun clitic in an object relative clause flanked periphrastically by both of Somali's negative markers *má...aán*. When this occurs, the three morphemes occur in only a single linear order, as shown in (26). Thus, the optionality of SPC/*aán* ordering seen in (24) is not possible when *má* is present.

(26)   *má + subject pronoun clitic + aán*

má=aan=aán	máanán	1SG (~ 1PL)
má=aad=aán	máadán	2SG (~ 2PL)
má=uu=aán	múusán	3SG.M/K
má=ay=aán	máayán ~ méeyán	3SG.F/T
má=aanu=aán	máannán	1PL.exc
má=aynu=aán	máynán ~ méynan	1PL.inc
má=aydin=aán	méydnán	2PL
má=ay=aán	máayán ~ méeyán	3PL

Sentence (27) shows a subject-object relative with periphrastic negation. The head noun is the subject of a declarative clause without focus. Accordingly, the main clause verb is again fully inflected, and its suffix is toneless.

(27) *Shaqáda   [máadán   qabanín]   wey*
     shaqa=da   ma=aad=an   qab-an-in   w=ay
     work=T.DEF NEG=2SG=NEG do-MID-PST.NEG   DEC=3SG.T
     adágtahay.
     adag-t-ah-ay
     difficult-3SG.T-be-PRES
     'The work that you didn't do is difficult.' (Z & I: 217)

Thus far, examples (25) and (27) have shown OO and OS relative clauses, respectively, both of which have a pronominal subject. A related example of an OO relative clause is given in (28) where the subject of both clauses is the ISP. Although the main clause object containing the relative clause is in focus, the focus marker is bare, as required by the presence of *la*.

(28) *Túugga   [aán sháley   la qabanín]   báa la*
     tuug=ga   aan shaley   la qab-an-in   baa la
     thief=K.DEF NEG yesterday ISP catch-MID-PST.NEG FOC ISP
     qabtey.
     qab-t-∅-ey
     catch-MID-3SG.M-PST
     'The thief that was not caught yesterday was caught.' (Z & I: 377)

Example (29) shows a OO relative clause whose subject is not pronominal. As expected, the presence of a resumptive subject pronoun clitic in such instances is optional, as indicated by parentheses.

(29) *Naágta   [aán(u)   Cali   arág] wáxay   ahayd   Caasha.*
     naag=ta   aan=u   Cali   arag wax=ay   ah-ay-d   Caasha
     woman=T.DEF NEG=3SG.M   Cali.SUBJ see   FOC=3SG.F   be-PST-3SG.F   Caasha
     'Caasha is the woman that Cali did not see.' (Livnat 1984: 107)

Turning to subject relative clauses, (30) shows a negative OS relative clause on *wíilkií* 'the boy.' As expected in a subject relative clause, there is no resumptive subject pronoun within the relative clause.

(30) *Wíilkií   [aán múuska   cunín]   wáan   arkay.*
     wiil-kii   aan muus=ka   cun-in   w=aan   ark-∅-ay
     boy-K.RDEF   NEG banana=K.DEF   eat-PST.NEG   DEC=1SG   see-1SG-PST
     'I saw the boy who didn't eat the banana.' (Antinucci & Puglielli 1984)

Example (31) shows a negative SS relative clause. The head noun containing the relative clause is the subject in a declarative main clause without focus marking. The relative clause verb, being the last element in the noun phrase, bears morphological subject marking.

(31) *Wíilka*   *[aán talyaániga   kú hadlini]*   *waa waláalkay.*
     wiil=ka   aan talyaani=ga   ku hadl-in=i   waa walaal-kay
     boy=K.DEF NEG Italian=K-DEF in speak-PST.NEG=SUBJ DEC brother-K.my
     'The boy who doesn't speak Italian is my brother.' (Antinucci & Puglielli 1984)

Sentence (32) differs slightly in that the head noun is the subject of a main clause with focus marking. However, it is the main clause predicate that is in focus.

(32) *Nínkií*   *[aán imán]*   *Cáli búu*   *ahaa.*
     nin-kii   aan im-an   Cali b=uu   ah-aa
     man-K.RDEF NEG come-NEG   Cali FOC=3SG.M be-3SG.M.PST
     'The man who didn't come was Cali.' (Livnat: 1984: 105)

Negative subject-subject relative clauses appear to be incompatible with subject focus. Rather, the sentiment entailed in such a clause is expressed with a declarative. Such an example is in (33) where the relative clause is subject marked, and a resumptive subject pronoun occurs on the declarative marker.

(33) *Nínkií*   *[aán dhimani]*   *wuu*   *soó noqdey.*
     nin-kii   aan dhim-an=i   w=uu   soo noq-d-∅-ey
     man-K.RDEF NEG   die-NEG=SUBJ   DEC=3SG.M VEN   return-MID-3SG.M-PST
     'The man who did not die returned.' (Bell 1953: 96)

14.1.4 Restrictive vs. non-restrictive

Whereas the restrictive relative clauses discussed thus far provide pertinent disambiguating information about their head noun, the non-restrictive (or appositive) relative clauses described in this section provide only supplemental information about an already defined entity. Non-restrictive relative clauses are recognizable in Somali by the presence of the relativizer *oo*. The examples provided below illustrate that most of the major structural and grammatical principles defined above for restrictive relative clauses also apply to non-restrictive relative clauses. Besides the presence of *oo*, the two relative clause types differ in that non-restrictive relative clauses i) must have a known or defined head and ii) can be located at a distance from the head noun that they modify.

Example (34) shows a non-restrictive subject-subject relative clause. As expected of Somali subject relative clauses, the relative clause verb takes reduced agreement. Because the relative clause modifies the non-focused subject of the main clause verb, it is morphologically subject marked. The main clause verb is fully inflected in the realis paradigm.

(34) *Saddéx nín   [oo socotó   ah]i   wéy   tageen.*
      saddex nin   oo   socota   ah=i   w=ey   tag-∅-ee-n
      three   man REL traveler   be.PRES.RED=SUBJ DEC=3PL   go-3-PST-PL
      'Three men, who are travelers, left.' (Z & I: 161)

Subject marking can also occur in a non-restrictive relative clause, as in (35). Here, the object relative clause has a non-pronominal subject that bears subject marking. The presence of a resumptive subject pronoun clitic is also grammatical, though not obligatory, as indicated by parentheses. The head noun of the relative clause is the focused object of the main clause verb. The relative clause verb is fully inflected and toned, while the main clause verb is fully inflected but toneless.

(35) *Barîiska   [oo (ay)   gabádhu   soó iibsataý]*
      bariis=ka   oo   ay   gabadh=u   soo iib-s-a-t-ay
      rice=K.DEF REL 3SG.F girl=T.DEF.SUBJ   VEN buy-WCAUS-MID-3SG.F-PST
      báy   karisay.
      b=ay   kar-i-s-ay
      FOC=3SG.F cook-WCAUS-3SG.F-PST
      'She cooked the rice that the girl bought.' (Orwin 1995: 189)

The example of an object-subject relative clause in (36) differs only slightly in that the relative clause does not have the ability to be subject marked as a whole, nor does it bear subject marking internally. As a subject relative clause, there is no possibility of subject marking, and there is no resumptive subject pronoun clitic. The relative clause verb requires reduced agreement, as otherwise expected.

(36) *Wáx walbá   [oo meésha   ká socdá]   wáan*
      wax wal=ba   oo   mees=sha   ka soc-d-a   w=aan
      thing every=INT REL place=T.DEF   in happen-MID-PRES.RED   DEC=1SG
      aqaannaa.
      aqaan-naa
      know-1SG.PRES
      'I know everything that is going on in that place.' (Z & I: 316)

Non-restrictive relative clauses modify known heads, meaning that they can often be expected to immediately follow a determiner. When this occurs, it is common for the relativizer *oo* to coalesce with the preceding determiner, as in (37).

(37) *Wáxaan dádk[oo   dhán] ú   sheégayaa...*
    wax=aan dad=k-oo   dhan u   sheeg-ay-∅-aa
    FOC=1SG person=K.DEF-REL every about tell-PROG-1SG-PRES
    'I am telling every person about ...' (halgan.net: 1607)

The relativizer *oo* also coalesces with a following subject pronoun clitic in otherwise expected combinations to form the following clusters: *oon* (1SG ~ 1PL), *ood* (2SG ~ 2PL), *ooy* (3SG, 3PL), *oonnu* (1PL.exc), and *ooynu* (1PL.inc). An example of such cluster in context is in (38).

(38) *Waa códkáaga   [ood   kú   cíil   baxdó].*
    waa cod-kaa=ga   oo=d   ku   ciil   bax-d-o
    DEC voice-your=K.DEF REL=2SG about anger come.out-2SG-IRR
    'It is your (own) voice that you are angry about.' (somaliland.org: 84525)

Coalescence is also possible between *oo* and the subordinate clause negative marker *aán*. This is seen in (39), though it is also notable that such coalescence is not obligatory, as in (40).

(39) *Waa sabáb weýn [oón   dheeldhéel gelín].*
    waa sabab weyn oo-n   dheeldheel gel-in
    DEC reason big   REL-NEG play   enter-PRES.NEG
    'It's a big reason not to play.' (somalilandpost: 2543)

(40) *Nínka   [oo aán báre   ahá]   báa yimí.*
    nin=ka   oo aan bare   ah-a   baa y-imi
    man=K.DEF REL NEG teacher be-PRES.NEG FOC 3SG-come-PST.RED
    'The man who is not a teacher came.' (Orwin 1995: 229)

One of the most striking and distinguishing characteristics of non-restrictive relative clauses compared to others is that the relative clause does not necessarily need to immediately follow the noun that it modifies. This is seen in (41) where the head noun *dukumentiyó* 'documents' is modified first by an immediately adjacent restrictive relative clause and thereafter by a non-restrictive relative clause. Relative clause coordination is discussed in greater detail in §15.3.[1]

---

1 When a restrictive relative clause is followed by another relative clause modifying the same head, they can be conjoined either with *ee* or with *oo*. Some have argued that this choice is predicated on

(41) Háse ahaáteen, sída   ay muujínayaan   dukumentiyó [ay
      hase ahaateen sida   ay muujin-ay-∅-aa-n   dukumenti-yo ay
      but however   according.to 3PL show-PROG-3-PRES-PL document-PL 3PL
      BBC-du   aragtaý]   [oo labáda   dál   ú
      BBC=d=u   arag-t-ay   oo laba=da   dal   u
      BBC=T.DEF=SUBJ see-3PL.T-PST.IRR REL two=T.DEF country to
      diréen   maxkamáda]...
      dir-∅-ee-n   maxkama=da
      sent-3PL-PST.IRR-PL court=T.DEF

      'However, according to the documents being shown which the BBC saw which
      sent two countries to court…' (bbc somali: 52687303)

14.1.5 Attributive relative clauses with nominal complements

In §9.4, it was shown that Somali can express attribution of a noun directly only by a closed class of approximately 40 lexical adjectives. In addition to this strategy and the associative constructions discussed in §9.5, another strategy to express attribution is via a subject relative clause. These attributive relative clauses are formed from a closed set of verbs taking a noun complement or otherwise by a hybrid verb.

Because attributive relative clauses are subject relative clauses, their verbs require reduced agreement, the details of which are discussed in §7.8. Also, because these modifying relative clauses are the last element of the larger noun phrase, there are a few instances in which we find evidence of subject marking on the relative clause verb. Throughout this section, relative clauses are indicated in square brackets.

The verbs involved in the formation of attributive relative clauses with a noun complement are *áh* 'be,' *léh* 'have,' and *la'* 'lack,' and also *qáb* 'hold, possess.'

14.1.5.1 with 'be'

Attributive relative clauses with *áh* 'be' take reduced agreement, resulting in a three-way inflectional distinction in the Simple Past (*ahaá* 1SG, 2SG, 3SG.M, 2PL, 3PL, *aháyd* 3SG.F, and *aháyn* 1PL). They further collapse onto a single form *áh* in the Simple Present. The nominal complement of these relative clause verbs can be definite or indefinite. The head noun and the nominal complement must match in their definiteness.

---

the definiteness of the head noun being modified (Saeed 1993b) or that *ee* vs. *oo* are optional variants with little difference in meaning (Zorc and Issa 1990). I hope to demonstrate in Chapter 15 that the distinction may be better stated relative to the role of the clause in disambiguation, or restriction vs. non-restriction of reference.

Example (42) shows a Simple Present relative clause verb with an indefinite noun and nominal complement while (43) shows a definite noun and nominal complement.

(42) *kób [abaár áh]*
    kob abaar ah
    area dryness be.PRES.RED
    'a dry area' (an area [that is] dry)

(43) *Ú yéedh nínka [Faransíiska áh].*
    u yeedh nin=ka Faransiis=ka ah
    to call-IMP man=K.DEF French=K.DEF be.PRES.RED
    'Call (to) the French man!'

The head noun can be made definite by any determiner, but a nominal complement takes only the definite determiner. This is seen in (44) where the head noun is modified by a demonstrative determiner while the nominal complement has a definite determiner.

(44) *Bahaláhán [dhágaxa áh] maxáa loolá*
    bahal-a-han dhagax-a ah ma=xaa lo=o=la
    animal-PL-K.DEM stone-K.DEF be.PRES.RED QM=FOC ISP=with=for
    jeedaa?
    jeed-∅-aa
    intend-3SG.M-PRES
    'What are these stone animals intended for?' (Z & O: 351)

Example (45) shows an attributive relative clause with a nominal complement whose verb is instead in the Simple Past.

(45) *Abwáanka ayáa tusaaloóyin ú soo qaatay dadáal*
    abwaan=ka ayaa tusaalo-oyin u soo qaat-∅-ay dadaal
    poet=K.DEF FOC example-PL with VEN cite-3SG.M-PST.RED effort
    [hodán ahaá].
    hodan ah-aa
    rich.person be-PST.RED
    'The poet cited examples of rich efforts...' (maroodijeex.com)

The relative clause verb 'be' can host the SUBJ marker when the noun phrase containing the relative clause is the subject of a main clause verb that is not in focus. Such modification by the SUBJ marker is seen in (46).

(46) meeláha   [caríiriga   ah]i
    meel-a=ha   cariiri=ga   ah=i
    place-PL=K.DEF narrow=K.DEF be.PRES.RED=SUBJ
    'the narrow places'

In the Simple Present, subject marking is realized on the verb as *ahi* or *ihi*. In the Simple Past, the forms are *ahaa* (with H tone loss alone), *ahaydi*, and *ahayni*.

There is a single negative form of the verb, *aháyn*, used in these relative clauses, as in (47). It is identical to that used for the Simple Past negative in main clauses. Negation may be further indicated within the relative clause by the subordinate clause negation marker *aán* at the left edge of the Verb Complex, as in (48).

(47) xaaláddéeda   [caádi ahayn]
    xaala-dee=da   caadi ah-ayn
    state-T.its=T.DEF normal be-NEG
    'an unusual state'

(48) úrur   [aán dówli   aháyn]
    urur   aan dowli   ah-ayn
    organization NEG government be-NEG
    'non-governmental organization'

The negative form of 'be' in a relative clause verb can also host the subject marker, as seen on *ahayni* in (49). As elsewhere, this is possible when the noun phrase containing the relative clause is the subject of a main clause verb that is not in focus.

(49) wíxií   [aán daacád ahayn]i
    wíx-ii   aán daacád ah-ayn=i
    thing-K.RDEF NEG honesty be-NEG=SUBJ
    'the dishonest thing'

14.1.5.2 with 'have'

Attributive relative clauses with *léh* 'have' exhibit the same behavior as defined just above for 'be.' There is a three-way inflectional distinction in the Simple Past (*laháa* 1SG, 2SG, 3SG.M, 2PL, 3PL, *laháyd* 3SG.F, and *laháyn* 1PL) but only a single form, *léh*, in the Simple Present. Example (50) shows a Simple Present verb, and (51) shows a Simple Past verb. The head noun and its complement must agree in definiteness.

(50) *meél [roób léh]*
    meel roob leh
    place rain have.PRES.RED
    'a rainy place'

(51) *ganacsadíhií [jáadka lahaá]*
    ganacsadi-hii jaad=ka lah-aa
    merchant-K.RDEF khat=K.DEF have-PST.RED
    'the khat merchant'

Example (52) shows subject marking on the relative clause verb. Subject-marked forms of these relative clause verbs are *lehi* or *lihi* in the Simple Present, and *lahaa, lahaydi*, and *lahayni* in the Simple Past.

(52) *baaritaannó [xóog leh]i*
    baaritaan-no xoog leh=i
    investigation-PL force have.PRES.RED=SUBJ
    'forceful investigations'

There is a single negative form of the verb, *laháyn*, used in these relative clauses. It can occur within the relative clause with or without the negative particle *aán*, as in (53) and (54), respectively.

(53) *díl [qíil laháyn]*
    dil qiil lah-ayn
    murder reason have-NEG
    'an unjustified murder'

(54) *ganacsí [aán xád laháyn]*
    ganacsi aan xad lah-ayn
    commerce NEG limit have-NEG
    'unlimited trade'

This negative verb can also host subject marking for the entire relative clause, becoming *lahayni*, as in (55).

(55) *Ká kelíya ee [aán xaddídáada lahayn]i waa Iláahaý.*
    ka keliya ee aan xaddidaada lah-ayn=i waa Ilaah-ay
    COM only REL NEG limitations=T.DEF have-NEG=SUBJ DEC God-K.my
    'The only one without limitations is my God.' (Somalibelievers: 120063)

14.1.5.3 with 'lack'

Attributive relative clauses with *la'* 'lack' require reduced agreement yielding *la'aá* (1SG, 2SG, 3SG.M, 2PL, 3PL), *la'aýd* (3SG.F), and *la'aýn* (1PL) in the Simple Past and a single form *lá'* in the Simple Present. For obvious reasons, these have no corresponding negative forms.

(56) *haweenéy [indhó la'aýd]*
 haween-ey indho la'-ay-d
 women-SG eyes lack-PST-3SG.F.RED
 'a blind woman'

Subject-marked forms are *la'aa*, *la'aydi*, and *la'ayni* in the Simple Past, and either *la'i* or *li'i* in the Simple Present.

(57) *sí [hagár li']i*
 si hagar li'=i
 way hesitation lack.PRES.RED=SUBJ
 'a confident way'

14.1.5.4 with 'hold, possess'

Attributive subject relative clauses are also formed with *qáb* 'hold, possess.' These differ in some respects from relative clauses with the irregular verbs discussed thus far in this section. The verb requires reduced agreement, but it does not collapse onto a single form in the Simple Present. Compare the following examples with different inflection on the relative clause verb. Example (58), in particular, shows a subject relative clause whose verb clearly exhibits reduced agreement.

(58) *cudurráda [xún qabá]*
 cudur-ra=da xun qab-a
 ailment-PL=T.DEF badness possess-PRES.RED
 'the bad diseases'

(59) *búlsho [caafimaád qabtá]*
 bulsho caafimaad qab-t-a
 society healthy possess-3SG.T-PRES.RED
 'a healthy society'

As in other instances, there is a single invariable form of the verb when it is inflected for negative. This is the same form of the negative as is found in main clauses.

(60) nín   [aán lixaádkíisa   qabín]
    nin   aan lixaad-kii-sa   qab-in
    man   NEG strength-K.his=T.DEF possess-NEG
    'a weak man' (a man not possessing his strength)

The negative relative clause verb can host the subject marker (yielding *qabini*) when the noun phrase containing the relative clause is the subject of a main clause verb that is not marked as in focus.

(61) Hawéenka   [aán áadka   tababarká   ú qabin]i
    haween=ka   aan aad=ka   tababar=ka   u qabin-i
    women=K-DEF NEG great.deal=K.DEF   training=K.DEF   of have-NEG=SUBJ
    'Women who do not have a great deal of training...' (7p.com: 118906)

14.1.6 Attributive relative clauses with hybrid verbs

Nouns can also be modified by an attributive relative clause whose verb is a hybrid verb. As discussed in §7.11, hybrid verbs are composed of an adjectival participle followed by an inflected form of *áh* 'be.' Recall from §7.1.10 that adjectival participles are derived from verbs by the stativizing extensions *-án* and *-óon*.

When 'to be' occurs in a subject relative clause with a nominal complement, (§14.1.5), it requires reduced agreement. This is shown in (62).

(62) rággií   [mujaahidiínta   ahaá]
    rag-gii   mujaahidiin=ta   ah-aa
    men-K.RDEF   mujaahidiin=T.DEF   be-PST.RED
    'the mujahideen'

However, when 'be' is involved in the formation of a hybrid verb in a relative clause, the verb is further truncated by the loss of the verb stem *ah*. This is illustrated in (63) which has the corresponding truncated form of 'be,' simply *aa*, when in a hybrid verb.

(63) nín [wanaagsánaá]
    nin wanaag-s-an-∅-aa
    man good-WCAUS-STV-be-PST.RED
    'a good man'

This behavior in the Simple Past serves as an important basis of comparison to what occurs in the Simple Present. In a subject relative clause with a nominal complement, there is a single truncated form of the verb *ah*, as in (64).

(64) nín [mas'úul áh]
nin mas'uul ah
man responsible be.PRES.RED
'a responsible man'

As suggested by Saeed (1988), and elsewhere since, one way to explain the absence of *ah* that occurs when the relative clause contains a hybrid verb, as in (65), is to draw a parallel to the truncation (i.e., loss) of the verb stem seen above in (63) under similar circumstances.

(65) nín [wanaagsán]
nin wanaag-s-an-∅
man good-WCAUS-STV-be.PRES.RED
'a good man'

Relative clause hybrid verbs inflect for negation via the suffix *-aýn*, as in (66).

(66) xafiiska [aán qabowaýn]
xafiis=ka aan qab-ow-ay-n
office=K.DEF NEG cold-INCH-be-NEG
'the non-cool office'

Subject marking on these relative clauses is via the addition of *-i* and H tone loss on the relative clause verb. The exception to this, however, is found in the Simple Present, where the subject marking is realized directly on the adjectival participle due to *ah* truncation. This is seen in (67).

(67) baabúurka [jaban]i
baabuur=ka jab-an-∅=i
truck=K.DEF broken-STV-be.PRES.RED=SUBJ
'the broken truck'

An adjectival participle can also be partially reduplicated in these constructions, as in *baabuuráda jajabán* 'the broken trucks.' Saeed (1999) states that partial reduplication of this type is aligned with plurality of the noun being modified. This has been called into question by Lampitelli (2015) who instead shows that reduplication of an adjectival participle is not obligatory when modifying a plural noun. For example, *baabuuráda jabán* would be perfectly grammatical without partial reduplication. I have also found that a partially reduplicated adjectival participle can modify a singular noun in order to emphasize and/or compare one noun to another. For example, the phrase *baabúurka jajabán* 'the broken truck,' containing a singular noun and reduplicated adjectival participle, is licit and can be used by a speaker to express the comparative brokenness between the truck being referenced and perhaps another broken truck beside it.

14.1.7 Indirect counting

An attributive relative clause is used to count nouns indirectly. Indirect counting involves a subject relative clause whose head is a numeric or quantifier. The counted noun is the nominal complement of the relative clause verb *áh*.

(68) *shán [géel áh]*
      five   camel be.PRES.RED
      'five camels'

(69) *xabbád [liín áh]*
      piece   orange be.PRES.RED
      'a piece of an orange'

Recall that direct counting typically applies to count nouns. A numeric at the head of a noun phrase is followed by the noun being counted and the two form an associative construction.

14.2 Complement clauses

Chapter 13 showed that Somali displays different syntax in the construction of its various subordinate clauses. There is a major division between the behavior of relative clauses (specifically subject relative clauses) vs. other dependent clauses. With the characteristics of relative clauses having been covered above, the remainder of this chapter is devoted to discussing the properties of complement clauses and adverbial clauses introduced by a subordinator.

Complement clauses are dependent clauses that function as an argument of a main clause verb. In this way, they differ from relative clauses, which instead modify a noun phrase within the main clause. Somali complement clauses are finite clauses and are identifiable by the presence of an obligatory complementizer, *ín*. Somali also has "infinitival complements," but these are distinct from complement clauses. Infinitival complements are non-finite clauses that are often translated like complement clauses but are formally different from them. They are selected by a closed set of verbs and do not require the *ín* complementizer. They are discussed separately in §7.4.

Complement clauses share several properties with other Somali subordinate clauses, including relative clauses. One of these shared properties is that no focus or clause type particle appears within them. Subordinate clause verbs are typically toned and some require irrealis paradigm inflection. An exception to this is when the clause functions as a non-focused subject of the main clause verb, which instead requires a toneless and realis inflection. Complement clauses bear a close resemblance to object relative clauses in this regard. They have indeed been analyzed by scholars like Antinucci et al. (1980), Lecarme (1984), and Saeed (1999) as being historically derived from object relative clauses on the head noun *ín* meaning 'part, amount, piece,' with this noun having since been grammaticalized as a complementizer. Such a perspective helps to explain certain particulars about them, such as their requirement for full agreement, the presence of H tone on their verbs, the possibility of irrealis paradigm inflection, and the ability for a subject pronoun clitic to appear within the complement clause itself. Recall that subject relative clauses instead require reduced agreement on their verbs and disallow subject pronoun clitics. Morphological subject marking is also found within complement clauses, just as it is in an object relative clause. Such marking is absent from subject relative clauses.

Some of these basic characteristics can be seen in (70) where the complement clause is the direct object of the main clause verb *rabaa* 'I want.' The complement clause verb takes the irrealis paradigm inflection with full agreement and its subject is expressed pronominally by a subject pronoun clitic that clusters with the complementizer. This example also shows that, due to their "weight," complement clauses are often, but not always, placed into focus by the post-verbal focus marker.

(70)   Wáxaan   rabaa   [ínaan   baakádán   ú diró
       wax=aan rab-∅-aa   in=aan   baaka-dan   u dir-o
       FOC=1SG want-1SG-PRES   COMP=1SG package-T.this to send-PRES.IRR
       Roóma].
       Rooma
       Rome
       'I want to send this package to Rome.' (Z & O: 37)

Example (71) shows that it is also possible for complement clause to be placed into focus by a pre-verbal focus marker.

(71)   [Ínaan   cabbeý],   báad   aragtey.
       in=aan   cabb-∅-ey   b=aad   arag-t-ey
       COMP=1SG   drink-1SG-PST   FOC=2SG   see-2SG-PST
       'That I drank is what you saw.' (Z & I: 163)

The examples thus far have shown that the complementizer may cluster with a subject pronoun clitic. The various combinations are given in (72).

(72) ín + subject pronoun clitic

ín=aan	ínaan	1SG (~ 1PL)
ín=aad	ínaad	2SG (~ 2PL)
ín=uu	ínuu	3SG.M/K
ín=ay	ínay ~ íney	3SG.F/T
ín=aannu	ínaannu	1PL.exc
ín=aynu	ínaynu ~ íneynu	1PL.inc
ín=aydin	ínaydin ~ íneydin	2PL
ín=ay	ínay ~ íney	3PL

When a subject noun phrase is present with the complement clause, it may intervene between the complementizer and the subject pronoun clitic, as in (73), or it may instead follow the SPC, as in (74).

(73) [ín dadáalkií Dawládda Soomaaliyeéd ay soó
in dadaal-kii dawlad=da Soomaaliy-eed ay soo
COMP effort-K.RDEF government-T.DEF Somali-ASSOC 3SG.T VEN
gashaý]
gash-ay
be.achieved.3SG.F-PST
'that the efforts of the Somali government have been achieved'
(somali-youth.org: 45)

(74) Wáan hubaa [ínay tártan isu dhów
w=aan hub-∅-aa in=ay tar-tan isu dhow
DEC=1SG be.sure-1SG-PRES COMP=3SG.T race-T.that RRP nearby
noqóneysó].
noqon-ey-s-o
become-PROG-3SG.T-IRR
'I am sure that the race's outcome will be close.' (Z & O: 626)

Similar to object relative clauses, however, the subject pronoun clitic need not be present as long as the complement clause subject is otherwise expressed. This is seen, for example, in (75).

(75) [ín xafiisku ká dheeraadó xisbinimáda]
in xafiis=k=u ka dheer-aad-o xisbinima=da
COMP office=K.DEF=SUBJ from be.distant-INCH-IRR party=T.DEF
'that the office must maintain a distance from the party.' (radiosomaliland: 29)

A complement clause in its entirety can function as the subject of the main clause. In such instances, it may be placed into subject focus. Just as in other instances of subject focus, and as shown in (76), this entails reduced agreement on the main clause verb, the absence of a subject pronoun clitic in the main clause, and that the main clause subject (here, the complement clause itself) does not bear morphological subject marking.

(76) Wáxaa waájib nagú áh [ínaan macrakáda ú
waxaa waajib na=gu ah in=aan macraka=da u
FOC duty 1PL.OBJ=for be.PRES.RED COMP=1PL battle=T.DEF to
rarnó gudáha dhúlka cadowgá].
rarn-n-o guda=ha dhul=ka cadow=ga
move-1PL-IRR inside=K.DEF land=K.DEF enemy=K.DEF
'That we move the battle into the land of the enemy is our duty.'
(radioandalus24: 362)

When a complement clause is the main clause subject, but not in focus, it can be subject marked and will be toneless and inflected for the realis paradigm. This is seen in (77) for both the main clause and complement clause verbs. This example also shows that a subject pronoun referring to a complement clause will take 3SG T-series agreement.

(77) Aníga sharáf báy ií tahay [ínaad imtixáanka
aniga sharaf b=ay i=i t-ah-ay in=aad imtixaan=ka
1SG honor FOC=3SG.T 1SG.OBJ=for 3SG.T-be-PRES COMP=2PL exam=K.DEF
wada baastaan].
wada baas-t-aa-n
all pass-2-PRES-PL
'It is an honor for me that you passed your exam.' (somaliland.org: 240246)

Like other subordinate clauses, negation must entail a negatively inflected verb and also typically requires the negative marker *aán*. When a subject pronoun clitic is not present within the complement clause, the negative marker and complementizer join one another, yielding *ínaán*, as seen in (78).

(78) [Ínaán xafíiska sigáar lagú cabbín] báa la
in-aan xafiis=ka sigaar la=gu cabb-in baa la
COMP-NEG office=K.DEF cigarette ISP=in drink-PRES.NEG FOC ISP
sheegay.
sheeg-ay
say-PST.RED
'It was stated that cigarettes are not to be smoked in the office.'
(Z & I: 379)

A subject pronoun clitic can also join a cluster of complementizer + negative marker. When this occurs, the subject pronoun will either be flanked by *ín...aán*, as in (79), or instead will be last in sequence, as in (80).

(79) *ín + subject pronoun clitic + aán*

ín=aan=aán	ínaanán	1SG (~ 1PL)
ín=aad=aán	ínaadán	2SG (~ 2PL)
ín=uu=aán	ínuusán	3SG.M/K
ín=ay=aán	ínayán/ínaysán ~ íneyán/íneysán	3SG.F/T
ín=aanu=aán	ínaannaán	1PL.exc
ín=aynu=aán	ínaynán ~ íneynán	1PL.inc
ín=aydin=aán	ínaydnán ~ íneydnán	2PL
ín=ay=aán	ínayán ~ íneyán	3PL

(80) *ín + aán + subject pronoun clitic*

ín-aán=aan	ínaánan	1SG (~ 1PL)
ín-aán=aad	ínaádan	2SG (~ 2PL)
ín-aán=uu	ínaánu	3SG.M/K
ín-aán=ay	ínaánay ~ ínaáney	3SG.F/T
ín-aán=aanu	ínaánnu	1PL.exc
ín-aán=aynu	ínaánayn ~ ínaáneyn	1PL.inc
ín-aán=aydin	ínaánayd ~ ínaáneyd	2PL
ín-aán=ay	ínaánay ~ ínaáney	3PL

Such clusters are shown in context in the following sentences. An *ín + SPC + aán* sequence is in (81), while the opposing order *ín + aán + SPC* is shown in (82).

(81) *Wáan ogay [ínuusán bíxi laháyn].*
w=aan og-∅-ay in=uu=aan bix-i lah-ayn
DEC=1SG know-1SG-PST COMP=3SG.M=NEG leave-INF have-PST.NEG
'I knew that he would not leave.'

(82) *Reeráha deegamádaás wáxaan fárayaa*
reer-a=ha deegam-a-daas wax=aan far-ay-∅-aa
family-PL=K.DEF community-PL-T.that FOC=1SG advise-PROG-1SG-PRES
[ínaánay wáxba samaynín].
in-aan=ay wax=ba sam-ayn-in
COMP-NEG=3PL thing=INT do-FACT-PST.NEG
'Families in that community, I am advising them to do nothing at all.'
(daadmadheedhnews.net: 13056)

14.3 Subordinating adverbial clauses

The adverbial clauses discussed below are formed by subordinate clauses, be they relative clauses or complement clauses. In some instances, adverbial clauses are formed by an object relative clause whose head noun has come to be grammaticalized as an adverb. For example, there are temporal adverbial clauses meaning 'when' that are constructed on the head *márka* 'the time.' Likewise, there are locative adverbial clauses meaning 'where' constructed on the head *xágga* 'the place.' There are other instances in which adverbial clauses with different functions are formed via a nonrestrictive relative clause introduced by the relativizer *oo*. Still others are more complex in that they are formed by complement clauses or otherwise entail an idiomatic phrase that has come to function adverbially. For example, *wáx kasta*, literally meaning 'each thing,' has also come to mean 'no matter what.'

In the sub-sections that follow, adverbial clauses are divided into five categories based on their function. These categories are time, purpose and/or reason, concession and condition, manner, and location. The aim has been to include examples and discussion concerning more commonly encountered adverbials. Due to the sheer diversity of these clauses and their construction, however, it would be impossible for this to be an exhaustive list. Also, because these adverbial clauses are formally subordinate clauses, they exhibit the same characteristics as those already described for relative clauses and complement clauses, depending on the particular way that they function within the main clause. The reader should consult sections above that are devoted to a particular subordinate clause type for more details on matters pertaining to verb inflection, subject marking, and the presence vs. absence of a subject pronoun clitic within the subordinate clause.

14.3.1 Time

Two of the most common temporal adverbial clauses are those derived from the nouns *már* 'time' and *ín* 'extent.' A simple example is in (83) where *márka* introduces an adverbial clause. As is common in such clauses, the adverbial is the head noun and functions formally as the oblique object of the relative clause verb. The head noun functions as an adverbial meaning 'when,' but one might translate the clause literally as 'the time at which a person writes something.'

(83) *Márka [qófi   wáx   qoró]...*
    marka qof=i   wax   qor-o
    when person=SUBJ thing write-IRR
    'When someone writes something...'

It is often the case that a pronominal subject expressed by a subject pronoun clitic will coalesce with the adverbial. This is seen in (84) where the adverbial *márka* is joined by the third person singular masculine subject pronoun clitic.

(84) *Márk[uu   ogaadaý]   ínuu*
     mark=uu   oga-a-d-ay   in=uu
     when=3SG.M know-MID-3SG.M-PST   COMP=3SG.M
     raystaý...
     ray-s-t-∅-ay
     succeed-WCAUS-MID-3SG.M-PST
     'When he realized that he had succeeded...'

Further subtleties can be added to temporal adverbials via the addition of other adverbials like *islá*, which might be translated as 'as soon as,' 'immediately,' or 'just now' (85), *káddib* (sometimes *ká dib* 'from the back'), meaning 'after' or 'next' (86), or relatedly *ká hór* ('from the front,' sometimes written *kahor*), meaning 'before' or 'ago' (87). Many others are also possible.

(85) *Islá   márkií [aad xúkunka   qabataý]...*
     isla   markii aad xukun=ka   qab-a-t-ay
     as.soon.as when   2SG control=K.DEF seize-MID-2SG-PST
     'As soon as you take control...' (muqdisho24.net: 12563)

(86) *káddib márkií [lagá   xiraý   xudduúdda   Jabuutí]*
     kaddib markii la=ga   xir-∅-ay   xudduud-da   Jabuuti
     after when   ISP=at detain-3SG.M-PST border=T.DEF Djibouti
     'after having been detained at the border with Djibouti' (allgalgaduud.com: 546)

(87) *ká   hór   márkií [uu   madaxweynáha   dálka*
     ka   hor   markii uu   madaxweyna=ha   dal=ka
     from before when   3SG.M president=K.DEF   country=K.DEF
     Túrkigu   gaadhaý]
     Turki=g=u   gaadh-∅-ay
     Turkey=K.DEF=SUBJ   arrive-3SG.M-PST
     'before the President of (the country of) Turkey arrived'
     (jubbalandnews.net: 6552)

There are closely related adverbial clauses formed on nouns such as *wáa* 'time' (88), *kól* 'instance, occasion' (89), and *xílli* 'season' (90).

(88) wáagií [aán caruúrta   ahaýn]
     waagii aan caruur=ta   ah-ayn
     when   NEG children=T.DEF be-NEG.PST
     'back when there were no children' (isbadaldoon.org: 44939)

(89) kólkií [ay   sugéeysaý]
     kolkii ay   sug-eey-s-ay
     while 3SG.F wait.FACT-3SG.F-PST
     'while she was waiting'

(90) xílli [ay   ká soó ráynayó   xaaládda]
     xilli ay   ka soo rayn-ay-o   xaalad=da
     while 3SG.T in VEN improve-PROG-IRR   situation=T.DEF
     'while they are improving the situation' (bbc.com: 451)

Other temporal adverbial clauses are formed on the noun *ín*, which is perhaps best translated as 'extent' in these instances, where 'extent' refers to time. Here, 'the extent that' functions adverbially, meaning 'when,' 'as,' 'since,' or 'while,' as in (91) through (93).

(91) ínt[aan   ká   bogsánayó]
     int=aan   ka   bog-s-an-ay-o
     while=1SG from recover-WCAUS-MID-PROG-IRR
     'while I am recovering from it' (Z & O: 69)

(92) íntií [aan ú wadnaý   isbitáalka]
     intii aan u wad-n-ay   isbitaal=ka
     while 1PL to carry-1PL-PST   hospital=K.DEF
     'as we carried him to the hospital'

(93) Ínt[aán   Cábdi imán]   an qadéynno.
     int-aan   Cabdi im-an   an qadeyn-no
     since-NEG Cabdi come-PRES.NEG   1PL have.lunch-1PL.OPT
     'Since Cabdi hasn't come, let's have lunch.' (Z & O: 331)

Another strategy for forming temporal adverbial clauses involves the creation of a non-restrictive relative clause with the relativizer *oo*. The basic properties of these relative clause are discussed in §14.1.4. This relativizer helps to establish a temporal relationship between two successive clauses, often being translated as 'while,' 'as,' or 'during.' Because these are subject relative clauses, they abide by different requirements than do the adverbial clauses formed by object relative clauses discussed above. Examples in context are in (94) and (95).

(94) *Aníg[oo   hurdá]   ayáa la xaday   lacágtii.*
     ani=g=oo   hurd-a   ayaa la xad-∅-ay   lacag-tii
     I=K.DEF=REL be.asleep-PRES.RED FOC ISP steal-3SG.M-PST money-T.RDEF
     'While I was asleep, the money was stolen.' (Z & O: 22)

(95) *Iság[oón   joogín]   báa baabúurkií lagá   soó*
     isa=g=oo=n   joog-in   baa baabuur-kii la=ga   soo
     he=K.DEF=REL=NEG stop-PST.NEG FOC car-K.RDEF ISP=from VEN
     qaadey.
     qaad-∅-ey
     take-3SG.M-PST
     'While he was not there, the car was taken from him.' (Z & O: 333)

The Arabic borrowing, *ilaá* 'until, since,' can sometimes be involved in subordination, but it also functions simply as a coordinating adverbial. See §15.5.

(96) *ilaá [uu   kú geeriyoodaý   dagáal]*
     ilaa uu   ku geeri-ood-∅-ay   dagaal
     until 3SG.M in die-EXP-3SG.M-PST fight
     'until he died in a fight'

14.3.2 Purpose and reason

Strategies for forming adverbial clauses that express purpose and reason can also be divided into different groups. Three adverbial clauses discussed in this section are formed by object relative clauses with no relativizer. Another type is formed by conjoining two clauses with *oo*. Two additional types involve complement clauses introduced by the complementizer *ín*.

Some adverbial clauses that express purpose and/or reason are built upon the head *sabábta* 'the reason.' These are often translated as 'because' or 'why' but would more literally be rendered 'the reason that' (97).

(97) *Máxay   tahay   sabábta [aad sídan   ugú*
     m=ax=ay   t-ah-ay   sabata aad si-dan   u-gu
     QM=FOC=3SG.T 3SG.T-be.PRES reason   2SG way-T.this for-in
     códaysaý]?
     cod-ay-s-ay
     vote-PROG-2SG-PST
     'Why are you voting on it this way?'

Purpose/reason adverbials are also built on the noun *sí* 'way, manner, method' followed by the adposition *ú*. The combination yields an adverbial clause meaning 'in order to,' 'since,' or 'so that.'

(98) *Sí   [aanán   ú   karsanín   cúnto], makhaayád báanu   tagney.*
     si   aan=an   u   karsan-in   cunto   makhaayad b=aanu tag-n-ey
     since 1PL=NEG for cook-PRES.NEG   food   restaurant FOC=1PL go-1PL-PST

   'Since we couldn't cook for ourselves, we went to a restaurant.' (Z & I: 252)

(99) *Sí   [uu   ú   yimaaddó]   waan   ú yeérayaa.*
     si   uu   u   y-imaad-do   w=aan u yeer-ay-∅-aa
     so.that 3SG with 3SG.M-come-IRR   DEC=1SG to call-PROG-1SG-PRES

   'I'm going to call (to) him so that he comes.' (Z & O: 712)

Another way to form purpose/reason adverbial is to join two clauses with *oo* such that a cause and effect relationship is established between them. Such conjunctions are translated as 'because,' 'so that,' or 'in order to.' This can be seen, for example, in sentence (100).

(100) *Súuqa   báan   tágayaa   oo hílib geél báan   soó*
      suuq=a   b=aan   tag-ay-∅-aa   oo hilib geel b=aan   soo
      market=K.DEF   FOC=1SG   go-PROG-1SG-PRES   SUB meat camel FOC=1SG   VEN
      iibínayaa.
      iib-in-ay-∅-aa
      buy-WCAUS-PROG-1SG-PRES

   'I am going to the market in order to buy camel meat.'

As discussed in §15.3, clausal conjunctions via *oo* have much in common with the formation of non-restrictive relative clauses. Though such conjunctions join two full clauses, they involve an element that is shared between both clauses upon which the latter clause is relativized. For example, in the case of (100), the shared element is *súuqa* 'the market.' As such, one might alternatively translate this example as 'I am going to the market at which I am going to buy camel meat.' Section 14.1.4 showed that non-restrictive relative clauses can be located at a distance from their head. Another example of this is in (101), where the shared element is the pronominal oblique object in the first clause and the subject of the second clause. An alternative translation would be 'Nothing is asked of us, the ones who are crazy.'

(101) *Wáx nalamá   weyddiiyó   oo   wáan   wada*
      wax na=la=ma   weyd-dii-yo   oo   w=aan   wada
      thing 1PL.OBJ=ISP=NEG ask-FACT-IRR   SUB DEC=1PL together
      waalánnahay.
      waal-an-n-ah-ay
      crazy-STV-1PL-be-PRES
      'Nothing is asked of us because we are crazy.' (Z & O: 671)

Also possible are adverbial clauses involving complement clauses. The first type, shown in (102), involves a complement clause focused by the post-verbal focus marker. The complement clause is governed by the adposition *ú* within the main clause Verb Complex. These are translated either as 'in order to' or 'so that.'

(102) *Bálse wáxaan ú qaaday   ínaan   cabbiró.*
      balse wax=aan u qaad-∅-ay   in=aan   cabbir-o
      just FOC=1SG to take-1SG-PST COMP=1SG measure-IRR
      'I took it in order to measure it.' (dalmarnews.net: 8718)

A related construction formed by *waa...ín* involves a declarative clause whose predicate is a complement clause. These entail a sense of necessity or obligation – 'it is that X' – and are typically translated 'must.'

(103) *Fulíntu   waa ín   ay   xílalkéeda   iyo*
      fulin=t=u   waa in   ay   xil-al-kee=da   iyo
      executive=T.DEF=SUBJ DEC COMP 3SG.T responsibility-PL-its=T.DEF   and
      hawláhéeda   gudataa.
      hawl-a-hee=da   gud-at-∅-aa
      function-PL-its=T.DEF fulfill-MID-3SG.T-PRES
      'The executive must carry out their responsibilities and functions.'
      (dharaaro.com: 145)

14.3.3 Concession and condition

There are, again, a few different strategies for forming concessive and conditional adverbial clauses involving subordination. One of these is via an object relative clause on a noun phrase whose head is *hád* 'moment.' These are often translated as 'if,' 'though,' or 'while,' though they would more literally be translated 'the moment that.'

(104) hádd[aad su'aaló   qabtáan]
      hadd=aad su'aal-o   qab-t-aa-n
      if=2SG   question-PL have-2-IRR-PL
      'if you have questions'

(105) háddii [ay   arríntaasi   dhábtahaý]
      haddii ay   arrin-taas-i   dhab-t-ah-ay
      though 3SG.T matter-T.this=SUBJ true-3SG.T-be.IRR
      'Though these things are true... (ceelwayne.com: 126)

Other variations on *hád* adverbials are *háddii kále* meaning 'otherwise' (i.e., 'another time') and *xatáa háddii* 'even if' (i.e., 'even that time').

(106) háddii kále   [guúl   lamá   gaadhín]
      haddii kale   guul   la=ma gaadh-in
      if   another success ISP=NEG arrive-PRES.NEG
      'otherwise, one would not be successful' (somaliland.org: 27370)

(107) xatáa háddii [aad dharka   dhigató]
      xataa haddii aad   dhar=ka   dhig-at-o
      even if   2SG   clothes=K.DEF put.on-MID-IRR
      'even if you put on your clothes' (somalilandpost: 11910)

Similar to what is described above for temporal adverbial clauses in §14.3.1, concessive and conditional adverbial clauses can also be formed by a non-restrictive subject relative clause introduced by the relativizer *oo*. When followed by a negative main clause, such clauses convey the meaning 'despite,' 'although,' or 'though.'

(108) Aníg[oo   Soomaáli áh],   báanán   kú
      ani=g=oo   Soomaali ah   ba=an-an   ku
      I=K.DEF=although   Somali   be.PRES.RED FOC=1SG-NEG in
      hadlín   af   Soomaáli.
      hadl-in   af   Soomaali
      speak-PRES.NEG language Somali
      'Although I am Somali, I do not speak Somali.' (Z & I: 362)

There are other concessive and conditional adverbial clauses constructed formally by a non-restrictive relative clause headed by the noun phrase *ín kastá*. These have literal meaning of 'every extent' but are best translated as 'no matter what,' 'although,' or 'despite.'

(109) ín   kastá [oo uu   cádowgu   badán yahaý]
       in   kasta oo uu   cadow=g=u   badan y-ah-ay
       extent every REL 3SG.K cadow=K.DEF=SUBJ many 3SG.K-be-PRES
       'although the enemy is large' (somalilandpatriots.com: 387)

The noun *ín* is also involved in a more complex and formulaic concessive adverbial, *ín…iyo ín kále* meaning 'whether or not.' This involves two conjoined relative clauses. The first expresses one option, and the second expresses the other with *ín kále*. The two are joined by *iyo* 'and.' Under this view, the sentence in (110) might instead be translated: 'I don't know the extent to which he comes and the extent of the other.'

(110) Ma ogí   ínuu   imánayó   iyo ín   kále.
       ma og-i   in=uu   iman-ay-o   iyo in   kale
       NEG know-PRES.NEG COMP=3SG.M come-PROG-IRR   and extent other
       'I don't know whether he is coming or not.' (Z & I: 329)

14.3.4 Manner

Many manner adverbials can be formed by a subject relative clause whose head is the noun *sí* 'way, manner.' The basic structure of these clauses is *sí…(áh)* where a noun, adjective, or adjectival participle intervenes between the head noun and the verb 'be.' Of course, it is important to bear in mind that this irregular verb is omitted in a subject relative clause when its complement is an adjective or adjectival participle. The possibilities are abundant for adverbial clauses formed in this way. For example, in (111), the adverbial *sí fudúd* 'easily' could be translated more literally as 'an easy way.'

(111) Sí [fudúd] báad   ú saméeysey.
       si fudud   b=aad   u sam-eey-s-ey
       way easy   FOC=2SG in do-FACT-2SG-PST
       'You did it easily.'

Other adverbials formed in this way include: *sí áad áh* 'a lot' (i.e., 'a way that is much'), *sí gáar áh* 'especially' (i.e., 'a way that is special'), *sí wálba* 'anyhow' (i.e., 'in any way'), and *sí kastá* 'somehow' (i.e., 'in every way'). There is also a more formulaic manner adverbial, *wáx kastá* 'whatever' (i.e., 'every thing'), that often functions as the head of a non-restrictive relative clause, as in (112).

(112) Wáx kastá oo uu saméeyába, wáxay isu
 wax kasta oo uu sam-ee-y-a=ba wax=ay isu
 thing every REL 3SG.M do-FACT-3SG.M-PST.RED=INT FOC=3PL RRP
 rógi xumaan.
 rog-i xum-∅-aa-n
 turn.out-INF be.bad-3-PRES-PL
 'Whatever he does, it turns out badly.' (Z & O: 377)

14.3.5 Location

Location adverbials involving subordination are also formed with an object relative clause. One type is formed on the noun *meél* 'place' and has the adverbial meaning 'wherever.' In (113), one could interpret the clause alternative as 'the place that you want to go.' The adverbial can be intensified, as in (114), becoming *meél wálba* meaning 'everywhere' or 'anywhere.' Another in this group is *meélna* 'nowhere.'

(113) meésh[aad doontó] ká socó]
 meesh=aad doon-t-o ka soc-o
 place=2SG want-2SG-IRR to proceed-IMP
 'go wherever you want'

(114) meél wálba [oo uu joogó]
 meel wal=ba oo uu joog-o
 place any=INT REL 3SG.M stop-IRR
 'anywhere he ends up'

15 Coordination and other adverbials

Earlier chapters have discussed the construction of noun phrases and the Verb Complex, as well as more complex clause level constituents (relative clauses, complement clauses, etc.) that involve subordination of different types. In this chapter, attention is turned to the ways that Somali coordinates these constituents. The chapter is divided into sections based on the type of coordinating element involved. Coordination can involve a coordinating conjunction, clitic, adverbial, or one of two coordinating particles *oo* and *ee* that play a role specifically in clausal coordination. Adverbials of different types are later discussed that involve neither subordination nor are necessarily implicated in coordination. This chapter closes by covering the formation of comparatives and superlatives.

15.1 Coordination with coordinators

This section deals with the coordination of constituents with coordinators. I use the term coordinator here in a general sense to describe a class of particles that function to join two phrasal or clausal constituents. Within this class, Somali has one conjunction particle *iyo* 'and' and two disjunction particles, *ama* and *misé*, both of which mean 'or,' but are used to join constituents under different circumstances. Last in this group is the contrastive coordinator *laakíin* 'but.'

15.1.1 Conjunction with *iyo*

The coordinating conjunction *iyo* has widespread use. Though other resources have stated that *iyo* functions only to join nominals (i.e., nouns and noun phrases), the examples in this section show that its use is much broader. Beginning with these simpler and better known uses, (1) shows the coordination of two bare nouns.

(1) Sáynab waa hoóyo dhashay   wíil iyo gabádh.
Saynab waa hooyo dhash-∅-ay   wiil iyo gabadh
Saynab DEC mother give.birth.to-2SG-PST boy and girl
'Saynab is the mother of a son and a daughter.' (weedhsan.com: 1)

In a similar manner, *iyo* joins two numeric nouns in forming complex numbers: *saddéx iyo labaátan* ('three and twenty') is the numeral 23.

In (2), two adjectival nouns modifying the same noun are joined together by *iyo* within an associative construction. If these were relative clauses, one might instead expect coordination via *oo*, as discussed in §15.3.

(2) *míd qurúx iyo macaanbá*
    mid qurux iyo macaan=ba
    one beauty and sweetness=INT
    'a thing of beauty and of sweetness'

The use of *iyo* quickly becomes more complex and extends beyond noun conjunction. For example, in (3), two verbs are conjoined by *iyo* within the same Verb Complex. That they are syntactically within the same VC is clear in that they share the same pronominal direct object.

(3) *Wúu   i   dhuftay   iyo haraatiyey.*
    w=uu   i   dhuf-t-∅-ay   iyo haraat-i-y-ey
    DEC=3SG.M 1SG.OBJ hit-MID-3SG.M-PST and strike-WCAUS-3SG.M-PST
    'He hit and kicked me.'

Example (4) shows two complement clauses, each introduced by the complementizer *ín*, that are conjoined by *iyo*. The connection between them is clear in that each has the same subject, referred to by the subject pronoun clitic *ay*.

(4) *ín[ay   heshó   kuwó   cusúb] iyo ín[ay   gácan kú*
    in=ay   hesh-o   ku-wo   cusub iyo in=ay   gacan ku
    COMP=3SG.F find-IRR one-PL new   and COMP=3SG.F   hand to
    siisó]
    sii-s-o
    give-WCAUS-IRR
    'that they find new ones and that they give them a hand' (wakaalada.com: 37)

The sentence in (5) shows conjoined non-restrictive relative clauses on the head *taasi* 'this (one).' Their bounds are indicated with square brackets. That the head of the second relative clause is the same as the first is clear from agreement on its verb, which is 3SG.F and reduced, as expected of a subject relative clause. These form a coordinate structure involving two clauses under one larger relative clause. As illustrated below in §15.3, other instances of clause level coordination involving non-restrictive relative clauses require each relative in sequence to be subordinated by its own relativizer.

(5) Taasi   [oo [werwér   badán] iyo [kugú   keéni   kartá]]
    taas=i   oo wer-wer   badan iyo ku=gu   keen-i   kar-t-a
    this=SUBJ REL Red-stress very   and 2SG.OBJ=to bring-INF be.able-2SG-RED
    daýn aánad   awoódi   karín.
    dayn aan=ad   awood-i   kar-in
    debt NEG=2SG   afford-INF be.able-PRES.NEG
    'This (which) can be very stressful and (which) can lead to debt you cannot afford.' (somalifashionista.com: 12)

Though a more exhaustive study may lead to further combinations of constituents joined by *iyo*, what should be clear here is that this coordinator is of more general use than previously reported in the literature. Saeed (1999), for example, describes *iyo* as being used only to join two "nominals." It is shown here, rather, that *iyo* has the ability to conjoin constituents of a variety of types provided that the constituents being conjoined are of the same type. While *iyo* can coordinate two relative clauses, this only occurs when the two are conjoined by a single relativizer within some larger constituent (e.g., two IPs within a CP). As illustrated in §15.3, when relative clauses are not embedded in such a way (e.g., as adjacent CPs), they are instead conjoined via *oo* or *ee*, the choice of which depends on the properties of the head being modified.

It is often stated that when multiple conjuncts are joined, *iyo* occurs only once, and specifically between the final two conjuncts. While there are certainly many cases in which this is true, as in (6), it is not ungrammatical for *iyo* to appear more than once, in between each conjunct, as in (7).

(6) sída   Rwanda, Uganda, iyo Ethiopia
    sida   Rwanda Uganda iyo Ethiopia
    such.as   Rwanda Uganda and Ethiopia
    'such as Rwanda, Uganda, and Ethiopia'

(7) Somaliland iyo dawládda   iyo dádkéeda
    Somaliland iyo dawlad=da   iyo dad-keed=da
    Somaliland and government=T.DEF   and people-K.its=T.DEF
    'Somaliland and the government and its people'

15.1.2 Disjunction with *ama*

Disjunctive coordination with *ama* is productive, having few apparent limitations on the types of conjuncts that it can conjoin. A number of possibilities are provided below, but, once again, this is not an exhaustive list. In the simplest of instances, it can join two nouns (8) or two morphologically simplex verbs (9).

(8) *guúsha   ama gúuldarráda*
    guush=a   ama guuldarra=da
    success=T.DEF or   failure=T.DEF
    'success or failure'

(9) *Tág ama jóog!*
    tag ama joog
    go   or stay
    'Go or stay!'

This coordinator also joins two verbs within the same Verb Complex. In (10), for example, both verbs share and are inflected for agreement with the same subject. A similar situation is found in (11) where the Verb Complex is instead formed by two phrasal verbs.

(10) *Hál márna   miyúu   tilmaamay   ama*
     hal mar=na   m=iy=uu   tilmaam-∅-ay   ama
     one time=CONJ QM=FOC=3SG.M point.out-3SG.M-PST or
     muujiyey   ín...
     muuj-i-y-ey   in
     demonstrate-WCAUS-3SG.M-PST COMP
     'Has he ever pointed out or demonstrated that...' (somalilandpost.net: 413)

(11) *Wasíirka   ayáa kú   tiraabaý   ama kú   qayliyaý...*
     wasiir=ka   ayaa ku   tiraab-ay   ama ku   qayl-iy-ay
     minister=K.DEF FOC about speak-PST.RED or about shout-WCAUS-PST.RED
     'The minister spoke about or shouted about...' (camuudnews.net: 9197)

The disjunctive coordinator is also used to conjoin successive complement clauses (12) and main clauses of different types. In (13), for example, *ama* joins an affirmative declarative clause with *waa* to a negative declarative clause with *má*.

(12) *ínuu   dhismáhaasi   waaró   ama ín   bádan*
     in=uu   dhisma-haas=i   waar-o   ama in   badan
     COMP=3SG.K building-K.that=SUBJ be.permanent-IRR or   COMP long
     taagnaadó
     taag-n-aad-o
     erect-STV-INCH-IRR
     'that that building is permanent, or that it is long standing'

(13) *Waan   imán   doonaa   ama máan   imán   doonó.*
    w=aan   im-an   doon-∅-aa   ama m=aan   im-an   doon-o
    DEC=1SG come-INF FUT-1SG-PRES or   NEG=1SG come-INF FUT-IRR
    'I will come, or I won't come.' (Z & I: 341)

Clauses of the same type and polarity can also be joined by *ama* (14), with a special case being those conjoined by *ama waa...ama waa* meaning 'either...or,' as shown in (15).

(14) *Hawádu   waa qabów ama waa kuláyl.*
    hawa=d=u   waa qabow ama waa kulayl
    weather=T.DEF=SUBJ DEC cold   or   DEC hot
    'The weather is cold, or it is hot.' (Z & I: 341)

(15) *Ama wuu   keéni   doonaa   ama wuu   soó díri.*
    ama wuu   keen-i   doon-∅-aa   ama w=uu   soo dir-i
    either DEC=3SG.M bring-INF FUT-3SG.M-PRES or DEC=3SG.M VEN send-INF
    'Either he will bring it or send it.'

Two relative clauses can also be joined disjunctively with *ama*. In (16), this is seen with two object relative clauses on *ímmisa*.

(16) *ímmisa   asxaábta   áh   ama eheláda   áh*
    immisa   asxaab=ta   ah   ama ehel-a=da   ah
    how.many friends=T.DEF be.PRES.RED or   relative-PL=T.DEF be.PRES.RED
    'how many friends or relatives' (qarninews.net: 11164)

Similar to what occurs for conjunctions with *iyo*, disjunctive coordination with *ama* can be between the final two elements being conjoined, as in (17). However, it is also possible for *ama* to appear between each element, as in (18).

(17) *shílalka   gurigá,   shaqadá,   ama márkii lá   wadó*
    shil-al=ka   guri=ga   shaqa=da   ama markii la   wad-o
    accident-PL=K.DEF house=K.DEF work=T.DEF or   while with drive-IRR
    gaáriga
    gaari=ga
    car=K.DEF
    'accidents at home, at work, or while driving' (galmudugnews.net: 604)

(18) ama Báwlos, ama Abólloos, ama dunída
 ama Bawlos ama Abolloos ama duni=da
 or Paul or Apollo or world=T.DEF

'either Paul, or Apollo, or the world' (codkanoloshacusub.info: 731)

15.1.3 Contrastive conjunction with *laakíin*

The contrastive conjunction *laakíin* 'but' is borrowed from Arabic. It is more limited in its distribution than the other coordinators discussed thus far in this section. It is used to join two clauses in contrast with one another, though it need not do so directly. In (19), *laakíin* joins two clauses with the same subject that contrast in polarity.

(19) Wuu   shaqéysan   jiray   laakíin hádda ma
 w=uu   shaq-eys-an   jir-∅-ay   laakiin hadda ma
 DEC=3SG.M do.work-FACT-INF used.to-3SG.M-PST but   now   NEG
 léh   sháqo.
 leh   shaqo
 have.PRES.RED work

'He used to work, but now (he) has no job.' (hablaha.com: 313)

Example (20) instead shows two contrastively conjoined clauses with different subjects. Sentences like this show that a difference in polarity is not always necessary with *laakíin*. Lastly, (21) shows *laakíin* can begin an independent clause, but one that is preceded, either directly or implicitly, by some exophoric proposition against which the contrast can be understood.

(20) Wáanu iskú   baahánahay   laakíin iyágaa nagá
 w=aanu is=ku baah-an-∅-ah-ay   laakiin iyag:aa na=ga
 DEC=1PL RRP=on need-STV-1PL-be-PRES but   they:FOC 1PL.OBJ=for
 baáhi   badán.
 baah-i   badan
 need-INF be.more

'We need one another, but they need us more.' (somalilandpatriots.com: 542)

(21) Laakíin xagáaga   báan   ú   jecéylyahay.
 laakiin xagaa=ga   b=aan u   jeceyl-∅-ah-ay
 but   summer=K.DEF FOC=1SG with like-1SG-be-PRES

'But, summer is my favorite.' (Z & I: 262)

The contrastive coordinator also occurs alongside other adverbials, as in *laakíin wéli* 'but still.'

(22) *Wáan   qadeeyay,   laakíin wéli waan*
    w=aan   qadee-y-ay   laakiin weli w=aan
    DEC=1PL eat.lunch-1SG-PST but   still DEC=1SG
    gaajáysnahay.
    gaaj-ays-n-∅-ah-ay
    hungry-FACT-STV-1SG-be-PRES
    'I have eaten lunch, but I am still hungry.' (Z & I: 342)

15.2 Coordination with clitics

Full clauses can also be conjoined conjunctively with *-na* or disjunctively with *-se*. These are "second position" clitics that obey Wackernagel's Law in that they are typically found at the right edge of the first phrasal constituent in the second of two conjoined clauses. Of course, phrases come in many shapes and sizes. If such a phrase is marked pre-verbally for focus, it is also possible for the clitic to join the focus marker directly, illustrating that a pre-verbal focus marker prosodifies with a preceding noun. If the second clause does not contain a full phrase, however, the clitic can join a function word preceding the Verb Complex.

15.2.1 Conjunction with *-na*

The conjunction clitic *-na* is shown in (23) where it join two clauses, having cliticized onto the noun *cíd* 'someone.' In (24), it cliticizes onto a pre-verbal focus marker when the first phrase in the second clause is in focus. This example and (25) also show that *-na* may co-occur with another coordinating conjunction.

(23) *Kólkaan   barqádií   soó noqday   cídna*
    kolk=aan   barqa-dii   soo noq-d-∅-ay   cid=na
    when=1SG   morning-T.RDEF VEN return-MID-1SG-PST person=CONJ
    meéshií   ugumá   imán.
    meesh-ii   u-gu-ma   im-an
    place-T.RDEF with-to-NEG   come-PST.NEG
    'When I returned in the morning, I did not find anyone there.' (Z & O: 384)

(24) *Maxámed báan   arkey   oo   salaán búuna   kuú*
     Maxamed b=aan   ark-∅-ey   oo   salaan b=uu=na   ku=u
     Maxamed FOC=1SG   see-1SG-PST   CONJ   greeting FOC=3SG.M=CONJ   2SG.OBJ=to
     soó   farey.
     soo   far-∅-PST
     VEN   sent-3SG.M-PST
     'I saw Maxamed, and he sent his greetings to you.' (Z & I: 340)

(25) *Isága   wúu   ku   dhuftay   iyo anígana*
     isa=ga   w=uu   ku   dhuf-t-∅-ay   iyo ani=ga=na
     he=K.DEF DEC=3SG.M 2SG.OBJ hit-MID-3SG.M-PST   and me=K.DEF=CONJ
     wúu   i   haraatiyey.
     w=uu   i   haraat-i-y-ey
     DEC=3SG.M 1SG.OBJ kick-WCAUS-3SG.M-PST
     'He hit you, and he kicked me.'

When the first phrase in the second of two conjoined clauses is complex, such as a noun modified by a relative clause, the conjunction clitic is still found phrase-finally. This is seen in (26), where the clitic joins a relative clause verb.

(26) *sída   uu   maamulúhu   sheégayna*
     sida   uu   maamulu=h=u   sheeg-∅-ay=na
     according.to 3SG.M   manager=K.DEF=SUBJ   say-3SG.M-PST=CONJ
     'and according to what the manager said'

Example (27) shows the same clitic in a situation where there is no noun phrase expressed in the second of two conjoined clauses. Here, *-na* cliticizes onto the declarative clause type marker.

(27) *Nínkii   wáa la fasaxay,   wúuna   baxay.*
     nin-kii   waa la fasax-∅-ay   w=uu=na   bax-∅-ay
     man-K.RDEF DEC ISP released-3SG.M-PST   DEC=3SG.M=CONJ   leave-3SG.M-PST
     'The man was released, and he left.' (salaanmedia.com: 698)

15.2.2 Disjunction with *-se*

The distribution of the disjunction clitic *-se* is analogous to that of *-na*. It can be found at the right edge of the first phrasal constituent in the second of two conjoined clauses. This can be on a simple noun phrase (28), as well as on more complex clusters, including those containing a function word (29).

(28) *Waan   idíin   sheegay   idínkuse   má*
     w=aan   idiin   sheeg-∅-ay idin=k=u=se   ma
     DEC=1SG to.2PL.OBJ tell-1SG-PST 2PL=K.DEF=SUBJ=DISJ NEG
     rumaysnín.
     rumays-nin
     believe-PST.NEG
     'I told you, but you did not believe it.'

(29) *Wuu   ií   sheegay   wáanse   illoóbi*
     w=uu   i=i   sheeg-∅-ay   w=aan=se   illoob-i
     DEC=3SG.M 1SG.OBJ=to say-3SG.M-PST DEC=1SG=DISJ forget-INF
     gaadhay.
     gaadh-∅-ay
     nearly.do-1SG-PST
     'He told me, but I almost forgot.'

The disjunction clitic also co-occurs alongside other coordinators. It joins the contrastive coordinator *laakíin* 'but,' yielding *laakíinse* in (30). This may be simply interpreted as 'or,' but sometimes instead as 'on the other hand.' It can similarly join the disjunctive coordinator *ama* 'or,' becoming *amase*, as in (31). Other disjunctions formed with *-se* include *bálse* 'but first' and *háddii kalése* 'otherwise.'

(30) *laakíinse má   ay   dégi   doonaan*
     laakiin=se ma   ay   deg-i   doon-∅-aa-n
     but=DISJ   NEG 3PL settle.down-INF FUT-3-PRES-PL
     'But, they will not settle down.' (codkanoloshacusub.info: 321)

(31) *Háddii ay   yaraató   amase ay   kú badató*
     haddii ay   yaraa-t-o   ama=se ay   ku bada-t-o
     if   3SG.M decrease-MID-IRR   or=DISJ 3SG.M in increase-MID-IRR
     dhíiga   labáduba   dhíb   wéeye.
     dhiig=a   laba=d=u=ba   dhib   weeye
     blood=K.DEF both=T.DEF=SUBJ=INT trouble DEC
     'If there is too little or too much in the blood, both are a problem.'
     (camuudnews.net: 55329)

The disjunction clitic occurs alongside the question particle *ma* and has become grammaticalized as the disjunctive coordinator *misé* (or *masé*), which is generally found only in forming questions. It can conjoin single words (32), but also larger phrases (33) and independent clauses (34).

(32) *Xaggée báad   doóneysaan,   fóoqa   misé*
     xaggee b=aad   doon-ey-s-aa-n   fooq=a   mise
     where   FOC=2PL want-PROG-2-PRES-PL   upstairs=K.DEF or
     hoósta?
     hoos=ta
     downstairs=T.DEF
     'Where would you like it, upstairs or downtairs?'

(33) *Wáqti horé misé wáqtiga   hádda?*
     waqti hore mise waqti=ga   hadda
     time   past or   time=K.DEF   now
     'Is it the past or present time?'

(34) *Fílimkani   ma kálar báa misé waa madów iyo caddaán?*
     filim-kan=i   ma kalar baa mise waa madow iyo caddaan
     film-K.this=SUBJ QM color FOC or   DEC black   and white
     'Is this film in color or is it in black and white?' (Z & O: 372)

Section 16.4 discusses that *misé* is also involved in the formation of one particular type of tag question: *misé maya?* meaning 'or not.'

15.3 Coordinating relative clauses

Chapter 14 showed that Somali relative clauses behave exceptionally in some ways when compared to other subordinate clauses like complement clauses or those introduced by a subordinating adverbial. This section shows that some of this exceptional behavior can be extended to the coordination of relative clauses. There is a distinction maintained between the coordination of restrictive vs. non-restrictive relative clauses. Recall that non-restrictive relative clauses require the relativizer *oo*, while restrictive relative clauses require no overt relativizer. The sub-sections that follow begin with the comparatively simpler case of coordinated relative clauses of the same type. They then turn to the coordination of restrictive relative clauses, for which there are two strategies that depend on the status of the head noun. It is important to note that the principles described in Chapter 14 concerning relative clauses of different types (i.e., subject vs. object, etc.) and the relationship of their head to the main clause also hold here. Thus, the examples provided in this section focus on coordination, rather than all possible aspects of relative clause behavior.

15.3.1 Non-restrictive coordination with *oo*

Section 14.1.4 showed that non-restrictive relative clauses are introduced by the relativizer *oo*. This requirement is maintained in a series of coordinated non-restrictive relative clauses where each successive relative clause must be introduced by its own relativizer. In this way, Somali signals that each characteristic contributed by the relative clause is not necessary for disambiguating its head.

Example (35) is an excerpt from a website discussing the symptoms of a soy allergy. It contains a sequence of two non-restrictive relative clauses. The first is a subject relative clause and the second is an oblique object relative clause on the same head *daréen yár* '(a) small reaction.' In this context, a reaction to the allergen is discussed. Knowing that there is, in fact, a reaction expected to take place, the additional information provided is about the degree and location of the reaction. Another way to translate this would be: 'a small reaction that is negative, that is from the body.'

(35) *daréen yár [oo diidmó áh]   [oo uu   jídhku   ká*
     dareen ya   oo diidmo ah   oo uu   jidh=k=u   ka
     reaction small REL negative be.PRES.RED REL 3SG.K body=K.DEF=SUBJ from
     bixiyó]
     bixi-yo
     come.out-IRR
     'a small negative reaction from the body' (naaf.no: 25)

Example (36) shows that the same behavior extends to more complex strings containing more than two non-restrictive relative clauses in sequence. Each of the three non-restrictive relative clauses on the same head *labá nín* 'two men' is introduced by *oo*.

(36) *labá nín [oo walaál áh]   [oo iskú áf   áh]   [oo*
     laba nin oo walaal ah   oo is=ku af   ah   oo
     two man REL sibling be.PRES.RED REL RRP=in language be.PRES.RED REL
     iskú   wadán áh]
     is=ku wadan ah
     is=in country be.PRES.RED
     'two men who are brothers, who are (speaking) the same language, who are in the same country' (fposts.com: 113)

Section 15.3.3 shows that it is also possible for a non-restrictive relative clause to modify a head at a distance, namely in the presence of an intervening restrictive relative clause.

15.3.2 Restrictive coordination with *ee*

The basic characteristics of restrictive relative clauses were discussed in §14.1. They differ most noticeably from non-restrictive relative clauses in that they immediately follow their head and do not require a relativizer. This generalization requires a slight adjustment when multiple relative clauses are coordinated, provided that at least one of them is restrictive. In this section, the coordination of multiple restrictive relative clauses is discussed. Focus then turns to sequences in which a restrictive relative clause is followed by a non-restrictive relative clause in §15.3.3. Restrictive relative clauses always come first in such a sequence.

Like when a single restrictive relative clause modifies some head, the first restrictive relative clause in a sequence of multiple restrictive relative clauses modifies its head directly with no relativizer. However, when a restrictive relative clause is followed by another relative clause modifying the same head, there are two possibilities for how they are conjoined, either with *ee* or with *oo*. This choice has elsewhere been said to be predicated on the definiteness of the head noun being modified (Saeed 1993b) or even that the use of *ee* vs. *oo* are optional variants with little difference in meaning (Zorc and Issa 1990). It would seem, however, that the distinction can more accurately be stated as one that is based on the relationship between the proposition entailed by the relative clause and its head, namely one of disambiguation, or restriction vs. non-restriction of reference.

When one restrictive relative clause is joined by one (or more) additional restrictive relative clauses, the latter clause(s) are introduced by the relativizer *ee*. It is shown in §15.3.3 that this can be directly compared to sequences of restrictive + non-restrictive relative clauses where a non-restrictive relative is instead introduced by *oo*.

A simple example like (37) shows that it is certainly the case that two restrictive relative clauses modifying the same "defined" head can be coordinated by *ee*. The first relative clause modifies its head directly with no relativizer, but the second requires *ee*.

(37) *dawládda*   *[federáalka   áh]*   *[ee Soomaaliyá]*
      dawlad=da   federaal=ka   ah   ee Soomaaliya
      government=T.DEF   federal=K.DEF be.PRES.RED REL Somalia
      'the federal government of Somalia'

An example like (38), however, shows that formal definiteness, as indicated by a determiner, is not necessarily a requirement for joining two restrictive relative clauses with *ee*.

(38) *Waa meél [róob badán] [ee qabów].*
waa meel roob badan ee qabow
DEC place rain much REL cold
'It is a place that is rainy and cold.'

When more than two restrictive relative clauses are coordinated on the same head, as in (39), each relative clauses after the first requires its own relativizer, which is once again *ee*.

(39) *ín   aanu xísbiga   [mucaáridka   áh]   [ee ugú adág]*
in   aanu xisbi=ga   mucaarid=ka   ah   ee ugu adag
COMP 1PL party=K.DEF opposition=K.DEF be.PRES.RED REL most strong
[ee hoggaamíya] [ee mustaqbálka] dálkan   ká taliya
ee hoggaamiya ee mustaqbalk=ka dal-kan   ka taliya
REL leading   REL future=K.DEF country-K.this of ruling
noqonó
noqon-ó
become-PRES.IRR
'that we become this country's strongest, leading, future ruling opposition party' (xogdoonnews.com: 4)

15.3.3 Restrictive/Non-restrictive coordination

In a sequence of multiple relative clauses on the same head, restrictives precede non-restrictives. A restrictive relative clause modifies the head directly, with any successive non-restrictive relative clause requiring the relativizer *oo*. A simple example is in (40) where two relative clauses modify *naág* 'woman.' Here, the interpretation is that the fact that the woman is tall is key, with the fact that she is thin being subsidiary from a standpoint of identifying the woman among others.

(40) *Waa naág [dhéer] [oo dhuubán].*
waa naag dheer oo dhuub-an
DEC woman tall REL thin-STV
'The tall woman is thin.'

The excerpt in (41) is more complex but follows the same principles. There is a sequence of two relative clauses, with the first being restrictive and the second non-restrictive. The excerpt pertains to a trip taken by the president of Djibouti, who travelled first to Mogadishu at the beginning of a longer trip. Both relative clauses have *socdáal* 'journey' as their head. The restrictive relative clause that directly modifies this head provides key information about the type of journey being embarked upon.

The second relative clause is supplemental information about the endpoint of the journey, which is a known destination in the context of the news report.

(41) *Muqdísho, wáxaana ú bilowdey socdáal [rásmi*
    Muqdisho, waxaa=na u bil-ow-d-ey socdaal rasmi
    Mogadishu FOC=CONJ on begin-INCH-3SG.M-PST journey official
    áh] [oo uu dálka kú yimíd].
    ah oo uu dal=ka ku y-imid
    be.PRES.RED REL 3SG.M country=KDEF to 3SG.M-come.PST
    'In Mogadishu, he began an official journey on which he came to the country.'
    (xamarcadde.com: 10)

When a sequence of restrictive relative clauses is followed by a non-restrictive relative clause, like in (42), *ee* conjoins the first two restrictives, after which *oo* conjoins a further non-restrictive to the string of restrictives.

(42) *guddoomiyáha [cusúb] [ee Góbolka Banaadír] [oo lagú*
    guddoomiya=ha cusub ee gobol=ka Banaadir oo la=gu
    governor=K.DEF new REL province=K.DEF Banaadir REL ISP=to
    wareejiyaý xafiisyáda dawladdá]
    wareej-i-y-ay xafiisy-a=da dawlad=da
    hand.over-WCAUS-3SG.M-PST office-PL=T.DEF government=T.DEF
    'the new governor of the province of Banaadir to whom the offices of the government were handed' (runtanews.net: 64)

15.4 Coordinating larger constituents

The coordinators *oo* and *ee* also play a role in conjoining larger constituents, though they differ somewhat in what constituents they conjoin and how they do so. Section 15.4.1 shows that *oo* conjoins two otherwise independent clauses that share a common argument. The clauses may be of different types, but they agree in modality. Clauses joined by *ee* in §15.4.2 also share a common element, though it may only be implied. They differ, however, in that there is a shift in modality between the two clauses.

15.4.1 with *oo*

The conjunction *oo* can, in fairly straightforward instances, conjoin two verbs (or Verb Complexes) that share the same subject within the same clause. In (43), two inflected verbs are coordinated within the same declarative clause marked by *waa*.

(43) *Wáan kacay oo baxay.*
    w=aan kac-∅-ay oo bax-∅-ay
    DEC=1SG get.up-1SG-PST CONJ leave-1SG-PST
    'I got up and left.'

Even simpler than this are commands involving two verbs like in (44). Here, *oo* joins two imperative mood verbs. The shared element could be seen as the object, namely the non-overt third person pronominal 'it,' which refers to some involved comestibles or meal.

(44) *Cún oo cáb!*
    cun oo cab
    eat.IMP CONJL cab.IMP
    'Eat and drink!'

A similar scenario is seen in (45) where two otherwise independent clauses, each of which has a focus marker, are conjoined by *oo*. The shared element between them is *nínkií* 'the man,' which is the focused subject of the first clause and the oblique object in the second.

(45) *Nínkií báa tagaý oo xáaskíisií báa lá*
    nin-kii baa tag-ay oo xaas-kiis-ii baa la
    man-K.RDEF FOC go-PRES.RED REL wife-K.his-K.RDEF FOC with
    socdaý.
    soc-d-ay
    go.along-3SG.F-PRES.RED
    'The man left, and his wife went along with him.'

Example (46) shows that the conjoined clauses need not necessarily be of the same type, though they must be of the same modality. Here, both clauses are declarative, though the first involves focus on an adverbial while the second is a declarative clause with *waa*.

(46) *Hálka búu imánayaa oo wáannu is*
    halka b=uu iman-ay-∅-aa oo wa=annu is
    here FOC=3SG.M come-PROG-3SG.M-PRES REL DEC=1PL RRP
    raácaynaa.
    raac-ay-n-aa
    follow-PROG-1PL-PRES
    'He is coming here, and we are following along together.' (Z & I: 339)

15.4.2 with *ee*

Full clauses joined by *ee* also have a shared element, but the clauses differ in their modality or polarity. For example, *ee* can join positive and negative declarative clause in instances like (47) and (48).

(47) Wáxba má cunín   ee wúu   baxay.
    wax=ba ma cun-in   ee w=uu   bax-∅-ay
    thing=INT NEG eat-PST.NEG REL DEC=3SG.M leave-3SG.M-PST
    'He ate nothing and he left.'

(48) Waáyo hay'adáha   caalamigú   má aha góle
    waayo hay'ad-a=ha   caalami=g=u   ma aha gole
    because organization-PL=K.DEF international=K.DEF=SUBJ NEG be entity
    sharcí ee waa caawiyeyaál.
    sharci ee waa caawi-ye-yaal
    law   REL DEC help-AGT-PL
    'It is not because the international organizations are legal entities, (but) that they are helpers.' (websomalia.com: 14)

Also possible are those that differ in modality, such as between potential and interrogative (49), or between negative and optative (50).

(49) Áydin tiraahdeen   ee má hubtaan?
    aydin t-iraah-d-ee-n   ee ma hub-t-aa-n
    you.PL 2PL-say-2-POT-PL REL QM be.sure-2-PRES-PL
    'You might say it, but are you sure?' (Z & O: 635)

(50) Makhaayáddaás máan   jeclí   ee yáynu   tegín.
    makhaayad-daas m=aan   jecl-i   ee y-aynu   teg-in
    restaurant-T.that NEG=1SG like-PRES.NEG REL OPT.NEG-1PL go-OPT.NEG
    'I don't like that restaurant, so let's not go.'

15.5 Coordinating adverbials

This section covers adverbials that coordinate clauses but that do not necessarily involve subordination. Subordinating adverbials are discussed separately in §14.3 alongside other surbordinate clauses. Given that there are so many adverbials that can be used to coordinate clauses, the goal of this section is not necessarily to provide an exhaustive list of possibilities, but rather to provide examples of some commonly encountered adverbials used in this way and to illustrate a variety of ways they can be constructed and used.

15.5.1 Time

There are coordinating time adverbials formed on temporal nouns like *wáa* 'time' and *béri* 'time,' that are modified by remote definite determiner and the adverb *hóre* 'first, former.' Among these are *wáagií hóre* 'formerly,' *bérigií hóre* 'in the old days,' and *sánnadkií hóre* 'years ago.'

(51) *Wáxa la yidhi,   wáagií   hóre,   ín*
     waxa la y-idhi   waa-gii   hore   in
     FOC ISP 3SG.M-say.PST time-K.RDEF formerly COMP
     'It was said, long ago, that...'

As one might imagine, adverbials like these are sometimes formulaic, being used in narration and in story-telling. One adverbial within this vein is *wáa báa wáxaa* 'once upon a time,' where *wáa* functions as the noun 'time,' rather than as a declarative marker.

(52) *Wáa báa, wáxaa jiray   labó nín oo saaxiibó dháw ahaá.*
     waa baa waxaa jir-∅-ay   labo nin oo saaxiib-o dhaw ah-aa
     time FOC FOC   exist-3SG.K-PST two men REL friend-PL close be-PST.RED
     'Once upon a time, there were two men who were close friends.'
     (warkall.net: 45897)

There are other time adverbials based on the Arabic borrowing *ilaá* 'until, by.' These include *ilaá hádda* 'until now' and *ilaá iyo háddeér* 'up until the present time.' Note that *ilaá* can also introduce a subordinate clause. See §14.3.1.

(53) *Somaliland wáxaan anígu   joogey   ilaá iyo 2008.*
     Somaliland wax=aan ani=g=u   joog-∅-ay   ilaa iyo 2008
     Somaliland FOC=1SG I=K.DEF=SUBJ   remain-1SG-PST   until CONJ 2008
     'I stayed in Somaliland up until 2008.' (saxafimedia.com: 450)

Other temporal adverbials of this type use the demonstrative *tán* 'this,' including *tán iyo* 'since then,' *tán iyo goórtaás* 'until that time,' and *tán iyo íntií* 'up until now.'

(54) *Tán iyo íntií colaáddu   bilaabatay   aákhirkií*
     tan iyo intii colaad=d=u   bilaab-at-∅-ay   aakhir-kii
     this and now conflict=T.DEF=SUBJ   begin-MID-3SG.T-PST end-K.RDEF
     bíshií   hóre
     bish-ii   hore
     month-T.RDEF   last
     'Up until when the conflict began at the end of last month' (alkhabiir.com: 520)

15.5.2 Purpose and reason

One purpose/reason adverbial is derived from the noun *waáyo* meaning 'topic' or 'problem,' which is rendered adverbially as 'because.'

(55) Waan   kuú   caráysnahay,   waáyo wáx xún báad
w=aan   ku=u   carays-n-∅-ah-ay   waayo wax xun b=aad
DEC=1SG 2SG.OBJ=with angry-STV-1SG-be-PRES because thing bad FOC=2SG
igú   tiri.
i=gu   t-iri
1SG.OBJ=about 2SG-say.PST

'I am angry with you because you said bad things about me.' (Z & I: 290)

Another coordinating adverbial meaning 'because' is *máxaa yeelay*. This is built upon the verb *yéel* 'cause (v.).' As such, the adverbial might literally be translated 'the cause being.'

(56) Waan   hór   joogsaday,   máxaa yeelay, wúu
w=aan   hor   joog-s-ad-∅-ay   maxaa yeelay w=uu
DEC=1SG from stop-WCAUS-MID-1SG-PST QM   cause DEC=3SG.M
eedaysnaa.
eed-ays-n-∅-aa
guilty-FACT-MID-3SG.M-PST

I resisted him because he was guilty.' (noloshacusub.org: 63)

There are other adverbials formed by associative constructions, like *sída darteéd* or closely related *sídaás darteéd*, using the nouns *sí* 'matter' and *dár* 'reason.' These might literally be translated 'the reason of the matter' and 'the reason of that matter,' respectively. A similar strategy is involved in forming *táa awgeéd* on the noun *áw* 'purpose' and *sída daraadeéd* on the noun *daraád* 'reason.'

(57) Sída   daraadeéd   wáxaan soó jeedínaynaa
sida   daraadeed   wax=aan soo jeed-in-ay-n-aa
matter that.purposes FOC=1PL VEN suggest-WCAUS-PROG-1PL-PRES

'It is for that reason (that) we are suggesting...' (somaliland.org: 47882)

(58) Táa awgeéd   wáxba   kamá   tagó.
taa awgeed   wax=ba   ka-ma   tag-o
that its.reason thing=INT from-NEG go-IRR

'It's so that I leave nothing behind.'

15.5.3 Concession

Coordinating concessive adverbials include *háse yeeshee* and *háse ahaatee*, both of which are typically translated 'however.' The verb in these adverbials is in the potential mood. Others of this type are *ín kastába* 'no matter what' and *sí kastába há ahaatee* 'nevertheless.'

(59) *Magaaládu wey yártahay, háse yeeshee áad*
    magaala=d=u w=ey yar-t-ah-ay hase yeeshee aad
    city=T.DEF=SUBJ DEC=3SG.T small-3SG.T-be-PRES whatever cause very
    béy ú baabúur badántahay.
    b=ey u baabuur badan-t-ah-ay
    FOC=3SG.T with car many-3SG.T-be-PRES
    'The city is small, however it has a lot of cars.' (Z & I: 343)

(60) *Sí kastába há ahaatee, danjirúhu wúxuu*
    si kastaba ha ahaatee danjiru=h=u wux=uu
    way whatever might be ambassador=K.DEF=SUBJ FOC=3SG.M
    dammaanád qaaday ín...
    dammaanad qaad-∅-ay in
    guarantee bring-3SG.M-PST COMP
    'Nevertheless, the ambassador guaranteed that...' (wadaniga.net: 5601)

15.5.4 Manner

It has been shown thus far that a number of adverbials can be formed on the noun *sí* 'matter.' This is indeed the case with coordinating manner adverbials, which include *sída kále* 'on the contrary' (i.e., 'the other manner'), *sída tán* 'like this' (i.e., 'in this manner'), and *sídaás* 'like that' (i.e., 'in that manner').

(61) *Síduu yaqaan waa sídaás.*
    si=d=uu y-aqaan waa sidaas
    way=T.DEF=3SG.M 3SG.M-know.PRES DEC this.way
    'The way that he knows it is like this.' (Z & O: 708)

Similar to this is *wáxa wéeye*. Its literal meaning is 'the thing is,' but it is often translated as 'that is to say.' It sometimes introduces a subordinate clause, but this is not always the case.

(62) *Márkaa, wáxa   wéeye, sída   uu   shárcigu*
    markaa waxa   weeye sida   uu   sharci=g=u
    now   the.thing it.is according.to 3SG.M law=K.DEF=SUBJ
    dhígayó...
    dhig-ay-o
    write.down-PROG-IRR
    'Now, the thing is, according to what the law is saying...' (somaliland.org: 1466)

15.6 Other adverbials

This final section on adverbials covers those adverbs that are neither involved in subordination nor coordination. These are once again divided into groups based on their general function. These groups are time, location, and, in a few instances, manner. Because most of these adverbs are derived from nouns, their behavior and distribution often parallel that of other nouns and noun phrases. Their location relative to the Verb Complex and to other noun phrases varies, often being manipulated for pragmatic purposes.

15.6.1 Time

Temporal adverbials on the noun *wéli* generally convey a sense of 'still' or 'yet' (63). The noun itself is difficult to translate into English, but perhaps the closest equivalent would be 'forever.'

(63) *Anígu   wéli meesháydií   ayáan   iská   degánahay.*
    ani=g=u   weli meesh-ay-dii   ay=aan   is=ka   deg-an-∅-ah-ay
    I=K.DEF=SUBJ still place-T.my-T.RDEF FOC=1SG RRP=in   live-STV-1SG-be-PRES
    'I still live in my place.' (maslaxside.net: 215)

Used in negative contexts, it might be translated 'never' or 'yet' (64).

(64) *Wéli lamá   arkín   waxáan   oo kále.*
    weli la=ma   ark-in   waxaan   oo kale
    never ISP=NEG   see-PRES.NEG   something REL other
    'Never has anyone seen something like this.' (Z & I: 382)

This adverbial is also sometimes accompanied by a possessive determiner, functioning formally as an oblique, as in (65). This sentence might more literally be translated: 'I don't come to this street in my ever.'

(65) *Daríiqán wéligeý maan imaaddó.*
    dariiq-an weli-gey m=aan imaad-do
    street-K.this ever-K.my NEG=1SG come-IRR
    'I never come to this street.' (Z & I: 279)

Another group of closely related time adverbials are built upon the noun *hád* 'time, moment.' These include *hádda* 'now' (i.e., 'the time'), *hádba* 'every time,' *hádda ká hór* 'previously' (i.e., 'before the time'), and *hád iyo góor* 'time and time again' or 'continuously.'

(66) *Hádda wáxa jirá xéer la yidhaa...*
    hadda wax=a jir-a xeer la y-idh-aa
    now thing=K.DEF exist-PRES.RED rule ISP 3SG.M-say-PST
    'Now, the thing that exists is a rule called...' (tooshnews.net: 537)

Yet another group of temporal adverbs have in common that they are derived from nouns by the suffix *-to*. These include *sháleyto* 'yesterday,' *berríto* 'tomorrow,' and *xáleyto* 'last night,' among others.

(67) *Má wada imanáysaan berríto?*
    ma wada iman-ay-s-aa-n berrito
    QM together come-PROG-2-PRES-PL tomorrow
    'Are you all coming tomorrow?'

A number of other adverbials fall into this group: *máanta* 'today,' *sáaka* 'this morning,' *cáawa* 'tonight,' *dóraad* 'the day before yesterday,' and *ímminka* 'now.' To make such an adverbial more specific, other adverbials can accompany these and other temporal adverbs: *maalín wálba* 'every day,' *bíshii dambé* 'last month,' etc.

15.6.2 Location

There are several location adverbials that do not involve subordination or coordination. Two discussed here are built upon nouns that refer to a place or location. These are *hál* and *xág*. The first of these is used adverbially when modified by a demonstrative determiner, e.g., *hálkán* 'here,' *hálkaás* 'there,' and *hálkoó* 'over there.'

(68) *Ma hálkaán kuugú keenaa?*
    ma halk=aan ku=u-gu keen-∅-aa
    QM here=1SG 2SG.OBJ=to-over bring-1SG-PRES
    'Shall I bring it to you over here?'

Those built instead upon *xág* are often involved in the formation of associative constructions where the second constituent in the construction is some directional word (but not always, as with *xágna* 'nowhere'). These include, but are not limited to *xágga dámbe* 'in back of,' *xágga hóre* 'in front of,' and *xágga sáre* 'above.' A similar strategy involves *xág* being joined by a possessive determiner, which together modify some thing or location: *suúqa xaggiísa* 'towards the market' (i.e., 'the market, its direction' or 'the direction of the market').

15.6.3 Manner

Section 9.7.2 showed that Somali uses the clitic *=ba* as an intensifier on noun phrases. Given that many adverbs are derived from nouns in the language, this clitic is also found associated with some adverbs like *wéliba* 'moreover,' *sí wálba* 'in every way,' *hádaba* 'again and again.' Another means of intensification is via *aád…ú* or *sí aád…ú*.

(69) Sí   wálba   ha   noqotee.
   si   walba   ha   noqo-t-ee
   way whatever 3SG become-3SG.T-OPT
   'Whatever might come to pass…'

(70) Wúxuu   kú bilowday   ciyaárta   sí   aád ú
   wux=uu   ku bil-ow-d-ay   ciyaar=ta   si   aad u
   FOC=3SG.M on start-INCH-3SG.M-PST game=T.DEF way very of
   wanaagsan.
   wanaag-s-an
   good-WCAUS-STV
   'He started the game very well.' (onechelsea.net: 1282)

15.7 Comparatives and superlatives

Comparatives and superlatives belong in this chapter alongside other adverbials in that they deal with the degree to which a quality associated with one entity relates to that of another. In Somali, these concepts are expressed by an adjectival participle or hybrid verb that is preceded by an adpositional particle (or two, in the case of superlatives) that governs the entity being described. Before delving into more specifics, (71) shows a simple example of the structure underlying a basic comparative.

(71) *Xaaláddu   way   ká   fiicántahay   sídií*
    xaalad=d=u   w=ay   ka   fiic-an-t-ah-ay   si-dii
    situation=T.DEF=SUBJ DEC=3SG.T COM good-STV-3SG.T-be-PRES way-T.RDEF
    ay   wáx ahaayeén.
    ay   wax ahaa-y-ee-n
    3PL.T thing be-3-IRR-PL
    'The situation is better than the way that things were.'

In (71), the two entities being compared are *xaaláddu* 'the (current) situation' and *sídií ay wáx ahayeén* 'the way that things were.' The goodness of the first (*fiicántahay*) is compared to that of the second via the adposition *ká*, which one can translate 'than.'

Variations on this structure are possible, such as that seen in (72), where the element being compared *lacág* 'money' is incorporated into the verb. One might conceive of a sentence like this as 'Her money was more than his.'

(72) *Iyádu   way   ká   lacág badnayd   isága.*
    iya=d=u   w=ay   ka   lacag badn-ay-d   isa=ga
    she=T.DEF=SUBJ DEC=3SG.F COM money more-be-3SG.F him=K.DEF
    'She had more money than him.' (Z & O: 42)

While the adposition *ká* is the basic means of comparison, there are two types of superlatives. The first of these, which I call the 'relative' superlative, is formed with the adposition *ú*, as in (73), and conveys the sense of 'most X,' but seemingly only in comparison to a limited set of others.

(73) *Wiilásha   wuu   ú   gaabányahay.*
    wiil-ash=a   w=uu   u   gaab-an-y-ah-ay
    boy-PL=T.DEF DEC=3SG.M REL.SUP short-STV-3SG.M-be-PRES
    'He is the shortest among the boys.' (Z & I: 239)

The second superlative, which I call the 'absolute' superlative, is instead formed with the adposition cluster *ugú*. Its use, as in (74), is somewhat more emphatic, meaning 'most X of all.'

(74) *Fiitamíinka   ugú   wanaagsán wáxa lagá   helaa*
    fiitamiin=ka   ugu   wanaagsan waxa la=ga   hel-∅-aa
    vitamin=K.DEF ABS.SUP goodness   FOC ISP=within find-3SG.M-PRES
    cuntáda.
    cunta=da
    food=T.DEF
    'One can find the best vitamins (of all) in foods.' (somalifashionista.com: 12)

16 Questions

The final chapter of this grammar covers questions of different types. The chapter is divided into four main sections. The first section deals with content questions formed with interrogative words or an interrogative pronoun. The response to such questions is expected to provide substantive information about some element being questioned (e.g., the who, what, or why). The second section covers choice questions. These differ from content questions in that the expected response is a pronominal or demonstrative whose primary function is one of disambiguation. The third section deals with polar, or yes/no, questions, and the last section covers question tags of different types.

16.1 Content questions

Content questions in Somali ask for specific information (who, what, when, where, why, how) about some entity that is co-referential with an interrogative pronoun or word. Questions of this type are formed by several different strategies. For example, those asking *who?* are the only content questions that involve an interrogative pronoun. Others involve a particular interrogative word. For example, one way to ask *when?* is via *goórma*, which one might translate as 'which time.' It is formed by the noun *goór* 'time' joined by the interrogative enclitic *=ma*.

There is no special syntax or movement involved in forming questions of this type, but the questioned constituent is often morphologically marked as in focus. As illustrated below, an interrogative word and focus marker may be prosodified separately from one another, but it is not uncommon for them to coalesce, particularly when the focus marker hosts a subject pronoun enclitic. These interrogatives tend to be fronted, and thus, they occur alongside a pre-verbal focus marker and seldom occur under post-verbal focus. Responses to content questions, since they often introduce discourse-new information, also often involve constituent focus, but this is not obligatory. Short, contentful responses without a focused constituent are also possible. Consider for example, the question in (1), wherein the interrogative word *goórma* is joined by a focus marker and subject pronoun clitic. The presence of the focus marker is clear in the H tone that it contributes.

(1) *Iyáda   goórmáan   árkayaa?*
    iya=da   goorm=aan   ark-ay-∅-aa
    her=T.DEF   when=FOC.1SG   see-PROG-1SG-PRES
    'When am I going to see her?'

A reasonable and complete response to this question is in (2), where the adverbial *degdég*, being the new information contributed as a result of the question, is in focus. A short response like that in (3) is also possible.

(2) *Degdég   báad   ú   árkaysaa.*
    degdeg   b=aad   u   ark-ay-s-aa
    immediately FOC=2SG with see-PROG-2SG-PRES
    'You will be seeing her immediately.'

(3) *Ín   yár   ká   díb.*
    amount small from after
    'In a little while.'

Questions and responses employing declarative clauses with *waa* and other clause types are also possible. Compare, for example, (4) and (5), where the first is a declarative clause and the second is an optative clause.

(4) *Gaádhigu   waa xaggeé?*
    gaadhi=g=u   waa xaggee
    car=K.DEF=SUBJ DEC where
    'Where is the car?'

(5) *Gaádhigu   gúriga   há yaalló!*
    gaadhi=g=u   guri=ga   ha y-aal-o
    car=K.DEF=SUBJ house=K.DEF 3SG 3SG-exist-IRR
    'May the car be at home!'

16.1.1 Who? / Whom? - *yáa, kúma/túma*

Content questions asking *who?* or *whom?* are unique in that they can be formed with the interrogative pronoun *yáa*. The interrogative pronoun occurs before the verb complex, though its position relative to other noun phrases that might be present varies for pragmatic reasons, e.g., for the purpose of topicalization. The interrogative pronoun can be thought of as composed of a pronominal element *y-* and the pre-verbal focus marker *báa*. Evidence in support of such a proposition is that questions containing the interrogative pronoun have no other overt focus or clause type marker. In addition, when the interrogative pronoun is the subject of the sentence, the verb requires reduced agreement and a suffixal H tone. These are requirements of the Subject Focus Condition (§11.3).[1]

---

[1] The interrogative pronoun is also used on its own when seeking repetition or clarification: *yáa?* 'huh?'

(6) Yáa   imánayaý?
    y=aa   iman-ay-ay
    QM=FOC come-PROG-PST
    'Who was coming?'

(7) Yáa   lacágta   iyága   amaahiyaý?
    y=aa lacag=ta   iya=ga   amaah-iy-ay
    QM=FOC money=T.DEF them=K.DEF loan-WCAUS-PST
    'Who loaned the money to them?'

(8) Gaádhiga yáa   farafareeyaý?
    gaadhi=ga y=aa farafar-eey-ay
    car=K.DEF QM=FOC touch-FACT-PST
    'Who touched the car?'

When the interrogative pronoun is instead referring to an object, it is joined by a co-referential subject pronoun clitic in the combinations shown in (9).

(9) *yáa + subject pronoun clitic*

y=báa=aan	yáan	1SG (~1PL)
y=báa=aad	yáad	2SG (~2PL)
y=báa=uu	yúu	3SG.M/K
y=báa=ay	yáy ~ yéy	3SG.F/T
y=báa=annu	yáannu	1PL.exc
y=báa=aynu	yáynu ~ yéynu	1PL.inc
y=báa=aydin	yáydin ~ yéydin	2PL
y=báa=ay	yáy ~ yéy	3PL

The requirement for reduced agreement and suffixal H tone does not hold when the interrogative pronoun is an object. This is in line with the Object Focus Condition (§11.4).

(10) Cáli yúu   dilay?
     Cali y=uu   dil-∅-ay
     Cali QM=FOC.3SG.M beat-3SG.M-PST
     'Whom did Cali beat?'

(11) Yáydin   ú   karíneysaan?
     y=aydin   u   kar-in-ey-s-aa-n
     QM=FOC.2PL for cook-WCAUS-PROG-2-PRES-PL
     'You (PL) are cooking for whom?'

(12) Yáad   ú   maláynaysaa   ínuu   bádin   doonó?
    y=aad   u   mal-ayn-ay-s-aa   in=uu   bad-in   doon-o
    QM=FOC.2SG about think-FACT-PROG-2-PRES COMP=3SG.M win-INF FUT-IRR
    'Who do you think will win?'

Forming negative questions of this type involves negative *aán* joining the interrogative, yielding *yaán*, as well as a negatively inflected verb.

(13) Yaán   shaqáda   tagéyn   bérri?
    y=aan   shaqa=da   tag-eyn   berri
    QM=NEG   work=T.DEF   go-PRES.NEG tomorrow
    'Who isn't going to work tomorrow?'

When used in a sentential frame, *kúma* and *túma* (corresponding to K-series and T-series grammatical gender, respectively), can also mean 'who?,' 'whom?,' or 'which one?' These are derived from subject-marked definite determiners and, therefore, are not compatible with subject focus. They can be employed in a very general way alongside a declarative (14) but can also be placed into object focus (15).

(14) Waa kúma?
    waa k=u=ma
    DEC T.DEF=SUBJ=QM
    'Who is it?'

(15) Túma   báad   lá   hádlaysay?
    t=u=ma   b=aad   la   hadl-ay-s-ay
    T.DEF=SUBJ=QM FOC=2SG   with speak-PROG-2SG-PST
    'Whom were you speaking with?' (Orwin 1995: 197)

16.1.2 When? - *goórma*

Content questions asking *when?* are formed by the question word *goórma* (which is derived from the noun *goór* 'time') to which the question clitic *=ma* has been added. This interrogative functions as a sentential object. As the constituent being questioned, *goórma* is placed into focus and, as appropriate for the object focus condition, it may co-occur with a subject pronoun clitic. When placed into focus by *ayáa*, *goórma* and *ayáa* are prosodified separately, with any subject pronoun clitic that might be present joining the latter.

(16) *Goórma ayáad imánaysaa?*
goor=ma ay=aad iman-ay-s-aa
time=QM FOC=2SG come-PROG-2SG-PRES
'When are you coming?'

However, when *goórma* is placed into focus by *báa*, the two often coalesce along with a subject pronoun clitic. The presence of the focus marker is made clear by the fact that there are two H tones on the resulting word.

(17) *Tán iyo goórmáad   shákí nagú   sií wádi*
tan iyo goor=m=aad   shaki na=gu   sii wad-i
this and when=QM=FOC.2SG doubt 1PL.OBJ=from ITV continue-INF
doontaa?
doon-t-aa
FUT-2SG-PRES
'Until when will your doubt of us continue?' (noloshacusub.net: 619)

The various combinations of *goórma* followed by a focus marker and a subject pronoun clitic are shown in (18).

(18) *goórma + báa + subject pronoun clitic*

goórma=báa=aan	goórmáan	1SG (~1PL)
goórma=báa=aad	goórmáad	2SG (~2PL)
goórma=báa=uu	goórmúu	3SG.M/K
goórma=báa=ay	goórmáy ~ goórméy	3SG.F/T
goórma=báa=annu	goórmáannu	1PL.exc
goórma=báa=aynu	goórmáynu ~ goórméynu	1PL.inc
goórma=báa=aydin	goórmáydin ~ goórméydin	2PL
goórma=báa=ay	goórmáy ~ goórméy	3PL

16.1.3 Where? - *xaggeé, halkeé, meesheé*

Content questions asking *where?* are formed in three closely-related ways that involve defined derivatives of the nouns *xág*, *hál*, and *meél*, all of which generally mean 'place' or 'area.' Like the content question words discussed thus far, these three interrogative words arguably involve focus marking where the interrogative word itself is the focused object. The forms encountered differ depending on the particular focus marker being used. For example, these words do not coalesce with the focus marker *ayáa*. Rather, alongside *ayáa*, they are realized *xaggeé*, *halkeé*, and *meesheé*, where they are modified by an interrogative determiner. As expected of object focus, the focus marker is joined by a subject pronoun clitic.

(19) *Xaggeé   ayáy   aadeen?*
     xag-gee   ay=ay   aad-∅-ee-n
     place-K.IDEF FOC=3PL go.to-3-PST-PL
     'Where did they go to?'

(20) *Halkeé   ayúu   ká   yimaadda   hummáagga*
     hal-kee   ay=uu   ka   y-imaad-da hummaag=ga
     place-K.IDEF FOC=3SG.K from 3SG.K-come-PRES pain=K.DEF
     naftú?
     naf=t=u
     soul=T.DEF=SUBJ
     'Where does the pain of one's soul come from?' (bulshodoon.net: 162)

The situation is somewhat less clear in other instances, such as when the interrogative words are focused by *báa*. These sometimes look just like instances involving *ayáa* above, where no coalescence occurs. This is seen in (21) and (22).

(21) *Xággeé   búu   ká   keenay   awoóddan?*
     xag-gee   b=uu   ka   keen-∅-ay awood-dan
     where-K.IDEF FOC=3SG.M from bring-3SG.M-PST power-T.this
     'From where did he gain such power?' (taleex.net: 16100)

(22) *Meesheé   báan   ká   fuulaa?*
     mee-shee   b=aan   ka   fuul-∅-aa
     place-K.IDEF FOC=1SG from board-1SG-PRES
     'From where should I board?' (Z & I: 287)

In other instances, it appears that coalescence has occurred between the interrogative word, determiner, a subject pronoun clitic, and arguably *báa*. However, the presence of the focus marker is apparent only tonally. Such instances of coalescence are possible, but not obligatory, with attested forms shown below.

(23)   *xág + determiner + báa + subject pronoun clitic*

xág+determiner=báa=aan	xággáan ~xággéen	1SG/1PL
xág+determiner=báa=aad	xággáad ~xággéed	2SG/2PL
xág+determiner=báa=uu	xággúu	3SG.M/K
xág+determiner=báa=ay	xággáy ~xággéy	3SG.F/T
xág+determiner=báa=annu	xággáannu ~xággéennu	1PL.exc
xág+determiner=báa=aynu	xággáynu ~xággéynu	1PL.inc
xág+determiner=báa=aydin	xággáydin ~xággéydin	2PL
xág+determiner=báa=ay	xággáy ~xággéy	3PL

(24) *hál + determiner + báa + subject pronoun clitic*

hál+determiner=báa=aan	hálkáan ~hálkéen	1SG/1PL
hál+determiner=báa=aad	hálkáad ~hálkéed	2SG/2PL
hál+determiner=báa=uu	hálkúu	3SG.M/K
hál+determiner=báa=ay	hálkáy ~hálkéy	3SG.F/T
hál+determiner=báa=annu	hálkáannu ~hálkéennu	1PL.exc
hál+determiner=báa=aynu	hálkáynu ~hálkéynu	1PL.inc
hál+determiner=báa=aydin	hálkáydin ~hálkéydin	2PL
hál+determiner=báa=ay	hálkáy ~hálkéy	3PL

Example (25) shows such an instance of coalescence.

(25) *Básku   hálkúu   istaagaa?*
      bas=ku   hal=k=uu   istaag-∅-aa
      bus=K.DEF=SUBJ place=K.DEF=FOC.3SG.K stop-3SG.K-PRES
      'Where does the bus stop?'

16.1.4 What? - *maxá(a)*

Content questions asking *what?* are formed on the basis of the interrogative word *max*. This word is likely derived from *ma + wáx*, which consists of the basic interrogative particle followed by the noun meaning 'thing.' Like other interrogative words, however, the full form of the interrogative *maxá(a)* is arguably formed by coalescence of *max* with the pre-verbal focus marker *báa*. This may result in expected characteristics of subject focus. Its final vowel varies between being short and long, similar to what occurs with the post-verbal focus marker *wáxa(a)*.

Maxá(a) occurs on its own in the formation of basic questions like *Maxáa dhacaý?* 'What happened?' and in simple sentences like (26). But, it can also be found in more complex sentences like (27).

(26) *Maxáa la   keeney?*
      maxaa la   keen-∅-ey
      what ISP bring-PST
      'What was brought?'

(27) Maxá   igá   fileysay   ínaan   kú   sameeyó?
      ma-xa   i=ga   fil-ey-s-ay   in=aan   ku   sam-eey-o
      QM-FOC 1SG.OBJ=from expect-FACT-2SG-PST COMP=1SG 2SG.OBJ do-FACT-IRR
      'Is that I do it for you what you were expecting?' (soomaalida.net: 425)

In some instances of object focus, a SPC may clicitize onto *maxá(a)* yielding the clusters shown in (28). Indeed, the basic question *Waa maxáy?* 'what is it?' includes such a cluster. In each of these clusters, there is a H tone on the first mora of the second syllable. Variation seen elsewhere in 1PL and 2PL forms, as well as in vowel quality, is also seen here.

(28) max + báa + subject pronoun clitic

max-báa=aan	maxáan	1SG/1PL
max-báa=aad	maxáad	2SG/2PL
max-báa=uu	maxúu ~ muxúu	3SG.M/K
max-báa=ay	maxáy ~ maxéy	3SG.F/T
max-báa=aannu	maxáannu	1PL.exc
max-báa=aynu	maxáyn ~ maxéyn	1PL.inc
max-báa=aydin	maxáyd ~ maxéyd	2PL
max-báa=ay	maxáy ~ maxéy	3PL

Examples of these clusters in context follow in (29) and (30). The first shows a questioned object complement clause in its typical position following the Verb Complex. The second, however, illustrates a similar clause that is fronted, as is sometimes done for the purpose of placing contrastive focus on a previously topical constituent (Tosco 2002).

(29) Maxáad   jecéshahay   [ínaad   cuntó]?
      max-aad   jece-sh-ah-ay   in=aad   cun-t-o
      QM-FOC.2SG like-2SG-be-PRES COMP=2SG eat-2SG-IRR
      'What would you like to eat?'

(30) [Ínaan   aqaannó] muxúu   kú ogaadey?
      in=aan   aqaan-no mux=uu   ku oga-ad-∅-ey
      COMP=1SG know-IRR QM-FOC.3SG.M by find.out-MID-3SG.M-PST
      'How did he discover that I know?' (Z & O: 23)

Negative questions formed with *maxá(a)* seem to be only marginally acceptable. They appear fairly infrequently in the internet corpora that I have consulted and when I have attempted to test their use, my speakers have considered them to be grammatical, but stilted or awkward. The form without a SPC, *maxaán* (max + báa + aán), occurs in examples like (31).

(31) *Maxaán wáx loogú qabán?*
    maxa=aan wax lo=o=gu qab-an
    QM.FOC=NEG thing ISP=to=about do-NEG
    'Why not do something about it?'

Related forms with an SPC are encountered even less frequently, e.g., *muxúusán* (max + báa + uu + aán) or *maxáanan* (max + báa + aán + aan), but again, my speakers find these to be odd. Nonetheless, possible examples of their use that my speakers find at least marginally acceptable are in (32) and (33).

(32) *Maxáanán kuú saméyn karín?*
    max-aan-an ku=u sam-ey-n kar-in
    QM-FOC.NEG=1SG 2SG.OBJ=for do-FACT-INF be.able-PST.NEG
    'What wasn't I able to do for you?'

(33) *Muxúusán waddáda kú arkín?*
    mux-uus-an wadda=da ku ark-in
    QM-FOC.3SG.M-NEG road=T.DEF on see-PST.NEG
    'What didn't he see on the road?'

16.1.5 Why? - *maxá(a)...ú*

The strategy employed for creating content questions meaning *why?* closely parallels that used just above for questions meaning *what?*. This involves a form of *maxá(a)...ú* where the adposition *ú* governs the question. This can perhaps be thought of as 'for what?' Like the other content questions discussed in this section, *maxá(a)...ú* entails pre-verbal focus. Given the nature of the construction, however, the interrogative word functions as an oblique object. Thus, variations due to subject focus are not applicable in forming these questions. As in other instances of object focus, it is possible for this interrogative word to occur without a subject pronoun clitic (34), but it may also occur with one (35). The clusters formed are identical to those shown in (28).

(34) *Maxáa nabádda   iyo xasiloonída   ú diiday   magaaláda*
    maxaa nabad=da   iyo xasilooni=da   u diid-ay   magaala=da
    what peace=T.DEF and stability=T.DEF for cease-PST city=T.DEF
    Muqdísho?
    Muqidsho
    Mogadishu
    'Why have peace and stability ceased in the city of Mogadishu?'
    (godaalonews.net: 6895)

(35) *Hálkan maxáad   ú timaaddaa   már walbá?*
    halkan max=aad u t-imaadd-aa mar wal=ba
    here   what=2SG for 2-come-PRES time every=INT
    'Why do you come here so often?'

In addition to forming *why?* questions with *maxá(a)...ú*, there is another question word *waáyo?* that can mean 'why?' or 'why not?' according to context. An appropriate response still entails content, often involving a purpose/reason clause.

16.1.6 How? - *sideé*

Content questions asking *how?* are formed by an interrogative word derived from the noun *sí* 'manner, way.' It can be followed either by the interrogative determiner or the definite determiner. One might think of it as 'which way?' Like other interrogatives, it can be placed into focus morphologically (36). More specifically, it functions as a focused object, but it may also occur in a declarative clause with *waa* (37).

(36) *Walaáshaá sideé báy   tahay?*
    walaash-aa sidee b=ay   t-ah-ay
    sister-T.your how FOC=3SG.F 3SG.F-be-PRES
    'How is your sister?'

(37) *Máanta hawádu   waa sideé?*
    maanta hawa=d=u   waa sidee
    today temperature=T.DEF=SUBJ DEC how
    'How is the temperature today?'

These examples reveal that the behavior of this interrogative closely parallels that of some interrogatives meaning *where?*, as described in §16.1.3. When on its own and in focus, it must be followed by a focus marker. Of course, as in other instances of object focus, the focus marker may host a subject pronoun clitic. There are instances in which the elements cluster together, as in (38).

(38) *sí + determiner + báa + subject pronoun clitic*

sí+determiner-báa=aan	sidáan ~sidéen	1SG/1PL
sí+determiner-báa=aad	sidáad ~sidéed	2SG/2PL
sí+determiner-báa=uu	sidúu	3SG.M/K
sí+determiner-báa=ay	sidáy ~sidéy	3SG.F/T
sí+determiner-báa=aannu	sidáannu ~sidéennu	1PL.exc
sí+determiner-báa=aynu	sidáyn ~sidéyn	1PL.inc
sí+determiner-báa=aydin	sidáyd ~sidéyd	2PL
sí+determiner-báa=ay	sidáy ~sidéy	3PL

Examples of these combinations involving *how?* in context are as follows:

(39) Márkaás mustaqbálkíisa   maámulkán   sidáad   ú aragtaa?
      markaas mustaqbal-kii=sa maamul-kan   sid=aad   u arag-t-aa
      then   future-K.its=T.DEF administration-K.this how=2SG as see-2SG-PRES
      'Then how do you see the future of this administration?' (geeska.net: 9648)

(40) Sidéennu   hálkan kú soó   gaarnay?
      sid=eennu   halkan ku soo   gaar-n-ay
      how=1PL.ex here   to VEN   reach-1PL-PST
      'How did we get here?'

16.1.7 How much? / How many? - *ímmisa*

To ask *how much?* or *how many?* involves the interrogative word *ímmisa*, primarily in Northern Somali. Its equivalent in Central and Southern varieties of Somali is *meéqo*. The behavior of *ímmisa* is generally like that of other interrogatives discussed above. The interrogative itself often serves as the head of a noun phrase where its function is to quantify another noun. This is seen in (41) where the phrase *ímmisa maalmoód* 'how many days' is a focused oblique object. As expected of object focus, the focus marker may be joined by a subject pronoun clitic. Of course, it can also appear on its own, as in (42), in such a way that it quantifies some unknown or understood entity.

(41) Ímmisa   maalmoód búu   aróosku
    immisa   maalm-ood b=uu   aroos=k=u
    how.many day-ASSOC FOC=3SG.K wedding=K.DEF=SUBJ
    socdaa?
    soc-d-∅-aa
    proceed-MID-3SG.K-PRES
    'For how many days will the wedding continue?' (Z & I: 533)

(42) *Ímmisa   báad   siisay?*
    immisa   b=aad   sii-s-ay
    how.many FOC=2SG give-2SG-PST
    'How many did you give?'

It is sometimes the case that *ímmisa* coalesces with a focus marker and an encliticized subject pronoun. The resulting forms are shown in (43).

(43) *ímmisa + báa + subject pronoun clitic*

ímmisa-báa=aan	ímmisáan	1SG/1PL
ímmisa-báa=aad	ímmisáad	2SG/2PL
ímmisa-báa=uu	ímmisúu	3SG.M/K
ímmisa-báa=ay	ímmisáy	3SG.F/T
ímmisa-báa=aannu	ímmisáannu	1PL.exc
ímmisa-báa=aynu	ímmisáyn	1PL.inc
ímmisa-báa=aydin	ímmisáyd	2PL
ímmisa-báa=ay	ímmisáy	3PL

That *ímmisa* is placed directly into focus in such clusters is clear from their tonal behavior, with an additional H tone being contributed by the focus marker. Examples of clusters like these in context are as follows:

(44) *Ímmisáad   qaadatay?*
    immis=aad   qaad-at-∅-ay
    how.many=2SG take-MID-2SG-PST
    'How many (of them) did you take?'

(45) *Ímmisáan   gunnáda   hawlgabká   ú   hélayaa?*
    immis=aan   gunna=da   hawlgab=ka   u   helay-∅-aa
    how.much=1SG benefit=T.DEF retirement=K.DEF with receive-PROG-1SG-PRES
    'How much retirement pension am I receiving?' (nyiostergotland.nu)

16.1.8 How long? / How much? / From where? - *inteé*

Last among Somali's interrogative content questions to be covered in this section is *inteé*, which means *how long?* or sometimes *how much?* or *from where?*. Its properties closely parallel many of those observed for the other interrogative words discussed above. It functions formally as an oblique object and is morphologically marked as in focus. In some instances it occurs on its own but is followed by focus marker. As expected of the object focus condition, the focus marker may be joined by a subject pronoun clitic.

(46) *Inteé   báy   dayuuráddu   díb ú   dhácaysaa?*
     intee   b=ay   dayuurad=d=u   dib u   dhac-ay-s-aa
     how.long FOC=3SG.T   flight=T.DEF=SUBJ late for occur-PROG-2SG-PRES
     'For how long will the flight be delayed?' (Z & O: 148)

(47) *Inteé   báad   wáx   qiimayseen?*
     intee   b=aad   wax   qiim-ay-s-ee-n
     how.long FOC=2SG   thing value-FACT-2SG-PST-PL
     'You were selling it for how much?'

The propensity for *inteé* to coalescence with *báa* and a subject pronoun clitic appears more limited than what is seen for other interrogative words. Most common are the 1SG (or 1PL) *intéen* and 2SG (or 2PL) *intéed*.

(48) *Intéed   súgaysey?*
     int=eed   sug-ay-s-ey
     how.long=2SG wait-PROG-2SG-PST
     'For how long have you been waiting?'

(49) *Intéen   ká   keenaa?*
     int=een   ka   keen-∅-aa?
     where=1SG   from bring-1SG-PRES
     'Where should I bring it from?'

16.2 Polar questions

Polar questions differ from content questions from a functional standpoint in that they generally are seeking a 'yes' or 'no' response, though further clarifying information may thereafter be contributed. From a structural standpoint, these questions differ from content questions in that they involve the interrogative clause type particle *ma*. Interrogative *ma* and its interaction with other morphemes were first introduced in

§12.3. This particle can appear on its own but also appears in clusters with a subject pronoun clitic and with other functional morphemes.

The status of interrogative *ma* is on par with declarative *waa* and with focus markers in that a main clause with *ma* does not necessarily require the presence of one of these other particles to be grammatical. It can appear on its own when the matter on which the question centers is topical.

(50) *Muqdísho máad tagtey?*
Muqdisho m=aad tag-t-ey
Mogadishu QM=2SG go-2SG-PST
'Did you go to Mogadishu?'

(51) *Ma kú maqley?*
ma ku maql-Ø-ey
QM 2SG.OBJ hear-3SG.M-PST
'Did he hear you?'

Responses to questions solely containing interrogative *ma* do not necessarily seek new information. Thus, in addition to the expected 'yes' or 'no,' further information can be expressed with a declarative *waa* clause. An example of this is seen in the question and answer pair in (52) and (53). It is possible to answer such questions with contrastive focus, granted that some new information is being offered about the questioned constituent. This is shown in (54).

(52) *Búugga méydin akhriseen?*
buug=ga m=eydin akhr-i-s-ee-n
book=K.DEF QM=2PL read-WCAUS-2-PST-PL
'Did you (PL) read the book?'

(53) *Háa, wáannu akhrinney.*
haa w=aannu akhr-in-n-ey
yes DEC=1PL read-WCAUS-1PL-PST
'Yes, we read it.'

(54) *Háa, búugga áf Faransiiská báannu akhrinney.*
haa buug=ga af Faransiik=ka b=aannu akhr-in-n-ey
yes book=K.DEF language French=K.DEF FOC=1PL read-WCAUS-1PL-PST
'Yes, we read the French book.'

Though interrogative *ma* can appear on its own, it can also appear in a clause with a focus marker in order to emphasize the particular information being sought. The way in which it does so differs for each focus marker. The details pertaining to *báa* are discussed in §11.1.1.3, while those concerning *ayáa* and *wáxaa* are in Sections 11.1.2.3

and 11.2.2, respectively. In (55), interrogative *ma* occurs alongside the pre-verbal focus marker *báa*. A simple declarative response like (56) is expected though, once again, an answer with focus that provides new, contrastive information would also be reasonable.

(55) *Iyádu   ma macállin báa?*
    iya=d=u   ma macallin baa
    she=T.DEF=SUBJ QM teacher FOC
    'Is she a teacher?'

(56) *Háa, waa macállin.*
    yes DEC teacher
    'Yes, she is a teacher.'

16.2.1 *miyáa* as a general question marker

In addition to interrogative *ma*, the word *miyáa* functions in some instances as a general interrogative marker. Recall from §11.1.2, however, that *miyáa* (arguably composed of *ma+ ayáa*) elsewhere has a narrower function as a focus marker in interrogative clauses. The matter has been the subject of considerable debate (see Andrzejewski 1975; Antinucci 1980; Livnat 1984; Saeed 1984, 1999, among others). While there are certainly many instances in which *miyáa* is undeniably involved in focus, this section shows that it is also used to form polar questions in clauses where focus cannot clearly be implicated.

One illustration of *miyáa* as a general question marker is seen in that it can occur in verbless sentences like (57). This is reminiscent of the behavior of the declarative particle *waa*, or even moreso like clause-final *wáaye* discussed in §12.1.1.

(57) *Cali   macállin miyáa?*
    Cali   macallin miyaa
    Cali.SUBJ teacher QM
    'Is Cali a teacher?' (Antinucci et al. 1980)

Another illustration of the general use of *miyáa* is that it occurs at the beginning of sentences like (58) and (59). In these instances, one could not reasonably argue that it marks a particular constituent as being in focus. That is, in instances of constituent focus discussed in §11.1.2, *miyáa* immediately follows the constituent that it places into focus.

(58) *Miyúu   dhintay?*
    miy=uu   dhin-t-∅-ay
    QM=3SG.M die-MID-3SG.M-PST
    'Did he die?' (Z & I: 153)

(59) *Miyáa la idin   ká   qaadey?*
    miyaa la idin   ka   qaad-∅-ey
    QM   ISP 2PL.OBJ from take-3SG.M-PST
    'Was it taken away from you?' (Z & I: 351)

Note that the choice of whether or not to include an SPC in these examples, as in the case of clusters discussed in §12.3 formed with *ma* alone, can generally be viewed as a matter of disambiguation (Saeed 1984: 163) or emphasis. Yet another clear demonstration that *miyáa* sometimes does not function like a focus marker can be seen in (60).

(60) *Cali   miyúu   yimi?*
    Cali   miy=uu   yimi
    Cali.SUBJ QM=3SG.M y-imi
    'Did Cali come?' (Saeed 1984: 163)

In (60), the subject of the sentence is 'Cali,' which is followed immediately by the purported focus marker. However, if focus were involved here, we would expect to observe characteristics of the subject focus condition (see §11.3). However, as seen here, an SPC is present, the verb does not require reduced agreement, and it is toneless. Furthermore, 'Cali' is subject-marked by the loss of H tone.

16.3 Choice questions

Choice questions share some similarities with the content questions discussed in §16.1. These questions are posed when seeking clarifying or disambiguating information about a particular set of potential referents. They are formed in one of two ways, either with an interrogative determiner (*-keé/-teé*) or with the interrogative clitic *-ma*. Both of these are also seen in forming interrogative words used for content questions. The difference with choice questions is that they may be short utterances, rather than full clauses. For example *ninkeé?* 'which man?,' might be asked to confirm (or reconfirm) which man out of a particular group of possible men that might be active in the discourse scenario is being asked about. Responses to such questions may also simply be short utterances, rather than full clauses, and they often include a demonstrative, locative adverbial, or other attributive information that aides in selecting the intended referent. More complete responses are also possible and may employ contrastive focus.

16.3.1 With an interrogative determiner

One type of choice question is formed with an interrogative determiner, *keé* or *teé*, the choice of which depends on the grammatical gender of the supposed referent. For plural referents, *kuweé* is used instead. The simplest of such questions involve just the declarative marker and the interrogative, for example *waa keé?* 'which one?' As introduced just above, they can be formed on a particular noun, as in *ninkeé?* 'which man?', but as seen in (61), they can form full clauses.

(61) *Ninkeé   báad   aragtey?*
      nin-kee   b=aad   arag-t-ey
      man-K.IDEF   FOC=2SG   see-2SG-PST
      'Which man did you see?'

A short but licit response to such a question would be *nínkaás* 'that man,' or even *waa nínkaás* 'it is that man.' There are a host of other possible responses, including ones that make use of contrastive focus to emphasize newly contributed information.

16.3.2 With the interrogative clitic =ma

Another type of choice question is formed with the interrogative enclitic *=ma*. This clitic attaches to the right edge of a noun or noun phrase and is used to confirm information about it. Its basic use conveys the idea of 'which X,' where X is the noun. For example, *gúrima?* 'which house?,' *naágma?* 'which woman?,' or *iyáma?* 'which of them?' These questions are not used to seek new information. Note that the enclitic *=ma* is not associated with H tone nor does it influence the H tone of the phrase to which it attaches. Responses to these questions are analogous to those discussed just above in §16.3.1 for choice questions formed with interrogative determiners.

16.3.3 With *meé*

There is also a type of choice question formed with *meé* that is used specifically to seek clarifying information about the location of some entity. The use of *meé* on its own is most general, as in (62), but there are three additional forms that encode gender and number for third person referents: *meéye* 'where is he/it?', *meédey* 'where is she/it?', and *meéyey* 'where are they?'

(62) *Madaxweyníhií meé?*
 madaxweyni-hii mee
 president-K.RDEF where
 'Where is the president?'

Like other choice questions, possible responses are diverse but typically involve a declarative clause with some locative adverbial or demonstrative.

16.4 Tag questions

16.4.1 *misé máya* - or not?

The question tag *misé máya* 'or not' is found appended to declarative statements as a means to clarify the sentiment expressed by offering a negative alternative. It is formed by the disjunction *misé* 'or,' which was discussed in §15.2.2, followed by the word for 'no,' *máya*.

(63) *Ma wada socón   karaan,   misé máya?*
 ma wada soc-on   kar-∅-aa-n   mise maya
 QM ADV walk-MID.INF be.able-3-PRES-PL or no
 'Can they walk together, or not?' (isbadaldoon.org: 122780)

(64) *Ma lalá   hadley,   misé máya?*
 ma la=la   hadl-∅-ey   mise maya
 QM ISP=with talk-3SG.M-PST or no
 'Has someone spoken with him, or not?'

16.4.2 *s(h)ów...má aha* - isn't it?

Another question tag *s(h)ów...má aha* asks 'isn't it?' following a declarative. In doing so, the question seeks to clarify the content of the declarative by offering some alternative. This tag is formed by the potential classifier *s(h)ów* and *má aha*, which one might translate 'is it not.' Recall from §12.5 that the pronunciation of this particle differs between dialects. Example (65) shows that the tag can occurs on its own if the entire proposition is being questioned. However, in (66), if a particular element of the proposition is being questioned, that element is flanked by the two elements of the tag.

(65) *Mágaciisu   waa Cáli, sów má aha?*
    magac-iis=u   waa Cali   sow ma aha
    name-K.his=SUBJ DEC Cali   POT NEG be
    'His name is Cali, isn't it?'

(66) *Nábigu   sów ka kú   aasán   másjidkíisa, má aha?*
    nabi=g=u   sow ka ku   aas-an   masjid-kiisa ma aha
    prophet=K.DEF=SUBJ POT at within bury-STV mosque-K.his NEG be
    'The prophet is buried within his mosque, isn't he?'

A Appendix - Suffixing verb paradigms

This appendix aims to provide a comprehensive list of inflectional paradigms for suffixing verbs. Three stem types for suffixing verbs – bare (underived), weak causative, and middle – were covered in detail in Chapter 7. Inflectional forms for other stem types are formed by the same principles as these three and are provided below, though without detailed description, for the purpose of quick reference and comparison. Prefixing and irregular verbs are not included here, as their inflectional forms are covered fully in Chapter 7.

The appendix is divided into sections according to stem type. Due to there being many combinations of derivational extensions that can be found in the language, there are more stem types possible than those given here. In the interest of space, however, paradigms are included for ten simple stem types. This includes bare (underived) stems and eight stems containing a single derivational extension. In addition, I include one common complex stem type where the weak causative and middle are found in the same stem. The location of each paradigm is as follows:

(1) *Appendix summary*

Bare (underived)	Section A.1
Experiencer	Section A.2
Inchoative	Section A.3
Reciprocal	Section A.4
Weak Causative	Section A.5
Factitive	Section A.6
Middle	Section A.7
Neuter	Section A.8
Strong Causative	Section A.9
Weak Causative & Middle	Section A.10

Because of the complexity of the inflectional system, paradigms are simplified to the extent possible. For each stem type, main clause (MC) vs. subordinate clause (SC) forms are given, wherever relevant. This involves an alternation from realis to irrealis paradigm in the Simple Present, Present Progressive, and other contexts derived from them. As discussed in detail in §7.10, there are other alternations due to the relationship of the subordinate clause to the main clause subject. Full and reduced agreement forms are also included for each paradigm, wherever relevant. Recall that reduced agreement is found in all instances of subject focus and in subject relative clauses.

A.1 Bare (underived) stems

The exemplar in this section for bare (underived) stems is *cún* 'eat.' Its infinitival form is *cúni* 'to eat.'

(2) *Simple Present*

	MC Full	MC Reduced	SC Full	SC Reduced
1SG	cunaa	cunaa	cunó	cuná
3SG.M	cunaa	cunaa	cunó	cuná
2SG	cuntaa	cunaa	cuntó/cuntíd	cuná
3SG.F	cuntaa	cuntaa	cuntó	cuntá
1PL	cunnaa	cunnaa	cunnó	cunná
2PL	cuntaan	cunaa	cuntáan	cuná
3PL	cunaan	cunaa	cunáan	cuná

(3) *Present Progressive*

	MC Full	MC Reduced	SC Full	SC Reduced
1SG	cúnayaa	cúnayaa	cúnayó	cúnayá
3SG.M	cúnayaa	cúnayaa	cúnayó	cúnayá
2SG	cúnaysaa	cúnayaa	cúnaysó/cúnaysíd	cúnayá
3SG.F	cúnaysaa	cúnaysaa	cúnaysó	cúnaysá
1PL	cúnaynaa	cúnaynaa	cúnaynó	cúnayná
2PL	cúnaysaan	cúnayaa	cúnaysáan	cúnayá
3PL	cúnayaan	cúnayaa	cúnayáan	cúnayá

(4) *Simple Past*

	MCs Full	MC Reduced	SC Full	SC Reduced
1SG	cunay	cunay	cunaý	cunaý
3SG.M	cunay	cunay	cunaý	cunaý
2SG	cuntay	cunay	cuntaý	cunaý
3SG.F	cuntay	cuntay	cuntaý	cuntaý
1PL	cunnay	cunnay	cunnaý	cunnaý
2PL	cunteen	cunay	cuntéen	cunaý
3PL	cuneen	cunay	cunéen	cunaý

The negative form of the Simple Past is the same for all combinations of person, number, and grammatical gender: *cunín*. There are two variants of the negative for the Past Progressive: *cúnéyn* and *cúneynín*.

(5) *Past Progressive*

	MC Full	MC Reduced	SC Full	SC Reduced
1SG	cúnayay	cúnayay	cúnayaý	cúnayaý
3SG.M	cúnayay	cúnayay	cúnayaý	cúnayaý
2SG	cúnaysay	cúnayay	cúnaysaý	cúnayaý
3SG.F	cúnaysay	cúnaysay	cúnaysaý	cúnaysaý
1PL	cúnaynay	cúnaynay	cúnaynaý	cúnaynaý
2PL	cúnayseen	cúnayay	cúnayséen	cúnayaý
3PL	cúnayeen	cúnayay	cúnayéen	cúnayaý

The Optative is an irrealis paradigm context, though H tone remains on the stem. There is a single negative form of the Optative for all person, number, and grammatical gender combinations: *cunín*.

(6) *Optative*

1SG/3SG.M	cúno
2SG/3SG.F	cúnto/cúntid
1PL	cúnno
2PL	cúnteen
3PL	cúneen

(7) *Past Habitual*

	MC Full	MC Reduced	SC Full	SC Reduced
1SG	cúni jiray	cúni jiray	cúni jiraý	cúni jiraý
3SG.M	cúni jiray	cúni jiray	cúni jiraý	cúni jiraý
2SG	cúni jirtay	cúni jiray	cúni jirtaý	cúni jiraý
3SG.F	cúni jirtay	cúni jirtay	cúni jirtaý	cúni jirtaý
1PL	cúni jirnay	cúni jirnay	cúni jirnaý	cúni jirnaý
2PL	cúni jirteen	cúni jiray	cúni jirtéen	cúni jiraý
3PL	cúni jireen	cúni jiray	cúni jiréen	cúni jiraý

(8) *Conditional*

	MC Full	MC Reduced	SC Full	SC Reduced
1SG	cúni lahaa	cúni lahaa	cúni lahaá	cúni lahaá
3SG.M	cúni lahaa	cúni lahaa	cúni lahaá	cúni lahaá
2SG	cúni lahayd	cúni lahaa	cúni lahaýd	cúni lahaá
3SG.F	cúni lahayd	cúni lahayd	cúni lahaýd	cúni lahaýd
1PL	cúni lahayn	cúni lahayn	cúni lahaýn	cúni lahaýn
2PL	cúni lahaydeen	cúni lahaa	cúni lahaydéen	cúni lahaá
3PL	cúni lahayeen	cúni lahaa	cúni lahayéen	cúni lahaá

(9) *Future*

	MC Full	MC Reduced	SC Full	SC Reduced
1SG	cúni doonaa	cúni doonaa	cúni doonó	cúni dooná
3SG.M	cúni doonaa	cúni doonaa	cúni doonó	cúni dooná
2SG	cúni doontaa	cúni doonaa	cúni doontó/cúni doontíd	cúni dooná
3SG.F	cúni doontaa	cúni doontaa	cúni doontó	cúni doontá
1PL	cúni doonnaa	cúni doonnaa	cúni doonnó	cúni doonná
2PL	cúni doontaan	cúni doonaa	cúni doontáan	cúni dooná
3PL	cúni doonaan	cúni doonaa	cúni doonáan	cúni dooná

(10) *Imperative*

	Affirmative	Negative
SG	cún	cunín
PL	cúna	cunína

(11) *Potential*

	Affirmative	Negative
1SG/3SG.M	cunee	cunéen
2SG/3SG.F	cuntee	cuntéen
1PL	cunnee	cunnéen
2PL	cunteen	cuntéen
3PL	cuneen	cunéen

A.2 Experiencer stems

The exemplar in this section for experiencer stem is *murugóod* 'be worried.' Its infinitival form is *murugóon* 'to be worried.'

(12) *Simple Present*

	MC Full	MC Reduced	SC Full	SC Reduced
1SG	murugoodaa	murugoodaa	murugoodó	murugoodá
3SG.M	murugoodaa	murugoodaa	murugoodó	murugoodá
2SG	murugootaa	murugoodaa	murugootó/murugootíd	murugoodá
3SG.F	murugootaa	murugootaa	murugootó	murugootá
1PL	murugoonnaa	murugoonnaa	murugoonnó	murugoonná
2PL	murugootaan	murugoodaa	murugootáan	murugoodá
3PL	murugoodaan	murugoodaa	murugoodáan	murugoodá

(13) *Present Progressive*

	MC Full	MC Reduced	SC Full	SC Reduced
1SG	murugoónayaa	murugoónayaa	murugoónayó	murugoónayá
3SG.M	murugoónayaa	murugoónayaa	murugoónayó	murugoónayá
2SG	murugoónaysaa	murugoónayaa	murugoónaysó/ murugoónaysíd	murugoónayá
3SG.F	murugoónaysaa	murugoónaysaa	murugoónaysó	murugoónaysá
1PL	murugoónaynaa	murugoónaynaa	murugoónaynó	murugoónayná
2PL	murugoónaysaan	murugoónayaa	murugoónaysáan	murugoónayá
3PL	murugoónayaan	murugoónayaa	murugoónayáan	murugoónayá

(14) *Simple Past*

	MC Full	MC Reduced	SC Full	SC Reduced
1SG	murugooday	murugooday	murugoodaý	murugoodaý
3SG.M	murugooday	murugooday	murugoodaý	murugoodaý
2SG	murugootay	murugooday	murugootaý	murugoodaý
3SG.F	murugootay	murugootay	murugootaý	murugootaý
1PL	murugoonnay	murugoonnay	murugoonnaý	murugoonnaý
2PL	murugooteen	murugooday	murugootéen	murugoodaý
3PL	murugoodeen	murugooday	murugoodéen	murugoodaý

The negative form of the Simple Past is the same for all combinations of person, number, and grammatical gender: *murugóon*. There are two variants of the negative for the Past Progressive: *murugóonéyn* and *murugóoneynín*.

(15) *Past Progressive*

	MC Full	MC Reduced	SC Full	SC Reduced
1SG	murugoónayay	murugoónayay	murugoónayaý	murugoónayaý
3SG.M	murugoónayay	murugoónayay	murugoónayaý	murugoónayaý
2SG	murugoónaysay	murugoónayay	murugoónaysaý	murugoónayaý
3SG.F	murugoónaysay	murugoónaysay	murugoónaysaý	murugóonaysaý
1PL	murugoónaynay	murugoónaynay	murugoónaynaý	murugoónaynaý
2PL	murugoónayseen	murugoónayay	murugoónayséen	murugoónayaý
3PL	murugoónayeen	murugoónayay	murugoónayéen	murugóonayaý

The Optative is an irrealis paradigm context, though H tone remains on the stem. There is a single negative form of the Optative for all person, number, and grammatical gender combinations: *murugóon*.

(16) *Optative*

1SG/3SG.M	murugóodo
2SG/3SG.F	murugóoto
1PL	murugóonno
2PL	murugóoteen
3PL	murugóodeen

(17) *Past Habitual*

	MC Full	MC Reduced	SC Full	SC Reduced
1SG	murugóon jiray	murugóon jiray	murugóon jiraý	murugóon jiraý
3SG.M	murugóon jiray	murugóon jiray	murugóon jiraý	murugóon jiraý
2SG	murugóon jirtay	murugóon jiray	murugóon jirtaý	murugóon jiraý
3SG.F	murugóon jirtay	murugóon jirtay	murugóon jirtaý	murugóon jirtaý
1PL	murugóon jirnay	murugóon jirnay	murugóon jirnaý	murugóon jirnaý
2PL	murugóon jirteen	murugóon jiray	murugóon jirtéen	murugóon jiraý
3PL	murugóon jireen	murugóon jiray	murugóon jiréen	murugóon jiraý

(18) *Conditional*

	MC Full	MC Reduced	SC Full	SC Reduced
1SG	murugóon lahaa	murugóon lahaa	murugóon lahaá	murugóon lahaá
3SG.M	murugóon lahaa	murugóon lahaa	murugóon lahaá	murugóon lahaá
2SG	murugóon lahayd	murugóon lahaa	murugóon laháyd	murugóon lahaá
3SG.F	murugóon lahayd	murugóon lahayd	murugóon laháyd	murugóon laháyd
1PL	murugóon lahayn	murugóon lahayn	murugóon laháyn	murugóon laháyn
2PL	murugóon lahaydeen	murugóon lahaa	murugóon lahaydéen	murugóon lahaá
3PL	murugóon lahayeen	murugóon lahaa	murugóon lahayéen	murugóon lahaá

(19) *Future*

	MC Full	MC Reduced	SC Full	SC Reduced
1SG	murugóon doonaa	murugóon doonaa	murugóon doonó	murugóon dooná
3SG.M	murugóon doonaa	murugóon doonaa	murugóon doonó	murugóon dooná
2SG	murugóon doontaa	murugóon doonaa	murugóon doontó/ murugóon doontíd	murugóon dooná
3SG.F	murugóon doontaa	murugóon doontaa	murugóon doontó	murugóon doontá
1PL	murugóon doonnaa	murugóon doonnaa	murugóon doonnó	murugóon doonná
2PL	murugóon doontaan	murugóon doonaa	murugóon doontáan	murugóon dooná
3PL	murugóon doonaan	murugóon doonaa	murugóon doonáan	murugóon dooná

(20) *Imperative*

	Affirmative	Negative
SG	murugóon	murugóonín
PL	murugóona	murugóonína

(21) *Potential*

	Affirmative	Negative
1SG/3SG.M	murugoodee	murugoodéen
2SG/3SG.F	murugootee	murugootéen
1PL	murugoonee	murugoonéen
2PL	murugooteen	murugootéen
3PL	murugoodeen	murugoodéen

A.3 Inchoative stems

The exemplar in this section for inchoative stems is *quwóob* 'become strong,' whose infinitival form is *quwoóbi* 'to become strong.' One should keep in mind that there is variation between between forms in *-ów/-óob* and *-áw/-áab* that depends on the root vowel.

(22) *Simple Present*

	MC Full	MC Reduced	SC Full	SC Reduced
1SG	quwoobaa	quwoobaa	quwoobó	quwoobá
3SG.M	quwoobaa	quwoobaa	quwoobó	quwoobá
2SG	quwowdaa	quwoobaa	quwowdó/quwowdíd	quwoobá
3SG.F	quwowdaa	quwowdaa	quwowdó	quwowdá
1PL	quwownaa	quwownaa	quwownó	quwowná
2PL	quwowdaan	quwowdaan	quwowdáan	quwoobá
3PL	quwoobaan	quwoobaan	quwoobáan	quwoobá

(23) *Present Progressive*

	MC Full	MC Reduced	SC Full	SC Reduced
1SG	quwoóbayaa	quwoóbayaa	quwoóbayó	quwoóbayá
3SG.M	quwoóbayaa	quwoóbayaa	quwoóbayó	quwoóbayá
2SG	quwoóbaysaa	quwoóbayaa	quwoóbaysó/quwoóbaysíd	quwoóbayá
3SG.F	quwoóbaysaa	quwoóbaysaa	quwoóbaysó	quwoóbaysá
1PL	quwoóbaynaa	quwoóbaynaa	quwoóbaynó	quwoóbayná
2PL	quwoóbaysaan	quwoóbayaa	quwoóbaysáan	quwoóbayá
3PL	quwoóbayaan	quwoóbayaa	quwoóbayáan	quwoóbayá

(24) *Simple Past*

	MC Full	MC Reduced	SC Full	SC Reduced
1SG	quwoobay	quwoobay	quwoobaý	quwoobaý
3SG.M	quwoobay	quwoobay	quwoobaý	quwoobaý
2SG	quwowday	quwoobay	quwowdaý	quwoobaý
3SG.F	quwowday	quwowday	quwowdaý	quwowdaý
1PL	quwownay	quwownay	quwownaý	quwownaý
2PL	quwowdeen	quwoobay	quwowdéen	quwoobaý
3PL	quwoobeen	quwoobay	quwoobéen	quwoobaý

The negative form of the Simple Past is the same for all combinations of person, number, and grammatical gender: *quwóobín*. There are two variants of the negative for the Past Progressive: *quwóobéyn* and *quwóobeynín*.

(25) *Past Progressive*

	MC Full	MC Reduced	SC Full	SC Reduced
1SG	quwoóbayay	quwoóbayay	quwoóbayaý	quwoóbayaý
3SG.M	quwoóbayay	quwoóbayay	quwoóbayaý	quwoóbayaý
2SG	quwoóbaysay	quwoóbayay	quwoóbaysaý	quwoóbayaý
3SG.F	quwoóbaysay	quwoóbaysay	quwoóbaysaý	quwoóbaysaý
1PL	quwoóbaynay	quwoóbaynay	quwoóbaynaý	quwoóbaynaý
2PL	quwoóbayseen	quwoóbayay	quwoóbayséen	quwoóbayaý
3PL	quwoóbayeen	quwoóbayay	quwoóbayéen	quwoóbayaý

The Optative is an irrealis paradigm context, though H tone remains on the stem. There is a single negative form of the Optative for all person, number, and grammatical gender combinations: *quwoobín*.

(26) *Optative*

1SG/3SG.M	quwóobo
2SG/3SG.F	quwówdo
1PL	quwówno
2PL	quwówdeen
3PL	quwóobeen

(27) *Past Habitual*

	MC Full	MC Reduced	SC Full	SC Reduced
1SG	quwoóbi jiray	quwoóbi jiray	quwoóbi jiraý	quwoóbi jiraý
3SG.M	quwoóbi jiray	quwoóbi jiray	quwoóbi jiraý	quwoóbi jiraý
2SG	quwoóbi jirtay	quwoóbi jiray	quwoóbi jirtaý	quwoóbi jiraý
3SG.F	quwoóbi jirtay	quwoóbi jirtay	quwoóbi jirtaý	quwoóbi jirtaý
1PL	quwoóbi jirnay	quwoóbi jirnay	quwoóbi jirnaý	quwoóbi jirnaý
2PL	quwoóbi jirteen	quwoóbi jiray	quwoóbi jirtéen	quwoóbi jiraý
3PL	quwoóbi jireen	quwoóbi jiray	quwoóbi jiréen	quwoóbi jiraý

(28) *Conditional*

	MC Full	MC Reduced	SC Full	SC Reduced
1SG	quwoóbi lahaa	quwoóbi lahaa	quwoóbi lahaá	quwoóbi lahaá
3SG.M	quwoóbi lahaa	quwoóbi lahaa	quwoóbi lahaá	quwoóbi lahaá
2SG	quwoóbi lahayd	quwoóbi lahaa	quwoóbi lahaýd	quwoóbi lahaá
3SG.F	quwoóbi lahayd	quwoóbi lahayd	quwoóbi lahaýd	quwoóbi lahaýd
1PL	quwoóbi lahayn	quwoóbi lahayn	quwoóbi lahaýn	quwoóbi lahaýn
2PL	quwoóbi lahaydeen	quwoóbi lahaa	quwoóbi lahaydéen	quwoóbi lahaá
3PL	quwoóbi lahayeen	quwoóbi lahaa	quwoóbi lahayéen	quwoóbi lahaá

(29) *Future*

	MC Full	MC Reduced	SC Full	SC Reduced
1SG	quwoóbi doonaa	quwoóbi doonaa	quwoóbi doonó	quwoóbi dooná
3SG.M	quwoóbi doonaa	quwoóbi doonaa	quwoóbi doonó	quwoóbi dooná
2SG	quwoóbi doontaa	quwoóbi doonaa	quwoóbi doontó/ quwoóbi doontíd	quwoóbi dooná
3SG.F	quwoóbi doontaa	quwoóbi doontaa	quwoóbi doontó	quwoóbi doontá
1PL	quwoóbi doonnaa	quwoóbi doonnaa	quwoóbi doonnó	quwoóbi doonná
2PL	quwoóbi doontaan	quwoóbi doonaa	quwoóbi doontáan	quwoóbi dooná
3PL	quwoóbi doonaan	quwoóbi doonaa	quwoóbi doonáan	quwoóbi dooná

(30) *Imperative*

	Affirmative	Negative
SG	quwów	quwóobín
PL	quwóoba	quwóobína

(31) *Potential*

	Affirmative	Negative
1SG/3SG.M	quwoobee	quwoobéen
2SG/3SG.F	quwowdee	quwowdéen
1PL	quwownee	quwownéen
2PL	quwowdeen	quwowdéen
3PL	quwoobeen	quwoobéen

A.4 Reciprocal stems

The exemplar in this section for reciprocal stems is *gaátan* 'stalk.' This is also its infinitival form.

(32) *Simple Present*

	MC Full	MC Reduced	SC Full	SC Reduced
1SG	gaatamaa	gaatamaa	gaatamó	gaatamá
3SG.M	gaatamaa	gaatamaa	gaatamó	gaatamá
2SG	gaatantaa	gaatamaa	gaatantó/gaatantíd	gaatamá
3SG.F	gaatantaa	gaatantaa	gaatantó	gaatantá
1PL	gaatannaa	gaatannaa	gaatannó	gaatanná
2PL	gaatantaan	gaatamaa	gaatantáan	gaatamá
3PL	gaatamaan	gaatamaa	gaatamáan	gaatamá

(33) *Present Progressive*

	MC Full	MC Reduced	SC Full	SC Reduced
1SG	gaatámayaa	gaatámayaa	gaatámayó	gaatámayá
3SG.M	gaatámayaa	gaatámayaa	gaatámayó	gaatámayá
2SG	gaatámaysaa	gaatámayaa	gaatámaysó/gaatámaysíd	gaatámayá
3SG.F	gaatámaysaa	gaatámaysaa	gaatámaysó	gaatámaysá
1PL	gaatámaynaa	gaatámaynaa	gaatámaynó	gaatámayná
2PL	gaatámaysaan	gaatámayaa	gaatámaysáan	gaatámayá
3PL	gaatámayaan	gaatámayaa	gaatámayáan	gaatámayá

(34) *Simple Past*

	MC Full	MC Reduced	SC Full	SC Reduced
1SG	gaatamay	gaatamay	gaatamaý	gaatamaý
3SG.M	gaatamay	gaatamay	gaatamaý	gaatamaý
2SG	gaatantay	gaatamay	gaatantaý	gaatamaý
3SG.F	gaatantay	gaatantay	gaatantaý	gaatantaý
1PL	gaatannay	gaatannay	gaatannaý	gaatannaý
2PL	gaatanteen	gaatamay	gaatantéen	gaatamaý
3PL	gaatameen	gaatamay	gaataméen	gaatamaý

The negative form of the Simple Past is the same for all combinations of person, number, and grammatical gender: *gáatan*. There are two variants of the negative for the Past Progressive: *gáataméyn* and *gáatameynín*.

(35) *Past Progressive*

	MC Full	MC Reduced	SC Full	SC Reduced
1SG	gaatámayay	gaatámayay	gaatámayaý	gaatámayaý
3SG.M	gaatámayay	gaatámayay	gaatámayaý	gaatámayaý
2SG	gaatámaysay	gaatámayay	gaatámaysaý	gaatámayaý
3SG.F	gaatámaysay	gaatámaysay	gaatámaysaý	gaatámaysáy
1PL	gaatámaynay	gaatámaynay	gaatámaynaý	gaatámaynaý
2PL	gaatámayseen	gaatámayay	gaatámayséen	gaatámayaý
3PL	gaatámayeen	gaatámayay	gaatámayéen	gaatámayaý

The Optative is an irrealis paradigm context, though H tone remains on the stem. There is a single negative form of the Optative for the relevant person and number combinations: *gáatan*.

(36) *Optative*

1SG/3SG.M	gáatamo
2SG/3SG.F	gáatanto
1PL	gáatanno
2PL	gáatanteen
3PL	gáatameen

(37) *Past Habitual*

	MC Full	MC Reduced	SC Full	SC Reduced
1SG	gáatan jiray	gáatan jiray	gáatan jiraý	gáatan jiraý
3SG.M	gáatan jiray	gáatan jiray	gáatan jiraý	gáatan jiraý
2SG	gáatan jirtay	gáatan jiray	gáatan jirtaý	gáatan jiraý
3SG.F	gáatan jirtay	gáatan jirtay	gáatan jirtaý	gáatan jirtaý
1PL	gáatan jirnay	gáatan jirnay	gáatan jirnaý	gáatan jirnaý
2PL	gáatan jirteen	gáatan jiray	gáatan jirtéen	gáatan jiraý
3PL	gáatan jireen	gáatan jiray	gáatan jiréen	gáatan jiraý

(38) *Conditional*

	MC Full	MC Reduced	SC Full	SC Reduced
1SG	gáatan lahaa	gáatan lahaa	gáatan lahaá	gáatan lahaá
3SG.M	gáatan lahaa	gáatan lahaa	gáatan lahaá	gáatan lahaá
2SG	gáatan lahayd	gáatan lahaa	gáatan lahaýd	gáatan lahaá
3SG.F	gáatan lahayd	gáatan lahayd	gáatan lahaýd	gáatan lahaýd
1PL	gáatan lahayn	gáatan lahayn	gáatan lahaýn	gáatan lahaýn
2PL	gáatan lahaydeen	gáatan lahaa	gáatan lahaydéen	gáatan lahaá
3PL	gáatan lahayeen	gáatan lahaa	gáatan lahayéen	gáatan lahaá

(39) *Future*

	MC Full	MC Reduced	SC Full	SC Reduced
1SG	gáatan doonaa	gáatan doonaa	gáatan doonó	gáatan dooná
3SG.M	gáatan doonaa	gáatan doonaa	gáatan doonó	gáatan dooná
2SG	gáatan doontaa	gáatan doonaa	gáatan doontó/ gáatan doontíd	gáatan dooná
3SG.F	gáatan doontaa	gáatan doontaa	gáatan doontó	gáatan doontá
1PL	gáatan doonnaa	gáatan doonnaa	gáatan doonnó	gáatan doonná
2PL	gáatan doontaan	gáatan doonaa	gáatan doontáan	gáatan dooná
3PL	gáatan doonaan	gáatan doonaa	gáatan doonáan	gáatan dooná

(40) *Imperative*

	Affirmative	Negative
SG	gáatan	gáatamín
PL	gáatama	gáatamína

(41) *Potential*

	Affirmative	Negative
1SG/3SG.M	gaatamee	gaataméen
2SG/3SG.F	gaatantee	gaatantéen
1PL	gaatannee	gaatannéen
2PL	gaatanteen	gaatantéen
3PL	gaatameen	gaataméen

A.5 Weak causative stems

The exemplar in this section for weak causative stems is *dhoófi* 'send abroad.' Its infinitival form is *dhoofín* 'to send abroad.'

(42) *Simple Present*

	MC Full	MC Reduced	SC Full	SC Reduced
1SG	dhoofiyaa	dhoofiyaa	dhoofiyó	dhoofiyá
3SG.M	dhoofiyaa	dhoofiyaa	dhoofiyó	dhoofiyá
2SG	dhoofisaa	dhoofiyaa	dhoofisó/dhoofisíd	dhoofiyá
3SG.F	dhoofisaa	dhoofisaa	dhoofisó	dhoofisá
1PL	dhoofinnaa	dhoofinnaa	dhoofinnó	dhoofinná
2PL	dhoofisaan	dhoofiyaa	dhoofisáan	dhoofiyá
3PL	dhoofiyaan	dhoofiyaa	dhoofiyáan	dhoofiyá

(43) *Present Progressive*

	MC Full	MC Reduced	SC Full	SC Reduced
1SG	dhoofínayaa	dhoofínayaa	dhoofínayó	dhoofínayá
3SG.M	dhoofínayaa	dhoofínayaa	dhoofínayó	dhoofínayá
2SG	dhoofínaysaa	dhoofínayaa	dhoofínaysó/dhoofínaysíd	dhoofínayá
3SG.F	dhoofínaysaa	dhoofínaysaa	dhoofínaysó	dhoofínaysá
1PL	dhoofínaynaa	dhoofínaynaa	dhoofínaynó	dhoofínayná
2PL	dhoofínaysaan	dhoofínayaa	dhoofínaysáan	dhoofínayá
3PL	dhoofínayaan	dhoofínayaa	dhoofínayáan	dhoofínayá

(44) *Simple Past*

	MC Full	MC Reduced	SC Full	SC Reduced
1SG	dhoofiyay	dhoofiyay	dhoofiyaý	dhoofiyaý
3SG.M	dhoofiyay	dhoofiyay	dhoofiyaý	dhoofiyaý
2SG	dhoofisay	dhoofiyay	dhoofisaý	dhoofiyaý
3SG.F	dhoofisay	dhoofisay	dhoofisaý	dhoofisaý
1PL	dhoofinnay	dhoofinnay	dhoofinnaý	dhoofinnaý
2PL	dhoofiseen	dhoofiyay	dhoofiséen	dhoofiyaý
3PL	dhoofiyeen	dhoofiyay	dhoofiyéen	dhoofiyaý

The negative form of the Simple Past is the same for all combinations of person, number, and grammatical gender: *dhoofin*. There are two variants of the negative for the Past Progressive: *dhoofínéyn* and *dhoofíneynín*.

(45) *Past Progressive*

	MC Full	MC Reduced	SC Full	SC Reduced
1SG	dhoofínayay	dhoofínayay	dhoofínayaý	dhoofínayaý
3SG.M	dhoofínayay	dhoofínayay	dhoofínayaý	dhoofínayaý
2SG	dhoofínaysay	dhoofínayay	dhoofínaysaý	dhoofínayaý
3SG.F	dhoofínaysay	dhoofínaysay	dhoofínaysaý	dhoofínaysaý
1PL	dhoofínaynay	dhoofínaynay	dhoofínaynaý	dhoofínaynaý
2PL	dhoofínayseen	dhoofínayay	dhoofínayséen	dhoofínayaý
3PL	dhoofínayeen	dhoofínayay	dhoofínayéen	dhoofínayaý

The Optative is an irrealis paradigm context, though H tone remains on the stem. There is a single negative form of the Optative for all person, number, and grammatical gender combinations: *dhoofín*.

(46) *Optative*

1SG/3SG.M	dhoofíyo
2SG/3SG.F	dhoofíso
1PL	dhoofínno
2PL	dhoofíseen
3PL	dhoofíyeen

(47) *Past Habitual*

	MC Full	MC Reduced	SC Full	SC Reduced
1SG	dhoofín jiray	dhoofín jiray	dhoofín jiraý	dhoofín jiraý
3SG.M	dhoofín jiray	dhoofín jiray	dhoofín jiraý	dhoofín jiraý
2SG	dhoofín jirtay	dhoofín jiray	dhoofín jirtaý	dhoofín jiraý
3SG.F	dhoofín jirtay	dhoofín jirtay	dhoofín jirtaý	dhoofín jirtaý
1PL	dhoofín jirnay	dhoofín jirnay	dhoofín jirnaý	dhoofín jirnaý
2PL	dhoofín jirteen	dhoofín jiray	dhoofín jirtéen	dhoofín jiraý
3PL	dhoofín jireen	dhoofín jiray	dhoofín jiréen	dhoofín jiraý

(48) *Conditional*

	MC Full	MC Reduced	SC Full	SC Reduced
1SG	dhoofín lahaa	dhoofín lahaa	dhoofín lahaá	dhoofín lahaá
3SG.M	dhoofín lahaa	dhoofín lahaa	dhoofín lahaá	dhoofín lahaá
2SG	dhoofín lahayd	dhoofín lahaa	dhoofín laháyd	dhoofín lahaá
3SG.F	dhoofín lahayd	dhoofín lahayd	dhoofín laháyd	dhoofín laháyd
1PL	dhoofín lahayn	dhoofín lahayn	dhoofín laháyn	dhoofín laháyn
2PL	dhoofín lahaydeen	dhoofín lahaa	dhoofín lahaydéen	dhoofín lahaá
3PL	dhoofín lahayeen	dhoofín lahaa	dhoofín lahayéen	dhoofín lahaá

(49) *Future*

	MC Full	MC Reduced	SC Full	SC Reduced
1SG	dhoofín doonaa	dhoofín doonaa	dhoofín doonó	dhoofín dooná
3SG.M	dhoofín doonaa	dhoofín doonaa	dhoofín doonó	dhoofín dooná
2SG	dhoofín doontaa	dhoofín doonaa	dhoofín doontó/ dhoofín doontíd	dhoofín dooná
3SG.F	dhoofín doontaa	dhoofín doontaa	dhoofín doontó	dhoofín doontá
1PL	dhoofín doonnaa	dhoofín doonnaa	dhoofín doonnó	dhoofín doonná
2PL	dhoofín doontaan	dhoofín doonaa	dhoofín doontáan	dhoofín dooná
3PL	dhoofín doonaan	dhoofín doonaa	dhoofín doonáan	dhoofín dooná

(50) *Imperative*

	Affirmative	Negative
SG	dhoofí	dhoofín
PL	dhoofíya	dhoofinína

(51) *Potential*

	Affirmative	Negative
1SG/3SG.M	dhoofiyee	dhoofiyéen
2SG/3SG.F	dhoofisee	dhoofiséen
1PL	dhoofinee	dhoofinéen
2PL	dhoofiseen	dhoofitéen
3PL	dhoofiyeen	dhoofiyéen

A.6 Factitive stems

The exemplar in this section for factitive stems is *adkéyn* 'strengthen.' This is also its infinitival form, though some speakers pronounce the suffix as *-áyn*.

(52) *Simple Present*

	MC Full	MC Reduced	SC Full	SC Reduced
1SG	adkeeyaa	adkeeyaa	adkeeyó	adkeeyá
3SG.M	adkeeyaa	adkeeyaa	adkeeyó	adkeeyá
2SG	adkeysaa	adkeeyaa	adkeysó/adkeysíd	adkeeyá
3SG.F	adkeysaa	adkeysaa	adkeysó	adkeysá
1PL	adkeynaa	adkeynaa	adkeynó	adkeyná
2PL	adkeysaan	adkeeyaa	adkeysáan	adkeeyá
3PL	adkeeyaan	adkeeyaa	adkeeyáan	adkeeyá

(53) *Present Progressive*

	MC Full	MC Reduced	SC Full	SC Reduced
1SG	adkéynayaa	adkéynayaa	adkéynayó	adkéynayá
3SG.M	adkéynayaa	adkéynayaa	adkéynayó	adkéynayá
2SG	adkéynaysaa	adkéynayaa	adkéynaysó/adkéynaysíd	adkéynayá
3SG.F	adkéynaysaa	adkéynaysaa	adkéynaysó	adkéynaysá
1PL	adkéynaynaa	adkéynaynaa	adkéynaynó	adkéynayná
2PL	adkéynaysaan	adkéynayaa	adkéynaysáan	adkéynayá
3PL	adkéynayaan	adkéynayaa	adkéynayáan	adkéynayá

(54) *Simple Past*

	MC Full	MC Reduced	SC Full	SC Reduced
1SG	adkeeyay	adkeeyay	adkeeyaý	adkeeyaý
3SG.M	adkeeyay	adkeeyay	adkeeyaý	adkeeyaý
2SG	adkeysay	adkeeyay	adkeysaý	adkeeyaý
3SG.F	adkeysay	adkeysay	adkeysaý	adkeysaý
1PL	adkeynay	adkeynay	adkeynaý	adkeynaý
2PL	adkeyseen	adkeeyay	adkeyséen	adkeeyaý
3PL	adkeeyeen	adkeeyay	adkeeyéen	adkeeyaý

The negative form of the Simple Past is the same for all combinations of person, number, and grammatical gender: *adkéyn*. There are two variants of the negative for the Past Progressive: *adkéynéyn* and *adkéyneynín*.

(55) *Past Progressive*

	MC Full	MC Reduced	SC Full	SC Reduced
1SG	adkéynayay	adkéynayay	adkéynayaý	adkéynayaý
3SG.M	adkéynayay	adkéynayay	adkéynayaý	adkéynayaý
2SG	adkéynaysay	adkéynayay	adkéynaysaý	adkéynayaý
3SG.F	adkéynaysay	adkéynaysay	adkéynaysaý	adkéynaysaý
1PL	adkéynaynay	adkéynaynay	adkéynaynaý	adkéynaynaý
2PL	adkéynayseen	adkéynayay	adkéynayséen	adkéynayaý
3PL	adkéynayeen	adkéynayay	adkéynayéen	adkéynayaý

The Optative is an irrealis paradigm context, though H tone remains on the stem. There is a single negative form of the Optative for all person, number, and grammatical gender combinations: *adkéyn*.

(56) *Optative*

1SG/3SG.M	adkéeyo
2SG/3SG.F	adkéyso
1PL	adkéyno
2PL	adkéyseen
3PL	adkéeyeen

(57) *Past Habitual*

	MC Full	MC Reduced	SC Full	SC Reduced
1SG	adkéyn jiray	adkéyn jiray	adkéyn jiraý	adkéyn jiraý
3SG.M	adkéyn jiray	adkéyn jiray	adkéyn jiraý	adkéyn jiraý
2SG	adkéyn jirtay	adkéyn jiray	adkéyn jirtaý	adkéyn jiraý
3SG.F	adkéyn jirtay	adkéyn jirtay	adkéyn jirtaý	adkéyn jirtaý
1PL	adkéyn jirnay	adkéyn jirnay	adkéyn jirnaý	adkéyn jirnaý
2PL	adkéyn jirteen	adkéyn jiray	adkéyn jirtéen	adkéyn jiraý
3PL	adkéyn jireen	adkéyn jiray	adkéyn jiréen	adkéyn jiraý

(58) *Conditional*

	MC Full	MC Reduced	SC Full	SC Reduced
1SG	adkéyn lahaa	adkéyn lahaa	adkéyn lahaá	adkéyn lahaá
3SG.M	adkéyn lahaa	adkéyn lahaa	adkéyn lahaá	adkéyn lahaá
2SG	adkéyn lahayd	adkéyn lahaa	adkéyn lahaýd	adkéyn lahaá
3SG.F	adkéyn lahayd	adkéyn lahayd	adkéyn lahaýd	adkéyn lahaýd
1PL	adkéyn lahayn	adkéyn lahayn	adkéyn lahaýn	adkéyn lahaýn
2PL	adkéyn lahaydeen	adkéyn lahaa	adkéyn lahaydéen	adkéyn lahaá
3PL	adkéyn lahayeen	adkéyn lahaa	adkéyn lahayéen	adkéyn lahaá

(59) *Future*

	MC Full	MC Reduced	SC Full	SC Reduced
1SG	adkéyn doonaa	adkéyn doonaa	adkéyn doonó	adkéyn dooná
3SG.M	adkéyn doonaa	adkéyn doonaa	adkéyn doonó	adkéyn dooná
2SG	adkéyn doontaa	adkéyn doonaa	adkéyn doontó/ adkéyn doontíd	adkéyn dooná
3SG.F	adkéyn doontaa	adkéyn doontaa	adkéyn doontó	adkéyn doontá
1PL	adkéyn doonnaa	adkéyn doonnaa	adkéyn doonnó	adkéyn doonná
2PL	adkéyn doontaan	adkéyn doonaa	adkéyn doontáan	adkéyn dooná
3PL	adkéyn doonaan	adkéyn doonaa	adkéyn doonáan	adkéyn dooná

(60) *Imperative*

	Affirmative	Negative
SG	adkéyn	adkéynín
PL	adkéyna	adkéynína

(61) *Potential*

	Affirmative	Negative
1SG/3SG.M	adkeeyee	adkeeyéen
2SG/3SG.F	adkeysee	adkeyséen
1PL	adkeynee	adkeynéen
2PL	adkeyseen	adkeyséen
3PL	adkeeyeen	adkeeyéen

A.7 Middle stems

The exemplar in this section for middle stems is *qabó* 'hold oneself.' Its infinitival form is *qabán* 'to hold oneself.'

(62) *Simple Present*

	MC Full	MC Reduced	SC Full	SC Reduced
1SG	qabtaa	qabtaa	qabtó	qabtá
3SG.M	qabtaa	qabtaa	qabtó	qabtá
2SG	qabataa	qabtaa	qabató/qabatíd	qabtá
3SG.F	qabataa	qabataa	qabató	qabatá
1PL	qabannaa	qabannaa	qabannó	qabanná
2PL	qabataan	qabtaa	qabatáan	qabtá
3PL	qabtaan	qabtaa	qabtáan	qabtá

(63) *Present Progressive*

	MC Full	MC Reduced	SC Full	SC Reduced
1SG	qabánayaa	qabánayaa	qabánayó	qabánayá
3SG.M	qabánayaa	qabánayaa	qabánayó	qabánayá
2SG	qabánaysaa	qabánayaa	qabánaysó/qabánaysíd	qabánayá
3SG.F	qabánaysaa	qabánaysaa	qabánaysó	qabánaysá
1PL	qabánaynaa	qabánaynaa	qabánaynó	qabánayná
2PL	qabánaysaan	qabánayaa	qabánaysáan	qabánayá
3PL	qabánayaan	qabánayaa	qabánayáan	qabánayá

(64) Simple Past

	MC Full	MC Reduced	SC Full	SC Reduced
1SG	qabtay	qabtay	qabtaý	qabtaý
3SG.M	qabtay	qabtay	qabtaý	qabtaý
2SG	qabatay	qabtay	qabataý	qabtaý
3SG.F	qabatay	qabatay	qabataý	qabataý
1PL	qabannay	qabannay	qabannaý	qabannaý
2PL	qabateen	qabtay	qabatéen	qabtaý
3PL	qabteen	qabtay	qabtéen	qabtaý

The negative form of the Simple Past is the same for all combinations of person, number, and grammatical gender: *qabán*. There are two variants of the negative for the Past Progressive: *qabánéyn* and *qabáneynín*.

(65) Past Progressive

	MC Full	MC Reduced	SC Full	SC Reduced
1SG	qabánayay	qabánayay	qabánayaý	qabánayaý
3SG.M	qabánayay	qabánayay	qabánayaý	qabánayaý
2SG	qabánaysay	qabánayay	qabánaysaý	qabánayaý
3SG.F	qabánaysay	qabánaysay	qabánaysaý	qabánaysaý
1PL	qabánaynay	qabánaynay	qabánaynaý	qabánaynaý
2PL	qabánayseen	qabánayay	qabánayséen	qabánayaý
3PL	qabánayeen	qabánayay	qabánayéen	qabánayaý

The Optative is an irrealis paradigm context, though H tone remains on the stem. There is a single negative form of the Optative for all person, number, and grammatical gender combinations: *qabán*.

(66) Optative

1SG/3SG.M	qabádo
2SG/3SG.F	qabáto
1PL	qabánno
2PL	qabáteen
3PL	qabádeen

(67) *Past Habitual*

	MC Full	MC Reduced	SC Full	SC Reduced
1SG	qabán jiray	qabán jiray	qabán jiraý	qabán jiraý
3SG.M	qabán jiray	qabán jiray	qabán jiraý	qabán jiraý
2SG	qabán jirtay	qabán jiray	qabán jirtaý	qabán jiraý
3SG.F	qabán jirtay	qabán jirtay	qabán jirtaý	qabán jirtaý
1PL	qabán jirnay	qabán jirnay	qabán jirnaý	qabán jirnaý
2PL	qabán jirteen	qabán jiray	qabán jirtéen	qabán jiraý
3PL	qabán jireen	qabán jiray	qabán jiréen	qabán jiraý

(68) *Conditional*

	MC Full	MC Reduced	SC Full	SC Reduced
1SG	qabán lahaa	qabán lahaa	qabán lahaá	qabán lahaá
3SG.M	qabán lahaa	qabán lahaa	qabán lahaá	qabán lahaá
2SG	qabán lahayd	qabán lahaa	qabán lahaýd	qabán lahaá
3SG.F	qabán lahayd	qabán lahayd	qabán lahaýd	qabán lahaýd
1PL	qabán lahayn	qabán lahayn	qabán lahaýn	qabán lahaýn
2PL	qabán lahaydeen	qabán lahaa	qabán lahaydéen	qabán lahaá
3PL	qabán lahayeen	qabán lahaa	qabán lahayéen	qabán lahaá

(69) *Future*

	MC Full	MC Reduced	SC Full	SC Reduced
1SG	qabán doonaa	qabán doonaa	qabán doonó	qabán dooná
3SG.M	qabán doonaa	qabán doonaa	qabán doonó	qabán dooná
2SG	qabán doontaa	qabán doonaa	qabán doontó/ qabán doontíd	qabán dooná
3SG.F	qabán doontaa	qabán doonaa	qabán doontó	qabán doontá
1PL	qabán doonnaa	qabán doonnaa	qabán doonnó	qabán doonná
2PL	qabán doontaan	qabán doonaa	qabán doontáan	qabán dooná
3PL	qabán doonaan	qabán doonaa	qabán doonáan	qabán dooná

(70) *Imperative*

	Affirmative	Negative
SG	qabó	qabán
PL	qabtá	qabanína

(71) *Potential*

	Affirmative	Negative
1SG/3SG.M	qabadee	qabadéen
2SG/3SG.F	qabatee	qabatéen
1PL	qabannee	qabannéen
2PL	qabateen	qabatéen
3PL	qabadeen	qabadéen

A.8 Neuter stems

The exemplar in this section for neuter stems is *beerán* 'be planted.' This is also its infinitival form.

(72) *Simple Present*

	MC Full	MC Reduced	SC Full	SC Reduced
1SG	beermaa	beermaa	beermó	beermá
3SG.M	beermaa	beermaa	beermó	beermá
2SG	beerantaa	beermaa	beerantó/beerantíd	beermá
3SG.F	beerantaa	beerantaa	beerantó	beerantá
1PL	beerannaa	beerannaa	beerannó	beeranná
2PL	beerantaan	beermaa	beerantáan	beermá
3PL	beermaan	beermaa	beermáan	beermá

(73) *Present Progressive*

	MC Full	MC Reduced	SC Full	SC Reduced
1SG	beérmayaa	beérmayaa	beérmayó	beérmayá
3SG.M	beérmayaa	beérmayaa	beérmayó	beérmayá
2SG	beérmaysaa	beérmayaa	beérmaysó/beérmaysíd	beérmayá
3SG.F	beérmaysaa	beérmaysaa	beérmaysó	beérmaysá
1PL	beérmaynaa	beérmaynaa	beérmaynó	beérmayná
2PL	beérmaysaan	beérmayaa	beérmaysáan	beérmayá
3PL	beérmayaan	beérmayaa	beérmayáan	beérmayá

(74) *Simple Past*

	MC Full	MC Reduced	SC Full	SC Reduced
1SG	beermay	beermay	beermaý	beermaý
3SG.M	beermay	beermay	beermaý	beermaý
2SG	beerantay	beermay	beerantaý	beermaý
3SG.F	beerantay	beerantay	beerantaý	beerantaý
1PL	beerannay	beerannay	beerannaý	beerannaý
2PL	beeranteen	beermay	beerantéen	beermaý
3PL	beermeen	beermay	beerméen	beermaý

The negative form of the Simple Past is the same for all combinations of person, number, and grammatical gender: *beerán*. There are two variants of the negative for the Past Progressive: *beerméyn* and *beerméynín*.

(75) *Past Progressive*

	MC Full	MC Reduced	SC Full	SC Reduced
1SG	beérmayay	beérmayay	beérmayaý	beérmayaý
3SG.M	beérmayay	beérmayay	beérmayaý	beérmayaý
2SG	beérmaysay	beérmayay	beérmaysaý	beérmayaý
3SG.F	beérmaysay	beérmaysay	beérmaysaý	beérmaysaý
1PL	beérmaynay	beérmaynay	beérmaynaý	beérmaynaý
2PL	beérmayseen	beérmayay	beérmayséen	beérmayaý
3PL	beérmayeen	beérmayay	beérmayéen	beérmayaý

The Optative is an irrealis paradigm context, though H tone remains on the stem. There is a single negative form of the Optative for all person, number, and grammatical gender combinations: *beerán*.

(76) *Optative*

1SG/3SG.M	beérmo
2SG/3SG.F	beeránto
1PL	beeránno
2PL	beeránteen
3PL	beérmeen

(77) *Past Habitual*

	MC Full	MC Reduced	SC Full	SC Reduced
1SG	beerán jiray	beerán jiray	beerán jiraý	beerán jiraý
3SG.M	beerán jiray	beerán jiray	beerán jiraý	beerán jiraý
2SG	beerán jirtay	beerán jiray	beerán jirtaý	beerán jiraý
3SG.F	beerán jirtay	beerán jirtay	beerán jirtaý	beerán jirtaý
1PL	beerán jirnay	beerán jirnay	beerán jirnaý	beerán jirnaý
2PL	beerán jirteen	beerán jiray	beerán jirtéen	beerán jiraý
3PL	beerán jireen	beerán jiray	beerán jiréen	beerán jiraý

(78) *Conditional*

	MC Full	MC Reduced	SC Full	SC Reduced
1SG	beerán lahaa	beerán lahaa	beerán lahaá	beerán lahaá
3SG.M	beerán lahaa	beerán lahaa	beerán lahaá	beerán lahaá
2SG	beerán lahayd	beerán lahaa	beerán lahaýd	beerán lahaá
3SG.F	beerán lahayd	beerán lahayd	beerán lahaýd	beerán lahaýd
1PL	beerán lahayn	beerán lahayn	beerán lahaýn	beerán lahaýn
2PL	beerán lahaydeen	beerán lahaa	beerán lahaydéen	beerán lahaá
3PL	beerán lahayeen	beerán lahaa	beerán lahayéen	beerán lahaá

(79) *Future*

	MC Full	MC Reduced	SC Full	SC Reduced
1SG	beerán doonaa	beerán doonaa	beerán doonó	beerán dooná
3SG.M	beerán doonaa	beerán doonaa	beerán doonó	beerán dooná
2SG	beerán doontaa	beerán doonaa	beerán doontó/ beerán doontíd	beerán dooná
3SG.F	beerán doontaa	beerán doontaa	beerán doontó	beerán doontá
1PL	beerán doonnaa	beerán doonnaa	beerán doonnó	beerán doonná
2PL	beerán doontaan	beerán doonaa	beerán doontáan	beerán dooná
3PL	beerán doonaan	beerán doonaa	beerán doonáan	beerán dooná

(80) *Imperative*

	Affirmative	Negative
SG	beerán	beermín
PL	beermá	beermína

(81) *Potential*

	Affirmative	Negative
1SG/3SG.M	beermee	beerméen
2SG/3SG.F	beerantee	beerantéen
1PL	beerannee	beerannéen
2PL	beeranteen	beerantéen
3PL	beermeen	beerméen

A.9 Strong causative stems

The exemplar in this section for strong causative stems is *cabsíi* 'make drink.' Its infinitival form is *cabsíin* 'to make drink.'

(82) *Simple Present*

	MC Full	MC Reduced	SC Full	SC Reduced
1SG	cabsiiyaa	cabsiiyaa	cabsiiyó	cabsiiyá
3SG.M	cabsiiyaa	cabsiiyaa	cabsiiyó	cabsiiyá
2SG	cabsiisaa	cabsiiyaa	cabsiisó/cabsiisíd	cabsiiyá
3SG.F	cabsiisaa	cabsiisaa	cabsiisó	cabsiisá
1PL	cabsiinnaa	cabsiinnaa	cabsiinnó	cabsiinná
2PL	cabsiisaan	cabsiiyaa	cabsiisáan	cabsiiyá
3PL	cabsiiyaan	cabsiiyaa	cabsiiyáan	cabsiiyá

(83) *Present Progressive*

	MC Full	MC Reduced	SC Full	SC Reduced
1SG	cabsiínayaa	cabsiínayaa	cabsiínayó	cabsiínayá
3SG.M	cabsiínayaa	cabsiínayaa	cabsiínayó	cabsiínayá
2SG	cabsiínaysaa	cabsiínayaa	cabsiínaysó/cabsiínaysíd	cabsiínayá
3SG.F	cabsiínaysaa	cabsiínaysaa	cabsiínaysó	cabsiínaysá
1PL	cabsiínaynaa	cabsiínaynaa	cabsiínaynó	cabsiínayná
2PL	cabsiínaysaan	cabsiínayaa	cabsiínaysáan	cabsiínayá
3PL	cabsiínayaan	cabsiínayaa	cabsiínayáan	cabsiínayá

(84) *Simple Past*

	MC Full	MC Reduced	SC Full	SC Reduced
1SG	cabsiiyay	cabsiiyay	cabsiiyaý	cabsiiyaý
3SG.M	cabsiiyay	cabsiiyay	cabsiiyaý	cabsiiyaý
2SG	cabsiisay	cabsiiyay	cabsiisaý	cabsiiyaý
3SG.F	cabsiisay	cabsiisay	cabsiisaý	cabsiisaý
1PL	cabsiinnay	cabsiinnay	cabsiinnaý	cabsiinnaý
2PL	cabsiiseen	cabsiiyay	cabsiiséen	cabsiiyaý
3PL	cabsiiyeen	cabsiiyay	cabsiiyéen	cabsiiyaý

The negative form of the Simple Past is the same for all combinations of person, number, and grammatical gender: *cabsíin*. There are two variants of the negative for the Past Progressive: *cabsíinéyn* and *cabsíineynín*.

(85) *Past Progressive*

	MC Full	MC Reduced	SC Full	SC Reduced
1SG	cabsíínayay	cabsíínayay	cabsíínayaý	cabsíínayaý
3SG.M	cabsíínayay	cabsíínayay	cabsíínayaý	cabsíínayaý
2SG	cabsíínaysay	cabsíínayay	cabsíínaysaý	cabsíínayaý
3SG.F	cabsíínaysay	cabsíínaysay	cabsíínaysaý	cabsíínaysaý
1PL	cabsíínaynay	cabsíínaynay	cabsíínaynaý	cabsíínaynaý
2PL	cabsíínayseen	cabsíínayay	cabsíínayséen	cabsíínayaý
3PL	cabsíínayeen	cabsíínayay	cabsíínayéen	cabsíínayaý

The Optative is an irrealis paradigm context, though H tone remains on the stem. There is a single negative form of the Optative for all person, number, and grammatical gender combinations: *cabsíin*.

(86) *Optative*

1SG/3SG.M	cabsíiyo
2SG/3SG.F	cabsíiso
1PL	cabsíinno
2PL	cabsíiseen
3PL	cabsíiyeen

(87) *Past Habitual*

	MC Full	MC Reduced	SC Full	SC Reduced
1SG	cabsíin jiray	cabsíin jiray	cabsíin jiraý	cabsíin jiraý
3SG.M	cabsíin jiray	cabsíin jiray	cabsíin jiraý	cabsíin jiraý
2SG	cabsíin jirtay	cabsíin jiray	cabsíin jirtaý	cabsíin jiraý
3SG.F	cabsíin jirtay	cabsíin jirtay	cabsíin jirtaý	cabsíin jirtaý
1PL	cabsíin jirnay	cabsíin jirnay	cabsíin jirnaý	cabsíin jirnaý
2PL	cabsíin jirteen	cabsíin jiray	cabsíin jirtéen	cabsíin jiraý
3PL	cabsíin jireen	cabsíin jiray	cabsíin jiréen	cabsíin jiraý

(88) *Conditional*

	MC Full	MC Reduced	SC Full	SC Reduced
1SG	cabsíin lahaa	cabsíin lahaa	cabsíin lahaá	cabsíin lahaá
3SG.M	cabsíin lahaa	cabsíin lahaa	cabsíin lahaá	cabsíin lahaá
2SG	cabsíin lahayd	cabsíin lahaa	cabsíin lahaýd	cabsíin lahaá
3SG.F	cabsíin lahayd	cabsíin lahayd	cabsíin lahaýd	cabsíin lahaýd
1PL	cabsíin lahayn	cabsíin lahayn	cabsíin lahaýn	cabsíin lahaýn
2PL	cabsíin lahaydeen	cabsíin lahaa	cabsíin lahaydéen	cabsíin lahaá
3PL	cabsíin lahayeen	cabsíin lahaa	cabsíin lahayéen	cabsíin lahaá

(89) *Future*

	MC Full	MC Reduced	SC Full	SC Reduced
1SG	cabsíin doonaa	cabsíin doonaa	cabsíin doonó	cabsíin dooná
3SG.M	cabsíin doonaa	cabsíin doonaa	cabsíin doonó	cabsíin dooná
2SG	cabsíin doontaa	cabsíin doonaa	cabsíin doontó/ cabsíin doontíd	cabsíin dooná
3SG.F	cabsíin doontaa	cabsíin doontaa	cabsíin doontó	cabsíin doontá
1PL	cabsíin doonnaa	cabsíin doonnaa	cabsíin doonnó	cabsíin doonná
2PL	cabsíin doontaan	cabsíin doonaa	cabsíin doontáan	cabsíin dooná
3PL	cabsíin doonaan	cabsíin doonaa	cabsíin doonáan	cabsíin dooná

(90) *Imperative*

	Affirmative	Negative
SG	cabsíi	cabsíin
PL	cabsíiya	cabsiinína

(91) *Potential*

	Affirmative	Negative
1SG/3SG.M	cabsiiyee	cabsiiyéen
2SG/3SG.F	cabsiisee	cabsiiséen
1PL	cabsiinnee	cabsiinnéen
2PL	cabsiiseen	cabsiiséen
3PL	cabsiiyeen	cabsiiyéen

A.10 Weak causative & middle stems

The exemplar in this section for weak causative & middle stems is *doorsán* 'to change.' This is its infinitival form.

(92) *Simple Present*

	MC Full	MC Reduced	SC Full	SC Reduced
1SG	doorsadaa	doorsadaa	doorsadó	doorsadá
3SG.M	doorsadaa	doorsadaa	doorsadó	doorsadá
2SG	doorsataa	doorsadaa	doorsató/doorsatíd	doorsadá
3SG.F	doorsataa	doorsataa	doorsató	doorsatá
1PL	doorsannaa	doorsannaa	doorsannó	doorsanná
2PL	doorsataan	doorsadaa	doorsatáan	doorsadá
3PL	doorsadaan	doorsadaa	doorsadáan	doorsadá

(93) *Present Progressive*

	MC Full	MC Reduced	SC Full	SC Reduced
1SG	doorsánayaa	doorsánayaa	doorsánayó	doorsánayá
3SG.M	doorsánayaa	doorsánayaa	doorsánayó	doorsánayá
2SG	doorsánaysaa	doorsánayaa	doorsánaysó/doorsánaysíd	doorsánayá
3SG.F	doorsánaysaa	doorsánaysaa	doorsánaysó	doorsánaysá
1PL	doorsánaynaa	doorsánaynaa	doorsánaynó	doorsánayná
2PL	doorsánaysaan	doorsánayaa	doorsánaysáan	doorsánayá
3PL	doorsánayaan	doorsánayaa	doorsánayáan	doorsánayá

(94) *Simple Past*

	MC Full	MC Reduced	SC Full	SC Reduced
1SG	doorsaday	doorsaday	doorsadaý	doorsadaý
3SG.M	doorsaday	doorsaday	doorsadaý	doorsadaý
2SG	doorsatay	doorsaday	doorsataý	doorsadaý
3SG.F	doorsatay	doorsatay	doorsataý	doorsataý
1PL	doorsannay	doorsannay	doorsannaý	doorsannaý
2PL	doorsateen	doorsaday	doorsatéen	doorsadaý
3PL	doorsadeen	doorsaday	doorsadéen	doorsadaý

The negative form of the Simple Past is the same for all combinations of person, number, and grammatical gender: *doorsán*. There are two variants of the negative for the Past Progressive: *doorsánéyn* and *doorsáneynín*.

(95) *Past Progressive*

	MC Full	MC Reduced	SC Full	SC Reduced
1SG	doorsánayay	doorsánayay	doorsánayaý	doorsánayaý
3SG.M	doorsánayay	doorsánayay	doorsánayaý	doorsánayaý
2SG	doorsánaysay	doorsánayay	doorsánaysaý	doorsánayaý
3SG.F	doorsánaysay	doorsánaysay	doorsánaysaý	doorsánaysaý
1PL	doorsánaynay	doorsánaynay	doorsánaynaý	doorsánaynaý
2PL	doorsánayseen	doorsánayay	doorsánayséen	doorsánayaý
3PL	doorsánayeen	doorsánayay	doorsánayéen	doorsánayaý

The Optative is an irrealis paradigm context, though H tone remains on the stem. There is a single negative form of the Optative for all person, number, and grammatical gender combinations: *doorsán*.

(96) *Optative*

1SG/3SG.M	doorsádo
2SG/3SG.F	doorsáto
1PL	doorsánno
2PL	doorsáteen
3PL	doorsádeen

(97) *Past Habitual*

	MC Full	MC Reduced	SC Full	SC Reduced
1SG	doorsán jiray	doorsán jiray	doorsán jiraý	doorsán jiraý
3SG.M	doorsán jiray	doorsán jiray	doorsán jiraý	doorsán jiraý
2SG	doorsán jirtay	doorsán jiray	doorsán jirtaý	doorsán jiraý
3SG.F	doorsán jirtay	doorsán jirtay	doorsán jirtaý	doorsán jirtaý
1PL	doorsán jirnay	doorsán jirnay	doorsán jirnaý	doorsán jirnaý
2PL	doorsán jirteen	doorsán jiray	doorsán jirtéen	doorsán jiraý
3PL	doorsán jireen	doorsán jiray	doorsán jiréen	doorsán jiraý

(98) *Conditional*

	MC Full	MC Reduced	SC Full	SC Reduced
1SG	doorsán lahaa	doorsán lahaa	doorsán lahaá	doorsán lahaá
3SG.M	doorsán lahaa	doorsán lahaa	doorsán lahaá	doorsán lahaá
2SG	doorsán lahayd	doorsán lahaa	doorsán lahaýd	doorsán lahaá
3SG.F	doorsán lahayd	doorsán lahayd	doorsán lahaýd	doorsán lahaýd
1PL	doorsán lahayn	doorsán lahayn	doorsán lahaýn	doorsán lahaýn
2PL	doorsán lahaydeen	doorsán lahaa	doorsán lahaydéen	doorsán lahaá
3PL	doorsán lahayeen	doorsán lahaa	doorsán lahayéen	doorsán lahaá

(99) *Future*

	MC Full	MC Reduced	SC Full	SC Reduced
1SG	doorsán doonaa	doorsán doonaa	doorsán doonó	doorsán dooná
3SG.M	doorsán doonaa	doorsán doonaa	doorsán doonó	doorsán dooná
2SG	doorsán doontaa	doorsán doonaa	doorsán doontó/ doorsán doontíd	doorsán dooná
3SG.F	doorsán doontaa	doorsán doontaa	doorsán doontó	doorsán doontá
1PL	doorsán doonnaa	doorsán doonnaa	doorsán doonnó	doorsán doonná
2PL	doorsán doontaan	doorsán doonaa	doorsán doontáan	doorsán dooná
3PL	doorsán doonaan	doorsán doonaa	doorsán doonáan	doorsán dooná

(100) *Imperative*

	Affirmative	Negative
SG	doorsó	doorsán
PL	doorsáda	doorsánína

(101) *Potential*

	Affirmative	Negative
1SG/3SG.M	doorsadee	doorsadéen
2SG/3SG.F	doorsatee	doorsatéen
1PL	doorsannee	doorsannéen
2PL	doorsateen	doorsatéen
3PL	doorsadeen	doorsadéen

Bibliography

Abdile, Mahdi, and Paivi Pirkkalainen. 2011. Homeland perception and recognition of the diaspora engagement: The case of the Somali diaspora. *Nordic Journal of African Studies* 20:48–70.
Abdinoor, Abdullahi. 2007. *Af-Soomaali aan ku hadalno*. Madison, WI: NALRC.
Abdullahi, Mohamed D. 1996. *Parlons somali*. Paris: L'Harmattan.
Abdullahi, Mohamed Diriye. 2000. Le somali, dialectes et histoire. Doctoral Dissertation, Université de Montréal.
Abo, Sharif Ahmed Omar. 2007. *Ilmaaytaan ha bartaan afaan Xamar (Let our children learn our dialect of Hamar)*. London: self-published.
Abu-Manga, Al-Amin, and Herrmann Jungraithmayr. 1988. On the middle voice in African languages (Fulfulde and Somali). *Journal of West African Languages* 18:65–72.
Ahmed, Ismail I. 2000. Remittances and their impact in postwar Somaliland. *Disasters* 24:380–389.
Ahmed, Jimale Ali. 1996. *Daybreak is near: Literature, clans, and the nation-state in Somalia*. Asmara: Red Sea Press.
Ajello, Roberto. 1984. Il focus nell'idioma degli ashraaf di shingaani. In *Aspetti morfologici, lessicali e della focalizzazione*, ed. Annarita Puglielli, 135–146. Rome: Ministero degli affari esteri-Dipartimento per la cooperazione allo sviluppo.
Ajello, Roberto. 1988. Theme constructions in Af Ashraaf and Standard Somali. In *Proceedings of the Third International Congress of Somali Studies*, ed. Annarita Puglielli, 78–89. Rome: Il Pensiero Scientifico Editore.
Ajello, Roberto. 1995. La focalizzazione in somalo. In *Scritti linguistici e filologici in onore di Tristano Bolelli*, ed. Roberto Ajello and Saverio Sani, 1–28. Pisa, Italy: Pacini.
Al-Sharmani, Mulki. 2006. Living transnationally: Diasporic Somali women in Cairo. *Journal of International Migration* 44:1–23.
Al-Sharmani, Mulki. 2008. Contemporary migration and transnational families: The case of Somali diaspora(s). *Migration and Refugee Moments in Middle East and North Eastern Africa*.
Ali, Mohamed Nuuh. 1985. History in the Horn of Africa, 1000 BC - 1500 (ad): Aspects of social and economic change between the Rift Valley and the Indian Ocean. Doctoral Dissertation, University of California - Los Angeles.
Andrzejewski, Bogumił W. 1955. The problem of vowel representation in the Isaaq dialect of Somali. *Bulletin of the School of Oriental and African Studies* 17:567–580.
Andrzejewski, Bogumił W. 1956. Accentual patterns in verbal forms in the Isaaq dialect of Somali. *Bulletin of the School of Oriental and African Studies* 18:103–129.
Andrzejewski, Bogumił W. 1960. Pronominal and prepositional particles in Northern Somali. *African Language Studies* 1:96–108.
Andrzejewski, Bogumił W. 1964. *The declensions of Somali nouns*. London: SOAS.
Andrzejewski, Bogumił W. 1968. Inflectional characteristics of the so-called 'weak verbs' in Somali. *African Language Studies* 9:1–51.
Andrzejewski, Bogumił W. 1969. Some observations on hybrid verbs in Somali. *African Language Studies* 10:47–89.
Andrzejewski, Bogumił W. 1971. The role of broadcasting in the adaptation of the Somali language to modern needs. In *Language use and social change: Problems of multilingualism with special reference to Eastern Africa*, ed. W. H. Whiteley, 262–273. London: International African Institute.
Andrzejewski, Bogumił W. 1975. The role of indicator particles in Somali. *Afroasiatic Linguistics* 1:123–191.
Andrzejewski, Bogumił W. 1977. The position of Somali among the languages of the world. Paper presented at the Somali Institute of Development and Administration & Management.

Andrzejewski, Bogumił W. 1978. The development of a national orthography in Somalia and the modernization of the Somali language. *Horn of Africa* 1:39–45.
Andrzejewski, Bogumił W. 1979. *The case system in Somali.* London: SOAS.
Andrzejewski, Bogumił W., and Ioan M. Lewis. 1964. *Somali poetry: An introduction.* London: Oxford University Press.
Andrzejewski, Bogumił W., Stefan Strelcyn, and Joseph Tubiana. 1966. *Somali: The writing of Somali.* Paris: UNESCO.
Angoujard, Jean-Pierre. 1989. (Dé)voisement en somali central. *Current Approaches to African Linguistics* 6:1–18.
Angoujard, Jean-Pierre, and Mohamed M. Hassan. 1991. Qualité vocalique, rythme et genre grammatical en somali. *Linguistique Africaine* 6:11–49.
Antinucci, Francesco. 1980. The syntax of indicator particles in Somali, part two: The construction of interrogative, negative, and negative-interrogative clauses. *Studies in African Linguistics* 11:1–37.
Antinucci, Francesco, and Axmed Faarax Cali. 1986. *Idaajaa.* Rome: Ministero Affari Esteri.
Antinucci, Francesco, Lucyna Gebert, and Annarita Puglielli. 1980. *Studi sulla lingua somala.* Università di Roma.
Antinucci, Francesco, and Annarita Puglielli. 1980. The syntax of indicator particles in Somali: Relative clause constructions. *Afroasiatic Linguistics* 7:85–102.
Antinucci, Francesco, and Annarita Puglielli. 1984. Relative clause construction in Somali: A comparison between the Northern and Coastal dialects. In *Current progress in Afro-Asiatic linguistics: Papers of the Third International Hamito-Semitic Congress, London, 1978*, ed. James Bynon, 17–31. Amsterdam: John Benjamins.
Appleyard, David L. 1990. Prepositional particles in Somali and their cognates in other Cushitic languages. *African Languages and Cultures* 3:15–31.
Appleyard, David L. 2001. The verb 'to say' as a verb 'recycling device' in Ethiopian languages. In *New data and new methods in Afroasiatic linguistics: Robert Hetzron in memoriam*, ed. Andrzej Zaborski, 1–11. Wiesbaden: Harrassowitz.
Appleyard, David L., and Martin Orwin. 2008. The Horn of Africa: Ethiopia, Eritrea, Djibouti, and Somalia. In *Language and national identity in Africa*, ed. Andrew Simpson, 267–290. Oxford: Oxford University Press.
Armstrong, Lilias E. 1934. *The phonetic structure of Somali.* Hants, UK: Gregg Press.
Aïm, Emmanuel. 1999. Cas d'harmonie et de disharmonie vocalique en somali. Master's thesis, Université Paris 7.
Banti, Giorgio. 1984a. The morphology of the nominative case in Somali. In *Discussion papers for the Fifth International Phonology Meeting*, ed. Wolfgang Dressler, Oskar E. Pfeiffer, and John R. Rennison, 27–31. Vienna: University of Vienna.
Banti, Giorgio. 1984b. Possessive affixes in the Somali area. In *Proceedings of the Second International Congress of Somali Studies*, ed. Thomas Labahn, 135–154. Hamburg: Helmut Buske.
Banti, Giorgio. 1985. *Lineamenti di fonologia, morfologia e sintassi del somalo e dei suoi dialetti.* Università di Roma.
Banti, Giorgio. 1988a. 'Adjectives' in East Cushitic. In *Cushitic-Omotic: Papers from the International Symposium on Cushitic and Omotic languages*, ed. Marianne Bechaus-Gerst and Fritz Serzisko, 202–259. Hamburg: Helmut Buske.
Banti, Giorgio. 1988b. Reflections on derivation from prefix-conjugated verbs in Somali. In *Proceedings of the Third International Congress of Somali Studies*, ed. Annarita Puglielli, 43–59. Rome: Il Pensiero Scientifico.
Banti, Giorgio. 1988c. Two Cushitic systems: Somali and Oromo nouns. In *Autosegmental studies on pitch accent*, ed. Harry van der Hulst and Norval Smith, 11–50. Berlin: de Gruyter.

Banti, Giorgio. 2011a. Internally-headed relative clauses in literary Somali. In *A country called Somalia: Culture, language and society of a vanishing state*, ed. Mara Frascarelli, 32–47. Rome: Università degli Studi Roma Tre.
Banti, Giorgio. 2011b. Somali. In *Encyclopaedia Aethiopica, vol. 4*, ed. Siegbert Uhlig, 693–696. Wiesbaden, Germany: Harrassowitz.
Banti, Giorgio. 2013. Strata on loanwords from Arabic and other Semitic languages in Northern Somali. In *Africa Arabic: Approaches to dialectology*, ed. Mena Lafkioui, 185–210. Berlin: Walter de Gruyter.
Banti, Giorgio. 2019. Expressing focus in Somali without the best-known focus markers. Paper presented at Workshop on Somali Grammar, University of Gothenburg.
Banti, Giorgio, and Francesco Giannattasio. 1996. Music and meter in Somali poetry. *African Languages and Cultures* Supplement 3:83–127.
Barillot, Xavier. 2002. Morphophonologie gabaritique et information consonantique latente en somali et dans les langues est-couchitiques. Doctoral Dissertation, Université Paris VII Denis Diderot.
Barillot, Xavier, Sabrina Bendjaballah, and Nicola Lampitelli. 2018. Verbal classes in Somali: Allomorphy has no classificatory function. *Journal of Linguistics* 54:3–43.
Barillot, Xavier, and Philippe Ségéral. 2005. On phonological processes in the "3rd conjugation" of Somali. *Folia Orientalia* 41:115–133.
Bell, Christopher Richard Vincent. 1953. *The Somali language*. Hants, UK: Gregg International.
Bendjaballah, Sabrina. 1998. La palatalisation en somali. *Linguistique Africaine* 21:1–48.
Bendjaballah, Sabrina, and David Le Gac. 2019. The acoustics of Somali voiced stops. Paper presented at the Workshop on Somali Grammar, University of Gothenburg.
Berchem, Jorg. 1991. *Referenzgrammatik des Somali*. Köln: Omimee Intercultural.
Biber, Douglas. 1982. Accent in the Central Somali nominal system. *Studies in African Linguistics* 13:1–10.
Biber, Douglas. 1984a. The diachronic development of preverbal case markers in Somali. *Journal of African Languages and Linguistics* 6:47–62.
Biber, Douglas. 1984b. Pragmatic roles in Central Somali narrative discourse. *Studies in African Linguistics* 15:1–26.
Bigelow, Martha A. 2010a. *Mogadishu on the Mississippi: Language, racialized identity, and education in a new land*. Malden, MA: Wiley and Sons.
Bigelow, Martha A. 2010b. Orality and literacy within the Somali diaspora. *Language Learning* 60:25–57.
Blevins, Juliette. 2004. *Evolutionary phonology: The emergence of sound patterns*. Cambridge: CUP.
Bourdin, Phillippe. 2002. The grammaticalization of deictic directionals into modulators of temporal distance. In *New reflections on grammaticalization*, ed. Ilse Wischer and Gabriele Diewald, 181–200. Philadelphia: John Benjamins.
Bourdin, Phillippe. 2005. The marking of directional deixis in Somali. *Typological Studies in Language* 64:13–42.
Bybee, Joan. 1998. Irrealis as a grammatical category. *Anthropological Linguistics* 40:257–271.
Cabredo Hofherr, Patricia. 2004. Impersonal pronouns in Somali, German, and French. Paper presented at Syntax of the World's Languages 1. Max Planck Institute.
Cabredo Hofherr, Patricia. 2007. Reciprocals in Somali. Paper presented at Reciprocals Cross-Linguistically. Berlin.
Callegari, Laura. 1988. I prestiti arabi nella lingua somala. Doctoral Dissertation, Istituto di Orientalistica, Università degli Studi di Torino.
Caney, John C. 1984. *The modernization of Somali vocabulary with particular reference to the period from 1972 to the present*. Hamburg: Helmut Buske.

Carcoforo, Enrico. 1912. *Elementi di somalo e ki-suahili parlati al benadir*. Milan: Ulrico Hoepli.
Cardona, Giorgio R. 1981. Profilo fonologico del somalo. In *Fonologia & Lessico - Studi Somali I*, ed. Giorgio R. Cardona and Francesco Agostini, 5–26. Rome: Ministero Affari Esteri, Roma.
Carter, Joy. 1984. *La soco Af-Soomaaliga*. Nairobi, Kenya: Mennonite Board of East Africa.
Casali, Roderic F. 2003. [ATR] value asymmetries and underlying vowel inventory structure in Niger-Congo and Nilo-Saharan. *Linguistic Typology* 7:307–382.
Casali, Roderic F. 2008. ATR harmony in African languages. *Language and Linguistics Compass* 2:496–549.
Casali, Roderic F. 2016. Some inventory-related asymmetries in the patterning of tongue root harmony systems. *Studies in African Linguistics* 45:95–140.
Cerulli, Enrico. 1964. Lingua somala in caratteri arabi. *Somalia: Scritti vari editi ed inediti* 3:115–151.
Comfort, Jade, and Mary Paster. 2009. Notes on Lower Jubba Maay. In *Selected proceedings of the 38th Annual Conference on African Linguistics: Linguistic theory and African language documentation*, ed. Masangu Matondo, Fiona McLaughlin, and Eric Potsdam, 204–216. Somerville, MA: Cascadilla.
Darmon, Chloe. 2012. Light verb constructions in Xamtanga. In *Selected proceedings of the 42nd Annual Conference on African Linguistics*, ed. Michael R. Marlo, Nikki B. Adams, Christopher R. Green, Michelle E. Morrison, and Tristan M. Purvis, 183–194. Somerville, MA: Cascadilla.
Dhoorre, Cabdulqaadir Salaad, and Mauro Tosco. 1998. Somali ideophones. *Journal of African Cultural Studies* 11:125–156.
Downing, Laura J., and Morgan Nilsson. 2019. Prosodic restructuring in Somali nominals. In *African linguistics across the disciplines: Selected papers from the 48th Annual Conference on African Linguistics*, ed. Samson Lotven, Silvina Bongiovanni, Phillip Weirich, Robert Botne, and Samuel G. Obeng, 125–142. Berlin: Language Science Press.
Eberhard, David M., Gary F. Simons, and Charles D. Fennig. 2019. *Ethnologue: Languages of the World, 22nd edition*. Dallas, TX: SIL International.
Edmondson, Jerold A., John H. Esling, and Jimmy G. Harris. 2004. Supraglottal cavity shape, linguistic register, and other phonetic features of Somali. Unpublished ms.
Ehret, Christopher. 2011. *History and the testimony of language*. Berkeley, CA: University of California Press.
Ehret, Christopher, and Mohamed Nuuh Ali. 1984. Soomaali classification. In *Proceedings of the Second International Congress of Somali Studies*, ed. Thomas Labahn, 201–269. Hamburg: Helmut Buske.
El-Somali-Mewis, Catherine. 1987. *Lehrbuch des Somali*. Hamburg: Helmut Buske.
Elliott, J.R. 2000. Realis and irrealis: Forms and concepts of the grammaticalisation of reality. *Linguistic Typology* 4:55–90.
Farnetani, Edda. 1981. Dai tratti ai parametri: introduzione all'analisi strumentale della lingua somala. In *Fonologia & Lessico - Studi Somali I*, ed. Giorgio R. Cardona and Francesco Agostini, 29–108. Rome: Ministero Affari Esteri, Roma.
Frascarelli, Mara. 2010a. Narrow focus, clefting and predicated inversion. *Lingua* 120:2121–2147.
Frascarelli, Mara. 2010b. Scope marking and focus in Somali. *Linguistic Variation Yearbook* 10:78–116.
Frascarelli, Mara, and Annarita Puglielli. 2003. Focus markers and universal grammar. In *Omotic and Cushitic language studies: Papers from the Fourth Cushitic Omotic Conference*, ed. Azeb Amha, 119–134. Köln: Rüdiger Köppe.
Frascarelli, Mara, and Annarita Puglielli. 2007. Focus in the Force-Fin system. In *Focus strategies in African languages: The interaction of focus and grammar in Niger-Congo and Afro-Asiatic*, ed. Enoch Aboh, Katharina Hartmann, and Malte Zimmermann, 333–358. Berlin: Mouton de Gruyter.

Frascarelli, Mara, and Annarita Puglielli. 2009. Information structure in Somali: Evidence from the syntax-phonology interface. *Brill's Annual of Afroasiatic Languages and Linguistics* 1:146–175.
Frid, Johan. 1995. Aspects of Somali tonology. Unpublished ms. Lund University.
Gabbard, Kevin. 2010. A phonological analysis of Somali and the guttural consonants. BA thesis, The Ohio State University.
Gabbard, Kevin. 2014. Two Somali dialects: Self-destructive feeding versus counter-bleeding. Paper presented at the 45th Annual Conference on African Linguistics, University of Kansas.
Gajraj, Priya, Shonali Sardesai, and Per Wam. 2005. Conflict in Somali: Drivers and dynamics. Unpublished ms.
Galaal, Muuse Xaaji Ismaaciil. 1954. Arabic script for Somali. *Islamic Quarterly* 1/2:114–118.
Gebert, Lucyna. 1986. Focus and word order in Somali. *Afrikanistiche Arbeitspapiere* 5:43–69.
Gebert, Lucyna. 1988. Notes on Somali verbal aspect. In *Proceedings of the Third International Congress of Somali Studies*, ed. Annarita Puglielli, 60–68. Rome:Il Pensiero Scientifico Editore.
Givón, Talmy. 1994. Irrealis and the subjunctive. *Studies in Language* 18:265–337.
Godon, Elsa. 1998. Aspects de la morphologie nominale du somali: la formation du pluriel. Master's thesis, Université Paris 7.
Green, Christopher R. 2019. Prosodic and morphosyntactic conditions on Somali cliticization. Paper presented at Workshop on Somali Grammar, University of Gothenburg.
Green, Christopher R., and Evan Jones. 2018. Notes on the morphology of Marka (Af-Ashraaf). In *Theory and description in African linguistics: Selected papers from the 47th Annual Conference on African Linguistics*, ed. Emily Clem, Peter Jenks, and Hannah Sande, 117–132. Berlin: Language Science Press.
Green, Christopher R., and Nicola Lampitelli. 2021. Prosodic conditions on complex exponence: A case study of the Somali subject marker. Unpublished ms.
Green, Christopher R., and Michelle E. Morrison. 2015. On the realization, representation, and prosodic function of Somali topic-marking. Paper presented at the 12th Old World Conference on Phonology.
Green, Christopher R., and Michelle E. Morrison. 2016. Somali wordhood and its relationship to prosodic structure. *Morphology* 26:3–32.
Green, Christopher R., and Michelle E. Morrison. 2018. On the morphophonology of domains in Somali verbs and nouns. *Brill's Journal of Afroasiatic Languages and Linguistics* 10:200–237.
Green, Christopher R., Michelle E. Morrison, Nikki B. Adams, Erin Smith Crabb, Evan Jones, and Valerie Novak. 2014. An annotated bibliography of reference and pedagogical resources for 'standard' Somali. *Electronic Journal of Africana Bibliography* 15:1–33.
Greenberg, Joseph. 1963. *The languages of Africa*. Bloomington, IN: Indiana University.
'Guri-Barwaaqo', Cabdiraxmaan C. Faarax. 2018. The behaviour of the suffixes -le, -ley, -ey and la in Somali. In *Papers from the linguistics workshop: Somali language and literature at the Hargeysa Cultural Centre, December 2015*, ed. Martin Orwin, 53–61. Hargeysa: Ponte Invisibile.
Hagi, Aves Osman, and Adbiwahid Osman Hagi. 1998. *Clan, sub-clan, and regional representation in the Somali government organization, 1960-1990: Statistical data and findings*. Self-published.
Hall, Beatrice L., R. M. R. Hall, and Martin D. Pam. 1973. African vowel harmony systems from the vantage point of Kalenjin. *Afrika und Übersee* 57:241–267.
Hall, T. A., and Silke Hamann. 2006. Towards a typology of stop assibilation. *Linguistics* 44:1195–1236.
Hamann, Silke, and Susanne Fuchs. 2008. How do voiced retroflex stops evolve: Evidence from typology and an articulatory study. *ZAS Papers in Linguistics* 49:97–130.
Hared, Mohamed Farah. 1992. Modernization and standardization in Somali press writing. Doctoral Dissertation, University of Southern California.

Hargreaves, Katherine. 2006. A computational implementation of Somali morphosyntax. Doctoral Dissertation, University of Manchester.

Hargreaves, Katherine, and Allan Ramsay. 2006. Local constraints on sentence markers and focus in Somali. In *Proceedings of the COLING/ACL 2006 Main Conference Poster Sessions*, 337–344. Sydney, Australia: Association for Computational Linguistics.

Hashi, Abdirahman A. 1998. *Essential Somali-English dictionary*. Addis Abeba, Ethiopia: Fiqi Educational Materials.

Hayward, Richard J., and John I. Saeed. 1984. NP focus in Somali and Dirayta: A comparison of *baa* and *pa*. In *Proceedings of the Second International Congress of Somali Studies*, ed. Thomas Labahn, 1–21. Hamburg: Helmut Buske.

Heine, Bernd. 1978. The Sam languages: A history of Rendille, Boni and Somali. *Afroasiatic Linguistics* 6:23–115.

Hetzron, Robert. 1965. The particle *baa* in Northern Somali. *Journal of African Languages* 4:118–130.

Hetzron, Robert. 1980. The limits of Cushitic. *Sprache und Beschichte in Afrika* 2:7–126.

Houssein, Charmarkeh. 2013. Diaspora, memory, and ethnic media: Media use by Somalis living in Canada. *Bildhaan* 12:87–105.

Hunter, Frederick M. 1880. *A grammar of the Somali language*. Byculla, India: The Education Society's Press.

Hyman, Larry M. 1981. Tonal accent in Somali. *Studies in African Linguistics* 12:169–203.

Hyman, Larry M. 2006. Word-prosodic typology. *Phonology* 23:225–257.

Hyman, Larry M. 2019a. Do all languages have word accent? In *Word stress: Theoretical and typological issues*, ed. Harry van der Hulst, 56–82. Cambridge: Cambridge University Press.

Hyman, Larry M. 2019b. Positional prominence vs. word accent. In *The study of word stress and accent: Theories, methods and data*, ed. Rob Goedemans, Jeffrey Heinz, and Harry van der Hulst, 60–75. Cambridge: Cambridge University Press.

Ismail, Abdirachid M. 2015. *Dialectologie du somali: problématiques et perspectives*. Riga, Latvia: Presses Académiques Francophones.

Ismail, Abdirachid Mohamed. 2011. Dialectologie du somali: problématiques et perspectives. Doctoral Dissertation, INALCO.

Issa-Salwe, Abdisalam M. 2006. The internet and the Somali diaspora: The web as a new means of expression. *Bildhaan* 6:54–67.

Iverson, Gregory, and Joseph C. Salmons. 2006. On the typology of final laryngeal neutralization: Evolutionary phonology and laryngeal realism. *Theoretical Linguistics* 32:5–36.

Johnson, John W. 1979. Somali prosodic systems. *Horn of Africa* 2:46–54.

Johnson, John W. 1984. Recent researches into the scansion of Somali oral poetry. In *Proceedings of the Second International Congress of Somali Studies*, ed. Thomas Labahn, 313–331. Hamburg: Helmut Buske.

Johnson, John W. 1988. Set theory in Somali poetics: Structures and implications. In *Proceedings of the Third International Congress of Somali Studies*, ed. Annarita Puglielli, 123–132. Rome: Il Pensiero Scientifico Editore.

Johnson, John W. 1996. Musico-moro-syllabic relationships in the scansion of Somali oral poetry. In *Voice and power: The culture of language in north-east Africa*, ed. R. J. Hayward and Ioan M. Lewis, 73–82. London: SOAS.

Kaldhol, Nina Hagen. 2017. The Oslo dialect of Somali: Tonal adaptations of Norwegian loanwords. Master's thesis, University of Oslo.

Kaldhol, Nina Hagen. 2019. Gender and tone assignment to nominal compounds in Somali. Paper presented at University of Gothenburg.

Kimper, Wendell, William Bennett, Christopher Green, and Kristine Yu. 2018. Acoustic correlates of harmony classes in Somali. In *Theory and description in African linguistics: Selected pa-*

pers from the 47th Annual Conference on African Linguistics, ed. Emily Clem, Peter Jenks, and Hannah Sande, 195–210. Berlin: Language Science Press.

Kirk, John W. C. 1905. *A grammar of the Somali language, with examples in prose and verse and an account of the Yibir and Midgan dialects*. London: Cambridge University Press.

Kleist, Nauja. 2004. Nomads, sailors, and refugees: A brief history of Somali migration. *Sussex Migration Working Papers* 23:1–14.

Kleist, Nauja. 2008. Mobilising 'The Diaspora': Somali transnational political engagement. *Journal of Ethnic and Migration Studies* 34:307–323.

Klingenheben, August. 1949. Ist das Somali eine Tonsprache? *Zeitschrift für Phonetik und allgemeine Sprachwissenschaft* 3:289–303.

Labahn, Thomas. 1982. *Sprache und Staat*. Hamburg: Helmut Buske.

Lahrouchi, Mohamed, and Nicola Lampitelli. 2014. On plurals, noun phrase and num(ber) in Moroccan Arabic and Djibouti Somali. In *The form of structure, the structure of form: Essays in honor of Jean Lowenstamm*, ed. Sabrina Bendjaballah, Noam Faust, Mohamed Lahrouchi, and Nicola Lampitelli, 303–314. Amsterdam: John Benjamins.

Laitin, David D. 1977. *Politics, language, and thought: The Somali experience*. Chicago: University of Chicago Press.

Lamberti, Marcello. 1984. The linguistic situation in the Somali Democratic Republic. In *Proceedings of the Second International Congress of Somali Studies*, ed. Thomas Labahn, 155–200. Hamburg: Helmut Buske.

Lamberti, Marcello. 1986. Die Somali-Dialekte: eine vergleichende Untersuchung. Doctoral Dissertation, University of Cologne.

Lampitelli, Nicola. 2011. Forme phonologique, exposants morphologiques et structure nominales: étude comparée de l'italien, du bosnien et du somali. Doctoral Dissertation, Université Paris Diderot.

Lampitelli, Nicola. 2013. The decomposition of Somali nouns. *Brill's Annual on Afroasiatic Languages and Linguistics* 5:117–158.

Lampitelli, Nicola. 2015. Somali. In *The Edinburgh handbook of evaluative morphology*, ed. Nicola Grandi and Livia Korvélyessy, 507–514. Edinburgh: Edinburgh University Press.

Lampitelli, Nicola. 2017. Pluralization, feminization and pitch accent in Djibouti Somali nouns. *Journal of African Languages and Linguistics* 38:89–132.

Lampitelli, Nicola. 2019. On nominal declensions and syntactic case. Paper presented at Workshop on Somali Grammar, University of Gothenburg.

de Larajasse, Fr. Evangelist. 1897. *Somali-English and English-Somali dictionary*. London: K. Paul, Trench, Trübner and Co.

de Larajasse, Fr. Evangelist, and Fr. Cyprien de Sampont. 1897. *Practical grammar of the Somali language, with a manual of sentences*. London: K. Paul, Trench, Trübner and Co.

Le Gac, David. 1997. L'intonation du GN en somali standard. Master's thesis, Université Paris 7.

Le Gac, David. 2001. Structure prosodique de la focalisation: le cas du somali et du français. Doctoral Dissertation, Université Paris 7.

Le Gac, David. 2002. Tonal alternations and prosodic structure in Somali. In *Proceedings of Speech Prosody 2002*, ed. Bernard Bel and Isabelle Marlien, 455–458. Aix-en-Provence: Laboratoire Parole et Langage, CNRS.

Le Gac, David. 2003a. Marques prosodiques de la focalisation contrastive en somali. In *Fonction et moyens d'expression de la focalisation à travers les langues*, ed. A. Lacheret-Dujour and J. Francois, 49–80. Leuven, Belgium: Peeters.

Le Gac, David. 2003b. Tonal alternations in Somali. In *Research in Afroasiatic grammar II*, ed. Jacqueline Lecarme, 287–304. Amsterdam, Philadelphia: John Benjamins.

Le Gac, David. 2016. Somali as a tone language. Paper presented at Speech Prosody 2016, Boston, MA.
Leben, William. 1973. Suprasegmental phonology. Doctoral Dissertation, MIT.
Lecarme, Jacqueline. 1984. On Somali complement constructions. In *Proceedings of the 2nd International Congress on Somali*, ed. Thomas Labahn, 37–54. Hamburg: Helmut Buske.
Lecarme, Jacqueline. 1991. Focus en somali: syntaxe et interpretation. *Linguistique Africaine* 7:34–64.
Lecarme, Jacqueline. 1994. Focus et effets 'verbe second' en somali. *Recherches Linguistiques de Vincennes* 23:25–44.
Lecarme, Jacqueline. 1995. L'accord restrictif en somali. *Langues Orientales Anciennes Philologie et Linguistique* 5-6:133–152.
Lecarme, Jacqueline. 1996. Tense in the nominal system: The Somali DP. In *Studies in Afroasiatic grammar*, ed. Jacqueline Lecarme, Jean Lowenstamm, and Ur Shlonsky, 159–178. The Hague: Holland Academic Graphics.
Lecarme, Jacqueline. 1999a. Focus in Somali. *Linguistik aktuell: The grammar of focus* 24:275–310.
Lecarme, Jacqueline. 1999b. Nominal tense and tense theory. *Empirical issues in formal syntax and semantics* 2:333–354.
Lecarme, Jacqueline. 2002. Gender 'polarity': Theoretical aspects of Somali nominal morphology. In *Many morphologies*, ed. Paul Boucher and Marc Plenat, 109–141. Somerville, MA: Cascadilla.
Lecarme, Jacqueline. 2008. Tense and modality in nominals. In *Time and modality*, ed. Jacqueline Guéron and Jacqueline Lecarme, 195–225. Springer.
Lewis, Ioan M. 1955. *The peoples of the Horn of Africa: Somali, Afar, and Saho*. London: International African Institute.
Lewis, Ioan M. 1958. The Gadabuursi Somali script. *Bulletin of the School of Oriental and African Studies* 21:134–156.
Lewis, Ioan M. 1999. *A pastoral democracy: A study of pastoralism and politicals among the Northern Somalis of the Horn of Africa*. New York: James Currey Publishers.
Lewis, Ioan M. 2002. *A modern history of the Somali: Nation and state in the Horn of Africa*, 4th edn. Oxford: James Currey.
Lewis, Ioan M. 2010. *Making the breaking states in Africa: The Somali experience*. Asmara: Red Sea Press.
Livnat, Michal A. 1983. The indicator particle *baa* in Somali. *Studies in the Linguistic Sciences* 13.
Livnat, Michal A. 1984. Focus constructions in Somali. Doctoral Dissertation, University of Illinois at Urbana-Champaign.
Maddieson, Ian, Sinisa Spajic, Bonny Sands, and Peter Ladefoged. 1993. Phonetic structures of Dahalo. *Afrikanistische Arbeitspapiere* 36:5–53.
Maffi, Luisa. 1984. Somali colour terminology: An outline. In *Proceedings of the Second International Congress on Somali*, ed. Thomas Labahn, 299–312. Hamburg: Helmut Buske.
Maffi, Luisa. 1990. Somali color term evolution: Grammatical and semantic evidence. *Anthropological Linguistics* 32:316–334.
Maino, Mario. 1951. L'alfabeto osmania in Somalia. *Rassegna di Studi Etiopici* 10:108–121.
Maino, Mario. 1953. *La lingua somala strumento di insegnamento professionale*. Alessandria: Ferrari, Occella and Co.
Maniscalco, Samuele. 2015. The gender system of Somali. Master's thesis, Humboldt Universität zu Berlin.
Mansur, Abdalla Omar, and Annarita Puglielli. 1999. *Barashada naxwaha Af Soomaaliga: A somali school grammar*. London: Haan.
Mansur, Cabdalla C. 1984. Some traces of Somali history in Maay dialect. In *Proceedings of the 2nd International Congress on Somali*, ed. Thomas Labahn. Hamburg: Helmut Buske.

Mauri, Caterina, and Andrea Sansò. 2012. What do languages encode when they encode reality status? *Language Sciences* 34:99–106.
Mauri, Caterina, and Andrea Sansò. 2016. The linguistic marking of (ir)realis and subjunctive. In *The Oxford handbook of modality and mood*, ed. Jan Nuyts and Johan van der Auwera, 166–195. Oxford: Oxford University Press.
Meinhof, Carl. 1912. *Die Sprachen der Hamiten*. Hamburg: L & R Friederischsen.
Mioni, Alberto M. 1988. Italian and English loanwords in Somali. In *Proceedings of the Third International Conference of Somali Studies*, ed. Annarita Puglielli, 36–42. Rome: Il Pensiero Scientifico Editore.
Mithun, Marianne. 1995. On the relativity of irreality. In *Modality in grammar and discourse*, ed. Joan Bybee and Suzanne Fleischman, 367–388. Amsterdam: John Benjamins.
Mohamoud, Hawa A. 2013. ATR harmony in Somali: Neutral vowels and dialectal variation. Master's thesis, Leiden University.
Moreno, Marcello Mario. 1953. Il dialetto Ašrâf di Mogadiscio. *Rassegna di studi etiopici* 12 and 13:107–138, 105–119.
Moreno, Marcello Mario. 1955. *Il somalo della Somalia: grammatica e testi del Benadir, Darod e Dighil*. Roma: Istituto Poligrafico dello Stato.
Morin, Didier. 1984. À propos des emprunts à l'arabe et au francais en afar et en somali à Djibouti. In *Proceedings of the 2nd International Congress on Somali*, ed. Thomas Labahn. Hamburg: Helmut Buske.
Morin, Didier. 1991. Marques et relations en somali: le problème des 'déclinaisons'. *Linguistique Africaine* 6:75–102.
Morin, Didier. 1995. *Des parole douces comme la soie: Introduction aux contes dans l'aire couchitique (bédja, afar, saho, somali)*. Leuven, Belgium: Peeters.
Morrison, Michelle E. 2016. Sóó and síí: Contrasting 'self' and 'other' in Somali deictics. Paper presented at the 47th Annual Conference on African Linguistics.
Morrison, Michelle E., and Abdullaziz A. Abokor. 2016. A comparative reference guide to Maay and other language varieties of southern Somalia. Unpublished ms. University of Maryland.
Mous, Maarten. 1993. *A grammar of Iraqw*. Hamburg: Helmut Buske.
Mous, Maarten. 2012. Cushitic. In *The Afroasiatic languages*, ed. Zygmunt Frajzyngier and Erin Shay, 342–422. Cambridge: Cambridge University Press.
Mukhtar, Mohamed H., and Omar M. Ahmed. 2007. *English-Maay dictionary*. London: Adonis and Abbey.
Nagano-Madsen, Yasuko, Laura Downing, and Morgan Nilsson. 2019. Aspects of Somali intonation. Paper presented at the Somali Grammar Workshop, University of Gothenburg.
Nespor, Marina, and Irene Vogel. 1985. *Prosodic phonology*. Dordrecht: Foris.
Nilsson, Morgan. 2016a. Somali gender polarity revisited. In *Diversity in African languages*, ed. Doris Payne, Pacchiarotti, and Mokaya Bosire, 451–466. Berlin: Language Science Press.
Nilsson, Morgan. 2016b. *Somali language and linguistics: A bibliography*. University of Gothenburg.
Nilsson, Morgan. 2017. Does tone mark case in Somali? Paper presented at the 14th International Conference of Africanists, Moscow.
Nilsson, Morgan. 2018. Grammatical gender and number in Somali nouns. In *Papers from the Linguistics Workshop: Somali Language and Literature at the Hargeysa Cultural Centre, December 2015*, ed. Martin Orwin, 27–52. Hargeysa, Somaliland: RedSea.
Nilsson, Morgan. 2019. On the non-canonicity of case in Somali. Paper presented at Workshop on Somali Grammar, University of Gothenburg.
Nilsson, Morgan, and Laura J. Downing. 2019. Somali vowel qualities and vowel harmony domains. Paper presented at NACAL 47, Paris.

Nimaan, Abdillahi, Pascal Nocera, and Jean-François Bonastre. 2006. Towards automatic transcription of Somali language. In *Proceedings of the Language Resource and Evaluation Conference (LREC)*, 131–134.

Olgac, Christina Rodell. 2001. Socialisation, language and learning in a Somali diasporic community in Rinkeby. *Africa and Asia* 1:69–78.

Orwin, Martin. 1991. Arabic loanwords in the Somali language. *Journal of the Anglo-Somali Society* 27–29.

Orwin, Martin. 1993. Phonation in Somali phonology. In *Anthropologie somaliénne*, ed. Mahamed Abdi, 251–257. University of Besançon.

Orwin, Martin. 1994. Aspects of Somali phonology. Doctoral Dissertation, University of London.

Orwin, Martin. 1995. *Colloquial Somali: A complete language course*. London: Routledge.

Orwin, Martin. 1996. A moraic model of the prosodic phonology of Somali. *African Languages and Cultures* Supplement 3:51–71.

Orwin, Martin. 2001. On consonants in Somali metrics. *Afrikanistische Arbeitspapiere* 65:103–127.

Orwin, Martin, N. Awde, and C. Xaaji. 1999. *Somali-English, English-Somali dictionary and phrasebook*. Hippocrene Books.

Orwin, Martin, and Mohamed Hashi Dhama Gaarriye. 2010. Virtual geminates in the metre of Somali poetry. In *Peace and Milk, Drought and War: Somali Culture, Society and Politics: Essays in Honour of I.M. Lewis*, ed. Markus V. Hoehne and Virginia Luling, 245–258. London: Hurst.

Orwin, Martin, and Maxamed Cabdullaahi Riiraash. 1997. An approach to relationships between Somali metre types. *African Languages and Cultures* 10:83–100.

Osman, Madina, and R. David Zorc. 1992. *Somali handbook*. Kensington, MD: Dunwoody.

Ouhalla, Jamal. 1993. Subject-extraction, negation and the anti-agreement effect. *Natural Language and Linguistic Theory* 11:477–518.

Palermo, Giovanni Maria da. 1914. *Grammatica della lingua somala*. Asmara: Tipografia Francescana.

Paster, Mary. 2007. Aspects of Maay phonology and morphology. *Studies in African Linguistics* 35:73–120.

Paster, Mary. 2010. Optional multiple plural marking in Maay. In *Current issues in linguistic theory 310: Variation and change in morphology*, ed. Franz Rainer. Amsterdam: John Benjamins.

Paster, Mary. 2018. Gender instability in Maay. In *Selected proceedings of the 45th Annual Conference on African Linguistics*, ed. Jason Kandybowicz and Harold Torrence, 205–218. Berlin: Language Science Press.

Paster, Mary, and Rodrigo Ranero. 2015. CASL introductory structural sketches for African languages: Maay. Technical Report 2.9b (DO0050). University of Maryland Center for Advanced Study of Language.

Pia, J. Joseph. 1965. Somali sounds and inflections. Doctoral Dissertation, Indiana University.

Prince, Alan. 1990. Quantitative consequences of rhythmic organization. *Chicago Linguistic Society* 355–398.

Puglielli, Annarita. 1981. La derivazione nominale in somalo. In *Aspetti morfologici, lessicali e della focalizzazione*, ed. Annarita Puglielli, 1–52. Rome: MAE, Departimento per la Cooperazione allo Sviluppo.

Puglielli, Annarita, and Biancamaria Bruno. 1988. Middle voice in Somali. In *Cushitic-Omotic: Papers from the International Symposium on Cushitic and Omotic languages*, ed. Marianne Bechaus-Gerst and Fritz Serzisko. Hamburg: Helmut Buske.

Puglielli, Annarita, and Cabdalla C. Mansur. 2012. *Qaamuuska Af-Soomaaliga*. Rome: RomaTrE.

Putman, Diana Briton, and Mohamood Cabdi Noor. 1993. The Somalis: Their history and culture. *Refugee Fact Sheet* 9.

Qoorsheel, Maxamud Jaamac. 2007. *English-Somali, Somali-English dictionary*. London: Simon Wallenberg.
Reinisch, Leo. 1903. *Die Somali Sprache*. Vienna: Alfred Hölder.
Rose, Sharon. 2017. ATR vowel harmony: New patterns and diagnostics. In *Proceedings of the 2017 Annual Meeting on Phonology*, ed. Gillian Gallagher, Maria Gouskova, and Sora Heng Yin.
Saeed, John I. 1982a. Central Somali: A grammatical outline. *Monographic Journals of the Near East: Afroasiatic Linguistics* 8.
Saeed, John I. 1982b. The syntactic status of quantifiers in Somali. *Bulletin of the School of Oriental and African Studies* 45:525–545.
Saeed, John I. 1984. *The syntax of focus and topic in Somali*. Hamburg: Helmut Buske.
Saeed, John I. 1988. An argument for the category adjective in Somali. In *Cushitic-Omotic: Papers from the International Symposium on Cushitic and Omotic Languages*, ed. M. Bechhause-Gerst and F. Serzisko, 567–579. Hamburg: Helmut Buske.
Saeed, John I. 1992. Dialectal variation in Somali. In *First International Congress of Somali Studies*, ed. H. A. Adam and C. L. Geshekter, 464. Scholars Press.
Saeed, John I. 1993a. Adpositional clitics and word order in Somali. *Transactions of the Philological Society* 91:63–93.
Saeed, John I. 1993b. *Somali reference grammar*. Kensington, MD: Dunwoody.
Saeed, John I. 1994. Syntactic typology and 'free word order' in Cushitic. *Teanga* 14:58–75.
Saeed, John I. 1995. The semantics of middle voice in Somali. *African Languages and Cultures* 8:61–85.
Saeed, John I. 1996. Head-marking and pronominal clitics in Somali. *African Languages and Cultures* Supplement:37–49.
Saeed, John I. 1999. *Somali*. Amsterdam: John Benjamins.
Saeed, John I. 2004. The focus structure of Somali. In *RRG 2004 book of proceedings-Linguistic theory and practice: Description, implementation and processing*, ed. Brian Nolan, 258–279. Dublin, Ireland: Institute of Technology Blanchardstown.
Saeed, John I. 2007. Somali morphology. In *Morphologies of Asia and Africa*, ed. Alan S. Kaye, 547–586. Eisenbrauns.
Samarin, William J. 1971. Salient and substantive pidginization. In *Pidginization and creolization of languages*, ed. Dell Hymes, 117–140. Cambridge: Cambridge University Press.
de Sampont, Fr. Cyprien. 1905. *Grammaire somalie*. London: Mission Catholique.
Sasse, Hans-Jürgen. 1978. The consonant phonemes of Proto-East-Cushitic (PEC): A first approximation. *Journal of Afroasiatic Linguistics* 7:1–67.
Sasse, Hans-Jürgen. 1984. The pragmatics of noun incorporation in Eastern Cushitic languages. In *Objects: Towards a theory of grammatical relations*, ed. Frans Plank, 243–268. London: Academic Press.
Schleicher, Adolf W. 1892. *Die Somali Sprache*. Berlin: Theodor Frölich.
Selkirk, Elisabeth O. 1978. On prosodic structure and its relation to syntactic structure. In *Nordic prosody*, ed. Thorstein Fretheim, 111–140. Trondeim: TAPIR.
Selkirk, Elisabeth O. 1981. On the nature of phonological representation. In *The cognitive representation of speech*, ed. John M. Anderson, John Laver, and Terry Myers, 379–388. Amsterdam: North-Holland.
Selkirk, Elisabeth O. 1984. *Phonology and syntax: The relation between sound and structure*. Cambridge, MA: MIT Press.
Serzisko, Fritz. 1992. Collective and transnumeral nouns in Somali. In *Proceedings of the First International Congress of Somali Studies*, ed. H. A. Adam and C. L. Geshekter, 516–530. Atlanta, GA: Scholars Press.

Ségéral, Philippe, and Tobias Scheer. 2001. Abstractness in phonology: The case of virtual geminates. In *Constraints and preferences*, ed. Katarzyna Dziubalska-Kołaczyk, 311–337. New York: Mouton de Gruyter.

Sheikh, Hassan, and Sally Healy. 2009. *Somalia's missing million: The Somali diaspora and its role in development*. United Nations Development Programme.

Soravia, Giulio. 1994. Gli imprestiti arabi in somalo. In *Sem-Cam-Iafet: atti della Giornata di Studi Camito-Semitici e Indoeuropei*, ed. Vermondo Brugnatelli, 199–224. Milan: Centro Studi Camito-Semitici.

Svolacchia, Marco, Lunella Mereu, and Annarita Puglielli. 1995. Aspects of discourse configurationality in Somali. In *Discourse configurational languages*, ed. Katalin Kiss, 65–98. New York: Oxford University Press.

Svolacchia, Marco, and Annarita Puglielli. 1999. Somali as a polysynthetic language. In *Boundaries of morphology and syntax*, ed. Lunella Mereu, 97–120. Amsterdam: John Benjamins.

Topintzi, Nina. 2014. *Onsets: Suprasegmental and prosodic behaviour*. Cambridge, UK: Cambridge University Press.

Tosco, Mauro. 1994. The historical reconstruction of a Southern Somali dialect: Proto-Karre-Boni. *Sprache und Geschichte in Afrika* 15:153–209.

Tosco, Mauro. 2000. Cushitic overview. *Journal of Ethiopian Studies* 33:108.

Tosco, Mauro. 2002. A whole lotta focusin' goin' on: Information packaging in Somali texts. *Studies in African Linguistics* 31:27–53.

Tosco, Mauro. 2004. Between zero and nothing: Transitivity and noun incorporation in Somali. *Studies in Language* 28:83–104.

Tosco, Mauro. 2008. A case of weak Romancisation: Italian in East Africa. In *Aspects of language contact: New theoretical, methodological, and empirical findings with special focus on Romancisation processes*, ed. Thomas Stolz, Dik Bakker, and Rosa Salas Palomo, 377–398. Berlin: Mouton de Gruyter.

Tosco, Mauro. 2010. Somali writings. In *5000 Jahre Schrift in Afrika*, ed. Anja Kootz and Helma Pasch. Afrikanistik Online.

Tosco, Mauro. 2012. The unity and diversity of Somali dialectal variants. In *The harmonization and standardization of Kenyan languages: Orthography and other aspects*, ed. Nathan Oyori Ogechi, Jane A. Ngala Oduor, and Peter Iribemwangi, 263–280. Cape Town: Centre for Advanced Studies of African Society.

Tosco, Mauro. 2015. Short notes on Somali previous scripts. In *Proceedings of the Conference on the 40th Anniversary of Somali Orthography*, ed. Cabdirashiid M. Ismaaciil, Cabdalla C. Mansuur, and Saynab A. Sharci, 189–217. Djibouti: Intergovernmental Academy of Somali Language.

US Central Intelligence Agency. 2020. The World Factbook 2020. https://www.cia.gov/library/publications/resources/the-world-factbook/index.html. Washington, DC: Central Intelligence Agency.

Vanhove, Martin. 2007. L'auxiliare di 'dire' dans les composés descriptifs en bedja. In *Proceedings of the XII Incontro Italiano di linguistica Camito-Semitica (Afroasiatica)*, ed. M. Moriggi, 221–231. Rubbettino.

Vasaturo, Laura. 2012. I prestiti arabi in somalo e swahili. Doctoral Dissertation, Università degli Studi di Napoli L'Orientale.

Warsame, Ali A. 2001. How a strong government backed an African language: The lessons of Somalia. *International Review of Education* 37:341–360.

Watson, Janet C. E. 2007. Syllabification patterns in Arabic dialects: long segments and mora sharing. *Phonology* 24:335–356.

Zaborski, Andzrej. 1967. Arabic loan-words in Somali: Preliminary survey. *Folia Orientalia* 8:125–175.

Zorc, R. David, and Abdullahi A. Issa. 1990. *Somali textbook*. Kensington, MD: Dunwoody.
Zorc, R. David, and Madina M. Osman. 1993. *Somali-English dictionary with English index, 3rd edition*. Kensington, MD: Dunwoody.

Index

A
Adjective 105, 158, 207, 362
Adposition 105, 222
Adverbial 278, 280
Alternation, tone 74, 105, 143, 241, 250
Alternation, vowel 74, 131, 134
Ambiguity 264, 270, 322, 334, 347, 422
Aspiration 28, 32, 36, 84, 88
Associative construction 106, 214, 226, 232, 233, 239, 241, 383

C
Cleft 335, 343
Clitic 236, 238, 245, 262, 404, 407, 422
Clusivity 235, 240, 258
Comparative 281
Complementizer 260, 340, 369, 370, 384
Compound 107
Coordinating conjunction 347, 383, 396

D
Deictic 105, 220
Dialects 3, 7–10, 32, 88, 186, 318, 325, 417, 424
Diphthong 48, 85, 88

E
Equative 316
Evidentiality 160, 197
Expletive subject 316

F
Feminine exponent 104
Focus marker 259, 411

G
Geminate 28, 45, 47, 65, 85
Grammatical gender 103, 119, 145, 161, 211, 239, 249

H
Headedness, phonological 63, 107, 211
Headedness, syntactic 212, 226, 249, 339, 348, 359, 384

I
Infinitival complement 164
Intensifier 275, 404

Interrogative determiner 411, 419, 422

L
Length contrast 25, 33, 40, 42, 62
Lexicalization 151, 219, 222, 228, 374
Loanwords 7, 12, 31, 39, 40, 43, 63, 86, 88, 126, 131, 232, 377, 388, 399

M
Metathesis 77, 98, 283
Metrical structure 81, 98
Middle 81, 141
Modernization 11

N
Negation 162, 252, 263, 266, 268, 296, 300, 364
Neutralization of contrast 66, 71
Noun incorporation 257
Number marking 15, 104, 165, 192, 203, 227

O
Orthography 7, 11, 38, 48, 49, 62, 225, 283

P
Passive 155
Phonotactics 53, 62, 77, 79, 84, 267
Phrasal verb 282, 284, 286
Pre-modifier form 109, 124, 239
Prosodification 95, 110, 167, 168, 170, 172, 285
Proto-Cushitic 328

R
Reduced agreement 160, 202, 209, 309, 310, 330, 332, 335, 339, 342, 360, 408
Reduplication 124, 368
Register 294
Relative clause 193, 229, 230, 246
Relativizer 347, 348, 359, 374, 376, 380, 385, 393, 394

S
Second position clitic 389
Spirantization 35
Standardization 11, 23
Stative 367
Stop contrast 28

Subject marking 195, 235, 244, 253, 318, 331, 353

T
Tag question 325
Tone 26, 147, 149
Tone bearing unit 101
Tone polarity 110
Topicalization 295, 408

V
V/Ø alternation 70, 77, 79, 98, 123, 154
Valency 151, 153, 155, 217, 219, 220, 225, 344
Variation 75, 80, 87, 104, 111, 145, 167, 168, 176, 178, 180, 212, 233, 234, 237, 238, 240, 241, 247, 258, 264, 285, 296, 299, 300, 303, 304, 306, 313, 316, 321, 324, 331, 347, 353, 357, 368, 371, 394, 405, 414
Verb Complex 66, 108, 384
Vowel harmony 25, 53

W
Weak Causative 70, 78, 81, 105, 141
Word order 255, 258, 293, 328–331, 344, 361

www.ingramcontent.com/pod-product-compliance
Lightning Source LLC
Chambersburg PA
CBHW081943230426
43669CB00019B/2911